Discover Caribbean Islands

Experience the best of the Caribbean Islands

This edition written and researched by

Ryan Ver Berkmoes,
Jean-Bernard Carillet, Paul Clammer, Michael Grosberg, Kevin Raub, Brendan Sainsbury, Andrea Schulte-Peevers, Polly Thomas, Luke Waterson, Karla Zimmerman

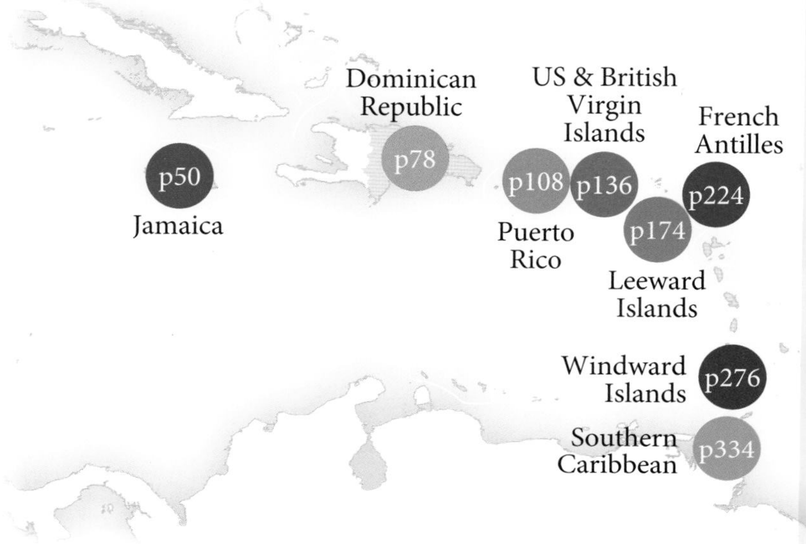

Dominican Republic p78

US & British Virgin Islands p136

French Antilles p224

Jamaica p50

Puerto Rico p108

Leeward Islands p174

Windward Islands p276

Southern Caribbean p334

Contents

Plan Your Trip

Discover

US & British Virgin Islands

Southern Caribbean

Contents

Discover Caribbean Islands

Southern Caribbean 334

Best of the Rest 391

In Focus

Survival Guide

This Is the Caribbean

Rocked by music, rolled by change, lapped by turquoise waters, blown by hurricanes – the Caribbean is not a place anyone could call static. It's a lively and intoxicating profusion of people and places spread over 7000 islands (fewer than 10% are inhabited). But, for all they share, there's also much that makes them different. Forming a huge swath around the Caribbean Sea, the namesake islands contradict in ways big and small. Can there be a greater contrast than between bustling Barbados and its neighbor, the seemingly unchanged-since-colonial-times Saint Vincent? Or between booming British-oriented St Kitts and its sleepy, Dutch-affiliated neighbor Sint Eustatius, just across a narrow channel?

You'll soon discover there is no typical Caribbean. Azure seas, white beaches, green forests so vivid they actually hurt the eyes – there is nothing subtle about the bold colors of the Caribbean. Swim below the waters for a color chart of darting fish and corals. Wander along the sand and stop at the paint-factory explosion that is a beach bar, from the garish decor to the rum punch in your glass. Hike into emerald wilderness and spot the accents of red orchids and yellow parrots.

All the colors are infectious. Like birds shedding dull adolescent plumage, visitors leave their wardrobes of gray and black behind when they step off the plane and don the Caribbean palette. Even the food is colorful, with rainbows of produce brightening up the local markets. You'll also see every color but dull at intense, costume-filled festivities like Carnival, celebrated throughout the region.

You can find any kind of island adventure here. With so many islands, beaches, cultures, flavors and waves to choose from you are bound to have a fabulous time. Doing nothing on the sand, partying at a resort, exploring a new port of call, hopping between islands, discovering wonders under the water or catching a perfect wave above, reveling in a centuries-old culture, and finding your inner pirate are all possible.

> "You can have any kind of island adventure here"

Soufrière (p297), St Lucia

Caribbean Islands

UNITED STATES OF AMERICA
Gulf of Mexico
Straits of Florida
Freeport
Little Abaco
New Plymouth
Sandy Point
Great Abaco
Nicolls Town
Eleuthera
Andros Town
NASSAU
THE BAHAMAS
Andros Island
Cat Island
San Salvador
Exuma Cays
Tropic of Cancer
HAVANA
Mars Bay
Long Island
Santa Clara
Archipiélago de Sabana-Camagüey
Crooked Island
Nueva Gerona
Acklins Island
TURKS & CAICO
Sancti Spiritus
CUBA
Isla de la Juventud
Great Inagua
Cockbu Town
Las Tunas
Bayamo
Guantánamo
Puerto Plata
Cayman Islands (UK)
Cayman Brac
Port-de-Paix
Santiago de Cuba
Gonaïves
Santiago
Caribbean Sea
GEORGE TOWN
Montego Bay
Ocho Rios
Port Antonio
Jérémie
PORT-AU-PRINCE
Ázua
Negril
JAMAICA
HAITI
Les Cayes
Jacmel
SANTO DOMING
Treasure Beach
KINGSTON
Barahona
DOMINICAN REPUBLIC
British Virgin Islands (UK)
Road Town
Anegada
St John
Tortola
Charlotte Amalie
The Valley
Anguilla (UK)
Marigot
Philipsburg
St-Martin/ Sint Maarten (FR & NETH)
Gustavia
St Barthélemy (FR)
Christiansted
St Croix
US Virgin Islands (US)
Codrington
Barbuda
ANTIGUA & BARBUDA
Aruba (NETH)
Windwardside
Saba (NETH)
Oranjestad
Sint Eustatius (NETH)
ST KITTS & NEVIS
St Kitts
BASSETERRE
Nevis
Charlestown
Saint John's
Antigua
Plymouth
Montserrat (UK)
Pointe-a-Pitre
La Désirade
Guadeloupe (FR)
Basse-Terre
0 100 km
0 50 miles

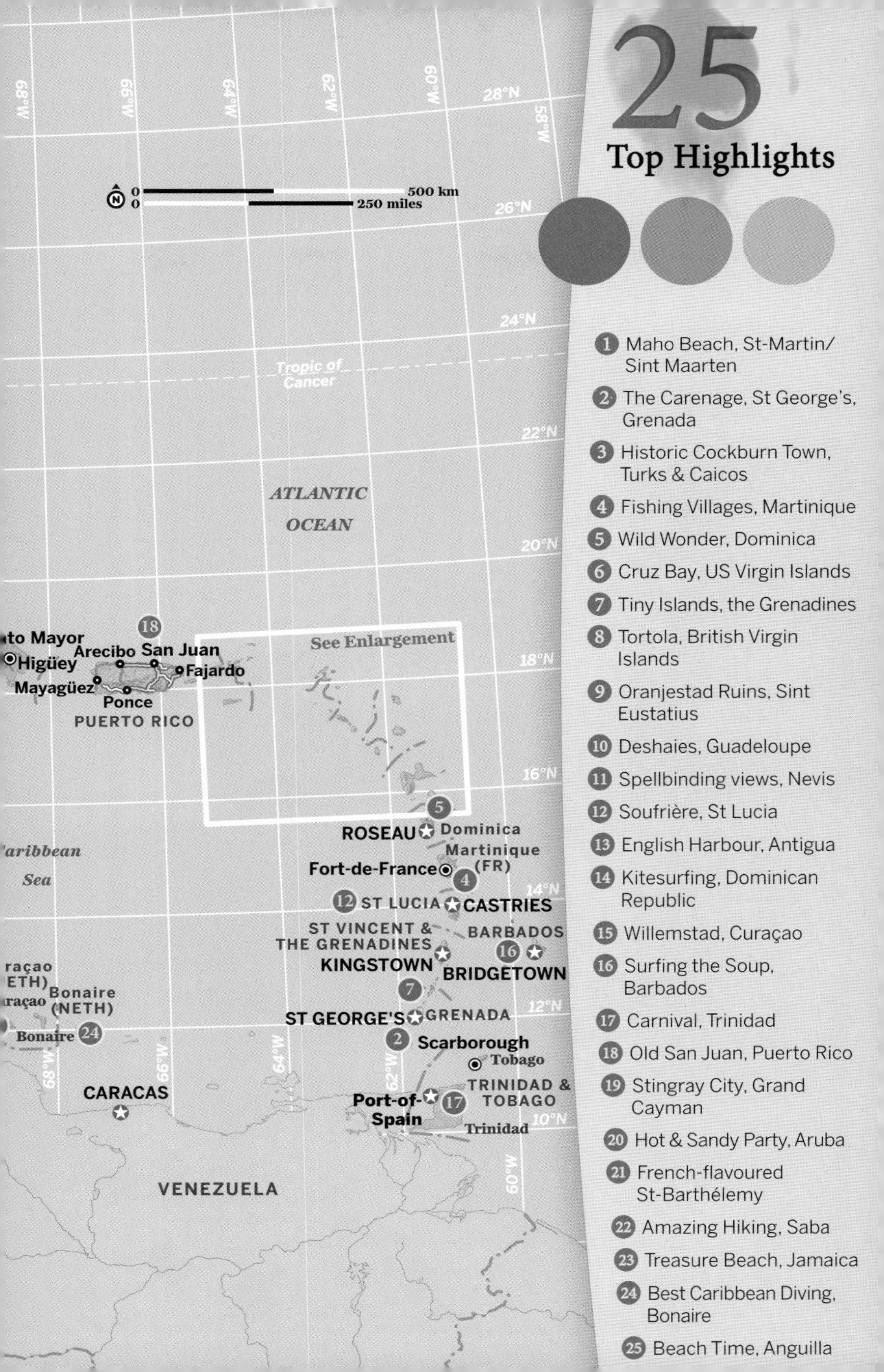

25
Top Highlights
1 Maho Beach, St-Martin/Sint Maarten
2 The Carenage, St George's, Grenada
3 Historic Cockburn Town, Turks & Caicos
4 Fishing Villages, Martinique
5 Wild Wonder, Dominica
6 Cruz Bay, US Virgin Islands
7 Tiny Islands, the Grenadines
8 Tortola, British Virgin Islands
9 Oranjestad Ruins, Sint Eustatius
10 Deshaies, Guadeloupe
11 Spellbinding views, Nevis
12 Soufrière, St Lucia
13 English Harbour, Antigua
14 Kitesurfing, Dominican Republic
15 Willemstad, Curaçao
16 Surfing the Soup, Barbados
17 Carnival, Trinidad
18 Old San Juan, Puerto Rico
19 Stingray City, Grand Cayman
20 Hot & Sandy Party, Aruba
21 French-flavoured St-Barthélemy
22 Amazing Hiking, Saba
23 Treasure Beach, Jamaica
24 Best Caribbean Diving, Bonaire
25 Beach Time, Anguilla
0 500 km
0 250 miles
Tropic of Cancer
ATLANTIC OCEAN
See Enlargement
San Juan
Arecibo
Higüey
Fajardo
Mayagüez
Ponce
PUERTO RICO
ROSEAU
Dominica
Martinique (FR)
Fort-de-France
ST LUCIA
CASTRIES
ST VINCENT & THE GRENADINES
KINGSTOWN
BARBADOS
BRIDGETOWN
ST GEORGE'S
GRENADA
Scarborough
Tobago
TRINIDAD & TOBAGO
Port-of-Spain
Trinidad
Bonaire (NETH)
Bonaire
CARACAS
VENEZUELA
Sea

25 The Caribbean Islands' Top Highlights

Maho Beach, St-Martin/Sint Maarten

Most island-goers would consider careening jumbo jets and large tracts of concrete runway to be noisy eyesores, but not on St-Martin/Sint Maarten. Clustered around Juliana International Airport – the area's transportation hub – you'll find a handful of bumpin' bars that cling to the sides of the runway while also abutting the turquoise waters. At Sunset Beach Bar (p231), arrival times are posted in chalk on a surfboard and aircraft landings are awaited with much anticipation as beach bums get blown into the blue from the backlash of jet propulsion.

1

FRANS LEMMENS/GETTY IMAGES ©

2

The Carenage, St George's, Grenada

One of the prettiest waterfronts in the Caribbean, this buzzing little horseshoe-shaped harbor (p310) is the perfect place to get a flavor of Grenada, with bobbing boats, busy cafes and shad spots where you can watch the world go by or admire the gorgeous old waterside buildings. Spreading up from the bay, the brightly colored rooftops and a glowering stone fort get a sceni backdrop courtesy of the green, misty peaks of the Grand Etang National Park.

Historic Cockburn Town, Turks & Caicos

Look no further for the old Caribbean than Cockburn Town (p398), the tiny national capital of the Turks and Caicos islands, where brightly painted colonial buildings line the roads and life goes on at a wonderfully slow pace miles away from the resorts of Providenciales. Wander down Duke St and Front St and pass whitewashed stone walls, traditional streetlamps and creaking old buildings, some of which have miraculously survived for over two centuries in this charming backwater.

3

The Best... White-Sand Beaches

ANSE DE GOUVERNEUR
St Barthélemy's gorgeous and secluded beach lines a U-shaped bay. (p243)

GRACE BAY BEACH
Lined with resorts in the Turks & Caicos, notably long and beautiful. (p392)

WHITE BAY
Wriggle your toes in the crazy-white sand in the British Virgin Islands. (p168)

BARBUDA
There's no such thing as a bad beach on this island. (p195)

The Best... Outdoor Adventure

SURFING, PUERTO RICO
Rincón has a wave riding scene once immortalized by the Beach Boys. (p131)

WINDSURFING, BARBADOS
The wind blows well and one of the world's great windsurf shops is here. (p317)

HIKING, MARTINIQUE
Hike along the base of the still-smoldering Mont Pelée, which blew in 1902. (p262)

HIKING, US VIRGIN ISLANDS
Feral donkeys watch as you hike along St John's trails. (p148)

SOBERKA RICHARD/HEMIS.FR/GETTY IMAGES ©

4 Fishing Villages, Martinique

The remedy to Martinique's often rampant development can be found in its charming fishing villages (p256), where life goes on much as it always has and the tourist dollar has still not made much of an impact. Surrounded by majestic forested hillsides and framed by crescent sand beaches, there's a particular string of these beauties on the island's southwestern corner – don't miss lovely Anse d'Arlet, friendly Petite Anse or stunning Grande Anse.

NICK LEDGER/GETTY IMAGES ©

5 Wild Wonder, Dominica

Before you die, visit Dominica (p280), one of the least developed and most unusual islands. Covered almost entirely by thick, virgin rainforest, it has a landscape quilted with innumerable shades of green. See beautiful scenes of misty waterfalls, chilly and boiling lakes, sulfur springs steaming through the earth, and valleys and gorges. The natural mosaic will tug at the hearts of artists, wanderers, romantics and anyone with a green bent.

6 Cruz Bay, US Virgin Islands

As the gateway to Virgin Islands National Park, Cruz Bay (p148) has trails from town that wind by shrub-nibbling wild donkeys and drop onto secluded beaches prime for snorkeling. All the activity can make a visitor thirsty, so it's a good thing Cruz Bay knows how to host a happy hour. Hippies, sea captains, retirees and reggae devotees all clink glasses at daily parties that spill out into the street.

7 Tiny Islands, the Grenadines

It's heard in offices the world over daily: 'I'm chucking it in and going to a tropical island!' In a world of package tourism, cruise ships and mega-resorts, the idea seems lost in a simpler time. Until you reach the Grenadines (p299). Starting with Bequia, multiple tiny islands stretch south, still mostly linked by wooden fishing boats. Hitch a ride, feel the wind in your face and head off to adventure.

Tortola, British Virgin Islands

Endowed with steady trade winds, tame currents and hundreds of protected bays, the British Virgin Islands are a sailor's fantasyland. Many visitors come expressly to hoist a jib and dawdle among the multiple isles, trying to determine which one serves the best rum-pineapple-and-coconut Painkiller. Tortola (p157), known as the charter-boat capital of the world, is the launching pad, so it's easy to get geared up. Don't know how to sail? Learn on the job with a sailing school.

8

The Best... Nightlife

JOST VAN DYKE, BVI
Party-hearty beach bars, one of which invented the Painkiller drink. (p166)

SOUTH FRIGATE BAY, ST KITTS
Compare the potency of the rum punches poured at the string of funky beach bars making up 'The Strip.' (p213)

SANTURCE
The heart of the best nightlife in San Juan – a heady mix of locals out for an evening of fun. (p121)

SOUTH COAST, BARBADOS
Beach bars and glitzy clubs coexist with the legendary weekend party at Oistins. (p323)

Oranjestad Ruins, Sint Eustatius

Like monuments to fallen empires, the ruins of Oranjestad (p204) are the whispers of a forgotten age, when rum, gold and slaves moved around the world with alacrity. Sint Eustatius' naturally deep harbor was the doorway to the New World, and during its golden era there were over 25,000 inhabitants representing a diverse spread of cultures and religions. Today, all that's left of this time are the stone skeletons of several imposing forts, mansions, a synagogue and a church.

The Best... Pampered Luxury

WEST COAST, BARBADOS
Called the Platinum Coast, the cloistered old resorts welcome new and old money alike. (p324)

ANGUILLA
The preferred retreat for those needing an escape from the spotlight. (p178)

MUSTIQUE
Even the name has mystique, the exclusive island with every comfort imaginable. (p307)

ST-BARTHÉLEMY
Jet-setters glitzed out with bling hobnob from December to April on this tiny island with continental airs. (p237)

9

10 Deshaies, Guadeloupe

This Basse-Terre village (p251) strikes just the right balance between working fishing port and sophisticated dining destination to keep its well-heeled visitors happy. Wooden houses line the tidy sand beach and colorful fishing boats bob up and down in the turquoise waters. Only the odd yacht in the distance gives you any indication of the smart crowd that flocks to Deshaies for its great restaurants, lively bars and fabulous nearby beaches.

11 Spellbinding Views, Nevis

Nevis (p215) is tailor-made for trading the beach lounger for the nature trail. Hit the higher ground on a ramble through luxuriant tropical forest, colorful gardens and cane fields clinging to the slopes of volcanic Mt Nevis. Walk through air perfumed by exotic flowers and along paths shaded by fruit-laden trees while keeping an eye out for the elusive vervet monkey. Panoramic views opening up between the foliage extend to other islands, including neighboring St Kitts, and will have you burning up the bytes in your digicam, fast.

12

Soufrière, St Lucia

Swim-up bars, lavish spas, infinity pools, gourmet restaurants... When it comes to upscale resorts, St Lucia is hard to beat and there's something for everybody. Some venues are straight from the pages of a glossy magazine, with luxurious units that ooze style and class, such as Ladera, Hotel Chocolat and Jade Mountain, near Soufrière (p297), while others specialize in all-inclusive packages. You don't need to remortgage the house to stay in one of them; special rates can be found on the hotels' websites or on booking sites.

HOLGER LEUE/GETTY IMAGES ©

13

English Harbour, Antigua

Antigua has been blessed with many splendors, including gorgeous beaches, crystalline waters and a deeply indented coastline with natural harbors. English Harbour (p193) boasts one of the preeminent historic sites in the Caribbean: Nelson's Dockyard. Travel back to the 18th century as you wander cobbled lanes and past restored old buildings. Still a working marina, it's one of the world's key yachting centers and attracts an international flotilla to its regattas.

Kitesurfing, Dominican Republic

Do your part for the environment: use wind-powered transportation. Year-round strong offshore breezes make Cabarete, on the north coast of the DR, one of the undisputed capitals for the burgeoning sport of kitesurfing (p100). Harnessing the wind's power to propel you over the choppy surface of the Atlantic isn't like another day at the beach. It takes training and muscles, not to mention faith, before you can try the moves of the pros from around the world who ply their trade here.

14

The Best... Beautiful Scenery

DOMINICA
A lake that literally boils, the aptly named Valley of Desolation and waterfalls splashing down. (p280)

MT SCENERY, SABA
Tiny Saba's volcanic peak has an ethereal beauty, which is particularly stunning at dusk. (p202)

CASCADA EL LIMÓN, DOMINICAN REPUBLIC
The 165ft-high waterfall is rough, rugged and surrounded by forest-covered peaks. (p96)

NORTHERN RANGE, TRINIDAD & TOBAGO
This chain of small coastal mountains hosts rich rainforests and stunning beaches. (p369)

The Best... Sounds of the Caribbean

TRINIDAD & TOBAGO
Electrifying and mesmerizing, steel-pan music will infect every molecule of your being. (p359)

BRITISH VIRGIN ISLANDS
When the sun sets and the moon waxes full, the music begins in Tortola. (p157)

DOMINICAN REPUBLIC
Test out your merengue moves with seriously talented dancers at one of Santo Domingo's nightclubs. (p82)

PUERTO RICO
Salsa is the sound of Puerto Rico; hear it in Old San Juan. (p112)

15

Willemstad, Curaçao

Curaçao's capital Willemstad (p351) is a bit of a holiday black hole: once you get sucked in, you might never leave. There's the Sint Annabaai ship channel, which cleaves the town in two and leads to one of the world's great harbors. Pause while strolling the Unesco-recognized colonial-era neighborhoods and watch huge freighters pass meters away. Old sailors' and workers' districts are being restored and reenergized, and Pietermaai – a faded area of old Dutch traders' mansions – is getting edgy new cafes and bars.

(TOP) FRANK VAN DEN BERGH/GETTY IMAGES ©; (MAIN) TORSTEN STAHLBERG/GETTY IMAGES ©

Surfing the Soup, Barbados

16

Like a monster wave breaking, Barbados (p317) has crashed onto the world surf scene. Although long the haunt of surf-happy locals, only recently has Barbados' east-side surf break, called the Soup Bowl, gone supernova. Sets travel thousands of miles across the rough Atlantic and form into huge waves that challenge the world's best. From September to December, faces found in surfing magazines stare wistfully out to sea from the very mellow beach village of Bathsheba. A slight calming from January to May brings out the hopefuls.

DONALD MICHAEL CHAMBERS/GETTY IMAGES ©

Carnival, Trinidad

17

Home to one of the world's biggest and best Carnivals (p359), Trinidad is party central, and its two days of fabulousness have inspired the most creative, dynamic music and dance culture in the Caribbean. Visit a pan-yard and let the rhythmic sweetness of steel pan vibrate through your body, check out the fireworks and drama of a soca concert or don a spangly, feathery costume and learn to 'wine your waist' like the locals during the two-day street parade.

Old San Juan, Puerto Rico

Even those limited to a quick visit find it easy to fall under the beguiling spell of Old San Juan (p114), with its cobblestone streets, pastel-painted colonial buildings and grand fortresses. Atop the ramparts of El Morro, the allure of this place is evident in every direction – from the labyrinth of crooked lanes to the endless sparkle of the Atlantic. By day, lose yourself in historical stories of blood and bombast; by night float along in crowds of giggling tourists, rowdy locals and syncopated salsa rhythms.

18

The Best... Old Colonial Towns

WILLEMSTAD, CURAÇAO
Little changed in a century, this old Dutch city dates back 300 years. (p351)

SINT EUSTATIUS
Once the busiest seaport in the world, it has scores of archaeological sites. (p203)

COCKBURN TOWN, TURKS & CAICOS
The real old Caribbean, the capital is totally undeveloped and absolutely charming. (p398)

OLD SAN JUAN
Huge forts, crooked streets and pastel facades; spend a few days here in awe. (p119)

BRIDGETOWN, BARBADOS
Explore the colonial streets of this Unesco-recognized town. (p317)

The Best... Wildlife Watching

BARBUDA
Observe one of the world's largest frigate bird colonies off the west coast of Barbuda. (p195)

SALT CAY, TURKS & CAICOS
One of the best places on earth to whale watch during the annual humpback migration. (p397)

BONAIRE
Take a break from the underwater thrills to spot pink flamingos. (p346)

Stingray City, Grand Cayman

19

Otherworldly looking stingrays languidly cruise the warm and shallow waters just off Grand Cayman's shore at famous Stingray City (p408). Years of free food have stoked a population of these creatures, who flit about cheerfully accepting handouts of squid from giggling, delighted onlookers. You can just stand in the water and stroke their astonishingly smooth and velvety skin while they swim around you, or go snorkeling and see them in their true habitat.

PHILIP COBLENTZ/GETTY IMAGES ©

BERT VAN WIJK/GETTY IMAGES ©

20 Hot & Sandy Party, Aruba

Hit the beach with 10,000 of your new best friends on Aruba (p338). Two legendary beaches, Eagle and Palm, stretch for miles and fulfill the sun-drenched fantasies of shivering hordes every winter. Wide, white and powdery, they face water that has enough surf to be interesting but not so much you'll be lost at sea. The beaches are backed by shady palms, and cheery holidaymakers stay at the long row of resorts just behind. The scene here is pulsing, vibrant and happy, with action that extends well into the night.

French-flavored St-Barthélemy

21

It's easy to dismiss St-Barth (p237) as the Caribbean capital of jet-setterdom, but there's much more to it. Within its craggy coves are small towns with stone walls that look like they've been plucked directly from the French countryside. This counterpoint of cultures plays out in the local food; scores of world-class restaurants dish out expertly crafted meals that meld the savoir faire and mastery of French cuisine with vivid bursts of bright island flavors.

22

Amazing Hiking, Saba

Rising dramatically out of the ocean, tiny Saba's volcanic peak (p199) can only be fully appreciated in person. Even the craftiest photographers can't correctly capture its beauty, especially ethereal when the setting sun casts flickering shadows across the forested terrain. Sign up for a trek with Crocodile James and wend your way through fascinatingly different climate zones as you ascend from the crashing waves up into the lazy clouds. From the top, you can stare out over the island's trademark white-green-brown architecture in the valleys below.

Treasure Beach, Jamaica

Down in Treasure Beach (p73), miles from the urban chaos of Kingston, you'll find a quiet stretch of sand where visitors, expats and Jamaican locals kick back every evening. Beers are passed around, reggae cracks over the air and a supreme sense of chilled-out-ed-ness – oh, let's just say it: 'irie' – descends onto the crowd. Music, food, Red Stripe, smiles – it all comes together here to create the laid-back Jamaican scene that many travelers dream of. Come for a day, stay for a week.

23

The Best... Relaxing at a Resort

ARUBA
Dozens of resorts sit right on the sand along a string of lovely beaches. (p338)

PUERTO RICO
The resort-lined beaches march down San Juan's coast like sets of breakers. (p112)

VIRGIN GORDA, BVI
A very laid-back place with dreamy resorts, especially around North Sound. (p163)

ST LUCIA
Magnificent inns and boutique hotels dot the beaches and verdant hills around Soufrière. (p297)

Best Caribbean Diving, Bonaire

Almost the entire coast of Bonaire (p346) is ringed by some of the healthiest coral reefs in the region. Sometimes it seems like half the population of the island are divers – and why shouldn't they be? The Unesco-recognized shore reefs can be reached right off your room's back deck at oodles of low-key diver-run hotels. All-you-can-breathe-in-a-week tank specials are common. Beyond the exquisite shore diving (more than half the 90 named sites are right off the beach) are more challenging sites for advanced divers.

The Best... Party

CARNIVAL, TRINIDAD
One of the world's biggest and best, two days of festival fabulousness. (p359)

NEGRIL, JAMAICA
Party till the sun comes up and goes back down. (p70)

OISTINS FISH FRY, BARBADOS
Vendors selling BBQ and rum mark this legendary weekly festival where the dance bars never close. (p323)

CHARLOTTE AMALIE, USVI
When the cruisers sail off at night, the fun dials up at a string of bars. (p140)

25

Beach Time, Anguilla

It's hard to go past the sandy coast and glistening water of Anguilla (p178). There's nothing better to do than spend days under the bright tropical sun on the beach, swinging in hammocks, splashing in the sea, and licking your fingers after gorging on ribs barbecued by limin' locals under windswept tents nearby. On weekends don't be surprised to find local artists jammin' at their favorite seaside haunts, like the world-famous Dune Preserve, home to Bankie Banx.

Caribbean Islands' Top Itineraries

Puerto Rico to US Virgin Islands No passport needed

5 DAYS

Enjoy some of the best of the Caribbean without leaving the US. Start with historic San Juan, then enjoy some of the region's best beaches on the little island of Vieques. Hit the lovely US Virgin Islands with their myriad diversions.

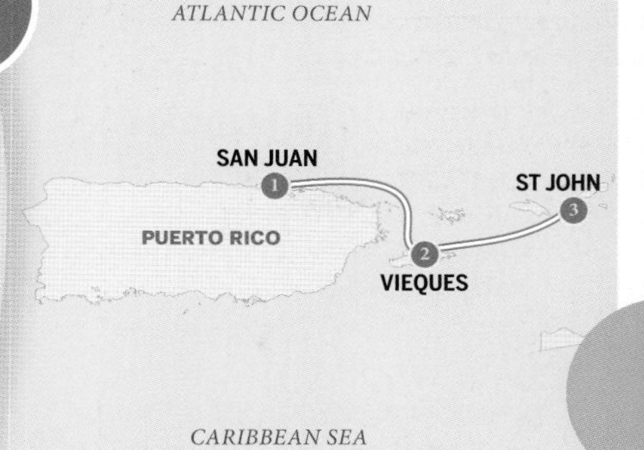

1 San Juan (p112)

Plunge into Old San Juan, the centuries-old bastion that combines modern vibrancy with some of the most historic sites in the hemisphere. Visit first-class museums, galleries, monuments and forts. After dark, book a table from a choice of restaurants that combine to give San Juan the hottest dining scene in the Caribbean. The next day head east to the rainforest at El Yunque; from here it's not far to Fajardo, where you get a ferry to Vieques.

SAN JUAN ➔ VIEQUES

Two hours, then **75 minutes**

2 Vieques (p124)

By night, don't miss the glowing Bioluminescent Bay of Vieques. By day, go exploring. For decades much of the island was an off-limits military site. The upside is that there are dozens of the region's best beaches that are virtually undeveloped within the Vieques National Wildlife Refuge. Spend the night wandering the waterfront cafes of Esperanza, which has the feel of The Next Big Thing.

VIEQUES ➔ ST JOHN

Plane **30 minutes**

St John (p148)

Spend a day at St John's North Shore beaches: Cinnamon Bay with windsurfing and trails through mill ruins; Maho Bay, where sea turtles swim; or Leinster Bay, where snorkelers can jump in amid rays and barracudas. Raise a toast to your beach in rollicking Cruz Bay.

Spend time on the South Shore at Salt Pond Bay, where cool hikes, groovy beach-combing and turtle-and-squid snorkeling await. Drink, dance and dine with the colorful characters in Coral Bay afterward.

Hike the Reef Bay trail, kayak along coastal reefs or take on another favorite activity. Hop on a ferry to check out St Thomas' East End. Here is the bulk of the island's resorts. Red Hook is the only town to speak of, though it's small and built mostly around the St John ferry dock and American Yacht Harbor marina. Have a rum punch with some colorful yachties.

Vieques (p124), Puerto Rico

DONALD NAUSBAUM/GETTY IMAGES ©

Cayman Islands to Jamaica
Fun, safe & wild

The contrasts of this itinerary make it appealing – enjoy an upscale citadel of capitalism and family-friendly holidays, Grand Cayman, then experience a true desert island nearby. Then go to the liveliest and wildest island in the Caribbean: Jamaica.

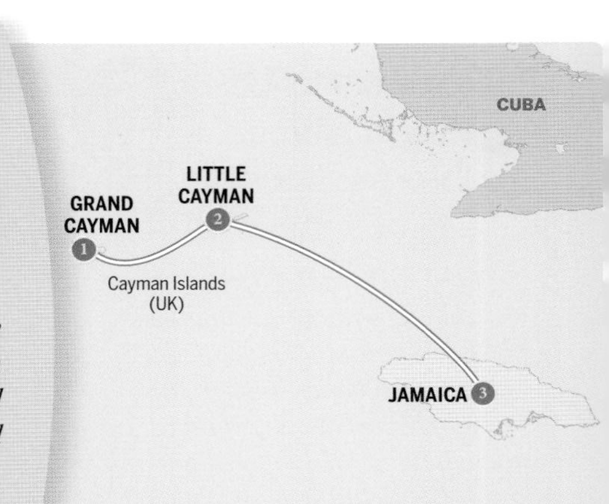

1 Grand Cayman (p401)

Find your perfect resort on Seven Mile Beach. Walk the length, although it's so lovely you're unlikely to feel short-changed when you learn it's somewhat under 6 miles long. Go snorkeling at Stingray City. Spend a day doing as little as possible. Sample some of the excellent restaurants. The bars close at 1am, so you'll get a good rest: you'll need it for Jamaica. Explore some of Grand Cayman's lesser-known attractions. Try the Botanic Park with its fierce-looking blue iguanas and Rum Point, which has a good beach and a very fun cafe.

GRAND CAYMAN ➜ LITTLE CAYMAN

Plane **30 minutes**

 Little Cayman (p409)

Fly to Little Cayman, where the 170 residents will be happy to see you. Laze on its desert-isle beaches and consider a world-class wall dive at Bloody Bay Marine Park. Choose from its several excellent yet low-key resorts. Watch out for iguanas.

LITTLE CAYMAN ➜ JAMAICA

Plane **Two hours**; Little Cayman to Grand Cayman then Kingstown.

3 Jamaica (p51)

Hit the sand in Montego Bay. (Some 80% of travelers choose the country's second-largest city, MoBay as everyone calls it, as their port of entry.) Laze on Doctor's Cave Beach, which is a pretty arc of sugary sand fronting a deep-blue gem studded with floating dive platforms and tourists sighing happily. Then take a raft trip down the Martha Brae, a swim in the Glistening Waters and a walk around historic Falmouth. The best place to orient yourself here is Water Sq, at the east end of Duke St. Named for an old circular stone reservoir dating to 1798, the square (actually a triangle) has a fountain topped by an old waterwheel. Now go straight to Treasure Beach and explore around the South Coast in areas like Black River and YS Falls, interspersed with relaxing on the beach. If you have a chance, don't miss sunrise over Blue Mountain Peak. The majestic, forest-covered mountains here throw the rest of the island into sharp relief. Their slopes, crags and fern forests seem light years from the capital's gritty streetscape, allowing you to hike old trails; perch on a mountaintop, and watch the valleys unfold out of the mist below.

Stingray City (p408), Grand Cayman

St Vincent to Tobago
Beaches, birds & more

Travel by water and air through the lush heart of the Caribbean's south end, always the warmest part in winter.

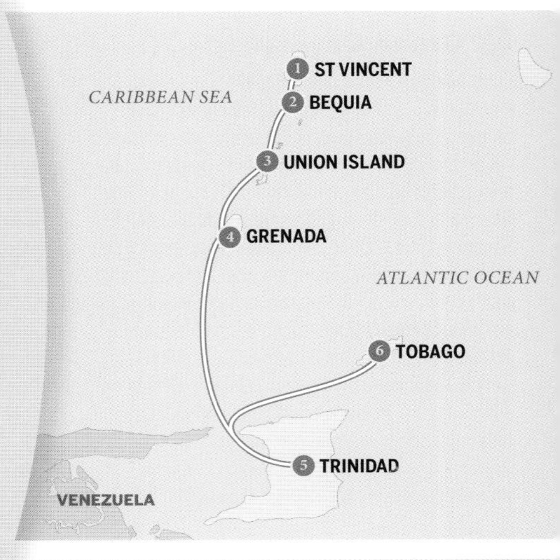

1 St Vincent (p300)

Still covered in rainforest and banana plantations, St Vincent is an island of boundless energy that is far removed from more affluent islands such as neighboring Barbados. Market days in Kingstown are chaotic as the streets teem with people. See some of the lush countryside that lured the makers of the *Pirates of the Caribbean* movies on a boat excursion to the Falls of Baleine.

ST VINCENT ➔ BEQUIA

One hour

2 Bequia (p303)

Catch a ferry for the one-hour ride to Bequia, the center of beach fun and nightlife in the Grenadines and quite possibly the best all-around little island in the Caribbean. Yachts anchor in Admiralty Bay and you can wander the shore choosing from great places for a sundowner and dinner. By day, there are some simply perfect beaches such as Lower Bay. Heading south through the Grenadines, you can go direct to Union Island, but why not make a day of it and stop off at Canouan or Mayreau?

BEQUIA ➔ UNION ISLAND

One to four hours

3 Union Island (p308)

A quiet yacht-filled port, Union Island is close to the amazing Tobago Cays, where you can snorkel or dive in an amazing underwater park. Leaving for Grenada, you first charter a boat and cross the aquatic border to Carriacou, the pint-sized sister island to Grenada. Then you hop the fast ferry to Grenada's St George's.

Jungle hillside, Tobago (p372)
DEBRA WISEBERG/GETTY IMAGES ©

UNION ISLAND ➔ GRENADA

Three hours Union Island to Carriacou one hour, then Carriacou to St George's two hours

4 Grenada (p308)

Immerse yourself in St George's, one of the Caribbean's most charming capital cities. Get yourself some beach time at the perfect sands of Mourne Rouge Bay. Save a day for hiking lush Grand Etang National Park, where the smells of fruit and spices such as nutmeg are intoxicating.

GRENADA ➔ PORT OF SPAIN, TRINIDAD

Plane **30 minutes**

5 Trinidad (p354)

Check out downtown Port of Spain and the nightlife. Head up to Maracas Bay to ride the waves. Take a boat tour of the Caroni Bird Sanctuary to see scarlet ibis and swim in Rio Seco falls.

TRINIDAD ➔ TOBAGO

2½ hours

6 Tobago (p372)

Spend the day relaxing on the sand, and learn to windsurf and snorkel or dive at the Speyside reefs at Pigeon Point. Head up the Caribbean coast and spend time on the beach in Castara, then hole up in a Charlotteville guesthouse, soaking up the rays on Pirate's Bay. Take a walk through the ancient Tobago Forest Reserve.

Guadeloupe to St Lucia
Ferry-hopping for pleasure

There are not many places in the Caribbean where you can visit so many different islands without leaving the ground (unless you're zip-lining). Start with the archipelago of Guadeloupe and finish with bipolar St Lucia. In between you'll love Dominica and Martinique.

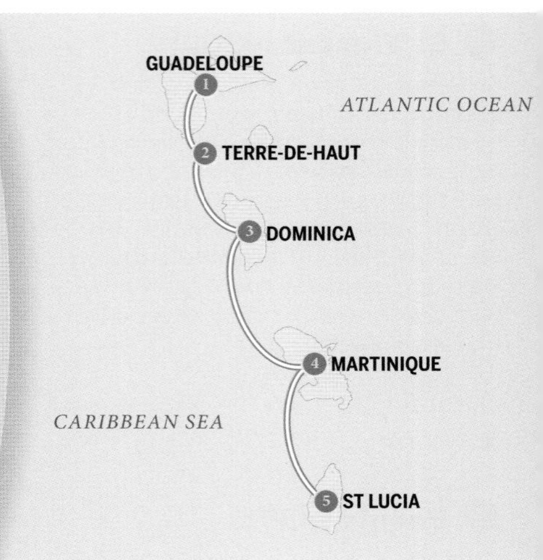

1 Guadeloupe (p243)

On Guadeloupe, prioritize beautiful Basse-Terre – drive the northern coast road and stop at the sublime beaches at Grande Anse and enjoy the relaxed atmosphere and good eating in Deshaies. Go diving at Pigeon Island and then return to Pointe-à-Pitre via the dramatic Route de la Traversée.

GUADELOUPE ➔ TERRE-DE-HAUT
One Hour

2 Terre-de-Haut (p252)

Explore a truly remote slice of the French Caribbean on a day trip. Lying 10km off Guadeloupe, Terre-de-Haut is the largest of the eight small islands that make up Les Saintes. Terre-de-Haut is unhurried and feels like a small slice of southern France transported to the Caribbean. Wander old Fort Napoléon.

TERRE-DE-HAUT ➔ DOMINICA
90 minutes

3 Dominica (p280)

Start at Dominica in the interesting capital, Roseau. Then lose yourself in the rainforest at Morne Trois Pitons National Park, a Unesco World Heritage site. On an island laced with waterfalls, the walk in the park to Middleham Falls is splendid. It can be enjoyed in less than half a day. Celebrate with a glass of bubbly – or at least the natural bubbles that tickle you while diving at Champagne Reef.

DOMINICA ➔ MARTINIQUE
90 minutes

4 Martinique (p256)

On Martinique, hit the beach at Les Salines, followed by diving and drinking in the lively fishing village of Ste-Luce. Then concentrate on the south: base yourself somewhere along the coast around Grande Anse or Diamant. Don't miss the stunning views of Rocher du Diamant from the coastal road, or the eating and activity options around Trois-Îlets.

MARTINIQUE ➔ ST LUCIA
90 minutes

5 St Lucia (p291)

St Lucia emerges like a virescent monolith from the Caribbean as you home in on the ferry. Stay in Soufrière, which has a dramatic position on a bay that's shadowed by the iconic peaks of the Pitons. Travel north to the lively city of Castries, then explore the old fishing village of Gros Islet and the Pigeon Island National Landmark, all scenically set on Rodney Bay. Spend time learning to kitesurf and, finally, sample the delights of the wild Atlantic-battered east coast.

Grand-Rivière (p263), Martinique

Sint Maarten to Bonaire
Discover the Dutch side of the Caribbean

The French provide the perfect accent on this Dutch adventure that begins in the northeast and ends in the dry southwest. Along the way enjoy some of the region's best beauty above and below the water.

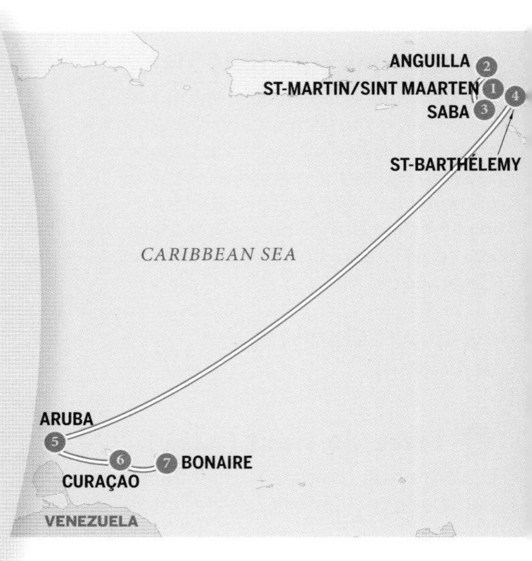

1 St-Martin/Sint Maarten (p228)

On St-Martin/Sint Maarten, head down to Philipsburg, which allows time for some retail therapy. Bounce over to the French side of the island and hang out in Grand Case, where your dining choices range from beach-shack casual to fine-French bistro. For beach time try the local favorite Friar's Bay. Or head further afield to Baie Longue or Le Galion. When you start feeling antsy, hit the lively bar scene at Maho Beach.

ST-MARTIN/SINT MAARTEN ➔ ANGUILLA

25 minutes

2 Anguilla (p178)

From Marigot, ferry over to Anguilla. Once there, choose between two beaches: popular Shoal Bay East or the quieter, windswept Junk's Hole. Head to the Valley for an early lunch at one of the local BBQ tents. Finish with a romantic dinner along Meads Bay and hit the quaint bar scene in Sandy Ground.

ANGUILLA ➔ SABA

Two hours Anguilla to Marigot 25 minutes, then Philipsburg to Saba 90 minutes

3 Saba (p198)

You'll be struck by Saba's volcanic beauty as you arrive by ferry. Explore the small town of Windwardside, then head out into the bush for a rugged hike up the aptly named Mt Scenery. Rent some diving gear and explore submerged pinnacles that teem with nurse sharks. Head back to St-Martin.

SABA ➔ ST-BARTHÉLEMY

2½ hours Saba to Philipsburg 1¾ hours, then on to St-Barthélemy 45 minutes

4 St-Barthélemy (p237)

The ferry to St-Barthélemy is famous for being a wild ride. Have lunch at the gorgeous French village of Gustavia, and then sun yourself on white-sand Anse de Colombier. Although St-Barth is fabled as a playground of the rich and famous, the beauty of the island is that this matters little once everybody's in T-shirts and shorts.

Houses in Punda (p351), Curaçao
FRANK VAN DEN BERGH/GETTY IMAGES ©

ST-BARTHÉLEMY ➲ ARUBA

Boat and Plane **Four hours** St-Barthélemy to Philipsburg, then fly to Aruba two hours

5 Aruba (p338)

Stay on relaxed Eagle Beach, Aruba's best. Assuming you're here for the sand – that's Aruba's real charm – then besides a day to explore the wet and wild northeast coast, Arikok National Wildlife Park and interesting Oranjestad, you should just play on the beach. And given the vast stretches of sand on the island, it won't be too hard to find the ideal plot for your beach blanket.

ARUBA ➲ CURAÇAO

Plane **30 minutes**

6 Curaçao (p351)

Unlike its neighbors, Curaçao is all about exploring. Stay in colonial Willemstad (a Unesco World Heritage site), which is one of the region's most interesting towns, then wander the coast north to Westpunt, where national parks, restored plantations and a bevy of hidden beaches await. You might even want to try some snorkeling or head to Spaanse Water, where the windsurfing will blow you away.

CURAÇAO ➲ BONAIRE

Plane **30 minutes**

7 Bonaire (p346)

You may not see much of Bonaire above sea level as you'll be underwater much of the time. One of the world's great diving locations, Bonaire's underwater splendor and 90 named dive sites will keep you busy. Explore the island, which has stark beauty, spotting flamingos and learning about an easily accessed past. The island's second city – a village really – Rincon, has a slow and inviting pace, while at the horizon-spanning salt flats in the south you can still see evidence of slavery and colonial trade. In the middle of it all, cute little Kralendijk combines eating, sleeping and fun.

Caribbean Month by Month

Top Events

Festival San Sebastián, January

Carnival, Trinidad, February

Reggae Sumfest, July

Crop-Over Festival, July

Pirates Week, November

January

New Year's is celebrated with huge gusto. Resorts are full, and people are partying. Weather across the region is balmy, but there's the odd cool day in the north.

Jamaica Jazz & Blues Festival

Internationally acclaimed acts jam Jamaica's Montego Bay in late January for three nights of mellow music under the stars (www.jamaicajazzandblues.com). It starts the jazz festival season across the region.

Festival San Sebastián

Puerto Rico's famous street party, Festival San Sebastián, draws big crowds to Old San Juan for a week in mid-January. There are parades, dancing and much more.

February

Carnival is a huge event in many Caribbean countries, where it is tied to the Lenten calendar. No country has a bigger Carnival than Trinidad, which prepares all year for its exuberant explosion.

Carnival, Trinidad

Preparing for the Caribbean's biggest street party is a year-long affair in Trinidad. Steel-pan and calypso competitions, elaborate costumes, mud-covered revelers and blasting soca music.

Bob Marley Birthday Bash

The love for the sound that plays in beach bars worldwide brings acolytes and reggae fans to the Bob Marley Museum in Jamaica on Bob Marley's birthday, February 6.

Master of the Ocean

Called a 'triathlon of the waves,' this thrilling competition has the world's best windsurfers, kitesurfers and surfers going board to board on Playa Encuentro in the

(left) November Pirates Week

Dominican Republic during the last week in February.

Republic of Fun

The Dominican Republic celebrates Carnival with great fervor every Sunday in February, with a huge blowout in Santo Domingo on the last weekend of the month or the first weekend of March. Santiago hosts an international *careta* (mask) competition.

Party Puerto Rico

Ponce's Carnival festivities are some of the best on Puerto Rico, with traditional masks, music and lots of drunken parades.

Parading in Dominica

Dominica's Carnival runs for two weeks leading up to Ash Wednesday, with a costume parade among its highlights. Look for parades with startling energy.

Dancing in Curaçao

Curaçao's Carnival begins right after New Year's Day and continues through to Lent. It's one of the larger ones in the region.

March

High season throughout the Caribbean. On Barbados, American college students invade for spring break. The influx of visitors is greeted by lovely weather everywhere.

St Patrick's Week

Not a day but a week on Montserrat. The Irish heritage here means the day o' green is huge. Costumes, food, drink, dance and concerts by the much-lauded Emerald Community Singers are highlights.

April

Easter signals more Carnivals. High season continues but rates begin to fall at resorts. Temperatures are climbing in the south but the Caribbean is mostly dry.

Simadan

Bonaire's harvest festival is held in the small town of Rincon in early April. This was the historic home of the slaves who were brought to the island to make salt and harvest food. Celebrations include traditional dance and food.

Antigua Sailing Week

The Caribbean's largest regatta, Antigua Sailing Week follows the Antigua Classic Yacht Regatta and involves a range of sailing and social events around Nelson's Dockyard and Falmouth Harbour.

Séu Parade

Curaçao's 'Feast of the Harvest' features parades with folk music and dancing on Easter Monday. People in rural areas go a little nuts; for them it outclasses Carnival.

Jamaica's Carnival

The Easter Carnival in Kingston brings people into the streets for music and an impressive costume parade (www.jamaicacarnival.com). Huge, as you'd expect.

Carnival

The two-week Sint Maarten Carnival, on the Dutch side, outclasses its counterpart on the French side. Activities begin in the second week after Easter.

June

June remains dry and relatively storm-free. Like May, it's not a peak time for visitors, except the savvy ones who value dry, sunny days and low hotel rates.

St Kitts Music Festival

Top-name calypso, soca, reggae, salsa, jazz and gospel performers from throughout the Caribbean gather on the small island during the three-day St Kitts Music Festival and pack out every venue – plus parks, stadiums and more. Reserve a room way in advance.

July

Summer holiday crowds start arriving, as do the very first tropical storms of the hurricane season. There's another tranche of carnivals and other special events.

 Crop-Over Festival

Marks the end of the sugarcane harvest in Barbados. Over three weeks from mid-July, there are calypso competitions, fairs and more, finishing with a costume parade and fireworks on Kadooment Day in August.

 Reggae Sumfest

The big mama of all reggae festivals, held in late July in Montego Bay, brings top acts together for an unforgettable party. Even if you're not attending, you're attending – festivities tend to take over MoBay.

 Vincy Mas

St Vincent's Carnival and biggest cultural event for the year, Vincy Mas, is held in late June and early July.

 Santo Domingo Merengue Festival

Santo Domingo hosts the country's largest and most raucous merengue festival. For two weeks at the end of July and the beginning of August, the world's top merengue bands play for the world's best merengue dancers all over the city.

 BVI Emancipation Festival

Held on Tortola, the nation's premier cultural event features beauty pageants, horse racing and 'rise and shine tramps' (3am parades led by reggae bands). The celebration marks the end of slavery (1834).

August

The summer high season continues and you can expect the first real storms of the hurricane season, although mostly that means heavy rains as opposed to big blows.

 Anguilla Summer Festival

Anguilla's 10-day-long Summer Festival takes place around the first week of August and is celebrated with boat races, music, dancing and more.

 Latin Music Festival

The Dominican Republic's huge, three-day festival, held at Santo Domingo's Olympic Stadium, attracts the top names in Latin music; dates vary.

 Grenada Carnival

Grenada's big annual event may be later than most islands' but that doesn't dim its festivities. The celebration is spirited and includes calypso and steel-pan competitions, costumed revelers, pageants and a big, grand-finale jump-up (nighttime street party).

October

Dominica comes to the rescue of what is otherwise a quiet month (other than a few passing squalls). Some family-run businesses close for the month.

World Creole Music Festival

Dominica's ode to Creole music attracts big-name Caribbean music and dance acts, and food vendors sell spicy goodness.

November

Hurricane season has mostly blown itself out and Christmas decorations are going up. Baseball season arrives in the Dominican Republic.

Tranquility Jazz Festival

Attracting big names as well as local talent, and culminating with a free jazz concert on the beach, Anguilla's Tranquility Jazz Festival draws jazz fans from far and wide.

Pirates Week

This wildly popular family-friendly extravaganza on Grand Cayman features a mock pirate invasion, music, dances, costumes, games and controlled mayhem. Book hotels in advance.

December

High season begins mid-month and incoming flights are full. Rates are up and everything is open. Carnival prep is reaching fever pitch on many islands.

Foxy's Old Year's Night Party

Hundreds of boats show up in Jost Van Dyke harbors on December 31. Every beach bar at this end of the British Virgin Islands is hopping.

St Kitts Carnival

The biggest event on St Kitts. Starting around mid-December, it offers a couple of weeks of music, dancing and steel pan.

Far left: April Antigua Sailing Week
Left: July Crop-Over Festival

What's New

For this new edition of Discover Caribbean Islands, our authors hunted down the fresh, the transformed, the hot and the happening. Here are a few of our favorites. For up-to-the-minute recommendations, see lonelyplanet.com/caribbean.

1 **FALMOUTH CRUISE PORT**
Jamaica now has a third major port of call for cruise ships. Go on heritage walks around the historic 18th-century town. (p69)

2 **SABA & SINT EUSTATIUS**
These two very small islands became 'special municipalities' of the Netherlands and have adopted the US dollar as their currency.

3 **ANTIGUA & BARBUDA PASSPORT SALE**
The nation started its own 'citizenship by investment' program (St Kitts & Nevis and Dominica already have such schemes). Pay enough money and you can obtain citizenship.

4 **MARTINIQUE**
Jardin Botanique du Carbet is a beautiful new botanical garden created around ruins from the colonial era. It's in the hills, just a short drive from Fort-de-France. (p261)

5 **CONDADO VANDERBILT HOTEL, SAN JUAN**
Signaling new energy on San Juan's beautiful beachfront, this enormous old hotel has been lavishly renovated. Its historic charms are now matched with modern luxury. (p120)

6 **SEABOURNE AIRLINES**
During a time when the major regional airline Liat has had financial problems, this Puerto Rico–based carrier is expanding fast across the region.

7 **KEMPINSKI RESORT, DOMINICA**
The island's government has cut a deal with Middle East developers for a new upscale resort on the north end of the island. It will be the first major resort on Dominica.

8 **NATIONAL GALLERY OF THE CAYMAN ISLANDS**
This art museum has made a huge move from a storefront in a strip mall to a beautiful new building on Grand Cayman. Its collection of regional works has never looked better. (p403)

Get Inspired

Books

- **Sugar in the Blood: A Family's Story of Slavery and Empire** Andrea Stuart writes about her family's haunting legacy as Barbados sugar barons.

- **The Banana Wars: United States Intervention in the Caribbean, 1898–1934** Lester D Langley shows the cost of meddling in the region.

- **The Slave Ship: A Human History** Marcus Rediker looks at the transportation of 12 million Africans to the US and Caribbean during slavery.

- **Banana: The Fate of the Fruit that Changed the World** Dan Koeppel explores the enormous impact – not always for the better – of this ubiquitous fruit.

- **Simone** Eduardo Lalo's prize-winning novel sets an almost hypnotic tone for its ramble through the city of San Juan.

Films

- **Marley** (2012) A superb documentary about the life of Bob Marley.

- **Better Mus Come** (2010) The most critically acclaimed Caribbean film in recent years, it dramatically re-creates 1970s Jamaica when political parties used rival gangs for influence.

- **The Harder They Come** (1973) This Jamaican movie is still the most famous film to have come out of the Caribbean in decades.

Music

- **Tito Puente: Babarabatiri** Includes the Puerto Rican salsa great's *Ran Kan Kan*.

- **Diamonds** Like everything else by Barbadian Rihanna, it went platinum on release.

Websites

- **Caribbean Cricket** (www.caribbeancricket.com) Bone up on batsmen, bowlers, sticky wickets and the region's favorite sport.

- **The Caribbean Writer** (www.thecaribbeanwriter.org) A journal of works by regional authors, highly readable.

Banana plantation, Bridgetown (p317)

Short on time?

This list will give you an instant insight into the Caribbean Islands.

Read *The Firm* John Grisham's page-turner about financial shenanigans in the Cayman Islands.

Watch Any *Pirates of the Caribbean* movie; get in a good mood and revel in the locations.

Listen The Lashing Dogs are a hot fungi band from Tortola.

Log on www.caribjournal.com is a news site that covers the region with an emphasis on events affecting tourism.

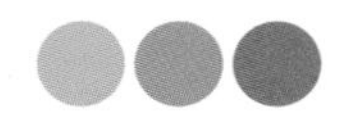

Need to Know

Currency
Eastern Caribbean dollar (EC$), US dollar (US$; accepted almost everywhere), Euro (€), Netherlands Antillean guilder (NAf/ANG; there are plans to replace this currency).

Language
English, Spanish, French

Visas
Citizens of Canada, the EU and the US don't need visas for visits of under 90 days throughout the region.

Money
ATMs are found in all touristed areas, except for the very smallest islands and towns.

Mobile Phones
Most mobile phones work; avoid roaming charges with easily bought local SIM cards. Puerto Rico and USVI included in US plans.

Wi-Fi
Common in hotels, usually free everywhere except pricey resorts.

Internet Access
Most people use wi-fi or their phone.

Tipping
Varies; 15% in restaurants is average. Watch for service charges added to bills.

When to Go

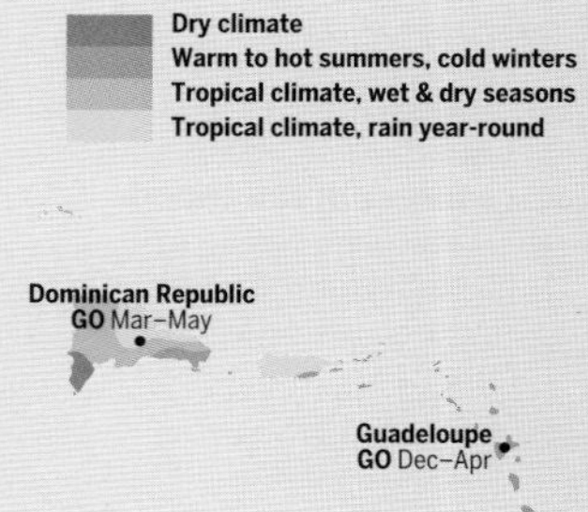

High Season (Dec–Apr)
- People fleeing the northern winter arrive in droves and prices peak.
- The region's driest time.
- Can be cold in the northern Caribbean.

Shoulder (May–Jun & Nov)
- The weather is good, rains are moderate.
- Warm temperatures elsewhere reduce visitor numbers.
- Best mix of affordable rates and good weather.

Low Season (Jul–Oct)
- Hurricane season; odds of being caught are small, but tropical storms are like clockwork.
- Good for eastern Caribbean's surf beaches.
- Room prices can be half or less than in high season.

Advance Planning
- **Six months before** Book your accommodations if you will be traveling in peak season. Do so earlier if you hope for special deals.
- **Three months before** Reserve rental cars and make reservations for special meals if traveling in a busy time.
- **One month before** Book special tours like kayaking on bioluminescent lakes or scuba classes.

Daily Costs

Budget less than US$150

- Room away from the beach: under US$100
- Meal at a locally popular restaurant: US$10
- Ride local buses: US$3

Midrange US$150–300

- Double room in the action: US$200
- Visit parks and beaches that are free, rent bikes or snorkel for US$10 per day
- Rental car for exploring: US$40 to US$60 a day

Top end over US$300

- Beautiful rooms at the best resorts in high season: US$400 and over
- Activities in beautiful places: US$100 and up
- World-renowned meals: US$100 per person and more

Exchange Rates

Australia	A$1	$EC2.52
Canada	C$1	$EC2.53
Europe	€1	$EC3.67
Japan	Y100	$EC2.64
New Zealand	NZ$1	$EC2.36
UK	£1	$EC4.63
USA	US$	$EC2.70

For current exchange rates see www.xe.com

What to Bring

- The Caribbean islands are casual, so bring light, comfy clothes: a bathing suit, T-shirt and shorts will be your wardrobe. Add long pants or a dress for nights out. A few essentials:
- **Sun hat** Buying at home ensures a better fit.
- **Quick-dry towel** A small one, for when the whim to swim hits.
- **Flashlight with batteries** For nighttime reading, blackouts.
- **Plastic resealable bags** Essential for keeping things (cameras, air tickets, passports) dry on boat trips.
- **Snorkeling mask with corrective lenses** Suddenly, reefs are in focus.

Arriving in the Caribbean

- Every airport will have taxis waiting for flights.
- Many hotels and resorts will meet your flight, usually for a modest fee.
- Car rental is easily arranged in advance, through major firms or local outfits. Don't expect cars to be available for walk-up rental in high season.
- Public transit that's convenient for arriving visitors at airports is uncommon.

Getting Around

- **Bikes** A good choice on flatter, quieter islands.
- **Walk** Some islands are so small, you can easily walk everywhere.
- **Rental cars** Always available from somebody; note variations in local road rules.
- **Public minivans or buses** Cheap; can be found in some form on most islands, ask locals.
- **Road conditions** Usually bad; travel can be slow, despite what seems to be short distances.
- **Charter taxis** On all islands, taxi drivers will give custom tours and arrange for cross-island transfers; agree to a fee in advance.
- **Ferries** Not common, only operate a few routes.
- **Flights** Between islands near each other, flying may require long detours and connections.

Sleeping

- **Exclusive resorts** Often found in remote and amazing locations.
- **Large beach resorts** Only some – not all – islands have huge beach resorts.
- **Hotels** Simple places found across the region.
- **Hostels & Camping** Not common.
- **Holiday rentals** Common on popular islands.

Be Forewarned

- **Water** Not always safe to drink.
- **Hurricanes** Most islands go years or decades without being hit by a hurricane. Watch the weather but the odds are small.
- **Seasonal closings** Small and family-run businesses may close for a period between August and November.
- **Safety** Some, but not all, islands have problems with crime. Ask locally and take precautions.

Jamaica

Jamaica, at first blush, is the Caribbean island many know best thanks to its relentless exposure. Is there a person out there who hasn't heard Bob Marley sing or seen Usain Bolt run?

But did you know there are Chinese Jamaicans and Jewish Jamaicans and white Jamaicans who speak patois as fluently as downtown Kingston yardies? Jamaica, perhaps more than any other Caribbean nation, also keeps one foot (and much of its cultural soul) rooted in Africa.

Jamaica packs in extremes. Long white beaches twinned with steep green mountains; relaxed resorts and adrenaline-charged ghettoes; sweet reggae and slack dancehall. It's a complicated national soundtrack, but one that is impossible not to groove along to.

Reach Falls (p63)
DOUG PEARSON/GETTY IMAGES ©

Jamaica Itineraries

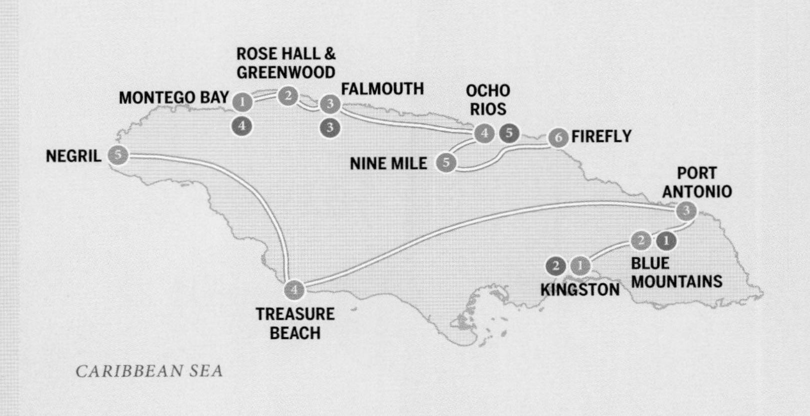

Four Days

1 Montego Bay (p65) The gateway to Jamaica for about 80% of international travelers. Hit Doctor's Cave Beach for water sports and head downtown to take in the architecture and the hustle of a real Jamaican city. Dinner on the Hip Strip is a must.

2 Rose Hall and Greenwood (p69) For an insight into how Jamaica came to be, a trip to these colonial great houses will take you back to the days of sugar plantations and slavery. Watch out for the ghost stories.

3 Falmouth (p69) Take a foodie walking tour around this historic town that's an open-air museum of colonial architecture (and a modern cruise-ship hub), then hang on until dark to swim in the luminescent Glistening Waters.

4 Ocho Rios (p63) Stay overnight in this modern tourist hub, with its great bars and restaurants, but pack your swimming gear to make the splashy ascent of the beautiful Dunn's River Falls, deservedly Jamaica's most popular waterfalls.

5 Nine Mile (p65) Reggae enthusiasts can take the rough road through stunning scenery to this tiny village where Bob Marley was born and is now buried, and visit his childhood home and mausoleum.

6 Firefly (p65) Follow the dramatic coast east to take in the views at Firefly, the beautiful house once home to Noel Coward, when Jamaica was a hub for the jet set in the golden age of Hollywood.

THIS LEG: 155 MILES

One Week

1 Kingston (p54) Dive in to the excitement of Jamaica's lively capital. It's got some of the best restaurants on the island, a reggae heritage that lives on in the live-music scene as well as the Bob Marley Museum and Trench Town Culture Yard, plus the extraordinary collection of the National Gallery of Jamaica.

2 Blue Mountains (p62) Get out of the city and into the cool air of the thickly forested Blue Mountains that overlook Kingston. Enjoy some locally grown coffee, then get up early to hike to the top of Blue Mountain peak – on a clear day you can see all the way to Cuba.

3 Port Antonio (p60) Make like Errol Flynn once did in the old banana centre of Port Antonio, set amid the rugged greenery of Portland Parish. Eat jerk in its spiritual home in nearby Boston Bay, and explore the wilds of gorgeous Reach Falls.

4 Treasure Beach (p73) This is where those in the know go to escape the crowds, a laid-back hideaway tucked into a sweet southern corner of the island. There's a handful of quiet beaches to charm you, and for the adventurous, crocodile-spotting boat trips on the nearby Black River.

5 Negril (p70) Jamaica tourism first made it big here, and you'll understand why when you sit with drink in hand on a seven-mile beach and take in the most famous sunset into the sea in the whole Caribbean. When you're done, finish up in Montego Bay.

THIS LEG: 370 MILES

Jamaica Highlights

1 Best Hike: Blue Mountain Peak (p62) Hike through the rainforest above Kingston for epic views to Cuba.

2 Best Culture: National Gallery of Jamaica (p54) An inspiring art collection in the heart of downtown Kingston.

3 Best History: Falmouth (p69) Take the heritage walking tour of the historic town.

4 Best Music: Reggae Sumfest (p66) Get your reggae on in Montego in July for the island's greatest music festival.

5 Best Natural Wonder: Dunn's River Falls (p63) Wade and climb up the cascading pools of Jamaica's most beautiful waterfall.

Ocho Rios (p63)
ALVARO LEIVA/GETTY IMAGES ©

Discover Jamaica

KINGSTON

POP 780,000

Whether you approach by air or by land, Kingston impresses you with its setting and overwhelms you with its sheer size, noise and traffic. This is the island's cultural and economic heart, where political deals are made, musicians come to follow in the footsteps of the greats, and you can be exposed to squalor and luxury within footsteps of each other. You want 'real' Jamaica? This is it.

Devon House (p56)
DOUGLAS PEARSON/GETTY IMAGES ©

Sights

DOWNTOWN

National Gallery of Jamaica Art Gallery

Map p57 (☎ guided tours 922-1561; www.natgalja.org.jm; 12 Ocean Blvd; admission J$400, 45min guided tour J$2000; ⏰10am-4:30pm Tue-Thu, to 4pm Fri, to 3pm Sat) The superlative collection of Jamaican art housed by the National Gallery is the finest on the island and should on no account be missed. As well as offering a distinctly Jamaican take on international artistic trends, the collection attests to the vitality of the country's artistic heritage as well as its present.

Trench Town Culture Yard Community Project

Trench Town, which began life as a much-prized housing project erected by the British in the 1930s, is widely credited as the birthplace of ska, rocksteady and reggae music. It has been immortalized in numerous reggae songs, not least Bob Marley's 'No Woman No Cry,' the poignant anthem penned by Marley's mentor, Vincent 'Tata' Ford, in a tiny bedroom at what is now the **Trench Town Museum** (**☎ 859-6741; www.trenchtowncultureyard.com; 6-10 Lower First St; yard & museum J$1000, with guided neighborhood tour J$1500; ⏰8am-6pm**).

UPTOWN

Bob Marley Museum Museum

Map p58 (☎ 876-927-9152; www.bobmarley-foundation.com/museum.html; 56 Hope Rd; adult/child J$2000/1000; ⏰9:30am-4pm Mon-Sat) The large, creaky, colonial-era wooden house on Hope Rd, where Bob Marley lived and recorded from 1975 until his death in 1981,

Jamaica

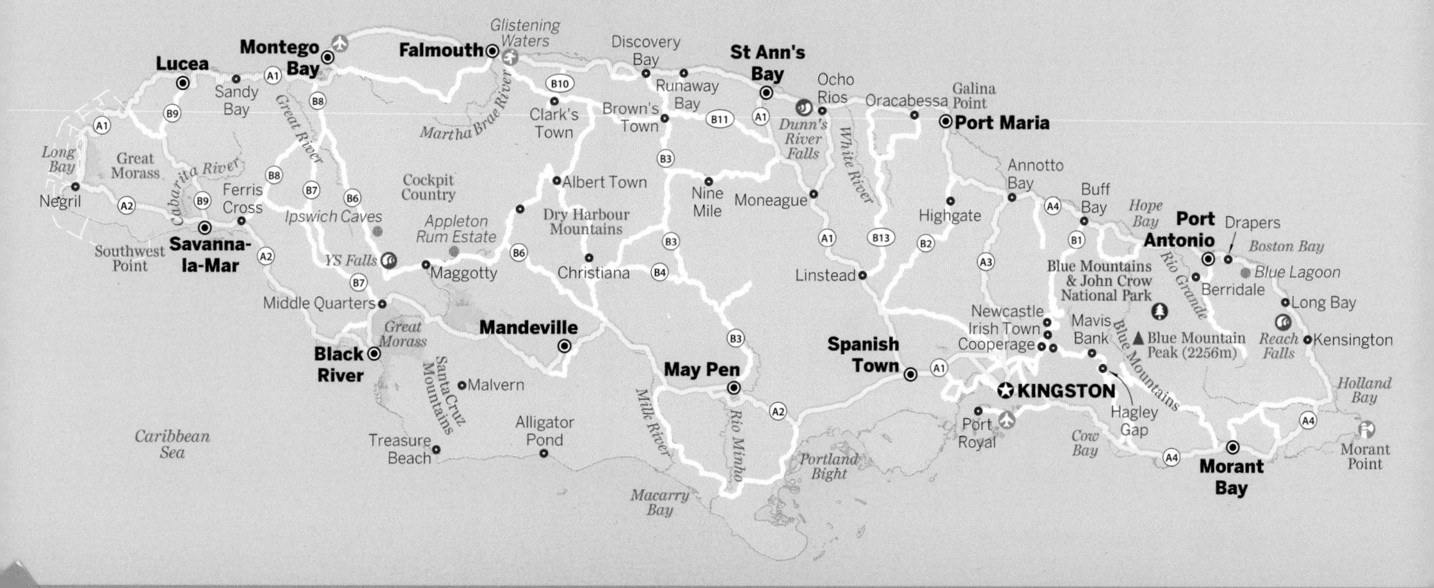
0 30 km
0 15 miles
Caribbean Sea
Glistening Waters
Lucea
Montego Bay
Falmouth
Discovery Bay
St Ann's Bay
Ocho Rios
Oracabessa
Galina Point
Port Maria
Sandy Bay
Runaway Bay
Brown's Town
Clark's Town
Martha Brae River
Great River
Long Bay
Great Morass
Cabarita River
Negril
Ferris Cross
Savanna-la-Mar
Southwest Point
Ipswich Caves
Cockpit Country
Appleton Rum Estate
YS Falls
Maggotty
Albert Town
Dry Harbour Mountains
Christiana
Nine Mile
Moneague
Dunn's River Falls
White River
Linstead
Highgate
Annotto Bay
Buff Bay
Hope Bay
Port Antonio
Drapers
Boston Bay
Blue Lagoon
Berridale
Rio Grande
Long Bay
Reach Falls
Kensington
Blue Mountains & John Crow National Park
Blue Mountain Peak (2256m)
Blue Mountains
Newcastle
Irish Town
Cooperage
Mavis Bank
Hagley Gap
KINGSTON
Port Royal
Cow Bay
Morant Bay
Holland Bay
Morant Point
Spanish Town
May Pen
Rio Minho
Milk River
Portland Bight
Macarry Bay
Middle Quarters
Great Morass
Mandeville
Black River
Santa Cruz Mountains
Malvern
Treasure Beach
Alligator Pond
Caribbean Sea
A1
A2
A3
A4
B1
B2
B3
B4
B6
B7
B8
B9
B10
B11
B13

is the city's most-visited site. Today the house functions as a tourist attraction, museum and shrine, and much remains as it was in Marley's day.

Devon House Museum
Map p58 (☎929-6602; www.devonhousejamaica.com; 26 Hope Rd; admission J$700; ⏱9am-4:30pm Tue-Sat) This beautiful colonial house was built in 1881 by George Stiebel, the first black millionaire in Jamaica. Antique lovers will enjoy the visit, whose highlights include some very ornate porcelain chandeliers. Note the trompe l'œil of palms in the entrance foyer and the roundabout chairs, designed to accommodate a man wearing a sword. Amid the grand surroundings, Stiebel even managed to discreetly tuck a gambling room away in the attic. Admission includes a mandatory guided tour.

Sleeping

Reggae Hostel Hostel **$**
(☎920-1596; www.reggaehostel.com; 8 Burlington Ave; dm US$15-30 d US$70; P ❄ @ 📶) Close to Halfway Tree, this excellent hostel has a relaxed, friendly vibe. Dorms are simple, with fans, while private rooms (one with its own bathroom) are spacious and have air-con. There's a communal kitchen, patio bar (with Sunday barbecue), and helpful staff. Highly sociable if you're looking for people to hook up with to go to a dancehall street party or weekend beach trip.

Mikuzi Guest House Guesthouse **$**
(☎978-4859, 813-0098; www.mikuzijamaica.com; 5 Upper Montrose Rd; r US$50-80, ste US$90; P ❄ 📶) Friendly, yellow colonial-era guesthouse with comfortable rooms – all bright colors and funky furnishings, most with kitchenettes. All but the 'backpacker rooms' have air-con. There's a cushion-strewn gazebo in the lush garden for relaxing in. It's just off Hope Rd, a stone's throw from the Bob Marley Museum, and has a sister outfit near Port Antonio.

Spanish Court Hotel Boutique Hotel **$$$**
Map p58 (☎926-0000; www.spanishcourthotel.com; 1 St Lucia Ave; r US$239-245, ste US$282-1212; P ❄ @ 📶 🏊) A favorite with the discerning business elite. Modern rooms have Jamaican-designed furniture and come with iPod docks. Relaxation options

Ports of Call

MONTEGO BAY

- Achieve tanning Zen at Doctor's Cave.
- Wince at the overproof rum in the Reggae Bar.
- Dive some serious sea walls at the Point.

OCHO RIOS

- Funk up the scene at friendly Turtle Beach.
- Pay tribute to Brother Bob at his birthplace in Nine Mile.
- Climb with dozens more to the legendary cascades of Dunn's River Falls.

FALMOUTH

- Soak in the atmosphere of Jamaica's best-preserved historic town.
- Take a food-themed walking tour for the best in local cuisine.

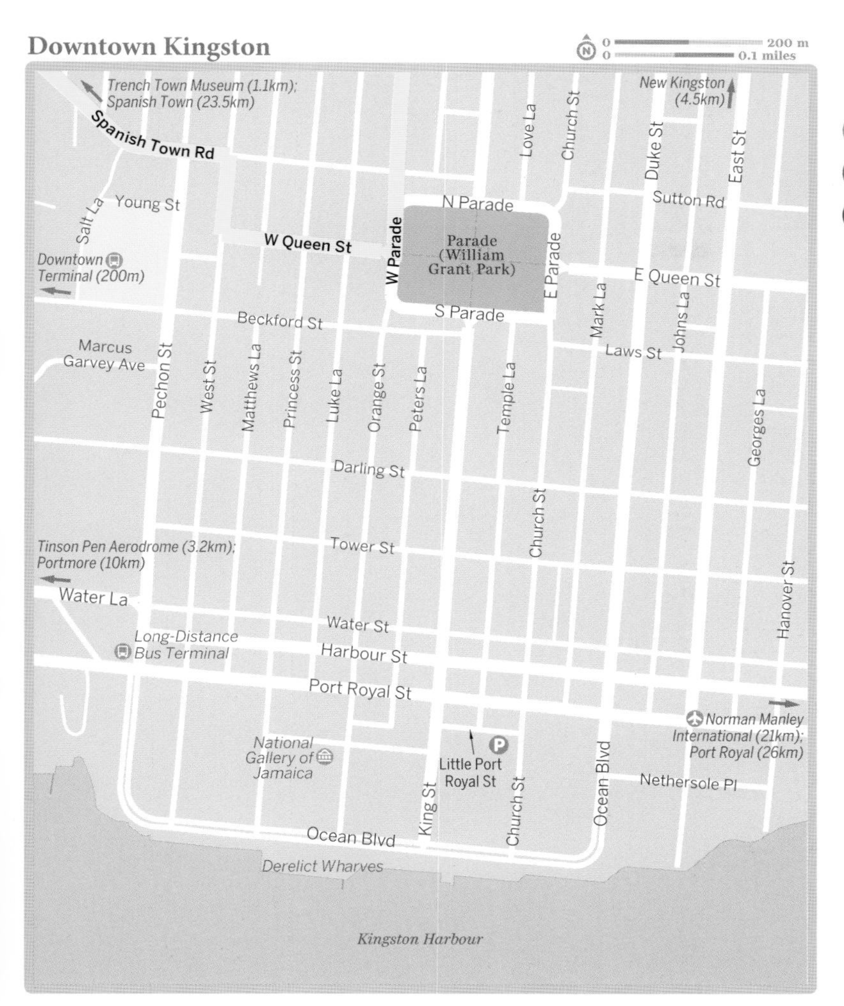

include the rooftop pool, gym and a spa with a full range of treatments. The Gallery Café serves a selection of gourmet coffees and snacks, while the restaurant has beautifully presented international and Jamaican dishes.

Eating

Sweetwood Jerk — Jerk $

Map p58 (Knutsford Blvd; jerk from J$400; lunch & dinner) This lively jerk center, opposite Pegasus Hotel, is popular with Uptown office staff and gets particularly busy after work. Spicy, flavorful meaty offerings can be enjoyed in the outdoor sitting area facing Emancipation Park. Accompaniments include festival, sweet potato and particularly good fried breadfruit. This is one of the few jerk joints in Jamaica to feature jerk lamb.

Sonya's Homestyle Cooking — Jamaican $$

Map p58 (968-6267; 17 Central Ave; mains around J$1200; 6:30am-6pm Mon-Fri, 7:30am-6pm Sat, 8:30am-7pm Sun) Famous for big

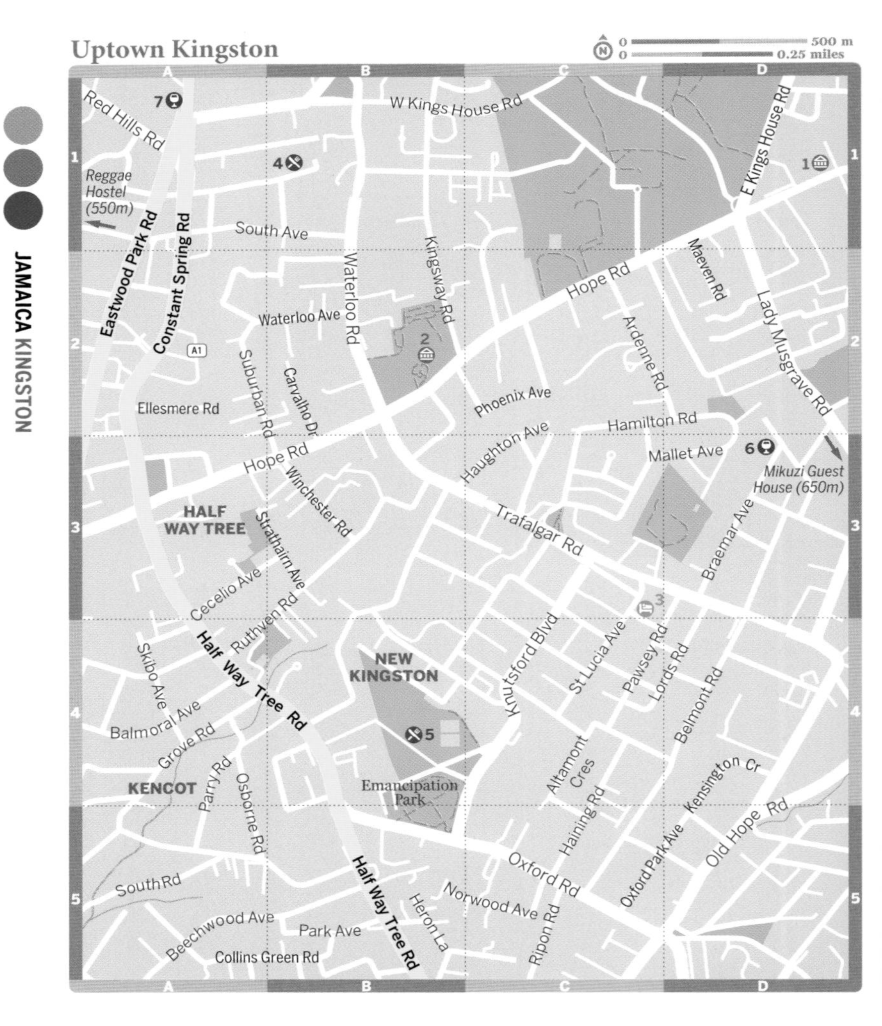

traditional Jamaican breakfasts, washed down with fresh juices; the Sunday buffet (8:30am to midday) is particularly popular. For lunches and early dinner, there's good pepper pot soup, curry goat, oxtail and beans, stew pork and fry chicken.

Drinking & Entertainment

Red Bones Blues Café Bar
Map p58 (www.facebook.com/RedbonesBlues-Cafe; 1 Argyle St; 11am-1am Mon-Fri, 7pm-1am Sat) This could easily become your favorite Kingston spot – it's a hip open-air bar with cool ambience and great music. There are quality live bands throughout the week, including blues, jazz and reggae, showcasing well-chosen local and international talent, as well as regular poetry slams. Oh, and the food is great too.

Tracks & Records Bar
Map p58 (906-3903; www.facebook.com/UBTracks; Market Pl, 67 Constant Spring Rd; 11:30am-11:30pm) Music meets athletics

Uptown Kingston

Sights
1 Bob Marley Museum D1
2 Devon House B2

Sleeping
3 Spanish Court Hotel C3

Eating
4 Sonya's Homestyle Cooking B1
5 Sweetwood Jerk B4

Drinking & Nightlife
6 Red Bones Blues Café D3
7 Tracks & Records A1

at this doubly-punning sports bar owned by Usain Bolt. The atmosphere is lively, with plenty of drinks and bar food, plus some surprisingly good karaoke, and live music on 'Behind the Screens' Tuesday.

Information

Dangers & Annoyances

Avoid Kingston during periods of political tension, when localized violence can spontaneously erupt. Most murders are drug-related or politically inspired and occur in the shantytowns of West Kingston. Parts of Spanish Town are heavily affected by gang violence. Beware of pickpocketing, especially at the market. Stick to the main streets – if in doubt ask your hotel concierge or manager to point out the trouble areas.

Emergency

Police (**922-9321**); headquarters (**11 East Queen St**); Half Way Tree (**142 Maxfield Ave**); Cross Roads (**Brentford Rd**)

Medical Services

Andrews Memorial Hospital (**926-7401; 27 Hope Rd**) Well-equipped private hospital with well-stocked pharmacy.

Getting There & Around

Air

Norman Manley International Airport (p76), 27km southeast of downtown, handles international flights.

Bus

Buses, coasters and route taxis run between Kingston and every point on the island. They arrive and depart from the **bus station** (**Beckford St**).

Essential Food & Drink

Jerk Jamaica's most well-known dish, jerk is actually a cooking method: smother food in a tongue-searing marinade, then smoke over a wood fire.

Seafood Snapper and parrotfish are popular. A favorite dish is escoveitched fish; pickled in vinegar then fried and simmered with peppers and onions.

Breadkinds A catchall term for starchy sides, from plantains and yam to pancake-shaped cassava bread (bammy) and johnnycakes (fried dumplings).

Saltfish & Ackee Jamaica's national dish, and a delicious breakfast besides. Ackee is a fleshy, somewhat bland fruit; saltfish is, well, salted fish. When mixed together they're delicious, somewhat resembling scrambled eggs.

Brown stew Not a soup, brown stew is another popular method of cooking that involves simmering meat, fish or vegetables in savory-sweet sauce.

Patties Baked pastry shells filled with spicy beef, chicken, vegetables or fish. Cheap and filling.

Rum Clear and light white rums, flavored rums, brain-bashing overproof rums (rum over 151 proof), deep dark rums, and the rare amber nectar of the finest premium rums.

Comfortable Knutsford Express (p77) buses run from its own bus terminal in New Kingston to Ocho Rios (J$1600, two hours) and Montego Bay (J$2450, four hours).

Car

Reputable companies with offices at Norman Manley International airport:

Avis (924-8293; www.avis.com)

Island Car Rentals (924-8075; www.islandcarrentals.com)

NORTHERN JAMAICA

Port Antonio

Cupping an unruffled bay and backing into the sleepy Rio Grande valley, Port Antonio is the perfect capital for Portland. The parish's only sizable town is largely untarnished by the duty-free, tourist-overfriendliness of Ocho Rios or Montego Bay.

Sights

Port Antonio's heart is the main square at the junction of West and Harbour Sts. It's centered on a **clock tower** and backed by a handsome red-brick Georgian **courthouse**. On the west side of the square is the clamorous and colorful **Musgrave Market**. Fort George St leads to the Titchfield Peninsula, where you'll find several dozen Victorian-style gingerbread houses.

Sleeping

Ivanhoe's Guesthouse $
(993-3043; 9 Queen St; r US$50-65;) Fantastic views across the whole of Port Antonio from breezy verandas, spotless white rooms and bargain rates are the hallmarks of this spot, the oldest guesthouse on historic Titchfield Hill. Meals are cooked to order.

DeMontevin Lodge Guesthouse $
(993-2604; 21 Fort George St; d US$50, d with shared bathroom US$40) This venerable

Left: Doctor's Cave Beach (p65)
Below: Rafting the Rio Grande Valley (p62)
(LEFT) HOLGER LEUE/GETTY IMAGES ©; (BELOW) DOUG PEARSON/GETTY IMAGES ©

Victorian guesthouse has a homey ambience that blends modern kitsch and antiques – the place could almost be the setting of a tropical Sherlock Holmes novel. The simple bedrooms (six with private bathrooms) are timeworn, but clean as a whistle.

Eating

Survival Beach Restaurant Jamaican $
(24 Allan Ave; mains US$5-10; breakfast, lunch & dinner;) In addition to the usual local fare, natural juices and the best jelly coconut in town, this choice shack serves a tasty dish made with coconut milk, pumpkin, Irish potato, garlic, scallion, thyme, okra, string beans and three kinds of peas, served with sides of cabbage and callaloo. Just ask for the vital I-tal stew.

Dickie's Best Kept Secret Fusion $$
(809-6276; dinner US$20-40; dinner) Dickie's – a tiny pointy-roofed seaside hut on western outskirts of Port Antonio – offers enormous five-course meals in rooms best described as Bob Marley meets Alice in Wonderland. They'll cook almost anything you want (provided they have the ingredients) but trust their suggestion – that anything will be delicious. Reservations essential.

Getting There & Around

A **transportation center** (Gideon Ave) extends along the waterfront. Buses, coasters and route taxis leave regularly for Port Maria (where you change for Ocho Rios) and Kingston.

Around Port Antonio

RIO GRANDE VALLEY

The Rio Grande rushes down from the Blue Mountains through a deeply cut gorge to the sea. The region is popular for **hiking**, but trails are confusing and demanding and should not be attempted without a guide.

Rafting is also a big draw. Passengers make the three-hour, 9.5km journey on poled bamboo rafts from Grant's Level or Rafter's Village, just east of Berridale, all the way to St Margaret's Bay. En route you'll pass through Lovers Lane, a moss-covered narrow stream where you're supposed to kiss and make a wish. Try **Rio Grande Experience** (993-5778; Berridale; per raft US$65).

BLUE LAGOON

The waters that launched Brooke Shields' movie career (and the site of a less-famous Jacques Cousteau dive), the Blue Lagoon, 11km east of Port Antonio, is by any measure one of the most beautiful spots in Jamaica. The 55m-deep 'Blue Hole' (as it is known locally) opens to the sea through a narrow funnel, but is fed by freshwater springs that come in at a depth of about 40m. Its color changes through every shade of jade and emerald during the day.

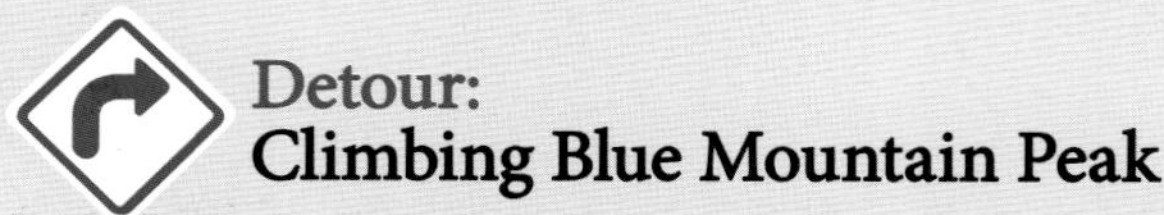

Detour: Climbing Blue Mountain Peak

Looming over Kingston, the crags and fern forests of the Blue Mountains seem light years from the capital's gritty streetscape. Here you can hike old Maroon trails, search for the streamertail hummingbird (Jamaica's national bird) or simply perch on a mountaintop, watching the valleys unfold out of the mist below.

By far the most popular hike is the steep, well-maintained trail to Blue Mountain Peak. From Penlyne Castle to the summit (2256m) is a 950m ascent and a three- or four-hour hike one way. It's not a serious challenge, but you need to be reasonably fit.

Overnighting at the Rasta-run **Jah B's Guesthouse** (377-5206; bobotamo@yahoo.com; dm/r J$20/30; P), the base for hikes to the peak, most hikers set off from Hagley Gap. It's about 12km away and you need to depart around 2am to reach the peak for sunrise. The first part of the trail – a series of steep, scree-covered switchbacks named Jacob's Ladder – is the toughest; following this painful bit of hiking it's basically a long, grinding ascent. You should arrive at the peak around 5:30am, while it's still dark. As the sun rises (and if the weather's clear) you can see Cuba, 144km away.

Don't hike without a guide at night. Numerous spur trails lead off and it's easy to get lost. Although hiking boots or tough walking shoes are best, sneakers will suffice, though your feet will likely get wet. At the top, temperatures can approach freezing before sunrise, so wear plenty of layers. Rain gear is essential, as the weather can change rapidly.

The area is part of the Blue Mountains and John Crown National Park, administered by the **Jamaica Conservation & Development Trust** (960-2848; www.jcdt.org.jm; 29 Dumbarton Ave, Kingston 10, who collect the US$5 park fee. From Kingston, head to Papine, from where Gordon Town Rd (B1) leads into the mountains. Follow the road past Mavis Bank (served by minibuses) and Hagley Gap. Penlyne Castle is reached via a 5km dirt road that ascends precipitously from Hagley Gap. Only 4WD vehicles with low-gear option can handle the dauntingly narrow and rugged road.

BOSTON BAY

Boston Bay is mainly known as the birthplace, and exemplar, of the art of jerk. Heavenly smelling chicken and pork sizzle away on smoky barbecue pits along the roadside.

One of the most unusual accommodations in Jamaica, **Great Huts** (**353-3388; www.greathuts.com; Boston Beach Lane; African-style hut per person US$55-80, treehouse US$163-255;**) perches on a scenic crag overlooking Boston Bay. There are four huts and tree houses, lavishly designed with Afrocentric flair. These two-story, open-air structures are romantic as hell.

REACH FALLS

All of Jamaica's tumbling cascades are refreshing, but this waterfall is downright rejuvenating. This peaceful spot is surrounded by virgin rainforest and features a series of cascades tumbling over limestone tiers from one hollowed, jade-colored pool to another.

Once you enter the **falls** (**adult/child US$10/5; 8:30am-4:30pm Wed-Sun**) a guide will offer his services. This is actually pretty crucial if you want to climb to the top pools, which we highly recommend.

A charter taxi from Port Antonio costs about US$60 round-trip.

Ocho Rios

In spite of sometimes feeling like a theme park, with cruise ships disgorging hordes of passengers, the area around the third-largest town in Jamaica features some of the most beautiful (and popular) natural attractions on the island. Along the north coast you will find pleasant white-sand beaches, clear waters, spectacular waterfalls and lush mountainous terrain.

Beaches

The main beach of Ocho Rios, popular with tourists, is the long crescent known variously as **Turtle Beach** and **Ocho Rios Bay** (**admission J$200; 8am-5pm**), stretching east from the Turtle Towers condominiums to the Renaissance Jamaica Grande Resort, fenced off and topped with barbed wire. There are changing rooms and palms for shade. **Fisherman's Beach** FREE has colorful fishing boats and eateries with fresh fish.

Sights

Dunn's River Falls Waterfall
(**876 974-2857; www.dunnsriverfallsja.com; adult/child US$20/12; 8:30am-4pm Sat-Tue, 7am-4pm Wed-Fri**) These famous falls, 3km west of town, are Jamaica's top-grossing tourist attraction. Great throngs of people can sometimes make it seem more like a theme park than a natural wonder, but this doesn't make the climb up the falls any less exhilarating. You clamber up great tiers of limestone that step down 180m in a series of beautiful cascades and pools. The water is refreshingly cool, with everything shaded by tall rainforest.

Activities

Virtually the entire shoreline east of Ocho Rios to Galina Point is fringed by a reef, and it's great for **snorkeling** and **diving**.

Resort Divers Diving
(**881-5760; www.resortdivers.com; Royal DeCameron Club Caribbean, Runaway Bay; 1-/2-tank dive US$50/95, snorkeling US$30**)

Tours

Chukka Caribbean Adventure Tours Adventure Tour
(**972-2506; www.chukkacaribbean.com/jamaica; tour incl lunch/high tea US$29/39**) Established adventure specialist offering horseback-riding tours, river tubing, zip-line canopy tours, ATV safaris, trips to Bob Marley's birthplace at Nine Mile and even dog-sleigh tours.

Sleeping

Reggae Hostel Guesthouse $
(**974-2607; www.reggaehostel.com; 19 Main St; r US$60, dm US$20;** P) A new offshoot of the popular Kingston hostel, this relaxed guesthouse is perfectly located in the centre of Ocho Rios. There's a good

mix of simple private rooms (air-con) and dorms (fan only), and a rooftop bar and lounge area that's ideal for socializing. The manager is a font of local knowledge for backpacker-friendly excursions.

Hibiscus Lodge Hotel **$$**
(974-2676; www.hibiscusjamaica.com; 83 Main St; r US$150-192; P) A stairway descends alongside a cliff overhang, past flowering gardens overflowing with bougainvillea, and down to a private sunning deck, perfect for a spontaneous jump in the sea. A small gallery of contemporary Jamaican art complements the main building. Rooms are modestly furnished; deluxe ones are worth the extra expense for the large private balconies. There's also a breezy bar and the **Almond Tree** (974-2813; Hibiscus Lodge, 83 Main St; meals J$1200-3000; breakfast, lunch & dinner) restaurant.

Eating

Ocho Rios Jerk Centre Jerk **$**
(974-2549; 16 DaCosta Dr; meals J$550-1000; lunch & dinner) Its deserved popularity further boosted by it being the official Knutsford Express stop, the liveliest jerk joint in town serves excellent jerk pork (J$390), chicken (J$390) and conch (J$850), as well as BBQ ribs. There are daily specials, the best being curry goat (J$450) and goat head soup (J$100). Grab a Red Stripe and watch sports on the big-screen TV while you're waiting for your jerk. 'Spicy Fridays' feature weekly DJ sets (free entry) and the last Friday of the month is Retro/Soca Nite.

Passage to India Indian **$$$**
(795-3182; Soni's Plaza, 50 Main St; meals J$1800-3200; lunch & dinner Tue-Sun, lunch Mon;) On the rooftop of a duty-free shopping center, offering respite from the crowds below in addition to very good northern Indian fare. The naan is crisp, the lassis flavorful, the curries sharp, and the menu divided into extensive chicken, mutton, seafood and vegetarian sections. Tandoori options are also on offer.

Drinking & Entertainment

Amnesia Dancehall
(876 974-2633; 70 Main St; admission J$350-550; Wed-Sun) A classic Jamaican dancehall, this remains the happening

Fruit stall, Boston Bay (p63)

scene. Theme nights include an oldies jam on Sunday, ladies' night on Thursday and an after-work party on Friday. It all leads up to Saturday's dress-to-impress all-night dance marathon. Expect lots of sweat, a tightly packed dance floor and some of the raunchiest dancing you've ever seen.

Shopping

Harmony Hall Art

(975-4222; www.harmonyhall.com; 10am-5:30pm Tue-Sun) Art gallery featuring the best of local art, located 7km east of Ocho Rios. Renowned for its Christmas, Easter and mid-November craft fairs, and regular exhibitions.

Information

There are numerous banks along Main St, including Scotiabank. All have foreign-exchange facilities and ATMs.

Tourist Information (974-7705; Shop 3, Ocean Village, Main St; 9am-5pm Mon-Thu, to 4pm Fri) Represents the Jamaica Tourist Board. Staff can help you suss out Ochi's transportation, lodging and attractions options.

Getting There & Away

Buses, minibuses and route taxis arrive and depart Ocho Rios at the transportation center (Evelyn Rd). During daylight hours there are frequent departures for Kingston and destinations along the north coast; there are fewer departures on Sunday. There is no set schedule and they depart when full. Knutsford Express (www.knutsfordexpress.com) has scheduled departures to Kingston (J$1200, two hours) and Montego Bay (J$1200, two hours).

Getting Around

Minibuses and route taxis ply Main St and the coast road (J$80 for short hauls, J$150 to Boscobel or Mammee Bay).

Around Ocho Rios

NINE MILE

In theory, **Nine Mile Museum** (999-7003; www.ninemilejamaica.com; admission J$1900; 9:30am-4:30pm) could be such a great attraction. The plain two-room house where Marley spent his early years is touching, as is his marble mausoleum, with its candles, Bible and stained-glass windows. Unfortunately, the site's relentless plastic commercialization, and the hoary tales from guides grubbing for tips, may quickly depress the casual visitor, and upset those who ever got a spiritual lift from the man's music. Adjust your expectations accordingly.

FIREFLY

Set amid wide lawns high atop a hill 5km east of Oracabessa, **Firefly** (997-7201, 994-0920; admission J$847; 9am-5pm Mon-Thu & Sat) was the home of Sir Noel Coward, the English playwright, songwriter, actor and wit. On display are Coward's original paintings and photographs of himself and a coterie of famous friends. The views take in Port Maria Bay and the coastline further west. Coward lies buried beneath a plain white marble slab on the wide lawns where he entertained stars of stage and screen.

MONTEGO BAY & AROUND

Montego Bay

There's a good chance MoBay (as everyone calls it) will be your introduction to Jamaica – some 80% of travelers choose the country's second-largest city as their port of entry. Montego has made an interesting progression from local port to tourist-packaged commodity to an intriguing, if not terribly attractive, blend of both.

Beaches

Doctor's Cave Beach Beach

(952-2566; www.doctorscavebathingclub.com; adult/child US$6/3; 8:30am-sunset) It may sound like a rocky hole inhabited by lab-coated troglodytes, but this is actually Montego Bay's most famous beach. A pretty arc of sugary sand fronts a deep-blue gem studded with floating dive platforms and speckled with tourists sighing happily. Er, *lots* of tourists – and a fair few Jamaicans as well. The upside is an admission charge keeps out most of the beach hustlers.

Cornwall Beach Beach

(979-0102; www.cornwallbeachja.com; admission $J350; 8am-6pm) Cornwall Beach has the most coolness cred out of Montego's beaches – if you're looking for a beach that feels like the spot where the cool locals hang out (well, the cool locals willing to shell out $J350), this is your spot. There's a nice shallow shelf for snorkeling, clear water for swimming and white sand for you to look good on. Every Wednesday an (open bar) beach party goes down here from 9pm til *oh-god-is-that-the-sun?*

Sights

Church Street Street

Many of the most interesting buildings in town are clustered along Church St, the most picturesque street in MoBay, although you shouldn't expect a quiet historic district – this thoroughfare is as alive and chaotic as anywhere else downtown.

Activities

For advanced divers, the **Point** north of the airport has a good wall dive. **Airport Reef**, off the southwestern edge of the airport, is considered by some to be the best site on the island, with masses of coral canyons, caves and tunnels and a DC-3 wreck that's become a multicolored fish mansion.

Besides boasting the sort of name you'd expect in a *Pirates of the Caribbean* movie, **Widowmakers Cave** is an incredible tunnel filled with sponges, barracuda and clouds of smaller fish that are as colorful as candy wrappers.

Resort Divers Diving

(973-6131; www.resortdivers.com; 2 Gloucester Ave; 1/2-tank dive US$50/95)

Festivals & Events

Montego Bay's most celebrated events are its two high-profile music festivals.

Jamaica Jazz & Blues Festival Music

(www.jamaicajazzandblues.com) Brings internationally acclaimed acts to Cinnamon Hill, near Rose Hall, in late January for three nights of music under the stars.

Red Stripe Reggae Sumfest Music

(www.reggaesumfest.com) Jamaica's premier reggae festival typically includes more than 50 world-class reggae artists. Held in July.

Sleeping

Polkerris B&B B&B $$

(876-877-7784; www.polvista.com; 31 Corniche Rd; r US$165-175; P) The best B&B in Jamaica? Maybe. The best B&B in Montego Bay? No question. Hanging above the Hip Strip like a beautiful apparition, Polkerris, run by a British expat and his Jamaican wife, is sublime in every detail.

There's the trickling waterfall, the inviting swimming pool, the view-embellished veranda, the stupendous breakfast and – most importantly – the one-of-the-family style service that

Montego Bay

Sights

1 Cornwall Beach B3
2 Doctor's Cave Beach B4

Activities, Courses & Tours

3 Montego Bay Yacht Club A6
4 Resort Divers C3

Sleeping

5 Polkerris B&B C4
6 Richmond Hill Inn D5

Eating

7 Nyam 'n' Jam B2
8 Pelican B4
9 Pork Pit C4

Drinking & Nightlife

10 Reggae Bar B4

Shopping

11 Fantasy Craft Market C3
12 Fort Montego Craft Market A1
13 Harbour Street Craft Market A2

Montego Bay

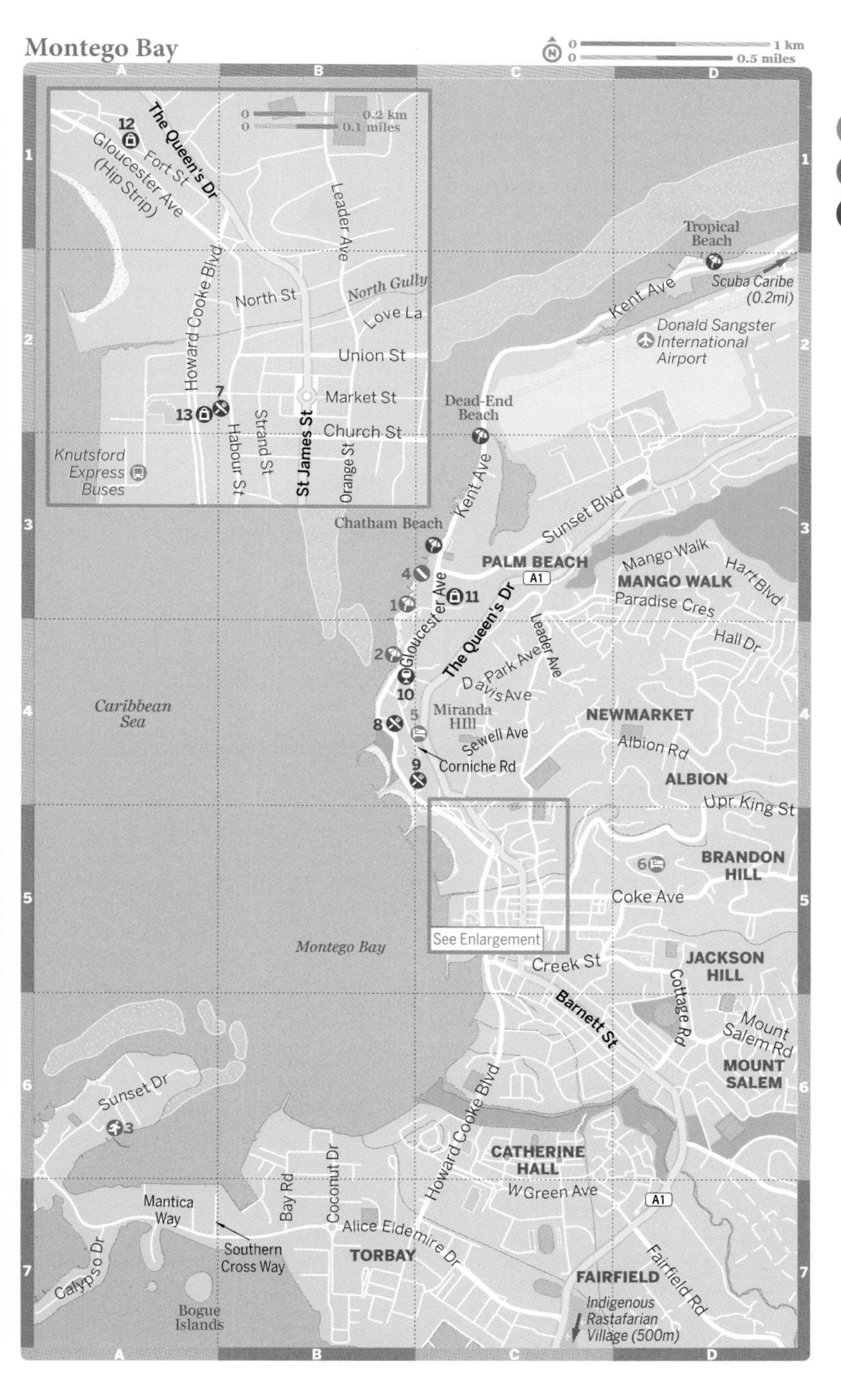

0 1 km
0 0.5 miles
0 0.2 km
0 0.1 miles
12
The Queen's Dr
Gloucester Ave (Hip Strip)
Fort St
Leader Ave
Howard Cooke Blvd
North St
North Gully
Love La
Union St
Market St
7
13
Church St
Habour St
Strand St
St James St
Orange St
Knutsford Express Buses
Tropical Beach
Scuba Caribe (0.2mi)
Kent Ave
Donald Sangster International Airport
Dead-End Beach
Sunset Blvd
Chatham Beach
PALM BEACH
A1
Mango Walk
MANGO WALK
Hart Blvd
Paradise Cres
Hall Dr
4
11
1
2
10
Gloucester Ave
The Queen's Dr
Park Ave
Leader Ave
Davis Ave
Miranda Hill
Sewell Ave
Corniche Rd
8
5
9
NEWMARKET
Albion Rd
ALBION
Upr King St
Caribbean Sea
6
BRANDON HILL
Coke Ave
See Enlargement
Montego Bay
Creek St
JACKSON HILL
Barnett St
Cottage Rd
Mount Salem Rd
MOUNT SALEM
Sunset Dr
3
Howard Cooke Blvd
CATHERINE HALL
W Green Ave
A1
Mantica Way
Bay Rd
Coconut Dr
Alice Eldemire Dr
Southern Cross Way
TORBAY
Calypso Dr
FAIRFIELD
Fairfield Rd
Bogue Islands
Indigenous Rastafarian Village (500m)

reminds you warmly that you're in the real Jamaica.

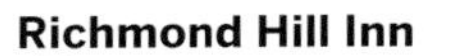

Richmond Hill Inn Hotel $$

(☎952-3859; www.richmond-hill-inn.com; Union St; s/d/ste US$85/115/189; P ❄ 📶 🏊) Stay in a historic Great House within Montego Bay's city limits. This spectacularly located gem atop a small hill once belonged to the Scotch Whiskey heirs and is bedizened with fine local art, antique furniture and the ghosts of prestigious former guests. Richard Nixon and James Bond in his third incarnation (Roger Moore) stayed here. Spacious rooms are a relative bargain.

Eating

Nyam 'n' Jam Jamaican $

(☎876-952-1922; 17 Harbour St; mains J$300-700; ⏰8am-11pm) On the cusp of the craft market, you can retreat into the red glow of a truly authentic Jamaican dining experience with none of the tourist get-out clauses of the Hip Strip. Settle down for snapper with a spicy sauce, jerk chicken or perhaps your first curried goat.

Pork Pit Jerk $

(☎952-1046; 27 Gloucester Ave; mains J$300-800; ⏰11am-11pm) 'Pit' is the operative word at this glorified food shack on the Hip Strip where a half-roasted chef slaves over a blackened barbecue fashioned from bamboo sticks laid over smoking hot coals. Notwithstanding, his meat-cooking travails send a delicious aroma wafting down Gloucester Ave and provide a perfect advert for the Pork Pit's obligatory jerk pork.

Get it scooped straight off the barbecue into a Styrofoam container and sit down at a picnic table under the Pork Pit's 300-year-old cotton tree. It's a MoBay rite of passage.

Pelican Jamaican $$$

(☎952-3171; Gloucester Ave; mains US$12-38; ⏰7am-11pm) Loved by upper-crust Jamaicans and tourists on away-days from the all-inclusive buffets, Pelican is goat-curry heaven, though the oxtail's not bad either. Opened the same year Jamaica gained independence (1962) and armed with the same chef since the early 1980s, this

Rastafarians

Dreadlocked Rastafarians are as synonymous with Jamaica as reggae. Developed in the 1930s, the creed evolved as an expression of poor, black Jamaicans seeking fulfillment, boosted by Marcus Garvey's 'back to Africa' zeal.

Central to Rastafarianism is the concept that the Africans are one of the displaced Twelve Tribes of Israel. Jamaica is Babylon, and their lot is in exile in a land that cannot be reformed. The crowning of Ras Tafari (Haile Selassie) as emperor of Abyssinia in 1930 fulfilled the prophecy of an African king and redeemer who would lead them from exile to the promised land of Zion, the black race's spiritual home.

Ganja smoking is a sacrament for many (if not all) Rastas, allowing them to gain wisdom and inner divinity through the ability to 'reason' more clearly. The parsing of Bible verses is an essential tradition, helping to see through the corrupting influences of Babylon. The growing of dreadlocks is an allegory for the mane of the Lion of Judah.

Despite its militant consciousness, the religion preaches love and nonviolence, and adherents live by strict biblical codes advocating a way of life in harmony with Old Testament traditions. Some Rastas are teetotalers who shun tobacco and keep to a strict diet of vegetarian I-tal food, prepared without salt; others, such as the 12 Tribes Rastafari, eat meat and drink beer.

seminal Hip Strip restaurant has fully earned its right to be called a MoBay institution.

Drinking & Nightlife

Reggae Bar Bar
(Gloucester Ave; noon-midnight) An upstairs bar in a two-story Hip Strip shack where the hustlers take time off from hustling to down a few Red Stripe beers to a back-beat of Bob Marley and the click of pool balls. Cheap, but not at all nasty.

Shopping

Craft Markets Markets
For the largest crafts selection head to the **Harbour Street Craft Market (Harbour St; 7am-7pm)**, which extends for three blocks between Barnett and Market Sts. **Fantasy Craft Market (8am-7pm)**, at the northern end of Gloucester Ave, and **Fort Montego Craft Market (8am-7pm)**, behind the fort, offer less variety and quality. You can expect a hard sell at all of these places, so bring your haggling skills and don't be afraid to walk away from something you don't like.

Information

Visitors can expect to be approached in none-too-subtle terms by locals offering their services (drugs and sex), which gets a bit wearying.

Cornwall Regional Hospital (952-5100; Mt Salem Rd) Has a 24-hour emergency ward.

Getting There & Around

Air

A tourist taxi to/from MoBay's Donald Sangster International Airport to Gloucester Ave costs US$10.

Boat

Cruise ships berth at the Montego Freeport, about 3km south of town. Taxis to downtown MoBay cost US$20.

Bus & Minibus

Comfortable **Knutsford Express (971-1822; www.knutsfordexpress.com)** buses run to Ocho Rios (J$1600, two hours) and Kingston (J$2450, four hours).

Public Transportation

Route taxis, recognizable by their red license plates, charge J$80 for trips between neighborhoods.

Rose Hall to Greenwood

Rose Hall Great House Great House
(953-2323; www.rosehall.com; adult/under 12yr US$20/10; 9am-6pm, last tour 5:15pm) This mansion, with its commanding hilltop position 3km east of Ironshore, is the most famous Great House in Jamaica.

Construction was begun by George Ashe in the 1750s and was completed in the 1770s by John Palmer, a wealthy plantation owner. Palmer and his wife Rose (after whom the house was named) hosted some of the most elaborate social gatherings on the island.

Greenwood Great House Great House
(953-1077; www.greenwoodgreathouse.com; adult/child US$20/10; 9am-6pm) This marvelous estate sits high on a hill 11km east of Ironshore. While the region's main attraction is Rose Hall, visiting Greenwood is a far more intimate and, frankly, interesting experience. The furnishings are more authentic, the tour less breakneck than Rose Hall's, and there's none of the silly ghost stories – although the exterior edifice is admittedly not as impressive.

Falmouth

Few other towns in Jamaica have retained their original architecture to the same degree as Falmouth, which has a faded Georgian splendor – now somewhat overshadowed by its huge cruise-ship dock.

Sights & Activities

Town Center Notable Buildings
The best place to orient yourself is **Water Sq**, at the east end of Duke St. Named for an old stone fountain that pumped freshwater before New York City had any such

luxury. Many of the wooden shop fronts in this area are attractively disheveled relics.

The Victorian market structure on the east side of Water Sq, which dominates central Falmouth, was once the site of slave auctions.

One block east of Water Sq is Seaboard St and the grandiose Georgian **courthouse** in Palladian style, fronted by a double curling staircase and Doric columns, with cannons to the side. The town council presides here.

On Cornwall St one of the most stately edifices is the restored **Baptist Manse** (cnr Market & Cornwall Sts), formerly the residence of nonconformist Baptist preacher William Knibb, who was instrumental in lobbying for passage of the Abolition Bill that ended slavery.

On July 31, 1838, slaves gathered outside **William Knibb Memorial Church** (cnr King & George Sts) for an all-night vigil, awaiting midnight and then the dawn of full freedom (to quote Knibbs: 'The monster is dead'), when slave shackles, a whip and an iron collar were symbolically buried in a coffin.

Falmouth Heritage Walks Ltd Historical

(☎876-407-2245; www.falmouthheritagewalks.com; 4 Lower Harbour St) This excellent Heritage Walking Tour (adult/child US$25/15) is a ramble around Falmouth's small urban grid punctuated with Tropical-Georgian architecture. The Food Tour (adult/child US$45/25) alternates cultural musings with tastings of street food, while the Jewish Cemetery Tour (adult/child US$15/10) visits a cemetery with gravestones etched in Hebrew. Walks usually take place on the days a cruise ship is in port.

Glistening Waters

Located in an estuary near Rock, about 1.6km east of Falmouth, the waters of Glistening Waters glow an eerie green when disturbed at night, due to the presence of microorganisms that produce photochemical reactions when disturbed. Needless to say, the swimming here is awesome, especially on starry nights, when it's hard to tell where the water ends and the sky begins. Half-hour **boat trips** are offered from **Glistening Waters Marina** (☎954-3229; per person US$25; 6:45-8:30pm).

NEGRIL & THE WEST

If the popular tourist image of Jamaica is sun, beach life, rum, sun, sea, sun, diving and sunsets, chances are the popular tourist is thinking of Negril – or thinking in particular of Jamaica's longest swath of sugary white-sand beach at Long Bay (also known as Seven Mile Beach).

Negril

POP 4200

In the 1970s Negril lured hippies with its offbeat beach life to a countercultural Shangri-la where anything went. To some extent anything still goes here, except the innocent – they left long ago.

The gorgeous, 11km-long swath of sand that is Long Bay is still kissed by serene waters into which the sun melts evening after evening in a riot of color. And the easily accessible coral reefs offer some of the best diving in the Caribbean. Yet these undeniable attractions have done just that: attract. In the last three decades Negril has exploded as a tourist venue. With tourism comes the hustle – you're very likely to watch the sunset in the cloying company of a ganja dealer or an aspiring tour-guide-cum-escort.

Beaches

Long Bay Beach

This blindingly white, world-famous, 11km-long beach is Negril's claim to fame. No matter how cynical you are, you gotta admit: this is one beautiful beach. It's a hell of a show: naked Europeans, tattooed Americans, gigolos and hustlers. Water-sports concessions line the beach. By night, music pumps from reggae bars and discos.

Sights & Activities

Negril Lighthouse Lighthouse

(West End Rd; 9am-sunset) FREE The gleaming white, 20m-tall Negril Lighthouse,

5km south of Negril Village, illuminates the westernmost point of Jamaica. Erected in 1894, the lighthouse is now solar powered and flashes every two seconds. The superintendent will gladly lead the way up the 103 stairs for a bird's-eye view of the coast.

Sleeping

Judy House Cottages & Rooms Cottages, Hostel $
(957-0671; judyhousenegril.com; Westland Mountain Rd; dm/s US$20/25;) Offering the seclusion of the Negril of yore, this lush tropical garden on a hill above the West End guards two self-contained cottages with kitchens (US$75 to US$85) and five additional rooms (three singles and a couple of dorms all with shared bathroom) aimed at backpackers on a budget. The luxury here isn't in the gilded bath taps, it's in the unscripted extras.

Blue Cave Castle Hotel $$
(957-4845; www.bluecavecastle.com; West End Rd; s/d US$60/125;) Winner of Negril's 'quirky hotel' prize is this mock castle that sits like a crenellated fortification warding off invaders on the cliffs of the West End. Fourteen fit-for-a-king rooms and a private grassy terrace create a less swashbuckling atmosphere inside. Lots of repeat visitors testify to fine, yet discreet service and a blissful ambiance. There's a swimming cave accessed via a slippery staircase.

Rockhouse Hotel $$$
(957-4373; www.rockhousehotel.com; West End Rd; r/studio/villa US$180/220/410;) One of the West End's most beautiful and well-run hotels, with luxury thatched rondavels (African huts) built of pine and stone, plus studio apartments that dramatically cling to the cliffside above a small cove. Decor is basic yet romantic, with net-draped poster beds and strong Caribbean colors.

Eating & Drinking

Cosmo's Seafood $
(957-4784; Norman Manley Blvd; mains J$300-1000; 10am-11pm) A tatty hippy outpost that sits like an island of good taste amid an ocean of insipid all-inclusive buffets. Cosmo's, in Negril-speak, is a synonym for

Greenwood Great House (p69)

'fantastic seafood.' Eschewing fine-dining for a few rough-hewn beachside tables, the plates of melt-in-your-mouth lobster and curried conch are deliciously spicy.

3 Dives Jerk Centre Jerk $

(☎957-0845; West End Rd; quarter-/half-chicken J$350/600; ⌚noon-midnight) This unimpressive shack, which looks like it'll blow away in the next category one hurricane, serves up what may be the best food in Negril. Let your nose and taste buds be the judge. Feast your eyes on those sizzling lobsters or that smoking jerk and be prepared for a loooong, totally worthwhile, wait. The fresh food is prepared before your eyes!

Norma's on the Beach at Sea Splash Jamaican $$

(☎957-4041; www.seasplash.com/normas-restaurant; Norman Manley Blvd; mains US$15-32; ⌚7:30am-10:30pm) This Negril branch of Norma Shirley's celebrated Jamaican culinary empire seems to have escaped the hype surrounding her Kingston flagship, but the 'new world Caribbean' food at this stylish beach restaurant is just as adventurous. Expect to find the likes of lobster, Cornish game hen, jerk chicken and pasta, as well as tricolor 'rasta pasta.'

Entertainment

Negril's reggae concerts are legendary, with performances every night in peak season, when there's sure to be talent in town. Big-name acts usually perform at **MXIII** (West End Rd), and at **Roots Bamboo** (☎957-4479; Norman Manley Blvd; ⌚Wed & Sun) on Long Bay. You'll see shows advertised on billboards and hear about them from megaphone-equipped cars.

Information

Negril has arguably the worst hustlers in Jamaica. On your first day on the beach they will mark you and approach with a sales pitch for tours, drugs, sex, etc. Most back off after a polite but firm 'no', but some are worryingly aggressive.

While police patrol the beach, and resort owners watch out for tourists, robberies occur in Negril. Don't walk between Long Bay and the West End at night. Try to avoid unlit stretches of beach after dark.

Jamaica Tourist Board/TPDCo (☎957-9314, 957-4803; Times Sq Plaza; ⌚9am-5pm Mon-Fri)

Negril Beach Medical Center (☎957-4888; fax 957-4347; Norman Manley Blvd; ⌚9am-5pm, doctors on call 24hr) Has a lab open 9:30am to 2pm Tuesday and Friday.

Treasure Beach (right)

Getting There & Away

Dozens of coasters and route taxis run between Negril and Montego Bay. The two-hour journey costs about J$400, including changing vehicles in Lucea. Be prepared for a hair-raising ride. Minibuses and route taxis also leave for Negril from Donald Sangster International Airport in Montego Bay (the price is negotiable, but expect to pay about US$10).

A licensed taxi between Montego Bay and Negril will cost at least US$65, but expect drivers to quote ridiculous rates and prepare for a lot of arguing.

Getting Around

Negril stretches along more than 16km of shoreline, and it can be a withering walk. Route taxis cruise Norman Manley Blvd and West End Rd; the fare between any two points should never be more than about J$150.

SOUTHERN JAMAICA

Treasure Beach

You'll be hard-pressed to find a more authentically charming and relaxing place in Jamaica. The sense of remoteness, the easy pace and the graciousness of the local farmers and fisherfolk attract travelers seeking an away-from-it-all, cares-to-the-wind lifestyle.

A bicycle is a good means of getting around quiet Treasure Beach; most hotels and guesthouses rent them out for a small fee. There is one main road connecting all of the beaches, plus many smaller cow paths and dirt trails.

Beaches

At the eastern 'bottom' of Treasure Beach you'll find **Great Bay**, a pretty, rural patchwork of fields and beach; **Jack Spratt Beach**, at the western edge of Jake's Place, is next along as you head north and west; here brightly painted wooden fishing boats are pulled up on the sand and there is invariably a fisherman or two on hand tending the nets. This is the safest beach for swimming.

The next beach to the west is **Frenchman's Beach**, watched over by a landmark 'buttonwood' tree that has long attracted the attention of poets, painters and woodcarvers who ply their wares. It's a great place to arrange trips to the Pelican Bar or Black River.

In the opposite direction from Jake's there's **Calabash Bay Beach**, with a few cook and rum shops and a sandy beach.

Sleeping

Nuestra Casa Guest House Guesthouse $

(965-0152; www.billysbay.com; d US$50;) Nuestra Casa is just gorgeous; it's a pretty house run by the lovely Roger and his mum Lillian, who together with their Jamaican staff are the epitome of hospitality.

Jake's Hotel Hotel $$$

(965-3000, in the UK 020-7440-4360, in the USA 800-688-7678; www.jakeshotel.com; r US$150-395; @) If you haven't been to Jake's, you haven't really been to Treasure Beach. This romance-drenched boutique hotel is the nexus of pretty much everything in the area – cooking courses, yoga classes and mosaic workshops all happen here. Furthermore, it's owned by Jason Henzell, son of film director Perry Henzell who conceived Jamaica's great seminal movie *The Harder They Come* in 1972.

Eating

Jack Sprat Café Fusion $$

(965-3583; mains US$7-20; 10am-11pm) Seafood and pizza aren't obvious bedfellows until you wander into Jack Sprat's, where they dare to put fresh lobster on their thick Italian-style pies. For many it's the start of a beautiful friendship enhanced by the dreamy location (candlelit tables beside a near perfect scimitar of sand) and bohemian interior (a dandy mix of retro reggae posters and old album covers).

Pelican Bar Jamaican **$$**
(**☎354-4218; mains US$5-15; ⏰morning-sunset**) Built on a submerged sandbar 1km out to sea, this thatch-roofed eatery on stilts provides Jamaica's most enjoyable spot for a drink. Getting there is half the fun: hire a local boat captain (you can book passage from Jake's for US$30).

Information

Breds (**☎965-9748; Kingfisher Plaza; ⏰9am-5pm**) Unofficial information center.

Getting There & Around

There is no direct public transport to Treasure Beach from Montego Bay, Negril or Kingston. Most hotels arrange transfers from MoBay for US$80 to US$100.

Black River

The waters of Black River's **Great Morass**, stained by tannins and dark as molasses, are a complex ecosystem and a vital preserve for more than 100 bird species. The morass also forms Jamaica's most significant refuge for crocodiles. Locals take to the waters in dugout canoes, tending funnel-shaped shrimp pots made of bamboo in the traditional manner of their West African forebears.

Tours are offered by **St Elizabeth River Safari** (**☎965-2229, 965-2374; ⏰tours 9am, 11am, 2pm & 3:30pm**) and **Irie Safaris** (**☎965-2211; Riverside Dr; ⏰tours every 90min 9am-4:30pm**) wharfside from a jetty just east of the bus station (Irie can also arrange **kayaking** trips in the area, which we highly recommend). At the time of research tours ran around US$20 to US$30.

SURVIVAL GUIDE

Directory A–Z

Accommodations

Jamaica offers something for all tastes and budgets, from small guesthouses and hotels to luxury resorts. If you're in a family or group, consider one of the hundreds of villas available to rent across the island (visit **Villas in Jamaica** (**☎974-2508, in the USA 800-845-5276; www.villasinjamaica.com**) for more). For better or worse Jamaica was the spawning ground for the all-inclusive resort. Guests pay a set price and (theoretically) pay nothing more once setting foot inside the resort – book in advance to avoid the rack rate.

We generally quote rates for the high season (mid-December to April). At other times rates can be 20% to 60% lower. Accommodations are categorized as follows:

$ less than US$90

$$ US$90 to US$200

$$$ more than US$200

Dangers & Annoyances

Although Jamaica can sometimes carry a fearsome reputation before it, the biggest problem you're likely to encounter is the army of hustlers who harass visitors in and around major tourist centers. Ganja (marijuana) is widely available in Jamaica, and you're almost certain to be approached by hustlers selling it, but be aware that it remains strictly illegal and if you get caught in possession, you will not be getting on your plane home, however small the amount.

Jamaica has an undoubtedly high murder rate, but the vast majority of violent crimes occur in ghettoes far from the tourist centers. Visitors are sometimes the victims of robbery

Practicalities

- **Electricity** 110V, 50Hz; standard US two- or three-pin plugs.
- **Newspapers & Magazines** The *Jamaica Gleaner* is the biggest newspaper, rivaled by the *Jamaica Observer*.
- **Smoking** Banned in public places (including bars and restaurants).
- **Weights & Measures** Metric system.

and scams. Still, the overwhelming majority of visitors will enjoy their vacations without incident.

Food

The following price categories are based on the cost of an average meal.

$ less than US$15

$$ US$15 to US$25

$$$ more than US$25

Gay & Lesbian Travelers

There's a gay scene in Jamaica, but it's an underground affair as the country is a largely homophobic society. Sexual acts between men are punishable by up to 10 years in prison, and many lyrics by big-name dancehall stars could be classified as anti-gay hate speech. Nonetheless, in the more heavily touristed areas, you can find more tolerant attitudes, and hotels that welcome gay travelers, including all-inclusives. Publicly, discretion is important and open displays of affection should be avoided. For more information check out Gay Jamaica Watch **(http://gayjamaicawatch.blogspot.com)** and J-FLAG **(www.jflag.org)**.

Language

English is the official language. The unofficial lingo is patois (*pa*-twah), a musical dialect with a staccato rhythm and cadence, laced with salty idioms and wonderfully witty compressed proverbs.

Money

The unit of currency is the Jamaican dollar (J$). Prices for hotels and valuable items are usually quoted in US dollars, which virtually forms a second currency. ATMs are widespread across the island, and credit cards are widely accepted.

Opening Hours

Bars Around noon until the last guest leaves.

Businesses 8:30am to 4:30pm Monday to Friday.

Restaurants Breakfast dawn to 11am, lunch noon to 2pm, dinner 5:30pm to 11pm.

Shops 8am or 9am to 5pm Monday to Friday, to noon Saturday.

Public Holidays

In addition to holidays observed throughout the region, Jamaica also has the following public holidays:

Ash Wednesday Six weeks before Easter

Labor Day May 23

Emancipation Day August 1

Independence Day August 6

National Heroes' Day October 19

Telephone

Jamaica's country code is ☎876. To call Jamaica from the US, dial ☎1-876 plus the seven-digit local number. From elsewhere dial your country's international dialing code, then ☎876 and the local number.

Black River (left)

DANITA DELIMONT/GETTY IMAGES ©

Below: Fried fish and dumplings (p432); **Right:** Sun-shower in the Blue Mountains (p62)

Visas

For stays of six months or less, no visas are required for citizens of the US, Canada, the EU, Australia, New Zealand, Japan and many Western countries.

 Getting There & Away

Air

The majority of international visitors arrive at Montego Bay's Donald Sangster International Airport (MBJ; ☎952-3124; www.mbjairport.com). In Kingston Norman Manley International Airport (KIN; ☎924-8452; www.nmia.aero) handles international flights. Both are well served by major international carriers from North America and Europe. Air Jamaica (☎922-3460; www.airjamaica.com) has excellent regional connections.

Sea

Jamaica is a popular port of call for cruise ships, who make stop-overs in Ocho Rios, Montego Bay and Falmouth. Yachters frequently visit from North America, docking at Errol Flynn Marina (☎993-3209, 715-6044; www.errolflynnmarina.com; Port Antonio, GPS N 18.168889°, W -76.450556°), Port Antonio, Montego Bay Yacht Club (☎979-8038) or the Royal Jamaican Yacht Club (☎924-8685; www.rjyc.org.jm; Norman Manley Dr, Kingston, GPS N 17.940939°, W -76.764939°), Kingston.

 Getting Around

Air

There are four domestic airports: Tinson Pen Aerodrome in Kingston, Ian Fleming International Airport (formerly Boscobel Airport) near Ocho Rios, Negril Aerodrome, and Ken Jones Aerodrome at Port Antonio. Montego Bay's Donald Sangster International Airport also receives domestic flights. Air Jamaica Express (☎922-3460; www.airjamaica.com) operates scheduled services between Kingston and Montego Bay. TimAir (☎952-2516; www.timair.net) offers air taxi charters.

Bicycle

Mountain bikes and 'beach cruisers' can be rented at most major resorts (US$10 to US$30 per day). Road conditions are hazardous and Jamaican drivers aren't considerate to cycli sts.

Public Transportation

Public transport options are myriad. The simplest are route taxis, cheap communal taxis reaching every part of the country, picking people up en route. Look for white taxis with red plates. 'Coasters' (private minibuses) between towns go when full, and serve virtually every corner of the island. Drivers usually have an unhealthy disregard for speed limits and other road rules. The most reliable (and expensive) way to get between major towns and cities are the air-conditioned buses of **Knutsford Express** (☎971-1822; **www.knutsfordexpress.com**).

Ferry

At the time of writing, a new tourist ferry between Ocho Rios, Montego Bay and Negril had just been announced, with services expected to commence by mid-2015.

Car

Car hire is a great way to explore Jamaica. All major car-rental agencies operate in Jamaica (with desks at international airports), plus many local firms. Rates begin at around US$45 per day, rising in high season. Most companies offer unlimited mileage, and accept deposits by credit card. Renters must be at least 21 years of age, and have a valid driver's license from their home country.

Drive on the left side of the road. Main roads are in reasonable condition, but secondary roads can often be poor. Beware other road users; driving is frequently bad and often dangerous.

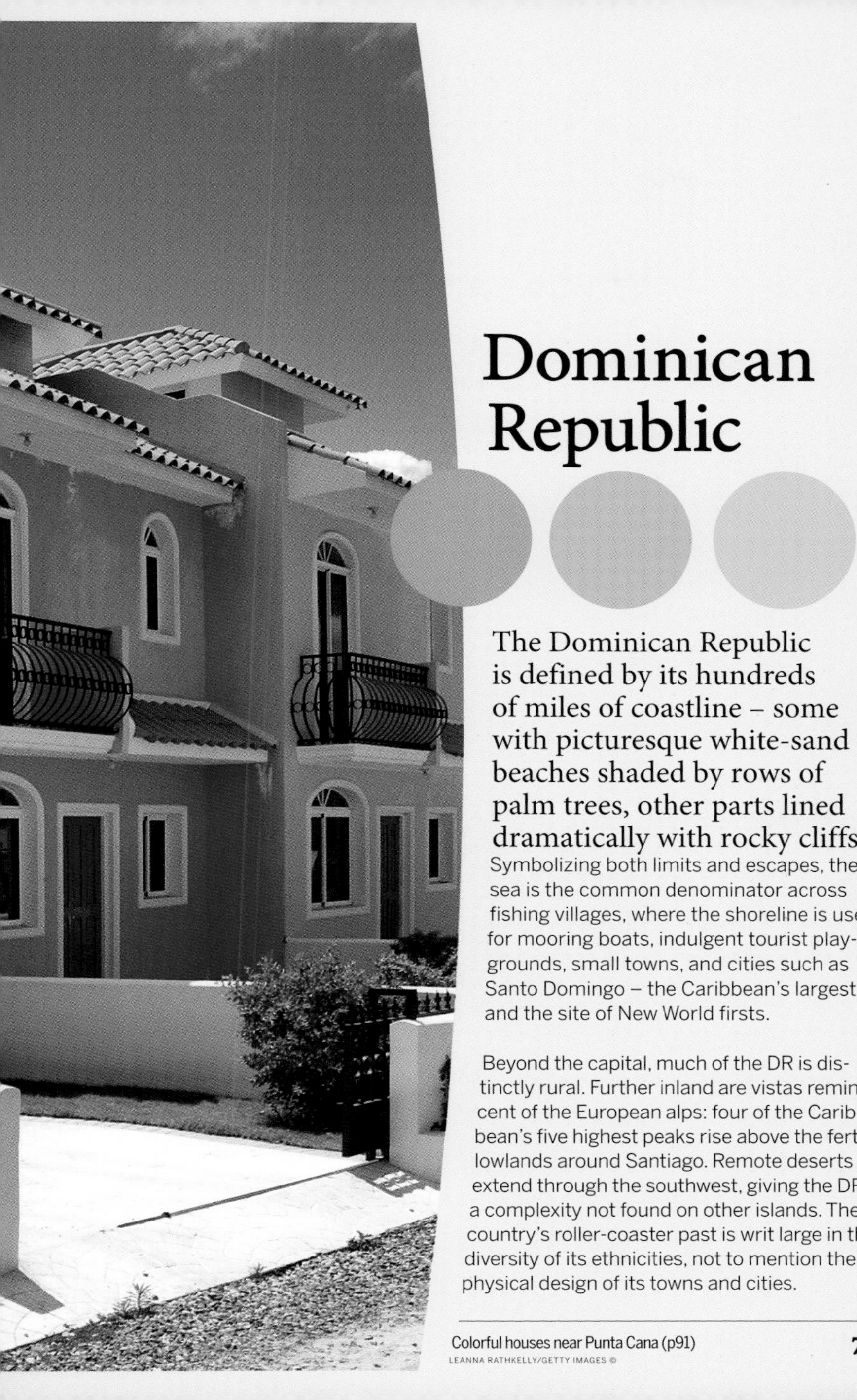

Dominican Republic

The Dominican Republic is defined by its hundreds of miles of coastline – some with picturesque white-sand beaches shaded by rows of palm trees, other parts lined dramatically with rocky cliffs. Symbolizing both limits and escapes, the sea is the common denominator across fishing villages, where the shoreline is used for mooring boats, indulgent tourist playgrounds, small towns, and cities such as Santo Domingo – the Caribbean's largest and the site of New World firsts.

Beyond the capital, much of the DR is distinctly rural. Further inland are vistas reminiscent of the European alps: four of the Caribbean's five highest peaks rise above the fertile lowlands around Santiago. Remote deserts extend through the southwest, giving the DR a complexity not found on other islands. The country's roller-coaster past is writ large in the diversity of its ethnicities, not to mention the physical design of its towns and cities.

Colorful houses near Punta Cana (p91)

Dominican Republic Itineraries

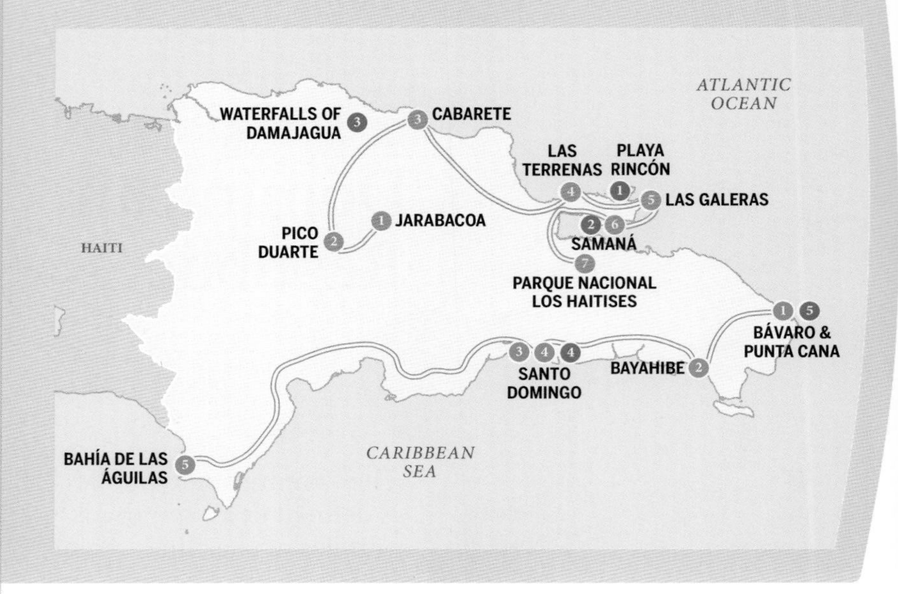

Seven Days

❶ **Bávaro and Punta Cana** (p91) Fly into the airport directly outside this resort area and base yourself at one of the beachfront properties for a little sun and sand and all-you-can-eat buffets for two or three days.

❷ **Bayahibe** (p91) Not far from here and accessible on a long day trip is this tiny town on the edge of a national park with the best scuba diving in the DR and a number of excursions including catamaran tours to Isla Saona, an island beach, and snorkeling trips.

❸ **Zona Colonial, Santo Domingo** (p82) Take a walk through history in the Zona Colonial, past beautifully restored mansions, churches and forts, many converted into evocative museums. But the past and present coexist in the former seat of Spain's 16th-century empire: pop into a shop selling CDs from the latest Dominican merengue star.

❹ **Santo Domingo night life** (p88) Get dressed to the nines, do some limbering up and get your dance moves on. Nightclubs in the seaside resort hotels host some of the best merengue and salsa bands this side of Havana. Downtown has trendy, sceney clubs for the fashionable set and the Zona Colonial is chockablock with spots.

❺ **Bahía de Las Águilas** (p90) Pick up a rental car in the city and hit the road for this stunning 10-km-long far-flung beach. Its remoteness and loneliness adds savor and spice to the adventure of reaching these postcard-perfect sands in an extreme corner of the Pedernales Peninsula.

➡ THIS LEG: 128 MILES

Ten Days

❶ **Jarabacoa** (p102) Go white-water rafting in the morning and visit the nearby waterfalls in the afternoon before spending a cool night in the countryside with mountain vistas in the distance.

❷ **Pico Duarte** (p100) Jarabacoa is also the gateway to Parque Nacionales Armando Bermúdez and the hike to Pico Duarte. Consider making the standard three-day hike to the summit, which at 3087m is the highest in the Caribbean.

❸ **Cabarete** (p100) Head out of the mountains to this laid-back beach town and water-sports mecca on the north coast. Active types will assuredly want to stay in or around Cabarete, east of Puerto Plata; it also has a happening bar and restaurant scene. Carve out several hours or days learning the ropes from the best in kitesurfing, windsurfing or just plain surfing. Of course, the beaches are equally alluring for doing absolutely nothing but sipping cocktails and making headway in a good book.

❹ **Las Terrenas** (p96) Continue further along the coast until you reach the Peninsula de Samaná and the cosmopolitan town of Las Terrenas. Kitesurfing and other water sports are deservedly popular here.

❺ **Las Galeras** (p94) Another nearby option is this sleepy fishing village at the far eastern end of the peninsula. Swaying palm trees back beaches ready-made for a movie set, and waves crash over hard-to-get-to cliffs.

❻ **Whale Watching, Samaná** (p94) If possible, plan your trip for mid-January to mid-March, when humpback whales migrate to the Bahía de Samaná and boat-based whale-watching tours are in full steam.

❼ **Parque Nacional Los Haitises** (p98) Or arrange a boat trip to see the mangroves and cave paintings at this park by the bayside town of Sabana de la Mar.

THIS LEG: 160 MILES

Dominican Republic Highlights

❶ **Best Beach: Playa Rincón** (p94) An ideal 3km of pitchperfect sands with a thick palm forest providing the backdrop.

❷ **Best Wildlife Viewing: Whale Watching** (p94) Witness 30-ton humpbacks breaching and diving in the Bahía de Samaná.

❸ **Best Outdoor Adventure: 27 Waterfalls of Damajagua** (p101) Adrenalin-pumping fun wading through clear pools, climbing rocks and leaping into roaring rapids.

❹ **Best Walking Tour: Zona Colonial, Santo Domingo** (p85) Wandering the cobblestone streets of the oldest city in the New World.

❺ **Best Resort Relaxing: Bávaro and Punta Cana** (p91) All-inclusive resorts on the choicest beachfront, famous for delivering carefree holidays.

Beachfront, Bávaro (p91)

Discover Dominican Republic

SANTO DOMINGO

POP 2 MILLION

Santo Domingo, or 'La Capital' as it's typically called, is a collage of cultures and neighborhoods. At the heart of the city is the Zona Colonial, where you'll find one of the oldest churches and the oldest surviving European fortress, among other New World firsts. Amid the cobblestone streets, it would be easy to forget Santo Domingo is in the Caribbean. But this is an intensely urban city, home not only to colonial-era architecture but also to hot clubs, vibrant cultural institutions and elegant restaurants.

Museo Alcázar de Colón (p84), Santo Domingo
DANITA DELIMONT/GETTY IMAGES ©

Sights & Activities

ZONA COLONIAL

Catedral Primada de América Church

(Nuestra Senora de la Anunciacion; ☎809-685-2302; Parque Colón; adult/child RD$60/free; ⏰8am-5pm Mon-Sat) The first stone of this cathedral, the oldest in operation in the western hemisphere, was set in 1514 by Diego Columbus, son of the great explorer (the ashes of both father and son are said to have once resided in the chapel's crypt). Construction however didn't begin in earnest until the arrival of the first bishop, Alejandro Geraldini, in 1521. From then until 1540, numerous architects worked on the church and adjoining buildings, which is why the vault is Gothic, the arches Romanesque and the ornamentation baroque. It's anyone's guess what the planned bell tower would have looked like: a shortage of funds curtailed construction, and the steeple, which undoubtedly would have offered a commanding view of the city, was never built.

Museo de las Casas Reales Museum

(Museum of the Royal Houses; ☎809-682-4202; Las Damas; adult/under 12yr RD$100/free; ⏰9am-5pm Tue-Sat, to 4pm Sun) Built in the Renaissance style during the 16th century, this building was the longtime seat of Spanish authority for the entire Caribbean region, housing the governor's office and the powerful Audiencia Real (Royal Court), among others. It showcases

Dominican Republic

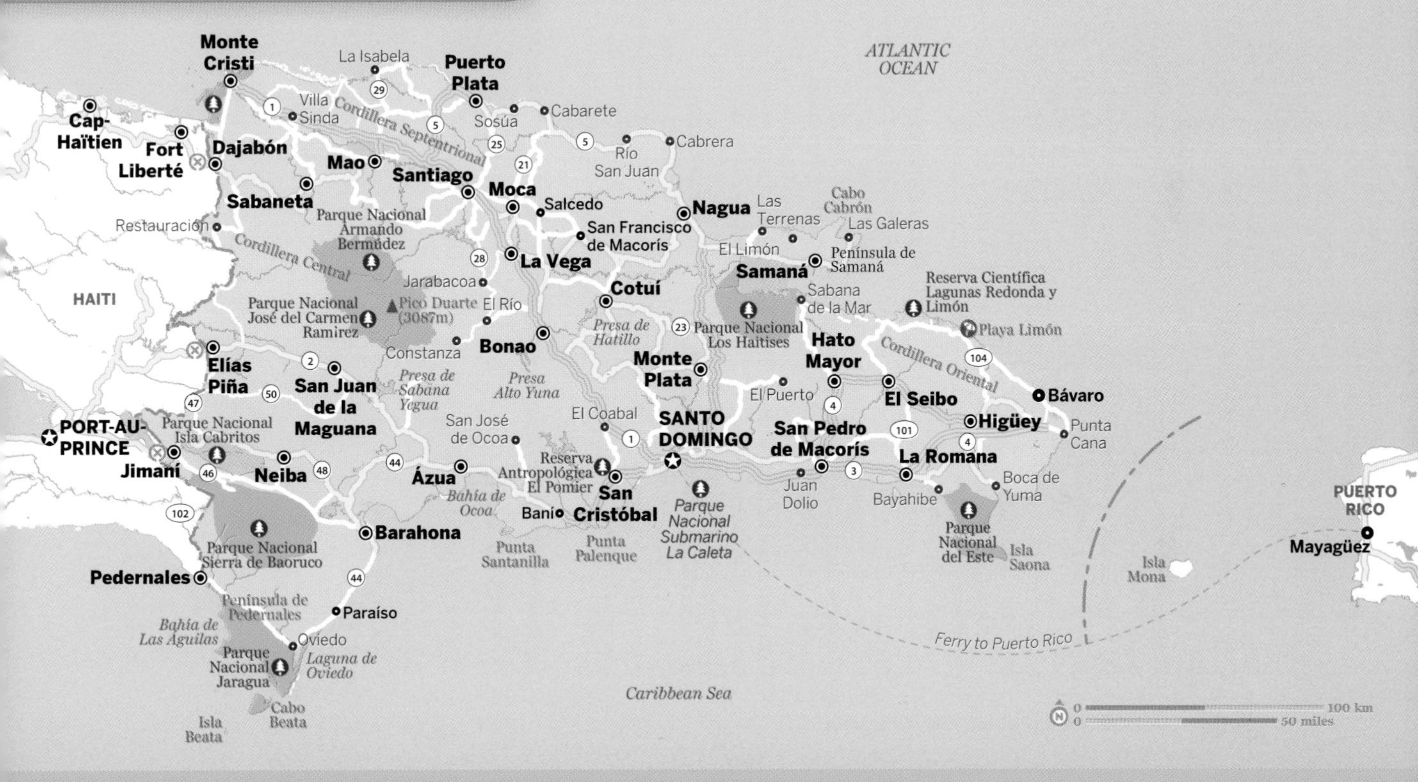

colonial-period objects, including many treasures recovered from Spanish galleons that foundered in nearby waters. Each room has been restored according to its original style, and the displays range from Taíno artifacts to dozens of hand-blown wine bottles and period furnishings.

Museo Alcázar de Colón Museum

(Museum Citadel of Columbus; ☎809-682-4750; Plaza España; adult/child RD$100/20; ⏰9am-5pm Tue-Sat, to 4pm Sun) Designed in the Gothic-Mudéjar transitional style, this was once the residence of Columbus' son, Diego, and his wife, Doña María de Toledo, during the early 16th century. The magnificent building we see today is the result of three historically authentic restorations: one in 1957, another in 1971 and a third in 1992. The building itself, as well as the household pieces on display (said to have belonged to the Columbus family), are definitely worth a look.

Convento de la Orden de los Predicadores Church

(Convent of the Order of Preachers; cnr Calle Duarte & Padre Billini; ⏰varies) Built in 1510 by Charles V, this is the first convent of the Dominican order founded in the Americas. It is also where Father Bartolomé de las Casas – the famous chronicler of Spanish atrocities committed against indigenous peoples – did most of his writing. The vault of the chapel, remarkable for its stone zodiac wheel carved with mythological and astrological representations, is worth a look.

Parque Colón Park

(cnr Calle El Conde & Isabel la Católica) Beside the Catedral Primada de América, this historic park contains several shade trees and a large statue of Admiral Columbus himself. It's the meeting place for local residents and is alive with tourists, townsfolk, hawkers, guides, taxi drivers, shoeshine boys, tourist police and thousands of pigeons.

Plaza España Plaza

The large, open area in front of the Alcázar de Colón has been made over many times. Running along its northwest side is **Calle la Atarazana**, fronted by a half dozen restaurants in buildings that served as warehouses through most of the 16th and 17th centuries.

Fortaleza Ozama Historical Site

(☎809-686-0222; Las Damas; admission RD$70; ⏰9am-6:30pm Mon-Sat, to 4pm Sun) This is the oldest colonial military edifice in the New World. Construction of the fortifi-

Ports of Call

There are a number of options even for a short visit in these ports.

SANTO DOMINGO

The city's most interesting sights are all located in the cobblestone blocks of the Zona Colonial only steps from the port. Take a walking tour of Zona Colonial, eat in a restaurant in Plaza España and walk part of the Malecón.

SAMANÁ

- Take a boat out to the island of Cayo Levantado.
- Hang out at a cafe at Las Terrenas.
- Ride a horse to Cascada El Limón.
- Sunbathe at Playa Rincón.

cation began in 1502 and continued in various stages for the next two centuries. Over the course of its history the fort has flown the flag of Spain, England, France, Haiti, Gran Columbia, the US and the DR. Until the 1970s, when it was opened to the public, it served as a military garrison and prison.

Near the door you'll find several guides (Spanish, English and French spoken, sometimes German and Italian).

Tours

Zona Colonial Walking Tours — Walking Tour

Interesting and informative walking tours of the Zona Colonial are offered daily by a number of official guides – look for men dressed in khakis and light-blue dress shirts hanging out at Parque Colón. Always ask to see their official state-tourism license and agree to a fee before setting out. Walks typically last 2½ hours and cost between US$20 and US$30.

Sleeping

The Zona Colonial is the most distinctive part of the city and therefore where most travelers prefer to stay. Gazcue, a quiet residential area southwest of Parque Independencia, has several midrange options and a handful of high-rise hotels with resort amenities line the Malecón.

ZONA COLONIAL

Portes 9 — B&B $

(☎849-943-2039; info@portes9.com; Calle Arzobispo Portes 9; r incl breakfast from US$55; ❄ 📶) Four tastefully furnished all-white wood-floored rooms with high ceilings make up this Spanish-owned B&B fronting a quiet plaza in the neighborhood's southeast corner. It's an intimate spot where guests socialize over breakfast.

Hotel Villa Colonial — Hotel $$

(☎809-221-1049; www.villacolonial.net; Calle Sánchez 157; s/d incl breakfast US$75/85; 📶 ≋) The French owner has created an idyllic oasis, an exceptionally sophisticated combination of European elegance with a colonial-era facade and an art-deco design. The rooms lining the narrow garden and pool area all have high ceilings and four-poster beds, as well as flatscreen TVs and bathrooms with ceramic-tile floors.

El Beaterío Guest House — Guesthouse $$

(☎809-687-8657; www.elbeaterio.com; Calle Duarte 8; s/d incl breakfast US$75/100; ❄ 📶) Take thee to this nunnery – if you're looking for austere elegance. Each of the 11 large rooms is sparsely furnished, but the wood-beamed ceilings and stone floors are truly special, and the tile-floored bathrooms are modern and well maintained.

Hostal Nicolás de Ovando — Historic Hotel $$$

(☎809-685-9955; www.mgallery.com; Las Damas; s US$220-336, d US$238-354, restaurant mains US$17-35; P ❄ 📶 ≋) Even heads of state must get a thrill when they learn they're sleeping in the former home of the first governor of the Americas. Oozing character, old-world charm and historic pedigree, the Nicolás de Ovando is as far from a chain hotel as you can get. Indisputably one of the nicest hotels in the city, it features 97 rooms packed with 21st-century amenities.

Eating

ZONA COLONIAL

Antica Pizzeria — Italian $$

(☎809-689-4040; cnr Billini & José Reyes; mains RD$350; ⏲5-11pm Mon, Wed & Thu, noon-midnight Fri-Sun) Sophisticated and stylish, with oversized framed poster reproductions of European Renaissance paintings decorating the triple-height ceilings, Antica wouldn't be out of place in a fashionable district of Rome. The Italian owner keeps a watchful eye on the kitchen and the exposed brick-oven pizza, which does excellent pies and a handful of pasta dishes.

Central Santo Domingo (Zona Colonial)

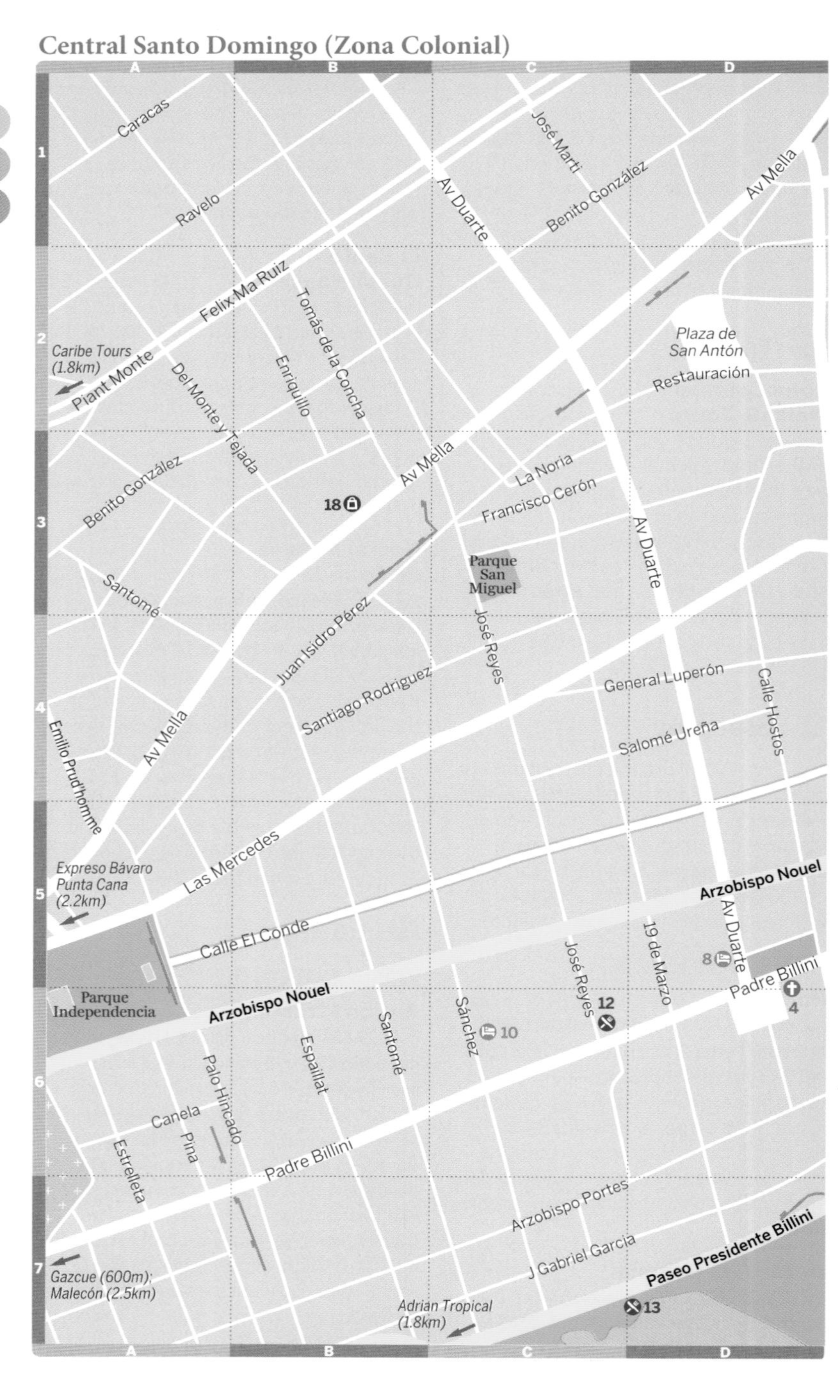

A
B
C
D
1
2
3
4
5
6
7
Caracas
Ravelo
José Martí
Av Duarte
Benito González
Av Mella
Felix Ma Ruiz
Tomás de la Concha
Enriquillo
Del Monte y Tejada
Caribe Tours (1.8km)
Piant Monte
Plaza de San Antón
Restauración
La Noria
Francisco Cerón
Benito González
18
Parque San Miguel
Santomé
Juan Isidro Pérez
José Reyes
Santiago Rodriguez
General Luperón
Salomé Ureña
Calle Hostos
Emilio Prud'homme
Las Mercedes
Expreso Bávaro Punta Cana (2.2km)
Arzobispo Nouel
Calle El Conde
19 de Marzo
8
Padre Billini
4
Parque Independencia
Arzobispo Nouel
12
Sánchez
10
Santomé
Espaillat
Palo Hincado
Canela
Pina
Estrelleta
Padre Billini
Arzobispo Portes
J Gabriel Garcia
Paseo Presidente Billini
Gazcue (600m); Malecón (2.5km)
Adrian Tropical (1.8km)
13

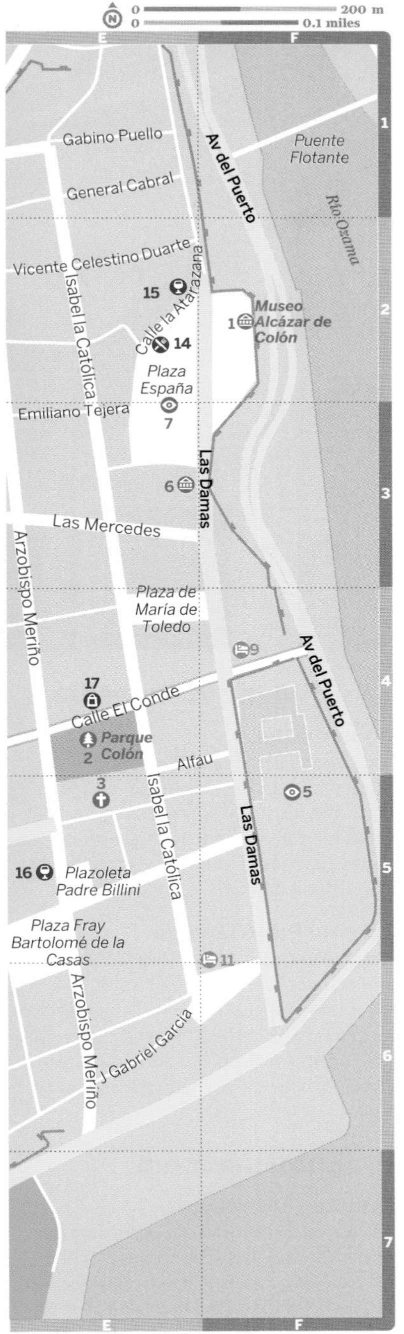

Central Santo Domingo (Zona Colonial)

Don't Miss Sights

1 Museo Alcázar de Colón F2
2 Parque Colón E4

Sights

3 Catedral Primada de América E5
4 Convento de la Orden de los Predicadores D5
5 Fortaleza Ozama F5
6 Museo de las Casas Reales E3
7 Plaza España E3

Sleeping

8 El Beaterío Guest House D5
9 Hostal Nicolás de Ovando F4
10 Hotel Villa Colonial C6
11 Portes 9 .... F5

Eating

12 Antica Pizzeria C6
13 D'Luis Parrillada D7
14 Pat'e Palo E2

Drinking & Nightlife

15 Canario Patio Lounge E2
16 Double's Bar E5

Shopping

17 Felipe & Co E4
18 Mercado Modelo B3

D'Luis Parrillada Dominican $$
(Paseo Presidente Billini; RD$350; 11am-late) This casual open-air place perched over the ocean only a few blocks from the Zona Colonial is one of only a few to take advantage of the Malecón's setting. The large menu includes fajitas, grilled and barbecue meats, sandwiches, seafood *cazuela* (RD$400) and little-found *pulpofongo* (*mofongo* with Creole-style cuttlefish; RD$330). Wonderful place for a drink too.

Pat'e Palo Spanish, Mediterranean $$$
(809-687-8089; Calle la Atarazana 25; mains RD$650-1200; noon-midnight) The most happening and deservedly longest surviving of Plaza España's restaurant row, Pat'e Palo is for anyone tired of the same old bland pasta and chicken. Large, both physically and in terms of its selection, the menu includes creatively designed dishes like foie gras with dark beer jam and risotto in squid ink and shrimp

brunoise with lobster tail and roasted arugula.

GAZCUE & MALECÓN

Il Cappucino Italian $$
(☎809-682-8006; Máximo Gómez 60; mains RD$400; ⌚8am-11:30pm; ❄ 📶) You might leave this oasis of comfort and sophistication on an otherwise gritty stretch feeling envious of the regulars who are welcomed like family. Nearly three-dozen types of really top-notch pizza and pasta, plus fish and meat dishes round out the menu.

Adrian Tropical Dominican $
(Av George Washington; mains RD$200; ⌚8am-11pm Mon-Fri, 24hr Sat & Sun; 👪) This popular family-friendly chain occupies a spectacular location overlooking the Caribbean. Waiters scurry throughout the two floors and outdoor dining area doling out Dominican specialties such as yucca or plantain *mofongo* as well as standard meat dishes.

Drinking & Nightlife

Double's Bar Bar
(Arzobispo Meriño; ⌚6pm-late) Good-looking 20-somethings grind away to loud pop and Latin music on weekend nights. Otherwise, groups can lounge around one of the couches or sidle up to the classic long wood bar.

Canario Patio Lounge Bar
(Calle la Atarazana 1; ⌚7pm-3am Tue-Sun) Owned by a Dominican salsa star, this bar, whose walls are covered in graffiti, is for grown-ups; if the salsa and merengue music gets too loud, step out into the beautiful courtyard. Quiet on weekday nights.

Entertainment

Estadio Quisqueya Sports
(☎809-540-5772; www.estadioquisqueya.com.do; cnr Avs Tiradentes & San Cristóbal; tickets RD$250-1000; ⌚games 5pm Sun, 8pm Tue, Wed, Fri & Sat) One of the best places to experi-

Left: Catedral Primada de América (p82); **Below:** Museo de las Casas Reales (p82)

ence Dominican baseball is at the home field of two of the DR's six professional teams, **Licey** (www.licey.com) and **Escogido** (www.escogido). Asking for the best seats available at the box office is likely to cost RD$1000 and put you within meters of the ballplayers and the between-innings dancers.

Shopping

Felipe & Co Handicrafts

(809-689-5812; Calle El Conde 105; 9am-8pm Mon-Sat, 10am-6pm Sun) This shop on Parque Colón, easily one of the best in the Zona Colonial, is stocked with charming high-quality handicrafts, such as ceramics, jewelry and handbags, and also a good selection of paintings.

Mercado Modelo Market

(Av Mella; 9am-5pm Mon-Sat, to noon Sun) Bargain hard at this crowded market, which sells everything from love potions to woodcarvings, jewelry and, of course, the ubiquitous 'Haitian style' paintings.

The market is housed in an aging two-story building just north of the Zona Colonial in a neighborhood of fairly run-down stores and souvenir shops.

Information

Medical Services

Clínica Abreu (809-687-4922; cnr Av Independencia & Beller; 24hr) Widely regarded as the best hospital in the city, this is where members of many of the embassies go.

Farmacia San Judas (809-685-8165; cnr Av Independencia & Pichardo; 24hr) Pharmacy offers free delivery.

Getting There & Away

Air

Aeropuerto Internacional Las Américas (p106) is 26km east of the city. The smaller Aeropuerto Internacional La Isabela Dr Joaquin Balaguer (p106), north of the city, handles mostly domestic carriers and air-taxi companies.

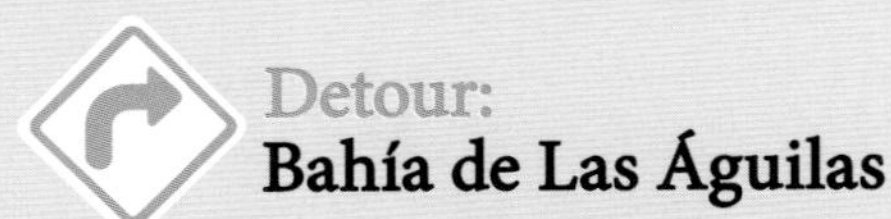

Detour: Bahía de Las Águilas

If you believe in fairy-tale utopian beaches, pristine Bahía de Las Águilas fits the bill. Located in the extremely remote southwestern corner of the DR, it's not on the way to anything else, but those who do make it are rewarded with 10km of nearly deserted beach forming a slow arc between two prominent capes.

To get there, take the paved (and signed!) road to Cabo Rojo, about 12km east of Pedernales. From here you can get to the beach by (really good) 4WD, but the far more spectacular alternative is to go by boat, where the ride is every bit as jaw-dropping as the destination.

Gorgeously located restaurant Rancho Tipico, in Las Cuevas, offers tours. The price for groups of one to five is RD$2000 per boat. **Ecotour Barahona** (☎809-856-2260; www.ecotourbarahona.com; apt 306, Carretera Enriquillo 8, Paraíso) runs a day trip which includes transport, lunch and snorkeling gear (US$119). The national park entrance fee is RD$100.

Bus

The country's two main bus companies – Caribe Tours (p107) and **Metro** (☎809-227-0101; www.metrotours.com.do; Calle Francisco Prats Ramírez) – have individual depots west of the Zona Colonial. Expreso Bávaro Punta Cana (p107) has a direct service between the Gazcue neighborhood (just off Av Máximo Gómez) in the capital and Bávaro, with a stop in La Romana (RD$400, three hours).

Car

Numerous car-rental companies have offices in Santo Domingo and at Las Américas airport.

Getting Around

To/From the Airport

There are no buses that connect directly to either of Santo Domingo's airports. From Las Américas, a taxi to the Zona Colonial costs US$40.

Bus

The cost of a bus ride from one end of the city to the other is around RD$12 (6:30am to 9:30pm). Most stops are marked with a sign and the word *parada* (stop). The routes tend to follow major thoroughfares.

Metro

Line 1 runs from La Feria near the Malecón to the far northern suburb of Villa Mella. Line 2 runs east–west along Av John F Kennedy, Expreso V Centenario and Av Padre Castellanos. Each ride costs RD$20.

Público

More numerous than buses are *públicos* (RD$12 per ride) – mostly beat-up minivans and private cars that follow the same main routes but stop anywhere that someone flags them down.

Taxi

Taxis in Santo Domingo don't have meters, so you should always agree on the price before climbing in. Standard fare is around RD$200 from one side of the city to the other. Within the Zona Colonial it should be even cheaper. You can always find cabs at Parque Colón and Parque Independencia, or call **Apolo Taxi** (☎809-537-7771).

THE SOUTHEAST

A Caribbean workhorse of sun and sand, the southeast is synonymous with go-big-or-go-home tourism where sprawling resort developments line the white sands and turquoise seas from Punta Cana to Bávaro. The fishing village of Bayahibe is the departure point for trips to the nearby islands in the Parque Nacional del Este and north of Bávaro is Playa Limón, an isolated stretch of beach backed by palm trees and, more unusually, a lagoon and several mountain peaks.

Bávaro & Punta Cana

In terms of their soft, white texture and their warm aquamarine waters the beaches from Punta Cana to El Macao rival those anywhere else in the Caribbean. Punta Cana, where the airport is located and used as shorthand for the region as a whole, is actually somewhat of a misnomer since the majority of resorts are scattered around the beaches of Bávaro and El Cortecito. **Playa del Macao**, around 9km north of **Playa Arena Gorda**, is a gorgeous stretch of beach; however, it's also the stop-off for a slew of all-terrain vehicle tours.

Activities

La Cana Golf Course Golf
(☎809-959-4653; www.puntacana.com; Punta Cana Resort & Club, Punta Cana; ⏰7:30am-6pm) Punta Cana's top golf course is located at the area's top resort. The 18-hole course, designed by Pete Dye, has several long par fives and stunning ocean views.

Tours

Every resort has a tour desk that can arrange all variety of trips, from snorkeling and deep-sea fishing to the popular Isla Saona trip, a large island with picturesque beaches off the southeastern tip of the DR. A handful of locals set up on El Cortecito beach offer one-hour **snorkeling trips** (US$25 per person) and **glass-bottom boat rides** (US$35 per person) to a nearby reef.

RH Tours and Excursions (☎809-552-1425; www.rhtours.com; El Cortecito; ⏰9am-5pm Mon-Sat) offers a number of day trips including Parque Nacional Los Haitises (US$128), Isla Saona (US$92 to US$118) and tours of Santo Domingo's Zona Colonial (US$77).

Sleeping

Bávaro Hostel Hostel $
(☎809-931-6767; www.bavarohostel.com; Av Alemania, Edificio Carimar 4A, Bávaro; dm US$22, r US$40-45; P ❄ 📶) This new hostel, mere meters from the beach, occupies several rooms in a four-story building in the heart of Los Corales and is run by an immensely friendly half-Dominican, half-English brother-sister team.

Paradisus Punta Cana Resort $$$
(☎809-687-9923; www.melia.com; Playa Bávaro; all-inclusive d from US$446; P ❄ @ 📶 🏊) Almost jungly and discerningly quiet, this resort feels nothing like most in the area. It attracts singles and families alike and takes appreciated steps to keep them separate where desired. The made-over standard rooms feel more urban art house than Caribbean and the 190 newer Reserve rooms feature lush courtyards, modern art, patios and spa tubs for two.

Punta Cana

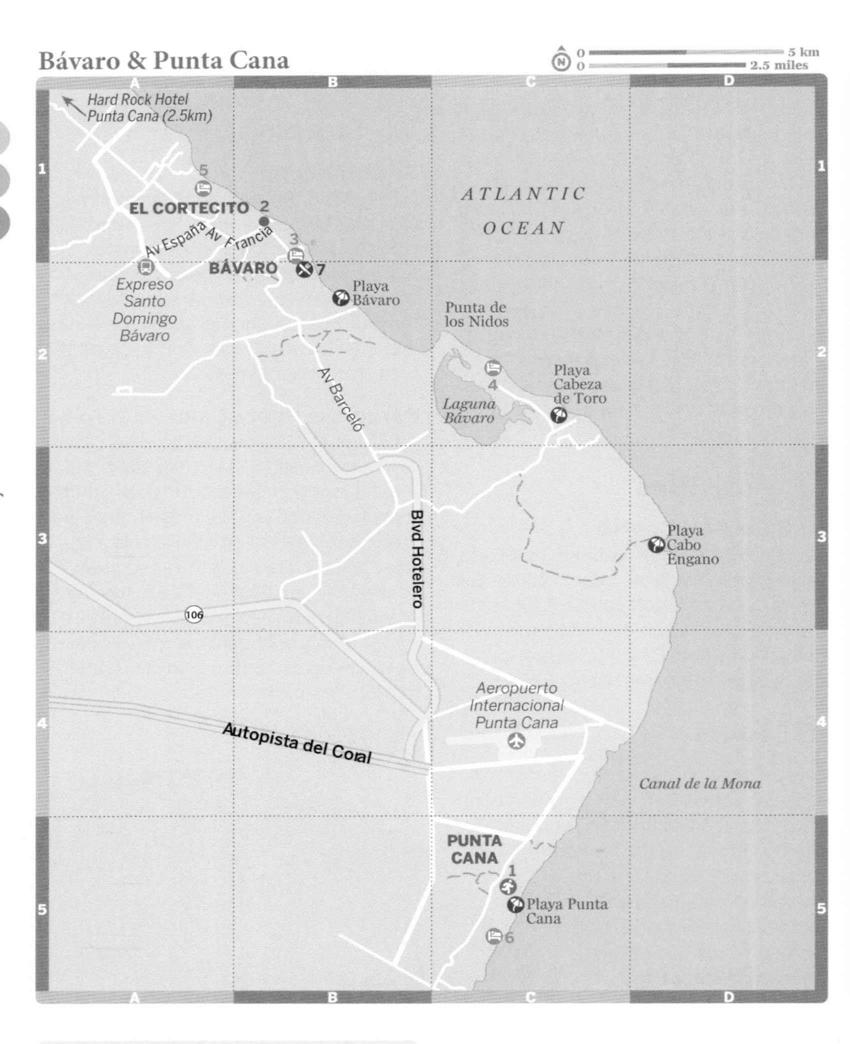

Bávaro & Punta Cana

Activities, Courses & Tours
1 La Cana Golf Course C5
2 RH Tours & Excursions B1

Sleeping
3 Bávaro Hostel B1
4 NaturaPark Beach Ecoresort & Spa C2
5 Paradisus Punta Cana A1
6 Puntacana Resort & Club C5

Eating
7 Ñam Ñam B2
Passion by Martín Berasategui ... (see 5)

Puntacana Resort & Club Resort **$$$**

(☎809-959-2714; www.puntacana.com; Punta Cana; d incl breakfast from US$382; P ❄ @ ☎ ≋) Famous for its part-time residents including Julio Iglesias, Oscar de la Renta and Mikhail Baryshnikov, this discerning and huge resort is also notable for its environmental efforts, especially the associated ecological park across the street from the entrance to the resort. Unlike all-inclusives, however, lunch, dinner and drinks aren't included in the rates.

NaturaPark Beach Ecoresort & Spa Hotel $$$

(809-221-2626; www.blau-hotels.com; Cabeza de Toro; d from US$218;) NaturaPark has a narrow beach outside the village of Cabeza de Toro, halfway between Bávaro and Punta Cana. From the Lincoln Logs–style recycled coconut wood lobby furniture to the beautiful free-growing mangroves on the property, it's all got a sustainable edge and the resort has won awards for reducing its environmental impact.

Eating

Ñam Ñam Cafe $$

(www.nam-nams.com; Plaza Sol Caribe, Bávaro; mains RD$119-549; 11am-3pm & 6-11pm Tue-Sun;) The friendly Belgradian couple behind this tiny Los Corales kitchen – they do it all themselves – know a thing or two about making your belly happy. The now-famous burgers, in regular, gourmet (minced with bacon and chili) and stuffed (with ham, cheese and mushrooms) versions: superb.

Passion by Martín Berasategui Basque $$$

(Paradisus Punta Cana, Bávaro ; 7-course prix-fixe guest/nonguest US$45/65; 6:30-10pm) Chef Martín Berasategui hails from San Sebastián in Spanish Basque country – not a bad place to eat for those who might not know – and he packed a few recipes in his gastro-luggage on his way to overseeing what is easily Punta Cana's most memorable dining experience.

Information

Medical Services

Hospitén Bávaro (www.hospiten.es; Carretera Higüey-Punta Cana) Best private hospital in Punta Cana, with English-, French- and German-speaking doctors and a 24-hour emergency room.

Money

Almost every major Dominican bank has at least one branch in the Bávaro area. Banco León, BanReservas and Scotiabank all have ATMs.

Getting There & Away

Air

Aeropuerto Internacional Punta Cana (PUJ; www.puntacanainternationalairport.com; Carretera Higuey-Punta Cana Km 45) is on the road to Punta Cana about 9km east of the turnoff to Bávaro.

For domestic air connections, **Dominican-Shuttles** (in Santo Domingo 809-738-3014; www.dominicanshuttles.com) has direct domestic flights on five- and 19-seat planes between Punta Cana and Samaná's Aeropuerto Internacional Arroyo Barril (one way $159, 8am Monday, Wednesday, Thursday, Friday and Sunday).

Several car agencies, including **Avis** (809-688-1354; www.avis.com.do; Aeropuerto Internacional Punta Cana) and **National/Alamo** (809-466-1083; Carr Bávaro (Av Barceló) Km 5), have small booths near baggage claim.

Resort minivans transport the majority of tourists to nearby resorts, but taxis are plentiful. Fares range from US$30 to US$80.

Bus

The bus terminal is at Bávaro's main intersection, near the Texaco gas station, almost 2km inland from El Cortecito.

Expreso Santo Domingo Bávaro (809-552-1678; Av Estados Unidos) has direct 1st class service between Bávaro and the capital (RD$400, three hours). Departure times are 7am, 9am, 11am, 1pm, 3pm and 4pm.

From the same terminal, **Sitrabapu** (809-552-0771; Av Estados Unidos) has departures to La Romana (RD$225, 1¼ hours) and Higüey (RD$130, one hour).

Getting Around

Local buses pass all the outdoor malls on the way to El Cortecito (RD$40). They are supposed to pass every 15 to 30 minutes but can sometimes take up to an hour.

There are numerous taxis in the area – look for stands at El Cortecito, Plaza Bávaro and at most all-inclusives. It's around US$8 minimum for pretty much any short trip within Bávaro.

Whale-Watching & Samaná

For sheer awe-inspiring impact, a whale-watching trip is hard to beat. Around 45,000 people travel to Samaná every year from January 15 to March 15 to see the majestic acrobatics of these massive creatures. Try to avoid coming during Carnaval, the busiest day of the year. **Whale Samaná** (809-538-2494; www.whalesamana.com; cnr Calle Mella & Av La Marina; adult/under 5yr/5-10yr RD$2500/free/RD$1250; office 9am-1pm & 3-6pm Jan-Mar, 9am-1pm Mon-Fri Apr-Dec), the most recommended outfit, is owned and operated by pioneering Canadian marine mammal specialist Kim Beddall. The daily tour leaves at 9am and lasts three to four hours.

Occupying the western third of **Cayo Levantado**, a lush island 7km from Samaná, is a gorgeous beach open to the public. Boatmen at the pier make the trip for RD$250 per person round-trip. The rest of the island is the property of the romantic and luxurious five-star **Gran Bahia Principe Cayo Levantado** (809-538-3232; www.bahia-principe.com; Cayo Levantado; all-inclusove r from RD$6400; @).

PENÍNSULA DE SAMANÁ

Laid-back and cosmopolitan, Samaná offers a European vibe as strong as espresso. Of course, the majority come to gasp at the North Atlantic humpback whales doing their migratory song and dance from mid-January to mid-March. Sophisticated Las Terrenas is the place for those that crave a lively social scene, and sleepy Las Galeras boasts several of the best and most secluded beaches in the DR.

Las Galeras

The road to this small fishing community 28km northeast of Samaná ends at a fish shack on the beach. So does everything else, metaphorically speaking. Las Galeras, as much as anywhere else on the peninsula, offers terrestrial and subaquatic adventures for those with wills strong enough to ignore the simple pleasure of doing nothing but lying around your bungalow.

Beaches

Playa Rincón Beach

Stretching uninterrupted for almost 3km of nearly white, soft sand and multihued water good for swimming, the beach even has a small stream at its far western end, great for a quick freshwater dip at the end of a long, sunny day. A thick palm forest provides the backdrop. Several small restaurants serve mostly seafood dishes and rent beach chairs, making this a great place to spend the entire day. Most people arrive by boat. If you join up with other beachgoers, it costs RD$500 to RD$1000 per person round-trip. A round-trip taxi to Rincón, including waiting time, should cost RD$1800.

Playas Frontón & Madama Beach

Preferred by some locals over Playa Rincón, Playa Frontón boasts some of the area's best snorkeling. Playa Madama is a small beach framed by high bluffs; keep in mind there's not much sunlight here in the afternoon.

Activities

Las Galeras Divers Diving
(☎809-538-0220; www.las-galeras-divers.com; Plaza Lusitania; ⏰8:30am-7pm) Las Galeras Divers is a well-respected, French-run dive shop at the main intersection. One-/two-tank dives including all equipment cost RD$2200/3400 (RD$400 less if you have your own).

Sleeping

Casa Por Qué No? B&B $$
(☎809-712-5631; casaporqueno@live.com; s/d incl breakfast US$45/55; ⏰closed May-Oct; P ❄ 📶) Pierre and Monick, the charming French-Canadian owners of this B&B, are consummate hosts and rent out two rooms on either side of their cozy home – each room has a separate entrance and hammock – only 25m or so north of the main intersection on your right as you're walking toward the beach.

Todo Blanco Boutique Hotel $$
(☎809-538-0201; www.hoteltodoblanco.com; r with/without air-con RD$3800/3700; P ❄ 📶) Living up to its 'All White' name, this whitewashed, well-established inn sits atop a small hillock a short walk from the end of the main drag in Las Galeras. Rooms are large and airy, with high ceilings, private terraces overlooking the sea, and pastel headboards, while the multilevel grounds are nicely appointed with gardens and a gazebo.

Eating

Rincón Rubi Caribbean, Seafood $$
(☎809-380-7295; Playa Rincón; mains RD$300-650; ⏰9am-4pm Dec-Mar, with reservation Apr-Nov) This dressed-up beach shack justifies the trip to long and beautiful Playa Rincón on whose eastern end it sits. Picnic-table-style seating is juiced up with bright tablecloths, and a single chalkboard relays the offerings: fresh fish, *langosta* (lobster), grilled chicken etc, all cooked up on a massive, open-air grill.

Le Taínos Fusion $$
(Calle Principal; mains RD$360-640; ⏰6-11pm Nov-Apr) The focal point of the center of town, this atmospheric eatery is the town's most cosmopolitan, with a small but exciting menu of all sorts of scrumptious dishes you don't see elsewhere, beautifully presented on massive plates fit for a king.

Humpback whale, Península de Samaná (left)

REINHARD DIRSCHERL/GETTY IMAGES ©

Getting There & Around

Gua-guas head to Samaná (RD$100, one hour, every 15 minutes from 6:30am to 5:45pm) from the beach end of Principal and also cruise slowly out of town picking up passengers. There are also three daily buses to Santo Domingo (RD$350, three hours, 5:30am, 1:15pm and 3:15pm).

Taxis (809-481-8526) are available at a stand just in front of the main town beach. Some sample one-way fares are Aeropuerto Catey (RD$3000), Las Terrenas (RD$2500) and Samaná (RD$1000).

Renting a car is an excellent way to explore the peninsula on your own. Try RP Rent-A-Car (**809-538-0249; Calle Principal; 8am-7pm Mon-Sat, to 1pm Sun**), on the way out of town.

Las Terrenas

POP 18,829

No longer a rustic fishing village, Las Terrenas is a cosmopolitan town, seemingly as much French and Italian as Dominican with a lively mix of styles and a vibrant social scene. A walk along the beach road in either direction leads to beachfront scattered with hotels, high palm trees and calm aquamarine waters.

Las Terrenas

GARDEL BERTRAND/HEMIS.FR/GETTY IMAGES ©

Sights

Cascada El Limón — Waterfall

Tucked away in surprisingly rough landscape, surrounded by peaks covered in lush greenery, is the 52m-high El Limón waterfall. A beautiful swimming hole at the bottom can be a perfect spot to wash off the sweat and mud from the trip here, though it's often too deep and cold for a dip. The departure point is the small town of El Limón, only a half-hour from Las Terrenas.

Activities

Las Terrenas has reasonably good **diving** and **snorkeling**. Favorite dive spots include a wreck in 28m of water, and Isla Las Ballenas, visible from shore, with a large underwater cave.

Second to Cabarete, Las Terrenas is nevertheless a good place to try out a wind sport. The beach at Punta Popy, only a kilometer or so east of the main intersection, is a popular place for **kitesurfers** and **windsurfers**.

LTK — Water Sports

(**809-801-5671; www.lasterrenas-kitesurf.com; Calle 27 de Febrero**) Recommended kitesurfing school run by a friendly Frenchman who speaks Spanish and English as well. It rents surfboards (per day US$15) and kitesurfing equipment (per day US$70) and provides lessons for both these activities.

Turtle Dive Center — Diving

(**829-903-0659; www.turtledivecenter.com; El Paseo shopping center; 10am-12:30pm & 4-7pm**) A highly recommended SSI-

Las Terrenas & Playa Bonita

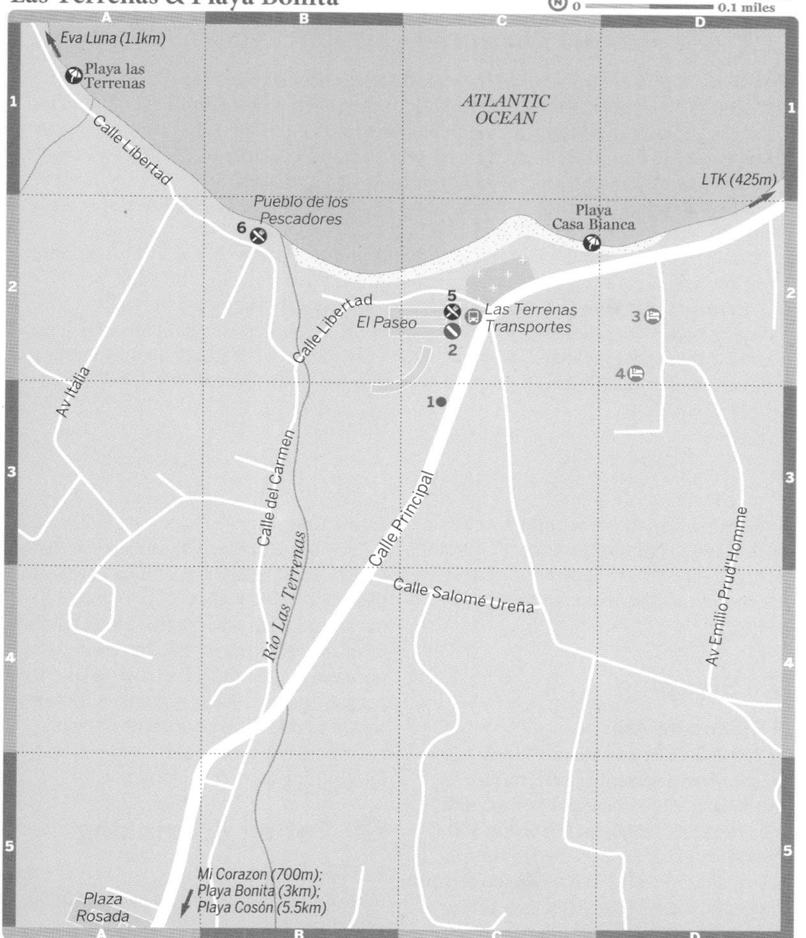

affiliated shop, run by a safety-first Frenchman. Also runs snorkeling trips to Playa Jackson (half/full day US$55/80) and Isla Las Ballenas (US$45).

Tours

Flora Tours Ecotours

(**809-923-2792; www.flora-tours.net; Calle Principal 278; 8:30am-12:30pm & 3:30-6:30pm Mon-Sat**) This French-run agency takes top honors in town for eco-sensitive tours to Parque Nacional Los Haitises

Las Terrenas & Playa Bonita

Activities, Courses & Tours
1 Flora Tours....C3
2 Turtle Dive Center....C2

Sleeping
3 Casa del Mar Neptunia....D2
4 El Rincon de Abi....D2

Eating
5 Brasserie Bárrio Latíno Cafe....C2
6 La Terrasse....B2

Detour: Parque Nacional Los Haitises

Meaning 'Land of the Mountains', **Parque Nacional Los Haitises (admission RD$100; 7am-8pm)** is a 1375-sq-km park at the southwestern end of the Bahía de Samaná containing scores of lush hills jutting some 30m to 50m from the water and coastal wetlands. The area receives a tremendous amount of rain, creating perfect conditions for subtropical humid forest plants and it's one of the most biodiverse regions in the Caribbean. Some of the park's series of limestone caves contain intriguing Taíno pictographs.

Tour outfits in Samaná and Las Terrenas offer trips here for around RD$2600 per person, including guide and transportation to, and inside, the park.

Paraíso Caño Hondo (809-248-5995; www.paraisocanohondo.com; s/d/tr incl breakfast RD$2040/3212/4437; P), one of the DR's most special places to stay, is near the park entrance. The Jivales River, which runs through the property, has been channeled into 10 magical waterfall-fed pools, perfect for a soak any time of the day.

and hard-to-access beaches, as well as more tranquil catamaran trips, culturally-sensitive quad tours to remote villages and mountain bike excursions of varying levels.

Sleeping

El Rincon de Abi — Hotel $

(809-240-6639; www.el-rincon-de-abi.com; Av Emilio Prud'Homme; d/tr incl breakfast from RD$1500/2000, bungalow without/with air-con RD$2000/2500, apt RD$4000-5000; P) This French-owned hotel is well maintained and full of cute colors and character. Even better, there's a somewhat established independent traveler vibe here. There's a nice communal outdoor kitchen, a spa bath, and a small pool.

Casa del Mar Neptunia — Hotel $

(809-240-6884; www.casasdelmarneptunia.com; Av Emilio Prud'Homme; s/d incl breakfast RD$1600/1900; P) New hands-on Canadian owners have whipped this humble abode into a charming little oasis of hospitality and calm. Homey and quiet with 12 large, airy rooms, it lacks some of the privacy of others on the same street, but makes up for it in value – your pesos will rarely go this far in Las Terrenas.

Eva Luna — Villa $$$

(809-978-5611; www.villa-evaluna.com; Calle Marico, Playa Las Ballenas; villas for 2/4 people US$120/220; P @) A paragon of understated luxury, these five Mexican-style villas come with fully equipped kitchens, gorgeously painted living rooms, and terraces where a delicious gourmet breakfast is served. The bedrooms are a bit cramped, but the serenity and exquisite decor more than make up for it.

Eating & Drinking

La Terrasse — French $$

(Pueblo de los Pescadores; mains RD$380-750; 11:30am-2:30pm & 6:30-11pm) The Dominican chef at this sophisticated French bistro deserves a few Michelin stars for his steak *au poivre* (RD$500) – you'll be genuflecting at his kitchen's door after it graces your lips – one of the most perfect meals in the entire Dominican Republic.

Brasserie Bárrio Latíno Cafe — Cafe $$

(809-240-6367; El Paseo shopping center, Calle Principal; breakfast RD$50-230, mains RD$150-420; breakfast, lunch & dinner;) Occupying the busiest corner in town – and milking that for all it's worth – this open-sided tropical *brasserie* has a large menu of international standards such as sandwiches, burgers, pastas and meat dishes.

Mi Corazon Fusion **$$$**
(809-240-5329; www.micorazon.com; Calle Duarte 7; mains RD$780-1040; 7-11pm Tue-Sun;) Las Terrenas may feel like a Franco-Italian enclave, but it's a Swiss-German trio that offers the area's top dining experience. Daniel, Lilo and Flo ensure your culinary ride here is a doozy: everything is made fresh on the premises and served in a romantic white-washed colonial-style courtyard, open to the stars and complete with a trickling fountain.

Information

Clínica Especializada Internacional (809-240-6701; Calle Fabio Abreu) This new private hospital, run by Cuban doctors, is the peninsula's most modern.

Getting There & Away

Air

International flights arrive at Aeropuerto Internacional El Catey, located 8km west of Sánchez and a 35-minute taxi ride (US$70) to Las Terrenas.

Aerodomca (in Santo Domingo 809-826-4141; www.aerodomca.com) offers sporadic, often cancelled services to Aeropuerto Internacional Arroyo Barril near Samaná from Punta Cana daily, departing at 2pm.

Bus

Las Terrenas Transportes (809-240-5302) operates coaches to Santo Domingo (RD$350, 2½ hours, 5am, 7am, 9am, 2pm and 3:30pm) and Puerto Plata (RD$300, three hours, 6:30am).

Guaguas to Samaná leave in front of Casa Linda on the corner of Calle Principal and the coastal road eight times daily (RD $100, 1¼ hours) between 7:15am and 5pm.

Trucks and *gua-guas* to El Limón 14km away (RD$50, 35 minutes, every 15 minutes from 7:15am to 6:15pm) leave from the same stop at Casa Linda.

Getting Around

You can walk to and from most places in Las Terrenas. Taxis charge US$15 each way to Playa Bonita and US$40 for the round trip to El Limón. *Motoconchos* are RD$100 to Playa Bonita.

Parque Nacional Los Haitises (left)

RAUL TOUZON/GETTY IMAGES ©

NORTH COAST

Within two hours' drive of Puerto Plata airport you'll find all the best the north coast has to offer – water sports and beach nightlife in Cabarete, mountain biking in the coastal hills, the celebrated 27 waterfalls of Damajagua, sleepy little Dominican towns where it's still possible to escape the tourist hordes, and mile after mile of that famous Caribbean sand.

Cabarete

POP 14,600

This one-time farming hamlet is now a sophisticated, grown-up and growing beach town and the adventure-sports capital of the country with a beach-dining experience on Playa Cabarete second to none (not to mention the best wind and waves on the island). Scores of kiters of all skill levels negotiate amid the waves and traffic at **Kite Beach**, 2km west of town. Another 2km further on is **Playa Encuentro**, a long narrow stretch of sand with the best surf in the area.

Activities

KITESURFING

Kite Beach has ideal conditions for this sport and a number of kitesurfing schools offer multiday courses – just to go out by yourself you'll need at least three to four days of instruction (two to three hours' instruction per day). **Laurel Eastman Kiteboarding** (809-571-0564; www.laureleastman.com; Cabarete) is a friendly, safety-conscious operation located at the high-end Millennium Resort.

Expect to pay US$200 to US$280 for four hours of beginner lessons, or anywhere from US$300 to US$500 for a three- to four-day course (around eight hours total).

SURFING

Some of the best waves for surfing on the entire island – reaching up to 4m – break over reefs 4km west of Cabarete on Playa Encuentro. Several outfits in town and on Playa Encuentro rent surfboards and offer instruction.

DIVING

The well-respected Sosúa-based dive shop **Northern Coast Diving** (809-571-1028; www.northerncoastdiving.com; Calle Pedro Clisante 8) has a representative in the offices of Iguana Mama and can organize excursions from Río San Juan in the east to Monte Cristi in the west.

Tours

Iguana Mama — Outdoor Adventures
(809-571-0908, cell 809-654-2325; www.iguanamama.com; Calle Principal, Cabarete) This very professional and family-run adventure-sports tour operator on the north coast is in a class of its own. Its specialties are mountain biking (from easy to insanely difficult, US$65) and canyoning. Trips to Damajagua (US$85) go to the 27th waterfall, and Iguana Mama pioneered several other canyoning trips in the area. There's also a variety of hiking trips and its Pico Duarte trek is handy if you want transportation to and from Cabarete (per person US$450).

Sleeping

Ali's Surf Camp — Surf Hotel $
(809-571-0733; www.alissurfcamp.com; s US$29-44, d US$33-66, apt US$75-120; P ❄ ⓦ ≋) On the edge of a lagoon a five-minute walk inland, this lushly landscaped property has small, colorful and rustic backpacker-style cabins; larger, modern rooms with kitchenettes in a two-story Victorian-style building; and, best of all, two colonial-style all-wood rooms with louvered windows in a 'tower' above the kitchen and dining area.

Swell Surf Camp — Surf Hotel $$
(809-571-0672; www.swellsurfcamp.com; week-long incl breakfast and 4 dinners dm/s/d US$425/635/1000; P ❄ ⓦ ≋) Designed with the discerning surfer in mind, Swell is far from a crash pad. The spare clean lines, plush bedding, modern photographs and funky furniture say 'boutique', but the pool, ping-pong and foosball tables and social vibe suggest otherwise. A huge wood communal table is the center of the hanging-out action.

Twenty-Seven Waterfalls of Damajagua

Travelers routinely describe the tour of the waterfalls at Damajagua as the coolest thing they did in the DR. We agree. Guides lead you up, swimming and climbing through the waterfalls. To get down you jump – as much as 8m – into the sparkling pools below.

It's mandatory to go with a guide and wear a helmet and life jacket, but there's no minimum group size. You'll need around four hours to make it to the 27th waterfall and back. The falls are open 8:30am to 4pm, but go early, before the crowds arrive.

You can go up to the seventh, 12th or 27th waterfall. Iguana Mama runs trips to the 27th for US$89. If you visit on your own, the entrance fee varies depending on your nationality and how far you go. Foreigners pay RD$600 to the highest waterfall, less to reach the lower ones.

Velero Beach Resort Hotel $$$
(809-571-9727; www.velerobeach.com; La Punta 1; r from US$175; P ❄ @ ≋) Distinguished by boutique-style rooms and its location down a small lane at the relatively traffic-free eastern end of town, Velero is an excellent choice. True to its four-star rating in service, professionalism and property maintenance, the Velero's only downside is its on a small spit of a beach, but the pool and lounge area more than make up for this.

Eating

Belgium Bakery Bakery, Sandwiches $$
(Plaza Popular Cabarete, Calle Principal; mains RD$260; 7am-7pm;) Hands down *the* place for breakfast in Cabarete: strong coffee, delicious bread and pastries and large omelets. Though it fronts a parking lot and not the beach, the outdoor patio seating is an ideal spot to while away several hours. Burgers, paninis and salads are served throughout the day.

Pomodoro Italian $$
(809-571-0085; mains RD$380; 3-11pm Mon-Fri, from 11:30am Sat & Sun;) Run by Lorenzo, an Italian jazz fiend (and the organizer of the Jazz Festival), Pomodoro serves the best crispy-crust pizza on the beach. It uses only quality toppings – including pungent, imported Italian cheese – and there's live jazz on Thursday nights (8pm to 10pm). It delivers.

Otra Cosa French $$$
(809-571-0607; otracosa_lapunta@hotmail.com; La Punta; mains RD$600; 6:30-11pm;) Located at a secluded spot with marvelous sea breezes at dusk, this French-Caribbean restaurant guarantees an incredible dining experience. You can listen to the surf and watch the moon rise over the water while sipping wine and feasting on dishes that are expertly prepared and *très délicieux*, such as seared tuna in ginger flambéed in rum (RD$650).

Drinking & Nightlife

Onno's Nightclub
(9am-late) This edgy, Dutch-owned restaurant and nightclub is a European and hipster hangout and serves good-value food on the beach. At night a DJ spins a decent set.

Lax Bar, Nightclub
(www.lax-cabarete.com; 9am-1am) This mellow bar and restaurant serves food until 10:30pm, when the DJ starts to spin. In many ways it's the social headquarters of Cabarete.

 Information

Servi-Med (809-571-0964; Calle Principal; 24hr) English, German and Spanish are spoken, and travel medical insurance and credit cards accepted.

Getting There & Around

None of the main bus companies services Cabarete. The closest depots are in Sosúa. The best place to arrange car rental is at Puerto Plata airport when you arrive.

Heaps of *gua-guas* ply this coastal road, including east to Río San Juan (RD$80, one hour) and west to Sosúa (RD$20, 20 minutes) and Puerto Plata (RD$50, 45 minutes). Transportation in town is dominated by *motoconchos*. A ride out to Encuentro should cost RD$100.

The motorcycle-shy can call a taxi (809-571-0767; www.taxisosuacabarete.com), which will cost RD$250 to Encuentro, US$35 to the airport or Puerto Plata. There's also a taxi stand in the middle of town.

CENTRAL HIGHLANDS

When you've overdosed on sun and sand, the cool mountainous playground of the central highlands is the place to come; where else can you sit at dusk, huddled in a sweater, watching the mist descend into the valley as the sun sets behind the mountains? Popular retreats, roaring rivers, soaring peaks and the only white-water rafting in the Caribbean, beckon.

Jarabacoa

POP 40,550 / ELEV 488M

Nestled in the low foothills of the Cordillera Central, Jarabacoa maintains an under-the-radar allure as the antithesis to the clichéd Caribbean vacation. Nighttime temperatures call for light sweaters, a roiling river winds past forested slopes that climb into the clouds, and outdoor adventurers can raft, hike, bike, horseback ride, go canyoning or simply explore rural life.

Sights

Three nearby waterfalls, **Salto de Jimenoa Uno**, **Salto de Jimenoa Dos** and **Salto de Baiguate**, are easy to visit if you've got your own transportation. If not, a *motoconcho* tour to all three will set you back around RD$1000, a taxi US$80 to US$100. Uno is the most picturesque and has a sandy beach and icy cold (and potentially dangerous) swimming hole.

Activities

The Río Yaque del Norte is the longest river in the country and **rafting** (US$50) a portion of it can be a fun day trip. The rapids are rated II and III

Kitesurfer, Cabarete (p100)

GREG JOHNSTON/GETTY IMAGES ©

and part of the thrill is the risk your raft may turn over, dumping you into a rock-infested river.

In addition to climbing Pico Duarte, there's a number of half-day and full-day **walks** you can take in the area. Or you can go **canyoning** (US$50) and spend a few hours rappelling, jumping, sliding and zip-lining down a mountain river.

Tours

Rancho Baiguate Adventure Tour

(809-574-6890; www.ranchobaiguate.com; Carretera a Constanza) Rancho Baiguate is recommended for safety and reliability. While its main clientele are Dominican groups from the capital and foreign guests from the all-inclusive resorts near Puerto Plata, independent travelers are always free to join any of the trips, usually by calling a day or two in advance (except for Pico Duarte, which should be arranged weeks in advance).

Sleeping

Rancho Baiguate Resort **$$**

(809-574-6890; www.ranchobaiguate.com; Carretera a Constanza; all-inclusive s US$77-107, d US$126-163, tr US$170-220, q US$252; P) A wonderful base to explore the mountains, Baiguate is a rustic resort set in an enormous 72-sq-km leafy compound. Ask for a room in the low-slung building along the river – large, comfortable, tile-floored rooms have private patios with wicker chairs.

Hotel Gran Jimenoa Hotel **$$**

(809-574-6304; www.granjimenoahotel.com; Av La Confluencia; s/d/tr incl breakfast from RD$1375/1870/2400; P@) Set several kilometers north of town directly on the roaring Río Jimenoa, this is the Cordillera Central's most upscale hotel. It's neither on the beach nor an all-inclusive hotel, but you could easily spend a week here without leaving the extensive grounds, which include a footbridge to a bar on the far bank of the river.

Eating

All of the accommodation options listed have their own restaurants. **Plaza La Confluencia**, a small, newly opened (and when we visited, not yet fully occupied) two-story shopping mall, has several places to eat.

Pizza & Pepperoni Pizza **$$**

(809-574-4348; Paseo de los Maestros; pizza RD$200-300; 11am-11pm) The straightforward name isn't entirely accurate: excellent pepperoni pizzas are on the menu, along with more than a dozen other varieties, but so are calzones, burgers, pasta, grilled meat and fish dishes. It has a modern outdoor dining area with TVs tuned to sports. Delivers.

Aroma de la Montana International **$$$**

(829-452-6879; www.jamacadedios.com; mains RD$600-1500; 10am-10pm Mon-Thu, to 11pm Fri & Sat) Sweeping, practically aerial views of the entirety of the Jarabacoa countryside are available anytime from the balcony seating. Lunchtime has a family atmosphere but there's a distinctly romantic candlelit vibe on weekend nights (reservations highly recommended), at least on the rotating top floor.

Getting There & Away

Caribe Tours (809-574-4796; José Duran, near Av Independencia) has the only 1st-class bus service between Jarabacoa and Santo Domingo (RD$280, 2½ hours, 7am, 10am, 1:30pm and 4:30pm).

Getting Around

The town of Jarabacoa is easily managed on foot, but to get to outlying hotels and sights you can easily flag down a *motoconcho* on any street corner during the day. If you prefer a cab, try **Jaroba Taxi** (809-574-4640), next to the Caribe Tours terminal.

SURVIVAL GUIDE

Directory A–Z

Accommodations

Room rates are for the high season (generally from December to March and July to August); low-season rates are 20% to 50% less than high-season rates.

Rooms booked a minimum of three days in advance on the internet can be shockingly cheap (especially so at the all-inclusive resorts).

Be sure the rate you are quoted already includes the 23% room tax.

We've listed accommodations rates in US$ or RD$, depending on which is most commonly quoted.

$ less than US$50/RD$2100

$$ US$50 to US$100/RD$2100 to RD$4200

$$$ more than US$100/RD$2400

Food

The following price categories refer to the cost of a meal with tax which includes a 18% sales tax (ITBIS) and a 10% service charge:

$ less than RD$214/US$5

$$ RD$214 to RD$640/US$5 to US$15

$$$ more than RD$640/US$15

Health

The DR is generally safe as long as you're reasonably careful about what you eat and drink. Only purified water should be used for drinking, brushing your teeth, and hand washing. It's worth noting there's a small risk of malaria and dengue fever in certain areas.

Money

There are one- and five-peso coins; notes are in denominations of 10, 20, 50, 100, 500 and 1000 pesos. Most midrange and top-end hotels list prices in US dollars but accept Dominican Republic pesos (RD$) at the going exchange rate. We've listed prices in the currency in which they're most commonly quoted on the ground.

ATMs

ATMs (available 24 hours) are common and are the best way to obtain Dominican Republic pesos and manage your money on the road. Most banks charge ATM fees of around RD$115.

Left: Waterfall near Jarabacoa (p102); **Below:** Broad-billed tody, Jarabacoa
(LEFT) DEMETRIO CARRASCO/GETTY IMAGES ©; (BELOW) CULTURA SCIENCE/JOUKO VAN DER KRUIJSSEN/GETTY IMAGES ©

Credit Cards

Visa and MasterCard are more common than Amex, but most cards are accepted in tourist areas. Some businesses add a credit-card surcharge (typically 16%).

Taxes & Tipping

There are two taxes on food and drink sales: an 18% sales tax (ITBIS) and a 10% service charge. There's a 23% tax on hotel rooms – ask if listed rates include taxes. It's customary to tip bellhops and housecleaners at resorts, and tour guides.

Opening Hours

Banks 9am to 4:30pm Monday to Friday, to 1pm Saturday.

Bars 6pm to late, to 2am in Santo Domingo.

Government offices 7:30am to 2:30pm Monday to Friday.

Restaurants 8am to 10pm Monday to Saturday (some closed between lunch and dinner).

Shops 9am to 7:30pm Monday to Saturday; some open half-day Sunday.

Supermarkets 8am to 10pm Monday to Saturday.

Public Holidays

In addition to holidays observed throughout the region, the Dominican Republic also has the following public holidays:

Epiphany/Three Kings Day January 6

Our Lady of Altagracia January 21

Duarte Day January 26

Independence Day February 27

Holy Thursday, Holy Friday, Easter Sunday March or April

Pan-American Day April 14

Labor Day May 1

Foundation of Sociedad la Trinitaria July 16

Restoration Day August 16

Our Lady of Mercedes September 24

Columbus Day October 12

UN Day October 24

All Saints' Day November 1

Practicalities

- **Electricity** 110 to 125 volts AC, 60-Hz, flat-pronged plugs; same system as USA and Canada.
- **Newspapers** *El Listín Diario*, *Hoy*, *Diario Libre* and *El Nacional* plus *International Herald Tribune*, the *New York Times* and the *Miami Herald* can be found in many tourist areas.
- **TV & Radio** About 150 radio stations, most playing merengue and *bachata*; seven local TV networks. Cable and satellite programming is very popular for baseball, movies and American soap operas.
- **Weights & Measures** Metric system used, except for gasoline (measured in gallons).

Telephone

Remember that you must dial ☎1 + 809 or 829 for all calls within the DR, even local ones. Toll-free numbers have ☎200 for their prefix (not the area code).

The easiest way to make a phone call in the DR is to pay per minute (average rates to USA US$0.20, to Europe US$0.50) at a Codetel Centro de Comunicaciones (Codetel) call center or an internet cafe. Phonecards can be used at public phones.

Local SIM cards can be used or cell phones can be set for roaming. There are GSM-suitable networks.

Visas

The majority of foreign travelers do not need a visa.

Getting There & Away

Entering the Dominican Republic

All foreign visitors must have a valid passport. A tourist card (you don't need to retain it for your return flight), valid for up to 30 days, is issued for US$10 upon arrival to visitors.

Air

Airports

Aeropuerto Internacional Las Américas (José Francisco Peña Gómez) (SDQ; ☎809-947-2220) The country's main international airport is located 20km east of Santo Domingo.

Aeropuerto Internacional Punta Cana (PUJ; ☎809-959-2473; www.puntacanainternationalairport.com) Serves Bávaro and Punta Cana, and is the busiest airport in the country.

Aeropuerto Internacional Gregorío Luperón (POP; ☎809-586-0107; www.puerto-plata-airport.com) Puerto Plata is served by this airport 18km east of town along the coastal highway (past Playa Dorada), and just a few kilometers west of Sosúa.

Aeropuerto Internacional Samaná El Catey (Presidente Juan Bosch) (AZS; ☎809-338-0094) Located around 40km west of Samaná.

Aeropuerto Internacional del Cibao (STI; ☎809-581-8072; www.aeropuertocibao.com.do) Serves Santiago and the interior, but an option worth considering for north coast destinations as well.

Aeropuerto Internacional La Isabela Dr Joaquín Balaguer (JBQ, Higüero; ☎809-826-4003) This airport is just north of Santo Domingo proper. It handles mostly domestic flights.

Sea

Caribbean Fantasy (www.acferries.com) Santo Domingo (☎809-688-4400; www.acferries.com); Mayagüez (☎787-832-4800; www.acferries.com); San Juan (☎787-622-4800; www.acferries.com) Offers a passenger and car ferry service between Santo Domingo and San Juan and Mayagüez, Puerto Rico (12 hours, three times weekly).

Getting Around

Air

Those with limited time should consider flying. Most one-way flights cost US$35 to US$170. The main domestic carriers and air-taxi companies include the following:

AeroDomca (☎809-826-4141; www.aerodomca.com) Scheduled daily flights between Punta

Cana and Arroyo Barril (one way US$300); charter flights can be booked elsewhere.

Air Century (☎809-826-4222; www.aircentury.com) Flights from La Isabela to Punta Cana, Puerto Plata, La Romana, Santiago and Samaná.

Dominican Shuttles (☎809-738-3014; www.dominicanshuttles.com) Flights between La Isabela and Punta Cana (US$99); two daily flights (US$99) between La Isabela and El Portillo.

Bus

First-Class Service

First-class buses have air-con and often TVs and a movie. Fares are low – the most expensive is less than US$10. Reservations aren't usually necessary.

Caribe Tours (☎809-221-4422; www.caribetours.com.do; cnr Avs 27 de Febrero & Leopoldo Navarro, Santo Domingo) One of the country's two main bus companies; has most departures and covers more destinations.

Metro (☎809-566-7126; www.metrotours.com.do; Calle Francisco Prats Ramírez, Santo Domingo) Metro serves nine cities, mostly along the Santo Domingo–Puerto Plata corridor. Fares tend to be slightly more expensive than Caribe Tours.

Expreso Bávaro Punta Cana (☎in Santo Domingo 809-682-9670; Juan Sánchez Ramirez 31) Direct service to Bávaro with a stop in La Romana. Departure times in both directions are 7am, 10am, 2pm and 4pm (RD$350, four hours).

Gua-guas

Gua-guas range from minivans to midsize buses with room for around 30 passengers. They stop all along the route to pick up and drop off passengers – wave to be picked up. Most pass every 15 to 30 minutes and cost RD$35 to RD$70. They rarely have signs, so ask a local if you're unsure which one to take.

Local Bus

Large cities such as Santo Domingo have public bus systems that operate as they do in most places around the world. *Públicos* pass much more frequently.

Car

Rental

If you plan to do any driving outside major cities, a 4WD is recommended. Daily rates from multinational agencies are US$40 to US$120, but if you make an internet reservation the discounts are substantial.

Road Rules

In theory, road rules are the same as for most countries in the Americas and the lights and signs are the same shape and color you find in the US or Canada. That said, driving in the DR is pretty much a free-for-all, a test of one's nerves and skill. Be alert for potholes, speed bumps and people walking along the roadside, especially near populated areas. Be particularly careful when driving at night – better yet, never drive at night.

Motoconchos

Motoconchos (motorcycle taxis) are the best and sometimes only way to get around in many towns. An average ride should set you back no more than RD$30, but you might have to negotiate to get a fair price.

Públicos

These are banged-up cars, minivans or small pickup trucks that pick up passengers along set routes in towns. *Públicos* (also called *conchos* or *carros*) don't have signs, but the drivers hold their hands out the window to solicit fares.

Taxis

Dominican taxis rarely cruise for passengers – instead they wait at designated *sitios* (stops). You also can phone a taxi service (or ask your hotel receptionist to call for you). Taxis do not have meters – agree on a price beforehand.

Puerto Rico

Puerto Rico

Perfect beaches, swashbuckling history and a vibrant, distinct culture make the sun-washed backyard of the United States a place fittingly hyped as the 'Island of Enchantment'. It's the Caribbean's only island where you can catch a wave before breakfast, hike a rainforest after lunch and race to the beat of a high-gloss, cosmopolitan city after dark.

Between blinking casinos and chirping frogs, Puerto Rico is also a land of dynamic contrasts, where the breezy gate of the Caribbean mixes with the hustle of contemporary America. Don't miss San Juan's beaches, historic forts, brilliant restaurants, urban grit and craps tables. But also take time for the off-beat islands off-shore, the misty mountains and roads that wander through an ever-changing landscape. There's a lot in this small package and you can expect a rich range of experiences in even a short visit.

Mural, Old San Juan (p114)

Puerto Rico Itineraries

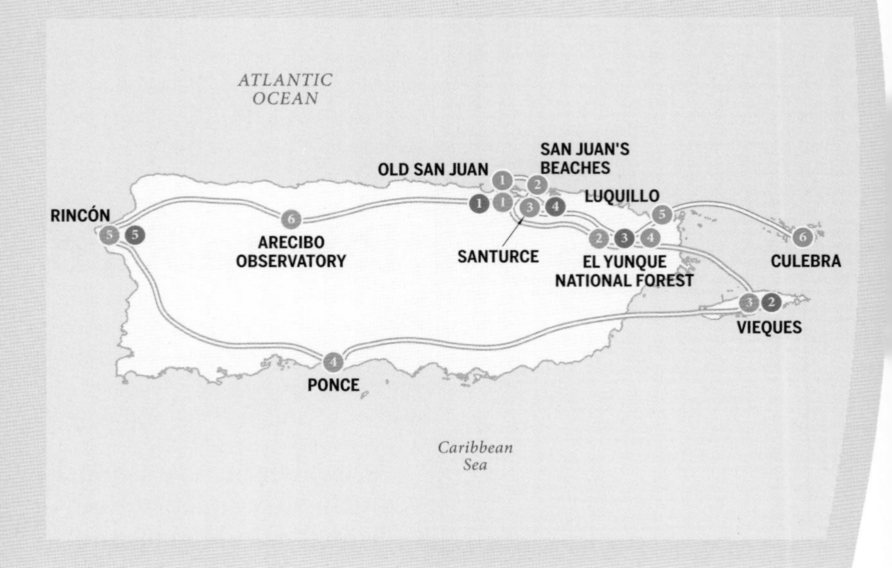

Four Days

❶ **Old San Juan** (p114) Spend a lazy day exploring one of the most interesting historic towns in the Americas. Escape the crowds on evocative little backstreets with timeless bars and cafes. Wander the old forts and make a discovery in the back corner of a museum. Sit on a square and feel urban rhythms unchanged in decades.

❷ **San Juan's Beaches** (p112) Much of San Juan faces the Atlantic and boasts a string of excellent urban beaches. You can pick your style: from stylish to active to chilled-out bum.

❸ **Santurce** (p117) This once stylish, then gritty neighborhood is now an enticing mélange of both qualities. Street art covers walls and there's a fascinating mix of hipster joints, old stand-bys and much-loved newcomers. Wander through a gallery, then join the crowds bar- and restaurant-hopping.

❹ **El Yunque National Forest** (p124) Driving Hwy 191 into the lush rainforest wonders, you'll climb ever higher into the misty peak and you can pick your stops for waterfalls and nature hikes. Consider stopping off at one of the adventure parks where you can zip-line through the trees.

❺ **Luquillo** (p124) Enjoy the popular beach and go nuts feeding at the food stands, where locals spend hours browsing and munching classic local treats.

❻ **Culebra** (p127) You'll have no shortage of options for a day trip or (better) a longer stay. Get a taste of funky island life and enjoy some sensational snorkeling.

THIS LEG: 60 MILES

Seven Days

❶ **San Juan** (p119) Dive into endlessly interesting Old San Juan, with first-class museums, galleries, monuments and forts. Find time to laze on a beach, then after dark, book a table for world-class dining in up-and-coming Santurce.

❷ **El Yunque National Forest** (p124) Enjoy a rainforest day trip to North America's best-preserved mountain rainforest. Get wet in a waterfall. This is a fine first stop on a clockwise itinerary around Puerto Rico.

❸ **Vieques** (p124) Try to decide which of this island's brilliant beaches is your favorite. Then revel in the funky local vibe, first in atmospheric Isabel Segunda, then south in Esperanza, the perfect place to enjoy the slow pace of the tropics while enjoying some fine places to stay, eat and drink. And don't miss the glowing wonder of Bioluminescent Bay.

❹ **Ponce** (p130) Explore the treats that await at Puerto Rico's second city: colonial buildings, a gaggle of museums and excellent restaurants. The drive south through the forested hills features coffee plantations and, if it's a weekend, be sure to stop in Guavate to sample smoky pork at one of the famed roadside *lechoneras* (eateries specializing in suckling pig).

❺ **Rincón** (p131) Add a rush to your trip surfing (or taking lessons) on perfect waves and soaking up the island's best sunsets with an icy rum drink in hand at this idyllic surfers' retreat. The drives along this part of the Puerto Rican coast are both lovely and far quieter than roads in the east.

❻ **Arecibo Observatory** (p124) Before arriving back in San Juan check out this vast and iconic research center where the mysteries of the universe are explored.

THIS LEG: 270 MILES

Puerto Rico Highlights

❶ **Best Exploring: Old San Juan** (p114) Crooked alleys, towering forts, pastel-painted facades and 500 years of history make this ancient city a must.

❷ **Best Beaches: Vieques** (p124) Snorkel and swim at myriad flawless beaches on this island where two-thirds of the land is protected.

❸ **Best Park: El Yunque National Forest** (p124) Explore drippy trails and misty waterfalls in the rainforest.

❹ **Best Eating: Santurce** (p117) Famous chefs and an ever-changing lineup of fab places to eat (from cafes to bistros) make wandering this neighborhood a must.

❺ **Best Surfing: Rincón** (p131) Paddle out to perfect breaks in this well-chilled wave-riding capital.

Vieques (p124)
OLIVER GERHARD/GETTY IMAGES ©

Discover Puerto Rico

SAN JUAN

POP 389,000

Established in 1521, San Juan is the second-oldest European-founded settlement in the Americas and the oldest under US jurisdiction. Shoehorned onto a tiny islet that guards the entrance to San Juan harbor, the old town was inaugurated almost a century before the Mayflower laid anchor in present-day Massachusetts, and is now a historic wonderland that juxtaposes historical authenticity with pulsating modern energy.

Beyond its timeworn 15ft-thick walls, San Juan is far more than a collection of well-polished colonial artifacts – it's also a mosaic of ever-evolving neighborhoods such as Santurce, which has a raw vitality fueled by galleries, superb restaurants and a bar scene that takes over the streets at night.

And then there's the beaches. Silky ribbons of sand line San Juan's northern edge from swanky Condado to resort-filled Isla Verde. You can land at the airport and be out splashing in the azure waters an hour later.

El Morro (p114)

 Beaches

San Juan has some of the best municipal beaches this side of Rio de Janeiro. Starting half a mile or so east of the Old Town, they vary from rustic to swanky in the space of 7½ miles.

Balneario Escambrón Beach

A sheltered arc of raked sand, decent surf breaks, plenty of local action and a 17th-century Spanish fort shimmering in the distance are the hallmarks of this fine beach only a stone's throw from Old San Juan and the busy tourist strip of Condado. Best of all, it's often uncrowded.

Playa Condado Beach

Hemmed in by hotels and rocky outcrops, Condado's narrow beaches are busier than Ocean Park's but less exclusive than Isla Verde's. Expect splashes of graffiti, boisterous games of volleyball and plenty of crashing Atlantic surf. The public beach

Puerto Rico

ATLANTIC OCEAN
0 50 km
0 25 miles
Punta Sardina
Punta Borinquen
Isabela
112
Aguadilla
Punta Gorda
2
Rincón
402
Cordillera Jaicoa
Río Culebrinas
Camuy
Hatillo
Montañas Guarionex
Arecibo
Puertro Arecibo
Arecibo Observatory
Cavernas del Río Camuy
129
Lares
Utuado
123
124
Montañas de Uroyan
Mayagüez
105
Maricao
135
525
131
518
120
366
365
Laguna de Joyunda
San Germán
2
Sabana Grande
Cordillera Central
100
101
Sierra Bermeja
116
Cabo Rojo (Punta Jagüey)
La Parguera
Punta Brea
Yauco
Guayanilla
Bosque Estatal de Guánica
Bahía de Tallaboa
Punta Las Tunas
Río Grande de Arecibo
Puerto del Tortuguero
Barceloneta
Punta Puerto Nuevo
Manatí
22
149
Ciales
149
Cerro Los Tres Picachos (3953ft)
Cerro de Punta (4389ft)
Cordillera Central
143
Adjuntas
Reserva Forestal Toro Negro
149
Ponce
Playa Ponce
Punta Cabullónes
Isla Caja de Muertos
Coamo
14
Santa Isabel
Cayo Berberia
52
2
888
San Juan
Cataño
26
Bayamón
Guaynabo
Río de Bayamón
1
167
722
1
Salinas
3
Cayos de Ratónes
53
Cayos de Barca
Guayama
Puerto Arroyo
Caguas
52
Guavate
179
7740
15
Sierra de Cayey
Patillas
Maunabo
Yabucoa
182
901
Punta Yeguas
Cabo Mala Pascua
Punta Vacía Talega
Loíza Aldea
Canóvanas
Río Grande
Punta Picúa
Luquillo
Fajardo
(Caribbean National Forest)
El Yunque (3496ft)
El Toro (3522ft)
Sierra de Luquillo
Naguabo
30
Humacao
3
Puerto Humacao
Punta Candelero
Pasaje de San Juan
Cayo Icacos
Isla Palominos
Isla Piñeros
Puerto Pasaje de Vieques
Punta Arenas
Esperanza
Bahía Mosquito
Isabel Segunda
Vieques
Punta Este
Cayo Norte
Culebra
Cayo Luis Peña
Dewey
Isla Culebrita
Sonda de Vieques
Caribbean Sea

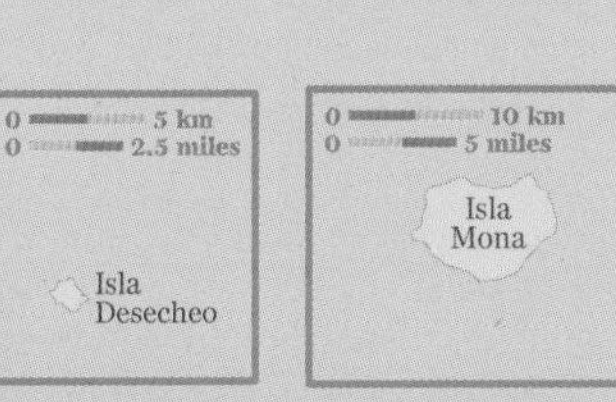

0 5 km
0 2.5 miles
Isla Desecheo
0 10 km
0 5 miles
Isla Mona

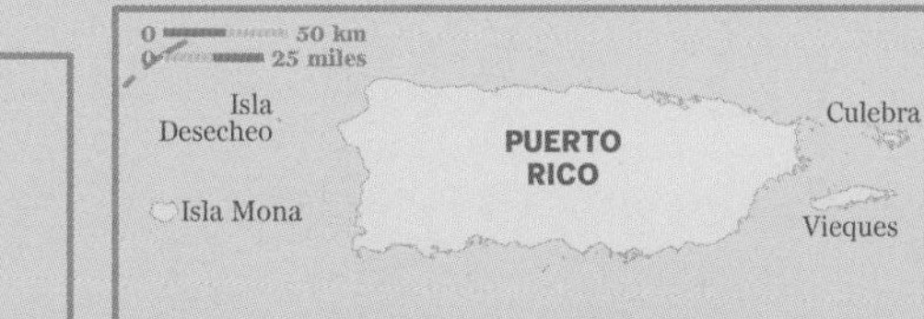

0 50 km
0 25 miles
Isla Desecheo
Isla Mona
PUERTO RICO
Culebra
Vieques

Port of Call – Old San Juan

Cruise ships dock at the huge port area on the south side of Old San Juan.

- Climb the ramparts of El Morro for great views.
- Explore the dripping jungles of El Yunque.
- Splash and gamble at the beaches and resorts.

is a small arc of sand, adjacent to the Dos Hermanos bridge.

Playa Isla Verde Beach
With its legions of tanned bodies and dexterous beach bums flexing their triceps around the volleyball net, Playa Isla Verde basks in its reputation as the Copacabana of Puerto Rico.

Sights

Most of San Juan's major attractions, including museums and art galleries, are in Old San Juan. Beaches dominate the appeal of Condado, Ocean Park and Isla Verde (as they should), while Santurce offers buzzy, gritty delights.

OLD SAN JUAN

Old San Juan is a colorful kaleidoscope of life, music, legend and history and would stand out like a flashing beacon in any country, let alone one as small as Puerto Rico. From the blue-toned, cobblestoned streets to the spectacle of more than 400 historically listed buildings to the stunning views from old walls, there is a plethora of visual treats great and small.

El Morro Fort
Map p115 (Fuerte San Felipe del Morro; ☎787-729-7423; www.nps.gov/saju; Calle del Morro; adult/child $3/free; ⏱9am-6pm) The star of Old San Juan, El Morro juts aggressively over bold headlands, glowering across the Atlantic at would-be conquerors. The 140ft walls (some up to 15ft thick) date back to 1539, and El Morro is said to be the oldest Spanish fort in the New World.

Displays document the construction of the fort, which took almost 200 years, as well as El Morro's role in rebuffing attacks on the island by the British, the Dutch and, later, the US military.

Fuerte San Cristóbal Fort
Map p115 (San Cristóbal Fort; ☎787-729-6777; www.nps.gov/saju; Av Muñoz Rivera; adult/child $3/free; ⏱9am-6pm) San Juan's second major fort is Fuerte San Cristóbal, one of the largest military installations the Spanish built in the Americas. In its prime, San Cristóbal covered 27 acres

Old San Juan

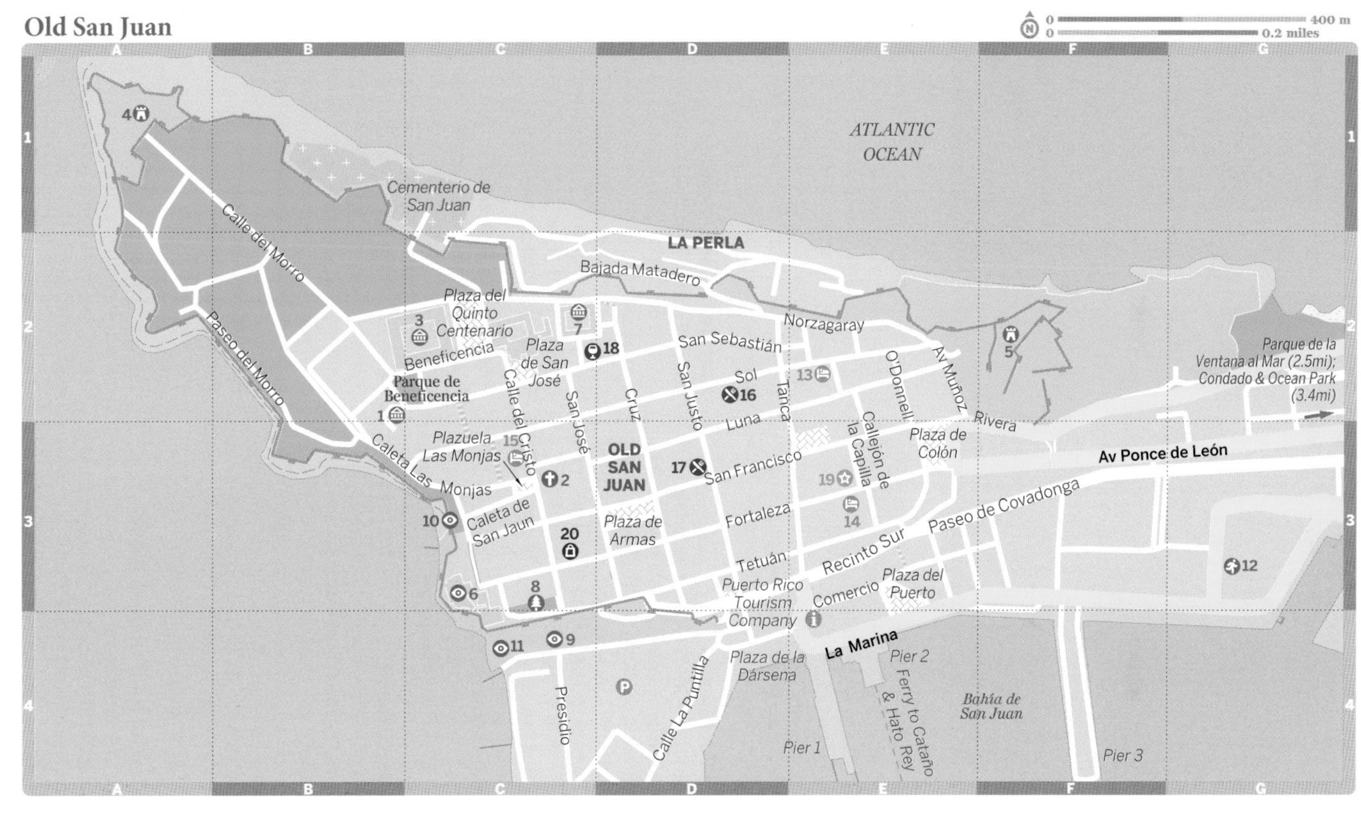
Old San Juan
0 400 m
0 0.2 miles
A
B
C
D
E
F
G
1
2
3
4
ATLANTIC OCEAN
Cementerio de San Juan
LA PERLA
Bajada Matadero
Calle del Morro
Paseo del Morro
Plaza del Quinto Centenario
Beneficencia
Parque de Beneficencia
Plaza de San José
Norzagaray
San Sebastián
Sol
Luna
San Francisco
Fortaleza
Tetuán
Recinto Sur
Comercio
Calle del Cristo
San José
Cruz
San Justo
Tanca
Callejón de la Capilla
O'Donnell
Av Muñoz Rivera
Plaza de Colón
Av Ponce de León
Paseo de Covadonga
Plazuela Las Monjas
Caleta Las Monjas
Caleta de San Jaun
OLD SAN JUAN
Plaza de Armas
Puerto Rico Tourism Company
Plaza del Puerto
La Marina
Plaza de la Dársena
Calle La Puntilla
Presidio
Pier 1
Pier 2
Pier 3
Ferry to Cataño & Hato Rey
Bahía de San Juan
Parque de la Ventana al Mar (2.5mi); Condado & Ocean Park (3.4mi)
1
2
3
4
5
6
7
8
9
10
11
12
13
14
15
16
17
18
19
20

Condado & Ocean Park

with a maze of six interconnected forts protecting a central core with 150ft walls, moats, booby-trapped bridges and tunnels. The fort has a fascinating museum, a store, military archives, a reproduction of a soldier's barracks, and stunning Atlantic and city views.

La Fortaleza Historic Site

Map p115 (787-721-7000; www.fortaleza.gobierno.pr; Recinto; suggested donation $3; tours 9am-3:30pm Mon-Fri) Guarded iron gates mark La Fortaleza, also known as El Palacio de Santa Catalina. This imposing building, dating from 1533, is the oldest executive mansion in continuous use in the western hemisphere. You can take a short guided tour that includes the mansion's Moorish gardens, the dungeon and the chapel.

Casa Blanca Historic Building

Map p115 (White House; 787-725-1454; San Sebastián; adult/child $2/1; 8:30am-4:20pm Tue-Sat) First constructed in 1524 as a residence for Puerto Rico's pioneering governor, Juan Ponce de León (who died before he could move in), the Casa Blanca is the oldest continuously occupied house in the western hemisphere.

Cuartel de Ballajá & Museo de las Américas Museum

Map p115 (off Norzagaray; 9am-noon & 1-4pm Tue-Sat, noon-5pm Sun) FREE Built in 1854 as a military barracks, the *cuartel* is a three-story edifice with large gates on two ends, ample balconies, a series of arches and a protected central courtyard that served as a plaza and covers a reservoir. The small ground-floor cafe is a good place to pause and soak up the monumental courtyard's atmosphere.

Parque de las Palomas Park

Map p115 (Pigeon Park) On the southern end of Calle del Cristo, Parque de las Palomas is in a tree-shaded cobblestone courtyard on the top of the city wall, with excellent views of Bahía de San Juan and the criss-crossing water traffic that includes Brobdingnagian cruise ships.

Paseo de la Princesa Promenade

Map p115 (Walkway of the Princess) Evoking a distinctly European feeling, the Paseo de la Princesa is a 19th-century esplanade just outside the city walls. Lined with antique streetlamps, trees, statues, benches, fruit vendors' carts and street entertainers, this romantic walkway ends at the magnificent **Raíces Fountain**.

Puerta de San Juan Gate

Map p115 (San Juan Gate) Spanish ships once anchored in the cove just off these ramparts to unload colonists and supplies, all of which entered the city through a tall red portal known as Puerta de San Juan. This tunnel through the wall dates from the 1630s.

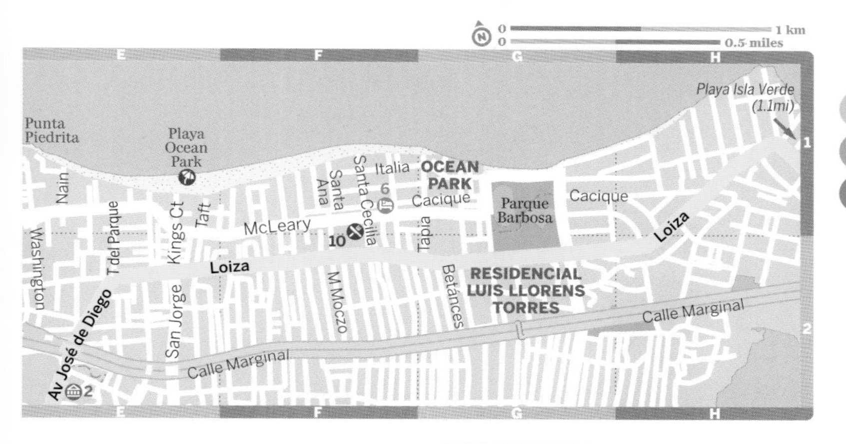

Museo de San Juan Museum
Map p115 (787-480-3530; 150 Norzagaray; by donation; 9am-4pm Tue-Sun) Located in a Spanish colonial building, the Museo de San Juan is the definitive take on the city's 500-year history. The well-laid-out exhibition showcases pictorial and photographic testimonies from the Caparra ruins to the modern-day shopping malls.

Catedral de San Juan Church
Map p115 (787-722-0861; www.catedralsanjuan.com; 153 Calle del Cristo; 8am-5pm) FREE It's noticeably smaller and more austere than other Spanish churches, but the cathedral nonetheless retains a simple earthy elegance dating from the 1500s.

SANTURCE

Much of Santurce's current vibrancy can be found in and around **La Placita de Santurce** (Map p116), the small square that's home to the **Santurce Mercado** and many cafes, as well as along Avenida Ponce de León.

As you can see from the stunning street art, the local art scene is hot, with small galleries and cultural spaces organizing all manner of shows and events.

Museo de Arte de Puerto Rico Museum
Map p116 (MAPR; 787-977-6277; www.mapr.org; 299 Av José de Diego; adult/student & senior $6/3; 10am-5pm Tue-Sat, to 8pm Wed, 11am-6pm Sun) San Juan boasts one of the largest and most celebrated art museums in the Caribbean. Housed in a splendid neoclassical building that was once the city's Municipal Hospital, MAPR boasts 18 exhibition halls spread over an area of 130,000 sq ft.

The artistic collection includes paintings, sculptures, posters and carvings from the 17th to the 21st century, chronicling such renowned Puerto Rican artists as José Campeche, Francisco Oller, Nick Quijano and Rafael Ferrer.

Condado & Ocean Park

Sights
1 La Placita de Santurce D2
2 Museo de Arte de Puerto Rico E2
3 Playa Condado D1

Activities, Courses & Tours
4 Caribe Aquatic Adventures B1

Sleeping
5 Alelí by the Sea D1
6 Andalucía Guest House F1
7 Condado Vanderbilt Hotel D1
8 La Concha C1

Eating
9 José Enrique D2
10 Kasalta's F1
11 Santaella D2

Drinking & Nightlife
La Placita de Santurce .... (see 1)

Activities

At most of the city's beaches, you'll find vendors that will rent you pretty much anything that floats, or simply take you for a ride: banana boats, wave runners, kayaks ($20 to $30 per hour), small catamarans (with captain; $60 to $70 per hour), jet skis, water skis and kneeboards. Or get airborne with some parasailing (from $60 per person).

Stick to the shore and cycling in San Juan can actually be good fun, as long as you know where to go. In fact, it is perfectly feasible to work your way safely along coastline from Old San Juan out as far as Isla Verde and beyond.

Acampa Outdoor Gear

(787-706-0695; www.acampapr.com; 1221 Av Jesús T Piñero, Caparra; tours $80-160; 10am-6pm Mon-Fri, 10:30am-5:30pm Sat) One of the best places in town to buy or rent outdoor gear. They also run a number of excellent tours all over the island, including hiking, mountaineering, kayaking and paddle-boarding.

Caribe Aquatic Adventures Diving, Snorkeling

Map p116 (787-281-8858; www.caribe-aquatic-adventures.com; snorkel/1-tank dive incl equipment from $50/90) This outfit does dives near San Juan, but also further afield around the islands off the coast of Fajardo (Icacos for snorkeling, and Palominos and Palominitos for diving). The dives from the shore at Balneario Escambrón are highly recommended.

Rent the Bicycle Bicycle Rental

Map p115 (787-602-9696; www.rentthebicycle.net; 100 Del Muelle, Old San Juan; per day rental from $27) Offers tours and rents sturdy banana-yellow cruiser bikes with lock and helmet. Rental bikes can be delivered to your hotel or you can arrange for pick-up after a one-way ride. The shop is near Pier 6; the staff are brilliant with advice.

Left: City Walls, Old San Juan (p114); Below: Fuerte San Cristóbal (p114)
(LEFT) WILLIAM RANDALL/GETTY IMAGES ©; (BELOW) BRYAN MULLENNIX/GETTY IMAGES ©

Festivals & Events

Fiesta de la Calle San Sebastián Cultural Festival
(mid-Jan) For a full week around the third weekend in January, Old San Juan's Calle San Sebastián, hums with semi-religious processions, music, food stalls and larger-than-ever crowds. During the day, it's folk art and crafts; at night, it's raucous revelry.

Fiesta de San Juan Bautista Cultural Festival
(late Jun) Celebration of the patron saint of San Juan and a summer solstice party, Latin style. Staged during the week preceding June 24, the heart of the action is in Old San Juan.

Sleeping

You'll find ample accommodations in San Juan, many right on the beaches. Old San Juan offers historical havens. You can find a huge range of rental condos in the high-rises along the beaches on airbnb.com and vrbo.com. Some are excellent value.

OLD SAN JUAN

Casablanca Hotel Hotel $$
Map p115 (787-725-3436; www.hotelcasablancapr.com; 316 Fortaleza; r $180-200;) This stylish hotel blends a luxurious mix of colonial and contemporary styles. Five floors of rooms (but no elevator) are swathed in vibrant fabrics, and some of the bathrooms sparkle with gorgeous mother-of-pearl sinks. Greet the morning on the roof deck.

Casa Sol B&B $$
Map p115 (787-399-0105, 787-980-9700; www.casasolbnb.com; Sol 316; r $140-210;) A great new addition in the heart of the old town, this charming B&B has five very nicely decorated rooms. The restored 19th-century building has a bright central courtyard with a skylight. The owners are generous with their local knowledge and often lead tours.

Hotel El Convento Hotel $$$
Map p115 (787-723-9020; www.elconvento.com; 100 Calle del Cristo; r $265-385, ste $650-1460; P ❄ @ ≋) Historic monument, tapas restaurant, meeting place, coffee bar and evocative colonial building…El Convento is Puerto Rico's most complete atmospheric and multifaceted hotel. Built in 1651 as the New World's first Carmelite convent, the 67 rooms are gorgeously decorated.

CONDADO & OCEAN PARK

Andalucía Guest House Guesthouse $$
Map p116 (787-309-3373; www.andaluciapr.com; 2011 McLeary; d from $100; P ❄ @) Within striking distance of Ocean Park's excellent restaurants and beaches, this comfortable guesthouse makes you feel like you're part of the neighborhood.

Alelí by the Sea Guesthouse $$
Map p116 (787-725-5313; alelibythesea@hotmail.com; 1125 Sea View; r $85-110; P ❄) A gift to budget-conscious travelers, this modest nine-room guesthouse is the final bastion of inexpensive seaside accommodations in Condado. Try for a room with an ocean view. There's a handy kitchen, and a spacious deck fronts the beach.

La Concha Resort $$$
Map p116 (787-721-7500; www.laconcharesort.com; 1077 Av Ashford; r $340-380; P ❄ @ ≋) Popular La Concha will wow you. Spacious and serene white rooms pop with flashes of color, and blue-lit showers exude an otherworldly underwater glow. Add in its three pools (one adults-only), a 24-hour casino and some very fine dining and you won't feel the need to venture far.

Condado Vanderbilt Hotel Hotel $$$
(787-721-5500; www.condadovanderbilt.com; 1055 Av Ashford; r from $350; P ❄ @ ≋) One of the most opulent hotels when it opened in 1919, the Condado Vanderbilt reopened in 2014 after a lavish restoration and expansion. Its 323 rooms, including 90 rooms in the original building, are large, and a high percentage of them are suites. Service is tops, with concierges stationed on every floor. Public spaces are opulent.

ISLA VERDE

El San Juan Resort & Casino Resort $$$
(787-791-1000; www.elsanjuanhotel.com; 6063 Av Isla Verde; r from $335; P ❄ @ ≋) Bedazzled by starburst chandeliers and animal-print sofas, the lobby is a theatrical backdrop for the fashion parade prancing in for the legendary nightly entertainment. It's renowned for its flashy casino and rollicking nightlife.

Eating

San Juan offers the finest dining in the Caribbean, with enough cutting-edge restaurants to justify a trip in its own right. Calle Fortaleza in Old

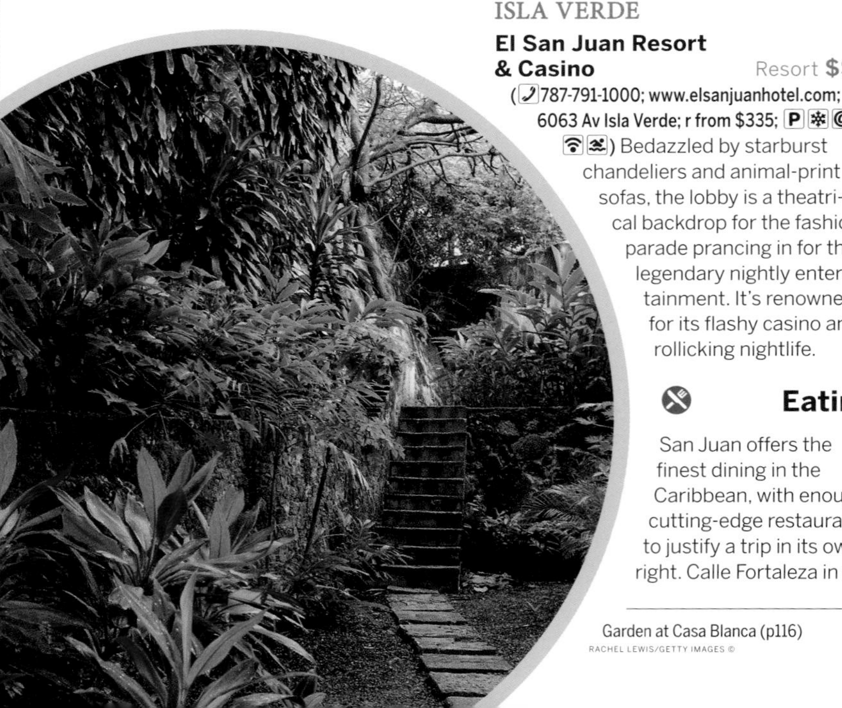

Garden at Casa Blanca (p116)
RACHEL LEWIS/GETTY IMAGES ©

San Juan is the eclectic heart of the city's 21st-century fusion-cuisine revolution.

OLD SAN JUAN

Finca Cialitos Cafe $

Map p115 (☎939-207-9998; www.fincacialitos.com; 150 San Justo; snacks from $3; ⏰9am-5pm Tue-Sun) Your best cup of San Juan coffee is at this funky find which calls itself the 'Cafe Espresso Art'. Beans for the brews here come from the family's coffee estate in the nearby lush hills and are roasted on site.

El Jibarito Puerto Rican $$

Map p115 (☎787-725-8375; 280 Sol; mains $10-25; ⏰10am-9pm) The kind of unpretentious place that you just know will serve a good and garlicky *mofongo* (mashed plantains) or *arroz con habichuelas* (rice and beans).

Marmalade Fusion $$$

Map p115 (☎787-724-3969; www.marmaladepr.com; 317 Fortaleza; mains $20-35; ⏰6-10pm;) The personal vision of noted chef Peter Schintler, Marmalade was one of the first restaurants to bring real foodie recognition to Old San Juan more than a decade ago.

OCEAN PARK

Kasalta's Cafe $$

Map p116 (☎787-727-7340; 1966 McLeary; mains $5-24; ⏰6am-10pm) Tucked into Ocean Park's residential enclave, this is the sort of authentic Puerto Rican bakery and diner that you'll find yourself crossing town to visit daily; the coffee is as legendary as the sweets that fill a long glass display case.

SANTURCE

San Juan's hottest neighborhood for eats has dozens of fine choices in and around La Placita de Santurce.

José Enrique Bistro $$$

Map p116 (☎787-725-3518; www.joseenriquepr.com; 176 Duffaut; meals from $35; ⏰11:30am-10pm Tue-Fri, 6:30-10pm Sat) Discreetly hidden in a yellow house lacking a sign, you'll have no problems finding one of the hemisphere's best restaurants – just follow the excited hordes in the know. No reservations, so be prepared to wait. The namesake chef is a multiple award winner and he combines local ingredients brilliantly.

Santaella Fusion $$$

Map p116 (☎787-725-1611; www.santaellapr.com; 219 Canals; meals from $35; ⏰11:30am-11pm Tue-Fri, 6:30-11pm Sat) One of San Juan's best restaurants, Santaella buzzes with excitement, inspired by the superb drinks at the bar and the sensational fare. Dishes range from tapas-small to full-size and include a varying line-up of simple creations that are a triumph of flavor. Book in advance.

Guavate

Puerto Ricans speak of Guavate in reverential tones. During the week it's just an unkempt strip of scruffy, shack-like restaurants abutting the Carite Forest. But on weekends a freewheeling atmosphere united around good food, spontaneous dancing and boisterous revelry earns it the designation as the 'Routa del Lechón', Hwy 184.

Considered the font of traditional Puerto Rican cooking, Guavate is the spiritual home of the island's ultimate culinary delicacy, *lechón asado,* or whole roast pig, locally reared and turning on a spit.

Visit on weekends between 2pm and 9pm, when old-fashioned troubadours entertain; if you can't choose a *lechónera,* try **El Rancho Original** (☎787-747-7296; Rte 184 Km 27.5; plates $6-7; ⏰10am-8pm Sat & Sun).

To get to Guavate from San Juan, follow expressway 52 to exit 31, halfway between Caguas and Cayey. Turn east onto Hwy 184.

Drinking & Entertainment

Wander Old San Juan for nightlife in all forms or hit a major resort for a club. Don't miss **La Placita de Santurce** (Map

Puerto Rico's Favorite Food & Drink

Mofongo The Commonwealth's delicious staple, *mofongo* is made from plantains mashed and cooked with garlic, spices, broth and bits of pork for richness and flavor. No two versions are the same.

Lechón Asado The heavenly smell of *lechón asado* (roast suckling pig) wafts from countless stalls and simple open-air restaurants. Succulent, juicy and lavishly seasoned, it's always popular. In fact, many make the pilgrimage to Guavate, where scores of outlets compete for business.

Rum As the home of Bacardi, the world's largest producer of rum, it's no surprise that Puerto Rico loves the spirit in its many forms, from crystal clear to amber, mild to complex.

p116; La Placita de Santurce; 5pm-late Thu & Fri), the wildly popular street party in its namesake neighborhood.

La Taberna Lúpulo Bar

Map p115 (787-721-3772; 150 San Sebastián; 6pm-2am Mon-Fri, from 3pm Sat & Sun) This beautiful old corner bar has been updated with Puerto Rico's best selection of microbrews. Windows are open to the street on both sides and the neighborhood has a relaxed, leafy charm.

Nuyorican Café Live Music

Map p115 (787-977-1276; www.nuyoricancafepr.com; 312 San Francisco, Old San Juan; 8pm-late) If you came to Puerto Rico in search of sizzling salsa music, you'll find it at the Nuyorican Café. San Juan's hottest night-spot – stuffed into an alley off Fortaleza, opposite a nameless drinking hole – is a congenial hub of live Latino sounds and hip-gyrating locals.

Shopping

The best arts and crafts shopping is in Old San Juan, though most schlocky T-shirt shops are there too. San Francisco and Fortaleza are the two main arteries in and out of the old city, both are packed cheek-by-jowl with shops. Running perpendicular at the west end of town, Calle del Cristo is home to many more chic establishments.

Olé Clothing

Map p115 (787-724-2445; 105 Fortaleza, Old San Juan; 9am-6pm Mon-Sat) Although beloved by tourists, this old-school hat shop is no tourist trap. As he has for generations, Guillermo Cristian Jeffs will custom-fit you for a truly authentic Panama hat (from $60) – not some faux hipster facsimile.

Information

Puerto Rico Tourism Company (PRTC; 800-223-6530, 787-721-2400; www.seepuertorico.com) LMM airport **(PRTC; 787-791-1014; near Terminal C; 9am-8pm)**; Old San Juan (**787-722-1709; Edificio Ochoa, 500 Tanca; 9am-6pm, extended hours in peak season)**

Getting There & Away

Air

International flights serve Luis Muñoz Marín International Airport (LMM; p134), which is close to all of San Juan. Some flights serving the islands of Culebra and Vieques use **Aeropuerto de Isla Grande (Fernando Luis Ribas Dominicci Airport; airport code SIG)**, in the city's Miramar district.

Público

Major *público* centers include LMM airport, two large stations in Río Piedras (Centro de Públicos Oeste and Centro de Públicos Este) and – to a lesser extent – Plaza de Colón in Old San Juan.

Getting Around

To/From the Airport

Fixed-price taxis serve LMM airport. The flat fees per carload (up to five passengers) include $10 to Isla Verde, $15 to Condado and Ocean Park, and $19 to Old San Juan. Add $1 for each piece of luggage, and $1 after 10pm. If you find others going your way you can share the costs.

Bus

AMA Metrobus (Autoridad Metropolitana de Autobuses, Metropolitan Bus Authority; ☎787-767-7979; www.dtop.gov.pr; fare $0.75; ⏲most routes 6am-10pm, reduced service Sun) operates San Juan's public buses. Buses are clean and air-conditioned, but the system is not easy for visitors. Route maps and info are hard to find and few stops have any indication of what buses stop there.

The routes taken most often by travelers (bus numbers are followed by associated route descriptions) include the following:

- **A5** Old San Juan, Stop 18, Isla Verde (via Loiza)
- **A9** Old San Juan, Sagrado Corazón (Tren Urbano station), Río Piedras
- **B40** Isla Verde, LMM airport, Río Piedras
- **C53** Old San Juan, Condado, Ocean Park (via McLeary), Isla Verde

Car

Try to avoid driving in the city. Roads are in poor condition, while haphazard local driving habits may jangle your nerves or crinkle your fender.

Taxi

Taxi fares are set in the main tourism zones. From Old San Juan, trips to Condado or Ocean Park cost $12, and $19 to Isla Verde. Journeys within Old San Juan cost $7.

Outside of the major tourist areas, cab drivers are supposed to use meters, but it rarely happens. Insist on it, or establish a price from the start.

Taxis line up at the east end of Fortaleza in Old San Juan; in other places you will likely need to call one. Try Metro Taxi (☎787-945-5555) or Rochdale Radio Taxi (☎787-721-1900).

AROUND SAN JUAN

You can be three-quarters of the way across the island and still within an hour or two's drive of San Juan (traffic permitting); so day trips from the capital can take you almost anywhere in the commonwealth.

Sights

Bacardí Rum Factory Landmark

(☎787-788-8400; www.casabacardi.org; Hwy 888 Km 2.6; ⏲tours 9am-4:15pm Mon-Sat, 10am-3:45pm Sun) FREE Called the 'Cathedral of Rum' because of its six-story distillation tower, the Bacardí Rum Factory covers 127 beautifully situated acres near the entrance to the Bahía de San Juan, across from Old San Juan. The free tour (every 30 minutes, lasting about one hour) includes two free drinks and a tram tour explaining the history of the distillery.

Playa Luquillo (p124)

MICHAEL RUNKEL/GETTY IMAGES ©

Arecibo Observatory Observatory
(☎878-2612; www.naic.edu; adult/child & senior US$6/4; ⌚9am-4pm Dec 15-Jan 15 & Jun-Jul, 9am-4pm Wed-Sun other times) The Puerto Ricans reverently refer to it as 'El Radar'. To everyone else it is simply the largest radio telescope in the world. Resembling an extraterrestrial spaceship grounded in the middle of karst country, the Arecibo Observatory looks like something out of a James Bond movie – probably because it is (007 fans will recognize the saucer-shaped dish and craning antennae from the 1995 film *Goldeneye*).

EL YUNQUE & EASTERN PUERTO RICO

The east coast is Puerto Rico shrink-wrapped; a tantalizing taste of almost everything the island has to offer. Here in the foothills the sprawling suburbs of San Juan blend caustically with the jungle-like quietness of El Yunque National Forest, the commonwealth's giant green lungs and biggest outdoor attraction.

Separated from mainland Puerto Rico by a 7-mile stretch of choppy ocean, the two islands of Culebra and Vieques sport a laid-back vibe and some of the Caribbean's best beaches.

El Yunque

Covering 28,000 acres of land in the Sierra de Luquillo, this verdant tropical rainforest is crisscrossed by an excellent network of signposted trails with waterfalls and sweeping views as highlights. Stop first at **El Portal Visitors Center** (☎787-888-1880; www.fs.usda.gov/elyunque; Hwy 191 Km 4.0; adult/child $4/free; ⌚9am-5pm) for information and details about its hikes. It has a short intro walk and some beautiful flora.

You can get here from San Juan on an organized trip, or by driving along Hwy 3 to the junction with Hwy 191 just past the settlement of Río Grande. You'll see numerous jungle adventure parks advertised where you can go sailing through the rainforest on a zip line.

Luquillo & Around

Luquillo is synonymous with its *balneario* (public beach), the fabulous **Playa Luquillo** (Balneario La Monserrate; parking $5). Set on a calm bay facing northwest and protected from the easterly trade winds, the public part of this beach makes a mile-long arc to a point of sand shaded by evocative coconut palms. Although crowds converge on weekends and holidays, Luquillo has always been more about atmosphere than solitude. Don't miss the famous food kiosks.

Eating

Luquillo Beach Kiosks Puerto Rican $
(Hwy 3, Playa Luquillo; dishes $3-20; ⌚hours vary, generally 11am-10pm) Luquillo's famous line of 60 or so beachfront *friquitines* (also known as *quioscos*, *kioskos* or just plain food stalls) along the western edge of Hwy 3 serve often-excellent food at very popular prices. It's a fine way to sample local food and snack culture, including scrumptious *surullitos* (fried cornmeal and cheese sticks).

Two recommended choices are **Vejigante** (kiosk 31) for creative local fare served with flair, and upscale **La Parilla** (kiosk 2), serving excellent seafood.

Getting There & Away

Públicos run from San Juan (US$5 to US$8) to and from the Luquillo plaza. Aside from that, you'll need your own wheels.

Vieques

POP 10,000

Measuring 21 miles long by 5 miles wide, Vieques is renowned for its gorgeous beaches, semi-wild horses and unforgettable bioluminescent bay.

Vieques was where Puerto Rico's most prickly political saga was played out in the public eye. For more than five decades the US Navy used more than two-thirds of the island for military target practice but withdrew in 2003 after years of protests.

Beaches

The beaches in the national wildlife refuge are as good as you'll find anywhere. Elsewhere you'll find numerous strips of sand where days can easily pass into weeks.

Playa Caracas Beach

(Southern Shore) Calm and clear Playa Caracas is reached on a paved road and has gazebos with picnic tables to shade bathers from the sun. Just west, **Playuela** is lesser known and has less shade,

ranza, has the highest concentration of phosphorescent dinoflagellates not only in Puerto Rico, but in the world.

A trip through the lagoon (take a tour) is nothing short of psychedelic, with hundreds of fish whipping up bright-green sparkles below the surface as your kayak or electric boat passes by (no gas-powered boats are permitted).

Local Knowledge

Name: Owen Smith

OCCUPATION: OWNER OF CASA DE AMISTAD GUESTHOUSE, VIEQUES

RESIDENCE: VIEQUES

1 WHAT ARE YOUR FAVORITE BEACHES … EQUES?

… n wildlife refuge beaches on the … ea. You can beach-hop and/or hike … other hidden beaches and stunning … at Playa Caracas and just keep going.

… ARE THE BEST HIDDEN … HES?

… direct you to both of these: Black Sand … lack lava sand mixed with sienna- … d creating a fascinating swirl design … ed by limestone cliffs; Playa Pata … nerly known as 'Secret Beach', has … and white sand and is surrounded by …

… AT'S THE BEST BEACH FOR … RKELING?

… Pier at Rompeolas. This is the best … experience you can get without actually … full diving gear. You can snorkel shallow … to see amazing things while swimming … close to the rocks along the pier.

… venture Adventure Tour

… **; www.viequesadventures. … 50)** You can't miss the … inescent waters from a clear canoe. Groups are small. It also does fly-fishing tours via kayak as well as mountain bike tours.

Sleeping

ESPERANZA

Trade Winds Guesthouse $

(☎787-741-8666; Calle Flamboyán; r $70) Situated on the far west end of the *malecón,* this popular guesthouse and inn has 10 rooms, most with air-con, including three terrace rooms that have a harbor view and catch the breeze.

Malecón House Inn $$$
(787-741-0663; www.maleconhouse.com; 105 Calle Flamboyán; r incl breakfast $160-250; P) With its travertine floors, beautiful fabrics and light wood furniture, this spacious 13-room upmarket inn is a gracious choice. Looking out over the water from a quiet section of the main street, two rooms have private seaside balconies.

ELSEWHERE ON THE ISLAND

Casa de Amistad Guesthouse $$
(787-741-3758; www.casadeamistad.com; 27 Calle Benitez Castaño; r $75-120; @) Everything a great holiday guesthouse should be. Right in the middle of Isabel Segunda, super-friendly Casa de Amistad has nine stylish rooms. The ferry is a five-minute walk and there are great restaurants close by.

Blue Horizon Boutique Resort Boutique Hotel $$$
(787-741-3318; www.bluehorizonboutiqueresort.com; off Hwy 997; r $200-400; P) Even though it's one of the island's few beachside resorts, the Blue Horizon still shines over the competition. With only 10 rooms harbored in separate bungalows wedged onto a stunning oceanside bluff west of Esperanza, the sense of elegance here – both natural and created – is breathtaking.

Eating & Drinking

ESPERANZA

Right on the Caribbean, Calle Flamboyán (aka the *malecón*) is lined with tourist-friendly cafes and bars. A little glitter is in the offing as celebrity chef Jose Enrique of San Juan will be operating the bar and restaurant at the hip new El Blok hotel at the strip's east end.

El Quenepo Seafood $$$
(787-741-1215; 148 Calle Flamboyán; mains $20-32; 5:30-10pm Mon-Sat) Upscale El Quenepo has a lovely interior and an equally delectable menu. The food is catch-of-the-day fresh – a family of seven brothers supplies the seafood – and the decor is stylish. Be sure to reserve.

ELSEWHERE ON THE ISLAND

Tin Box Fusion $$
(787-741-7700; off Hwy 996; mains $8-20; 9am-2pm Sun & 5-9pm daily) The local Duffy family knows how to have fun and more importantly it knows how its patrons want to have fun. There's an eclectic collection of comfort foods here such as ribs, burgers, tacos and more.

Arecibo Observatory (p124)
TIM DRAPER/GETTY IMAGES ©

Getting To Vieques & Culebra

AIR

Vieques and Culebra get frequent air service from San Juan ($65 to $100 one way) and Ceiba ($30 to $45 one way) and are linked with each other ($65 to $90 one way).

Air Flamenco (www.airflamenco.net)

Air Sunshine (www.airsunshine.com)

Cape Air (800-352-0714; www.flycapeair.com)

Vieques Air Link (www.viequesairlink.com)

FERRY

The most popular and by far the cheapest way to Culebra from the mainland, the **Maritime Transportation Authority** (ATM; 787-863-0705) public ferries suffer from a bad rep given to them by tourists who consider cruise ships the standard of comfort.

In reality it's simple: get to the ferry terminal in Fajardo (about one to two hours east of San Juan, a five-passenger taxi costs $80) at least an hour early and buy your ticket (there are no reservations). Schedules vary by day, but there are usually at least three round-trips taking up to two hours each way. Check times locally or at tourist info websites.

On busy weekends, daytrippers may get bumped by island residents.

Al's Mar Azul Bar

(787-741-3400; Calle Plinio Peterson; 11am-late) In Isabel Segunda, locals come to play pool, and expats come to drink... and drink. Visitors teeter somewhere in between. Those in the know head to the narrow deck out back for sunset and stars. Food is greasy and filling.

Getting Around

Vieques is a small island, but a car or 4WD will be useful for exploring the hidden beaches. *Públicos* and taxis congregate at the ferry terminal, the airport and on 'the strip' in Esperanza.

Culebra

POP 2000

Welcome to Culebra – the island that time forgot; mainland Puerto Rico's weird, wonderful and distinctly wacky smaller cousin that lies glistening like a bejeweled Eden to the east.

Situated 17 miles from mainland Puerto Rico, the culturally isolated island is home to an offbeat mix of folks willing to dodge the manic intricacies of modern life. Long feted for its diamond-dust beaches and world-class diving reefs, the place is simply beautiful.

Beaches

Playa Flamenco Beach

(Hwy 251) Stretching for a mile around a sheltered, horseshoe-shaped bay, Playa Flamenco is not just Culebra's best beach, it is also generally regarded as the finest in Puerto Rico and the Caribbean. Backed by low scrub and trees rather than craning palms, rustic Flamenco gets very crowded on weekends. It has a range of amenities.

Playa Zoni Beach

(Hwy 250) Head to the eastern end of the island and you'll eventually run out of road at Playa Zoni. From the airport junction, it's a straightforward 3-mile drive through

Puerto Rico's Status

A commonwealth of the United States of America, Puerto Rico is a semi-autonomous territory whose constitutional status has long been a major point of contention. Puerto Ricans enjoy many protections and benefits that US citizens have, but they are not allowed to participate in federal elections and have only a nonvoting 'Resident Commissioner' in the US House of Representatives.

A non-binding resolution in 2012 showed that the majority of the island's voters favor statehood with the US. President Obama has committed to funding an 'official' referendum that would decide Puerto Rico's political fate. The cost, a mere $2.5 million, is subject to congressional debate. A bill that would link a majority vote for statehood with a mandated admission process to the US as the 51st state spent 2013 wandering through Congress. Its fate depends on tepid Republican party support, since the consensus is that Puerto Rico would elect Democrats and that would have a major impact on the politically divided and deadlocked US Congress.

rolling hills. Zoni is long and straight, with beautiful islands in the distance. A short walk will guarantee you solitude.

Playa Tamarindo Beach

On an isolated bit of coast west of Punta Melones, this is a very good snorkeling beach; it overlooks the fish-filled waters of the **Luis Peña Marine Preserve**. It's accessible by foot by either turning off the Dewey–Flamenco Beach road at the bottom of the hill just before the lagoon, or from an unmarked trail west off the Flamenco parking lot.

Activities

Despite damage from the US Navy testing era and endemic climate-change pressures, Culebra has some of Puerto Rico's most amazing dive spots, including sunken ships, coral reefs, drop-offs and caves.

Good snorkeling can be accessed from many beaches. **Tamarindo** is a good example of the bounty on offer: it teems with a spectacular variety of fish and features a 50ft wall of coral, all protected by the **Luis Peña Marine Preserve**.

Culebra Divers and Culebra Bike Shop rent snorkeling equipment; most boat captains will also arrange snorkel tours.

Aquatic Adventures Diving, Snorkeling

(515-290-2310; www.diveculebra.com; Calle Fulladoza; snorkeling/2-tank dives from $60/95; 9am-5pm) Located just above Dinghy Dock (handy for a post-dive cocktail), this fine shop leads four-hour dive and snorkeling tours that leave about 10am. Trips include lunch.

Sleeping & Eating

Several places to stay in budget-friendly Culebra are a short walk from the ferry dock in Dewey, otherwise you'll find options island-wide.

Villa Flamenco Beach Apartments **$$**

(787-383-0985, 787-742-0023; www.villaflamencobeach.com; off Hwy 251; r $135-180; P ❄) Gentle waves lulling you to sleep, a night sky replete with twinkling stars, and one of the best beaches on the planet (Playa Flamenco) just outside your window: this six-unit place is a winner.

Villa Fulladoza Apartments **$$**

(787-742-3576; www.villafulladoza.wix.com/culebra; Calle Fulladoza; apt $75-120;) Super-cute and vividly turquoise and

s a frenzy of expats
peers and acts as the
grapevine.

Around

natural attractions are not
u will need to organize a ride,
taxi, or bicycle. *Público* vans
waiting at the ferry dock and

**l (787-742-3514; www.
n; Hwy 250)** Rents small cars
from $75), golf carts (from
(from $35). A short walk
ee transport to/from the

RN & WESTERN RICO

ge of scenery awaits you
ern coast – particularly
city, Ponce. The central
their coffee plantations
denuded plains that
ations in the 1800s. Now
atch the eye – outside of
rms of Ponce – until you
rvana of Rincón.

ALEKSANDAR KOLUNDZIJA/GETTY IMAGES ©

Ponce

POP 160,000

Central Ponce has outstanding colonial architecture and a dozen or so museums. Three miles south, the seashore-hugging restaurant-lined boardwalk of La Guancha Paseo Tablado is another fine draw.

Sights & Activities

Plaza Las Delicias Square

Within this elegant square you'll discover the heart of Ponce and two of the city's landmark buildings, **Parque de Bombas** and **Catedral Nuestra Señora de Guadalupe**. The **Fuente de los Leones** (Fountain of Lions), a photogenic fountain rescued from the 1939 World's Fair in New York, is the square's most captivating attraction.

Museo de Arte de Ponce Art Gallery

(MAP; 787-848-0505; www.museoarteponce.org; 2325 Av Las Américas; adult/senior & student $6/3; 10am-6pm Wed-Mon) A $30-million renovation celebrates the museum's 50th anniversary and the smart curation – some 850 paintings, 800 sculptures and 500 prints presented in provocative historical and thematic juxtapositions – represents five centuries of Western art.

Sleeping

Hotel Bélgica Hotel $

(787-844-3255; www.hotelbelgica.com; 122 Villa; r $80-90;) Just off the southwest corner of Plaza Las Delicias, this traveler-favorite has a creaking colonial ambience, with 15ft ceilings and wrought-iron balconies. The hallways are a bit of a maze and dimly lit, but the place is charming, with delightful old furniture in many of the 20 rooms.

Hotel Meliá Hotel $$

(800-44-UTELL, 787-842-0260; www.hotelmeliapr.com; 75 Cristina, cnr Plaza Las Delicias; r incl continental breakfast $100-140; P) Just east of the plaza, this independent, historic hotel has rich colonial charm. The grand lobby is more plush than the rooms, but everything is clean and functional, and the building is monumental.

Parque de Bombas

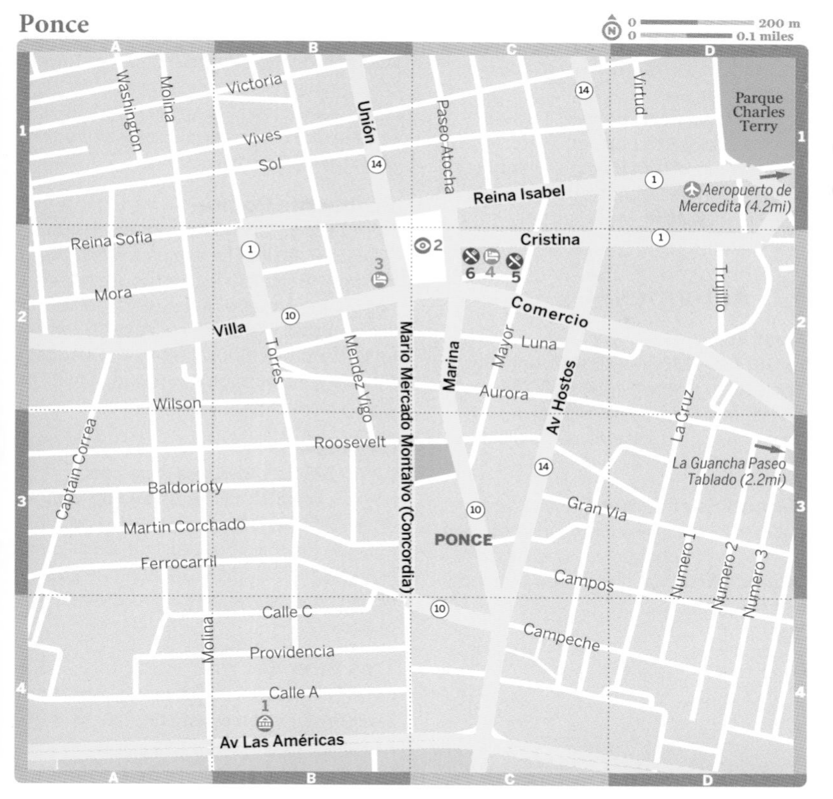

Eating

Cesar's Comida Criolla

Caribbean $

(near cnr Mayor & Cristina; dishes $2-14; lunch) The ultimate hole-in-the-wall joint for *comida criolla* (traditional Puerto Rican cuisine), this spot doles out oodles of pork, chicken and seafood (most served with rice and beans).

King's Cream

Ice Cream $

(9223 Marina; cones $1-3; 8am-12am) On warm evenings lines stretch down the sidewalk of this institution, located across from Parque de Bombas.

Getting There & Around

The *público* terminal is three blocks north of the plaza, near Plaza del Mercado, with connections to all major towns. There are plenty of long-haul vans headed to Río Piedras in San Juan (about US$20) and Mayagüez (about US$10).

You'll need your own wheels to get around.

Ponce

Sights

1 Museo de Arte de Ponce B4
2 Plaza Las Delicias C2

Sleeping

3 Hotel Bélgica B2
4 Hotel Meliá C2

Eating

5 Cesar's Comida Criolla C2
6 King's Cream C2

Rincón

POP 15,000

Shoehorned far out in the island's most psychedelic corner, Rincón is Puerto

Rico at its most unguarded; a place where the sunsets shimmer scarlet and the waiters are more likely to call you 'dude' than 'sir'.

Not surprisingly, Rincón's waves are often close to perfect. The crème de la crème is Tres Palmas, a white-tipped monster that is often dubbed the 'temple' of big-wave surfing in the Caribbean.

Activities

Surf 787 Surfing

(787-448-0032; www.surf787.com) The coolest kid on the block, Surf 787 has a suite of packages, all-inclusive surf vacations, adult getaways and a kids' surf camp.

Rincon Surf School Surfing, Yoga

(787-823-0610; www.rinconsurfschool.com) Rincon Surf School often does lessons at Sandy Beach and is a good option for beginning adults.

Sleeping

Accommodation is either south of town (marginally better-connected to the center) or north of town via Hwy 413 (where steep hills and twisting lanes give an extra degree of isolation).

Beside the Pointe Hotel $

(787-823-8550; www.besidethepointe.com; r $75-125; P) The social centerpiece of Sandy Beach, this guesthouse has a happening bar and restaurant, rooms that are outfitted like small apartments, and lots of unpretentious character. Despite the seafront location few rooms have good views.

Casa Islena Hotel $$

(787-823-1525; www.casa-islena.com; Hwy 413, Beach Rd; r incl breakfast $125-205; P @) A high-class option in the heart of Rincón's best surfing, Casa Islena is an elegant, Mediterranean-style guesthouse on a magnificent, moody stretch of ocean.

Tres Sirenas Guesthouse $$$

(787-823-0558; www.tressirenas.com; 26 Sea Beach Drive; r inc breakfast $150-280;) All things weighed up, this is Rincón's best guesthouse. A stone's throw from two of the bigger, more luxurious municipality hotels, true indulgence awaits you at this serene end-of-street detached house.

Drinking & Nightlife

Calypso Tropical Café Cafe, Bar

(787-823-4151; cnr Hwy 413 & lighthouse road; noon-midnight) The Calypso is everything you'd expect a beach-side surfers' bar to be.

Surfer, Puerto Rico

Getting There & Around

If you are coming from San Juan, you can fly into Mayagüez.

The **público stand** is just off Plaza de Recreo on Nueva. Expect to pay about $5 if you are headed north to Aguadilla or $3 to go south to Mayagüez (you can access San Juan – four or more hours – from either of these cities). Both trips take about 40 minutes.

The only reliable way to get around the area is by rented car, taxi, irregular *públicos* or – if you're energetic and careful – walking.

SURVIVAL GUIDE

Directory A–Z

Accommodations

You can find all types of accommodation in Puerto Rico – from huge resorts to humble guesthouses to remote mountain retreats. Compared to the rest of the Caribbean, however, you won't find as many all-inclusive resorts. Hostels are also rare, as are chain motels that are common in the US. There are a burgeoning number of B&Bs, a previously unknown category on the island.

The following price ranges refer to a double room with bathroom in high season. Unless otherwise stated a tax of 9% to 15% is included in the price.

$ less than US$80

$$ US$80 to US$200

$$$ more than US$200

Food

The following price ranges refer to a standard one- or two-course meal. Tipping is extra.

$ less than US$15

$$ US$15 to US$30

$$$ more than US$30

Health

Tap water in Puerto Rico is safe to drink.

Language

Both English and Spanish are official languages, although Spanish is primarily spoken. You'll get by in urban centers with English alone.

Practicalities

- **Electricity** Puerto Rico has the 110V AC system used in the USA.
- **Time** Puerto Rico is on Atlantic Standard Time. Clocks in this time zone read an hour later than the Eastern Standard Time zone, which encompasses such US cities as New York. There is no Daylight Saving Time observed on the island.
- **Tipping** Tipping in restaurants averages 15% to 20%.
- **Weights & Measures** The imperial system with two exceptions: distances on road signs are in kilometers and gas (petrol) is pumped in liters.

Money

The US dollar is used.

Opening Hours

Banks 8am to 4pm Monday to Friday, 9:30am to noon Saturday.

Bars 2pm to 2am, often later in San Juan.

Government offices 8:30am to 4:30pm Monday to Friday.

Post offices 8am to 4pm Monday to Friday, 8am to 1pm Saturday.

Shops 9am to 6pm Monday to Saturday, 11am to 5pm Sunday, later in malls.

Public Holidays

In addition to holidays observed throughout the region, Puerto Rico also has the following public holidays:

Three Kings Day (Feast of the Epiphany) January 6

Eugenio María de Hostos' Birthday January 10; honors the island educator, writer and patriot

Martin Luther King Jr Day Third Monday in January

Presidents' Day Third Monday in February

Below: Fishing boats at sunset; **Right:** Old San Juan (p114)

Emancipation Day March 22; island slaves were freed on this date in 1873

Palm Sunday Sunday before Easter

Jose de Diego Day April 18

Memorial Day Last Monday in May

Independence Day/Fourth of July July 4

Luis Muñoz Rivera's Birthday July 18; honors the island patriot and political leader

Constitution Day July 25

Jose Celso Barbosa's Birthday July 27; honors the father of the Puerto Rican statehood movement

Labor Day First Monday in September

Columbus Day Second Monday in October

Thanksgiving Fourth Thursday in November

Telephone

The country code for Puerto Rico is ☎1. The island is included in American cell phone plans so users avoid roaming charges.

Visas

- Visitors from other countries must have a valid passport.
- You need a visa to enter Puerto Rico if you need a visa to enter the US.
- Countries participating in the Visa Waiver Program – the EU, Australia, New Zealand and much of Latin America – don't need visas to visit Puerto Rico.

Getting There & Away

Entering Puerto Rico

US nationals don't need a passport for travel to Puerto Rico.

Air

Puerto Rico is well served with flights from the US as well as the rest of the Caribbean. Most people arrive and depart via **Luis Muñoz Marín International Airport** (SJU; www.aeropuertosju.com) in San Juan.

Sea

A new ferry service connects the Dominican Republic with Puerto Rico. America Cruise Ferries (☎Mayaguez 787-832-4800, San Juan 787-622-4800; www.acferries.com; one-way adults from $90, cars from $250) is running the large *Caribbean Fantasy* from the Don Diego port near Santo Domingo in the Dominican Republic. It serves San Juan (13 hours) two days a week and Mayaguez (12 hours) in the west one day a week. The ferry is large and luxurious (it has extra-cost cabins).

San Juan is the second-largest port for cruise ships in the western hemisphere (after Miami).

Getting Around

Air

The only service of interest to visitors are the many flights linking the main island to Culebra and Vieques.

Boat

Public ferries run from Fajardo to Vieques and Culebra.

Car

Driving is currently the most convenient way to get around the countryside, see small towns, cross sprawling suburbs and explore wide, open spaces.

Although drivers are more aggressive than those in the United States, and road conditions can be very poor, Puerto Rico has the same basic rules of the road as the US.

All major car rental firms have offices in San Juan and rates can be very competitive. Two local firms worth considering:

Charlie Car Rental (☎787-728-2418; www.charliecars.com) Has offices in San Juan plus Aguadilla and Caguas.

Target (☎787-728-1447, 800-934-6457; www.targetrentacar.com) Large local firm has offices across San Juan plus numerous other cities.

Público

Públicos (large vans that pick up and drop off passengers with great frequency and little haste) run between major cities and towns, but it's a very slow (though cheap) way to travel. The longest ride on the island will not cost more than $15, though something around $4 or less is more common.

US & British Virgin Islands

Hmm, which isle to choose for hammock-strewn beaches and conch fritters?

Easy: any one, though each differs in personality.

The US Virgin Islands (USVI) hold the lion's share of population and development. St Thomas has more resorts and water sports than you can shake a beach towel at. St John cloaks two-thirds of its area in parkland and sublime shores, ripe for hiking and snorkeling. The largest Virgin, St Croix, pleases divers and drinkers with extraordinary scuba sites and rum factories.

The British Virgin Islands (BVI) closely resemble their US counterparts, though they're quirkier and less developed. Main island Tortola is known for its full moon parties and sailing prowess. Billionaires and yachties swoon over Virgin Gorda and its magical rocks. And who can resist little Jost Van Dyke, the 'barefoot island' where Main St is a calypso-wafting beach?

Virgin Gorda (p163)

Virgin Islands Itineraries

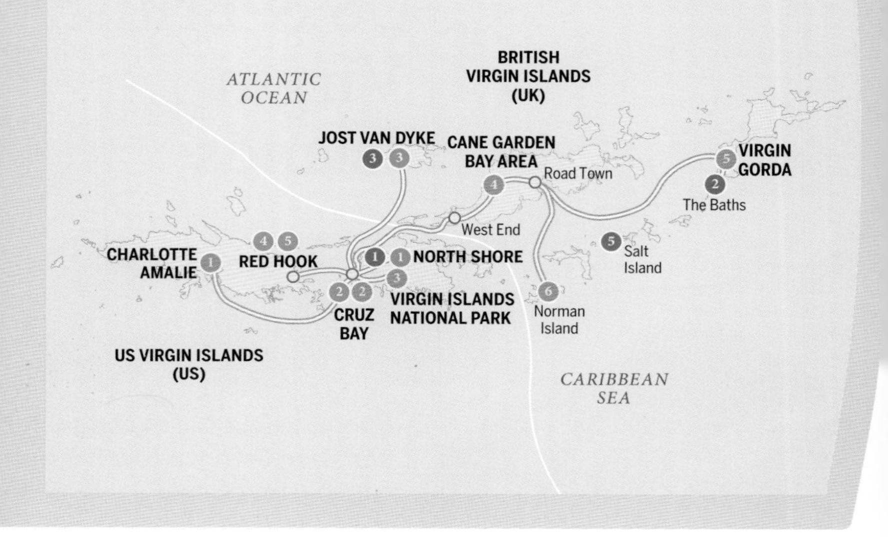

Three Days

❶ **North Shore** (p151) Spend the day on a gorgeous beach in the heart of the St John's protected parkland. Lengthy Cinnamon Bay has the most going on: an archaeological museum, stand-up paddleboarding and trails through mill ruins. At Honeymoon Beach you can kayak, nap in a hammock, then walk back to town on a trail through the bird-flittering forest.

❷ **Cruz Bay** (p148) When happy hour strikes, pick a bar in St John's festive main town – perhaps mango-tinged microbrews at the Tap Room or US$1 beers at Woody's Seafood Saloon. Loads of restaurants await for dinner.

❸ **Jost Van Dyke** (p166) Make a day trip to the wee island. Take the ferry (a 45-minute trip) to Great Harbour in the morning. Drop by Foxy's, the Soggy Dollar and other famed, rum-pouring beach bars, then return to St John on the evening ferry. Or visit Jost via a boat/snorkeling trip with a company like Low Key Watersports. Remember, Jost is in the BVI, so you'll need your passport.

❹ **Virgin Islands Ecotours** (p146) This company also operates on St John, but a more adventurous option – and one that provides an opportunity to take in another island – is to ferry over to Red Hook, St Thomas and kayak through the nearby mangrove lagoon.

❺ **Duffy's Love Shack** (p148) Celebrate your feats with a flaming drink (or one served in a coconut husk) before returning home.

THIS LEG: ABOUT 14 MILES

Seven Days

1 Charlotte Amalie (p140) You'll likely fly in to the airport here, so why not take a look around for the afternoon? Shopping is the big to-do. Or get acquainted with hot-spiced callaloo soup and other West Indian dishes at Gladys' Cafe.

2 Cruz Bay (p148) Many travelers consider St John to be the gem of the Caribbean. Happy-go-lucky Cruz Bay is the island's well-provisioned hub and a fine place to settle in for three days, thanks to sweet lodging and eating options. Outfitters can arrange diving, kayaking and hiking trips. Happy hours rock hard.

3 Virgin Islands National Park (p148) Most of St John is protected forest and shoreline. Get info from the park visitor center about where to hike and snorkel. Then head out to explore fish-frenzied reefs and trails that wind by petroglyphs.

4 Cane Garden Bay Area (p159) Take the ferry to West End, Tortola, and spend the rest of the week cruising the British Virgin Islands. Villas dot the hills surrounding Cane Garden Bay, a good-time spot where live music pumps nightly and palmy beaches beckon by day.

5 Virgin Gorda (p163) Ferries run almost hourly to the BVI's most beloved island. From the dock all roads lead to the Baths, a jumble of lofty boulders that you can hike around via a water trail.

6 Outlying Islands (p167) Hop aboard a day sail excursion and glide to barely inhabited Norman and Cooper islands, where life is reduced to the pleasures of snorkeling, diving and napping under a shade tree.

THIS LEG: ABOUT 40 MILES

Virgin Islands Highlights

1 Best Beach: Cinnamon Bay (p152) The mile-long strand adds archaeological sites and hiking trails to its water sports.

2 Best Natural Wonder: The Baths (p164) Huge volcanic boulders at the sea's edge offer an ethereal trek through sunlight-shafted grottoes.

3 Best Cocktails: Soggy Dollar Bar (p169) Wriggle your feet in the crazy-white sand while swilling a Painkiller.

4 Best Sunset: Freedom City Beach Bar & Surf Shop (p156) Catch an unobstructed view as the mango-colored orb sinks beneath the waves.

5 Best Diving & Snorkeling: RMS Rhone (p167) The 1867 shipwreck rests in shallow water and offers easy access.

Queen angelfish
ARMANDO F. JENIK/GETTY IMAGES ©

Discover US & British Virgin Islands

US VIRGIN ISLANDS

POP 110,300

Consistent 80°F (27°C) weather, ridiculously white sands and a rum-infused taste of West Indian culture – the US Virgin Islands (USVI) earn a gold star for 'tropical'. Americans don't even have to use a passport to join the fun, as these are US territories. Get ready for reggae rhythms, curried meats and mango-sweetened microbrews. It's still a world away, mon.

Magens Bay

DANITA DELIMONT/GETTY IMAGES ©

St Thomas

POP 52,000

Most visitors arrive at the US Virgin Islands via St Thomas, and the place knows how to strike a first impression. Jungly cliffs poke high in the sky, red-hipped roofs blossom over the hills, and all around the turquoise, yacht-dotted sea laps. St Thomas is the most commercialized of the Virgins, with cruise-ship traffic and big resorts galore, but it's also a fine island to sharpen your knife and fork, and kayak through mangrove lagoons.

CHARLOTTE AMALIE

With two to six Love Boats docking in town daily, Charlotte Amalie (a-*mall*-ya) is one of the most popular cruise ship destinations in the Caribbean. Downtown buzzes with visitors swarming the jewelry shops and boutiques by day. By early evening, the masses clear out, the shops shutter, and the narrow streets become shadowy. Sure, the scene can overwhelm, but why not take a deep breath and focus on having a good meal and on your proximity to white-sand beaches?

Beaches

Magens Bay Beach

(www.magensbayauthority.com; adult/child US$4/2; 8am-6pm; ) The sugary mile that fringes heart-shaped Magens Bay makes almost every travel publication's list of beautiful beaches. The seas here are calm, the bay broad and the surrounding green hills dramatic, and tourists mob the place to soak it all up. The beach has lifeguards, picnic tables, changing facilities, a taxi stand, food vendors and water-sports

US & British Virgin Islands

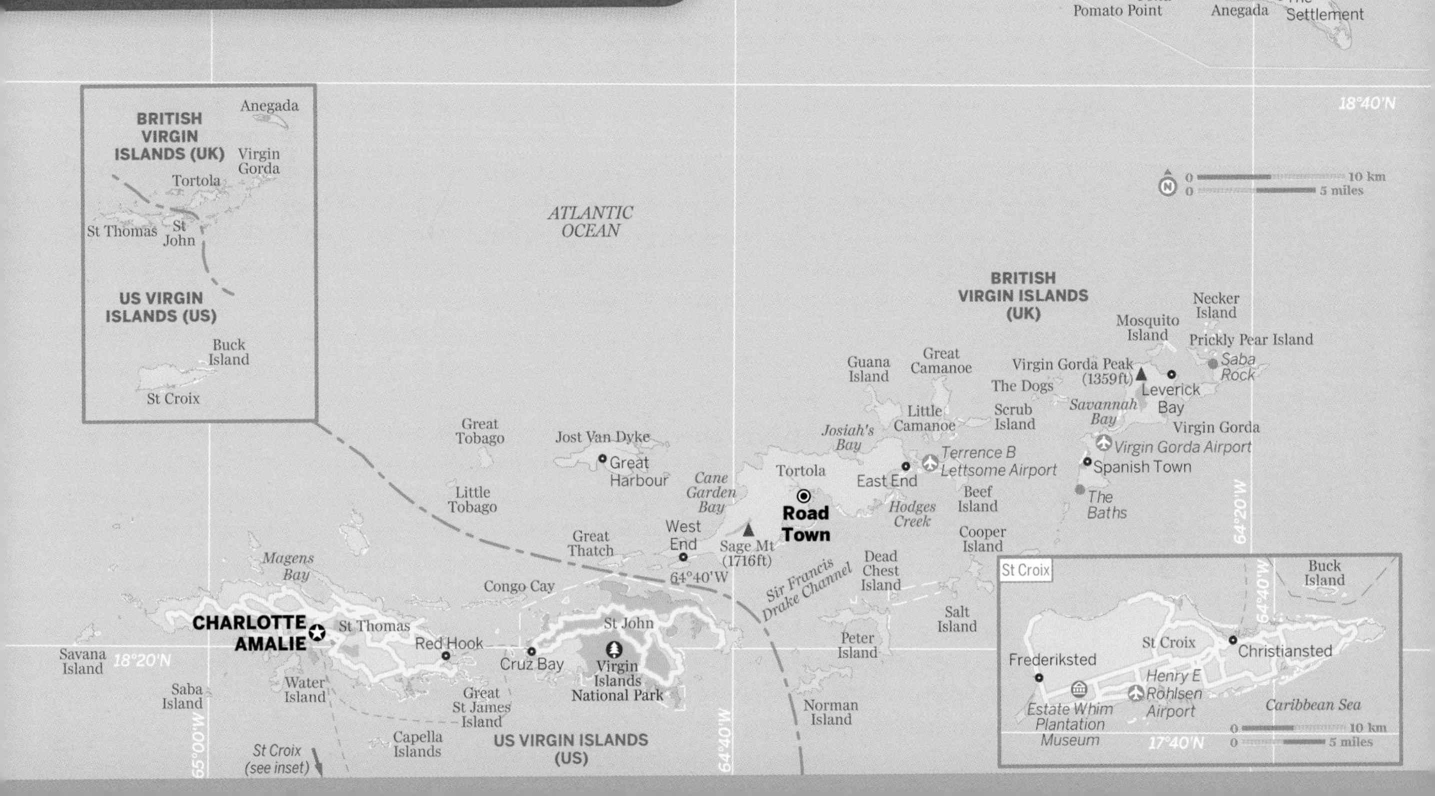

Ports of Call

CHARLOTTE AMALIE, ST THOMAS

- Major cruise ship stop; up to six ships daily.
- There are two docks, each about 1 mile from downtown: shop-filled Havensight to the east, and less-commercial Crown Bay to the west.
- Most visitors beeline to the historic downtown district, filled with duty-free shops and good local restaurants.
- Other excursions include Magens Bay Beach (p140) (an easy taxi ride) and St John (ferry to the neighboring island and visit the national park).

ROAD TOWN, TORTOLA

- Receives one or two ships daily.
- The dock is downtown, where a smattering of craft vendors and restaurants await.
- Top excursions are taking the ferry to Virgin Gorda, taxiing to Cane Garden Bay (p160) or Brewers Bay (p160), or day-sailing to outer islands to snorkel around fishy reefs.

FREDERIKSTED, ST CROIX

- Receives a ship or two per week.
- The dock is downtown. It's a small village and easy to walk around the shops and restaurants.
- Island van tours are popular (around $40 per person, including entry fees). They stop by the Cruzan Rum Distillery (p156) and Estate Whim Plantation Museum (p156) en route to Christiansted.
- Active types can take a rainforest trail ride from Freedom City Cycles (p155).

operators renting kayaks, paddleboards and paddle boats (US$20 to US$30 per hour). Magens Bay is 3 miles north of Charlotte Amalie.

Sights

Water Island Island

Sometimes called the 'Fourth Virgin,' Water Island floats spitting distance from Charlotte Amalie. But with only about 100 residents and very few cars or shops, it feels far more remote. **Honeymoon Beach** offers fine swimming and snorkeling – it's a 10-minute walk from the ferry dock. A couple of food stands sell drinks, sandwiches and fish tacos. Get here via the **ferry** (☎690-4159; one way US$5) that departs roughly every hour from outside Tickle's Dockside Pub at Crown Bay Marina.

Sleeping

Green Iguana Hotel $$

(☎340-776-7654; www.thegreeniguana.com; 1002 Blackbeard's Hill; r US$150-200; ❄@✆) Up the hill behind Blackbeard's Castle, this welcoming place is set in lush gardens and overlooks St Thomas Harbor. The nine rooms come in several configurations, but all have free wi-fi, satellite TV, a microwave and refrigerator; some also have a fully equipped kitchen and private balcony. While it's more plain than luxurious, the Iguana is good value if you don't mind the steep walk.

Crystal Palace B&B **$$**

(☎340-777-2277, 866-502-2277; www.crystalpalaceusvi.com; 12 Crystal Gade; r with shared/private bathroom US$139/169; ❄📶) Ronnie Lockhart owns this five-room property in a colonial mansion that has been in his family for generations. Two rooms have private bathrooms; the other three share a bathroom. Antique West Indian decor pervades, and there's a view-tastic patio on which to eat the continental breakfast or swill a drink from the honor bar.

Ronnie is a fountain of local lore; he'll pick you up at the airport or ferry dock for free.

Miller Manor Guesthouse **$$**

(☎340-774-1535, 888-229-0762; www.millermanor.com; 2527 Prindsesse Gade, Frenchman's Hill; r with shared bathroom US$90-110, with private bathroom US$140-160; ❄📶) This 26-room hillside establishment has the feel of your Aunt Josie's summer place. A 150-year-old Danish townhouse anchors the complex, with a bar overlooking the

Charlotte Amalie

Sleeping
1 Crystal Palace A2
2 Green Iguana C1

Eating
3 Gladys' Cafe A4
4 Greenhouse A4

Shopping
5 AH Riise B3
6 Pirates in Paradise B3
7 Vendors' Plaza C3

Charlotte Amalie

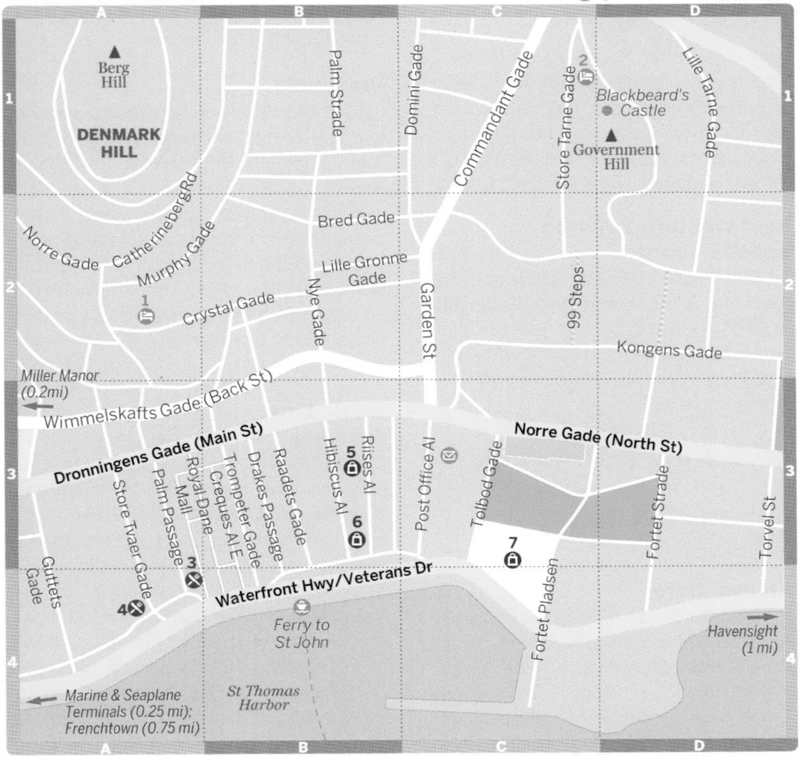

Island Insights

- Handy resources for ferry schedules, taxi rates and local listings include *St Thomas/St John This Week*, *St Croix This Week* and *BVI Welcome Guide*. The magazines are readily available at lodgings, airports and ferry terminals.
- Many attractions are open only when cruise ships are in port. For schedules check www.vinow.com (for USVI) and www.bviports.org/?cruiseship (for BVI). Tuesdays and Wednesdays typically see the most traffic.
- It's wise to call ahead and make dinner reservations for midrange and top-end restaurants.

town and harbor. Rooms range from singles with a shared bathroom to large rooms with water-view balconies. While the manor is in a safe neighborhood, the dicey Savan district lies between here and the heart of town. Take a cab at night.

Best Western Emerald Beach Resort Hotel **$$**
(☎340-777-8800, 800-233-4936; www.emerald-beach.com; 8070 Lindbergh Bay; r US$215-300; ❄@🛜🏊) This property, near the airport, offers 90 snazzy rooms, with private beachfront balconies, flat-screen TVs and free in-room wi-fi.

Eating & Drinking

DOWNTOWN CHARLOTTE AMALIE

Gladys' Cafe Caribbean **$$**
(☎340-774-6604; www.gladyscafe.com; 5600 Royal Dane Mall; mains US$14-22; ⏰7am-4pm Mon-Sat, 8am-2:30pm Sun) With the stereo blaring beside her, Gladys belts out Tina Turner tunes while serving some of the best West Indian food around. Locals and tourists pile in for her callaloo, fungi, Ole Wife (triggerfish), fried plantains and sweet potatoes. Gladys' homemade hot sauces (for sale at the front) make a fine souvenir.

Greenhouse Burgers, Seafood **$$**
(☎340-774-7998; www.thegreenhouserestaurant.com; cnr Waterfront Hwy & Store Tvaer Gade; mains US$12-29; ⏰11am-9pm; 🛜) Cavernous, open-air Greenhouse overlooks the harbor and rocks hard during happy hour (4:30pm to 7pm, when drinks are two for the price of one). The cuisine is predictable American pub fare, but the menu is extensive, with burgers, pizzas and seafood. When everything else downtown closes early, Greenhouse is the one reliable place still open.

FRENCHTOWN

The cute fisherman's neighborhood is a 1.25-mile walk west on Waterfront Hwy (turn left just past the post office). Or take a taxi for US$4 per person.

Pie Whole Italian **$$**
(☎340-642-5074; www.piewholepizza.com; 24a Honduras, Frenchtown; mains US$13-17; ⏰11am-3pm & 5-11pm Mon-Fri, 5-11pm Sat) Six tables and 10 bar stools comprise this cozy eatery. The 13-inch, crisp-crusted, brick-oven pizzas are the claim to fame. Super-fresh ingredients, ie spinach and ricotta or mozzarella and basil, top the white or wheat crust. Several house-made pastas and a robust beer list raise Pie Whole well beyond the norm.

Hook, Line & Sinker Burgers, Seafood **$$**
(☎340-776-9708; www.hooklineandsinkervi.com; Frenchtown; mains US$13-26; ⏰11:30am-11pm Mon-Sat, 10am-2:30pm Sun) This open-air, mom-and-pop operation feels like a real sea shack, where you smell the salt water, feel the ocean breeze and see sailors unload their boats dockside. The menu mixes sandwiches, salads, pastas and seafood mains, such as the almond-crusted yellowtail, with plenty of beers to wash it down.

Epernay Bistro & Wine Bar Wine Bar
(340-774-5348; 24a Honduras, Frenchtown; 5pm-1am Mon-Thu, 5pm-2am Fri, 6pm-2am Sat) Guess what they pour here? Epernay is a popular hangout for St Thomian professionals and snowbirds. Friday evening happy hour is the biggest scene.

HAVENSIGHT

Havensight is a 1-mile walk east on Waterfront Hwy. It's the neighborhood that holds the main cruise ship dock, and it bursts with casual restaurants.

Sheryl's Diamond Delight Caribbean $$
(715-8528; 9713 Estate Thomas; mains US$11-22; 7am- 6pm Mon-Sat, 10am-3pm Sun) Follow the locals and visit Sheryl in her pink-painted, buffet-style eatery, where you can tuck into authentic island dishes such as bullfoot soup, conch in butter sauce, and saltfish and okra. She also sells yummy banana bread, coconut tarts and other island pastries from her bakery case. She's located across from the Havensight cruise dock.

Shopping

Jewelry is the big deal in town. US citizens can leave with a whopping US$1600 in tax-free, duty-free goods.

AH Riise Jewelry
(www.ahriise.com; 37 Main St) This is the famous store that most visitors beeline to, where you can buy everything from watches and jewels to tobacco and liquor. There's another outlet at Havensight.

Vendors' Plaza Market
(cnr Tolbod Gade & Waterfront Hwy; 9am-5pm) Sellers hawk fruit smoothies, batik dresses, T-shirts, Prada knock-offs and other typical Caribbean trinkets under blue-canopied stalls beside Emancipation Garden.

Pirates in Paradise Souvenirs
(38A Waterfront Hwy; 10am-4pm;) Argh! Here's your treasure trove of pirate gear, including eye patches and fake doubloons.

Getting There & Around

Air

Cyril E King Airport (STT; www.viport.com) is located 2.5 miles west of Charlotte Amalie. Taxis (ie multipassenger vans) are readily available. The fare to downtown is US$7; it's US$11 to US$15 to Red Hook. Luggage costs US$2 extra per piece.

Boat

The **Marine Terminal** (Waterfront Hwy) is a 10-minute walk west of downtown. It's a hub for ferries to Tortola and Virgin Gorda, as well as seaplanes to St Croix. A ferry to St John (one way US$13, 45 minutes) departs downtown at the foot of Raadet's Gade at 10am, 1pm and 5:30pm daily.

Charlotte Amalie also has two cruise-ship terminals: Havensight (1 mile east of downtown) and Crown Bay (1 mile west of downtown).

Bus

'Dollar' buses (aka 'safaris') stop along the main road. These vehicles are open-air trucks with benches in back that hold 20 people. Flag them down by flapping your hand, and press the buzzer to stop them when you reach your destination. The fare is US$2.

Car

Most rental agencies have outlets at the airport. Prices start around US$60 per day.

Avis (800-331-1084; www.avis.com)

Budget (800-626-4516, 776-5774; www.budgetstt.com)

Dependable Car Rentals (800-522-3076; www.dependablecar.com)

Discount Car Rentals (776-4858, 877-478-2833; www.discountcar.vi)

Hertz (800-654-3131; www.hertz.com)

Taxi

Rates are set by the government. Prices are listed in the free tourist guide.

Many taxis are vans that carry up to 12 passengers. Other taxis are open-air trucks with benches in back that carry 20 people (much like the 'dollar buses'). Taxis service multiple destinations and may stop to pick up passengers

along the way, so their rates are usually charged on a per-person basis. The following are per-person rates from downtown.

Frenchtown US$4

Havensight US$6

Magens Bay US$10

Red Hook US$13

RED HOOK & EAST END

The East End holds the bulk of the island's resorts. Red Hook is the only town to speak of, though it's small and built mostly around the St John ferry dock and American Yacht Harbor marina.

Beaches

Secret Harbour Beach Beach

This west-facing beach in front of the eponymous resort could hardly be more tranquil. It's an excellent place to snorkel with equipment rented from the resort's water-sports operation.

Sights & Activities

Coral World Ocean Park Aquarium

(340-775-1555; www.coralworldvi.com; 6450 Estate Smith Bay; adult/child US$19/10; 9am-4pm;) This aquarium, at Coki Point, is one of St Thomas' most popular attractions. Pick up a schedule when entering – staff feed the sea creatures and give talks about marine biology throughout the day. Many of the creatures have been rescued (for example the sea turtles were orphans, and the sea lions were in harm's way in Uruguay, where fishermen were shooting them as pests).

The site has restaurants and gift shops, along with changing rooms if you want to visit nearby Coki Beach.

Virgin Islands Ecotours Kayaking

(340-779-2155, 877-845-2925; www.viecotours.com; 2½hr tours adult/child US$69/39; 10am & 2pm) Virgin Islands Ecotours offers a guided kayak-and-snorkeling expedition where you'll paddle through a

Left: Colonial architecture, Charlotte Amalie (p140); Below: A colorful lorikeet

mangrove lagoon to a coral rubble beach and reef. Tours depart just east of the intersection of Rtes 30 and 32, at the entrance to the Inner Mangrove Lagoon Sanctuary. There's also a three-hour tour that adds hiking to the mix.

Sleeping

Bolongo Bay Beach Resort Resort $$$

(340-775-1800, 800-524-4746; www.bolongobay.com; 7150 Bolongo Bay; r US$250-415;) Family-owned Bolongo is a fun, casual resort. Its beach offers a full array of free water sports. The rooms won't win any awards for size or decor, but who cares? You'll be outside. Oceanview rooms are on the 2nd and 3rd floors, while beachfront rooms are on the 1st floor – all have sea views and private patios. The 'value' rooms are in a building across the street.

Secret Harbour Beach Resort Resort $$$

(340-775-6550; www.secretharbourvi.com; 6280 Estate Nazareth; ste US$350-650;) Secret Harbour is a family favorite. Of the 70-plus suites, more than half sit on the beach and the rest are up a hill behind the beach, with sea views. Suites come in three main sizes: studio (660 sq ft), one bedroom (935 sq ft) and two bedroom (1360 sq ft). All have a kitchen and a balcony or patio.

Eating & Drinking

Lots of party-hearty bars and restaurants cluster in Red Hook near the ferry dock.

Latitude 18 Burgers, Seafood $$

(340-777-4552; Vessup Bay Marina; mains US$20-30; 11am-1am) This funky sea ramblers' place is a patio protected by

The Best... Local Cuisine

1 Sugar Mill Restaurant (p161)

2 Harvey's (p154)

3 Gladys' Cafe (p144)

4 Ruby Roti Queen Restaurant (p158)

5 Palm's Delight (p161)

6 Sheryl's Diamond Delight (p145)

a roof of old sails and tarps. Locals rave about the flavorful dishes coming from the little kitchen, such as seared tuna roll with papaya salad. Most nights Latitude brings in fiddlin' bands that fire up the crowd. It's located down a bumpy dirt road around the south side of Vessup Bay.

Duffy's Love Shack Bar
(www.duffysloveshack.com; 650 Red Hook Plaza; 11:30am-midnight) It may be a frame shack in the middle of a paved parking lot, but Duffy's creates its legendary atmosphere with high-volume rock and crowds in shorts and tank tops. The food is classic, burger-based pub fare. The big attractions here are the people-watching and killer cocktails, such as the 64oz 'shark tank' or the flaming 'volcano.' Cash only.

Getting There & Around

Red Hook's ferry dock bustles, with most traffic headed to St John; passenger ferries (US$7 one way, 20 minutes) to Cruz Bay depart on the hour. Ferries also go to Tortola's West End four times daily. Taxis queue outside the marine terminal; it's US$13 to Charlotte Amalie.

St John

POP 4300

Two-thirds of St John is a protected national park, with gnarled trees and spiky cacti spilling over its edges. There are no airports or cruise-ship docks, and the usual Caribbean resorts are few and far between. It's blissfully low-key compared to its neighbor St Thomas.

Hiking and snorkeling are the big to-dos. Trails wind by petroglyphs and sugar-mill ruins, and several drop out onto beaches prime for swimming with turtles and spotted eagle rays.

CRUZ BAY

Nicknamed 'Love City,' St John's main town indeed wafts a carefree, spring-break party vibe. Hippies, sea captains, American retirees and reggae worshippers hoist happy-hour drinks in equal measure, and everyone wears a silly grin at their great good fortune for being here. Cruz Bay is also the place to organize your hiking, snorkeling, kayaking and other activities, and to fuel up in the surprisingly good restaurant mix. Everything grooves within walking distance of the ferry docks.

Sights

Virgin Islands National Park Park
(www.nps.gov/viis; visitor center 8am-4:30pm) FREE Virgin Islands National Park covers two-thirds of St John, plus 5650 acres underwater. It's a tremendous resource, offering miles of shoreline, pristine reefs and 20 hiking trails. The park visitor center sits on the dock across from the Mongoose Junction shopping arcade. It's an essential first stop to obtain free guides on hiking trails, snorkeling spots, bird-watching lists, petroglyph sites and daily ranger-led activities. Green iguanas, geckoes, hawksbill turtles, wild donkeys and an assortment of other feral animals roam the landscape.

Activities

Pick up the free *Trail Guide for Safe Hiking* and *Where's the Best Snorkeling?* brochures at the park visitor center. Several moderate trails leave from behind the center.

Virgin Islands Ecotours — Kayaking, Snorkeling

(**340-779-2155, 877-845-2925; www.viecotours.com; 3hr tours adult/child US$89/69**) This groovy company, which also operates on St Thomas, offers guided jaunts from the park visitor center and Caneel Bay. Some trips are kid-friendly (Caneel Bay), some are strenuous (Henley Cay).

Arawak Expeditions — Kayaking, Snorkeling

(**340-693-8312, 800-238-8687; www.arawakexp.com; half-/full-day trips US$75/110**) Well-planned paddling trips depart out of Cruz Bay; snorkel gear costs extra (US$7).

Low Key Watersports — Diving, Boat Trips

(**340-693-8999; www.divelowkey.com; Wharfside Village; 2-tank dive US$100; 8am-6pm**) This is a great dive-training facility and has some of the most experienced instructors in the islands. It offers wreck dives to the RMS *Rhone*, as well as night dives and dive packages. It also has dinghy rentals and powerboat rentals. Trips to the BVI go to either the Baths or Jost Van Dyke.

Reef Bay Hike — Hiking

(**340-779-8700; per person US$30; 9:30am-3pm Mon & Thu year-round, plus Tue & Fri Dec-Apr**) This hike, guided by rangers from Virgin Islands National Park, is a 3-mile downhill trek through tropical forests, leading past petroglyphs and plantation ruins to a swimming beach at Reef Bay, where a boat runs you back to Cruz Bay (hence the fee). It's very popular, and the park recommends reserving at least two weeks in advance. Departure is from the park visitor center, from which a taxi takes you to the trailhead.

Sleeping

St John Inn — Hotel $$

(**340-693-8688, 800-666-7688; www.stjohninn.com; r US$200-250;**) Rooms at the uberpopular St John Inn are decked out with bright-hued walls, tiled floors and handcrafted wood furniture. A homey atmosphere pervades, and guests grill fresh fish on the communal barbecue, laze on the sun deck or dip in the small pool. Free continental breakfast, evening rum punch, beach chairs and snorkel gear are included. The inn also rents cheap cell phones.

Diving off St John

STEVE SIMONSEN/GETTY IMAGES ©

Cruz Bay Boutique Hotel Hotel **$$**
(📞340-642-1702; www.cruzbayhotel.com; King St; r US$195; ❄📶) It's the closest lodging to the ferry dock, smack in the heart of Cruz Bay. The seven tidy white rooms are located above Da Livio restaurant, and are good value for the island, which is why they book up fast. Free continental breakfast is part of the deal.

Garden by the Sea B&B B&B **$$**
(📞340-779-4731; www.gardenbythesea.com; r US$250-275; ❄📶) B&B-ers swoon over this place. The owners live on-site and have splashed the three rooms in bright hues of sea green, lavender and blueberry, each with a sturdy, four-post canopy bed and private bathroom. Solar panels provide the electricity. Cash or traveler's checks only.

Eating

Jake's Breakfast **$**
(📞340-777-7115; www.jakesstjohn.com; Lumberyard; mains US$10-16; 🕒7:30am-2pm) Breakfast is Jake's forte, including well-stuffed omelets, crispy home fries and strong coffee. Ceiling fans whir, newspapers rustle and reggae drifts from the speakers – then the couple next to you orders a triple shot of Jack Daniel's to accompany their pancakes. Jake's is that kind of place. The open-air cafe is up the hill across from the BVI ferry dock.

Lime Inn Seafood **$$**
(📞340-776-6425; www.thelimeinn.com; King St; mains US$24-34; 🕒11:30am-3pm Mon-Fri, 5:30-10pm Mon-Sat) Lime Inn is a travelers' favorite for quality cuisine, ambience and service at moderate prices. The New England clam chowder, shrimp dijon and chocolatey desserts earn rave reviews. Reservations are a good idea.

Da Livio Italian **$$**
(📞340-779-8900; www.dalivio.it; King St; mains US$17-35; 🕒5:30-10pm, closed Mon May-Nov) Fork into authentic northern Italian food lovingly cooked by a chef-transplant from the motherland. Staff makes all the pasta, gnocchi and bread from scratch, and it goes down nicely with the hearty wines. Corks dot the ceiling, and the black-and-white decor gives the trattoria a sleek-casual ambience.

Waters off St John (p148)

Uncle Joe's BBQ Barbecue $$

(340-693-8806; mains US$16-18; 11:30am-9pm) Locals and visitors go wild tearing into the barbecue chicken, ribs and corn on the cob at this open-air restaurant across from the post office. The chef grills the meats outside, perfuming the entire harbor-front with their tangy goodness. Cash only.

Drinking

Tap Room Microbrewery

(www.stjohnbrewers.com/taproom.html; Mongoose Junction; 11am-midnight Mon-Sat, from noon Sun;) St John Brewers taps its sunny, citrusy suds here (the actual brewing takes place stateside). Join the locals hanging off the bar stools and sip a flagship Mango Pale Ale, or try the alcohol-free options, including house-made root beer, ginger beer and Green Flash energy drink.

Good sandwich-y pub grub is available if you get hungry.

Woody's Seafood Saloon Bar

(www.woodysseafood.com; Centerline Rd; 11am-1am) St John's daily party starts here at 3pm, when the price on domestic beers drops precipitously (US$1 for a bottle of Coors). By 4pm the tanned crowd in the tiny place has spilled over onto the sidewalk. Bartenders pass beers out a streetside window. Woody's actually serves some reasonable pub food; try the grilled fish or corn-crusted scallops.

Joe's Rum Hut Bar

(www.joesrumhut.com; Wharfside Village; 11am-1am) Around 11am, a bartender materializes with rum and a whopping bowl of limes at this beachfront boozer. After that, it's all about sitting at the open-air counter, clinking the ice in your mojito and watching the boats bob in the bay out front. Joe's is tucked in the Wharfside Village mall, on the 1st floor fronting the water.

Shopping

Friends of the Park Store Souvenirs

(Mongoose Junction; 9am-6pm) Looking for paper made out of local donkey poo? Thought so. It's here, along with shelves of other ecofriendly wares and seaglass jewelry. Proceeds go to the Virgin Islands National Park.

Getting There & Around

Boat

Boats from St Thomas and the British Virgin Islands arrive at separate docks, though they are within steps of each other. Main routes:

Red Hook, St Thomas US$7 one way, 20 minutes, hourly (big pieces of luggage cost US$4 extra)

Charlotte Amalie, St Thomas US$13 one way, 45 minutes, three daily

West End, Tortola US$30 one way, 45 minutes, three daily

Jost Van Dyke US$70 round trip, 45 minutes, two daily (except none Thursday)

Car

Most rental agencies provide 4WDs and SUVs to handle the rugged terrain. Costs hover near US$80 per day.

Cool Breeze Jeep/Car Rental (340-776-6588; www.coolbreezecarrental.com)

Denzil Clyne Car Rental (340-776-6715)

St John Car Rental (340-776-6103; www.stjohncarrental.com)

Taxi

Rates are set. From downtown it costs per person US$7 to US$9 to Cinnamon Bay, and US$9 to US$16 to Coral Bay. Call the **St John Taxi Commission** (340-774-3130) for pickups.

NORTH SHORE

Life's a beach on the tranquil North Shore. A rental car is the easiest way to see the area via North Shore (Rte 20) and Centerline (Rte 10) Rds, but taxis will also drop you at the beaches.

Beaches

Cinnamon Bay Beach

Mile-long Cinnamon Bay is St John's biggest beach and arguably its best. It has showers, toilets, a restaurant, a grocery store, a taxi stand, a campground and – something you don't see at every beach – an archaeological museum of Taino relics. The Water Sports Center rents sailboats, windsurf boards, stand-up paddleboards and sea kayaks (US$20 to US$35 per hour). It also offers lessons and leads guided paddling jaunts. Across the highway, a short hiking trail winds by the ruins of an old sugar factory.

Honeymoon Beach Beach

Honeymoon is a mile hike from the park visitor center along the Lind Point Trail. The handsome, white-sand strand is often empty and quiet – except on days when charter boats arrive between mid-morning and mid-afternoon. A hut onsite sells snacks and rents chairs, hammocks, kayaks and other water-sports gear.

Trunk Bay Beach

(adult/child US$4/free) This long, gently arching beach is the most popular strand on the island and the only one that charges a fee. The beach has lifeguards, showers, toilets, picnic facilities, snorkel rental, a snack bar and a taxi stand. No question, the sandy stretch is scenic, but it often gets packed. Everyone comes here to swim the underwater snorkeling trail, though experienced snorkelers will likely not be impressed by the murkiness or quality of what's on offer beneath the surface.

Sights

Annaberg Sugar Mill Ruins Historic Site

(www.nps.gov/viis; North Shore Rd; 9am-4pm, demonstrations 10am-2pm Tue-Fri) FREE Part of the national park, these ruins near Leinster Bay are the most intact sugar plantation ruins in the Virgin Islands. A 30-minute, self-directed walking tour leads you through the slave quarters, village, windmill, rum still and dungeon. The schooner drawings on the dungeon wall may date back more than 100 years.

When you're finished milling around, hop on the **Leinster Bay Trail** that starts near the picnic area and ends at, yep, Leinster Bay. It's 1.6 miles, round trip.

St Croix

POP 54,000

St Croix is the Virgins' big boy – it's more than twice the size of St Thomas – and it sports an exceptional topography spanning mountains, a spooky rainforest and a fertile coastal plain that, once upon a time, earned it the nickname 'Garden of the Antilles' for its sugarcane-growing prowess. Today the island is known for its scuba diving, rum making, marine sanctuary and 18th-century forts.

CHRISTIANSTED

Christiansted evokes a melancholy whiff of the past. Cannon-covered Fort Christiansvaern rises up on the waterfront. It abuts Kings Wharf, the commercial landing where, for more than 250 years, ships landed with slaves and set off with sugar or molasses. Today the wharf is fronted by a boardwalk of restaurants, dive shops and bars. It all comes together as a well-provisioned base from which to explore the island.

Sights

Christiansted National Historic Site Historic Site

(340-773-1460; www.nps.gov/chri; admission US$3; 9am-5pm) This historic site includes several structures. The most impressive is **Fort Christiansvaern** (1749), a four-point citadel occupying the deep-yellow buildings on the town's east side. Built out of Danish bricks (brought over as ships' ballast), the fort protected citizens from the onslaught of pirates, hurricanes and slave revolts. Cannons on the ramparts, an echoey claustrophobic dungeon and latrines with top-notch sea views await inside. Nearby, the three-story neoclassical **Danish West India and Guinea Company Warehouse** served as company headquarters; slaves were auctioned in its central courtyard.

Buck Island Reef National Monument Island
(www.nps.gov/buis) For such a small land mass – 1 mile long by 0.5 miles wide – Buck Island draws big crowds. It's not so much what's on top but what's underneath that fascinates: an 18,800-acre fish-frenzied coral reef system surrounding the island, protected as Buck Island Reef National Monument. The sea gardens and a marked underwater trail create captivating snorkeling on the island's east side. Most visitors glide here aboard tour boats departing from Christiansted, 5 miles to the west.

Activities

Christiansted is chock-full of operators that book Buck Island excursions and diving trips. St Croix is a diver's mecca thanks to two unique features: one, it's surrounded by a massive barrier reef, so turtles, rays and other sea creatures are prevalent; and two, a spectacular wall runs along the island's north shore, dropping at a 60-degree slope to a depth of more than 12,000ft.

Big Beard's Adventures Boat Trips
(☎340-773-4482; www.bigbeards.com; Queen Cross St by Kings Wharf) Makes trips to Buck Island aboard catamaran sailboats.

Cane Bay Dive Shop East Diving
(☎340-718-9913; www.canebayscuba.com; boardwalk at Pan Am Pavilion) Specializes in dives at the spectacular Cane Bay Drop-Off on the north shore and can arrange transportation there.

Ay-Ay Eco-Hikes Hiking
(☎340-772-4079; ayaytours@gmail.com; 3hr hikes US$50-65) Herbalist Ras Lumumba offers tours to Maroon Ridge, Annaly Bay, Salt River Bay and more.

Local Knowledge

Name: Chuck Pishko

OCCUPATION: VOLUNTEER, VIRGIN ISLANDS NATIONAL PARK

RESIDENCE: ST JOHN

1 HOW LONG HAVE YOU VOLUNTEERED AT THE PARK?
Ten years. I've been a guide on the Reef Bay and Cinnamon Bay hikes. I currently work in the visitor center.

2 WHAT'S THE BEST THING TO DO ON ST JOHN IF YOUR TIME IS LIMITED?
There are some excellent hikes from the visitor center. The Lind Point Trail is shaded and not too strenuous. It goes through the forest and passes by two beaches. Solomon Beach comes first – it's secluded and rocky. Honeymoon Beach is next. It's more open and has restrooms, snacks and water-sports rentals. It's 1.1 miles to Honeymoon on the trail.

3 ANY OTHER GOOD HIKES NEARBY?
If you have more time and are looking for something more demanding, try the 2.4-mile Caneel Hill Trail. It also begins near the visitor center. It goes to splendid overlooks where you can take beautiful photos. It's steep – you gain about 700 feet in elevation up Caneel Hill and there's another gain up Margaret Hill. The hike takes around three hours.

4 WHAT'S AN EASY-TO-REACH PLACE TO GO SNORKELING?
At Honeymoon Beach you can see moray eels, lots of reef fish like sergeant majors, and turtles.

5 WHAT OTHER BEACHES DO YOU RECOMMEND?
Cinnamon Bay has a couple of nice little additions. There's an archaeological museum with Carib ceremonial artifacts. There's also a short, well-signed trail that goes through an old sugar estate.

Sleeping

King's Alley
Hotel $$

(340-773-0103; 57 King St; d US$179;) King's Alley has 35 recently refurbished rooms above a gallery of shops and restaurants right on the harbor. The set-up imitates a 19th-century Danish great house with colonial-style mahogany furniture and vaulted ceilings to match. The big, handsome rooms have French doors that open onto tiny but pretty balconies. It's the hotel business people use, though the wi-fi is sporadic.

Hotel on the Cay
Hotel $$

(340-773-2035; www.hotelonthecay.com; r US$140-190; @) This hotel sits just offshore on its own little island called Protestant Cay, accessible by a five-minute ferry ride (free for guests). It's good value for the spacious rooms with full kitchenettes, cooking utensils and bright furnishings, even if they're a bit faded. Private balconies let you take in cool breezes, hear waves lap the shore and watch pelicans dive-bomb for fish.

Hotel St Croix
Hotel $$

(340-773-0210; www.hotel-st-croix.com; 1 Strand St; r US$200-300;) This downtown property is set in a 250-year-old Danish mansion. The 23 rooms have been beautifully renovated with West Indian antique decor, new beds, flat-screen satellite TVs and in-room internet access, and the place now has a boutique-hotel vibe. The good news is it's in the heart of Christiansted's entertainment district, right by the boardwalk; the bad news is the area can be noisy.

Eating & Drinking

Harvey's
Caribbean $$

(340-773-3433; 11B Company St; mains US$11-23; 11am-4pm Mon-Sat) At breezy, 10-table Harvey's, a classic tropical cafe, you half expect Humphrey Bogart from *Casablanca* to walk in and order a drink at the bar. Conch in butter sauce, delicate grouper, sweet potato–based Cruzan stuffing, rice and peas and many more West Indian dishes arrive heaped on plates. Look for the mural outside of NBA star Tim Duncan; he used to wait tables here.

Savant
International $$

(340-713-8666; www.savantstx.com; 4C Hospital St; mains US$17-30; 6-10pm Mon-Sat;) Cozy, low-lit Savant serves upscale fusion cookery in a colonial townhouse. The ever-changing menu combines spicy Caribbean, Mexican and Thai recipes; sweat over them indoors in the air-con or outdoors in the courtyard. Reservations recommended.

Tavern 1844
Pub

(340-773-1844; www.tavern1844.net; cnr Company St & Queen Cross St; 5:30pm-12:30am Tue-Sat) Lots of hop-heads line up at this cozy bar, where 75 different microbrews (mostly

Annaberg Sugar Mill ruins (p152)
ALEKSANDAR KOLUNDZIJA/GETTY IMAGES ©

bottled) await. Fat burgers come with a pail of fries to help soak up the suds.

Fort Christian Brew Pub Microbrewery
(www.fortchristianbrewpub.com; 55 King's Alley; 11am-midnight;) Right on the boardwalk overlooking yachts bobbing in the sea, this open-air pub is primo for sampling the VI Brewing Company's small-batch suds. Try the flagship Blackbeard Ale.

Getting There & Around

Air

Henry E Rohlsen Airport (STX; www.viport.com), 8 miles southwest of Christiansted, handles flights from the US, many connecting via San Juan, Puerto Rico or St Thomas. Taxis from the airport to Christiansted cost US$16 per person.

Seaborne Airlines (www.seaborneairlines.com) flies seaplanes between St Thomas and St Croix – a sweet little ride (one way US$90, 20 minutes). They land in Christiansted's downtown harbor.

Car

Rentals cost about US$55 per day. Many companies will pick you up at the airport or seaplane dock.

Budget (340-778-9636; www.budgetstcroix.com)

Centerline Car Rentals (340-778-0450, 888-288-8755; www.ccrvi.com)

Hertz (340-778-1402; www.rentacarstcroix.com)

Taxi

Rates are set by territorial law. It costs US$24 to go between Christiansted and Frederiksted.

FREDERIKSTED

St Croix's second-banana town is a motionless patch of colonial buildings snoring beside the sea. Other than the occasional boatload of visitors, it'll be you and that lizard sunning itself who will have the gritty outpost to yourselves. With its out-of-the-mainstream, laissez-faire ambience, Frederiksted is the center for gay life on St Croix.

Sights & Activities

Frederiksted Pier & Waterfront Park Park
The palm-lined seafront has benches where you can sit and watch the cruise-ship scene. During quiet times (ie when cruise ships aren't here), snorkelers and divers gravitate to the pier's pilings, which attract an extensive collection of marine life, including schools of sea horses. The **Sunset Jazz Festival** (5:30pm 3rd Fri of month) FREE brings throngs of locals and visitors to the park.

Freedom City Cycles Cycling
(340-277-2433; www.freedomcitycycles.com; 2 Strand St; 2½hr tours US$60) Pedal past sugar-plantation ruins, beaches and tide pools; more difficult rides bounce over rainforest trails. Bicycle rentals (US$5 per hour) are available for DIY adventures.

N2 The Blue Diving
(340-772-3483; www.n2theblue.com; 202 Customs House St) It specializes in west-end wreck dives and Frederiksted Pier dives (including colorful night dives).

Freedom City Surf Shop Surfing
(340-227-0682; Frederiksted Beach; 11am-8pm) The congenial owners rent beach chairs and snorkel gear, but their specialty is stand-up paddleboard rentals and lessons (US$30 per hour).

Sleeping

Sand Castle on the Beach Hotel $$
(340-772-1205, 800-524-2018; www.sandcastleonthebeach.com; 127 Estate Smithfield; r/ste from US$159/269;) Right on the beach about a mile south of Frederiksted, 21-room Sand Castle is one of the few gay- and lesbian-oriented hotels in the Virgin Islands. The motel-like rooms come with kitchenettes; most have sea views. Continental breakfast is included.

Eating & Drinking

Freedom City Beach Bar Burgers, Seafood $
(☎340-713-5159; Frederiksted Beach; mains US$10-16; ⌚11am-8pm) Two sisters run this superfriendly enterprise. The bar whips up lovely burgers, tacos and cilantro-lime rice bowls tossed with sweet corn and black beans. The surf shop (p155) next door sells shaved ice treats and rents beach. Stay for sunset – the colors are dazzling.

Polly's at the Pier Cafe $
(☎340-719-9434; 3 Strand St; mains US$5-10; ⌚7am-6pm Mon-Fri, 8am-5pm Sat & Sun; 📶) Polly's serves coffee, tea, sandwiches and omelets a stone's throw from the pier. It also scoops several flavors of local Armstrong's ice cream. Savor it in the cafe's open, airy, island-bohemian ambiance.

Lost Dog Pub Pub
(☎340-772-3526; 14 King St; ⌚11am-midnight) Friendly expats hang out at The Dog to sip cold beer, chow pizza and rock out to the jukebox. Think of something clever to write on the wall before the night is done.

AROUND FREDERIKSTED

A couple of key sights lie south of Frederiksted on Centerline Rd (Rte 70).

Only a few of Whim Plantation's original 150 acres survive at **Estate Whim Plantation Museum** (☎340-772-0598; www.stcroixlandmarks.com; Centerline Rd; adult/child US$10/5; ⌚10am-4pm Wed-Sat), but the grounds thoroughly evoke the colonial days when sugarcane ruled St Croix. Guided tours leave every 30 minutes, or wander by the crumbling stone windmill and chimney on your own.

To find out how the islands' popular elixir gets made, stop by **Cruzan Rum Distillery** (☎340-692-2280; www.cruzanrum.com; 3A Estate Diamond, Rte 64; adult/child $5/1; ⌚9am-4pm Mon-Fri, 10am-2pm Sat & Sun) for a tour. The journey through gingerbread-smelling (from molasses and yeast), oak-barrel-stacked warehouses takes 20 minutes, after which you get to sip the good stuff. The factory is about 2 miles east of Whim Plantation.

Trunk Bay (p152)

KEN BROWN/GETTY IMAGES ©

BRITISH VIRGIN ISLANDS

POP 29,000

The British Virgin Islands (BVI) are territories of Her Majesty's land, but aside from scattered offerings of fish and chips, there's little that's overtly British. Most travelers come to hoist a jib and dawdle among the 50-plus isles. With steady trade winds, calm currents, protected bays and pirate-ship bars, this is one of the world's sailing hot spots.

Tortola

POP 24,000

Among Tortola's sharp peaks and bougainvillea-clad hillsides you'll find a mash-up of play places. Take surfing lessons, join fire jugglers at a full-moon party, dive on shipwrecks, and by all means go sailing amid the festive surrounding isles.

About 80% of the BVI's 29,000 citizens live and work on Tortola. It's the BVI's governmental and commercial center, plus its air and ferry hub.

ROAD TOWN

Let's be honest: the BVI's capital is nothing special – no mega sights to see or scenery to drop your jaw. But there's nothing wrong with Road Town, either (perhaps excepting all the traffic). It's a perfectly decent place to spend a day or night, and most visitors do exactly that when they charter their own boat or take the ferries to the outlying islands.

Activities

Day-sail boats are rife. Most go to the Baths, Cooper Island, Salt Island and Norman Island.

Caribbean Images Tours Snorkeling, Boat Trips

(www.snorkelbvi.com; Prospect Reef Marina; half/full day from US$85/110) Fun trips aboard a 34ft dive boat. Adventurous types can go via a seven-person rigid hull inflatable boat for farther-flung jaunts. Departures are from Prospect Reef Marina, about a mile southwest of the ferry terminal on Waterfront Dr.

Lionheart Snorkeling, Boat Trips

(www.aristocatcharters.com; Village Cay Marina; full day US$120) Glide out in a 48ft catamaran.

Sleeping

Village Cay Hotel & Marina Hotel $$

(☎284-494-2771; www.villagecayhotelandmarina.com; Wickhams Cay 1; r US$135-200; ❄@🛜🏊) Located in the middle of Road Town overlooking the bay's yacht slips, Village Cay is a sweet place to rest your head, especially if you want to schmooze with fellow boaters. The 23 rooms, suites and condos have first-class amenities for less than you'll find elsewhere in town. It books up fast. If nothing else, come for a drink at the pierside bar-restaurant.

Hummingbird House B&B $$

(☎284-494-0039; www.hummingbirdbvi.com; Pasea; r US$150-165; ❄@🛜🏊) Tile floors, batik decor and thick towels fill the four breezy rooms run by long-time UK transplant Yvonne. Breakfast is a full-cooked affair served poolside. There's a surcharge to use the air-con (per night US$10). Hummingbird is located in the leafy Pasea neighborhood, a 25-minute walk or US$5 cab ride northeast from town. It's near the Moorings, so lots of boaters stay here.

Maria's by the Sea Hotel $$

(☎284-494-2595; www.mariasbythesea.com; Wickhams Cay 1; r US$160-230; ❄@🛜🏊) Maria's is on the harbor (no beach) at Wickhams Cay 1. If you like watching the coming and going of charter yachts from a seaside pool and sundeck, this expansive three-story operation may be for you. All rooms have a balcony and kitchenette. Rooms in the original wing have tropical but plain-Jane decor. Rooms in the new wing have modern, business-y furnishings.

Road Town

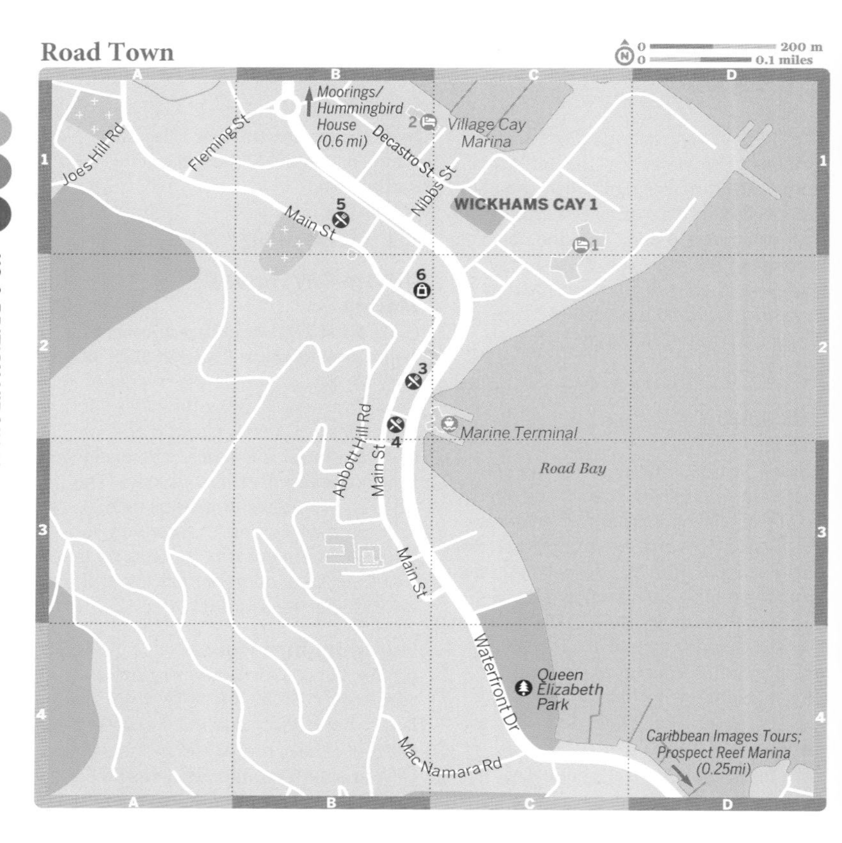

Road Town

Activities, Courses & Tours
Lionheart .... (see 2)

Sleeping
1 Maria's by the Sea C1
2 Village Cay Hotel & Marina B1

Eating
3 Capriccio di Mare B2
4 Dove B2
5 Ruby Roti Queen Restaurant B1

Shopping
6 Sunny Caribbee Spice Shop B2

Eating & Drinking

Ruby Roti Queen Restaurant — Indian $

(284-441-0770; Main St; mains US$5-9; 10am-9pm Mon-Sat) Ruby may well cook the best roti in the islands at her cute little six-table restaurant above Serendipity Bookshop. Fiery hot sauce sets off the chicken, goat, shrimp or chickpea-filled rolls. Flowery garlands hang from the entrance, Bollywood videos blare on TV, and pots of dhal (spiced lentils), pumpkin and eggplant waft from the kitchen for additional sustenance.

Capriccio di Mare — Italian $$

(284-494-5369; Waterfront Dr; mains US$11-19; 8am-9pm Mon-Sat) Set on the porch of a classic West Indian house across from the ferry dock, this Italian cafe draws both locals and travelers. Breakfast includes pastries and cappuccino. Lunch and dinner feature salads, pasta dishes and pizza, with plenty of wines to wash it all down.

Dove French $$$

(☎284-494-0313; www.thedovebvi.com; 67 Main St; mains US$25-33; ⏲6-10pm Tue-Sat) The cozy, French-flaired Dove, set in a historic house, is pretty much the top address in town. The menu changes but you might see pan-roasted duck, dry aged steaks, charcuterie platters, even some sushi. For something lighter, head upstairs to the wine bar for tapas. Oh, did we mention the wine? The list at the Dove is supposedly the BVI's largest.

Shopping

Sunny Caribbee Spice Shop Souvenirs

(www.sunnycaribbee.com; Main St; ⏲10am-5pm Mon-Sat) It's a favorite for its colorful array of island-made seasonings such as 'rum peppers' and 'mango magic.' Spices are also packaged as hangover cures and bad-spirit repellents.

Getting There & Around

Air

Terrence B Lettsome Airport (EIS; ☎284-494-3701) is on Beef Island, at Tortola's East End. It is a 25-minute drive from Road Town. A taxi costs US$27.

Boat

Road Town's **marine terminal** is the busy hub for ferries to Virgin Gorda and St Thomas' Charlotte Amalie, with multiple trips daily. Boats to Anegada depart three days weekly. There's another, smaller terminal on Tortola's West End (a 20-minute drive) that has ferries to Jost Van Dyke, St John and St Thomas' Red Hook.

Car

High-season rates begin at US$60 per day, and can run as high as US$90. **Itgo Car Rental** (☎284-494-5150; www.itgobvi.com) is a good indie agency, located at Wickhams Cay 1.

Taxi

Taxis are widely available; many queue at the marine terminal. Rates are government-set.

CANE GARDEN BAY AREA

A turquoise cove ringed by steep green hills, Cane Garden Bay is just the kind of place Jimmy Buffett would immortalize in song – which he did in 1978's 'Mañana.' The perfect 1-mile beach and throngs of rum-serving bars and restaurants make it Tortola's most popular party zone.

Road Town store (p157)

RICHARD CUMMINS/GETTY IMAGES ©

South of Cane Garden Bay is a series of picturesque bays. Speckled amid clumps of shoreside holiday villas are small West Indian settlements. When you stay out here you're living among locals.

Beaches

Cane Garden Bay — Beach

Cane Garden Bay is probably on the postcard that drew you to the BVI in the first place. The gently sloping crescent of sand hosts plenty of beachside bars and watersports vendors. It's a popular yacht anchorage, and becomes a full-on madhouse when cruise ships arrive in Road Town and shuttle passengers over for the day.

Brewers Bay — Beach

This palm-fringed beauty just east of Cane Garden Bay has excellent snorkeling and a tranquil scene – possibly because getting here involves an expensive cab ride or a brake-smoking, DIY drive down steep switchbacks. Nicole's beach bar rents chairs and sells snacks. Brewers is usually quiet when Cane Garden Bay is mobbed.

Sights

Callwood Rum Distillery — Distillery

(Cane Garden Bay; 7:30am-5pm) FREE Just off the North Coast Rd at the west end of Cane Garden Bay, this is the oldest continuously operated distillery in the Eastern Caribbean. The Callwood family has been producing Arundel rum here for more than 300 years, using copper vats and wooden aging casks. A small store sells the delicious local liquor, pours samples (four shots US$1) and offers tours through the atmospheric structure. There's a small fee to take photos.

Green VI Glass Studio — Arts Studio

(www.facebook.com/greenvi; Cane Garden Bay; 10am-4pm Mon-Sat) This nonprofit group recycles glass from local restaurants and turns it into cool jewelry, bowls, suncatchers and other artworks. Glassblowers give demonstrations. The studio is behind Myett's restaurant.

North Shore Shell Museum — Museum

(Carrot Bay; admission free but donation requested; hrs vary) It's more of a folk art gallery/junk shop than museum, but it's funky by whatever name you call it. The hours vary depending on when the proprietor, Egbert Donovan, is around to show you through. He'll also encourage you to buy something or to eat in the upstairs restaurant.

Sleeping

Mongoose Apartments — Apartment $$

(284-495-4421; www.mongooseapartments.com; Cane Garden Bay; apt US$200-240;) Each of the six large units has a living room, a full kitchen (including a blender for frosty drinks), a bathroom and bedroom as well as a private balcony.

Village Cay Marina (p157)

The common area has books and board games, and the beach – where lounge chairs and kayaks await guests – is a two-minute walk through a coconut palm grove. There's a $20 surcharge to use the air-conditioning.

Heritage Inn Apartment **$$**
(☎284-494-5842; www.heritageinnbvi.com; Windy Hill; 1-/2-bedroom apt US$225/360; ❄ ≋) High on Windy Hill between Cane Garden Bay and Carrot Bay, this property has nine spacious apartments that seem to hang out in thin air. If you like the feel of a self-contained oasis with a pool, sundeck, and bar-restaurant with awesome views, Heritage Inn is for you.

Icis Villas Apartment **$$**
(☎284-494-6979; www.icisvillas.com; Brewers Bay; 1-/2-bedroom apt US$180/290; ❄ ≋) Icis' one- to three-bedroom units aren't villas in the luxury sense. It's more like a small hotel with a shady courtyard and pool, conveniently located a five-minute walk from Brewers Bay beach. Most units have a kitchen. A fresh fruit and muffin-laden continental breakfast is included.

Eating & Drinking

Palm's Delight Caribbean **$$**
(☎284-495-4863; Carrot Bay; mains US$11-22; ⏱6-10pm) Located right on the water's edge, this family-style West Indian restaurant serves up great pâtes, rotis, fish Creole and local ambience. Friday nights provide a lively scene, with families eating on the patio and a bar crowd watching cricket or baseball on the TV.

Quito's Gazebo Caribbean **$$**
(☎284-495-4837; www.facebook.com/quitosgazebo; Cane Garden Bay; mains US$16-33; ⏱noon-2am Mon-Sat) This beachside bar-restaurant takes its name from its owner, Quito Rymer, whose band has toured with Ziggy Marley. You can dance up a storm to Quito's reggae rhythms, and hundreds pack the restaurant on weekends to do just that. Rotis and fresh salads make for popular light lunches. At night, grilled items such as snapper fill the menu.

Sugar Mill Restaurant Caribbean **$$$**
(☎284-495-4355; www.sugarmillhotel.com; Apple Bay; mains US$28-40; ⏱7-9pm) Foodies salivate over the mod Caribbean concoctions such as poached lobster and eggplant Creole. Owners Jeff and Jinx Morgan, contributing writers for *Bon Appétit* magazine, oversee the constantly changing menu that's served in the restored, candlelit boiling house of the plantation's rum distillery. Wines, cocktails and decadent desserts complete the sensory experience. Reservations are a must. Apple Bay is 2.5 miles southwest of Cane Garden Bay.

Bomba's Surfside Shack Bar
(☎284-495-4148; Cappoons Bay; ⏱noon-late) Bomba started his bar-restaurant more than 30 years ago to feed the surfers who still ride the waves curling out front. Today the shack is famous for its monthly full-moon parties that serve psychoactive mushroom tea (mushrooms grow wild on Tortola and are legal). Full moon or not, the bar is a sight to behold, built from a mishmash of license plates, surfboards, bras and graffiti-covered signposts. Cappoons Bay is about 3 miles southwest of Cane Garden Bay.

Getting There & Around

Cane Garden Bay has a taxi stand. It costs US$24 to or from Road Town and takes 25 minutes over the mountainous road. It's the same price to Brewers Bay. It's US$27 to Apple Bay and Cappoons Bay.

EAST END

Tortola's eastern end is a mix of steep mountains, remote bays and thickly settled West Indian communities. Art and surfing take pride of place. The BVI's main airport welcomes travelers here.

Beaches

Josiah's Bay Beach
An undeveloped gem on the north shore near the East End, Josiah's Bay is a dramatic strand at the foot of a valley that

Below: Snorkelling at The Baths (p164); **Right:** Boulders at Devil's Bay (p164)
(RIGHT) HOLGER LEUE/GETTY IMAGES ©; (BELOW) M SWIET/GETTY IMAGES ©

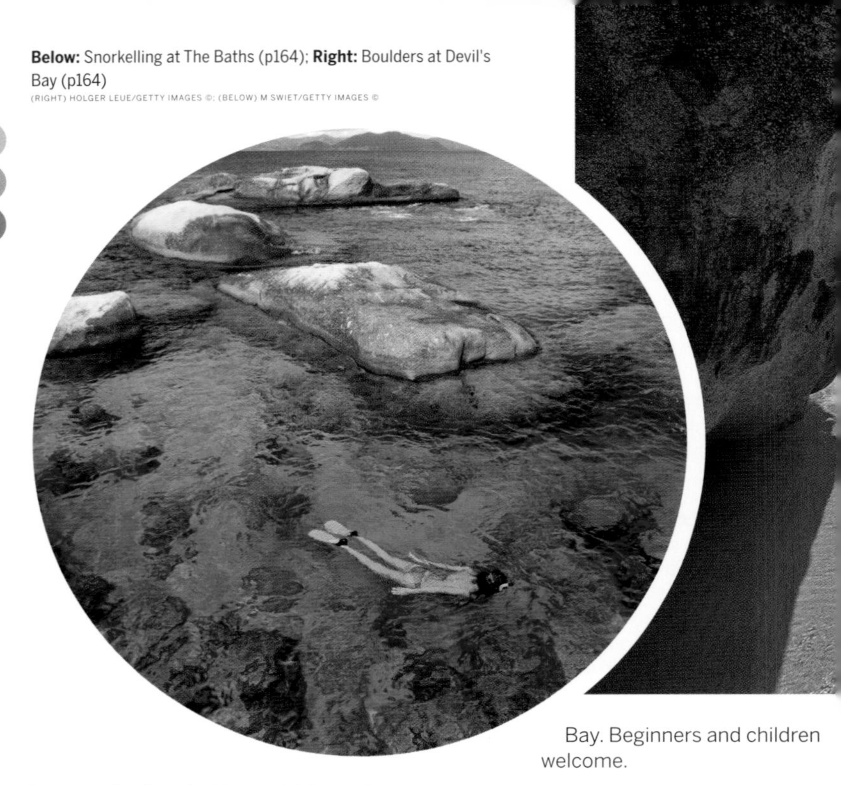

has excellent surf with a point break in winter. Many say it offers Tortola's best surfing. Lifeguards patrol the water, and a couple of beach bars serve cold Red Stripes and snacks; they also rent boards.

Sights & Activities

Aragorn's Studio Arts Center
(www.aragornsstudio.com; Trellis Bay; ⌚9am-6pm) Local metal sculptor Aragorn Dick-Read started his studio under the sea-grape trees fronting Trellis Bay, the broad beach just east of the airport. It grew to include space for potters, coconut carvers and batik makers, many of whom you can see at work in the now-sprawling arts center. Aragorn also hosts family-friendly full-moon parties.

Surf School BVI Surfing
(☎284-343-0002; www.facebook.com/surfschoolbvi; Josiah's Bay; 👪) Excellent instructors teach you how to hang ten at Josiah's Bay. Beginners and children welcome.

Eating

Trellis Bay Kitchen Cafe $
(www.adventures-bvi.com; Trellis Bay; mains US$8-18; ⌚7am-7pm; 📶) Stop in for all-day breakfasts, such as pancakes, omelets, porridge or English-style, baked bean-laden plates; or for West Indian dishes, including curried goat, crab cakes, steamed mahi mahi and rotis. It's a good place to hang out and use the free wi-fi while waiting for a flight at the nearby airport.

Entertainment

Fireball Full Moon Party Traditional Music
(www.adventures-bvi.com; Trellis Bay; 👪) Aragorn's Studio and the surrounding businesses combine to put on the Fireball Full Moon Party each month, which is an artsy, family-friendly event (unlike the island's other moon bashes). The party

kicks off around 7pm with fungi music, stilt walkers and fire jugglers. At 9pm Aragorn sets his steel 'fireball sculptures' ablaze on the ocean – a must to see.

Getting There & Around

Terrence B Lettsome Airport (p159) is on Beef Island, connected via bridge to Tortola. It is a 25-minute drive to Road Town. A small dock lies within walking distance of the airport at Trellis Bay, where water taxis depart for Virgin Gorda's resorts. Josiah's Bay is a good 15-minute drive (US$20 taxi ride) from the airport.

Virgin Gorda

POP 4000

Virgin Gorda is the BVI's rich, plump beauty. The otherworldly, granite megaliths at the Baths put on the main show, but gorgeous beaches unfurl all around the island. Movie stars live here (oh hey, Morgan Freeman), and billionaires own the isles floating just offshore (lookin' at you, Richard Branson). Somehow, Virgin Gorda keeps a level head and remains a slowpoke, chicken-dotted destination sans rampant commercialism.

SPANISH TOWN & THE VALLEY

Spanish Town isn't a town so much as a long road with businesses strung along it. It's the commercial center of Virgin Gorda, with its hub at the boat-bobbing Yacht Harbour. Overall the settlement is a sleepy place, but the mix of islanders, yachties and land travelers eating and drinking together creates a festive vibe.

'The Valley' is the long rolling plain that covers the island's southern half, including Spanish Town.

Beaches

Spring Bay Beach

FREE An excellent beach with national-park designation, Spring Bay abuts the Baths to the north. The beauty here is having a Baths-like setting but without the crowds. Hulking boulders dot the fine

Top British Virgin Islands Snorkel Sites

The Caves at Norman Island See lobsters hiding, coral flowering, and sergeant majors and barracudas swimming around. It's good for newbie snorkelers as the water is usually calm.

The Indians Loads of colorful fish dart around these rock pinnacles that rise up from the water near Norman Island. It's a great spot for experienced snorkelers.

The Rhone Another site for those with experience, this shipwreck by Salt Island is best known as a dive site, but you can snorkel the southern end and see the propeller and stern, which are in relatively shallow water.

Cooper Island It's beloved by beginners, as you can swim in from the beach, it's shallow, and you'll see lots of small fish.

white sand. There's clear water and good snorkeling off the area called 'the Crawl' (a large pool enclosed by boulders and protected from the sea). Sea-grape trees shade a scattering of picnic tables, but that's the extent of the facilities.

To get here, watch for the Spring Bay sign just before Guavaberry Spring Bay Homes on the road to the Baths; turn off to reach a parking area.

Sights & Activities

The Baths Park

(admission US$3; sunrise-sunset) This collection of sky-high boulders marks a national park and the BVI's most popular tourist attraction. The rocks – volcanic lava leftovers from up to 70 million years ago – form a series of grottoes that flood with sea water. The area makes for unique swimming and snorkeling, but the coolest part is the trail through the 'Caves' to Devil's Bay. During the 20-minute trek, you'll clamber over boulders, slosh through tidal pools and squeeze into impossibly narrow passages. Then you'll drop onto a sugar-sand beach.

While the Baths and environs stir the imagination, the places are often overrun with tourists. By 9am each morning fleets of yachts have moored off the coast, and visitors have been shuttled in from resorts and cruise ships. All you have to do, though, is come at sunrise or late in the afternoon, and you'll get a lot more elbow room.

The Baths' beach has bathrooms with showers, a snack shack and snorkel gear rental (US$10). Taxis run constantly between the park and ferry dock.

Dive BVI Diving, Boat Trips

(www.divebvi.com; 1-/2-tank dives US$85/120) This shop, with outlets at both Yacht Harbour and Leverick Bay, has several fast boats that take you diving at any of the BVI sites. It also offers full-day boating/snorkeling trips (US$100 per person) aboard a catamaran.

Sleeping

Guavaberry Spring Bay Homes Apartment $$

(284-495-5227; www.guavaberryspringbay.com; apt US$250-320; @ wifi) A short walk from the Baths and plopped amid similar hulking boulders, Guavaberry's circular cottages come with one or two bedrooms, a kitchen, a dining area and a sun porch. The setting amazes. There's a common area with wi-fi (for a small fee), games, books and cable TV, and a commissary stocked with alcohol, snacks and meals to cook in your cottage.

Fischer's Cove Beach Hotel Hotel $$

(284-495-5252; www.fischerscove.com; d/cottage US$165/245) Surrounded by gardens and just a few steps from the beach, Fischer's Cove has eight triangular-shaped cottages and a main hotel building with 12 no-frills studios. The cottages have full kitchens, but no phones, TVs or air-con (they're also located by a drainage ditch). The hotel units do have phones and TVs, and a few also have air-con.

It's a 15-minute walk south from the ferry dock.

Bayview Vacation Apartments — Apartments $$

(284-495-5329; www.bayviewbvi.com; apt US$140-165;) Each of these apartments, behind Chez Bamboo restaurant, has two bedrooms, a full kitchen, dining facilities and an airy living room. It has a plain-Jane ambience, with faded rattan furnishings, but it can be a good deal, especially if you have three or four people.

Eating & Drinking

LSL Bake Shop & Deli — Bakery $

(sandwiches US$5-8; 7am-6pm Mon-Fri, to 4pm Sat & Sun) LSL's deli sandwiches are stacked high with meaty goodness, but you're here for the bread pudding, raisin rolls, guava tarts and other sublime treats. What's more, prices are among the island's lowest. Take a picnic to the Baths. LSL is located in the Yacht Harbour mall.

Mermaid's Dockside Bar & Grill — Seafood $$

(284-495-6663; www.mermaiddockside.com; mains US$18-28; 9am-11pm) Mermaid's is indeed dockside, on a breezy pier over the true-blue water. It specializes in seafood with Spanish flair. Staff members grill your mahimahi, snapper or other fish right on the dock and plate it alongside rice and pigeon peas and lots of veggies. Sunset vistas compliment the casual, open-air vibe. It's located on the road leading west from the roundabout.

CocoMaya — International $$

(284-495-6344; www.cocomayarestaurant.com; US$24-34; 3-10pm Mon-Sat) Slick, loungey CocoMaya seems more apt for the big city than the beach. But on the sand it is, near Fischer's Cove, creating dishes with an Asian and Latin twist. Small plates include hoisin-sauced duck tacos and vegetable gyoza (dumplings), while large plates bring pan-fried snapper and pad thai. Vegetarians and gluten-free diners will find more choices than usual.

Top of the Baths — International $$

(284-495-5497; www.topofthebaths.com; mains US$14-24; 8am-7pm) Yes, it sits above the Baths and yes, it's touristy. But the hilltop view kills and the comfort food (say, Amaretto French toast for breakfast and conch burgers for lunch) is decent. Plus there's a little swimming pool to dip into.

Virgin Gorda (p163)

Detour: Anegada

The easternmost Virgin floats just 12 miles away from its brethren, but you'll think you've landed on another planet. Anegada's pancake-flat, desert landscape looks that different, and its wee clutch of restaurants and guesthouses are that baked-in-the-sun mellow. Flamingos ripple the salt ponds, and ridiculously blue water laps at beaches with whimsical names such as **Loblolly Bay** and **Flash of Beauty**.

Eating an Anegada lobster is a traveler rite of passage. Every restaurant serves the massive crustaceans, usually grilled on the beach in a converted oil drum. Crack into one at **Lobster Trap** (284-495-9466; mains $22-50; 11am-2pm & 7:30-9pm), where owner/chef Wilfred pulls the spiny critters straight from the sea, out of his dock-side snare. Make reservations by 4pm.

If you want to stay awhile, try **Cow Wreck Beach Resort** (284-495-8047; www.cowwreckbeach.com; apt US$250-350;), where three cottages front a perfect, hammock-strewn beach. Or at least stop in to the bar-restaurant for Chef Bell's conch fritters.

Road Town Fast Ferry (284-494-2323; www.tortolafastferry.com; round-trip US$55) sails between Road Town, Tortola, and Anegada on Monday, Wednesday and Friday. The trip takes 1½ hours each way. VI Airlink (p172) and **Island Birds** (www.islandbirds.com) fly the route starting at US$100 round-trip.

Getting There & Around

Air

Virgin Gorda Airport (VIJ; 284-495-5621) is on the Valley's east side, about 1 mile from Spanish Town. A taxi into town costs US$5. The airport is teeny, though well-used by small regional airlines.

Boat

Ferries sail between Spanish Town and Road Town, Tortola almost every hour during the daytime (round-trip US$30, 30 minutes) via two companies:

Smith's Ferry/Tortola Fast Ferry (284-494-4454; www.bviferryservices.com)

Speedy's (284-495-5240; www.bviferries.com)

Speedy's also provides direct service between Spanish Town and Charlotte Amalie, St Thomas on Tuesday, Thursday and Saturday (round-trip US$70, 90 minutes).

Car

You'll pay US$65 to US$90 per day for a 4WD vehicle. Companies that will pick you up at the ferry or airport:

Mahogany Car Rentals (284-495-5469; www.mahoganycarrentalsbvi.com)

Speedy's Car Rental (284-495-5240; www.bviferries.com)

Taxi

Taxi fares are set. The rate from the ferry dock to the Baths is US$8 to US$10 round-trip. Reliable companies:

Andy's Taxis (284-495-5252, 284-495-5160)

Mahogany Taxi Service (284-495-5469)

Jost Van Dyke

POP 300

Jost (pronounced 'yoast') is a little island with a big personality. It may only take up 4 sq miles of teal-blue sea, but its reputation has spread thousands of miles beyond. A lot of that is due to calypsonian and philosopher Foxy Callwood, the island's main man.

In the late 1960s, free-spirited boaters found Jost's shores, and Foxy built a bar to greet them. Soon folks such as Jimmy

Buffett and Keith Richards were dropping by for a drink.

Despite its fame, Jost remains an unspoiled oasis of green hills fringed by blinding white sand. There's a small clutch of restaurants, beach bars and guesthouses, but little else.

GREAT HARBOUR

In Jost's foremost settlement, Main St is a beach lined with hammocks and open-air bar-restaurants – which might give you a hint as to the vibe here.

Other than hanging out, there's not much to do besides stop by **JVD Scuba** (284-495-0271; www.jostvandykescuba.com), which can set you up with hiking-and-snorkeling ecotours and dives.

Sleeping & Eating

Ali Baba's Guesthouse **$$**
(284-495-9280; www.alibabasheavenlyroomsbvi.com; r US$140-160;) This popular restaurant offers three 'heavenly rooms' on its 2nd floor. The compact, whitewashed, wicker-furnished units face the beach and have a wind-cooled balcony from which to view the action. Given the location, noise can sometimes be an issue. Patrons flock in to the lazy, open-air restaurant (mains US$22 to US$37, open 8am to 11pm) for fresh fish and the Monday-night pig roast.

Sea Crest Inn Apartments **$$**
(284-495-9024, 340-775-6389; www.seacrestinn.net; apt US$150-165;) Each of the four large studio apartments at this family-run property has a kitchenette, a TV, a queen-size bed, private bathroom and balcony. In the morning, sip complimentary coffee on the deck overlooking the harbor. It's just east of Foxy's Bar.

Foxy's Bar Burgers, Seafood **$$**
(284-495-9258; www.foxysbar.com; mains US$22-44; 11:30am-11pm) Calypso signer Foxy Callwood single-handedly put Jost on the map with this legendary beach bar. The menu is a mix of rotis, seafood and darn good burgers. Foxy even has his own microbrewery and rum distillery on-site, so fresh booze accompany the fare. The best time to catch him crooning is around 10am. At night, local bands rock the stage (usually Thursday through Saturday).

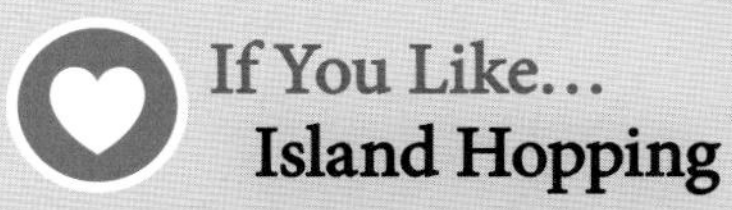

If You Like... Island Hopping

If you like Jost Van Dyke, glide over to these groovy isles that lure boaters. If you don't have your own vessel, hook up with a Tortola or Virgin Gorda day-sail tour.

NORMAN ISLAND

Since 1843, writers have alleged that treasure is buried on Norman Island, supposedly the prototype for Robert Louis Stevenson's book *Treasure Island*. Today adventurers come for two raucous beach bars. The **William Thornton** (Willy T; 284-340-8603; www.williamthornton.com; noon-1am) is a schooner converted into a bar-restaurant and moored in the bight. On the beach, **Pirate's Bight** (284-443-1305; www.piratesbight.com; noon-1am) is an open-air pavilion. Both have good food, loud music and a party-hearty crowd.

COOPER ISLAND

Lying about 4 miles south of Tortola, Cooper Island is a moderately hilly cay and is virtually undeveloped except for the **Cooper Island Beach Club** (284-495-9084, 800-542-4624; www.cooperislandbeachclub.com; r US$265; closed Sep), whose restaurant and two bars make it a popular anchorage for cruising yachts. Snorkelers and divers also swarm to the island's surrounding sites.

SALT ISLAND

The salt making which gave the island its name still goes on here, but the RMS *Rhone* is the big attraction. The *Rhone* crashed against the rocks off the southwest coast during a hurricane in 1867. Now a national park, the steamer's remains are extensive, making it one of the Caribbean's best wreck dives.

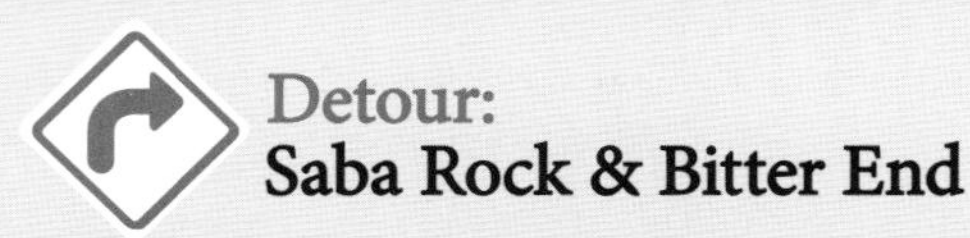

Detour: Saba Rock & Bitter End

On a fleck of island just offshore in Virgin Gorda's North Sound, **Saba Rock** (284-495-9966, 284-495-7711; www.sabarock.com; r US$150-295;) is a charismatic boutique hotel with eight rooms and a bar-restaurant (open 11am to 9pm) that is a very cool place for a drink. Lots of yachties drift in, especially during happy hour. Wander around and examine the shipwreck booty on-site, and take in views of Richard Branson's Necker Island (nearby to the north). Also keep an eye out for big fish and turtles lurking in the water by the tables. The hotel operates a ferry from Gun Creek to the island. The 10-minute jaunt is free, though the driver expects a tip; call 284-495-7711 to arrange pickup. Gun Creek is a US$30 taxi ride from Spanish Town.

Active types can head onward to **Bitter End Yacht Club & Resort** (284-494-2746, 800-872-2392; www.beyc.com; d incl meals from US$850; @), a quick zip from Saba Rock via the free ferry. Bitter End offers the mother lode of water-sports gear and instruction. Sailing, windsurfing and kiteboarding are all world-class here.

An alternate way to reach Bitter End is from Tortola. **North Sound Express** (284-495-2138; one way US$35) runs ferries from Trellis Bay/Beef Island six times daily. Call to make reservations; it's a 30-minute trip.

Corsairs Pizza, Seafood **$$**
(284-495-9294; www.corsairsbvi.com; mains US$25-40; 9:30am-11pm) Corsairs provides a variation on the usual seafood theme with a menu of pizzas and pastas, along with eclectic Tex-Mex, Thai and other fusion dishes. Most incorporate seafood in some fashion, including fish tacos, shrimp fettuccine and coconut pumpkin–sauced lobster. After dinner – and a few stiff drinks – join Corairs' limbo contest.

Getting There & Around

Boat

Most visitors arrive by yacht. Landlubbers can get here by ferry from Tortola or St John. Ferries land at the pier on the west side of Great Harbour. It's about a 10-minute walk from the pier to the town center.

New Horizon Ferry (284-495-9278; www.newhorizonferry.com; round-trip US$25) Sails five times daily to/from Tortola's West End (twice in the morning, three times in the afternoon); 25-minute trip; cash only.

Inter Island (284-495-4166; www.interislandboatservices.com; round-trip US$70) Sails twice daily to/from Red Hook, St Thomas, and Cruz Bay, St John. It leaves Jost at 9:15am and 4pm (times vary on Friday and Sunday). No service on Thursday.

Taxi

Taxis wait by the ferry dock. Fares are set. It costs US$10 per person to White Bay.

WHITE BAY

Jost's most striking beach – with its crazy-white sand and good-time bars – is a hilly, 1-mile walk from Great Harbour.

Sleeping & Eating

Perfect Pineapple Guesthouse **$$**
(284-495-9401; www.perfectpineapple.com; ste from US$160, mains US12-22;) Foxy Callwood's son Greg owns this property set on a steep hill back from the beach. The three one-bedroom suites each have a full kitchen and private porch with ocean views. There are also a couple of larger cottages on-site. The family owns Gertrude's restaurant down on the beach if you don't want to cook your own meals.

Drinking

Soggy Dollar Bar Bar

(284-495-9888; www.soggydollar.com; 9am-11pm) The infamous Soggy Dollar takes its name from the sailors swimming ashore to spend wet bills. It's also the bar that invented the Painkiller, the BVIs' delicious-yet-lethal cocktail of rum, coconut, pineapple, orange juice and nutmeg. This place is always hopping. Be sure to play the ring game, and find out how addictive swinging a metal circle onto a hook can be.

SURVIVAL GUIDE

Directory A–Z

Accommodations

High season is from mid-December through April, when rooms are costly and advance reservations essential. Three-night minimum stay requirements are common.

Prices listed in this chapter for double occupancy during high season and, unless stated otherwise, do not include taxes (10% in USVI, 7% in BVI). Most properties also levy a surcharge (for energy or other services), adding 8% to 15% more to the bill. Price ranges are:

$ less than US$100

$$ US$100 to US$300

$$$ more than US$300

Food

The following price indicators denote the cost of a main dish.

$ less than US$15

$$ US$15 to US$35

$$$ more than US$35

Health

Pesky mosquitoes and no see 'ums (tiny sand flies) bite throughout the islands, so slather on insect repellent. Tap water is safe to drink.

Internet Access

- Most lodgings have free wi-fi, though it can be slow. Relatively few bars and restaurants offer wi-fi.
- A few internet cafes can be found near the cruise-ship docks and marinas on St Thomas (at Havensight) and Tortola (in Road Town).

View from a cruise ship, Charlotte Amalie (p140)

Language

English is the official language. Islanders also speak a local Creole dialect. Many immigrants from Puerto Rico and the Dominican Republic also speak Spanish.

Money

Currency The US dollar (US$) is used in both the USVI and BVI.

ATMs Banks with ATMs hooked into worldwide networks (Plus, Cirrus, Exchange etc) are in the main towns on St Thomas, St John, St Croix, Tortola and Virgin Gorda. For other islands, you'll need to cash up beforehand.

Credit Cards Visa and Mastercard are widely accepted, American Express less so.

Opening Hours

Typical normal opening times are as follows:

Banks 9am to 3pm Monday to Thursday, to 5pm Friday.

Bars & pubs Noon to midnight.

Restaurants Breakfast 7am to 11am, lunch 11am to 2pm, dinner 5pm to 9pm daily; some restaurants open for brunch 10am to 2pm Sunday.

Shops 9am to 5pm Monday to Saturday.

Public Holidays

USVI

New Year's Day January 1

Three Kings Day (Feast of the Epiphany) January 6

Martin Luther King Jr's Birthday Third Monday in January

Presidents' Day Third Monday in February

Transfer Day March 31

Holy Thursday & Good Friday Before Easter (in March or April)

Easter Monday Day after Easter

Memorial Day Last Monday in May

Emancipation Day July 3

Independence Day (Fourth of July) July 4

Hurricane Supplication Day Fourth Monday in July

Labor Day First Monday in September

Columbus Day Second Monday in October

Liberty Day November 1

Veterans' Day November 11

Thanksgiving Day Fourth Thursday in November

Christmas Day & Boxing Day December 25 and 26

BVI

New Year's Day January 1

HL Stoutt's Birthday First Monday in March

Commonwealth Day Second Monday in March

Good Friday Friday before Easter (in March or April)

Easter Monday Day after Easter

Whit Monday May or June (date varies)

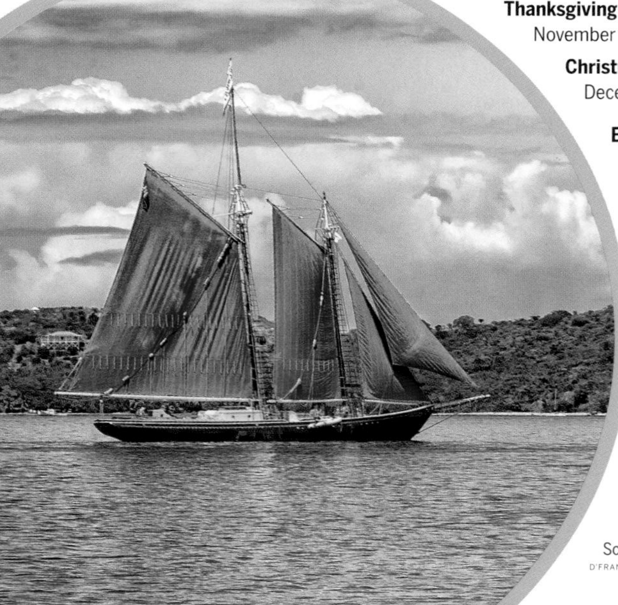

Schooner off St John (p148)

Sovereign's Birthday Mid-June (date varies)

Territory Day July 1

BVI Festival Days First Monday to Wednesday in August

St Ursula's Day October 21

Christmas Day & Boxing Day December 25 and 26

Telephone

USVI

Country code ☎1

Area code ☎340

Dialing USVI phone numbers consist of a three-digit area code, followed by a seven-digit local number. If you are calling from abroad, dial all 10 digits preceded by 1. If you are calling locally, just dial the seven-digit number.

Cell phones AT&T and Sprint are the islands' main service providers. If you use these companies at home, it's possible you may not have a roaming fee, but check in advance. Otherwise expect big roaming charges. It's difficult to find local SIM cards.

BVI

Country code ☎1

Area code ☎284

Dialing If calling from abroad, dial 1 + area code + seven-digit local number (use the latter only within the BVI).

Cell phones CCT Global (www.cctwireless.com), Lime (www.lime.com) and Digicel (www.digicelbvi.com) provide local service. SIM cards are easy to get at local shops.

Tourist Information

BVI Tourism Board (www.bvitourism.com) Official site with comprehensive lodging and activity info.

USVI Department of Tourism (www.visitusvi.com) Official tourism site with a 'hot deals' page.

Visas

Visitors from most Western countries do not need a visa to enter the USVI if they are staying less than 90 days, or to enter the BVI for 30 days or less.

Practicalities

- **Electricity** 120 volts is standard throughout the Virgins. Plugs are North American–style with two (flat) or three (two flat, one round) pins.
- **Smoking** Smoking is banned in all restaurants, bars and other public venues throughout the Virgins.
- **Time** GMT -4. Relative to New York and the eastern time zone: the Virgins are one hour ahead in winter, and in the same time zone in summer (due to Daylight Saving Time).
- **Tipping** In restaurants, 15% to 20% tip is the norm; 10% to 15% in taxis. A tip of 10% to 20% is reasonable for dive-boat operators and yacht crews.
- **Weights & Measures** All islands use imperial measurements. Distances are in feet and miles; gasoline is measured in gallons.

Getting There & Away

Air

Airports

St Thomas has the Virgin Islands' main airport. Tortola and St Croix are smaller gateways. Each facility has ATMs, food concessions, car rentals and taxis.

Cyril E King Airport (p145) On St Thomas.

Henry E Rohlsen Airport (p155) On St Croix.

Terrence B Lettsome Airport (p159) On Tortola.

Airlines

American Airlines, Delta, JetBlue, Spirit Airlines, United and US Airways all fly to the USVI. Hubs with nonstop flights include New York, Boston, Philadelphia and Atlanta. Many flights transit through Miami or San Juan, Puerto Rico. Only small, regional carriers fly to the BVI (often via San Juan).

Regional airlines serving the Virgins from around the Caribbean:

Air Sunshine (www.airsunshine.com) To/from San Juan daily.

BVI Airways (www.gobvi.com) To/from St-Martin/Sint Maarten and Dominica three times weekly (via Tortola only).

Cape Air (www.capeair.com) To/from San Juan daily.

LIAT (www.liatairline.com) To/from Antigua, Anguilla, St Kitts and St-Martin/Sint Maarten several times weekly.

Seaborne Airlines (www.seaborneairlines.com) The busiest local carrier. To/from San Juan daily, with connections to Dominica, St Kitts and Nevis.

Sea

Yacht

Lots of yachts drift into the Virgin Islands. The busiest marinas include the following:

St Thomas American Yacht Harbor, Red Hook

Tortola The Moorings, Road Town

Virgin Gorda Yacht Harbour, Spanish Town

Passports

USVI

US citizens do not need a passport to visit the US Virgin Islands, but all other nationalities do. Note that when departing the USVI, everyone must clear immigration and customs before boarding the plane. US citizens will be asked to show photo identification (such as a driver's license) and proof of citizenship (such as a birth certificate). If traveling to any other Caribbean country (besides Puerto Rico), US citizens must have a valid passport to re-enter the US.

BVI

Everyone needs a passport to enter the BVI by air. US citizens who enter the BVI by boat can opt for using the less-expensive passport card; see the **Western Hemisphere Travel Initiative** (www.getyouhome.gov) for more. All other nationalities need a passport to enter by boat.

Getting Around

Air

Air Sunshine (p172) flies between St Thomas and Tortola/Virgin Gorda daily.

Seaborne (www.seaborneairlines.com) operates seaplanes between the downtown harbors of St Thomas' Charlotte Amalie and St Croix's Christiansted.

VI Airlink (www.viairlink.com) buzzes between Tortola, Virgin Gorda, Anegada and St Thomas three times per week.

Boat

There are excellent ferry connections between the USVI and BVI. The free tourist magazines publish full schedules. Note ferries run until about 5pm only between the two territories.

Ferry companies:

Inter Island (340-776-6597; www.interislandboatservices.com)

Native Son (284-495-4617; www.nativesonferry.com)

Road Town Fast Ferry (284-494-2323; www.roadtownfastferry.com)

Smith's Ferry/Tortola Fast Ferry (284-494-4454; www.bviferryservices.com)

Speedy's (284-495-5240; www.bviferries.com)

The most common routes include the following:

St Thomas (Charlotte Amalie) to Tortola (Road Town) Road Town Fast Ferry is the only company that goes direct. US$35 one way, 45 minutes, several daily.

St Thomas (Charlotte Amalie) to Virgin Gorda (Spanish Town) Speedy's goes direct. US$40 one way, 90 minutes, Tuesday, Thursday and Saturday.

St Thomas (Red Hook) to Tortola (West End) Native Son goes direct. US$35 one way, 30 minutes, four daily.

St John (Cruz Bay) to Tortola (West End) Inter Island goes direct. US$30 one way, 45 minutes, three daily.

St Thomas (Red Hook)/St John (Cruz Bay) to Jost Van Dyke Inter Island sails the route. US$70 round-trip, 45 minutes, twice daily (except none Thursday).

Within the USVI

Between St Thomas and St John:

From Red Hook Passenger ferries (US$7 one way, 20 minutes) run on the hour to Cruz Bay, between roughly 7am and midnight. They return from Cruz Bay on the hour, too.

From Charlotte Amalie Passenger ferries (US$13 one way, 45 minutes) run three times a day to Cruz Bay from Charlotte Amalie's waterfront (at the foot of Raadet's Gade, *not* from the Marine Terminal), departing at 10am, 1pm and 5:30pm.

Within the BVI

Main routes:

Tortola (Road Town) to Virgin Gorda (Spanish Town) Between Speedy's and Smith's, there's a ferry almost every hour during the daytime (round-trip US$30, 30 minutes).

Tortola (West End) to Jost Van Dyke New Horizon (p168) sails five times daily (round-trip US$25, 25 minutes, cash only).

BVI Departure Tax

Travelers must pay a US$20 departure tax to leave the BVI by air. The tax is US$15 to leave by ferry. This is not included in the ticket price, and must be paid separately at the airport or ferry terminal (usually at a window by the departure lounge).

Car

Rule No 1: drive on the left-hand side of the road in both the USVI and BVI. Roads are steep, winding and incredibly potholed. See individual destinations for car-rental details.

Taxi

All of the islands have taxis that are easily accessible in the main tourist areas. Most vehicles are vans that carry up to 12 passengers; sometimes they're open-air pickup trucks with bench seats and awnings. Rates are set, with prices listed in the free tourist guides.

Swimmers off Virgin Gorda (p163)

Leeward Islands

The Leeward Islands – Anguilla, Saba, Sint Eustatius, St Kitts & Nevis, Antigua & Barbuda – are a natural mosaic that for centuries has tugged mightily at the hearts of explorers, buccaneers, traders and boaters. On this string of islands stretching south in an arc east of Puerto Rico, dreamy beaches flanked by crooked palms and lapped by cerulean waters are only the beginning. Sure, give your soul a vacation on the beach for a few days, but then tear yourself away and explore. Beat your path through dense rainforest to reach volcanic peaks for painterly panoramas or plunge below the waterline for mesmerizing close-ups of coral and tropical fish. Commune with colonial ghosts at ruined military forts or former sugar plantations, then connect back with the present over rum punches, roadside barbecues and jamming beach parties. Just don't expect casinos, condo complexes or big malls – this is the Caribbean unplugged.

English Harbour and Nelson's Dockyard, (p193) Antigua
PETER PHIPP/GETTY IMAGES ©

Leeward Islands Itineraries

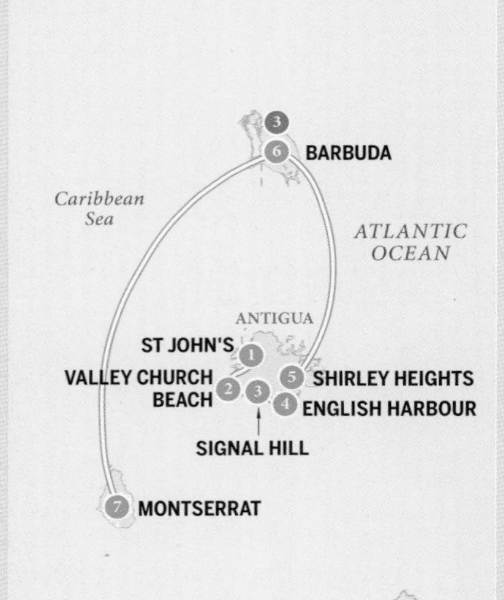

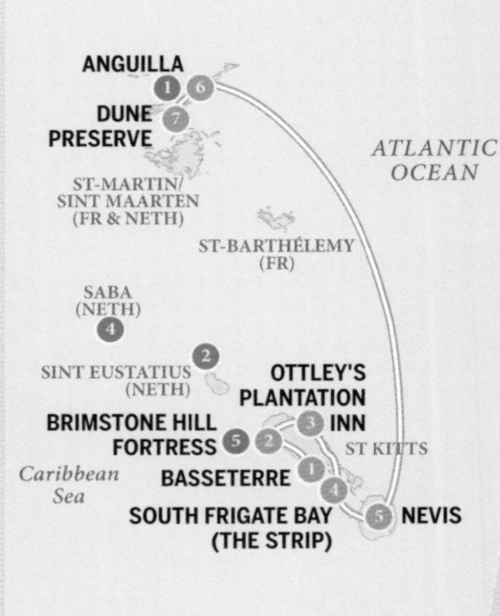

One Week

❶ **St John's, Antigua** (p186) This itinerary focuses on Antigua with day trips to Barbuda and Montserrat. Start with the colorful capital of St John's, stopping by the Public Market for great photo ops and pineapples.

❷ **Valley Church Beach** (p190) Pick this or any of the other pearls from the necklace of sparkling beaches between Jolly Harbour and Old Road Town and polish it with a leisurely lunch and rum-punch sundowners at a funky beach bar.

❸ **Signal Hill** (p191) Work off all those lobster dinners by exploring Antigua's rich eco-diversity on foot. The trek up Signal Hill is among the most rewarding, especially if you let Dassa of Footprint Rainforest Hiking Tours guide you.

❹ **English Harbour** (p193) Flash back to colonial times at the still-working Georgian marina at Nelson's Dockyard, then hit Happy Hour at the Mad Mongoose and wrap up with dinner at locally adored Trappas.

❺ **Shirley Heights** (p193) Head up the hill above English Harbour for wildly popular Sunday afternoon barbecue parties and stunning views of sea, sunset and sails as a steel-band plays its gentle rhythms.

❻ **Barbuda** (p195) Escape – by boat or by helicopter – to this still virtually untouched island paradise with its footprint-free beaches and squawking frigate bird colony.

❼ **Montserrat** (p412) See how this 'modern-day Pompeii' is recovering from the 1995 volcano eruption that left two-thirds of the island covered by ash and debris. A scenic flight over the 'Exclusion Zone' is ideal to fully comprehend the extent of the devastation.

➡ THIS LEG: 240 MILES

Two Weeks

1 Basseterre, St Kitts (p207) Continue your Leeward Islands exploration by flying to St Kitts. Start by strolling around its cute and vibrant capital, browsing the duty-free shops and fueling up on fried snapper and fresh fruit juice at El Fredo's.

2 Brimstone Hill Fortress (p211) Indulge in a blast from the past at the only Unesco World Heritage site in the Leeward Islands. Views from the mighty bastion in its aerie atop an 800ft volcanic cone are nothing short of spellbinding. On clear days, you can even spot little Saba in the distance.

3 Ottley's Plantation Inn (p212) This charmingly restored sugar estate with its majestic Great House and manicured lawns dotted with tidy stone cottages keeps the legacy of the colonial era alive.

4 South Frigate Bay (The Strip) (p213) If this row of classic, ramshackle Caribbean beach bars on South Frigate Bay don't get you into the spirit of this relaxed island, nothing will. Wriggle your toes in the sand as you watch the sunset, cold Carib in hand.

5 Nevis (p215) Catch the ferry to this egg-shaped emerald isle where you can wander in the footsteps of Alexander Hamilton and Horatio Nelson, have a Killer Bee at Sunshine's and a swim on secluded Lovers' Beach.

6 Anguilla (p178) Wrap up your two-week vacation by hopping over to this ritzy isle for a couple of days of serious tropical slothdom on some of the Caribbean's most blissful beaches such as powdery Shoal Bay East and sweeping Rendezvous Bay.

7 Dune Preserve (p183) Make a pilgrimage to the quintessential beach haunt personally stitched together by local reggae star Bankie Banx, who still performs live here alongside other local musicians. Beware Bankie's balance-reducing 'Dune Shine' potion.

THIS LEG: 200 MILES

Leeward Islands Highlights

1 Best Beach: Shoal Bay East, Anguilla (p183) This sublime, sugary beach will bring a tear to your holiday-hungry eye.

2 Best Diving: Sint Eustatius (p203) Crystal-clear waters shelter an underwater paradise before the fall.

3 Best Tour: Frigate Bird Sanctuary, Barbuda (p197) Observe frigate birds eat, sleep, mate and roost among the mangroves in this serene sanctuary.

4 Best Hike: Mt Scenery, Saba (p202) Conquer the tallest point of the Netherlands on this fairy-tale island.

5 Best Historic Site: Brimstone Hill Fortress, St Kitts (p211) Marvel at British colonial might when scaling this superbly preserved citadel that kept enemies at bay for nearly 200 years.

Frigate bird (p197)

Discover Leeward Islands

ANGUILLA

POP 15,750

Something old, something new, something borrowed, something blue – wedding bells immediately come to mind, but what about Anguilla? As rabid consumerism devours many Caribbean hot spots, this limestone bump in the sea has, thus far, maintained its charming clapboard shacks (something old) while weaving postmodern vacation properties (something new) into the mix. Prepare to discover a melting pot of cultures (something borrowed) set along mind-blowing beaches (something very, very blue).

Eel-shaped Anguilla is, however, no shoestring destination – authenticity comes at a premium here. Far from being St-Barth's stunt-double, Anguilla actually flaunts its down-to-earth charms to the jetset subset who crave a vacation off the radar.

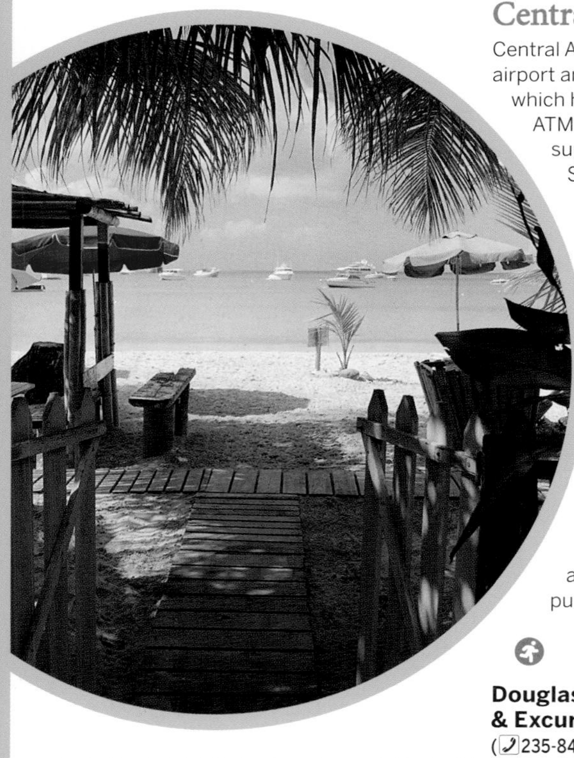

Beachway, Anguilla

MELANIE ACEVEDO/GETTY IMAGES ©

Central Anguilla

Central Anguilla is home to the tiny airport and the Valley, the island's capital, which has a smattering of banks with ATMs, restaurants, a gas station and supermarkets. The closest beach is Sandy Ground, about 3 miles to the southwest, which is also the epicenter of Anguilla's (fairly subdued) nightlife. The murky salt pond behind the beach was commercially harvested until the 1970s.

Beaches

Sandy Ground Beach

(Sandy Ground Rd, Sandy Ground Village) This golden, narrow beach fronting bobbing yachts and a pier may not be the best for swimming but its beach bars and restaurants still draw plenty of punters, especially on weekends.

Activities

Douglas Carty Diving & Excursions Diving

(☎235-8438; www.dougcarty.com) Native divemaster Doug can practically call each fish, shark and turtle by name, and they'll come.

Leeward Islands

Ports of Call

ST JOHN'S, ANTIGUA

- Cruise ships dock at Heritage Quay right in town.
- If you're not on a prebooked shore excursion, grab a cab for some R&R at a secluded beach south of Jolly Harbour or, if you're into yachts or history, head straight on to English Harbour with its Georgian-era heritage.

BASSETERRE, ST KITTS

- Ships moor dockside in Port Zante right next to a duty-free mall and the cute downtown area.
- A ride on the St Kitts Scenic Railway is a popular shore excursion, but DIY-types might prefer an island tour by cab, stopping at Brimstone Hill Fortress, lunch at Ottley's Plantation Inn and sundowners on 'the Strip'.

CHARLESTOWN, NEVIS

- Nevis doesn't have a dock that can accommodate enormous boats. Passengers are brought to port by tender from small ships anchored offshore, or as part of excursions from St Kitts.
- With its museums and historic buildings, Charlestown is good for a couple of hours of wandering.

He doesn't have an office, so you need to book ahead by phone or email.

Sleeping

Lodging options in the center of the island are as budget as things get on Anguilla and include nice but fairly low-frills B&Bs, inns and small hotels.

Lloyd's — B&B $

(497-2351; www.lloyds.ai; Crocus Hill, the Valley; s/d incl breakfast & tax US$99/145;) Owned by a prominent local family, Lloyd's was the first guesthouse to open on Anguilla in 1959. Today, the vintage-flair B&B in a banana-yellow clapboard building is a bargain-hunter's dream. Mornings start with cooked-to-order breakfast served in a spacious common area that gives way to smallish, low-frills rooms splashed in bright colors.

Sydans Apartments & Villas — Apartment $

(497-3180; www.inns.ai/sydans; Sandy Ground Rd, Sandy Ground; r US$85-105;) Anne Edwards presides over 10 basic apartments with separate bedrooms and full kitchens set around a convivial courtyard and within stumbling distance (and earshot) of the beach and its bars and restaurants. Units facing the salt pond are quieter and great for bird-watchers.

La Vue Boutique Inn — Inn $$

(497-6623; www.lavueanguilla.com; Back St, South Hill, Sandy Ground; 1-/2-bedroom ste incl breakfast & tax US$200/322;) This good-value hilltop abode gets a big thumbs up for its terrific views and super-helpful staff. Enjoy sweeping views of Sandy Ground Beach from your private balcony, perhaps with a drink or snack prepared in your kitchenette. The onsite restaurant, Flavours, does upscale Caribbean fare and has live jazz on Thursdays.

Eating & Drinking

Self-caterers flock to **JW Proctor Supermarket** (The Quarter, the Valley; 8am-8:30pm Mon-Fri, to 9:30pm Sat) and **Albert Lakes Marketplace** (Stoney Ground, the Valley; 8am-8pm Mon-Fri, to 9pm Sat).

Hungry's Good Food Caribbean $
(235-8907; www.hungrysgoodfood.com; the Valley; mains US$3-15; noon-10pm Mon-Sat) Chefs Irad and Papy have helmed some of the island's top kitchens and now serve up homemade soups, fresh salads, a dozen quesadilla varieties and delicious pasta to working locals and clued-in visitors from their colorful food truck parked opposite St Gerard's Church near the post office.

E's Oven Caribbean $$
(498-8258; South Hill Rd, South Hill, Sandy Ground; mains US$12-32; lunch & dinner Wed-Mon;) E's earns top marks across the board for great local food and competitive prices. Insiders phone ahead to preorder the famous roast chicken, but even if it's all gone, coconut-encrusted grouper, curried goat or creole conch fill the belly nicely.

Pumphouse International $$
(497-5154; www.pumphouse-anguilla.com; Sandy Ground Rd, Sandy Ground; mains US$11-28; 5pm-2am;) This former salt plant is one of Anguilla's most chilled-out spots with great pizza, burgers, beer by the bucket and other drink specials. Live bands, trivia quizzes, DJ nights and other events draw a big party crowd almost nightly.

Veya Fusion $$$
(498-8392; www.veya-axa.com; off Sir Emile Gumbs Dr, Sandy Ground; mains US$28-48; dinner Mon-Sat Nov-May, Mon-Fri mid-Oct-Nov & Jun-Aug) 'Cuisine of the sun' is the motto at this stellar Caribbean-Asian gourmet outpost with Zen-style ambiance amid tropical gardens with a koi pond and waterfalls. Dishes cycle on and off the menu but may include such palate teasers as vanilla-cured duck with guava sauce or jerk-spiced tuna with rum-coffee glaze. Enjoy them at a romantic table on the wraparound porch.

Elvis' Beach Bar Bar
(498-0101; Sandy Ground Rd, Sandy Ground; mains US$5-16; noon-late Wed-Mon) The beer is cold, the margaritas strong and the rum punch tastily laced with amaretto at Elvis' salty beach bar, which also has a menu of decent Mexican food. Belly up to the 16ft-boat-turned-bar or rock out to live bands until the wee hours during high-octane weekend beach parties.

Information

Banks with ATMs are located in the Valley and dispense both US and EC dollars.

Anguilla Tourist Board (497-2759, in USA 800-553-4939; ivisitanguilla.com; Coronation Ave, the Valley)

Anguilla's Heritage Trail

After perfecting your Caribbean tan, soak up some local history by following the Heritage Trail. Start at the privately run **Heritage Collection Museum** (497-4092; Liberty Rd, next to East End Salt Pond; adult/child US$5/3; 10am-5pm Mon-Sat), where artifacts, photos and maps chronicle milestones spanning from Anguilla's Arawak origins to royal visits and the 1967 island revolution. Ask owner-curator Colville Petty for a copy of the *Anguilla's Heritage Trail* pamphlet, then set out on the self-drive tour of 10 historical spots scattered around the island, including plantation houses, caves, a salt mill, an Amerindian well and archaeological sites. Limestone markers point to individual sites.

Prickly Pear

Lonely Prickly Pear sits off the coast of Anguilla just far enough to feel like a tiny colony in its own right. This windswept limestone bump above the waves features nothing but creamy beige sand ambushed by curls of rolling turquoise waves.

Prickly Pear has excellent snorkeling conditions. Tour boats leave Sandy Ground for Prickly Pear at around 10am, returning around 4pm; the cost averages US$80, including lunch, drinks and snorkeling gear.

The island is easily accessible by catamaran or sailboat on a day-trip tour from either Anguilla or St-Martin/Sint Maarten.

Western Anguilla

Long Bay Village and West End Village are home to Anguilla's most celebrated sands and lavish resorts.

Beaches

Meads Bay Beach
(Long Bay Village) Unplug from reality at this majestic beach, which gets busy around the Viceroy resort but has plenty of quiet spots further east along with such much-loved beach bars as Blanchard's.

Rendezvous Bay Beach
(Long Bay Village) This famous pearly white crescent is usually lapped by calm waters and is perfect for an extended stroll with a rum-punch stop at Bankie Banx's Dune Preserve.

Cove Bay Beach
(West End Village) Cove Bay has shallow, clear and mostly calm water but no amenities except for a rollicking beach bar. **Seaside Stables** (**☎235-3667; www.seasidestablesanguilla.com**) offers horseback rides along the beach from US$75.

Shoal Bay West Beach
(West End Village) The island road ends at this divine and usually deserted sweep of white powdery sand with fabulous offshore snorkeling.

Activities

CuisinArt Golf Club Golf
(**☎498-5602; www.cuisinartresort.com; Rendezvous Bay, West End Village; green fee 9/18 holes US$170/270**) Tee off with breathtaking views of St-Martin/Sint Maarten at this 18-hole, 7063yd course designed by Greg Norman.

Sleeping

Anacaona Hotel **$$**
(**☎497-6827; http://anacaonahotel.com; Albert Hughes Dr, West End Village; r from US$265; P ❄ @ ≋**) This locally run boutique hotel, set within a flourishing garden, is only a five-minute walk from dreamy Meads Bay beach. Lovely, accommodating staff look after the 27 units and also host the popular 'Antillean Night' featuring a local Mayoumba folklore troupe.

Anguilla Great House Hotel **$$**
(**☎497-6061, in USA 800-583-9247; www.anguillagreathouse.com; Rendezvous Bay, West End Village; s/d from US$290/310; P ❄**) This Caribbean-flavored cluster of cottages on glorious Rendezvous Bay has cheerfully if simply furnished rooms and staff that's generous with the smiles. Cool hangouts such as the Dune Preserve bar are within stumbling distance.

Cap Juluca Luxury Hotel **$$$**
(**☎497-6779, in USA 888-858-5822; www.capjuluca.com; Maundays Bay, West End Village; r from US$995; P ❄ @ ≋**) With its domed Greco-Moorish villas and excellent restaurants dotted along a sandy arc, Cap Juluca is easily one of Anguilla's most seductive resorts. After a facelift, it's roaring to recapture most-fave status with its demanding clientele, celebs included.

CuisinArt Golf Resort & Spa
Luxury Resort $$$

(☎498-2000, in USA 800-943-3210; www.cuisinartresort.com; Rendezvous Bay, West End Village; ste from US$875; P ❄ 📶 🏊) Nothing to do with the namesake kitchen appliance brand, this whitewashed top-notch resort sits on a divine stretch of beach and features tons of leisure facilities along with a trio of restaurants supplied by produce grown in the huge on-site hydroponic greenhouse (tours available).

Viceroy Anguilla
Luxury Hotel $$$

(☎497-7000; www.viceroyhotelsandresorts.com/anguilla; Meads Bay, Long Bay Village; ste from US$800; P ❄ @ 📶 🏊) The luxe apartment blocks of this blufftop campus are as angular as George Clooney's chin, but suites are a lot smoother thanks to such organic touches as driftwood lamps and petrified-wood tables. With its full complement of services and facilities, there's little incentive to leave the resort's grounds.

Eating & Drinking

Blanchard's Beach Shack
International $

(☎498-6100; www.blanchardsrestaurant.com; John Hodge Rd, Meads Bay, Long Bay Village; dishes US$4-25; 🕒11:30am-8:30pm Mon-Sat; P 📶) This charismatic barefoot beach bar is an island budget favorite right next to the fine-dining restaurant run by the same couple. Wriggle your toes in the sand while munching on tacos, burgers, salads or sandwiches, all made-to-order with fresh ingredients.

B&D's
Barbecue $

(John Hodge Rd, Long Bay Village; chicken/ribs/lobster US$8/9/30; 🕒dinner Fri & Sat) For more than 20 years this family-run roadside barbecue has dished up fingerlickin' platters of chicken, ribs and lobster to a cult following of locals and clued-in visitors. The johnnycakes are the biggest and flakiest around.

Smokey's at the Cove
Caribbean $$

(☎497-6582; www.smokeysatthecove.com; Cove Bay, West End Village; mains US$6-28; 🕒food 11am-9pm, party til late; 📶) Break up a day of swimming in Cove Bay with a 'Frisky Parrot' or grilled snapper at this chill nosh spot, then stay for the happy-feet-inducing local bands, which perform nightly (except Thursday) as well as on weekend afternoons.

Eastern Anguilla

Anguilla's quiet and unpretentious eastern end has its own share of blissful beaches as well as Island Harbour, a working fishing village with brightly colored boats bobbing in the bay.

Beaches

Shoal Bay East
Beach

(Shoal Bay Village) This 2-mile-long silvery strand caressed by glassy turquoise waters with thoughtfully placed snorkeling reefs is the ultimate Caribbean beach.

Banking on Bankie

Imagine if a reggae star was given a huge pile of driftwood and old boats and got to build his very own tree house on the beach. The result would be **Dune Preserve** (www.thedunepreserve.com; Rendezvous Bay, West End Village; 🕒whenever), the grooviest place on Anguilla. Hometown star Bankie Banx has jammed and limed in this Rendezvous Bay spot for a quarter century, founding the Moonsplash Festival, one of the top music festivals in the region, in 1991. There's live music several nights a week and, if you're lucky, you'll hear Bankie or his son Omar themselves. After trying the signature 'Dune Shine', a mindbending mix of ginger, pineapple juice, white rum and bitters, you may want to linger forever. To get there, turn off at the CuisinArt resort, go past the entrance and take the first left turn.

Junk's Hole Beach

(Junk's Hole) At the end of a bumpy, unpaved road, this silent stretch of windswept sand flanked by crooked palms is perfect for living out your castaway fantasies.

Activities

Shoal Bay Scuba Diving

(☎497-4371, 235-1482; www.shoalbayscuba.com; 2-tank boat dive US$90) This professional diving operation has high-quality equipment, good boats and divemasters familiar with every underwater crack and crevice.

Sleeping

Milly's Inn Inn $

(☎497-4274, 581-5398; www.millysinn.ai; Bay View Rd, Shoal Bay Village; d US$150-160;) Run with aplomb by the charming Milly, this four-unit villa is a hit with value-conscious travelers. The hillside location ensures good views and refreshing breezes with the heavenly beach only a short walk away. Self-caterers can whip up entire gourmet meals in their well-equipped kitchen.

Arawak Beach Inn Hotel $$

(☎497-4888; www.arawakbeach.com; Island Harbour; d US$245-415;) Hugging the rock-strewn western edge of Island Harbour, this convivial English-owned inn consists of a row of hexagonal candy-colored two-story cottages with lots of space and private porches for observing nose-diving pelicans.

Shoal Bay Villas Apartment $$$

(☎497-2051; www.sbvillas.ai; Bay View Rd, Shoal Bay Village; ste US$365-585;) With its front yard of white-sand perfection, this recently expanded genteel retreat encapsulates the laid-back Caribbean lifestyle. Each of the 15 comfortable units comes with prim tropical decor, a kitchen and sea-facing patio or balcony.

Left: Anguilla coastline; **Below:** Lobster dinner, Anguilla
(LEFT) PATRICE HAUSER/GETTY IMAGES ©; (BELOW) MELANIE ACEVEDO/GETTY IMAGES ©

Eating & Drinking

Uncle Ernie's Fast Food $
(☎497-3907; www.uncleerniesbeachbar.com; Shoal Bay East beach, Shoal Bay Village; mains US$6-10; ⏲10am-6pm) Ernie may have passed on but his bright green and purple beach shack continues to enjoy a cultish following among beachaholics needing a break from the Caribbean sun. The menu is straightforward (the ribs are recommended) and, at US$2 per can, the beer is indeed a local bargain.

Hibernia Restaurant Fusion $$$
(☎497-4290; www.hiberniarestaurant.com; Harbour Ridge Dr, Island Harbour; mains US$34-46; ⏲lunch Tue-Sat, dinner Tue-Sun, closed Aug-Oct) Hibernia's owners Raoul and Mary hail from France and Ireland and share passions for art, Asia and Anguilla. Their culinary retreat presents a harmonious alchemy of all these influences as reflected in the Caribbean-Zen flair, the French-Caribbean-Asian fusion cooking and the idiosyncratic decor. The wine list is tops, too. It's been a winning concept for more than 25 years. Reservations required.

Palm Grove (Nat's Place) Seafood $$$
(☎235-6528; Junk's Hole; mains US$20-40; ⏲lunch, call ahead to confirm) At this off-the-radar beachfront Shangri-la, owner-chef Nat magically churns out gourmet-level fish and seafood without the benefit of electrical power. Be sure to order a side of the flaky johnnycakes for sopping up the sauces and juices. It's at the end of a bumpy dirt road.

Scilly Cay Seafood $$$
(☎497-5123; Island Harbour; mains US$25-40; ⏲noon-3pm Wed & Sun, closed Sep-Oct & in rough weather) This atoll in Island Harbour is barely big enough for the funky namesake restaurant, which serves grilled lobster, crayfish and chicken along with its potent beverage. After lunch, have a

digestive snooze below the palm trees, snorkel around the reef or enjoy the reggae band. To get there, wave at the island from the pier and someone will sail out to get you.

ANTIGUA & BARBUDA

POP 90,150

On Antigua, life is a beach. Its corrugated coasts cradle scores of perfect little strands lapped by beguiling blue water, while the sheltered bays have provided refuge for everyone from Admiral Nelson to pirates and yachties. If you can tear yourself away from that towel, you'll discover that there's a distinct English accent to this classic Caribbean island with its narrow roads, candy-colored villages and fine historic sights.

If life on Antigua is a beach, Barbuda *is* a beach: one smooth, pink-tinged strand hemming the reef-filled waters. Birds, especially the huffing and puffing frigates, greatly outnumber residents on this perfect Caribbean dream island.

Antigua

Antigua's capital, St John's, is tucked into a sheltered bay, about 5 miles west of the airport. Most hotels and resorts cluster north of here along Dickenson Bay and south in historic English Harbour. The best beaches hem the west coast between Jolly Harbour and Old Road Town. The wind-swept east is sparsely settled and has only a few beaches.

ST JOHN'S & NORTHERN ANTIGUA

Intriguingly shabby, the island capital and commercial center is worth a spin for its cafes, restaurants, shops, cute museum and bustling market. The town all but shuts down at night and on Sundays. North of here, the middle market of Antigua's holidaymakers finds fun in the sun along Dickenson Bay, which has good swimming and plenty of aquatic activities.

Beaches

Dickenson Bay Beach

The closest beach to St John's is a fairly thin strip of golden sand fringed by calm waters and busy resorts with bars, restaurants and water-sports facilities. At its south end, it segues into tranquil and facility-free **Runaway Beach**.

Jabberwock Beach Beach

(Hodges Bay) This breezy white sandy beach is largely the domain of windsurfers and kitesurfers.

Sights

Museum of Antigua & Barbuda Museum

(☎462-1469; www.antiguamuseums.org; cnr Market & Long Sts; adult/child EC$8/free; ⏰8:30am-4pm Mon-Fri, 10am-2pm Sat) In the stately 1750

Devil's Bridge (p189)

St John's

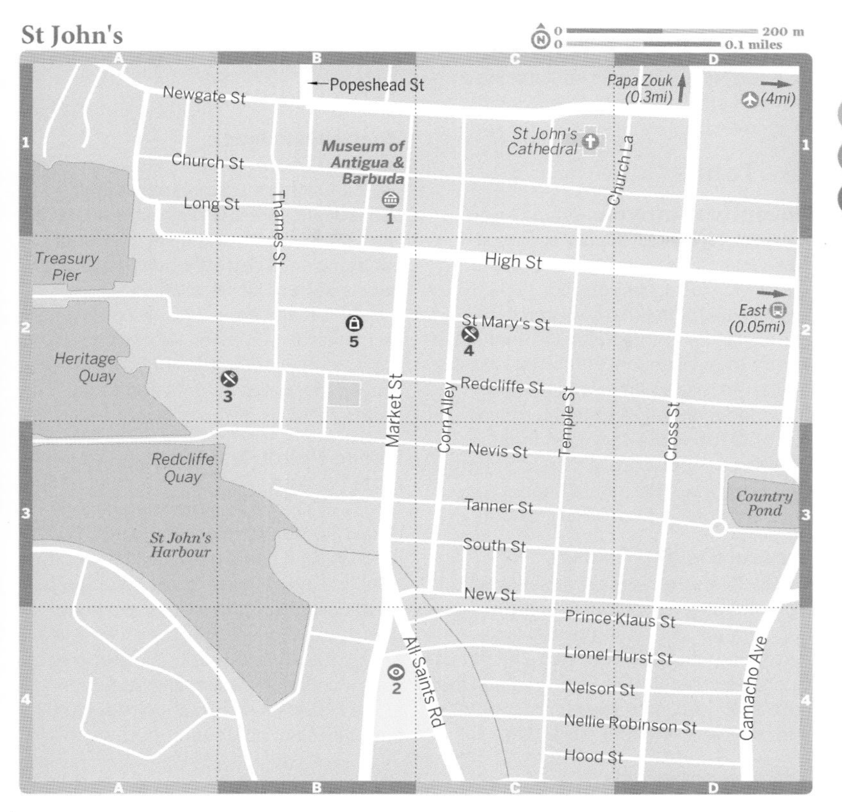

courthouse, this modest museum traces the history of Antigua from its geologic origins to its political independence in 1981. The hodgepodge of objects includes an Arawak canoe, models of sugar plantations and the cricket bat of hometown hero Viv Richards.

Activities

Tony's Water Sports Water Sports
(☎462-6326; next to Sandal's Resort, Dickenson Bay) Run by the son of local calypso great King Short Shirt, Tony's gets you waterborne with Hobie Cats, jet skis, banana boats and water skis.

Windsurf Antigua Windsurfing
(☎461-9463; www.windsurfantigua.net; Jabberwock Beach, Hodges Bay) Local windsurfing guru Patrick Scales guarantees to get beginners up and onto the water in one session (US$90 for two hours). Boards can be delivered islandwide. Prebooking advised.

Kite Antigua Kitesurfing
(☎720-5483; www.kitesurfantigua.com; Jabberwock Beach, Hodges Bay) Offers a four-hour

St John's

Don't Miss Sights
1 Museum of Antigua & Barbuda B1

Sights
2 Public Market B4

Eating
3 C&C Wine Bar B2
4 Roti King C2

Shopping
5 Best of Books B2

introductory kitesurfing course (from US$220) and a 10-hour clinic (from US$500) and also rents equipment to experienced riders (per hour US$30). Prebooking advised.

Tours

Adventure Antigua Adventure Tour
(☎726-6355; www.adventureantigua.com) Run by Eli Fuller, a former Olympian and third-generation local. His Eco-Tour (US$115) is a day spent boating, swimming and snorkeling amid the pristine waters of the North Sound National Park while learning about the area's rich flora and fauna. A second tour, the Xtreme Circumnav (US$170) aboard a 45ft speedboat, includes a snorkel trip, a stop at Stingray City and a swim at remote Rendezvous Bay. Book online for a 10% discount.

Treasure Island Cruises Cruise
(☎461-8675; www.treasureislandcruises.ag) Operates a variety of tours aboard a 70ft catamaran that combine sailing, snorkeling, entertainment and a barbecue. Options include the Circumnavigation tour (US$120), the Cades Reef tour (US$120) and the Bird Island tour (US$100).

Sleeping

Most people skip St John's and head to the coast for lodging.

Buccaneer Beach Club Apartment $$
(☎562-6785; www.buccaneerbeach.com; Marina Bay Rd, Dickenson Bay; apt from US$210; ❄@📶🏊) This beachfront cluster of candy-colored cottages hugging a large pool is perfect for families and self-caterers. It sits amid a lovely palm-and-orchid garden on a tiny sugary beach on the quiet end of Dickenson Bay with easy access to the restaurants and water-sports facilities of the adjacent resorts.

Ocean Point Residence Hotel & Spa Hotel $$
(☎562-8330; www.oceanpointantigua.com; Hodges Bay Main Rd, Hodges Bay; d from $150; P❄📶🏊) It could use a facelift, but this rambling, good-value resort definitely has great bone structure thanks to a huge pool, two lovely secluded beaches and a breezy Italian restaurant. The property caters both to travelers and students at the nearby medical school, but loud partying is not an issue.

Betty's Hope distillery (right)

RIEGER BERTRAND/HEMIS/CORBIS ©

Detour: Eastern Antigua

Sparsely populated eastern Antigua gets few visitors. Here's a brief rundown of what they're missing:

Ponder Antigua's colonial past while poking around the stone windmills, the Great House and the distillery of **Betty's Hope** (near Pares; 9am-4pm Mon-Sat) FREE, the island's first sugar plantation, built in 1674. Interpretative signs provide information about the sugar-making process and glimpses into daily life at the plantation. It straddles a quiet hill south of Pares, off the road to Long Bay. Continuing east, you'll soon reach the turnoff to Seatons, home of **Stingray City Antigua** (562-7297; www.stingraycityantigua.com; Seatons; around US$50; contact for schedule), where you can feed and swim with friendly stingrays and snorkel around a coral reef. Just before Long Bay itself, a rough 1-mile dirt road (better with a 4WD) veers off to **Devil's Bridge** (near Willikies, Long Bay), a windswept bluff ringed by rugged cliffs shaped by the relentless crashing of powerful waves. If the tide is right, you can see the powerful blowhole at the far end in action. Views from the bluff are especially dramatic at sunset.

Eating & Drinking

Self-caterers can stock up on seasonal bounty at the **Public Market** (Market St; 6am-6pm Mon-Sat) in St John's, which is busiest on Saturday mornings.

C&C Wine Bar International $
(470-7025; Redcliffe Quay, St John's; dishes US$3-13; lunch & dinner Tue-Sun;) The C's stand for Cutie and Claudine, the adorable proprietors of this cozy courtyard bar specializing in South African wines that are matched by such tasty nibbles as coconut shrimp and daily blackboard specials. 'Lasagne Thursdays' and 'Karaoke Saturdays' are especially busy.

Roti King Caribbean $
(cnr St Mary's St & Corn Alley, St John's; meals US$5-9; 8:30am-midnight Mon-Sat) This little shack does brisk business all day long with its mouthwatering roti bulging with curried chicken, shrimp, veggies or conch. Try them with a homemade juice.

Papa Zouk Seafood $$
(464-6044; Hilda Davis Dr, St John's; mains US$15; dinner Mon-Sat) This ramshackle Creole joint is famous for its fish soup, vast rum selection and high-energy vibe. Try the signature Ti Punch, a habit-forming concoction made with marinated rum.

Cecilia's High Point Cafe Mediterranean $$$
(562-4487; www.highpointantigua.com; Dutchman's Bay; mains US$22-37; dinner Mon, lunch Thu-Mon, closed Jun & Jul; P) Cecilia, the Swedish amazon and ex–Helmut Newton model who presides over this charming beachfront cottage, is on a first-name basis with many of the rich and famous that flock to her lair for light and fabulous Mediterranean-style fare.

Coconut Grove Caribbean $$$
(462-1538; www.coconutgroveantigua.net; Marina Bay Rd, Dickenson Bay; mains US$24-40; breakfast, lunch & dinner;) This beachy daytime hangout morphs into an elegant candlelit affair for dinner. The lobster thermidor medallions in mustard-brandy sauce is a top menu pick or go local and try the jerk pork tenderloin. The rum punch tastes deceitfully mellow.

Shopping

Duty-free shops cluster in Heritage Quay just off the cruise-ship pier, but don't expect major bargains except on booze and cigarettes. It segues into the Vendors' Mall, a cacophonous maze of trinkets and T-shirts. Adjacent Redcliffe Quay has more upscale galleries and boutiques.

Best of Books (562-3198; St Mary's St; 8:30am-5:30pm) has a great selection of novels.

Information

There are ATMs at the airport and in downtown St John's.

Antigua Tourist Office (562-7600; www.antigua-barbuda.org; ACB Financial Centre, High St; 10am-4pm Mon-Fri (varies)) Few brochures and not terribly helpful staff.

JOLLY HARBOUR TO CADES BAY

A short drive south of St John's, Jolly Harbour is a busy marina and dockside condominium village with a big supermarket, an ATM, a pharmacy and a few restaurants and bars. South of here, the coastal road wears a necklace of some of Antigua's best beaches, which are popular with locals on weekends but otherwise often deserted. Down in Cades Bay, the road passes a pineapple farm before cutting through rainforest as Fig Tree Dr which culminates in Swetes. From here, you're back in St John's in 20 minutes.

Beaches

Hermitage Bay Beach

(off Valley Rd, Jennings Village) This dreamy secluded arc punctuates the end of a 2½-mile-long road (the last two are graded dirt road). Wave-tossed shells litter the white sand that remains largely crowd-free despite being next to an ultra-posh resort. Turn off the main road at the Sleeping Indian sign in Jennings, about 1.5 miles north of Jolly Harbour.

Valley Church Beach Beach

(Valley Rd, Valley Church Village) There's often nary a soul on this long palm-lined beach with calm and shallow aquamarine waters and powdery white sand. Look for the turn-off to the Nest, the resident beach bar-restaurant (open 11am to sunset).

Ffryes Beach Beach

(Valley Rd, Bolans Village) This long, sea-grape-shaded sandy ribbon has barbecue facilities, showers and toilets and is

Half Moon Bay (p193)

TEMMUZ CAN ARSIRAY/GETTY IMAGES ©

popular with local families on weekends. Grab a cocktail in time for sunset from Dennis Cocktail Bar & Restaurant. Behind it ensues the gentle arc of **Little Ffryes Beach**, overlooked by the all-inclusive Cocobay Resort.

Turner's Beach Beach

(Valley Rd, Johnson's Point) Popular with the beach-bum brigade, this buzzing beach is anchored by a shell-decorated restaurant-bar (mains US$8 to $24) and has water-sports rentals and souvenir vendors.

Morris Bay Beach Beach

(Valley Rd, Old Road Village) Hemmed in by coconut palms, Morris Bay is locally beloved for its calm waters, and it stretches all the way to the posh Curtain Bluff Resort, which has water-sports facilities.

Activities

Jolly Dive Diving

(☎462-8305; www.jollydive.com; Jolly Harbour Dr; 2-tank dive US$100) This dive shop has a fine reputation and hits nearby reefs, wrecks and dropoffs.

Footsteps Rainforest Hiking Hiking

(☎460-1234, 773-2345; www.hikingantigua.com; Fig Tree Dr; over/under 16yr US$45/25; ⏲tours 9am Tue & Thu & by arrangement) Local Rasta Dassa knows every nook and cranny of Antigua and is happy to share his extensive knowledge of the island's flora, fauna and history on fun and educational guided hikes. The trek up Signal Hill is his signature tour but he's happy to customize any other route. Tours depart from the Fig Tree Studio Art Gallery.

Antigua Rainforest Company Zip-Lining

(☎562-6363; www.antiguarainforest.com; Fig Tree Dr; adults US$69-115; ⏲Mon-Sat) Channel your inner Tarzan (or Jane) while roaring through the treetops suspended on zip lines. The 2½-hour 'Full Course' includes 12 zips, short hikes between suspension bridges and a challenge course. Call ahead for timings, since it's only open if a cruise ship is in port.

Local Knowledge

Dassa Spencer & Sallie Harker

OCCUPATION: OWNERS OF FOOTSTEPS RAINFOREST HIKING TOURS & FIG TREE STUDIO ART GALLERY

RESIDENCE: ANTIGUA

1 WHAT'S THE ONE HIKE THAT PEOPLE SHOULDN'T MISS?

The hike up Signal Hill. It goes mostly through the jungle but from the top you have a 360-degree view of the island. In colonial times, flags were hoisted here to communicate with the British commanders down in Nelson's Dockyard (p193).

2 WHAT'S YOUR FAVORITE BEACH?

Half Moon Bay (p193) is a lovely beach. It has a very natural curved shape, soft sand and calm water. It's great for families and there's also a little local bar where you can get a drink.

3 WHAT'S AN INTERESTING PLACE THAT'S OFF THE TOURIST RADAR?

Sea View Farm Village has a lot of local potters who make traditional African-style coil pottery. The pottery is not fired in a kiln but in an open fire called raku. You can just go and visit them and ask them about the techniques.

4 WHAT'S YOUR FAVORITE FOOD EXPERIENCE?

Seafood Friday at the Copper & Lumber Store Hotel (p194) down in English Harbour is a lot of fun. It's nothing fancy but very good value and gets a good mix of tourists and locals mingling on the lawn.

5 AND YOUR FAVORITE PARTY SPOT?

We like to go to Shirley Heights (p193) for the Sunday barbecue and steel band. But it's always a good time to come up here for the views, and there are also vendors selling local crafts and jewelry.

Sleeping

Reefview Apartments
Apartment $$

(☎560-4354; www.reefviewapartments.com; Valley Rd, Cades Bay; apt from US$179; ❄ 📶) These spacious and uncluttered apartments with full kitchen deliver glorious views of Cades Bay. Even bigger assets, though, are your warm and charming hosts Nick and Karoll, who are always on hand with insider tips and advice. Rates include airport transfer and a welcome drink.

Sugar Ridge
Hotel $$$

(☎562-7700; www.sugarridgeantigua.com; Valley Rd, Jolly Harbour; r incl breakfast from US$550; ❄ 📶 🏊) A short drive south of Jolly Harbour, this hilltop charmer has lovely views from its 60 colonial-meets-contemporary rooms, the nicest of which have big verandas, four-poster beds and private plunge pools. Three onsite pools, two restaurants and a posh Aveda spa provide ample diversion and the beach is only a short, free shuttle ride away.

Eating

Dennis Cocktail Bar & Restaurant
Caribbean $$

(☎462-6740; www.denniscocktailbar.webs.com; Valley Rd, Ffryes Beach; burgers US$9, mains US$17-35; ⏰noon-late Tue-Sun; P 👪) Dennis Thomas says he learned to cook from his mom. She certainly taught him well, if the steady stream of customers vying for such soulful dishes as goat curry, Creole chicken, slow-cooked pork ribs or grilled lobster are any indication. The sublime location on a rise overlooking two beaches doesn't hurt either.

OJ's
Caribbean $$

(☎460-0184; Valley Rd, Crab Hill Village; sandwiches US$7-10, mains US$13-30; ⏰11am-11pm) With its rustic nautical decor, hammocks and waterfront tables, OJ's is your quintessential beach-bum hangout. Regulars swear by the grilled snapper, lobster salad and wicked rum punch. Live entertainment on Friday and Sunday nights.

Miracle's South Coast Restaurant
Caribbean $$

(☎732-1682; Valley Rd, Jolly Harbour; mains US$13-28; ⏰noon-2am; 👪) Don't be fooled by the humble roadside cottage look: Megan and Ollie whip up delicious lobster salad, grilled snapper, jerk chicken and other local dishes. Service may be slow, giving you plenty of time to nurse your beer on the wooden deck. Takeaway available.

Carmichaels
Fusion $$$

(☎562-7700; Valley Rd, Jolly Harbour; mains US$22-37; ⏰lunch & dinner) This fine-dining outpost where head chef Matt whips up a creative blend of Carib-Continental cuisine boasts a dramatic setting in its aerie above the

Nelson's Dockyard (right)

Sugar Ridge Hotel. Bring a swimsuit for a predinner dip in the infinity pool.

ENGLISH HARBOUR

Nowhere does Antigua flaunt its maritime heritage more than in English Harbour. It sits on two sheltered bays, Falmouth Bay and English Harbour, where salty boats and ritzy yachts bob in the water. The era when the British Navy was based here is still encapsulated in the beautifully restored Nelson's Dockyards, the island's top historical attraction.

Detour: Fig Tree Drive

Old Road, a village that juxtaposes a fair amount of poverty with two swank resorts (Curtain Bluff and Carlisle Bay), marks the start of 5-mile-long (badly potholed) Fig Tree Dr, which winds through rainforest, past big old mango and giant-leaved banana trees (called 'figs' locally) and roadside stands selling fruit, jam and juices. Stop for a short hike to the historic Wallings' Reservoir or a peek inside the charming **Fig Tree Studio Art Gallery** (**☎460-1234; www.figtreestudioart.com; Fig Tree Dr; ⏰9:30am-5:30pm Mon-Sat Nov-Jun**) where local artist Sallie Harker showcases her own and regional art work.

Beaches

Rendezvous Bay Beach

After a 90-minute walk through the rainforest, you'll have earned bragging rights for making it to one of Antigua's loveliest beaches. Because of its remoteness, it usually delivers footprint-free solitude. The path is not signposted, so either ask for detailed directions locally or sign up with a guide.

Galleon Beach Beach

(**English Harbour**) Galleon has plenty of facilities, calm waters and a snorkeling reef close to shore. Take the turn-off from the Shirley Heights road or catch the **water taxi** (**EC$10; ⏰9am-6pm**) from the Copper & Lumber Store Hotel.

Pigeon Point Beach Beach

(**Falmouth**) This tree-shaded community beach has showers, bathrooms, a playground and a bar but only so-so snorkeling. The access road turns off just before the Nelson's Dockyard parking lot.

Half Moon Bay Beach

(**near St Phillips**) Water the color of Blue Curacao laps this undeveloped, shadeless white crescent in the remote southeast. Bodysurfers head to the north end, snorkelers to the south, and everyone meets at the funky beach bar for sundowners.

Sights

Nelson's Dockyard Historic Site

(**☎481-5028; www.nationalparksantigua.com; Dockyard Dr, English Harbour; adult/under 12yr EC$18/free; ⏰9am-5pm; P**) This extensively restored Georgian-era marina has been in operation since 1745 and is Antigua's top sightseeing draw. Once home of the British Royal Navy, it was abandoned in 1889 following a decline in the island's economic and strategic importance. The Dockyard Museum in the brick-and-stone naval officers' residence relates tidbits about the history of the island, the dockyard and life at the forts. Among the many trinkets on display is a telescope once used by Nelson himself.

Shirley Heights Fort

(**☎481-5028; www.nationalparksantigua.com; Shirley Heights Rd, English Harbour**) For fabulous views of English Harbour and out to Guadalupe, head up the hill to these 18th-century military fortifications whose ruins are fun to poke around. Some buildings have been restored and house a restaurant bar; its legendary Sunday barbecue party with live bands has drawn revelers from around the island for three decades. Admission to the barbeque is EC$20.

Fort Berkeley Fort

(English Harbour) Though ruined, this fort, built in 1704 to defend English Harbour, still has enough walls and a cannon to evoke the challenges of the colonial era. It's a 10-minute stroll from the back of the Copper & Lumber Store Hotel.

Dows Hill Interpretation Centre Museum

(481-5045; www.nationalparksantigua.com; Shirley Heights Rd, English Harbour; admission EC$13, free with Nelson's Dockyard ticket; 9am-5pm) For a primer on Antigua history from the Amerindian era to the present, watch the 15-minute multimedia presentation at this interpretative center, then take in lovely views of English Harbour from the viewing platform.

Activities

Dockyard Divers Diving

(729-3040; www.dockyard-divers.com; Nelson's Dockyard, English Harbour; 2-tank dive US$89, snorkeling trip US$35) This well-established outfit offers dive and snorkeling trips to caves, reefs and sunken wrecks. Snorkeling gear rents for US$10 per day.

Sleeping

Ocean Inn B&B $

(463-7950; www.theoceaninn.com; English Harbour; r incl breakfast US$110-170;) For five-star views at three-star prices, secure a room at this charming inn on flowery, terraced grounds above English Harbour. The nicest are the cottages with private veranda; the cheapest, the breezy 'ocean budget rooms' with shared bathroom. Avoid the windowless room 5. Nice touch: the honor bar.

Copper & Lumber Store Hotel Hotel $$

(460-1058; www.copperandlumberhotel.com; Nelson's Dockyard, English Harbour; ste US$115-325; P) This graciously restored hotel was built in the 1780s to store the copper and lumber needed for ship repairs. It now has 14 studios and suites, each named after one of Nelson's ships. Everything drips with colonial vintage flair courtesy of four-poster beds, brick walls, wooden beams and mock gas lamps.

Weekends are rung in with the legendary 'Seafood Friday', a tasty

Shirley Heights (p193)

M TIMOTHY O'KEEFE/GETTY IMAGES ©

barbecue on the hotel lawn that brings out locals and visitors in droves.

Inn at English Harbour Boutique Hotel **$$$**
(☎460-1014; www.theinnantigua.com; Freeman's Bay, English Harbour; ste incl tax & service from US$732;) Enjoy sublime sunsets, cold Carib in hand, from the private terrace of your lusciously furnished suite or beach cabana at this peaceful and romantic retreat from reality. Though colonial-style in looks and flair, all the expected 21st-century amenities are accounted for, both in rooms and the public areas.

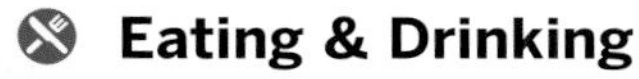

Eating & Drinking

Trappas International **$$**
(☎562-3534; Dockyard Dr, English Harbour; mains US$18; 6-10pm Mon-Sat;) It's often standing-room only when expats, locals and yachties descend for Simon and Caroline's dependable upscale comfort food served amid 'we're all friends here' vibe. Regulars swear by the fried calamari, Simon's special cheese burger and creative curries treated to an aromatic balm of local spices. The bar is a lively meet-and-greet zone.

Caribbean Taste Caribbean **$$**
(☎562-3049; off Dockyard Dr, English Harbour; mains US$9-25; lunch & dinner Mon-Sat) For authentic local food, point your compass to Gretel's cheerily painted cottage just off the main road to Nelson's Dockyard. The chalkboard menu lists such flavor-packed staples as conch stew and goat curry along with changing specials that might include octopus ceviche or Creole snapper.

Abracadabra Italian **$$**
(☎460-1732; www.theabracadabra.com; Dockyard Dr, English Harbour; mains US$13-33; dinner Mon-Sat;) Fondly known as 'Abra,' Salvatore's outpost is all things to all people: a restaurant where you can devour homemade pastas or the signature suckling pig, a chilled bar and lounge, and, on Saturday's, an energetic open-air dance club. Pure magic!

Mad Mongoose Bar
(☎463-7900; www.madmongooseantigua.com; English Harbour; mains US$15-27; 11am-late daily Nov-Apr, Fri-Mon May-Oct;) This Rasta-colored yachtie and expat favorite is the place to come for a rollicking good time. The long bar and pool tables are conducive to making new friends, as are the rum-fuelled live-music jams on Fridays. If you need to restore balance to the brain, there's a full menu of snacks and meals to choose from.

Barbuda

Barbuda's only village, sleepy Codrington, is home to most residents and the minuscule airport. It's about 3.5 miles north of the ferry landing on the eastern edge of the lagoon with its famous frigate bird colony.

Beaches

There is no such thing as a bad beach in Barbuda. All of them are hypnotic strips of pristine powdery white sand perfect for strolling, swimming, chilling and picnicking. The longest one is **17-Mile-Beach**, also known as Palm Beach, which stretches along the western side of the narrow strip of land hemming in Codrington Lagoon. **Coco Point** in the south, next to the eponymous luxury resort, is just as sublime.

Sights

Two Foot Bay National Park Cave
(Highland Rd) FREE Barbuda is riddled with mysterious caves, some of which are so well hidden you'll need a guide to locate them. Not so with Indian Cave in this national park on the northeastern coast. The three-chambered hole-in-the-ground features Arawak petroglyphs and a bat chamber. Look for the entrance atop a small bluff opposite a stone ruin.

Martello Tower Tower
FREE A short walk northwest of the ferry harbor, near River Beach, this 56ft-high fortified lookout station built by the

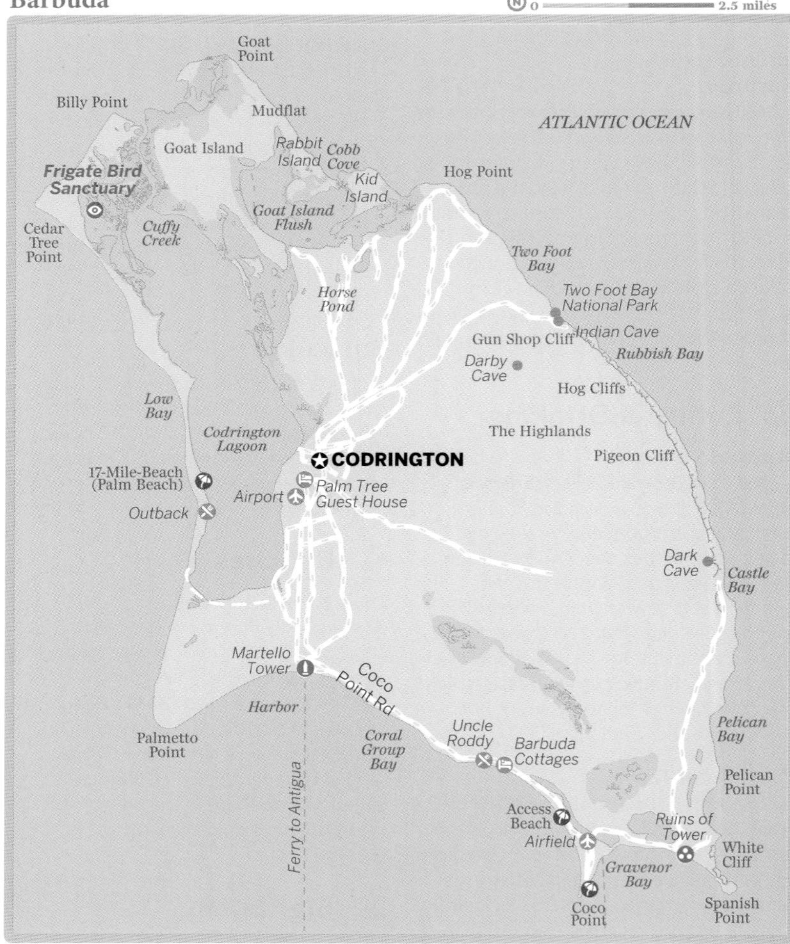

British looks just like an old sugar mill from afar.

Tours

Several locals offer island tours. Try **John Taxi Service** (779-4652, 788-5378) and **Barbuda Outback Tours** (721-1972, 721-3280) or check with the tourist office for a referral.

Barbuda Day Tour Boat Trips
(764-2291, 560-7989; www.barbudaexpress.com; adult/3-12yr US$169/85) This day trip, operated by Barbuda Express, includes the 90-minute ferry ride and visits to the Codrington Lagoon Frigate Bird Sanctuary and the Arawak caves as well as lobster lunch and a beach-splashing session.

Caribbean Helicopters Scenic Flights
(562-8687; www.caribbeanhelicopters.com; VC Bird International Airport, Runway 10; per passenger US$385; 9am, 9:45am, 10:30am) See Barbuda like a frigate bird on these airborne tours that depart from Antigua

and include the flight as well as a lobster lunch. The entire trip takes 4½ hours and includes time to swim and explore the lagoon.

Sleeping

Lodging on Barbuda is largely limited to two luxe resorts and a handful of locally run guesthouses.

Palm Tree Guest House Guesthouse $
(784-4331; Codrington; d/ste US$80/130;) This well-maintained guesthouse close to central Codrington has eight spacious rooms, each with a small fridge and cable TV, as well as a two-bedroom suite with kitchen. The gracious owner, Cerene, also operates a restaurant in town.

Barbuda Cottages Apartment $$$
(722-3050; www.barbudacottages.com; Coral Group Bay; cottage US$250-375, 4-night min; closed Aug-Oct) The lovely Kelcina presides over this little slice of paradise where you'll fall asleep to the ocean breezes in a solar-powered villa within a Frisbee toss of pearly Coral Group Bay beach. Each unit has its own kitchen, but the adjacent restaurant-bar makes tempting culinary treats.

Eating & Drinking

Barbuda's bars and restaurants keep erratic hours or must be booked in advance.

Uncle Roddy Caribbean $$
(785-3268; Coral Group Bay; meals EC$30-75; 11am-10pm Mon-Sat) Roddy's solar-powered beach bar is perfect for spending a relaxing day with grilled lobster and the signature Barbuda Smash. Make reservations 24 hours in advance as Roddy only buys supplies as needed. Bring bug spray to combat pesky sand flies.

Outback Caribbean $$
(721-3280; Palm Beach; mains EC$35-80; noon-3pm) This casual hangout on gorgeous Palm Beach doles out such finger-lickin' proteins as chicken, fish and lobster tickled to perfection on the open grill. Prices include free pick-up from the Codrington pier.

Information

Barbuda Tourist Office (562-7066; Codrington; 8am-4:30pm Mon-Thu, to 3pm Fri) Near the Codrington jetty, this office has maps and brochures and friendly staff who can set you up with a local guide.

Frigate Bird Sanctuary

Expansive Codrington Lagoon National Park, off Barbuda's northwest coast, supports the **Frigate Bird Sanctuary** (http://nationalparksbarbuda.com; sea taxi US$70 (4 people max), national park admission US$2), one of the world's largest colonies of frigate birds, with some 5000 of these black-feathered critters roosting amid the scrubby mangroves. The most popular time to visit this sanctuary is during mating season (September to April; December is peak time). While the male frigate birds line up in the bushes, arch their heads back and puff out their pouches with an air of machismo, the females take to the sky. When one spots a suitor that impresses her, she'll land and initiate a mating ritual. The lagoon, which also hosts lots of other bird species, can only be visited by licensed sea taxi from the Codrington jetty. Make arrangements a day in advance through your hotel or the tourist office.

SABA

POP 1800

A 'special municipality' of the Netherlands, tranquil Saba is as vertiginous as its motherland is flat. There's something otherworldly about this spiky volcanic peak that sits but a hop, skip and jump from St-Martin/Sint Maarten. Dense forest drapes its peaks and valleys, making it look like Ireland, while the traditional red-roofed houses with their green shutters and white gingerbread trim seem plucked from a Brothers' Grimm fairy tale. Below the waterline lies a colorful kingdom of coral teeming with sharks, turtles and luminous tropical fish. There is no crime, little traffic and a close-knit local community that's genuinely happy to be here – and to see you in their earthly 'Garden of Eden'.

Flat Point

The aptly named Flat Point is precisely that: a flat point (Saba's only one, in fact), and the perfect place to plunk down an airport. The **Juancho E Yrausquin Airport** has the world's shortest commercial runway (400m) and by the time you figure out how to pronounce the airport's name, you'll have already landed on St-Martin/Sint Maarten. Planes departing Saba don't actually lift off the ground; rather, the runway suddenly stops and the aircraft drives over a sheer cliff and glides away.

If you have a little time to kill before leaving, or after you arrive, leave your luggage in the waiting area and head down to the **tide pools** beside the airport. You'll find dramatic waves crashing against the thick beads of volcanic rock.

Windwardside

The quaint hamlet of Windwardside is Saba's commercial heart and features all of the traveler necessities: banks, a bakery, a grocery store, dive shops, the tourist office and several restaurants. The 'suburb' of Booby Hill is worth the short trek out to check out the stellar views.

Saba

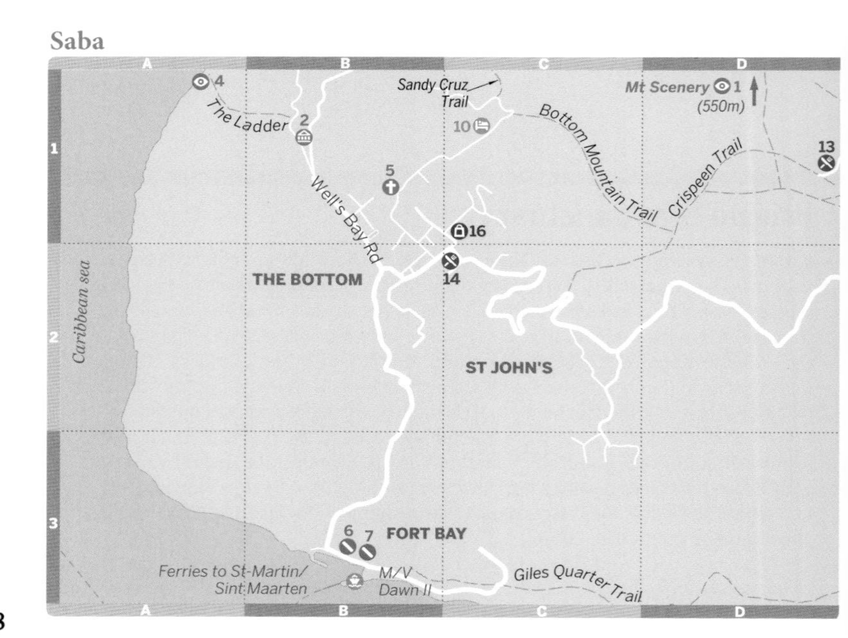

Sights

Harry L Johnson Museum Museum
(Windwardside; admission US$2; 11am-4pm Mon-Fri) Surrounded by wildflowers, this pint-sized museum occupies a 160-year-old sea-captain's cottage and is crammed with an eclectic collection. Highlights include vintage photographs of Dutch royalty, Saba's first telephone, the Steinway piano hoisted up 'The Ladder' by eight strong Saban lads, and an old rock oven. A museum guide is on hand to bring the stories behind these objects to life.

Activities

DIVING

Saba's otherworldly beauty extends to 25 diverse dive sites, including sheer wall dives and submerged pinnacles. Since 1987, the area has been protected as the Saba Marine Park by the nonprofit **Saba Conservation Foundation** (Fort Bay; 8am-noon & 1-5pm Mon-Fri, 8am-noon Sat). All divers must go through a dive operator and pay a US$3 fee per dive. Of Saba's three diving outfits, **Sea Saba** (416-2246; www.seasaba.com; Windwardside; 9am-5pm Mon-Sat) and **Saba Divers** (416-2741; www.sabadivers.com; 9am-5pm Mon-Sat) (both PADI five-star centers) are based in Windwardside, while **Saba Deep Dive Center** (416-3347; www.sabadeep.com; Fort Bay) is down south by the port in Fort Bay. All offer several boat dives daily and the gamut of courses and certifications.

For snorkelers, Well's Bay and the adjacent Torrens Point are popular spots, and there's even a marked underwater trail. Ladder Bay is also popular, but it's a good 30-minute hike down to the shore from the road and double that back up.

HIKING

Saba is a hiker's paradise with many of the century-old trails once used by the earliest settlers to get from village to village. Before setting out, drop by the **Trail Shop** (416-2630; Windwardside; 9:30am-4:30pm Mon-Fri, 10am-2pm Sat & Sun) for maps, nature books and the latest on trail conditions. When you're hiking, dress in layers, wear sturdy walking shoes and bring water. Some hikers

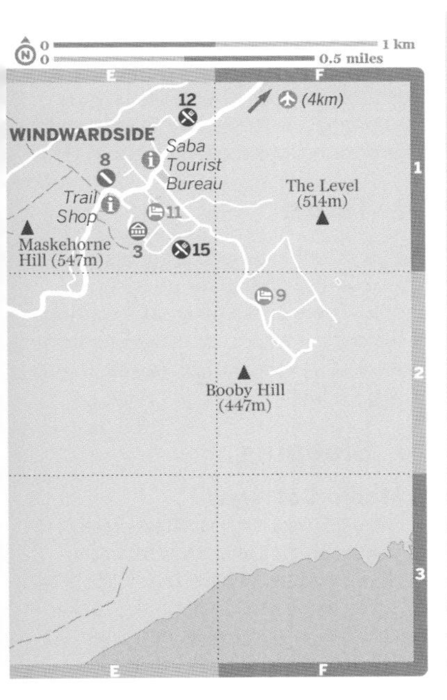

Saba

Don't Miss Sights
1 Mt Scenery ... D1

Sights
2 Abandoned Customs House ... B1
3 Harry L Johnson Museum ... E1
4 Ladder Bay ... A1
5 Sacred Heart Church ... B1

Activities, Courses & Tours
6 Saba Conservation Foundation ... B3
7 Saba Deep Dive Center ... B3
Saba Divers ... (see 11)
8 Sea Saba ... E1

Sleeping
9 El Momo Cottages ... F2
10 Queen's Garden Resort ... C1
11 Scout's Place ... E1

Eating
12 Brigadoon ... E1
13 Rainforest Restaurant ... D1
14 Saba Coffee House ... C2
Scout's Place ... (see 11)
15 Tropics Cafe ... E1

Shopping
16 Saba Artisan Foundation ... C1

Below: Homes in Windwardside (p198); Right: Mt Scenery (p202)
(BELOW) MAURICIO HANDLER/GETTY IMAGES ©; (RIGHT) FRANS LEMMENS/WWW.FRANSLEMMENS.COM/CORBIS ©

might appreciate a walking stick (available for free at the Trail Shop) to navigate steep and slippery sections.

Some 15 marked routes cut across seven ecosystems, including coastal meadows, rainforests and cloud forests. You'll see an extraordinary bounty of orchids, elephant trees, wild plantains, massive ferns and other flora as well as lots of birds and such endemic critters as the Anoles lizard and the (harmless) Racer snake. After Mt Scenery, the most popular hikes are the moderately strenuous Sulphur Mine Trail, which offers views of the airport landing strip, and the long but easy Sandy Cruz Trail, which leads past the deserted old village ruins of Mary's Point.

The only trail you shouldn't attempt without a guide is the North Coast Trail. All of the others are accessible to reasonably fit hikers, although they're much more fun in the company of ranger and guide extraordinaire James Johnson (aka 'Crocodile James'). The eighth-generation Saban will not only entertain you but open your eyes to the island's extraordinary ecodiversity. Contact him at jamesjohnsonsaba@yahoo.com.

Tours

Cabbies double as island guides with tours costing US$50 for up to four people. There are usually taxis waiting at the port or airport or order one from George at ☎416-3367 or Wayne at ☎416-7170.

Sleeping

El Momo Cottages Hotel $

(☎416-2265; www.elmomocottages.com; Booby Hill, Windwardside; d with shared bathroom US$75, with private bathroom US$95-115;)

This cluster of rustic cottages is tucked into a steep, rugged hillside smothered in juicy tropical foliage. A top budget pick

for nature-lovers, it also offers such perks as a pool with hammocks and a bar and, of course, breathtaking views, especially from the aptly named 'Cottage in the Sky'. Optional breakfast is US$9.

Scout's Place Hotel **$$**
(☎416-2740; www.sabadivers.com; Windwardside; d incl service & breakfast US$129-159; ❄📶) This charmingly funky 14-room hotel feels as warm and welcoming as a hug from an old friend. Operated by the same couple who runs Saba Divers, it features three room categories of which the nicest are the Cottage Rooms with their ocean-view balconies. All are cheerfully painted, equipped with kitchenettes and furnished in traditional Saba style.

Eating & Drinking

Call ahead for dinner reservations as many restaurants only cook enough food for guests with reservations.

Tropics Cafe International **$**
(Windwardside; mains US$5-18; 🕐7am-9:30pm Sat-Thu, Fri til late; 📶) Edging the swimming pool of the popular Juliana's Hotel, Tropics is a relaxed hangout with lots of special events. There's two-for-one beers from 4pm to 6pm daily, an eco-movie on Wednesdays and a tapas pool party on Sunday afternoons. On Fridays, the weekend is rung in with free Jell-O shots and 'Tropitastic' cocktails.

Brigadoon International **$$**
(☎416-2380; Windwardside; mains US$13-45; 🕐6:30-11pm Wed-Mon) Even Brig first-timers will soon feel like regulars thanks to host Trisha's disarming Texan charm. Her husband Michael, meanwhile, works his magic over the stoves, creating an eclectic assortment of international dishes – fresh lobster to garlicky falafel. Carnivores invade for the Thursday prime-rib special, and on Saturdays, it's the sushi-lovers' turn.

The Mystique of Mt Scenery

Mt Scenery (887m), the tippy top of Saba, is officially the highest point in the Netherlands. It's covered by Elfin Forest (cloud forest) with 200-year-old mountain mahogany trees smothered in orchids, bromeliads and other epiphytes. The trail starts behind the Trail Shop (p199) in Windwardside and climbs 1064 stairs – expect a serious thigh-and-glute workout! The best time to get started is about 9am or 10am, so you can reach the summit around noon, the least cloudy part of the day. The view will make the pain well worth it.

Scout's Place International $$
(416-2740; www.sabadivers.com; Windwardside; dinner mains incl tax & service US$14-25; breakfast, lunch & dinner;) This newly slicked up adjunct to the eponymous hotel is the unofficial 'club house' of Saba's young and forever young, especially during Friday night karaoke. The kitchen does great Caribbean breakfasts, fat burgers and all sorts of other soul-sustaining fare along with kick-ass cocktails such as the Saba Spice.

Rainforest Restaurant International $$$
(416-3348; www.ecolodge-saba.com; Ecolodge Rendez-Vous, Crispeen Trail; mains US$20-27; breakfast & lunch Tue-Sun, dinner Thu & Fri, brunch Sun) Cleanse your soul with a candlelit meal at this hideaway deep in the forest. Much of the food is homegrown and finds its destination in a wide range of global favorites from fragrant curries to hearty English breakfasts. It's part of the Ecolodge Rendez-Vous, a solar-paneled retreat.

Information

Saba Tourist Bureau (416-2231; www.sabatourism.com; Windwardside; 8am-5pm Mon-Thu, 8-4:30pm Fri) Glenn, Desiree and Zuleyka are an inexhaustible font of knowledge and happy to ensure memorable stays with free advice, maps and brochures.

The Bottom

Although home to Saba's administrative and governmental buildings, the island's capital is at no risk of being staid on account of the 400 students of Saba Medical College located in the village.

Sights

Sacred Heart Church Church
Locals refer to this stone church as 'Saba's Sistine Chapel' thanks to local artist Heleen Cornet's colorful and stunningly detailed altar mural that infuses Biblical scenes with a Saban rainforest twist.

Sleeping & Eating

Queen's Garden Resort Hotel $$$
(416-3494; www.queensaba.com; Troy Hill Dr, the Bottom; ste from US$250, dinner mains US$25-38; P) A class act altogether with divine views over the Bottom, the rainforest and the dancing waves, the hillside 'Queen' has indeed welcomed visiting royalty. The 12 spacious suites are filled with elegant Caribbean furnishings, such lifestyle essentials as iPod docking stations, wine fridges and – get this! – a private spa. The restaurant makes for a romantic soiree.

Saba Coffee House Cafe $
(416-3636; the Bottom; mains US$3-9; 7am-5:30pm Mon-Sat, 11am-2pm Sun;) Stop by for a relaxed refueling session at this contemporary coffee roastery which is often flooded by bleary-eyed medical students in need of a strong java. Fresh pastries, inventive panini, homemade soups and daily lunch specials provide sustenance.

Shopping

Saba Artisan Foundation Souvenirs

(☎416-3260; ⊙8:30am-4pm Mon-Thu, to 3:30pm Fri) This small guild of women produces an eclectic assortment of Saba-specific souvenirs, including clothing, bags and pillows made from fabrics hand-screened and sewn onsite. Homemade jams, potent Saba Spice liqueur and dainty Saba lace are also on the shelves. If you're interested in seeing how the latter is made, swing by the Eugenius Centre in Windwardside on a Thursday afternoon to see the 'Lace Ladies' in action.

Ladder Bay

Before Fort Bay became Saba's official port, everything – from a Steinway piano to Queen Beatrix herself – was hauled up to the Bottom via the **Ladder** (West coast), a vertical staircase of more than 800 steps. The area is now a moderately difficult trail that heads past an **abandoned customs house** (Ladder Bay, Saba) and affords hikers beautiful views.

SINT EUSTATIUS

POP 3900

Pop quiz: which Caribbean island was once the busiest seaport in the world but is unfamiliar to most people today?

Yup: Sint Eustatius (or Statia, as locals say) was the darling of the Caribbean in the 18th century when it became a tax-free haven under the Dutch and the busiest trading port for cargo bouncing between Europe and the American colonies. By the 1790s, more than 3500 ships landed in what was nicknamed 'Golden Rock' every year and the island population exceeded 30,000 people. The party ended in 1796 when the French took over Statia and instituted heavy taxes, thereby driving the merchants away.

Today, the island has a cult following among scuba divers and hikers and those who enjoy sun-kissed days of blissful nothingness. Statia's sole town – and capital – Oranjestad is a sleepy and unprepossessing collection of cottages and vestiges of a bygone era. It is divided into Upper Town and Lower Town down by the waterfront. The rest of the island is made up of rugged, rural terrain. Formerly part of the now-dissolved Netherlands Antilles, Statia became a 'special municipality' of the Netherlands in 2010 and adopted the US dollar as its currency in 2011.

Beaches

Lower Town Beach Beach

No one visits Statia for its beaches, but if you fancy a quick dip, head down to the

Diver off Sint Eustatius

narrow strip of grayish sand where you can snorkel among the 18th-century ruins of a breakwater and warehouses.

Sights

Fort Oranje Fort

(Fort Oranje Straat, Upper Town; 24hr) FREE Soak up history and sweeping views from this extensively restored fort, a mighty citadel complete with cannons, triple bastions and cobblestone parade grounds. The current stone structure was built by the British in 1703, replacing the original wooden fort the French erected in 1629.

Sint Eustatius Museum Museum

(318-2288; cnr Van Peereweg & De Graafweg; adult/child US$5/3; 9am-5pm Mon-Thu, to 3pm Fri, to noon Sat) This eclectic collection gives meaning to the Statian tag line 'The Historic Gem.' Along with period rooms in the style of an upper-class colonial-era villa, the museum also showcases pre-Columbian artifacts and exhibits on slavery, Statia's Jewish community, nautical history and colonial relics.

Miriam Schmidt Botanical Gardens Gardens

(318-2884; www.statiapark.org; suggested donation US$5; sunrise-sunset) The semi-wild botanical gardens grow across the southern slopes of the island's dormant volcano, the Quill. Though still a work in progress, a visit here is a fragrant introduction to the island's rich flora. A Sensory Garden, Palm Garden and Kitchen Garden are already completed along with the short Bird Observation Trail and a Look-out Garden with views of St Kitts. It's about 5km east of Oranjestad; a taxi ride is US$15.

Activities

DIVING & SNORKELING

Among clued-in aficionados, Statia's diving is regarded as among the best in the Caribbean. Protected as the Statia Marine Park since 1996, its waters are blessed with coral reefs, drop-offs, canyons and wrecks inhabited by a host of underwater creatures from ethereal seahorses to giant octopuses, plus stingrays, barracudas, coral, lobster, tropical fish...the list could go on forever. Also submerged

Fort Oranje

in the clear waters is plenty of colonial detritus, including anchors and cannons. Whales come through between January and April. There's also decent snorkeling among submerged 18th-century ruins off the beach in Lower Town.

Diving is only allowed through the two local dive shops, the recently upgraded **Scubaqua Dive Center** (318-5450; www.scubaqua.com; Lower Town, Oranjestad) and the **Golden Rock Dive Center** (318-2964; www.goldenrockdive.com; Lower Town, Orangestad), both in Lower Town. Each operates all manner of day and night dives as well as PADI certification courses. Divers must purchase a dive tag for US$4 per dive or US$20 per year to help maintain the pristine conditions. There are two recompression chambers on Statia.

HIKING

After diving, exploring the island's bountiful nature on foot is the second-most popular pastime on Statia. Staff at the St Eustatius National Parks Foundation (p206) in Lower Town have free maps and brochures with trail descriptions as well as the latest on trail conditions. They also organize guided tours and sell the 'trail tag' (US$6) to help maintain the trail system.

The Quill Hiking

Statia's landmark dormant volcano, the Quill (derived from the Dutch word for pit or hole) soars 1972ft (601m) above the island's rolling terrain. It was designated a national park in 1998 and is the most popular hiking destination. From the trailhead at the end of Rosemary Laan in Oranjestad (a cab ride from the airport is US$10, from town US$8), it takes about 45 minutes to ascend the moderately steep but densely canopied trail to the crater rim.

There's a viewpoint down into the jungly crater, but for close-ups you need to continue down a very steep and slippery half-mile trail to the bottom. There are two other trails heading north and south of the rim, but these are very rough and steep and should not be attempted without a guide.

Salute to America

A plaque in the courtyard of Fort Oranje, commissioned by US President Franklin D Roosevelt, commemorates Statia's most famous moment in history. On November 16, 1776, the American war vessel *Andrew Doria* sailed into the harbor and fired a 13-gun salute (one for each of the rebellious colonies). Statia's governor gave orders to fire Fort Oranje's cannons in a counter-salute, thereby becoming the first foreign nation to recognize the sovereignty of the new United States of America.

Tours

Local taxi drivers know Statia like the back of their hands and charge US$20 per person (US$40 minimum) for a 90-minute island tour.

Sleeping

Country Inn Guesthouse Guesthouse $

(318-2484; www.countryinn-statia.com; Passionfruit Rd 3; d incl tax US$70;) Near the airport, Iris Pompier's little inn offers excellent value in half a dozen simple but tidy and clean rooms in a white-washed building surrounded by nicely landscaped grounds. It's about a 20-minute walk or a quick hitch from town. Cash only.

Statia Lodge Apartment $$

(318-1900; www.statialodge.com; White Wall; 1-/2-bedroom bungalows incl tax & service US$165/260;) The cluster of 10 nicely furnished wooden bungalows with kitchens sits on a windswept bluff about a 15-minute ride south of Oranjestad. Knock back a couple of cold ones on your terrace or at the bar by the L-shaped waterfront pool. Small bungalows include a complimentary scooter, the large ones a car.

Old Gin House Hotel **$$$**
(☎318-2319; www.oldginhouse.com; Lower Town, Oranjestaad; d incl tax, service & breakfast from US$228; P ❄ 📶 🏊) This stately (cotton seed) ginning station has been restored to its 17th-century glory and makes for a romantic spot to unpack and unwind. Most of the traditionally furnished rooms are in a yellow two-story complex behind the historic structure and come with comfy mahogany sleigh beds. The nicest units, though, are the two new oceanfront suites across the street.

Eating

Blue Bead Bar & Restaurant Italian **$$**
(☎318-2873; Lower Town, Oranjestad; mains US$13-28; ⏲noon-2pm & 6-9pm Thu-Mon; 📶) The large and brightly painted deck is a fine perch from which to enjoy sunset drinks followed by an early dinner of pizza, pasta, salad or seafood. The pizzas especially get kudos for their thin crusts and generous and creative toppings. On Saturday nights, the place is a popular hangout for local families.

Ocean View Terrace Caribbean **$$**
(☎318-2934; www.restaurantoceanview.com; Fort Oranje Straat; sandwiches US$3-7.50, mains US$11-25; ⏲noon-1:30pm Mon-Fri, 6:30-9pm Mon-Sat; 📶) Lauris Redan's lair is swarmed by office jockeys and politicians from the adjacent Government Building at lunch time but is also a fine rest stop after a sightseeing spin around Fort Oranje. Sit on the terrace overlooking the fort or in the shady courtyard to refuel on burgers and sandwiches or go local with curried pork or conch stew.

Information

First Caribbean Bank (cnr Fort Oranjestraat & Emmaweg, Upper Town) Near Fort Orange; has an ATM.

Sint Eustatius Tourist Bureau (☎318-2433; www.statiatourism.com; Fort Oranje, Upper Town; ⏲8am-noon & 1-5pm Mon-Thu, to 4:30pm Fri) Has maps and a few brochures. The airport branch is usually staffed whenever flights are arriving or departing.

St Eustatius National Parks Foundation (Stenapa; ☎318-2884; www.statiapark.org; Lower Town; ⏲7am-5pm Mon-Fri) This nonprofit organization was started in 1998 to protect Statia's ample natural resources. It manages the Statia National Marine Park, the Quill National Park and the Miriam Schmidt Botanical Gardens. Stop by the office to pick up free maps, brochures and advice about exploring Statia above and below the waterline.

ST KITTS & NEVIS

POP 51,000

St Kitts & Nevis is a relaxed twin-island nation that wraps palm-shaded beaches, jungle-draped dormant volcanoes and plenty of vestiges from a turbulent past into one tidy package.

St Kitts

St Kitts definitely has a beat, and it's not just the one blasting from the many minibuses hauling folks hither and yon. Its capital, Basseterre, is a fascinating place to wander and very much the commercial heart of the island. Locals bustle shop to shop while the only explicitly tourist-geared businesses cluster at the cruise-ship dock.

After the demise of its sugar industry, St Kitts has indeed put most of its economic eggs into the cruise-ship basket with 2013 seeing around 600,000 passengers descending upon the island. Many head straight to the north where the past is present – sometimes breathtakingly, sometimes heartbreakingly – in abandoned sugarcane fields, ramshackle villages, manicured plantation inns and the Unesco-recognized Brimstone Hill Fortress National Park. Hedonistic pleasures, meanwhile, rule the island's still largely undeveloped south whose funky bars on glorious beaches invite rum-fueled tanning sessions. For now the idyll is fairly intact as the financial crisis has delayed mega-construction projects, including ritzy hotels and residential areas, a golf course and a marina.

BASSETERRE

St Kitts' bustling capital, Basseterre (pronounced '*bass-tear*'), has a compact downtown next to the cruise-ship terminal. At its center stands the Circus, a roundabout anchored by a Victorian-style green clock tower. Nearby, locals 'lime' on grassy Independence Square, a former slave market framed by Georgian-era brick houses and a dignified cathedral.

Sights & Activities

National Museum — Museum

Map p207 (466-2744; www.stkittsheritage.com; Bay Rd, Basseterre; adult/child EC$8/free; 9:15am-5pm Mon-Fri, to 1pm Sat) This modest museum is a good place to start your explorations of St Kitts. Displays deal with colonial and sugar history, the road to independence and local lifestyle and traditions. It's housed in the 1894 Treasury Building, a stately pile built from hand-cut volcanic limestone.

Immaculate Conception Cathedral — Church

Map p207 (Independence Square, Basseterre; varies) This hulking gray-stone house of worship has a barrel-vaulted wooden ceiling evoking a ship's hull. Sunlight filters through elaborate stained-glass windows above an altar made of multihued marble.

Basseterre

Sights
1 Immaculate Conception Cathedral C1
2 National Museum B2

Activities, Courses & Tours
3 Kenneth's Dive Center D2

Sleeping
4 Seaview Inn B2

Eating
5 Ballahoo B2
6 El Fredo's D2
7 Public Market A2

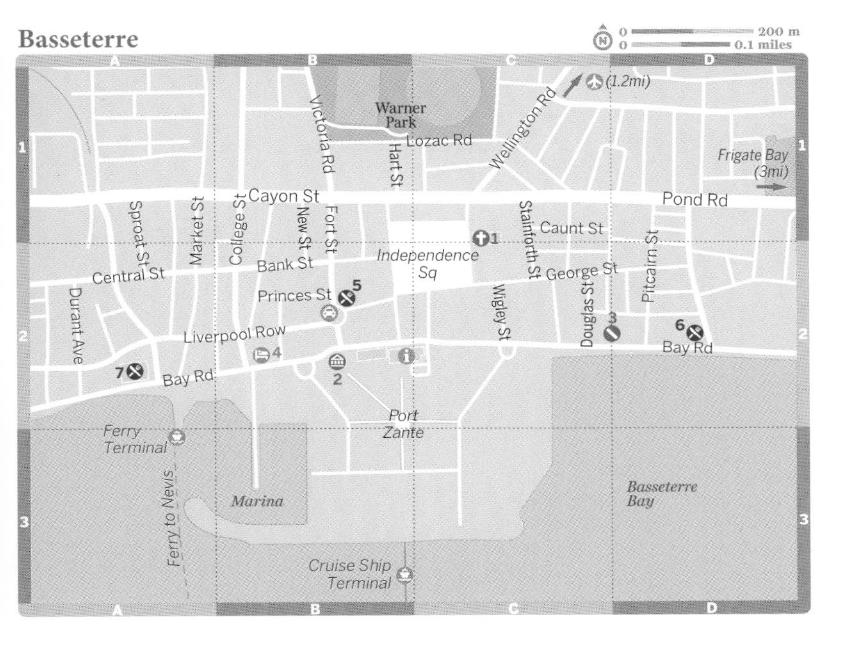

St Kitts & Nevis

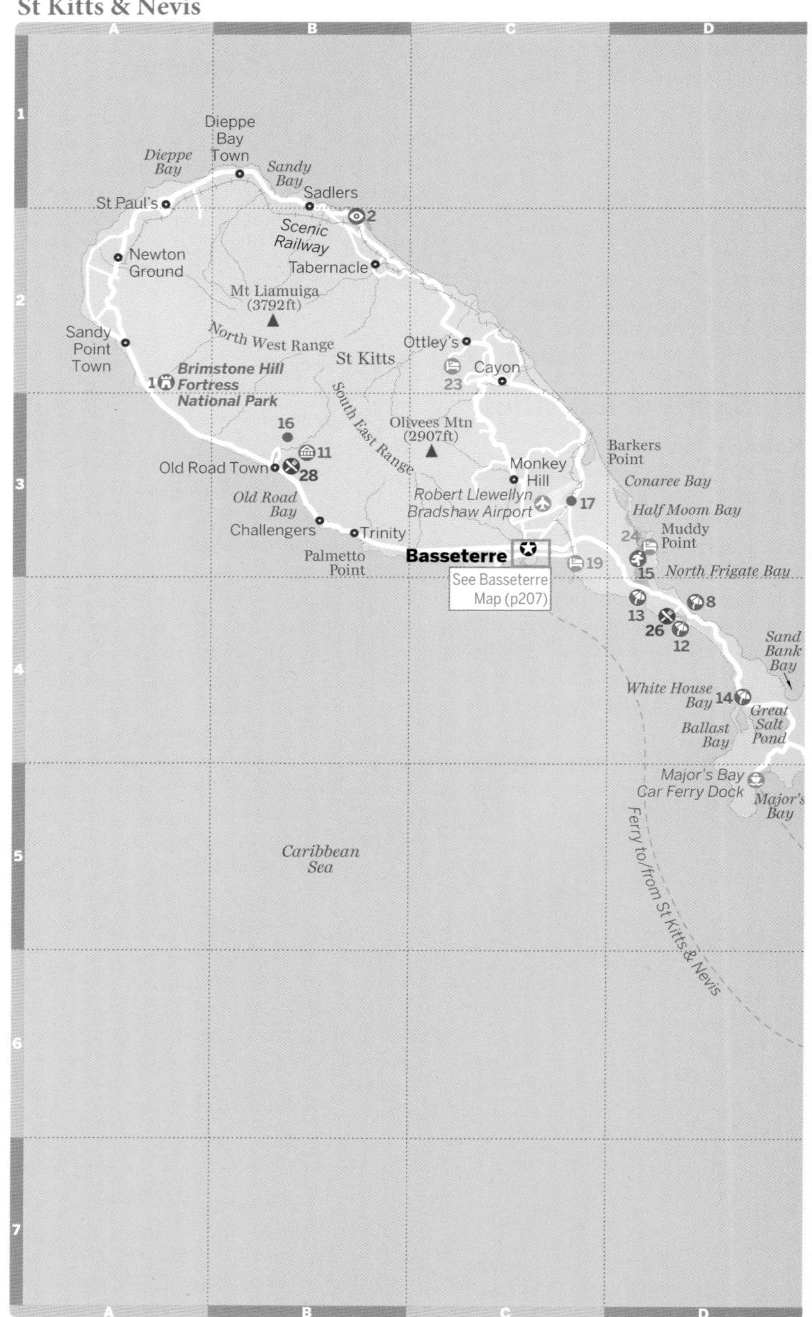

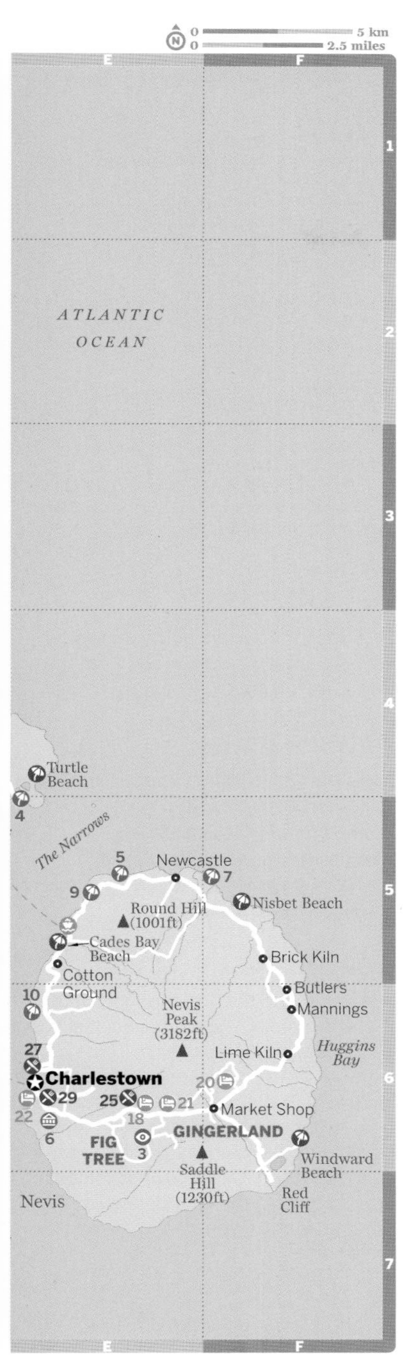

Kenneth's Dive Center — Diving

Map p207 (☎465-2670; www.kennethdivecenter.com; Bay Rd, Basseterre) The island's oldest dive shop offers boat dives and PADI certification courses and has counted astronaut Buzz Aldrin among its clients.

Tours

Blue Water Safaris — Boat Trips

(☎466-4933; www.bluewatersafaris.com; sunset/half-/full-day cruise US$50/61/95) The full-day catamaran cruise goes to Nevis with a snorkeling stop, lunch on Pinney's Beach and an open bar thrown in. There's also a half-day cruise and a two-hour sunset spin with a chance of spotting the elusive green flash optical phenomenon just before the sun dips below the horizon. Boats leave from Port Zante.

Sleeping

Bird Rock Beach Hotel — Hotel $

Map p208 (☎465-8914; www.birdrockbeach.com; S Pelican Dr, Bird Rock Village; r US$90-110, 2-/3-bedroom ste US$170/240; P ❄ 📶 🏊) This good-value pick sits on beautifully kept flowery grounds above a protected cove with good swimming, snorkeling and a dive shop. All rooms have ocean-view balconies and full kitchens. It's in a residential area a short drive south of Basseterre.

Seaview Inn — Guesthouse $

Map p207 (☎466-1635; Bay Rd, Basseterre; r US$75; P ❄ 📶) The 10 dark, cramped but reasonably clean rooms of this walk-up near the ferry terminal don't invite lingering but they are certainly cheap and the only lodging option right in town. Grab a cold one from the bar and settle down for some fine people-watching (*sans* sea views) on the wraparound porch.

Eating & Drinking

Central Basseterre brims with small eateries but food usually sells out by 2pm. For fresh produce, try the **Public Market** Map p207 (Bay Rd, Basseterre; 🕑Wed-Sat mornings) or head to the ferry terminal on Mondays when organic produce from fertile Dominica arrives.

St Kitts & Nevis

Don't Miss Sights
1 Brimstone Hill Fortress National Park ... A2

Sights
2 Black Rocks ... B2
3 Botanical Gardens of Nevis ... E6
4 Cockleshell Beach ... E5
5 Lovers Beach ... E5
6 Museum of Nevis History ... E6
7 Nisbet Beach ... F5
8 North Friar's Bay ... D4
9 Oualie Beach ... E5
10 Pinney's Beach ... E6
11 Romney Manor ... B3
12 South Friar's Bay ... D4
13 South Frigate Bay ... D4
14 White House Bay ... D4

Activities, Courses & Tours
Four Seasons Golf Course ... (see 10)
Mountain Bike Nevis ... (see 9)
15 Royal St Kitts Golf Club ... D3
Scuba Safaris ... (see 9)
16 Sky Safari ... B3
17 St Kitts Scenic Railway ... C3

Sleeping
18 Banyan Tree ... E6
19 Bird Rock Beach Hotel ... C3
Four Seasons ... (see 10)
20 Golden Rock Inn ... F6
21 Hermitage ... E6
22 JP's Guest House ... E6
23 Ottley's Plantation Inn ... C2
Oualie Beach Resort ... (see 9)
Rock Haven B&B ... (see 13)
24 St Kitts Marriott Resort ... D3
Timothy Beach Resort ... (see 13)

Eating
25 Bananas Restaurant ... E6
26 Carambola Beach Club ... D4
Mr X's Shiggidy Shack Bar & Grill (see 13)
27 Octagon Mermaid ... E6
Patsy's Beach Bar & Grill ... (see 13)
Spice Mill Restaurant ... (see 4)
28 Sprat Net Bar & Grill ... B3
Sunshine's ... (see 10)
29 Wilma's Diner ... E6

El Fredo's Caribbean **$**
Map p207 (466-8871; cnr Bay & Sanddown Rds, Basseterre; mains EC$20-35; 11am-4pm Mon-Sat) At lunchtime this locals' haunt does brisk business with delectable Kittitian favorites such as Creole-style snapper, conch stew or curried goat, all paired with a potpourri of provisions (starchy sides). The setting here is classic Caribbean cool but the homemade sauce is hot!

Ballahoo International **$$**
Map p207 (465-4197; www.ballahoo.com; Circus, Basseterre; mains EC$25-70; 8am-10pm Mon-Sat;) A dependable nosh spot any time of day, Ballahoo has great people-watching from terrace tables overlooking the Circus roundabout. The menu hopscotches around the world, with lobster sandwiches, Caesar salad, beef curry and fettuccine marinara all making appearances.

Shopping

Aside from liquor and cigarettes, genuine bargains are as rare as tulips in Tonga in duty-free Port Zante next to the cruise-ship dock. For a more authentic experience, stroll into town and see what the locals are buying.

Information

Banks with ATMs orbit the Circus but only the one at the Marriott dispenses US dollars.

Tourist Office (**465-4040; www.stkittstourism.kn; Pelican Mall, Bay Rd; 7:30am-4:30pm Mon-Fri**) Small office that can answer questions. Sometimes.

NORTHERN ST KITTS

A drive around the northern part of the island is a must. The entire circuit is about 35 miles and can easily fill half a day, especially with an extended stop at the landmark Brimstone Hill Fortress. Beyond here lowlands covered with abandoned sugarcane fields run up the hills to Mt Liamuiga, the 3792ft dormant volcano that dominates the interior. A guide is recommended if you want to hike to the crater rim.

Sights

Brimstone Hill Fortress National Park
Fort

Map p208 (465-2609; www.brimstonehillfortress.org; foreign visitors adult/child US$10/5; 9:30am-5:30pm) St Kitts' historical highlight became a Unesco World Heritage site in 1999 for being an exceptionally well-preserved example of 17th- and 18th-century military architecture. Far larger than it looks from below, this vast old military stronghold was built by the British with slave labor and offers insight into the violent and tumultuous past of the former Caribbean colonies. Budget at least an hour, better yet two, to explore this rambling compound.

Romney Manor
Historic Building

Map p208 (465-6253; www.caribellebatik-stkitts.com; Old Road Town; 8:30am-4pm Mon-Fri) This 17th-century sugar estate with its fecund gardens once belonged to the great-great-great-grandfather of Thomas Jefferson. Since 1964 it has been the home of **Caribelle Batik**, which sells handmade batik wraps, dresses, wall hangings and other items. As you drive up, note the black stones with Amerindian **petroglyphs** just past the nursery.

Black Rocks
Natural Landmark

Map p208 (near Sadlers Village) Wind and water have chiseled black lava belched up eons ago by Mt Liamuiga into fanciful coastal rock formations. Coming from the north, turn off the main road about on

The Best...
Leeward Island Historic Sites

1 Nelson's Dockyard (p193), Antigua

2 Brimstone Hill Fortress (p211), St Kitts

3 Fort Oranje (p204), Sint Eustatius

4 Alexander Hamilton Museum (p215), Nevis

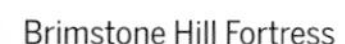

Brimstone Hill Fortress

eighth of a mile past an old stone church in a field.

Tours

St Kitts Scenic Railway Tour

Map p208 (465-7263; www.stkittsscenicrailway.com; Needsmust Estate Train Terminal; adult/child from US$89/44.50; Dec-Apr) This cheerfully painted tourist train makes a three-hour northern island loop along 18 miles of tracks of the old narrow-gauge sugar railway, followed by a 12-mile bus ride. The upper deck is great for sightseeing and the lower one has air-con. Trains only run if a cruise ship is in port. Independent travelers should call for departure times. The terminal is near the airport.

Sky Safari Zip-Lining

Map p208 (466-4259; www.skysafaristkitts.com; Wingfield Rd, Old Road Town; full/half tour US$89/45; call for hours) 'Speed junkies' will leap at the chance to whoosh through the rainforest treetops at speeds of up to 50mph while suspended on cables. The longest of the five lines runs 1350ft and puts you 250ft above the ground. It's as close to flying as you can get without growing wings. Note that it's only open on cruise-ship days.

Sleeping & Eating

Ottley's Plantation Inn Hotel $$$

Map p208 (465-7234, in the US 800-772-3039; www.ottleys.com; Ottley's village; r incl breakfast US$268-433, cottages US$700; P) Veering off the main road in the scruffy village of Ottley's, a meandering driveway ends at this immaculately restored vestige of colonial times. The Great House gives way to a sprawling manicured lawn dotted with cottages with antique-filled rooms and, in some cases, private plunge pools. The wonderful jungle trail is also open to nonguests, as is the alfresco Royal Palm restaurant, which is a popular lunch stop on island tours (mains US$14 to US$28).

Sprat Net Bar & Grill Caribbean $$

Map p208 (465-7535; Old Road Town; mains EC$30-110; 6pm-11:30pm Wed & Fri, to 11pm Thu & Sat, to 10pm Sun; P) Around sunset visitors and local families drop by this Kittitian waterfront institution for humungous platters of grilled chicken, fish and lobster served on plastic plates.

St Kitts Scenic Railway

M TIMOTHY O'KEEFE/GETTY IMAGES ©

Hunker down at a picnic table amid nautical decor and watch the kitchen staff in action. Bands get the crowd onto the dance floor on Wednesdays.

FRIGATE BAY & SOUTHERN ST KITTS

Frigate Bay, some 3 miles southeast of Basseterre, is an isthmus dividing the calm Caribbean side and the surf-lashed Atlantic side, which is dominated by the hulking Marriott resort. The area teems with good restaurants but the key draw is 'the Strip', a row of funky beach bars along South Frigate Bay. Beyond here, St Kitts' south is scrubby wild terrain filled with five-star beaches, grassy hills and salt ponds. The main road has potholes big enough to swallow small goats.

The Best... Leeward Island Beaches

1 Shoal Bay East (p183), Anguilla

2 Lovers Beach (p216), Nevis

3 Half Moon Bay (p193), Antigua

4 *Any* beach on Barbuda (p195)

5 South Friar's Bay (p213), St Kitts

Beaches

South Frigate Bay Beach

In season, the party never stops along the Strip, a bar-backed golden sweep of sand with mellow, kid-friendly waves.

South Friar's Bay Beach

There's excellent tanning and snorkeling along this lovely beach backed by palm trees and sea grapes and bookended by two restaurants: the snazzy Carambola and the funky Shipwreck Bar & Grill.

North Friar's Bay Beach

There's not so much as a cold-beer vendor in sight on this utterly wild Atlantic-side beach, which often has great body-surfing swells (beware of strong currents and rogue waves). Park along the road and look for the narrow access trails.

White House Bay Beach

This facility-free beach has St Kitts' best snorkeling thanks to offshore reefs and a couple of sunken wrecks.

Cockleshell Beach Beach

Enjoy great views of Nevis on this pretty but busy crescent, which offers calm and shallow waters and bars, restaurants and water-sports concessionaires. **Banana Bay**, the next beach over (behind the Spice Mill restaurant), is quieter.

Activities

Royal St Kitts Golf Club Golf

Map p208 (☎866-785-4653; www.royalstkittsgolfclub.com; 858 Zenway Blvd, Frigate Bay; green fee 9/18 holes US$95/165) Tee up in a spectacular setting between the Caribbean and Atlantic at this 18-hole, par 71 championship course designed by Tom McBroom.

Sleeping

Timothy Beach Resort Hotel **$$**

Map p208 (☎465-8597; www.timothybeach.com; South Frigate Bay Beach, Frigate Bay; r US$150-225, 1-/2-bedroom ste US$250/370; P ❄ ☜ ≋) The only resort right on a Caribbean-side beach, this low-key pad with 60 rooms and suites punctuates the south end of the Frigate Bay party 'Strip'. Larger units have full kitchens and sleep up to four adults and three kids. The cheapest face the hill (avoid!), but most others have large balconies with water views.

Rock Haven B&B B&B **$$**

Map p208 (☎465-5503; www.rock-haven.com; Scenic Dr, Frigate Bay; ste incl breakfast US$189-208; P ❄ ☜) This lovely Caribbean home is a great find for those not in need of buckets of privacy. It has just two artfully decorated suites, one with a full kitchen and a flower-filled patio. The warm host,

Judith, makes memorable breakfasts and can happily help you plan your stay.

St Kitts Marriott Resort Resort $$$

Map p208 (466-1200; www.marriott.com; Frigate Bay Rd, Frigate Bay; r from US$350;) This hulking resort on a wide sandy beach exudes cookie-cutter sophistication and is like a small village unto itself with garden villas dotted around multiple pools, restaurants and bars, a gym, a spa, a nightclub, duty-free shops and even a casino. It's the perfect choice for those who need all the comforts of home in a blue-sky locale.

Eating & Drinking

Patsy's Beach Bar & Grill Caribbean $

Map p208 (the Strip, South Frigate Bay; burgers US$4-6, mains US$10-20; 11am-10pm or later;) Beach gourmets flock to Patsy's for her famous barbecued ribs and mouth-watering shrimp pasta served in her cheerfully painted outpost towards the northern end of the Strip.

Mr X's Shiggidy Shack Bar & Grill Caribbean $

Map p208 (762-3983; the Strip, South Frigate Bay; mains US$5-19; 10am-midnight Sun-Fri, 10am-2am Sat;) Lanterns on battered picnic tables on the sand put you in instant party mood at this high-energy joint popular with expats and tourists. On some nights, bands hook up to the generator and jam; on others, karaoke drives many to drink (more). Thursday is bonfire night.

Carambola Beach Club International $$$

Map p208 (465-9090; www.carambolabeachclub.com; South Friar's Bay; mains lunch US$14-18, dinner US$25-44; 6-9pm Wed-Sun, lunch on cruise-ship days;) If you like your beach bars sophisticated instead of funky, saunter up to this snazzy club on one of St Kitts' dreamiest sandy patches. The stylish restaurant features pastas, salads and sushi for lunch and more elaborate fish and meat dishes for dinner. Note that lunch is only served on cruise-ship days but you're free to use the beach anyway.

Spice Mill Restaurant Fusion $$$

(765-6706; www.spicemillrestaurant.com; Cockleshell Beach; mains lunch US$11-22, dinner US$29-45; lunch Fri-Mon, dinner Fri-Wed;) With its shingle roof, crayfish-trap lamps and dugout canoe bar, Spice Mill gives the rustic beach shack a hipster makeover. The menu is just as zeitgeist-compatible, with local produce and fresh fish and seafood getting a flavorful workout with international spices and homemade rubs and hot sauces.

Stone windmill ruins, Nevis

Nevis

Coin-shaped Nevis (pronounced 'nay-vis') is a smaller, neater version of St Kitts, sprinkled with rustic charm and infused with a keen historical awareness and appreciation. Many visitors come here just for the day but those in the know stay much longer.

There's nothing brash about this sweet and unhurried island, whose blissfully uncrowded beaches fringe a forested interior that rises to majestic, often cloud-shrouded, Mt Nevis (3182ft). The coastal lowlands support bougainvillea, hibiscus and other flowering bushes that attract numerous hummingbirds. It's this lush landscape that makes Nevis so popular with bikers, hikers, birders and other nature and outdoor fans. History buffs, meanwhile, can snoop around the legacy of Horatio Nelson and Alexander Hamilton.

CHARLESTOWN

The ferry from St Kitts docks right in pint-size Charlestown, Nevis' cute capital, where banks and businesses coexist with tourist facilities and gingerbread Victorians. It's a fun spot for a stroll and is rarely crowded. The closest beach, lovely Pinney's, is a 15-minute jaunt north.

Sights

Alexander Hamilton Museum Museum

(469-5786; www.nevis-nhcs.org; Main St, Charlestown; adult/child US$5/2; 9am-4pm Mon-Fri, 9am-noon Sat) American statesman Alexander Hamilton (1757–1804) was many things in his short life: soldier, lawyer, author of the *Federalist Papers,* US founding father, the country's first Secretary of State and, finally, the victim of a fatal duel with his political nemesis Aaron Burr. He was also born – scandalously out of wedlock – on Nevis, near this modest museum that chronicles his rags-to-riches career. The adjacent cafe is a lovely, shaded rest spot.

> **Nevis Heritage Trail**
>
> Charlestown is the starting point of the **Nevis Heritage Trail**, which links 25 sites of historical importance, including churches, sugar estates, military installations and natural sites. Look for the blue and green markers or pick up a leaflet at the tourist office or the museums.

Museum of Nevis History Museum

(www.nevis-nhcs.org; Bldg Hill Rd, Charlestown; adult/child US$5/2; 8:30am-4pm Mon-Fri, 10am-1pm Sat) This small museum documents facets of island history (Amerindian origins, colonization, slavery, sugar) but mostly trains its focus on Horatio Nelson, the British sea captain who married a local woman in 1787 and met his demise at the Battle of Trafalgar in 1805. An endearing collection of maps, paintings, documents, busts, vases and other memorabilia help tell his story.

Sleeping & Eating

JP's Guest House Guesthouse $

(469-0319; jpwalters@caribsurf.com; Lower Prince William St, Charlestown; r US$72;) Two minutes from the ferry dock, this tidy upstairs place in a modern building has 10 rooms that are a tad twee but spotless and outfitted with cable TV and a fridge. Self-caterers can make use of the communal kettle and microwave.

Wilma's Diner Caribbean $

(663-8010; Main St, Charlestown; mains US$8-15; 11am-3pm Mon-Sat) The gracious Wilma is a wizard in the kitchen and dishes out a changing menu of authentic local dishes in her quaint and tidy cottage next to the police station.

Octagon Mermaid Caribbean $

(469-0673; Samuel Hunkins Blvd, Charlestown; dishes US$4-8) For a big dose of local

Below: Divers off Saba (p198); Right: Pinney's Beach
(RIGHT) PETER PHIPP/GETTY IMAGES ©; (BELOW) MAURICIO HANDLER/GETTY IMAGES ©

color, belly up to this outdoor bar on the waterfront, which also has cheap, simple lunches (salt fish, johnnycakes, chicken stew etc) and fresh homemade juices.

Information

Plenty of banks with ATMs line up on Main St.

Nevis Tourist Office (469-7550; www.nevisisland.com; Main St, Charlestown; 8am-5pm Mon-Fri) Two minutes from the ferry pier with knowledgeable staff and a good range of maps and brochures.

NORTHERN NEVIS

North of Charlestown are Nevis' best beaches and the massive Four Seasons, the island's only five-star resort.

Beaches

Pinney's Beach Beach

This 4-mile-long stretch of tan sand has decent snorkeling right offshore. Despite several beach bars and the Four Seasons, quiet patches abound.

Oualie Beach Beach

Family-friendly Oualie has grayish sand, shallow water and sunset views of St Kitts. The eponymous resort provides sustenance, beach chairs and water-based activities.

Lovers Beach Beach

Curtained off by sea grapes, mile-long Lovers Beach has white sands but its lack of facilities keeps it nearly deserted. Currents and a steep drop make the water less suitable for kids.

Nisbet Beach Beach

This palm-lined strip of soft white sand next to the namesake resort is open to all. Windy conditions can make the sea quite choppy.

Activities

Mountain Bike Nevis Water Sports, Cycling
(469-9682; www.bikenevis.com; Oualie Beach Resort; 10am-5pm) Nevis is a bikers' delight, and this quality shop rents out all manner of two-wheelers for road and mountain explorations. It also offers biking tours and kayak, board and boat rentals.

Scuba Safaris Diving
(469-9518; www.scubanevis.com; Oualie Beach Resort) This five-star PADI outfit runs boat dives to coral reefs and wrecks around Nevis and St Kitts and also offers certification courses and snorkel safaris.

Four Seasons Golf Course Golf
(9/18 holes US$150/235) The acclaimed 18-hole, par 71 course was designed by Robert Trent Jones II.

Sleeping

Oualie Beach Resort Resort $$
(469-9735; www.oualiebeach.com; Oualie Beach; r US$177-324; P) Tailor-made for families and active types, characterful Oualie sits on a lovely palm-studded beach lapped by tranquil waters and has its own boat dock as well as a spa and bike and water-sports rentals. The restaurant is only so-so but the bar is a popular locals' hangout and gets hopping nightly, sometimes with live music.

Four Seasons Luxury Hotel $$$
(469-1111; www.fourseasons.com/nevis; Pinney's Beach; r from US$500; P @) This luxury abode on the manicured grounds of a former sugar and coconut plantation has 196 rooms discreetly set in low-rise cottages along Pinney's Beach. Rooms are dressed in soothing yellows and blues and outfitted with all expected amenities.

Wrap up a day on the beach in the tropical spa or hit the balls on a tennis court or championship 18-hole golf course.

 Eating & Drinking

Sunshine's Caribbean **$$**

(469-5817; www.sunshinesnevis.com; Pinney's Beach; mains lunch US$8-15, dinner US$15-30; 11am-late; P) This Rasta-run rum-and-reggae joint has been getting people in a party mood for decades. A cold Carib goes well with the tasty sandwiches and seafood platters but the signature 'Killer Bee' rum punch demands your respect: its 'sting' has been documented by hundreds of photos decorating the walls.

SOUTH NEVIS

The circular road traverses the lush southern part of Nevis between cloud-shrouded Mt Nevis and Saddle Hill, skirting crumbling sugar-mill stacks and plantation-estates-turned-hotels. In the east, the population thins out and the sloping, green flatlands – once sugarcane plantations – run down to the turbulent Atlantic. It's a desolate and dramatic landscape.

 Sights

Botanical Gardens of Nevis Gardens

(469-3509; www.botanicalgardennevis.com; St John (Figtree) Parish; adult/child US$13/9; 9am-5pm Mon-Sat, closed mid-Aug–mid-Oct) It's easy to spend a couple of hours wandering around this lush symphony of orchids, palms, water-lily ponds, bamboo groves and other global flora interspersed with sculpture and fountains. In the Rainforest Conservatory parrots patrol the huge tropical plants, waterfalls and Mayan-style sculpture. A Thai restaurant serves lunches and refreshments.

 Tours

Sunrise Tours Hiking

(669-1227; www.nevisnaturetours.com) For a delightful and informative nature experience, hit the trail in the company of Nevis native and environmentalist Lynell Liburd whose hiking menu ranges from a gentle village walk to the strenuous trek up Mt Nevis.

 Sleeping & Eating

Banyan Tree B&B **$$**

(469-3449; www.banyantreebandb.com; Morning Star Village; r/cottage incl tax & breakfast US$150/200; closed mid-Nov–mid-Apr;) This darling retreat tucked beneath the leafy skirts of Mt Nevis combines everything that's special about Nevis into a tidy package: stunning nature, fall-over-backwards hospitality and laid-back ambience. Over home-cooked breakfast ask your delightful artist hosts Anne and John for insider tips on special hikes, galleries or beaches or browse their extensive library for ideas. No phone or TV.

Golden Rock Inn Hotel **$$$**

(469-3346; www.goldenrocknevis.com; Gingerland; d from US$220, lunch US$11-19, dinner US$22-32; closed mid-Aug–mid-Oct; P) The owner's great-great-great-great-grandfather built this lava-stone estate by hand in the 1810s. The 11 cottages are tucked into a terraced hillside amid jungly vegetation and drenched in cheerful Caribbean colors. The overall ambience of funky perfection extends to the popular restaurant. Several hiking trails leave right from the grounds.

Hermitage Hotel **$$$**

(469-3477; www.hermitagenevis.com; Gingerland; r incl breakfast US$255-425; P) Country comfort and Caribbean flair combine effortlessly at this cluster of candy-colored gingerbread stone cottages set amid beautiful gardens on a former plantation. Even if you're not staying, swing by for breakfast, lunch or dinner to soak up the serene setting.

Bananas Restaurant International **$$**

(469-1891; Morning Star Village; mains lunch US$16-30, dinner US$18-35; lunch & dinner Mon-Sat; P) A torchlit walkway leads to this enchanting hideaway handbuilt by British transplant and former dancer Gillian Smith. Enjoy the tranquil vibe ensconced on the veranda, slurping smooth tropical drinks and tucking into food inspired by her travels around the world. Local treats such as conch gratin, salt fish or goat water round out the menu. Reservations advised.

SURVIVAL GUIDE

Directory A–Z

Accommodations

Unless noted, lodging rates in this chapter refer to double rooms with private bathrooms in peak season (December to April) without tax and service. Rates drop as much as 50% in low season.

Anguilla

Finding lodging below US$300 is a tall order on luxe Anguilla. Unless noted rates quoted do not include 20% tax and service or the daily US$1 per person tourism fee. Price ranges:

$ less than US$200

$$ US$200 to US$400

$$$ more than US$400

Antigua & Barbuda

Antigua is expensive and besides a few guesthouses and moderately priced properties, resort-type complexes (often all-inclusive) dominate the market. Overnighting on Barbuda means either more or less roughing it in a basic guesthouse in or around Codrington or forking over megabucks for a luxury abode. The combined tax and service charge is 20.5%. Price ranges:

$ under US$125

$$ US$125 to US$250

$$$ more than US$250

Saba

Saba's accommodations range from ecolodges to luxe hotels and are quite reasonable. The government room tax of 5% and a daily US$1 nature fee are added to the bill. Some hotels also tack on a 10% to 15% service charge. Price ranges:

$ less than US$100

$$ US$100 to US$150

$$$ more than US$150

Practicalities

- **Electricity** North American–style two- and three-pin sockets dominate on all islands; however, Anguilla, Saba and Sint Eustatius are on 110V/60hz while St Kitts & Nevis and Antigua & Barbuda are on 220V/60hz, although many hotels on the latter provide both.
- **Time** The Leeward Islands are in the Atlantic Time Zone, which is four hours behind UTC/GMT. The region does not observe daylight-savings time.
- **Weights & Measures** Saba and Sint Eustatius use the metric system; Anguilla, Antigua & Barbuda and St Kitts & Nevis the imperial system.

Sint Eustatius

Most of Statia's accommodations are midrange. Service and taxes are included in the listed room rates. Price ranges:

$ less than US$100

$$ US$100 to US$200

$$$ more than US$200

St Kitts & Nevis

There are large resorts on both islands, but most accommodations are still small-scale hotels, plantation inns, guesthouses and apartment rentals. Tax and a service charge add 22% to the bill. Price ranges:

$ less than US$100

$$ US$100 to US$200

$$$ more than US$200

Food

The following price indicators refer to the average cost of one main course, not including applicable taxes and service charges or a tip:

$ less than US$10

$$ US$10 to US$20

$$$ more than US$20

Health

There are no compulsory vaccinations for travel to the Leeward Islands, although the Center for Disease control recommends being up-to-date on your routine vaccinations and getting inoculated against food- and water-borne Hepatitis A. Drinking bottled water is recommended. All islands have medical centers that can help with emergencies. The region's best hospital is Mt St John's in St John's on Antigua.

Money

Anguilla Although the Eastern Caribbean dollar (EC$) is the official currency, the US dollar is preferred.

Antigua & Barbuda Official currency is the Eastern Caribbean dollar (EC$) but US dollars are widely accepted. Except at local establishments, prices are often quoted in US dollars.

Saba The US dollar has been the island's official currency since 2011.

Sint Eustatius As on Saba, only US dollars are in use since 2011.

St Kitts & Nevis The official currency is the Eastern Caribbean dollar (EC$) but US dollars are accepted almost everywhere, although ATMs don't dispense them.

Opening hours

Hours listed in this chapter apply during the peak season (December to April), but they are only guidelines since many establishments are bound to open and close on a whim.

Banks 8am to 5pm Monday to Thursday, to 4pm Friday.

Bars noon to 11pm or midnight.

Shops 9am to 5pm Monday to Friday, to 1pm or 2pm Saturday, some close for lunch.

Supermarkets 8:30am to 7pm Monday to Thursday, to 8pm Saturday, to 1pm Sunday.

Public Holidays

In addition to the holidays observed throughout the region, the islands celebrate the following public holidays:

Anguilla

Anguilla Day May 30

Queen's Birthday June 11

August Monday (Emancipation Day) First Monday in August

August Thursday First Thursday in August

Constitution Day August 6

Separation Day December 19

A restored house at Hermitage (p218)

Antigua & Barbuda

Labour Day First Monday in May

Carnival Monday & Tuesday First Monday and Tuesday in August

Antigua & Barbuda Independence Day November 1

VC Bird Day December 9

Saba

Queen's Birthday April 30

Labor Day May 1

Ascension 40 days after Easter

Sint Eustatius

Queen's Birthday April 30

Labor Day/Ascension Day May 1

Emancipation Day July 1

Antillean Day October 21

Statia Day November 16

St Kitts & Nevis

Labour Day First Monday in May

Emancipation Day First Monday in August

National Hero's Day September 17

Independence Day September 19

Telephone

Local phone numbers on all Leeward Islands consist of seven digits. If you are calling locally, simply dial the local number. To call the island from North America, dial 1 + the island country code + the local number. From elsewhere, dial your country's international dialing code + the island country code + the local number.

Country codes:

Anguilla ☎264

Antigua & Barbuda ☎268

Saba ☎599

Sint Eustatius ☎599

St Kitts & Nevis ☎869

Getting There & Away

Anguilla

Air Anguilla's tiny Clayton J Lloyd International airport on the edge of the Valley is served by Cape Air from San Juan (Puerto Rico), by LIAT from Antigua and by Winair from Sint Maarten.

Sea Ferries make the 25-minute run from Marigot Bay on St-Martin/Sint Maarten to Blowing Point some 4 miles southwest of the Valley every 30 to 45 minutes from 8:15am to 7pm, with return ferries operating from 7:30am to 6:15pm. No reservations are necessary; simply show up at the ferry terminal. The one-way fare per person is US$15. Boats also connect Blowing Point four times daily directly with Juliana Airport on St-Martin/Sint Maarten for US$55 (plus departure tax).

Departure tax is US$20 plus a US$3 security fee (US$5 for day trips to/from St-Martin/Sint Maarten).

Antigua & Barbuda

Air VC Bird International Airport is about 5 miles east of St John's. American Airlines, Delta, US Air, United Airlines and Air Canada have direct flight from various North American gateway cities to Antigua. British Airways and Virgin Atlantic operate direct flights from the UK. LIAT and Caribbean Airlines are the main regional carriers. **Montserrat Airways** (☎**664-491-3434; www.flymontserrat.com**) flies to Montserrat and Nevis.

Sea St John's is a major port-of-call for cruise ships with up to five behemoths mooring at Heritage Quay simultaneously in peak season. The on-and-off-again **ferry service** (☎**778-9786; return EC$300**) to Montserrat was on again at the time of writing. Call for the latest schedule.

Departure tax is included in all tickets.

Saba

Note that bad weather (heavy wind is worse than rain) may cancel travel to and from Saba. Check ahead.

Air Saba is served several times daily by Winair from St-Martin/Sint Maarten.

Sea Two ferries make the 90-minute rides between St-Martin/Sint Maarten and Saba. Based at Fort Bay on Saba, the **M/V Dawn II** (☎**416-2299; www.sabactransport.com; same-day return adult/2-11yr US$68/35**) leaves at 7am on Tuesdays, Thursdays and Saturdays for the Dock Maarten Marina in Phillipsburg and returns to Saba at 4:30pm.

The M/V Edge (☎545-2640; www.stmaarten-activities.com; day trip adult/2-12yr US$80/40) leaves on day trips for Saba at 9am from Simpson Bay Resort on St-Martin/Sint Maarten, returning at 3:30pm.

The departure tax is US$10.

Sint Eustatius

Air Up to five Winair puddle-jumpers make the 20-minute trip from St-Martin/Sint Maarten to Statia's teensy airport daily.

The departure tax is US$15.

St Kitts & Nevis

Air St Kitts' Robert L Bradshaw International Airport (SKM; ☎465-8121; Basseterre) is on the northern outskirts of Basseterre. It is served seasonally by Air Canada, American Airlines, Delta, US Airways and British Airways. Year-round regional services to Antigua, Anguilla, St Thomas, St-Martin/Sint Maarten and Tortola are provided by LIAT. Winair flies to Nevis and St-Martin/Sint Maarten.

Nevis' diminutive Vance W Armory International Airport, on the northeastern edge of the island, is only served by regional airlines.

Departure tax is included in all airline tickets.

Getting Around

Anguilla

Car Anguilla has no public transport. Car-rental agencies issue the compulsory local driving permit for US$20. Driving is on the left-hand side of the road, but steering wheels can confusingly be on either the left or the right side. Avis, Hertz and Thrifty have offices on the island; local outfits include Island Car Rental (☎497-2723; www.island car.ai; Airport Rd) and Carib Rent a Car (☎497-6020; caribcarrental@anguillanet.com; Meads Bay).

Taxi Anguilla is divided into 10 taxi zones with fares depending on how many zones you travel through (ie one zone US$10, 10 zones US$36). Surcharges apply for rides after 6pm or for more than two persons. Two-hour island tours for two people cost US$55. Drivers only accept US dollars.

Antigua & Barbuda

Air In season, ABM Air (☎562-7183; www.antigua-flights.com) operates charter and daily scheduled flights between Antigua's VC Bird International Airport and Codrington Airport on Barbuda. Transfers and tours may also be arranged through Caribbean Helicopters (p196).

Heritage Quay, St John's

WALTER BIBIKOW/GETTY IMAGES ©

Boat Bumpy 90-minute catamaran rides operated by Barbuda Express (☎560-7989; www.barbudaexpress.com; Heritage Quay, St John's; round trip adult/7-12yr/3-6yr EC$260/200/120) link St John's with the River Wharf Landing in southern Barbuda. Boats leave at 9am (noon Sunday) and return from Barbuda at 3:45pm (2:30pm Sunday). There is no service on Mondays. In peak season, it's best to buy tickets in advance. Inclement weather may cancel service, so call ahead to confirm. The company also operates guided day tours (p196) to Barbuda.

Bus Antigua's 'public' transportation is operated by private minivans that travel along the main roads. Buses to the south and west leave from the West Bus Station opposite the Public Market in St John's, buses to the north and the east leave from the East Bus Station on Independence Ave. Barbuda has no buses.

Car International car-rental companies with outlets at the airport include Avis, Dollar and Hertz. Big's Car Rental (☎562-4901; www.bigscarrental.net; English Harbour) is a local outfit in English Harbour. All can issue the compulsory local drivers' license for US$20, which is valid on both islands. Driving is on the left, the steering wheel is on the right. For car rentals on Barbuda, try Evans Thomas (☎460-0408) or Shorelines Rentals (☎770-0166).

Taxi Taxis are plentiful and fares are government-regulated. On Antigua, the one-way trip from St John's to English Harbour, for instance, costs US$24. Private island tours are charged at about US$24 per hour for up to four people with a two-hour minimum. On Barbuda, taxis wait at the ferry dock, but you may prefer to prearrange a transfer or an island tour through your hotel, the Barbuda tourist office or by contacting a driver directly. Try Lynton Thomas (☎460-0081), John Taxi Service (☎788-5378) or D&D Taxi (☎724-2829).

Saba

There is no bus service on Saba. Most travelers hitchhike, walk or use taxis. Cab fares are fixed and drivers meet arriving flights. Otherwise, ask anyone to call you one. Renting a vehicle is not recommended for short stays.

Sint Eustatius

Statia has no buses, but Oranjestad itself is small enough to explore on foot. Taxis take you further afield; rates are fixed but should be confirmed before the ride. The dispatch is at ☎318-2620. If you want your own wheels, try Rainbow Car Rental (☎318-2811) or Rivers Car Rental (☎318-2309); the latter also rents scooters. You only need your home license and driving is on the right side of the road. Hitchhiking is common practice on Statia, although the usual precautions apply.

St Kitts & Nevis

Boat Several companies operate passenger ferries linking Basseterre on St Kitts and Charlestown on Nevis in about 45 minutes for EC$25 (child EC$15), plus the EC$1 port tax. Boats depart at least once hourly between 7am and 9pm. Tickets are sold from about 30 minutes before sailings. In peak times, arrive early as some boats sell out. Drivers can use the Seabridge car ferry (☎765-7053; Major's Bay; car & driver EC$75, additional passenger EC$20) which makes the trip from Major's Bay in southern St Kitts to Cades Bay on Nevis in 20 minutes roughly every two hours. For the current schedule, ask at your hotel, check www.sknvibes.com/travel/ferry.cfm or text 'Ferry' to ☎7568.

Bus There is no public transportation on either island, but privately operated minivans serve communities on an erratic schedule along the main roads. All have license plates starting with a 'H' and can be flagged down.

Car To hire your own wheels, you need a local driver's license (US$24) valid on both islands and issued by the rental companies. Driving is on the left side of the road, the steering wheel is on the right and speed limits are posted in miles per hour.

French Antilles

The French Antilles (St-Martin/ Sint Maarten, St-Barthélemy, Guadeloupe, Martinique, which are overseas French territories) form a fascinating quartet, with each island offering travelers something different while retaining its rich Franco-Caribbean culture and identity. Tiny St-Barth is a fabulous mix of sophistication, elegance and barefoot luxury, while Guadeloupe and Martinique have a fascinating Creole and French heritage. With its dual personality, St-Martin/ Sint Maarten is sure to captivate you. What they all have in common is mind-blowing beaches, from deserted to packed, from calm to rough, and all offering a number of high-energy distractions. There are jungle and coastal walks, boat excursions, windsurfing, kayaking, diving and snorkeling to keep you buzzing. Have we missed something? Oh yes. If food (and wine, and rum) is your true love, then you'll also find your bliss here.

St-Barthélemy (p237)

French Antilles Itineraries

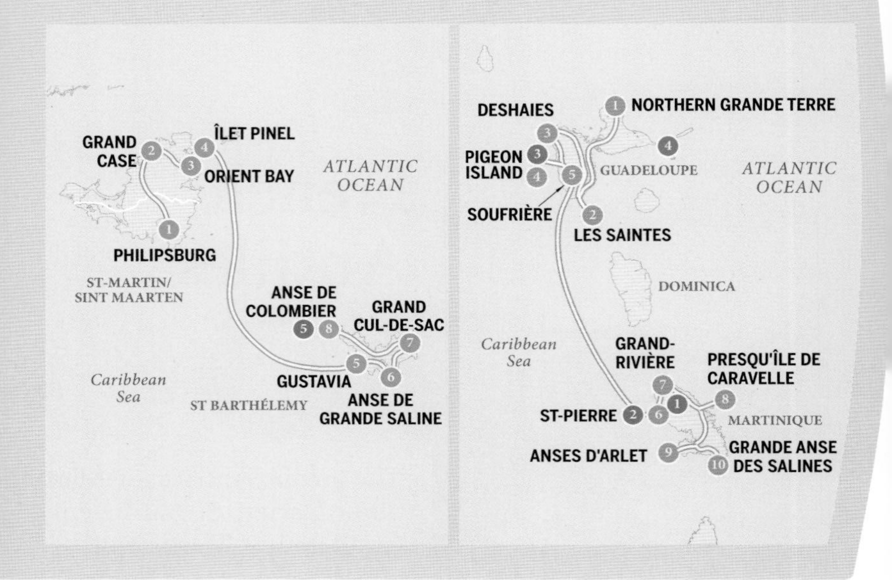

Five Days

1 Philipsburg, Sint Maarten (p228) Stroll around Dutch Sint Maarten's principal town, browsing the duty-free shops. Loads of restaurants await for lunch on the boardwalk.

2 Grand Case, St-Martin (p233) Gorge on sticky ribs at a beachside *lolo* shack in the 'Gourmet Capital of the Caribbean' or go for a shmancy dinner that will transport your taste buds all the way to Paris.

3 Orient Bay, St-Martin (p236) Spend the day sunning, taking a long beach walk and a swim in the turquoise water. A leisurely lunch and rum-punch sundowners at a funky beach bar are de rigueur.

4 Îlet Pinel, St-Martin (p236) Dedicate a day to the boat excursion to this little islet that's just 1km offshore.

5 Gustavia, St-Barth (p238) On day four make the short hop over to St-Barth. Strut your stuff window-shopping and yacht-ogling in Gustavia, the picturesque capital. When you tire of stylish clothes and fashion accessories, enjoy the town's top-notch restaurants and waterfront cafes.

6 Anse de Grande Saline, St-Barth (p243) Lay your towel on this perfect stretch of beach which is the quintessential tropical paradise.

7 Grand Cul-de-Sac, St-Barth (p241) Looking for a new high? Make a beeline for this windswept beach that's the St-Barth kitesurfing and windsurfing epicenter.

8 Anse de Colombier, St-Barth (p240) End your trip splashing around the jeweled waters of this idyllic stretch of sand that's accessible on foot only.

THIS LEG: 90KM

Two Weeks

1 Northern Grande-Terre, Guadeloupe (p248) After following our five-day itinerary, continue your exploration by flying to Guadeloupe. Spend a day or two driving around the northern half of Grande-Terre.

2 Les Saintes, Guadeloupe (p252) Take the ferry to this quaint archipelago where you should allow at least two days to soak up the laid-back atmosphere.

3 Deshaies, Guadeloupe (p251) Back on 'mainland' Guadeloupe, move on to this charmingly beautiful seaside town. Nourish your inner gourmet and encounter boaties from around the world.

4 Pigeon Island, Guadeloupe (p255) It's time to slip below the ocean's surface. This protected area is renowned for its underwater geography, exuberant corals and technicolor marine species.

5 Soufrière, Guadeloupe (p255) Another day could be taken up by the classic hike through the rainforest to the misty summit of this active volcano.

6 St-Pierre, Martinique (p260) It's time to change scene. Fly to Martinique and head to St-Pierre. See the devastation of Mont Pelée firsthand in this former capital of Martinique, as the volcano broods in the distance.

7 Grand-Rivière, Martinique (p263) Slow down the pace at this serene, laid-back fishing village that feels like the world's end.

8 Presqu'île de Caravelle, Martinique (p263) Soak up the sun and sand by day – and the gourmet flavors by night – on this lovely peninsula.

9 Anses d'Arlet (p267) Enjoy a day on the beach overlooked by an 18th-century church and the surrounding hillside in this peaceful village.

10 Grande Anse des Salines (p269) Wrap up your two-week vacation by wandering one of the island's most beautiful beaches; be sure to sample a coconut sorbet.

THIS LEG: 770KM

French Antilles Highlights

1 Best Hike: Mont Pelée (p262) Earn bragging rights for having conquered this still-active volcano.

2 Best Cultural Experience: Ruins (p260), **St-Pierre** Wander the ruins of the 'Pompeii of the Caribbean.'

3 Best Diving & Snorkeling: Réserve Cousteau (p255) A superb playground for snorkelers and novice divers. Plunge below the waterline for mesmerizing close-ups of corals and tropical fish.

4 Best Natural Wonder: Pointe des Châteaux (p248) Admire panoramic views of the coast from this windswept peninsula.

5 Best Beach: Anse de Colombier (p240) An intimate paradise, accessible by boat or on foot.

Ruins (p260), St-Pierre

Discover the French Antilles

ST-MARTIN/SINT MAARTEN

Two nations, one island. How strange it feels to visit a half-Dutch, half-French territory, with two very distinct personalities. For visitors, it's a great opportunity to enjoy the best of both worlds. First and foremost, get your tan. With 37 picture-perfect beaches that are spread out all over the island, your vacation here is sure to be a dream. The usual assortment of water sports are also available, from scuba diving and snorkeling to windsurfing and yachting. Be sure to save some energy for some serious shopping and partying. When it's time to relax, dozens of well-equipped resorts await. One thing is sure: whatever side of the island you choose to stay, you'll never get bored.

Beachfront, Philipsburg
PETER PHIPP/GETTY IMAGES ©

Sint Maarten

POP 41,000

Sint Maarten is completely different from its French sibling, which is part of its charm and appeal. With its appropriately tourist-friendly nightlife, flashy shopping centers, tacky casinos, numerous condo units and sprawling resorts, it can sometimes feel overdeveloped and artificial, but you'll also find a few gems in the form of picturesque beaches near Philipsburg, the bustling capital.

PHILIPSBURG

POP 18,000

Philipsburg, the capital of Sint Maarten's Dutch side, is a gridiron town along a wide arcing bay that mostly functions as an outdoor shopping mall for cruise-goers. There are some older buildings mixed among the new, but overall the town is far more commercial than quaint. Most of the action is along Frontstreet, the bayfront road, which is lined with boutiques, jewelry shops, restaurants, casinos and duty-free shops.

Activities

Trisport Outdoors
(**☎588-6009; www.trisportsxm.com; Bobby's Marina**) This versatile outfit has a range of bike tours (from US$49), kayak outings, snorkeling excursions and coastal hikes.

French Antilles

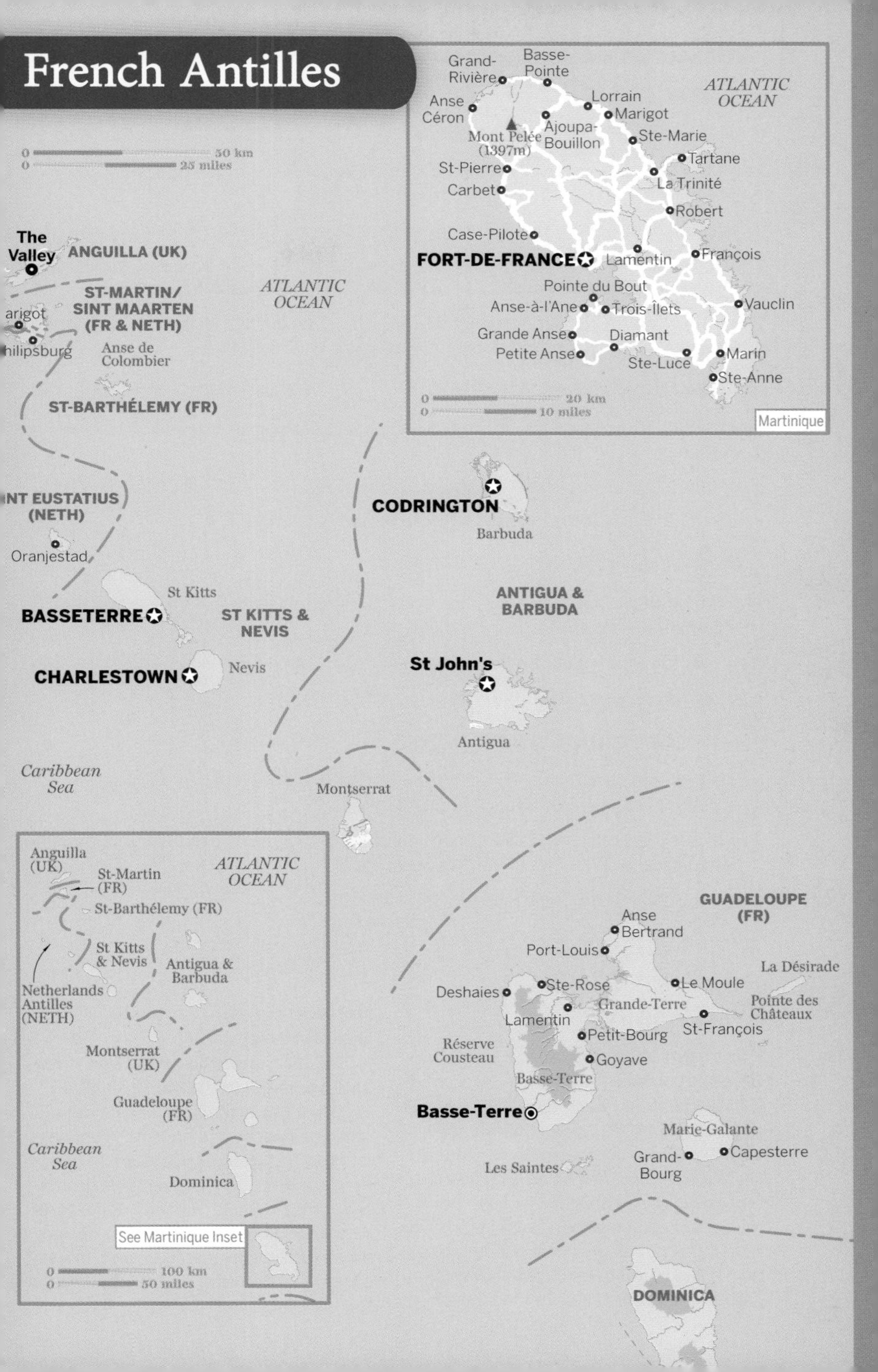

0 50 km
0 25 miles
The Valley
ANGUILLA (UK)
ST-MARTIN/
SINT MAARTEN
(FR & NETH)
arigot
hilipsburg
Anse de
Colombier
ST-BARTHÉLEMY (FR)
ATLANTIC
OCEAN
NT EUSTATIUS
(NETH)
Oranjestad
St Kitts
BASSETERRE
ST KITTS &
NEVIS
CHARLESTOWN
Nevis
CODRINGTON
Barbuda
ANTIGUA &
BARBUDA
St John's
Antigua
Caribbean
Sea
Montserrat
GUADELOUPE
(FR)
Anse
Bertrand
Port-Louis
La Désirade
Deshaies
Ste-Rose
Le Moule
Grande-Terre
Pointe des
Châteaux
Lamentin
St-François
Petit-Bourg
Réserve
Cousteau
Goyave
Basse-Terre
Basse-Terre
Marie-Galante
Grand-
Bourg
Capesterre
Les Saintes
DOMINICA
Grand-
Rivière
Basse-
Pointe
Anse
Céron
Lorrain
Marigot
ATLANTIC
OCEAN
Ajoupa-
Bouillon
Mont Pelée
(1397m)
Ste-Marie
Tartane
St-Pierre
Carbet
La Trinité
Robert
Case-Pilote
FORT-DE-FRANCE
Lamentin
François
Pointe du Bout
Anse-à-l'Ane
Trois-Îlets
Vauclin
Grande Anse
Diamant
Petite Anse
Ste-Luce
Marin
Ste-Anne
0 20 km
0 10 miles
Martinique
Anguilla
(UK)
St-Martin
(FR)
St-Barthélemy (FR)
ATLANTIC
OCEAN
St Kitts
& Nevis
Antigua &
Barbuda
Netherlands
Antilles
(NETH)
Montserrat
(UK)
Guadeloupe
(FR)
Caribbean
Sea
Dominica
See Martinique Inset
0 100 km
0 50 miles

Ports of Call

PHILIPSBURG (SINT MAARTEN)

- Most cruise ships drop anchor off Philipsburg or dock in the marina at the southern tip of the Philipsburg harbor.
- After alighting in Philipsburg, spend your half-day ogling souvenirs on the main drag.
- Hire a car and head to Grand Case (St-Martin) for succulent fusion fare.
- Stop at the Dutch side's Sunset Bar & Grill (p231) to sip a cocktail as the jumbo jets make a dramatic (and noisy) landing right over your head.

GUSTAVIA (ST-BARTHÉLEMY)

- (Small) cruise ships anchor in Gustavia harbor and bring passengers ashore on tenders.
- Rent a car and sunbathe at Anse de Grande Saline or Anse de Colombier.
- Sample a glass of rum at Le Select (p239) in Gustavia.

POINTE-À-PITRE (GUADELOUPE)

- Cruise ships dock at Pointe-à-Pitre. It's a 15-minute walk from the cruise terminal into town.
- Visit the Musée St-John Perse (p244) and the Musée Schoelcher (p244).
- Divers and snorkelers should head to Malendure.

FORT-DE-FRANCE (MARTINIQUE)

- All cruise ships land at Pointe Simon in Fort-de-France. This is within easy walking distance of the city center.
- In Fort-de-France, visit the Grand Marché (p257) and the beautiful Bibliothèque Schoelcher (p257).
- Take a taxi to the superb Jardin de Balata (p258).

Sleeping

Pasanggrahan Royal Guest House Hotel $$
(542-3588; www.pasanhotel.net; 19 Frontstreet; d from US$181; ❄ wi-fi) One of this historical building's many charms is its lived-in, slightly dog-eared condition. The restaurant and lobby are in a former governor's residence that feels like a Cuban plantation house. It occupies a prime spot on the beach and Frontstreet. Rooms were upgraded in 2013 but rates remain the same.

Holland House Beach Hotel Hotel $$
(542-2572; www.hhbh.com; 43 Frontstreet; d incl breakfast from US$240; P ❄ @ wi-fi) This well-managed hotel opens directly onto the beach. The building is soulless and the communal spaces are in need of a touch-up, but the spacious rooms are comfortably furnished and feature hardwood floors, subtle trendy design details, balconies, cable TV and, in most cases, a kitchenette. Top-floor suites have the best views.

Eating & Drinking

Greenhouse International $$
(542-2941; www.thegreenhouserestaurant.com; Kanal Steeg; mains US$10-30; 11am-9pm) After (or before) window-shopping on Frontstreet, recharge the batteries in this Philipsburg icon with charismatic staff. Don't miss its happy hour from 4:30pm to 7pm, which has two-for-one drinks as well as half-price snacks. It has the most eclectic menu in town. Here you can wrap your mandibles around burgers, sandwiches, salads, steaks, ribs, chicken and seafood.

Ocean Lounge Restaurant & Bar International $$$
(542-2572; Board Walk, Holland House Beach Hotel; mains US$18-40; breakfast, lunch & dinner) Spiffing setting, with a breezy terrace opening onto the seafront – a great place for quaffing a sunset beverage or enjoying a fine meal. Lunch can be a relatively simple affair, with a selection of burgers and grilled dishes. For dinner, try one of the chef's zesty versions of fish, meat or lobster. He also prepares a to-die-for West Indian risotto.

Information

Banks and ATMs can be found along Frontstreet, and all deal in US dollars.

Sint Maarten Tourist Bureau (542-2337; www.vacationstmaarten.com; Juancho Yrausquin Blvd 6; 8am-5pm Mon-Fri)

MAHO BAY

Calling all plane-spotters! Beautiful Maho beach is situated at the end of Juliana airport's runway and is famous for its unrivaled plane-spotting opportunties.

Eating & Drinking

Sunset Bar & Grill Restaurant/Bar $
(545-2084; www.sunsetsxm.com; 2 Beacon Hill Rd; mains US$10-20; breakfast, lunch & dinner;) Sunset Beach Bar is almost a rite of passage for aviation buffs, due to its strategic position at the end of the runway. Where else in the world can you sip an ice-cold beer while snapping photos of a jumbo jet soaring overhead? Awesome! Hint: check in early at the airport, then catch a taxi to the bar.

The Best... Beaches

1 Friar's Bay (p233)
2 Anse Marcel (p236)
3 Anse de Colombier (p240)
4 Grande Anse (p251)
5 Anse Noire (p265)
6 Grande Anse des Salines (p269)

SIMPSON BAY

Although close to the airport runway, beautiful Simpson Bay has some of the most captivating crystal tidewater out of all the beaches on the island.

Activities

Aqua Mania Adventures Water Sports
(544-2640, 544-2631; www.stmaarten-activities.com; Simpson Bay Resort) Has snorkeling trips, sunset lagoon cruises, deep-sea fishing outings and day trips to Pinel and Tintamarre islands.

Eating & Drinking

Karakter Restaurant/Bar $$
(Simpson Bay; mains US$10-21; breakfast, lunch & dinner) Not your average beach bar and restaurant, Karakter is wedged between the beach and the airport's runway and occupies a dilapidated bus-turned-bar meters from the turquoise water. Come for the good fun, great mix of people, wicked cocktails and flavorsome tapas – not to mention live music certain evenings.

Detour: Loterie Farm

A must for hikers, foodies and those in search of a hideaway, the **Loterie Farm** (**0590-87-86-16; www.loteriefarm.com; Rte Pic Paradis; swimming pool €20, mains €12-28; 9am-dinner Tue-Sun**) is an excellent place to spend the afternoon. This 53-hectare private nature reserve nestled in the hillside of Pic Paradis features a couple of well-marked walking trails, a large swimming pool and a great bar-restaurant that gets rave reviews. The cherry on the cake: a zip line over the forest canopy that will appeal to Tarzan types. The farm is on the way to Pic Paradis; look for the sign between Colombier and Grand Case.

St-Martin

POP 36,000

While the Dutch side embraces every Caribbean cliché, the French half clings to its European roots. Noticeably devoid of casinos and skyscraping timeshares, the quieter French side is a charming mix of white-sand beaches, cluttered town centers and stretches of bucolic mountainside.

MARIGOT

POP 12,500

The capital of French St-Martin, this bustling port town is dominated by a stone fort high up on the hill. A distinctive European flavor is palpable here – there's a produce market, a gaggle of *boulangeries* (bakeries), and a few buildings with iron-wrought balconies and belle epoque lamp-posts.

Sights

Fort Louis — Ruin

Fort Louis was constructed in 1767 by order of French King Louis XVI to protect Marigot from marauding British and Dutch pirates. It's been abandoned for centuries and contains only remnants from bygone eras, but the view alone is worth the 15-minute hike up to the ruins.

Produce Market — Market

(Blvd de France; sunrise-2pm Wed & Sat) The produce market on Marigot's waterfront has tropical fruit such as passionfruit and bananas as well as local root vegetables. There are also plenty of souvenir stalls.

Sleeping & Eating

Centr'Hotel — Hotel $

(**0590-87-86-51; www.centrhotel.fr; Rue du Général de Gaulle; s €55-70, d €60-75;**) A stone's throw from the waterfront, this 30-room hotel has all the hallmarks of a great deal; renovated, spruce rooms with modernized bathrooms, a super central location and a tab that won't burn a hole in your pocket.

Sarafina — Bakery $

(**0590-29-73-69; Blvd de France; mains €3-10; 6am-7:30pm Tue-Sat, 6am-2pm Sun**) In the heart of Marigot, Serafina lures peckish pedestrians off the sun-soaked streets with its authentic spread of French baked goods that come in sweet and savory forms. Wash it all down with a smooth espresso and you're good to go. It also serves up crepes and waffles as well as a wide assortment of tasty sandwiches. Deadly.

Enoch's Place — Caribbean $

(Front de Mer; mains €10-13; lunch & dinner Mon-Sat) Tasty, filling, cheap Creole food. No surprise, it's a hit. For a true local (if lowbrow) experience, try this bustling eatery strategically positioned on a corner of the Marigot open-air market. If you've never tried oxtail stew or conch salad here's a great place to savor the real deal, made fresh daily.

Ô Plongeoir — International $$

(**0590-87-94-71; Marina Fort Louis; mains €14-20; lunch & dinner Mon-Sat**) At the far end of Port St-Louis, this open-air joint is a great place to sit back with a coffee and spy on Anguilla in the distance. The food is excellent as well – it serves up creative

French cuisine with an Asian twist. We loved the deeply flavorful red tuna tartare.

Information

Banks with ATMs and exchange offices are easy to find in the center.

Tourist Office (☎0590-87-57-21; www.iledesaintmartin.org; Route de Sandy Ground; ⏰8:30am-1pm & 2:30-5:30pm Mon-Fri, 8am-noon Sat) Has brochures and maps.

FRIAR'S BAY

Friar's Bay, north of Marigot, is a postcard-worthy cove with a broad sandy beach. This popular local swimming spot is just beyond the residential neighborhood of St-Louis; the road leading in is signposted.

Eating

Friar's Bay Beach Café — French, Seafood $$$

(☎0590-49-16-87; Friar's Bay; mains €14-29; ⏰breakfast 9-11am, lunch noon-5pm, bar 9am-6:30pm) This snazzy little complex occupies a privileged spot on the beach – if the terrace was any nearer to the water you'd have to swim to dinner. Enjoy large leafy salads, sparkingly fresh fish dishes, as well as French classics. Be sure to look at the specials on the blackboard, too. There's live music on Friday evenings.

TERRES BASSES

Terres Basses (pronounced *'tair boss'*), also called the French Lowlands, is a verdant clump of lush, low-lying acreage connected to the larger part of the island by two thin strips of land. This quiet area is dominated by three gorgeous beaches and consists mostly of large private villas.

Beaches

Baie Longue — Beach

Long Bay, or Baie Longue, embraces two splendid miles of seemingly endless white sand and rocky outcrops. It's very wide and well off the beaten path, making it a great place for long strolls and quiet sunsets. To get there, after Cupecoy head to Baie aux Prunes then enter the seemingly private entrance and take an immediate left.

Baie aux Prunes (Plum Bay) — Beach

The remote and unspoiled Baie aux Prunes is a gently curving bay with polished shell-like grains of golden sand. The beach is popular for swimming and sunbathing.

The bay can be reached by turning right 1.3km south of Baie Rouge and immediately taking the signposted left fork.

Baie Rouge — Beach

Baie Rouge is a long, beautiful sandy strand with good swimming. Although this golden-sand beach is just 150m from the main road, it retains an inviting natural setting. For the best snorkeling, swim to the right toward the rocky outcrop and arch.

Sleeping & Eating

La Samanna — Resort $$$

(☎0590-87-64-00, in the US 0800-913-1800; www.lasamanna.com; Baie Longue; d from US$700; ❄@📶🏊) Tropical luxury at its best. Following a renovation in 2012, La Samanna is now one of the most attractive places to stay on the island. If you're not bowled over by features such as the magnificent beach and the alluring spa, you certainly will be by the two pools, the high-quality restaurants and the smartly finished villas and rooms.

GRAND CASE

The small beachside town of Grand Case has not been dubbed the 'Gourmet Capital of the Caribbean' for nothing.

> **Happy Bay**
>
> If you thought Friar's Bay was a quaint little speck of sand, head to the northernmost point of the beach and you'll discover a dirt path that twists over a bumpy headland to perfectly deserted Happy Bay. Equidistant from Marigot and Grand Case, this surprisingly serene strip of powdery sand is completely bare (as are those who like to hang out here).

Each evening, a ritual of sorts takes place on Grand Case's beachfront road, with restaurants placing their menus and chalkboard specials out front, and would-be diners strolling along the strip until they find a place that strikes their fancy.

While dining is the premier attraction here, there's also a decent beach and several affordable places to hang your hat.

Activities

Scoobidoo Boat Trips
(☎0590-52-02-53; www.scoobidoo.com; Grand Case) Scoobidoo offers excellent catamaran trips that go to Prickly Pear in Anguilla, Tintamarre or St-Barthélemy for around €96 per person. It also offers sunset cruises and snorkeling trips (€50 per person). Boats may also leave from Anse Marcel, depending on the trip.

Octopus Diving Diving, Snorkeling
(☎0590-29-11-27; www.octopusdiving.com; 15 Blvd de Grand Case) This well-established operator offers dive trips (from US$100) and snorkeling excursions (US$45) to various sites around the island. Also rents snorkeling gear (US$10 per day).

Sleeping

Hotel Hevea Guesthouse $$
(☎0690-29-36-71; www.hotelhevea.com; 163 Blvd de Grand Case; s €64-90, d €75-105; ❄📶) Following a full refit in 2013, this sweet establishment is looking excellent, with an assortment of colorful, well-equipped rooms, an inviting patio and friendly owners. Best of all, it's ideally positioned on Grand Case's beachfront road. A great budget option.

Grand Case Beach Club Hotel $$$
(☎0590-87-51-87; www.grandcasebeachclub.com; 21 Rue de Petite Plage; d incl breakfast from US$400; ❄📶🏊) On the quiet northeast end of the beach, this gently sprawling resort has a range of renovated, spick-and-span rooms in a cluster of two-story, motel-like buildings facing the sea. Plus, there's an on-site pool, a water-sports center, a well-regarded restaurant and superb snorkeling a few fin-strokes away.

Left: Anse Noire (p265); Below: Zip-lining, St-Martin (p232)
(LEFT) :BRUNO DE HOGUES/GETTY IMAGES ©; (BELOW) JOE KLEMENTOVICH/GETTY IMAGES ©

Online promotional deals provide real value.

Eating & Drinking

Lolos Barbecue $

(Blvd de Grand Case; mains €5-15; lunch & dinner) The big draw here for penny-pinchers is the collection of *lolos* between the main drag and ocean. These Creole barbecue shacks sit clustered around wooden picnic tables. Five unique establishments comprise this steamy jungle of smoking grills. Try succulent ribs, cod fritters, grilled fish or chicken legs, with a side of rice and peas. An iconic St-Martin experience.

Sunset Beach Café Caribbean $$

(0590-29-43-90; Grand Case Beach Club, Route de Petite Plage; mains lunch €10-18, dinner €16-29; breakfast, lunch & dinner) In a town that abounds with ocean views, this hotel restaurant, which literally hangs over the glittering water, takes first prize. Whether for a leisurely lunch or dinner on the breezy terrace, well-executed classics such as grilled sea bream and beef fillet share the menu with salads, juicy burgers and sandwiches.

Le Pressoir French $$$

(0590-87-76-62; www.lepressoir-sxm.com; Blvd de Grand Case; mains €25-35; dinner Mon-Sat) Set in a beautiful bright yellow house with charming clapboard shutters – one of the last remaining traditional Creole houses – this fantastic restaurant gets loads of well-deserved praise for its warm atmosphere and scrumptious dishes. Prices are steep, but this is the place to splurge.

L'Estaminet French $$$

(0590-29-00-25; 139 Blvd de Grand Case; mains €23-30; dinner Tue-Sun) Take your taste buds on a gustatory adventure through the twisted mind of the owner and chef. The kitchen presents an artful combination of old and new French cuisine, the ultrafresh products' natural

Îlet Pinel

This little islet just 1km from French Cul-de-Sac is a great spot to spend a sun-soaked afternoon. Totally undeveloped (it's protected by the national forest system), Pinel is the domain of day-trippers, who are deposited on the island's calm west-facing beach, where there's good swimming, snorkeling and three drink-wielding restaurants.

It's easy to get to Pinel – simply go to the dock at the road's end in French Cul-de-Sac, where you can catch a small boat that departs roughly every 30 minutes. The five-minute ride costs €5 round-trip and runs 10am to 5pm.

flavors enhanced by imaginative seasoning and beautiful presentation. If the menu features the Estaminet chocolate variation, do yourself a favor and indulge.

ANSE MARCEL & PETITE CAYES

Magical Anse Marcel is first glimpsed from high up in the mountains as you gently descend into this hidden bay. This quiet port is the stomping ground for wealthier vacationers, as some of St-Martin/Sint Maarten's fancier properties are located here. One of the island's top hidden beaches, Petites Cayes is accessible via a small trail at the north end of Anse Marcel. Follow the path along the rugged headland – it's a bit of a walk, but definitely worth it.

ORIENT BAY (LA BAIE ORIENTALE)

Although this most perfect of beaches has become something of a tourist settlement, it still retains a breezy Caribbean atmosphere. Snorkel-friendly reefs protect 5.5km of inviting white-sand beach. Restaurants, bars, water sports and resorts all call Orient Bay home.

Activities

Wind Adventures Water Sports
(**☎0590-29-41-57; www.wind-adventures.com; Orient Beach**) This water-sports center offers a wide range of activities, including windsurfing, kitesurfing, SUP boarding, kayaking and sailing.

Sleeping

L'Hoste Hotel Hotel **$$$**
(**☎0590-87-42-08; www.hostehotel.com; Parc de La Baie Orientale; d incl breakfast €210-340;**) Set slightly away from the sand, L'Hoste is the best bang for your buck near the booming Orient Beach. There are signs of wear and tear in the rooms but they get the job done, and in this location for this price, you won't hear anyone complaining. There's a three-night minimum stay.

La Plantation Hotel **$$$**
(**☎0590-29-58-00; www.la-plantation.com; Orient Bay; d incl breakfast €215-375;**) Although it's a five-minute walk away from the beach, this colonial-style hotel is one of the best deals at Orient Bay, with a clutch of trim, spacious and well-appointed Creole-style villas that are scattered on a landscaped slope. There's on on-site restaurant.

Eating & Drinking

Kakao Beach Bar & Restaurant International **$$**
(**☎0590-87-43-26; www.kakaobeach.com; Orient Bay; mains €13-20; 9am-4pm**) Complete a perfect morning in beach paradise with a tropical cocktail and lunch at this bustling venture. With its wooden decking terrace and first-class views of the turquoise surf, dining really does not get better than this. Cuisine is lots of salads, pasta and grills.

Waikiki Beach International **$$$**
(**☎0590-87-43-19; www.waikikibeachsxm.com; Orient Bay; mains €16-35; 9am-5pm**) This furiously fashionable restaurant awash with teak fittings is right on the beach. The point here is to see and be seen, and

in high season getting a table can be a titanic struggle. It specializes in meat dishes, grilled fish and sushi, all beautifully presented. Don't miss the signature Sunday night parties that stretch out across the sand.

OYSTER POND

The Dutch–French border slices straight across Oyster Pond, which actually isn't a pond at all but a stunning sunken bay nestled between two jagged hills. Most of the area's accommodations fall on the French side, while the Dutch half features condos and vacation rentals.

Sleeping & Eating

Les Balcons d'Oyster Pond Cottages **$$**

(0590-29-43-39; www.lesbalcons.com; 15 Ave du Lagon; bungalow €120-140;) Run by Carine and David, a lovely French couple, this place is one of the best deals on the island. Sitting on the French side, this charming collection of villas gently spreads across a scrubby hill, and offers excellent views of the bay and quiet marina below. Each cottage has a completely different decor. Another plus is the pool.

Quai Ouest French **$$**

(0690-73-76-01; Marina; mains €10-18; lunch Tue-Sat, dinner Mon-Sat) With a prime spot on the Oyster Pond waterfront, this eatery is known for its delectable French fare, grilled meats and tartare, along with plenty of daily specials. The roasted Camembert and duck breast in mushroom sauce will linger long on the palate. Come early for a good table at sunset.

ST-BARTHÉLEMY

POP 8900

This is it, the one. Picture this: dramatic sky-scraping mountains, isolated stretches of powder-soft sand, windswept cliffs, scrubby green hills and turquoise bays dotted with myriad sailboats. With such a dreamlike setting, St-Barth is, unsurprisingly, a destination of choice for the rich, famous and beautiful, who enjoy the sublime laid-back tempo and opulent hotels. But does St-Barth have anything to offer those of us who haven't won an Oscar? You bet. All beaches are easily accessible, public and free. And when working on your tan ceases to do it for you, you can indulge in fine dining, shopping, kitesurfing, sailing, diving and snorkeling. And it doesn't have to cost a fortune to stay here: try to visit the island off season, and you'll get fantastic deals. All in all, St-Barth is an expensive destination, but it's sure to be a highlight in your Caribbean sojourn.

Shell Beach (p238), Gustavia

Gustavia

POP 1500

About 50 years ago, it was a windswept fishing village; today this stunning port town is nothing short of majestic. Although relatively small when compared to other capitals in the Caribbean, Gustavia has plenty of places to 'see and be seen,' with myriad high-end boutiques, upmarket restaurants and a couple of historical sights.

 Beaches

Shell Beach Beach

A short stroll from the harbor, Shell Beach is an ideal Caribbean strand and is great for swimmers. As its name suggests, it's awash with seashells. Come late afternoon – as the sun-low sky deepens to orange, this beach might be just heaven. There's a beach restaurant.

 Sights

There aren't loads of sights on St-Barth, but it's worth stopping by the Office Territorial du Tourisme to grab its small pamphlet, which offers a nuanced caption to some of the older structures in Gusta-

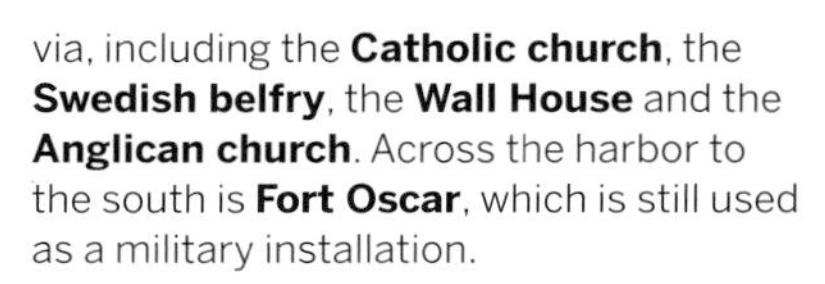

via, including the **Catholic church**, the **Swedish belfry**, the **Wall House** and the **Anglican church**. Across the harbor to the south is **Fort Oscar**, which is still used as a military installation.

Fort Gustave Ruin

The site of this ruined fort has a couple of cannons and a slightly bottle-shaped lighthouse, but most people come for the fine view of Gustavia and the harbor. A plaque points out local sights and landmarks.

 Activities

There are about 20 dive sites around St-Barth.

Saint-Barth Plongée Diving, Snorkeling

(☎0690-41-96-66; www.st-barth-plongee.com; Quai de la Collectivité) Reputable outfit run by qualified instructors offers trips that feel personalized due to a 10-person maximum. It charges €80 for an introductory dive and €70 for a single dive. Snorkeling trips (€40) are also on offer. These folks have decades of experience in St-Barth waters.

Gustavia Harbor

RICHARD CUMMINS/GETTY IMAGES ©

Sleeping

Sunset Hotel
Hotel $

(☎0590-27-77-21; www.st-barths.com/sunset-hotel; Rue de la République; s €115-138, d €138-158; ❄📶) If you're looking to save and be close to the action, this jolly venture with a handy location is a bonanza. It shelters 10 impeccable rooms with all mod cons; the pricier ones have a stunning view of the harbor and sunset but also get a bit of street noise. Skip breakfast. Book well in advance.

Eating & Drinking

Le Select
Fast Food $

(☎0590-27-86-87; cnr Rue de la France & Rue du Général de Gaulle; mains €5-16; ⊙lunch & dinner Mon-Sat) Located in the heart of Gustavia, Le Select is almost a rite of passage in St-Barth. It completely lacks glamor but has charm to spare and a gregarious atmosphere. A great budget bite, it dishes up burgers (go for the signature Marius special!) and simple meals at blessedly low prices. The bar here is a lively meet-and-greet zone.

La Cantina
International $

(☎0590-27-55-66; Rue du Bord de Mer; mains €12-16; ⊙breakfast, lunch & dinner) On the waterfront, this casual joint is no place to escape the crowds, but the food is tasty and great value. Choose from a fine selection of burgers, salads and other simple dishes. It's also a supremely chill place to sip a tropical potion and nibble on tapas while ogling yachts you wished you owned.

L'Isoletta
Italian $$

(☎0590-52-02-02; Rue du Roi Oscar II; mains €12-40; ⊙lunch & dinner) This upscale deli serves up an excellent assortment of Italian classics – pizzas and paninis are mainstays but the highlights are foccaccias and salads that are so irresistible that we would (and, on at least one occasion, did) cross the island just to try one. It's all watched over by a dynamic staff, and there's an agreeable terrace. Takeaway is available.

The Other Side of St-Barth

Pull back the island's satin curtains and link up with Hélène Bernier, whose family has called St-Barth home for 10 generations. Hélène runs **Easytime** (☎0690-63-46-09; www.stbartheasytime.com; Gustavia), a small tour operator that specializes in showing visitors the real faces of the island. During a **half-day tour** you'll uncover hidden viewpoints, local snack shops and colorful artists' studios. Check the website for details.

Eddy's
Fusion $$

(☎0590-27-54-17; Rue du Samuel Fahlberg; mains €19-25; ⊙dinner Mon-Sat) This handsome restaurant with an exotic feel – think tropical plants and wooden furniture – is a perennial favorite with locals and tourists in the know. The menu is among the most imaginative on the island and blends French, Caribbean and Asian influences. If only it had harbor views, life would be perfect.

Pipiri Palace
International $$

(☎0590-27-53-20; Rue du Général de Gaulle; mains €17-35; ⊙lunch & dinner Mon-Sat) A longstanding institution, Pipiri Palace distinguishes itself with its atmospheric decor – think a large Creole cottage pillowed in luxuriant greenery. Lunches are relatively simple affairs, with an emphasis on fresh meal-size salads, simple grills and daily specials. The dinner menu is more artful. Choose from a table inside or out on the enticing veranda.

Dõ Brazil
International $$$

(☎0590-29-06-66; www.dobrazil.com; Shell Beach; mains €24-45; ⊙lunch & dinner, bar 10am-7pm) This trendy bar and restaurant enjoys a wonderfully scenic beachfront setting. Tasty international dishes (think mahi mahi on a kebab, flavorful chicken in honey sauce or juicy burgers), jungle-chic decor and regular fits of live music will help you quickly forget that the menu is at times overpriced. Views face west and south, ensuring glorious sunset watching.

Shopping

Gustavia is a duty-free port and features the most exclusive labels in the world: Hermes, Bulgari, Rolex etc. But there is also a slew of small, locally owned boutiques and labels, such as Made in Saint-Barth and Ligne Saint-Barth, which sells name-branded sweatshirts, cloth bags and cosmetics.

Information

You'll find banks with ATMs in the center.

Comité Territorial du Tourisme (0590-27-87-27; www.saintbarth-tourisme.com; Quai Général de Gaulle; 8:30am-6pm Mon-Fri, 8:30am-noon Sat) Will help with accommodations, restaurant recommendations, island tours and activities. Has a map for a self-guided Gustavia walking tour.

Flamands

A small village on the northwestern side of the island, Flamands retains a pleasant rural character. The village stretches along a curving bay whose long, broad white-sand beach and clear waters are very popular with beachgoers. The catch? There's no shade. There's easy beach access with streetside parking at the westernmost end of Anse des Flamands.

Sleeping & Eating

Auberge de la Petite Anse Bungalow **$$**

(0590-27-64-89; www.auberge-petite-anse.com; Anse des Flamands; cottages s/d €160/210;) As the snaking stone road starts to peter out at the far end of Flamands, little Auberge de la Petite Anse will emerge. Its clump of semidetached bungalows squats on a small ledge over the cerulean waters many feet below (views!). Fancy a dip? Head to Anse Flamands beach, a mere five-minute walk away. Brilliant value, especially in low season.

La Langouste Seafood **$$**

(0590-27-63-61; Hôtel Baie des Anges; mains €15-29; lunch & dinner) In the Hôtel Baie des Anges, this Flamands icon is famous for one thing and one thing only: fresh *langouste* (lobster), best enjoyed on the oh-so-cute veranda overlooking the pool and the sea. Knock it down with a well-chosen French wine, and you'll be in heaven.

Anse de Colombier

This is the tropical paradise we've been daydreaming about all winter: a dazzling secluded white-sand beach that's fronted by turquoise waters and backed by undulating hills. It's reached by boat or via a scenic 20-minute walk that begins at the end of the road in La Petite Anse, just beyond Flamands. The sandy bay is ideal for swimming, and there's excellent snorkeling on the north side.

St-Jean

A number of hotels and restaurants line the main stretch of road in this tourist-heavy village, making parking difficult. Once you're off the road, the beach is delightful, the hotels comfortable and the dining eclectic, ranging from delis to tragically hip, techno-infused attitude factories. As the beach is situated at the end of St-Barth airport's runway, it's a great spot to watch the hair-raising takeoffs and landings.

Activities

Carib Waterplay Water Sports

(0690-61-80-81; www.caribewaterplay.net; St-Jean) This small outfit on the beach rents out kayaks, SUP boards (€20 per hour) and snorkeling gear (€10 per hour).

Sleeping & Eating

Hotel Le Village St Barth Hotel **$$**

(0590-27-61-39; www.villagestjeanhotel.com; St-Jean; d incl breakfast €280-550;) Comfort, charm and atmosphere: this place has it all. Accommodations vary from standard hotel rooms to deluxe cottages with kitchenettes and patios, ensuring good value on any budget – for St-Barth, that is. The dazzling infinity pool has mesmerizing ocean views. It's a five-minute walk uphill from the beach.

Eden Rock Luxury Hotel **$$$**

(**☎0590-29-79-99; www.edenrockhotel.com; St-Jean; cottage €750, ste €1300-2700; ❄ 📶**) St-Barth's first hotel stretches out and over a rocky promontory down to the white-coral St-Jean beach below. Each cottage is luxuriously appointed and enjoys an unbeatable view. There are also eight suites opening onto the beach. Amenities include two restaurants – the beachfront Sand Bar and the swooningly romantic On The Rocks – and a bar. What's missing? A spa.

Lorient

Lorient, the site of St-Barth's first French settlement (1648), is a small village fronted by a lovely white-sand beach. The town has a charming collection of old stone structures, including a small Caribbean-style convent and one of the island's three Catholic churches.

Sleeping

Les Mouettes Bungalow **$**

(**☎0590-27-77-91; www.lesmouetteshotel.com; bungalow €165-255; ❄ 📶**) For budget-conscious beach lovers, it's hard to imagine a more appealing spot. Opening right onto Lorient's flaxen sands, this retreat is cooled by trade winds and has a laid-back atmosphere. The seven bungalows are more utilitarian than charming and have sparkling bathrooms and full kitchenettes. One weak point: some bungalows are a bit close to the main road.

Grand Cul-de-Sac & Pointe Milou

Beautiful Grand Cul-de-Sac yawns across a large horseshoe-like bay, and has a sandy beach with good conditions for water sports. Fronting the open cove are several hotels and restaurants.

This is the island's main windsurfing center with a large protected cove that's ideal for beginners, and some nice wave action beyond the reef for those who are more advanced.

St-Barth and the Eden Rock from above

NATASHA SIOSS/GETTY IMAGES ©

Activities

Ouanalao Dive Diving, Water Sports

(**☎0590-27-61-37, 0690-63-74-34; www.ouanalaodive.com; Grand Cul-de-Sac)** Right on the beach, this professional outfit caters just as well to beginners as it does to advanced divers. Two-tank/introductory dives cost €140/85. There are special rates for multiday diving. It also rents out snorkeling gear (€15), SUP boards and canoes.

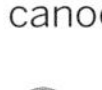

Sleeping & Eating

Christopher Hotel Hotel $$$

(**☎0590-27-63-63; www.hotelchristopher.com; Pointe Milou; d incl breakfast from €520;** ❄ 📶 🏊) The Christopher is back with a vengeance. After a serious makeover in 2012, it now ranks as one of the swankiest options on the island, with 42 rooms and suites. It incorporates two restaurants, a small spa and a bar. Note: there's no beach but you can cool off in the huge, gleaming pool. There's a three-night minimum stay.

Le Sereno Luxury Hotel $$$

(**☎0590-29-83-00; www.lesereno.com; Grand Cul-de-Sac; d from €730;** ❄ 📶 🏊) On a lovely stretch of beach, this classy boutique hotel with cutting-edge modern decor is one of our favorite upmarket places on the island. Pass through the entryway before uncovering a mesmerizing decked pool and cache of top-notch amenities, including a well-respected restaurant. Two quibbles, though: not all rooms have sea views, and the spa is modest.

Hotel Guanahani & Spa Luxury Hotel $$$

(**☎0590-52-90-00; www.leguanahani.com; Grand Cul-de-Sac; ste from €850;** ❄ 📶 🏊) The ultimate retreat and, with 67 renovated rooms, the island's largest hotel, this stunning resort is a hidden village of splendid bungalows flung across jungly grounds. It features a host of amenities, including two swimming pools, a spa, three restaurants, tennis courts, a kids club and a water-sports center. The icing on the cake: two beaches, both with different orientations.

O'Corail International $

(**☎0590-29-33-27; Grand Cul-de-Sac; mains €13-24; ⊙breakfast & lunch Tue-Sun;** 📶) Taste the salt of the sea in the breeze blowing through this sassy beachfront restaurant's terrace dining area and in the smacking-fresh fish dishes served here. The menu also features burgers, grilled meats and daily specials. The service is quite slow when it's crowded, but you'll be too busy watching the kitesurfers frolicking in the waves to care.

Le Ti St Barth French $$$

(**☎0590-27-97-71; www.letistbarth.com; Pointe Milou; mains €32-45; ⊙dinner Mon-**

Musée Schoelcher (p244), Pointe-à-Pitre

Sat) Like an evening in Baz Luhrmann's *Moulin Rouge*, Le Ti St Barth is a sumptuous jumble of wrought-iron chandeliers and gushing velvet drapes. The menu features a mix of upscale barbecue options, and in the late evening a local DJ swings by to give the place a li'l edge. It's located between Lorient and Marigot.

Anse de Gouverneur

Anse de Gouverneur is a gorgeous, sandy beach lining a U-shaped bay that's embraced by high cliffs at both ends. It's one of the broadest and most secluded spots in the region, and it's splendid for sunbathing and picnics. The lack of visitors – even in high season – means you'll often see sunbathers in their birthday suits.

Anse de Grande Saline

A long, lovely beach, broad and secluded, Anse de Grande Saline is the most photogenic of all St-Barth's beaches. This virgin swath of flaxen sand is excellent for working on your tan and frolicking in the crashing surf, but note that there's no shade. Anse de Grande Saline is also a favorite spot for nudists and gay visitors.

Sleeping & Eating

Fleur de Lune B&B **$**

(**0590-27-70-57, 0690-56-59-59; www.saintbarthgitefleurdelune.com; Anse de Grande Saline; d incl breakfast €140-250;**) A short amble from the beach, this B&B is the epitome of a refined cocoon, reveling quietly in minimalist lines, soothing color accents and well-thought-out decorative touches. Evening meals – available on request – are a great way to meet other guests. It's worth noting that off-season rates include use of a car – bargain! There's a two-night minimum stay.

Salines Garden Cottages Guesthouse **$**

(**0590-51-04-44; www.salinesgarden.com; Grande Saline; d incl breakfast €160-210;**) Salines Garden is one of the best deals on the island. Nestled slightly inland on the Grande Saline's parched terrain, five semidetached cottages huddle around a small plunge pool shaded by thick stalks of bamboo. Each unit is styled with knickknacks and drapery from a far-flung destination. The French owner, Jean-Phillipe, creates an inviting and friendly ambience. Minimum three nights.

Le Grain de Sel Creole **$**

(**0590-52-46-05; Anse de Grande Saline; mains €14-28; lunch & dinner)** Bedecked with stone pillars and hidden behind thirsty desert shrubs, Le Grain de Sel is a fantastic spot to savor traditional French and Creole meals before hitting the powdery sand for the day. The chef prepares a colorful assortment of palate pleasers, such as homemade burgers, conch fricassée and delicious lychee-mango ice cream.

GUADELOUPE

POP 405,500

Guadeloupe is a fascinating archipelago of islands, with each island offering travelers something different while retaining its rich Franco-Caribbean culture and identity. Guadeloupe's two main islands look like the wings of a butterfly and are joined together by a mangrove swamp. Grande-Terre, the eastern of the two islands, has a string of beach towns that offer visitors marvelous stretches of sand to laze on and plenty of activities, while mountainous Basse-Terre, the western of the two, is home to the wonderful Guadeloupe National Park, which is crowned by the spectacular La Soufrière volcano.

South of the 'mainland' of Guadeloupe are a number of small islands that give a taste of Guadeloupe's yesteryear.

Grande-Terre

The southern coast of Grande-Terre, with its reef-protected waters, is Guadeloupe's main resort area. The eastern side of the island is largely open to the Atlantic, with crashing surf, and in comparison with the southern coast is barely touched by tourism. Northern Grande-Terre doesn't have much in the way of accommodations but it's probably the best place to spend a day driving around – sea cliffs on one side and swaying fields of sugarcane on the other. Pointe-à-Pitre, the island's biggest city, is in the southeastern corner.

POINTE-À-PITRE

POP 17,300

From the outskirts, Pointe-à-Pitre looks pretty uninviting – a concrete jungle of high-rises and sprawling traffic. Venture into the center, though, and you'll find a much more attractive old town with peeling colonial architecture and palm-fringed streets. The town hub is Place de la Victoire, an open space punctuated with tall royal palms.

Sights

Musée St-John Perse Museum
(**☎0590-90-01-92; 9 Rue de Nozières; adult/child €2.50/1.50; ⏰9am-5pm Mon-Fri, 8:30am-12:30pm Sat**) This three-level municipal museum occupies an attractive 19th-century colonial building and is dedicated to the renowned poet and Nobel laureate Alexis Leger (1887–1975), better known as St-John Perse. The house offers a glimpse of a period Creole home and displays on Perse's life and work.

Musée Schoelcher Museum
(**☎0590-82-08-04; 24 Rue Peynier; adult/under 18yr €2/1; ⏰9am-5pm Mon-Fri**) Occupying an interesting period building, this museum is dedicated to abolitionist Victor Schoelcher. The main exhibits in the museum are art pieces that belonged to Schoelcher, and artifacts relating to slavery.

Festivals & Events

Carnival Carnival
Starts warming up in January with roving groups of steel-band musicians and dancers, but officially runs between the traditional weeklong Mardi Gras period, which ends on Ash Wednesday (46 days before Easter).

Sleeping

Gwada Hostel Hostel $
(**☎0590-55-67-86, 0690-11-89-74; www.e-gwada.net; 636 Rue de la Chapelle, Mare Gaillard; campsite s/d €15/26, dm €27, s/d with shared bathroom €35/64; P 📶 🏊**) Finding its groove at

Fishing, Grand-Terre (p243)

FRILET PATRICK/HEMIS.FR/GETTY IMAGES ©

Pointe-à-Pitre

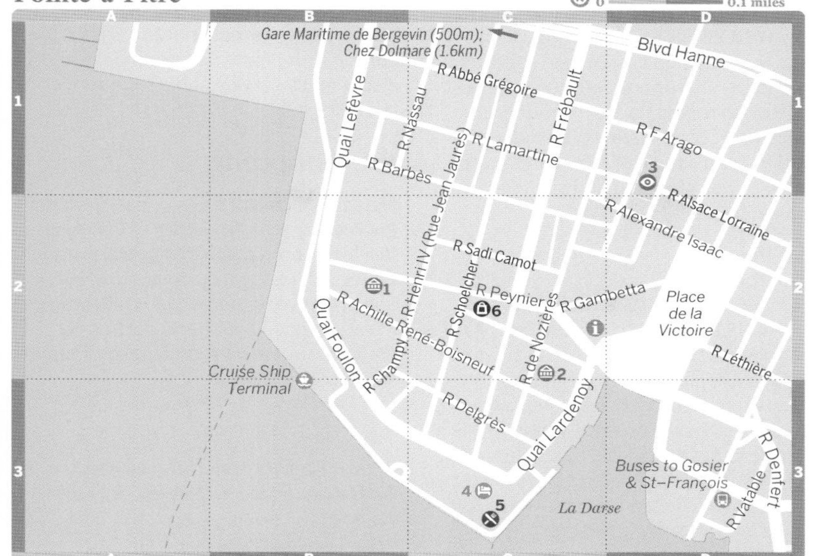

the budget-friendly side of Grande-Terre's overpriced accommodations spectrum, this hostel is a great place to call home during your Guadeloupean foray. Run by the informative and well-traveled Jean, it harbors several rooms, a dorm and even a tiny campground. Meals are available. It's in a residential area in Mare Gaillard, about 13km east of Pointe-à-Pitre.

La Case En Mer B&B **$$**

(**☎0590-26-45-13; www.im-caraibes.com/les-ilets; Îlet Boissard; d incl breakfast €85-100;** ❄📶) In search of an escape? This lovely B&B on a quiet islet, a two-minute boat ride from the shore, offers guests the chance to unplug in two cocoon-like rooms that are set amid beautifully landscaped gardens, with the added bonus of a Jacuzzi. Dinner costs €25, and the affable owners speak good English. There's a three-night minimum.

Hôtel Saint-John Perse Hotel **$$**

(**☎0590-82-51-57; www.saint-john-perse.com; s/d incl breakfast €85/100;** ❄📶) This midrange option is totally unexciting, but it's centrally located and extremely convenient if you're catching an early-morning boat. It has 44 rooms with shared balconies overlooking the harbor. There is free luggage storage for guests who want to travel light to the outlying islands.

Pointe-à-Pitre

Sights

1 Musée Schoelcher B2
2 Musée St-John Perse C2
3 Palais de Justice D1

Sleeping

4 Hôtel Saint-John Perse C3

Eating

5 La Canne à Sucre C3

Shopping

6 Marché Couvert C2

Eating & Drinking

Pointe-à-Pitre's middle class seems to spontaneously vanish from the city at dusk – they're all usually to be found at the Marina de Bas-du-Fort, a mile or so to the west of town. Here a number of lively restaurants and drinking holes surround a harbor full of sailboats and yachts.

Chez Dolmare
Seafood $$

(☎0590-91-21-32; Port de Pêche de Lauricisque; mains €11-15; ⏰lunch Mon-Sat) You'll find the best seafood in town here, and it's no wonder – this unpretentious locale is at the small fishing harbor of Lauricisque, northwest of the center. The menu is limited to a couple of daily specials, but they're well prepared and sizzling-hot value. Takeaway is available.

Le Pirate Caribéen
Seafood $$

(☎0590-90-73-00; Marina de Bas-du-Fort; mains €15-25, menus €18-30; ⏰8-1am; 📶) This marina institution is housed in an atmospheric all-wood building that's slightly set back from the waterfront. It has served up endless plates of *ouassous* (freshwater crayfish), salads, steak, pasta and fresh fish for 15 years. It's also a good place to hang out and just enjoy the fashionable buzz with a fresh beer in hand.

La Canne à Sucre
International $$$

(☎0590-90-38-83; www.lacanneasucre.com; 1 Quai Foulon; mains €17-26; ⏰lunch Mon-Sat, dinner Tue-Sat) The only stylish restaurant in town, La Canne à Sucre gives you the best views over Pointe-à-Pitre's busy harbor from its terraced seating. The excellent food blends international and French cuisine with Creole flavors, and there's also friendly service and a sumptuous dessert list.

Shopping

Marché Couvert
Market

(cnr Rues Peynier & Schoelcher; ⏰6am-4pm Mon-Sat) A good place to buy island handicrafts, including straw dolls, straw hats and primitive African-style woodcarvings. It's also a good spot to pick up locally grown coffee and a wide array of fragrant spices.

Information

Change Caraïbes (www.changecaraibes.com; 21 Rue Frebault; ⏰8am-4:45pm Mon-Fri) A money exchange.

Tourist Office (☎0590-82-09-30; www.lesilesdeguadeloupe.com; 5 Sq de la Banque; ⏰8am-5pm Mon-Fri, to noon Sat) The friendly staff speak good English and there's a lot of information about activities, walking and hotels to be had here.

Petite Terre islands, a boat trip from St-François (right)

GARDEL BERTRAND/HEMIS.FR/GETTY IMAGES ©

Getting There & Away

Boat

All ferries leave from the Gare Maritime de Bergevin, 1km northwest of Hôtel Saint-John Perse.

Bus

Buses to places in Basse-Terre leave from the northwest side of town near the Gare Maritime de Bergevin. Buses to Gosier, Ste-Anne and St-François leave from Rue Dubouchage at the east side of the harbor in Pointe-à-Pitre.

ST-FRANÇOIS

POP 14,300

St-François is a town with two distinct identities. The west side of town is a sleepy provincial backwater that's quite spread out, while the east side feels a lot like the small upscale marina that it is. The center of the action is the deep U-shaped harbor, which is lined with a handful of restaurants, hotels, boutiques and marina facilities. Just north of the marina there's a golf course.

For active types, there's a wide range of water sports on offer, from surfing and scuba diving to kitesurfing and snorkeling.

St-François is also a major jumping-off point for trips to Guadeloupe's smaller islands.

Beaches

Plage des Raisins Clairs Beach

On the western outskirts of town, Plage des Raisins Clairs is not the most stunning beach on Grande-Terre but it's safe for swimming. There's a gradual slope, no drop-off, a long stretch of relatively shallow water and plenty of shade.

Activities

Paradoxe Croisières Boat Trips

(**☎0590-88-41-73; Marina de St-François; adult/under 12yr €80/60**) Runs day trips to the small islands of Petite Terre for a spot of iguana-watching, beach lounging, lunch and snorkeling. Boats leave at 8am and return to St-François at 5:30pm.

Sleeping

Sunset Surf Camp Guesthouse $$

(**☎0590-21-51-10, 0690-41-66-69; www.sunsetsurfcamp.com; Route Touristique; s €40-70, d €76; P @ ☎ ≋**) Consistently rated highly by travelers, this efficiently run oasis about 2km west from the center sets the standard – well-organised rooms (but no air-con), a festive atmosphere, a pool, a tropical garden, enticing communal areas *and* charming owners. Reasonable rates, free bikes, good breakfasts (€10) and scrumptious dinners (twice weekly; €25) clinch the deal. Surfing lessons available.

La Maison Calebasse B&B $$$

(**☎0690-34-07-77; www.lamaisoncalebasse.com; Ste Madeleine; d incl breakfast €179; P ❄ ☎ ≋**) Tricky to find, but well worth the search, this gleaming villa is nestled amid sugarcane fields about 2.5km north of St-François. Brigitte, your affable host, has applied all her flair to the decor; choose from the gîtes (rented by the week) and an exceptionally bright room with a handsomely designed bathroom. Dinner is €23. A bijou hideaway.

Hôtel Amaudo Hotel $$$

(**☎0590-88-87-00; www.amaudo.fr; Anse à la Barque; d €145-155; ❄ ☎ ≋**) This special little place is in the hamlet of Anse à la Barque, a short distance to the west of St-François itself. It's a beautiful spot, with all of the communal areas attractively done in a colonial style and all 10 rooms having fantastic sea views and private outdoor areas. No beach, but the lovely pool offers adequate compensation.

Eating

Le Mabouya Dans La Bouteille Fusion $$$

(**☎0590-21-31-14; www.lemabouya.fr; 17 Salines Est; mains €22-29; ⏱dinner Wed-Mon**) Don't make any other plans for the evening – this romantic restaurant is one to linger at. The all-wood surrounds boast a kind of rustic charm. Chefs fuse French, Creole and other 'exotic' flavors into healthful dishes that would delight the *Yoga Journal* crowd. The caramelized lamb with rosemary is a standout, and creative desserts will satisfy the most discriminating foodies.

Iguane Café French $$$
(0590-88-61-37; www.iguane-cafe.com; Chemin rural La Coulée; mains €25-31, menus €45-82; lunch Sun, dinner Wed-Mon) For a true culinary experience, Iguane Café is hard to beat. On the road out of St-François toward Pointe des Châteaux you'll find what is probably Guadeloupe's finest restaurant. The food ranges from complicated seafood dishes to delectable meats. If you've got a sweet tooth, try the cocoa sorbet. Deadly.

Les Frères de la Côte Seafood $$$
(0590-88-59-43; 1 Rue de la Liberté; mains €19-24, lunch menu €16, menus €32-36; lunch Sat-Tue & Thu, dinner daily) Fish landed at the dock down the road are turned into works of simple culinary art in this respectable eatery. The *escalope de poisson au foie gras* (fish cutlet with foie gras) packs a punch, while the boxfish salad with citrus fruits is for connoisseurs. For meat-cravers, there are several carnivorous options.

POINTE DES CHÂTEAUX

Just a 20-minute drive from St-François is windswept Pointe des Châteaux, the easternmost point of Grande-Terre. This peninsula, which resembles a giant geographical finger poked toward La Désirade, stands out from the rest of Guadeloupe. The landscape is stark, with limestone cliffs pounded by crashing waves and eye-popping views of the jagged nearshore islets and the island of La Désirade. A walk up a sandy path to the large cross takes about 10 minutes and is a good place to look back at Guadeloupe. And for sunbathers, **Plage des Salines** beckons. Protected by a reef, this sweeping ribbon of white sand with no facilities (and no shade) offers calm waters.

NORTHERN GRANDE-TERRE

Once you've left St-François, the real wilderness of Grande-Terre begins to unfold, and a sense of escapism becomes tangible. The northern half of Grande-Terre is a rural area of grazing cattle and cane fields; the roads are gently winding but easy to drive. Adjust your camera setting to 'panoramic' and shoot spectacular natural wonders and a smattering of delightful beaches.

Beaches

Anse Laborde Beach
Make a beeline for this oft-overlooked beach that lies about 1.5km north of Anse-Bertrand. Strong riptides make it dangerous for swimming, but the peace you find sitting here under a tree may be as good as it gets on northern Grande-Terre.

Anse Souffleur Beach
(Port-Louis) This long, gently arching beach on northern Grande-Terre is picture-postcard every-

Porte d'Enfer (right), Grand-Terre
DANITA DELIMONT/GETTY IMAGES ©

where you look. Here, the long pale-sand beach has lapis lazuli waters on one side and a fringe of palm trees on the other. You won't find a better place for sunbathing. The beach's charms are no secret, but it never feels crowded.

Sights

Porte d'Enfer Lake

The 'Port of Hell,' as it's called, is actually a long and narrow lagoon that could be mistaken for a river from the viewpoint further down the road. It's a great place to picnic, swim or snorkel, but bring your own gear. The water crashing at the mouth of the lagoon would be the gates of hell for anyone foolish enough to venture beyond the calm waters.

Pointe de la Grande Vigie Viewpoint

The island's northernmost point, Pointe de la Grande Vigie offers scenic views from its high sea cliffs. A rocky path – walkable in flip-flops but better in tennis shoes – makes a loop from the parking lot to the cliffs and has some fantastic views. On a clear day you can see Antigua to the north and Montserrat to the northwest, both about 75km away.

Sleeping & Eating

Domaine de la Grande Vigie Bungalow $$

(0590-22-14-74; www.domainedelagrandevigie.com; Pointe de la Grande Vigie; d €106;) First, the perks: a decked swimming pool with sweeping views of the ocean. Your money goes far with these well-equipped bungalows scattered amid a garden overflowing with blossoming tropical vegetation. They're amply sized and well spaced out. You're nowhere near the beach, but the pool compensates nicely. It's a short drive south of Pointe de la Grande Vigie.

Hostellerie des Châteaux Hotel $$

(0590-85-54-08; www.hostellerie-des-chateaux.com; Pointe des Châteaux; d incl breakfast €95-120;) Set on a spacious lawn inland from the road to Pointe des Châteaux, this is a wonderful place for escape there are just four rooms and four bungalows on the grounds giving total privacy in sublime surroundings. Note that it's not on the beach. The on-site restaurant is open to the public and has great views.

Local Knowledge

Name: Petian Accaries

OCCUPATION: DIVE INSTRUCTOR

RESIDENCE: LES SAINTES

1 WHAT'S THE BEST DIVE AREA IN THE FRENCH ANTILLES?

Les Saintes, without a doubt. Here you'll find the most diverse, pristine and colorful dive sites.

2 ARE THE FRENCH ANTILLES SUITABLE FOR NEWBIE DIVERS?

The French Antilles are a great place to learn to dive. There are plenty of sites for all levels of proficiency, including the fabulous Réserve Cousteau on Guadeloupe. You don't need to go deep to enjoy the underwater scenery, and the water is always warm.

3 WHAT'S THE NOT-TO-BE-MISSED DIVE SITE FOR EXPERIENCED DIVERS?

The Sec Pâté, which is a seamount in the channel between Les Saintes and Basse-Terre, is a memorable dive, with outstanding topography – it's an underwater volcano – and tonnes of reef species that can be easily approached.

4 ON LAND, WHAT'S YOUR FAVORITE PLACE TO RECHARGE THE BATTERIES?

I love Basse-Terre on Guadeloupe, because it remains a wild territory, with thick tropical forests, mysterious mountains and gushing waterfalls.

5 WHERE ARE THE BEST BEACHES?

Marie Galante offers lots of secluded beaches. I also have a soft spot for Grande Anse near Deshaies and Plage de Pompierre in Les Saintes.

Below: Iguana, Terre-de-Haut (p252); **Right:** Terre-de-Haut, Les Saintes (p252)
(RIGHT) SOBERKA RICHARD/HEMIS.FR/GETTY IMAGES ©; (BELOW) DANITA DELIMONT/GETTY IMAGES ©

Au Coin des Bons Amis Creole **$**
(Anse Laborde; mains €8-10; lunch) Right on Anse Laborde beach, this place raises the bar in beach-shack cuisine. You'll be surprised such good stuff can come from such an unprepossessing place. Excellent grilled freshwater prawns and tasty catch-of-the-day grilled fish are just some of the few specialties on offer. It's a great bang for your buck, and the cherry on top: lovely sea views.

Chez Coco Creole **$$**
(0690-31-97-74; Porte d'Enfer; mains €12-20; lunch) A seductive setting complete with a breezy wooden terrace is the draw at this delightful joint close to the lagoon at Porte d'Enfer. The menu abounds in local flavor, everything from grilled fish to skewered conch. Coconut sorbet for dessert is a must.

Basse-Terre

Basse-Terre is Guadeloupe's trump card. The bigger of the two main islands (and yes, they are separate entities despite being joined by a road), it's also by far the more dramatic, boasting soaring peaks and thick rainforest within the huge Parc National de la Guadeloupe as well as some excellent beaches and one of the best dive sites in the Caribbean around Pigeon Island. The northwestern corner of Basse-Terre is the most scenic. Starting from the west side of Route de la Traversée, most of the west coast is rocky and many of the drives snake along the tops of towering sea cliffs. They are interspersed with attractive swimming beaches. Whatever you do in Guadeloupe, do not miss Basse-Terre.

ROUTE DE LA TRAVERSÉE

The road that heads across the center of the island, the Route de la Traversée (D23), slices through the Parc National

de la Guadeloupe, a 17,300-hectare forest reserve that occupies the interior of Basse-Terre. It's a lovely mountain drive that passes fern-covered hillsides, thick bamboo stands and enormous mahogany and gum trees.

Don't miss the **Cascade aux Écrevisses** **(Rte de la Traversée)**, an idyllic little jungle waterfall that drops into a broad pool. From the parking area the waterfall is just a three-minute walk on a paved trail. The roadside pull-off is clearly marked on the D23.

At **Maison de la Forêt** **(Rte de la Traversée; 8:30am-1pm & 1:30-4:30pm Mon-Sat, 9am-1:15pm Sun)**, 2km further west, there's a staffed exhibit center with a few simple displays on the forest in French and pamphlets in English, including a basic map that shows the parking areas for trailheads and picnic areas. A map board and the beginning of an enjoyable 20-minute loop trail are at the back of the center. The Bras David trail takes an hour, and is an enjoyable if muddy way to get deeper into the jungle.

DESHAIES

POP 4400

This charmingly sleepy spot has just the right blend of traditional fishing village and good selection of eating and drinking options to keep visitors happy. There's a sweet little beach framed by green hills all around, but as Deshaies is a working fishing port, the best beach for swimming and sunbathing is at nearby Grande Anse.

Thanks to its sheltered bay, the village is a popular stop with yachters and sailors and has an international feeling.

Beaches

Grande Anse Beach

This superb golden-sand beach with no hotel development in sight is just 2km north of Deshaies. This is one of Basse-Terre's longest and prettiest stretches of sand. The entire place is no secret though, and you won't be alone, but it's easy to escape the crowds by walking down the bay. There are a number of beachside restaurants.

Detour: Les Saintes

These tiny islands to the south of Basse-Terre are many people's highlight of Guadeloupe, as they allow visitors to enjoy a slice of the old Caribbean, far from the development and urban sprawl that has affected much of the region. These tiny charmers are a real secret – many day-trippers come over from Basse-Terre, but very few people spend any real time here exploring these gems. Don't miss your chance.

Lying 10km off Guadeloupe is Terre-de-Haut, the largest of the eight small islands that make up Les Saintes. The island's only village is Bourg des Saintes, which has plenty of great restaurants and excellent places to stay, including **LoBleu Hotel** (0590-92-40-00; www.lobleuhotel.com; Fond de Curé; s €114-135, d €122-145;) and **Les Petits Saints** (0590-99-50-99; www.petitssaints.com; La Savane; d incl breakfast €140-180;). There's no shortage of splendid beaches, including **Plage de Pompierre**, **Anse Crawen** and **Anse Rodrigue**. Diving is outstanding; one recommended dive shop is **Pisquettes Diving** (0590-99-88-80; www.pisquettes.fr; Bourg des Saintes).

There are multiple daily ferries to Terre-de-Haut from Trois-Rivières (on Basse-Terre) and Pointe-à-Pitre, and less frequently from St-François (on Grande-Terre); see p275.

Plage de Clugny Beach

Between Grande Anse and Ste-Rose, at the very tip of Basse-Terre, is this dazzling stretch of golden sand lapped by jade waters that just beg to be swum in. It has views toward a dramatic islet in the bay, and beyond that, to Montserrat. Bar one little terrace restaurant at the far end of the beach, Plage de Clugny is totally undeveloped. Be very careful as the water can be rough.

Sleeping

Tendacayou Ecolodge & Spa Boutique Hotel $$$

(0590-28-42-72; www.tendacayou.com; Matouba, Hauts de Deshaies; d incl breakfast €170-310;) Thumbs up, way up, for this bijou hideaway run with flair by a French architect and his wife. Located high above town, 11 bungalows are deployed on creatively landscaped grounds in a sea of spruce greenery. No expense has been spared in dousing guests in sassy swank – natural materials, a spa and a gourmet restaurant. English is spoken. Heaven.

Le Rayon Vert Hotel $$$

(0590-28-43-23; www.hotels-deshaies.com; La Coque Ferry; d incl breakfast €170-200;) Between Deshaies and Pointe-Noire, this sunset-friendly seducer has gone upmarket since a freshen-up a few years ago, but it has retained its reasonable prices and is a great place to enjoy a small-scale resort without breaking the bank. The 22 rooms exemplify functional simplicity and enjoy fabulous sea views. Amenities include a pool and a restaurant. Minimum four nights.

Domaine de la Pointe Batterie Luxury Hotel $$$

(0590-28-57-03; www.pointe-batterie.com; Chemin de la Batterie; studios/villas €159/249;) A terraced property just outside of Deshaies; every luxurious room here has a sea view and the villas each have a small private pool. The entire complex is set in beautiful gardens, and the on-site spa, one of the main attractions of the hotel, means that you can spend days here being pampered. There's a three-night minimum stay.

Eating & Drinking

Le Coin des Pêcheurs Creole, Seafood **$$**
(☎0590-28-47-75; Rue de la Vague Bleue; mains €14-20, menu €18; ⏲lunch & dinner Wed-Mon) This colorful beach restaurant has a great position overlooking the bay. With such breathtaking surroundings, many alfrescoholics would go back to this breezy veranda by the sea for the location alone; but the well-priced Creole-eclectic fare is delightful too, especially the *brochette de poisson* (skewered fish) and the conch fricassée. There's also a takeaway counter.

La Savane French, International **$$**
(☎0590-91-39-58; Blvd des Poissonniers; mains €18-23; ⏲lunch Sun, dinner Thu-Tue) Ignore the tacky gorilla sculpture at the entrance – this restaurant wins plaudits for its high-quality cuisine and divine location right on the seafront, with a terrace from which to drink it all in. Classic French food such as veal kidneys in mustard sauce and lamb fillet with rosemary anchors the menu. Wonderful desserts round out the offerings.

La Table du Poisson Rouge International **$$$**
(☎0590-28-42-72; www.tendacayou.com; Tendacayou Ecolodge & Spa, Matouba, Hauts de Deshaies; mains €19-27, dinner menu €30; ⏲lunch & dinner Wed-Sun) This elegant restaurant within the Tendacayou Ecolodge & Spa is an atmospheric place just perfect for that special meal. And you could lose yourself in the homemade *moelleux au chocolat* (chocolate cake) that arrives at the end of the meal. Judging by the tuna tataki in granadilla sauce, the beautifully presented mains are just as yummy though.

STE-ROSE

POP 19,800

Ste-Rose was once a simple little village, primarily involved with fishing and agriculture. While sugarcane is still an important crop in the area, Ste-Rose is increasingly becoming a tourist destination in its own right, not least because it's the main launching pad for boat excursions to Grand Cul-de-Sac Marin. This marine park is dotted with idyllic islets ringed by sandy beaches, mangrove swamps and healthy reefs. Don't miss it.

Sights & Activities

Musée du Rhum Museum
(Rum Museum; ☎0590-28-70-04; www.musee-du-rhum.fr; Viard; adult/child €6/4; ⏲9am-5pm Mon-Sat) Those who want to understand how the ambrosia called rum starts in the sugarcane fields and ends on their palates should really head to this excellent museum, which has thorough explanations in English. It's at the site of the Reimonenq Distillery, about 500m inland from the N2 in the village of Bellevue, just

Tropical rum punch
HOLGER LEUE/GETTY IMAGES ©

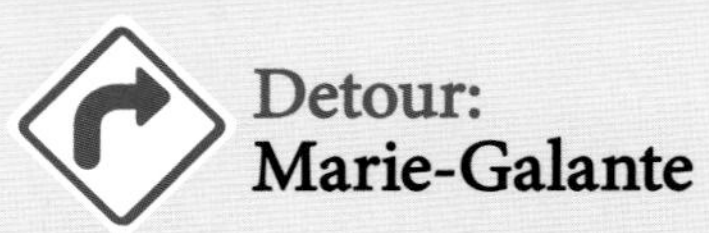

Detour: Marie-Galante

If a refuge from the troubles of the world is what you seek, look no further: Marie-Galante is your answer.

Marie-Galante is a rural and agricultural island beloved by those who enjoy the quieter pleasures in life and particularly by beach-lovers who want to escape the crowds. Compared with the archipelago's other islands, Marie-Galante is relatively flat, its dual limestone plateaus rising only 150m.

Rum distilleries are among the island's main sights. The **Distillerie Poisson** (0590-97-03-79; Habitation Edouard, Rameau, Grand-Bourg; 7am-1pm Mon-Sat) FREE, midway between St-Louis and Grand-Bourg, bottles the island's best-known rum under the Père Labat label. All of the distilleries have gift shops and rum is definitely one of the best gifts to bring back from Guadeloupe.

Idyllic beaches include **Plage de la Feuillère** and **Plage de Petite Anse**, just west of Capesterre, as well as **Plage de Vieux-Fort** and **Plage de l'Anse Canot**, which both lie north of St-Louis. Diving is also available.

Plan at least two days to do the island justice. It has excellent accommodations, including **Au Village de Ménard** (0590-97-09-45; www.villagedemenard.com; Section Vieux Fort; d €80-95;).

Regular ferries run to Pointe-à-Pitre, St-François, Les Saintes and La Désirade.

southeast of Ste-Rose. Exhibits include an old distillery, cane-extraction gears and a vapor machine dating from 1707.

BleuBlancVert Boat Tour
(0690-63-82-43; www.bleublancvert.com; Ste-Rose; half-day adult/child €35/15) This well-regarded operator runs half-day lagoon and mangrove tours on a motorized raft. The guide imparts environmental and geological knowledge, and you'll have the opportunity to snorkel along the barrier reef. Operates small groups only (four people maximum). Prices include drinks.

Nico Excursions Boat Tour
(0590-28-72-47, 0690-53-09-65; www.nicoexcursions.com; Ste-Rose; half-day €35) This reputable outfit runs very popular half-day trips to nearby islands and reefs, including Îlet Blanc, with a maximum of 12 people. It includes swimming and snorkel stops.

Eating

Chez Clara Creole, French $$
(0590-28-72-99; Blvd St Charles, Bord de Mer; mains €16-21, menu €18; lunch Thu-Tue, dinner Mon, Tue & Thu-Sat) Across the road from the small fishing harbor, this casually gracious eatery is held in high regard by tourists. Enjoy classics such as tuna tartare, veal cutlet and lamb steak. It's such a shame that service is so slow.

CHUTES DU CARBET

Unless it's overcast, the drive up to the Chutes du Carbet lookout gives a view of two magnificent waterfalls plunging down a sheer mountain face.

Starting from St-Sauveur on the N1, the road runs 8.5km inland, making for a nice 15-minute drive up through a rainforest. Nearly 3km before the end of the road is a marked stop at the trailhead to **Grand Étang**, a placid lake circled by a loop trail. It's just a five-minute walk from the roadside parking area down to the edge of the lake, and it takes about an hour more to stroll the lake's perimeter.

The road ends at the **Chutes du Carbet** (adult/child €2/0.80; 8am-4:30pm) lookout. From here you can see the two highest waterfalls from the upper parking lot, where a signboard marks the trailhead to the base of the falls. The well-trodden walk to the second-highest waterfall (110m) takes 20 minutes; it's about a two-hour hike to the highest waterfall (115m).

PLAGE DE MALENDURE & PIGEON ISLAND

This long stretch of beachside towns and villages is a mecca for divers who come to dive and snorkel at the superb Réserve Cousteau around little Pigeon Island and to relax on Plage de Malendure's dark-sand beaches. The entire area is backed by steep hills.

Sights & Activities

Réserve Cousteau Marine Park

Jacques Cousteau brought Pigeon Island to international attention by declaring it to be one of the world's top dive areas. The waters surrounding the island are now protected as an underwater park. The majority of the dive sites around Pigeon Island are very scenic, with big schools of fish and coral reefs that are shallow enough for good snorkeling. It's only a 10- to 15-minute boat ride to the dive sites.

Les Heures Saines Diving

(**☎0590-98-86-63; www.heures-saines.gp; Le Rocher de Malendure, Bouillante)** This extremely versatile operation is based under Le Rocher de Malendure restaurant. In addition to the standard dive offerings, it offers Soufrière hikes, canyoning and dolphin-watching trips.

PPK-Plaisir Plongée Karukera Diving

(**☎0590-98-82-43; www.ppk-plongee-guadeloupe.com; Plage de Malendure, Bouillante)** This efficiently run dive shop gets good reviews. An introductory/single dive costs €45/35. Also fits snorkeling in during its dive outings (€15).

Canopée Hiking

(**☎0590-26-95-59; www.canopeeguadeloupe.com; Plage de Malendure, Bouillante)** This is the area's best canyoning and hiking operation, offering a huge number of trips into the nearby mountains from half-day walks (€35) to more challenging canyoning outings (from €55).

Gwada Pagaie Kayaking

(**☎0690-93-91-71, 0590-10-20-29; www.gwadapagaie.com; Plage de Malendure, Bouillante)** Wanna see the Réserve Cousteau from a different perspective? With a kayak, you can reach Pigeon Island at your own pace. This outfit rents kayaks for €25/35 per half-/full day. A map of the marine park is provided, as well as life jackets; bring a picnic.

Climbing La Soufrière

There are a couple of ways to get to La Soufrière, the active 1467m volcano that looms above the southern half of the island.

The most direct route is to follow the N3 from Basse-Terre in the direction of St-Claude. From St-Claude, signs point to La Soufrière, 6km to the northeast on the D11. The road ends at Bains Jaunes, which is the trailhead for a couple of **walks**, including one to Chute de Galion, a scenic 40m waterfall on the Galion River. For an adventurous 1¾-hour hike to La Soufrière's sulfurous, moonscapelike summit, a well-beaten trail starts at the end of the parking lot. It travels along a gravel bed and continues steeply up the mountain through a cover of low shrubs and thick ferns. In addition to a close-up view of the steaming volcano, the hike offers some fine vistas of the island. Start early in the morning.

Detour: La Désirade

La Désirade is Guadeloupe's least-developed and least-visited island. Even the nicest beaches are nearly deserted; for the ultimate do-nothing vacation it's a place that's hard to beat.

Looking somewhat like an overturned boat when viewed from Guadeloupe, La Désirade is only 11km long and 2km wide, with a central plateau that rises 273m at its highest point. There are only three settlements, at Beauséjour, Le Souffleur and Baie Mahault. You can overnight at **Hôtel Oasis** (0590-20-01-00; www.oasisladesirade.com; Beauséjour; s/d incl breakfast €48/52;).

There are regular ferries to/from St-François, Les Saintes and Marie-Galantel; see p275.

Sleeping & Eating

Le Jardin Tropical Hotel $$
(0590-98-77-23; www.guadeloupehebergement.fr; Rue de Poirier; d from €80; P) Le Jardin Tropical stands out because of its friendly owners (when they're around), a pool that feels nearly private and an ace location on a greenery-shrouded hillside. The bungalow rooms are sparkling clean, simply furnished and good value, and all have outdoor patios, kitchens and unsurpassable sea views. Dinner meals are available (€10 to €16). There's a two-night minimum stay.

La Touna Seafood $$
(0590-98-70-10; www.la-touna.com; Pigeon; mains €14-25, menus €22-28; lunch & dinner Tue-Sat, lunch Sun;) This superfriendly, stylish place on the seafront has a sumptuous Creole menu with a French twist and specializes in fresh seafood (there's a lobster tank here where you can choose your dinner). The terrace has great views toward Pigeon Island and is a lovely cool place to round off your meal with a ti-punch to the sound of the waves.

Le Rocher de Malendure International $$$
(0590-98-70-84; Bouillante; mains €16-34, menus €19-32; lunch & dinner Thu-Tue) The best-established restaurant in Bouillante, this sprawling complex is actually built on the eponymous rock, and has incredible views on all sides. The restaurant offers everything from beef fillet to the fresh lobsters it keeps in a small pool.

MARTINIQUE

POP 400,000

Volcanic in origin, Martinique is a mountainous stunner crowned by the still-smoldering Mont Pelée, which wiped out Martinique's former capital of St-Pierre in 1902.

Martinique offers a striking diversity of landscapes and atmospheres. While it suffers from uncontrolled urban sprawl in some places, particularly in and around the busy capital, Fort-de-France, life – and travel – becomes more sedate as one heads north or south through some of the island's delicious scenery. The rainforested, mountainous northern part is the most spectacular, but the south has its fair share of natural wonders, including lovely bays and miles of luscious beaches.

It's also a fantastic playground for outdoorsy types, with a host of activities readily available, both on land and at sea.

Fort-de-France

POP 90,500

Fort-de-France is the mercantile and political capital of Martinique, and the largest city in the French West Indies. While it's a busy commercial center and has some decent shopping and an attractive historic fort, most people simply pass through. If you do, it is worth dedicating a few hours to wandering around the handful of historic sites, markets and museums the city has to offer.

Sights

Bibliothèque Schoelcher
Notable Building

(Rue de la Liberté; admission free; 1-5:30pm Mon, 8:30am-5:30pm Tue-Thu, 8:30am-5pm Fri, 8:30am-noon Sat) Fort-de-France's most visible landmark, the Bibliothèque Schoelcher is an elaborate, colorful building with a Byzantine dome and an interesting ornate interior. The library was built in Paris and displayed at the 1889 World Exposition. It was then dismantled, shipped in pieces to Fort-de-France and reassembled in its current location.

Cathédrale St-Louis
Cathedral

(Rue Schoelcher; dawn-dusk) With its neo-Byzantine style and 57m steeple, the Cathédrale St-Louis is one of the city's most distinguished landmarks. Built in 1895, the church fronts a small square and is picturesquely framed by two royal palms.

Island Insights

A few Creole staples:

Acras A universally popular hors d'oeuvre in Martinique and Guadeloupe, *acras* are fish, seafood or vegetables tempura. *Acras de morue* (cod) and *crevettes* (shrimp) are the most common and are both delicious.

Boudin créole Blood sausage.

Ti-punch Short for *petit punch;* this ubiquitous and strong cocktail is a mix of rum, lime and cane syrup – but mainly rum.

Blaff This is the local term for white fish marinated in lime juice, garlic and peppers and then poached.

Grand Marché
Market

(Rue Blénac; 5am-dusk Mon-Sat) This market is not as lively as you might expect, but it's a great place to stock up on crafts, souvenirs, spices, fruits and veggies.

Grand Marché, Fort-de-France

PATRICE COPPEE/GETTY IMAGES ©

Jardin de Balata Gardens
(☎0596-64-48-73; www.jardindebalata.fr; Route de la Trace; adult/child €13.10/7.50; ⏰9am-4:30pm) On the west side of the N3, about 10km north of Fort-de-France, is this mature botanical garden in a rainforest setting. One of Martinique's best attractions, it will please anyone with even a passing interest in botany. The hour-long walk around the garden is clearly marked, and a series of tree walks will keep kids interested. An audioguide in English is available. To get there from Fort-de-France, take a taxi or a bus (Line 25).

Festivals & Events

Mardi Gras Carnival Carnival
A spirited festival during the five-day period leading up to Ash Wednesday.

Sleeping & Eating

L'Impératrice Hotel $$
(☎0596-63-06-82; www.limperatricehotel.fr; 15 Rue de la Liberté; s €101-121, d €117-157; ❄📶) This hotel is by far the best in town, right in the middle of things and with a sleek art-deco feel to its facade. All 23 rooms are excellent, with laminate floors, dark-wood furniture, sparkling bathrooms and all modern comforts. Ask for a room on the upper floors; if you can, go for room 53, which has the best views.

Le Vieux Foyaal Creole $$
(☎0596-77-05-49; 22 Rue Garnier Pagès; mains €14-24; ⏰lunch & dinner Mon-Sat) Brimming with good cheer, this restaurant in a street running parallel to the seafront is that easy-to-miss 'secret spot' that local gourmands like to recommend. Everything is fresh and tasty – unfussy market cuisine at its best. Its plant-filled patio at the back is a haven of peace. Live dinnertime jazz on Thursday cranks the hip atmosphere up a notch.

Djol Dou Creole $$
(☎0596-63-10-84; 25 Rue Garnier Pagès; mains €12-15; ⏰lunch Mon-Sat, dinner Sat) For Creole fare at unbeatable prices, you can't do better than this family-run restaurant in a street running parallel to the seafront. More original items on the menu include *souris d'agneau au curcuma* (lamb in a turmeric sauce) and fish stew, as well as a couple of veggie options (soya steak, anyone?).

Le Foyaal International $$
(☎0596-63-00-38; Rue Ernest Deproge; mains €14-22, menus €15-20; ⏰8am-midnight) A focal point of life in Fort-de-France, this smart complex includes a buzzing brasserie serving everything from sandwiches to beef carpaccio, an upstairs restaurant serving gourmet food, and a next-door takeaway making crepes and wraps to go. Two downsides: it's on a noisy thoroughfare and service is lackadaisical.

Jardin de Balata

Fort-de-France

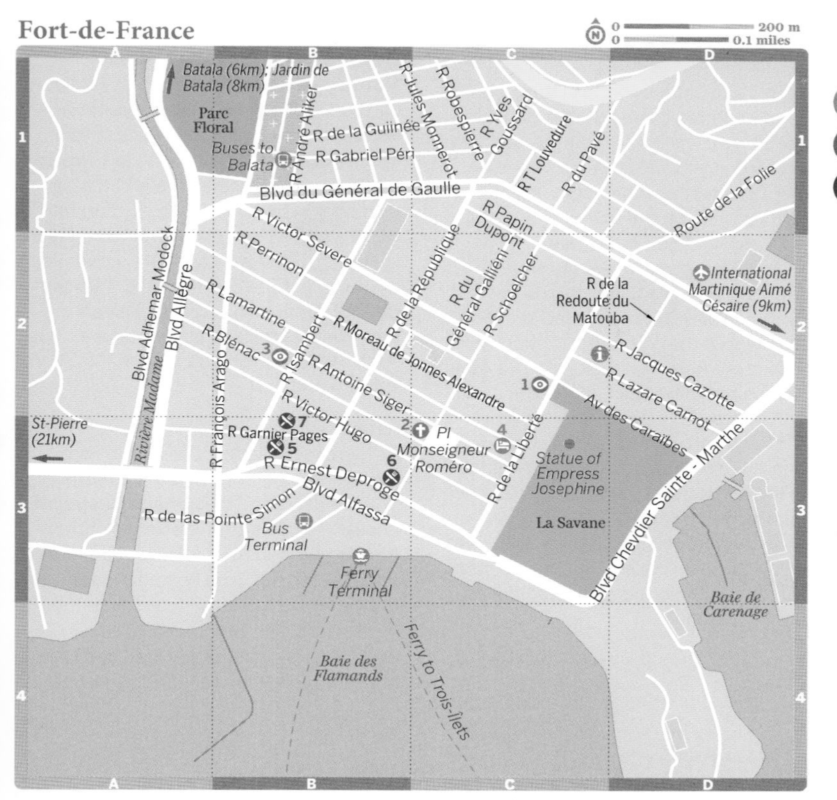

Information

Banks with ATMs are easy to find in the center.

Tourist Information

Tourist Office (☎0596-60-27-73; www.tourismefdf.com; 76 Rue Lazare Carnot; ⏰8am-5pm Mon-Fri, 9am-noon Sat) Has some useful brochures in English on activities and accommodations, and can arrange English-language walking tours.

Getting There & Around

To/From the Airport

The Martinique Aimé Césaire International Airport is just a 15-minute drive from Fort-de-France. Taxis are readily available at the airport (about €30 to Fort-de-France).

Fort-de-France

Sights
1 Bibliothèque Schoelcher C2
2 Cathédrale St-Louis C3
3 Grand Marché B2

Sleeping
4 L'Impératrice C3

Eating
5 Djol Dou B3
6 Le Foyaal B3
7 Le Vieux Foyaal B3

Boat

There are boats from Fort-de-France to Trois-Îlets, Anse Mitan and Pointe du Bout. The ferries dock at the quay fronting the minibus parking lot.

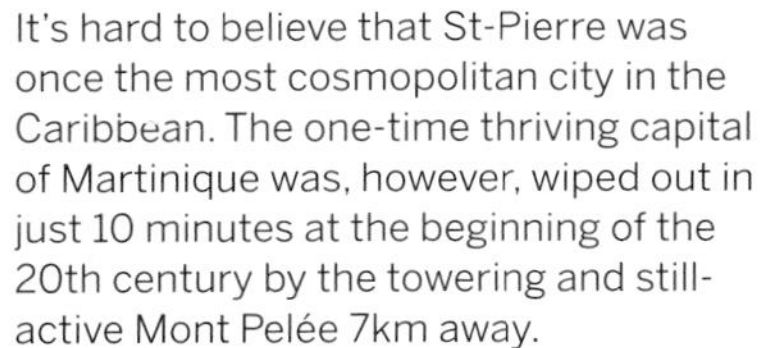

St-Pierre

POP 4500

It's hard to believe that St-Pierre was once the most cosmopolitan city in the Caribbean. The one-time thriving capital of Martinique was, however, wiped out in just 10 minutes at the beginning of the 20th century by the towering and still-active Mont Pelée 7km away.

Though a shadow of its former self, St-Pierre is an attractive place to wander. There are many blackened ruins throughout the city, some of which are little more than foundations, while others remain partially intact.

A beach of soft, dark-gray sand fronts the town and extends to the south. There are sailboats and fishing boats in the harbor, and the sunsets here are postcard-perfect.

If you want to escape the crowds and enjoy the quiet pace of life in a traditional Caribbean town, this is a great place to base yourself.

Sights

Centre de Découverte des Sciences de la Terre Museum

(**☎0596-52-82-42; www.cdst.e-monsite.com; Route du Prêcheur; adult/child €5/3; ⏰9am-4pm Tue-Sun)** Just 1.5km north of town, the earth-science museum looks like a big white box set on top of some columns. It hosts a permanent exhibit on Mont Pelée, in French. Documentaries are screened all day long, but the one to watch is *Volcans des Antilles,* which recounts Pelée's eruption and the dire consequences. It's subtitled in English and shown at 9:30am, 1:30pm and 4pm.

Ruins Ruin

St-Pierre's most impressive ruins are those of the old 18th-century **theater**. While most of the theater was destroyed, enough remains to give a sense of the former grandeur of this building, which once seated 800 and hosted theater troupes from mainland France. On the northeast side of the theater you can enter the tiny, thick-walled **jail cell** that housed Cyparis, one of the town's only

Bibliothèque Schoelcher (p257)

Island Insights

At the end of the 19th century, St-Pierre – then the capital of Martinique – was a flourishing port city. Mont Pelée, the island's highest mountain at 1397m, was just a scenic backdrop to the city.

In the spring of 1902, sulfurous steam vents on Mont Pelée began emitting gases, and a crater lake started to fill with boiling water. Authorities dismissed it all as the normal cycle of the volcano, which had experienced harmless periods of activity in the past.

But at 8am on Sunday May 8, 1902, Mont Pelée exploded into a glowing burst of superheated gas and burning ash, with a force 40 times stronger than the later nuclear blast over Hiroshima. Between the suffocating gases and the fiery inferno, St-Pierre was laid to waste within minutes.

Of the city's 30,000 inhabitants, there were just three survivors. One of them, a prisoner named Cyparis, escaped with only minor burns – ironically, he owed his life to having been locked in a tomblike solitary-confinement cell at the local jail.

Pelée continued to smolder for months, but by 1904 people began to resettle the town, building among the crumbled ruins.

survivors. Another area rich in ruins is the **Quartier du Figuier**, along Rue Bouillé.

Jardin Botanique du Carbet Gardens

(☎0596-52-76-08; www.jardinbotaniqueducarbet.com; Anse Latouche; adult/child €7.50/4; ⏲9:30am-4pm) Appealing to a wider audience than just plant-lovers and gardeners, this botanical garden on the southern outskirts of St-Pierre is definitely worth an hour or so for anyone interested in tropical flora and colonial history. The ruins of a sugar mill dating from the 18th century are truly atmospheric.

Distillerie Depaz Distillery

(☎0596-78-13-14; www.depaz.fr; Plantation de la Montagne Pelée; ⏲10am-5pm Mon-Fri, 9am-4pm Sat) FREE Learn how rum is made at this operation perched on a hillside amid sugarcane fields on the northern outskirts of St-Pierre. This interesting place offers self-guided tours, with signs in English. In the tasting room you can sample different rums, including *rhum vieux* (vintage rum), the Mercedes of Martinique rums, which truly rivals cognac. There's an on-site restaurant.

Activities

St-Pierre's trump card is diving, with a fantastic collection of wrecks lying just offshore – a number of ships sank in the 1902 eruption. The catch? They lie deep, and most of them are accessible to experienced divers only. For beginners, there are some excellent canyon dives. Further north, Îlet La Perle is an exposed seamount that consistently sizzles with fish action, in less than 25m of water.

Tropicasub Diving

(☎0596-78-38-03, 0696-24-24-30; www.tropicasub.com; Anse Latouche; ⏲Tue-Sun) One of the most experienced dive operators in the area is Tropicasub, on the southern outskirts of town. Introductory dives go for €55 while single dives cost €50. Certification courses and dive packages are also available.

Sleeping & Eating

Hôtel de l'Anse Hotel $

(☎0596-78-30-82, 0696-38-91-70; Anse Latouche; d €45-55, bungalow €60; P ❄ ᯤ) On the southern fringes of town, this well-priced abode is in an atmospheric heritage

Hiking Mont Pelée

Mont Pelée is the island's most famous natural attraction and a must-do for walkers. There are strenuous trails leading up both the northern and southern flanks of Mont Pelée. The shortest and steepest is up the southern flank, beginning at Refuge de L'Aileron in Morne Rouge (it's signposted), and takes about four hours round-trip.

Early morning is the best time to climb the volcano, as you stand a better chance of clear views.

building that offers nine impeccably simple and airy rooms. The upstairs rooms are a tad smaller but have more charm. There are also three cozy bungalows.

Hôtel Villa Saint-Pierre Hotel $$
(0596-78-68-45; www.hotel-villastpierre.fr; Rue Bouillé; d incl breakfast €135-145; P ❄) The best place in town is right on the waterfront and has a small beach just meters from the front door. The nine modern and comfortable rooms, complete with locally made wood furniture, have an almost boutique feel to them, and the welcome is friendly. Rooms with a sea view are inundated with natural light – well worth the extra €10.

Le Guérin Creole $
(0596-78-18-07; Rue Bouillé; menu €15; lunch Mon-Sat) There's no contest about the most popular lunch spot in town, within the market (upstairs). There can be a wait during the lunch rush, but with some of the best *acras* (deep-fried balls of dough filled with fish or shrimp) and *boudin créole* (blood sausage) on the island, the wait is worth it.

Chez-Marie Claire Creole $
(0596-69-48-21; Rue Bouillé; mains €10-13, menus €12-17; lunch Mon-Sat) This restaurant sits at the top of some steps inside the covered market. Diners can look down on the bustle below while eating Creole dishes such as stewed beef and freshwater crayfish. It's a friendly place, and the cook often comes by to make sure that guests enjoyed their meal.

La Lanterne French, Creole $$
(0596-76-60-36; www.restaurantlalanterne.com; Habitation Latouche; mains €16-22, menu €21; lunch daily, dinner Fri & Sat) Concealed in a wonderfully overgrown garden, this venue is known for its tantalizing French-Creole menu, served in snug surrounds complete with elegant furnishings and tropical plants. From conch stew and marlin in mustard sauce to chicken flambéed in vintage rum, the kitchen always seems to get it right. At the entrance of Jardin Botanique du Carbet.

Information

Tourist Office (0596-78-10-39; 8am-4pm Mon-Fri, 9am-noon Sat) Offers guided tours of St-Pierre in French (though some guides speak some English) at 9:30am and 2:30pm Monday to Friday.

Anse Céron & Around

From St-Pierre, the N2 turns inland but the D10 continues north for 13km along the coast and makes a scenic side drive. The shoreline is rocky for much of the way and the landscape is lush. The road ends at Anse Céron, a nice black-sand beach backed by the thick jungle rolling off the base of Mont Pelée. Anse Céron faces **Îlet la Perle**, a rounded rock off the northwest coast. A very steep one-lane route continues for 1.6km to the north and ends at **Anse Couleuvre**, another stunning gray-sand beach. From there, it's an easy 15-minute walk to **Anse Lévrier** on a well-defined path. It takes another 10 minutes to reach **Anse à Voile**, a gem of solitude. Very few visitors make it to this wild cove which feels like the world's end.

From Anse à Voile, it's possible to hike around the undeveloped northern tip of the island to Grand-Rivière – a six-hour, 20km adventure with panoramic views that will be etched in your memory forever.

Grand-Rivière

POP 840

Grand-Rivière is an unspoiled fishing village scenically tucked beneath coastal cliffs at the northern tip of Martinique. Mont Pelée forms a rugged backdrop to the south, while there's a fine view of neighboring Dominica to the north. The road dead-ends at the sea, where there's a fish market and rows of brightly colored fishing boats lined up on a little black-sand beach.

Activities

Au Fil des Anses Boat Tour

(☎0696-44-50-66, 0696-38-90-68; Grand Rivière; full day adult/child €60/35) Run by the friendly Omer, this well-run operation offers good-value boat excursions that take you to various scenic spots along the wild coast between Grand Rivière and Le Prêcheur for swimming, snorkeling and trying your hand at fishing. The itinerary is flexible.

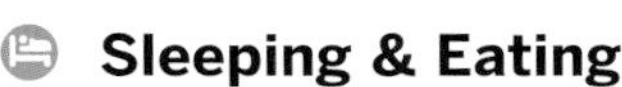

Sleeping & Eating

Chez Tante Arlette Creole, Seafood **$$$**

(☎0596-55-75-75; www.tantearlette.com; 3 Rue Lucy de Fossarieu; mains €20-45; ⌚lunch Tue-Sun, dinner available for hotel guests; 📶) This longstanding favorite is the best place in northern Martinique to try out authentic Creole food, such as *acras de titiris* (fried fish), but there's also a well-crafted seafood menu if your tummy and palate are timid. How does grilled lobster sound? You may like it enough to enquire about accommodations in one of the three rooms upstairs (from €65).

Presqu'île de Caravelle

This charming peninsula has some gorgeous stretches of beach and a wild and untamed feel in parts. A gently twisting road with spectacular views runs through sugarcane fields to the peninsula's main village, charming **Tartane**, and then on to Baie du Galion. On the north side of the peninsula are a couple of protected beaches.

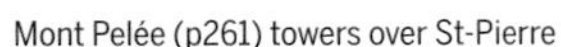

Mont Pelée (p261) towers over St-Pierre

Beaches

Anse de Tartane Beach

Fronting the village of Tartane, this long strand of soft beige sand has lots of fishing shacks, a fish market and colorful *gommier* (gum tree) boats. It can get crowded on weekends.

La Brèche Beach

On the eastern outskirts of Tartane, this crescent of sand shaded by manchineel trees is a stunning beach to sun yourself on. The color of the sand? Brown-gray. It has picnic tables and a beach restaurant.

Anse l'Étang Beach

This gently shelving, palm-fringed beach is one of the island's most appealing. It's not suitable for swimming, though, because the waters are rough, with lots of wave action. It's popular with surfers.

Sights

Château Dubuc Ruin

(☎0596-58-09-00; Presqu'île de Caravelle; adult/child €4/2; ⏰9am-4:30pm) Set on the tip of the peninsula are the deteriorated ruins of a 17th-century estate. These sprawling grounds have some of the most extensive plantation ruins in Martinique, and there's a very small museum. The master of the estate gained notoriety by using a lantern to lure ships into wrecking off the coast, and then gathering the loot. Several **hiking trails** start at the parking lot, including a 30-minute walk to the site of a historic lighthouse and stellar views.

Sleeping

Hotel Le Manguier Hotel **$$**

(☎0596-58-48-95; www.hotel-martinique-lemanguier.com; Tartane; d incl breakfast €82-102; ❄📶🏊) A great-value port of call. This charming collection of whitewashed units is perched high above the athletic grounds in the center of Tartane. The simple but comfortable rooms have small outdoor hot-plate kitchens and great balconies, many of which face the Atlantic Ocean. There's a small pool, and breakfast is served with a sea view.

Hotel Restaurant Caravelle Hotel **$$**

(☎0596-58-07-32; www.hotel-la-caravelle-martinique.com; Rte du Château Dubuc; d €84-135; ❄) This small, friendly, family-run hotel is a great choice. There is a hibiscus-covered terrace with glorious views of the Atlantic, and the public areas are all beautifully furnished and well looked after. Rooms are very pleasant and come in several different sizes, including studios that have

Lighthouse, Caravelle peninsula (p263)

Detour: Anse Dufour & Anse Noire

Few visitors have heard about Anse Dufour and Anse Noire, two little morsels of paradise that locals would like to keep for themselves. Approximately halfway between Anse Mitan and Grande Anse, a secondary road peels off the D7 and plunges straight to Anse Dufour 2km below. You'll be smitten by the mellow tranquillity of this fishing hamlet, which has a golden-sand beach and a handful of Creole restaurants.

If you're after an even more intimate, more secluded strip of sand, head to lovely Anse Noire to the north; it can be reached via cement stairs in less than 10 minutes. This tiny, dreamlike cove lapped by jade waters offers a small patch of black sand studded with palm trees. Swimming and snorkeling are excellent. Kayaking is another great way to explore the nearby bays at a gentle pace. Contact **Kayak de l'Anse Noire** (0696-34-86-36; Anse Noire; 1hr €6, half-day €13), which is right on the beach.

well-equipped kitchenettes on a spacious front porch with great views. There's an on-site restaurant.

Eating

Ti Carbet Creole $
(0696-27-17-01; Tartane; mains €9-11; lunch) Sweet! This local treasure could hardly be better situated: it overlooks Plage de la Brèche, on the eastern outskirts of Tartane. It concocts good, fresh food at competitive prices given the enviable location. You won't get much variety but tasty staples usually include grilled fish, octopus stew and curried chicken.

La Table de Mamy Nounou French, Creole $$
(0596-58-07-32; Hôtel Restaurant Caravelle, Rte du Château Dubuc; mains €13-29, menu €28; lunch & dinner Wed-Mon) This much-lauded restaurant at the Hotel Restaurant Caravelle is a winner, thanks to its breezy veranda with lovely sea views, sophisticated mains and wonderful homemade desserts. Stand-out dishes might include *grenadin de porcelet* (larded fillet of suckling pig) and lamb with aromatic herbs. The flambéed banana dessert is a treat.

Le Phare French $$
(0596-58-08-48; Anse Bonneville; mains €15-23, menus €16-20; lunch Tue-Sun, dinner Tue-Sat) In a terrific hilltop setting next to the end of the road that leads to Château Dubuc, the Phare is famous for the insane views of Anse Bonneville and the sea from its open-air deck; you may never have a tuna tartare or a kangaroo fillet with a view to rival this one.

Grande Anse

POP 600

The pleasant little village of Grande Anse is set along a beachfront road lined with brightly painted boats and a string of restaurants. The main street is for pedestrians only, making it more enjoyable to stroll along the beach.

Beaches

Plage de Grande Anse Beach
This long stretch of golden sand is nice to look at, but not so nice to tan on (due to fishing boats and no privacy). There are often sailboats moored offshore. The water is usually calm, with just enough wave action to remind you it's the sea.

Below: The Guadeloupe speciality of blaff (marinated fish; p432); **Right:** Grande Anse (p265)
(RIGHT) DONALD NAUSBAUM/GETTY IMAGES ©; (BELOW) FENOT ERIC/GETTY IMAGES ©

Activities

Alpha Plongée Diving, Snorkeling
(**☎0696-81-93-42; www.alpha-plongee.com; 138 Rue Robert Deloy**) This low-key diving venture specializes in small groups and offers an intimate feel to its aquatic adventures. Single dive trips cost €45 while introductory dives are also €45. Certification courses and dive packages are available. Also offers *randonnée palmée* (guided snorkeling tours; €20) and rents snorkeling gear (€10 per day).

L'Arlésienne Boat Tours
(**☎0696-82-54-41; Quai de Grande Anse; half-/full-day tour €30/55**) This operator offers an interesting tour that takes in the bays and coves between Grande Anse and Le Diamant. It's an ideal way to gain an overview of the coast's delights. There is a stop for a swim in a lovely little cove. Trips to northern Martinique can also be arranged.

Eating

Ti Sable International $$
(**☎0596-68-62-44; www.tisablemartinique.com; Grande Anse; mains €13-23; lunch & dinner;** wi-fi) Head to this surprisingly hip complex at the northern end of the beach for a lovely waterside eating experience. The food (a scrumptious assortment of fish dishes, exotic salads and barbecued meats) is a touch overpriced, but it's still worth it for the setting. On Sundays Ti Sable lays on an excellent lunch buffet (€28) and there's live music in the evening.

Chez Évelyne Creole $$
(**☎0596-48-39-38; Grande Anse; menus €14-30; lunch Tue-Sun**) This ramshackle eatery at the southern end of the beach has very reasonably priced set menus, and serves up all the Creole favorites, garnished with locally grown vegetables. Best of all, it has tables on the sand and photogenic views of the turquoise sea.

Anses d'Arlet

POP 3200

Anses d'Arlet is without a doubt the most charming fishing village in southern Martinique; it retains an undiscovered feel, as there's just one small guesthouse here and (for the moment) very little else. There's a handsome coastal road crowned by an 18th-century Roman Catholic church whose doors open almost directly onto the beach, and the entire scene is framed with steep, verdant hills.

Sleeping & Eating

Résidence Madinakay Hotel $

(**0596-68-70-76; 3 Allée des Arlésiens; d €60;**) Right in the thick of things and just across the road from the beach, this small hotel is excellent value for money. Run by the helpful Raymond de Laval, the eight studios are fairly unexciting but they are clean and equipped with all the necessary comforts. Complaints? We're nit-picking, but the rooms don't have sea views.

Chez Fredo Creole $$

(**0696-81-07-22; Rue des Pêcheurs, Petite Anse; mains €13-15; lunch daily, dinner Tue-Sun**) Worth a mention for its breezy terrace, memorable sea views, jovial atmosphere and convenient location across from Petite Anse beach, Chez Fredo is a popular hangout for locals and tourists alike. No culinary acrobatics in this few-frills haunt, just keep-the-faith Creole staples at puny prices. There's live music on Thurdays, Fridays and Saturdays. Takes cash only.

Valy et Le Pêcheur Creole $$

(**0696-93-60-87; Anses d'Arlet; mains €10-20, menus €16-35; lunch Wed-Mon**) This beachside kiosk is run by a dynamic crew who serve excellent local specialties, among them pork ribs, conch fricassée and braised chicken. Servings are large and the ramshackle tables right on the beach could just be our favorites along this stretch of coast.

Le Diamant

POP 3400

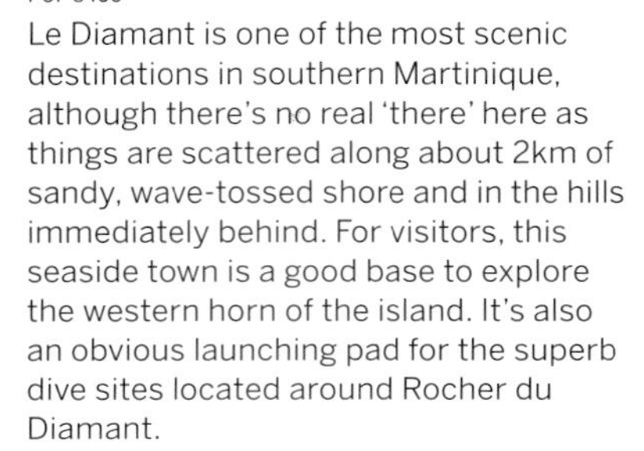

Le Diamant is one of the most scenic destinations in southern Martinique, although there's no real 'there' here as things are scattered along about 2km of sandy, wave-tossed shore and in the hills immediately behind. For visitors, this seaside town is a good base to explore the western horn of the island. It's also an obvious launching pad for the superb dive sites located around Rocher du Diamant.

Beaches

Plage du Diamant Beach

The beautiful strand of white sand stretches for 2km beside town. Swimming is not recommended, as the waves can be very strong, but it's the picture-perfect place for sunbathing, beachcombing, having a picnic lunch or simply enjoying the view of Rocher du Diamant.

Sights & Activities

Rocher du Diamant Natural Landmark

This 176m-high volcanic islet that's just 1.5km offshore from the village is a very popular dive site, with interesting cave formations but tricky water conditions. Various companies also organise boat excursions that take in the islet.

Antilles Sub Diamond Rock Diving

(**0596-76-10-65, 0696-82-14-35; www.plongee-martinique.fr; Hôtel Diamond Rock, Pointe de la Cherry**) A small outfit capably managed by a French couple; known for friendly service and small groups. Has introductory dives (€60), three-dive packages (€135), certifications courses and snorkeling trips.

Sleeping & Eating

L'Anse Bleue Bungalow **$$**

(**0596-76-21-91; www.hotel-anse-bleue.com; La Dizac; d €70, bungalow €85;**) This place is very simple, but somehow manages to get things just right – there are 25 delightful little bungalows spread out across spacious grounds, a decent-sized pool, a superb on-site restaurant and a peaceful location – all adding up to make this one of our favorite hotels in Martinique. It also has five cheaper, fuss-free rooms, all with sea views.

New Cap International **$$**

(**0596-76-12-99; Anse Caffard; mains €13-20; lunch & dinner Wed-Mon;**) A very relaxing spot. Picture a lovely beachfront location, ample views of Rocher du Diamant and a varied menu. Choose from frondy salads, meat and fish dishes, and daily specials chalked up on the blackboard. A wonderful *tarte au citron* (lemon tart) will finish you off sweetly. It's at Anse Caffard, about 3km west of Le Diamant.

Chez Lucie Creole **$$**

(**0596-76-40-10; 64 Rue Justin Roc; mains €15-22; lunch Wed-Mon, dinner Mon & Wed-Sat**) When this place opened in 1902, its owners couldn't have guessed it would have such a long life. The broad menu offers all sorts of tempting goodies, starting with codfish fritters, which you might follow with a tender veal escalope. It's a touch overpriced, but it's still worth it for the terrace overlooking the beach at the back. The menu is translated in English.

Presqu'île de Ste-Anne

The southeastern corner of Martinique forms a magnificient peninsula which has plenty to set your heart aflutter: liberally sprinkled with grandiose bays, turquoise waters and superb beaches, it's a powerful fix for any beach addict.

The southernmost town on Martinique, Ste-Anne has an attractive seaside setting with painted wooden houses and numerous trinket shops. Despite the large number of visitors that flock to the town on weekends and during the winter season, Ste-Anne remains a casual, low-key place, with abundant near-shore reef formations that make for good snorkeling.

For some serious sunbathing, make your way to Grande Anse des Salines, at the undeveloped southern tip of the island.

A 15-minute drive – and just 6km east as the crow flies – to the northeast transports you to yet another world, along the Atlantic-battered east coast, where you can experience Martinique from a different perspective. Near Cap Chevalier you'll find some great isolated beaches.

Beaches

Pointe Marin — Beach

Ste-Anne's most popular swimming beach is the long, lovely strand that stretches along the peninsula 800m north of the town center.

Grande Anse des Salines — Beach

This is it – that celebrity of all the beaches in southern Martinique. Immense, crystalline and glossy, it doesn't disappoint the bevy of swimmers who dabble in its gorgeous depths – nor the loads of sun worshippers who lay themselves out like sardines on the ribbon of golden sand.

Les Salines gets its name from Étang des Salines, the large salt pond that backs it; it's about 5km south of Ste-Anne along the D9. There are food vans and snack shops along the beach.

Anse Michel — Beach

The steady winds that buffet this part of the coast mixed with the reef-sheltered lagoon are the perfect combination for kitesurfing and windsurfing. It also offers excellent sunbathing and swimming opportunities.

Activities

Natiyabel — Diving, Kayaking

(**☎0696-36-63-01; www.natiyabel.com; Bourg, Ste-Anne**) This well-run dive center organizes a variety of dive trips and certification. Introductory/single dives cost €50/45. Snorkeling is €15. Kayaks are available for rent (€15 per half-day).

Alize Fun-Lagon Evasion — Water Sports

(**☎0696-91-71-06; www.alizefun.com; Anse Michel**) To brush up on your windsurfing or kitesurfing skills, or try a first lesson (from €95), contact this small outfit right on the beach. It also rents kayaks (€16 per hour) and can arrange guided kayak tours to nearby islets.

Taxi Cap — Boat Trips

(**☎0696-45-44-60, 0596-74-76-61; taxi.cap@wanadoo.fr; Cap Chevalier; adult/child €38/15**) The best way to discover the iridescent lagoon, the nearby islets and the mangrove is by joining a boat excursion. Taxi Cap runs regular day trips that include drinks and lunch.

Hawksbill turtle

Sleeping

Salines Studio Hotel $$
(0596-76-90-92, 0596-76-82-81; salinestudios@hotmail.fr; 7 Rue J-M Tjibaou, Ste-Anne; d €70-80;) Like most plain Janes, this one is dependable, low-key and quiet. It resembles a typical motel and would best suit budget travelers looking for kitchenette studios. It's on the main drag, right in the center.

Eating & Drinking

Le Coin des Grillades Seafood $$
(0596-85-86-67; Rue du Capitaine Constant, Ste-Anne; mains €12-17; lunch Tue-Sun, dinner Wed, Fri & Sat) Next to the market, this modest eatery balances a relaxed atmosphere, wallet-friendly prices, and quality food with a just-right, flavorful bite. It's renowned for its excellent locally caught seafood and grilled fish dishes – the conch on a kebab is memorable.

Le Paradisio International $$
(0596-76-92-87; Anse Michel; mains €17-26; lunch) There is a sophisticated vibe at this surprisingly hip eatery that's slightly set back from the beach (no sea view, alas). The French-influenced food is excellent, relying on fresh ingredients and creative preparations.

Paille Coco Creole $$
(0596-76-75-43; Rue J-M Tjibaou, Ste-Anne; mains €14-21, menu €18; 10am-4pm;) It's the location that's the pull here, rather than the food. Salads, fish dishes and meaty mains won't knock your socks off but you're literally hanging over the beach, with dizzying views of the turquoise water.

La Dunette Bar
(0596-76-73-90; www.ladunette.com; Rue J-M Tjibaou, Ste-Anne; daily) In the center of town, this hotel restaurant is one of the best spots to grab a drink and catch up with friends. The location alone – a wooden deck and a pontoon overlooking the water – will guarantee memorable sunset cocktails. There's live music on Thursday, Friday and Saturday evenings.

Parc National de la Guadeloupe, Basse-Terre (p250)

KARSTEN BIDSTRUP/GETTY IMAGES ©

SURVIVAL GUIDE

Directory A–Z

Accommodations

St-Martin/Sint Maarten

There are plenty of places to hang your hat on the island, but it's best to book in advance, especially during high season. Most of the lodging on the Dutch side is being turned into timeshares or large-scale resorts, while French properties tend to be much more quiet and quaint.

Prices for a double room in high season (December to April):

$ less than US$150

$$ US$150 to US$300

$$$ more than US$300

St-Barthélemy

St-Barth's largest hotel has a mere 70 rooms and the island's second biggest has barely half that number. The others are small, with usually less than a dozen rooms. Private villas are also available. During high season, everything books up fast.

There's no easy way to do St-Barth on the cheap, but in low season you can scout out great deals.

The following indicators apply for a high-season (mid-December to mid-April) room:

$ less than €200

$$ €200 to €400

$$$ more than €400

Guadeloupe & Martinique

Most hotels in Guadeloupe and Martinique are midsized and midrange, and prices are reasonable by the standards of the region. You'll also find private guesthouses *(chambres d'hôte)* or freestanding houses and cottages to rent (gîtes), but they generally require booking by the week.

The following price categories are based on the cost of a double room in high season (from December to April and July to August).

$ less than €60

$$ €60 to €150

$$$ more than €150

Food

The following price indicators are for the cost of a main course:

St-Martin/Sint Maarten

$ less than US$15

$$ US$15 to US$25

$$$ more than US$25

St-Barthélemy

$ less than €20

$$ €20 to €30

$$$ more than €30

Guadeloupe & Martinique

$ less than €12

$$ €12 to €20

$$$ more than €20

Health

As in much of the Caribbean, dengue fever has made an unwelcome reappearance in Martinique, Guadeloupe, Sint Maarten/St-Martin and St-Barthélemy. Dengue is transmitted by mosquito bites, so wear long sleeves and cover your legs in the evening.

In Martinique, beware of manchineel trees found on some beaches, as rainwater dripping off them can cause skin rashes and blistering. They're usually marked with a band of red paint.

Medical care in the French Antilles is very good, with excellent medical facilities and plenty of pharmacies in almost every region.

Languages

St-Martin French, English, Papiamento

Sint Maarten Dutch, English, Papiamento

St-Barthélemy French

Guadeloupe French, Creole

Martinique French, Creole

Money

St-Martin/Sint-Maarten On the French side, everything is priced in euros, while on the Dutch side items are always posted in US dollars. If you are paying with cash, it never hurts to ask the businesses on the eurocentric French side if they'll take one-for-one dollars to euros –

often times you'll get a reluctant-yet-positive response. ATMs blanket the island and credit cards are widely accepted.

St-Barthélemy The currency used in St-Barth is the euro. US dollars are sometimes accepted. ATMs are easy to find in Gustavia.

Guadeloupe & Martinique Guadeloupe and Martinique, as departments of France, use the euro. Hotels, larger restaurants and car-rental agencies accept Visa and MasterCard. ATMs are common across both islands.

Opening Hours

St-Martin/Sint Maarten

Banks 8am to 3pm Monday to Friday

Restaurants lunch 11:30am to 2:30pm, dinner 5pm to 11pm; French restaurants tend to open for dinner slightly later

St-Barthélemy

Banks 8am to noon and 2pm to 3:30pm Monday to Friday

Restaurants lunch 11:30am to 2:30pm, dinner 7pm to 11pm

Shops 9am to noon and 2pm to 6pm Monday to Friday

Guadeloupe & Martinique

Bars 6pm to midnight.

Restaurants Lunch noon to 2pm Monday to Saturday, dinner 7pm to 10pm, many closed one day per week.

Shops 9am to 7pm Monday to Saturday.

Public Holidays

In addition to the holidays observed throughout the region, the islands celebrate the following public holidays:

St-Martin/Sint Maarten

Queen's Day April 30 (Dutch side)

Labor Day May 1

Government Holiday The day after the last Carnival parade, about a month after Easter (Dutch side)

Ascension Thursday Fortieth day after Easter

Pentecost Monday Eighth Monday after Easter (French side)

Bastille Day July 14 (French side)

Assumption Day August 15 (French side)

Sint Maarten Day November 11 (both sides)

Ship off Terre-de-Haut, Les Saintes (p252)

PITAMITZ SERGIO/HEMIS.FR/GETTY IMAGES ©

St-Barthélemy

Easter Sunday Late March/early April

Labor Day May 1

Ascension Thursday Fortieth day after Easter

Pentecost Monday Seventh Monday after Easter

Bastille Day July 14

Assumption Day August 15

All Saints' Day (Toussaints) November 1

All Souls Day November 2

Armistice Day November 11

Guadeloupe & Martinique

Easter Sunday Late March/early April

Ascension Thursday Fortieth day after Easter

Pentecost Monday Eighth Monday after Easter

Labor Day May 1

Victory Day May 8

Slavery Abolition Day May 22 (Martinique)

Slavery Abolition Day May 27 (Guadeloupe)

Bastille Day July 14

Schoelcher Day July 21

Assumption Day August 15

All Saints Day November 1

Armistice Day November 11

Telephone

Local phone numbers on St-Barthélemy, Guadeloupe, Martinique and St-Martin consist of 10 digits (seven digits in Sint Maarten). If you are calling locally, simply dial the local number. To call the island from North America, dial 1 + the island country code + the local number (dropping the initial zero). From elsewhere, dial your country's international dialing code + the island country code + the local number (without the initial zero).

Country codes:

St-Martin ☎590

Sint Maarten ☎1721

St-Barthélemy ☎590

Guadeloupe ☎590

Martinique ☎596

Visas

Citizens of the US, Canada, Australia, New Zealand and many other Western countries can stay in St-Martin/Sint Maarten, St-Barthélemy, Guadeloupe and Martinique for up to 90 days without a visa by showing a valid passport. Citizens of the EU can stay indefinitely, and just need an official identity card or a valid passport to enter the country.

Practicalities

- **Electricity** 220V, 60Hz AC in St-Martin/Sint Maarten; 220V, 50Hz AC in St-Barthélemy, Guadeloupe and Martinique; standard European two-pin plugs are used in all four islands.
- **Tipping** Bar on St-Martin/Sint Maarten, tipping is not customary in the French Antilles.
- **Weights & Measures** The metric system.

Getting There & Away

St-Martin/Sint Maarten

Air There are two airports on the island: **Juliana International Airport** (☎546-7542; www.sxmairport.com; Sint Maarten) and **St-Martin Grand Case** (www.saintmartin-airport.com; Grand Case, St-Martin). All international flights arrive at Juliana Airport and it is a major hub for the region. Prop planes head from St-Martin Grand Case to Anguilla, St-Barthélemy, Guadeloupe and Martinique.

Major airlines fly to the island from the US, including Air Canada, American, Delta, JetBlue and US Airways. Air France connects the island with Paris and KLM has flights from Amsterdam.

From Juliana International Airport, there are regional services to Anguilla, Antigua, Curaçao, Dominica, Guadeloupe, Saba, San Juan, Sint Eustatius, St Kitts & Nevis, St-Barthélemy, St Croix, St Thomas, Tortola and Trinidad. Regional airlines serving Sint Maarten include **Air Sunshine** (www.airsunshine.com), **LIAT** (www.liatairline.com), **Winair** (www.fly-winair.com), **Air Antilles Express** (www.airantilles.com), **Insel Air** (www.fly-inselair.com) and **St Barth Commuter** (www.stbarthcommuter.com).

Sea The M/V Dawn II (www.sabactransport.com; same-day return adult/2-11yr US$68/35) ferry runs three times a week between Philipsburg and Saba. The M/V Edge (www.stmaarten-activities.com; day trip adult/child US$75/38) leaves on day trips for Saba from Simpson Bay Resort, returning at 3:30pm. The Voyager (☎0590-87-10-68; www.voy12.com) ferry has regular services from Marigot and Oyster Pond in St-Martin to St-Barthélemy. The one way/return fare is €60/88. Ferries also make the 25-minute journey from Marigot Bay to Blowing Point in Anguilla an average of once every 45 minutes during daylight hours. The one-way fare is US$20.

St-Barthélemy

Air St-Barth's only airport, Aéroport de St-Barthélemy (SBH; ☎0590-27-65-41), has the second-shortest runway in the world (the shortest is on Saba). Only teeny-tiny puddle jumpers can land on the island. There are frequent flights to/from Antigua, Guadeloupe, San Juan, Sint Maarten/St-Martin and St Thomas. Airlines serving St-Barthélemy include Air Antilles Express (www.airantilles.com), Air Caraïbes (www.aircaraibes.com), St-Barth Commuter (www.stbarthcommuter.com), Tradewind Aviation (www.tradewindaviation.com) and Winair (www.fly-winair.com).

Sea The Voyager (☎0590-87-10-68; www.voy12.com) ferry has regular services between Gustavia and Marigot (St-Martin), and between Gustavia and Oyster Pond (St-Martin). From Marigot, the journey is 1½ hours; from Oyster Pond, the ride is only 40 minutes. The one way/return fare is €60/88. Great Bay Express (☎542-0032; Bobby's Marina) also offers daily services between Gustavia and Philipsburg. The return fare is US$124. Day-trip tickets are significantly cheaper than returning on different days.

Guadeloupe

Air Guadeloupe's only international airport is Guadeloupe Pôle Caraïbes Airport (☎0590-21-14-98; www.guadeloupe.aeroport.fr; Les Abymes), which is north of Pointe-à-Pitre, 6km from the city center.

A number of airlines serve Guadeloupe, including Air Canada (from Montreal), Air France (from Paris), American Airlines (from San Juan and Miami) and Corsair (from Paris). There are direct regional services to Antigua, Barbados, Dominica, Fort-de-France, Port-au-Prince, St-Barthélemy, St-Martin/Sint Maarten, Santo Domingo and Trinidad & Tobago. Regional airlines serving Guadeloupe include Air Caraïbes (www.aircaraibes.com), Air Antilles Express (www.airantilles.com), Liat (www.liat.com) and Winair (www.fly-winair.com).

Sea L'Express des Îles (☎0825-35-90-00; www.express-des-iles.com; Gare Maritime, Bergevin) operates large, modern catamarans from Gare Maritime Bergevin in Pointe-à-Pitre to Roseau, Dominica (one way/round-trip €79/119, 1½ hours), continuing to Fort-de-France, Martinique (one way/round-trip €79/119, three hours) and then sometimes continuing to Castries, St Lucia (one way/round-trip €79/119, 4½

Beachfront, Philipsburg (p228), Sint Maarten
ADRIAN BEESLEY/GETTY IMAGES ©

hours). There are three to five weekly departures in both directions. Jeans for Freedom (☎0825-01-01-25; www.jeansforfreedom.com) operates services between Pointe-à-Pitre and St-Pierre in Martinique (one way €79). There are one to three weekly services depending on season.

Martinique

Air The island's only airport is Aéroport International Martinique Aimé Césaire (FDF; ☎0596-42-18-77; www.martinique.aeroport.fr; Le Lamentin), near the town of Lamentin in the southeast of Martinique, a short distance from Fort-de-France.

A number of airlines serve Martinique, including Air Canada (from Montreal), Air France (from Paris), American Airlines (from San Juan and Miami) and Corsair (from Paris). There are direct regional services to Dominica, Guadeloupe, Port-au-Prince (Haiti), San Juan, St-Barthélemy, St Lucia, St-Martin/Sint Maarten and Santo Domingo. Regional airlines serving Martinique include Air Caraïbes (www.aircaraibes.com), Air Antilles Express (www.airantilles.com) and Liat (www.liatairline.com).

Sea L'Express des Îles (☎0825-35-90-00; www.express-des-iles.com) operates large, modern catamarans between Fort-de-France and Pointe-à-Pitre, Guadeloupe (one way/round-trip €79/119, three hours), with a stop at Roseau in Dominica (one way/round-trip €79/119, 1½ hours). In the other direction there are departures from Fort-de-France to Castries in St Lucia (one way/round-trip €79/119, 80 minutes). There are three to five weekly crossings in both directions. Jeans for Freedom (☎0825-01-01-25; www.jeansforfreedom.com) operates services between St-Pierre and Pointe-à-Pitre (one way €79). There are one to three weekly services depending on season.

Getting Around

Boat

Guadeloupe

Ferries are the principal way to get between the islands of Guadeloupe. Multiple ferry operators run services between Grande-Terre and Terre-de-Haut, Marie-Galante and La Désirade. There are also ferries from Trois-Rivières on Basse-Terre to Terre-de-Haut in Les Saintes. Prices tend to be similar, though shop around on the ground for the best deal.

Babou One (☎0690-26-60-69, 0590-47-50-31; www.babouone.fr)

CTM Deher (☎0590-92-06-39; www.ctmdeher.com)

L'Archipel 1/L'Iguana Beach (☎0690-50-05-10, 0590-22-26-31)

L'Express des Îles (☎0825-35-90-00; www.express-des-iles.com)

Val Ferry (☎059-57-45-74; www.valferry.fr)

Martinique

A regular *vedette* (ferry) between Martinique's main resort areas and Fort-de-France provides a nice alternative to dealing with heavy bus and car traffic; it also allows you to avoid the hassles of city parking and is quicker to boot.

Vedettes Madinina (☎0596-63-06-46; www.vedettes.madinina.pagesperso-orange.fr) runs a boat between Anse Mitan, Anse-à-l'Ane, Pointe du Bout and Trois-Îlets daily from 6:20am to 6:30pm, and then every hour or so.

Bus

St-Martin/Sint Maarten, Guadeloupe and Martinique have a fairly reliable bus system but it's not the most convenient way of getting around. Traveling by bus may be an option to consider for shorter distances – and for visitors with a lot of extra time in their itinerary.

St-Barthélemy has no public transport.

Car & Motorcycle

Car hire is extremely popular in St-Martin/Sint Maarten, St-Barth, Guadeloupe and Martinique. No other form of transportation allows you to explore the islands' secret backwaters and enjoy as much freedom as a set of motorized wheels.

All major car rental agencies have a desk at airports. There are also a number of independent operators. Prices between December and April hover around €60 per day for cars, while low-season prices drop to a less outrageous €30 to €40 for a small car. Nearly all companies use an unlimited-kilometers rate. Most companies require a credit card, primarily so that you can leave a *caution* (deposit).

A driver's license from your home country is valid in all of the four islands.

Driving is on the right side of the road. Traffic regulations and road signs are of European standards.

Windward Islands

The English-speaking Windward Islands offer every experience one could want in the Caribbean and more.

In many ways, Dominica is the 'non-Caribbean' Caribbean island. Beaches are few, as are resorts; instead this volcanic island is blanketed by untamed rainforest that begs exploration. Rising like an emerald tooth from the Caribbean Sea, St Lucia grabs your attention with its arresting Pitons. In hills above small beaches, you'll find varied and interesting boutique hotels and resorts.

St Vincent and the Grenadines offer the sort of adventure that defines a Caribbean trip: hopping boats between islands ringed with untouched beaches and few other visitors. Grenada might offer the best of all worlds: gorgeous beaches, a neat little capital and a lush interior brimming with fragrant bounty.

Finally, Barbados is rich with island life and culture and has more beaches, nightlife and nature than you can ever digest.

Soufrière and the Pitons (p297)

Windward Islands Itineraries

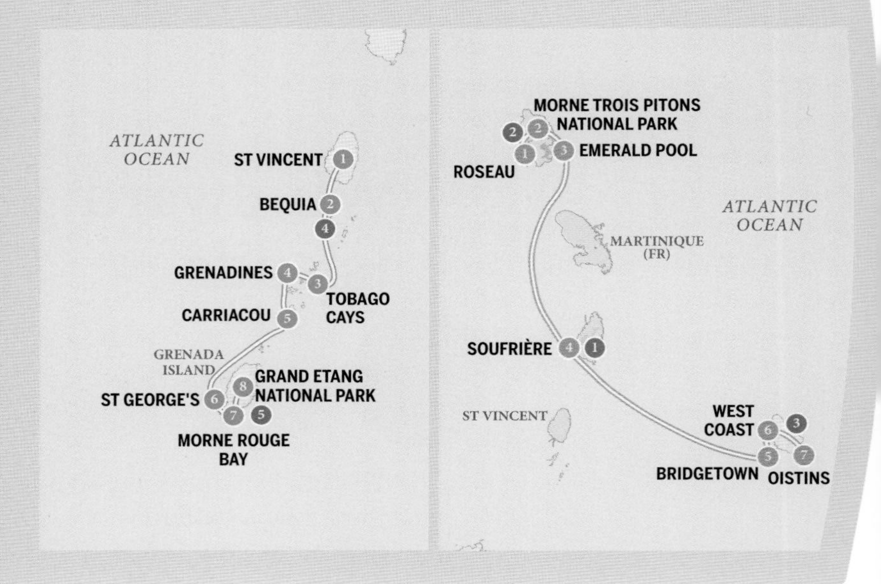

Seven Days

1. **St Vincent** (p300) Cruise the cobblestone streets of SVG's biggest city and capital, Kingstown, a vibrant mélange of lively markets, personable shops and open-air partying. Then get a boat tour up the coast to the beautiful waters at the Falls of Baleine on St Vincent.

2. **Bequia** (p303) Toss away your return ticket when you reach this idyllic island. Spend at least two nights lounging around its silken beaches and in the bars and restaurants around Admiralty Bay.

3. **Tobago Cays** (p308) Cruise on a day trip to these five picture-perfect islands that offer the snorkeling experience of a lifetime.

4. **Grenadines** (p308) Get a ticket for a ferry, hitch a ride on a passing fishing boat or charter a yacht and make your way down to Union Island, where you can relax watching boat masts bob in the marina.

5. **Carriacou** (p316) Hire a boat to take you from SVG to Grenada and enjoy a wildly scenic one-hour ride as you change counties.

6. **St George's** (p309) Save at least half a day for one of the Caribbean's prettiest capitals.

7. **Morne Rouge Bay** (p312) Get a room and sink your toes into the soft white sand and super-blue water.

8. **Grand Etang National Park** (p314) On your last day, hike the trails and check out the volcanic lake at this park which brims with jungle and luscious fruit and spice trees.

THIS LEG: 120 MILES

Ten Days

1 **Roseau** (p280) Start your adventure in this fun port town, with vintage buildings, a lively market and good sunsets. Head to nearby Wotten Waven for a soak in a hot-spring-fed spa.

2 **Morne Trois Pitons National Park** (p285) Count the shades of green amid the breathtaking scenery of this national park in the wild and beautiful hills that span the island. Hike to a waterfall.

3 **Emerald Pool** (p288) Take a refreshing dip into crystal-clear water, which reflects the shades of its verdant setting. Afterwards, soak up the mist on the wave-pounded Atlantic coast.

4 **Soufrière** (p297) Take a short flight to St Lucia and head south to the cute little fishing village of Soufrière, which has a world-class setting. Hit a local beach such as Anse Chastanet and snorkel and swim amid the stunning beauty of the Pitons. The next day, explore old plantations and take a hike on the Tet Paul Nature Trail.

5 **Bridgetown** (p317) Another short flight brings you to Barbados. The main city, Bridgetown, is one of the most intriguing in the hemisphere and has been named a Unesco World Heritage site for its hundreds of old colonial buildings and rich history.

6 **West Coast** (p324) Enjoy a day exploring the reefs and beaches of the island's posh West Coast. At night wander Holetown for drinks and a meal, whether sandy-toed casual or stylishly deluxe.

7 **Oistins** (p323) Revel in one of the Caribbean's great parties, the Oistins Fish Fry. Dance your weekend night away at one of the all-night bars.

THIS LEG: 250 MILES

Windward Islands Highlights

1 **Best Resorts: St Lucia** (p291) Revel in all manner of characterful places to unwind around Soufrière, some on the beach, some amid chocolate.

2 **Best Nature: Dominica** (p280) Soak off the island's amazing nature hikes in myriad hot springs hidden in the hills.

3 **Best Beaches: Barbados** (p317) The south and west coasts have the kind of dreamy sand that you fly for hours to enjoy.

4 **Best Island Escapes: St Vincent & the Grenadines** (p299) On little islands like Bequia you'll find it hard to ever leave.

5 **Best Smells: Grenada** (p308) On an island where nutmeg, cocoa, cinnamon, bananas, passionfruit, orchids and more grow profusely, breathe deep!

Lifeguard hut, Barbados (p317)

Discover the Windward Islands

DOMINICA

POP 71,700

Much of volcanic Dominica is blanketed by untamed rainforest that's a verdant backdrop to experiences such as an intense trek to a bubbling lake, soothing your muscles in hot sulfur springs, getting pummeled by a waterfall, snorkeling in a glass of 'champagne,' swimming up a narrow gorge – the list goes on.

Dominica has been spared mass tourism, in large part because there are very few sandy beaches, no flashy resorts and no direct international flights.

Roseau

POP 16,300

Roseau (*rose*-oh) is Dominica's compact, noisy, chaotic but vibrant capital, situated on the coast and the Roseau River. Reggae music blares through the narrow streets while people zip around in the daytime, but at night the city all but empties. Roseau's streets are lined with historic stone-and-wood buildings in states ranging from ramshackle to elegant.

Roseau is best explored on foot. The most historic section is the French Quarter, south of bustling King George V St.

Sights

Botanic Gardens Gardens

(www.da-academy.org/dagardens.html; 6am-7pm) The beautiful 40-acre botanic gardens teem with mature banyan, century palms and ficus trees along with flowering tropical shrubs. It's a great place for a wander and a picnic on the expansive lawns. A must-see is the **Parrot Conservation and Research Centre**, an aviary housing rare Jaco and Sisserou parrots. '**Jack's Walk**,' the short but steep and winding half-mile trail to the top of Morne Bruce, starts behind the aviary.

Old Market Square

(off King George V St; 10am-4pm) This cobblestone plaza has been the center of action in Roseau for the last 300 years. It's been

Springs near Boiling Lake (p285), Wotten Waven

Windward Islands

DOMINICA
Portsmouth
Dublanc
Marigot
Castle Bruce
Mero
Roseau
Delices
Scotts Head
Marigot
St-Pierre
MARTINIQUE (FR)
François
Cap Estate
Rodney Bay
CASTRIES
Marquis
Canaries
Dennery
Soufrière
ST LUCIA
Laborie
Vieux Fort
ST VINCENT
Chateaubelair
Georgetown
Barrouallie
KINGSTOWN
Port Elizabeth
Bequia
Isle A Quatre
Mustique
Canouan
Mayreau
Union Island
Palm Island
Petit St Vincent
Carriacou
Petite Martinique
Argyle
Ronde Island
Sauteurs
GRENADA
Grenville
ST GEORGE'S
Lance aux Épines

BARBADOS
Spring Hall
Speightstown
Bathsheba
Holetown
BRIDGETOWN
Oistins
0
50 km
0
25 miles

Ports of Call

ROSEAU

- The cruise-ship dock is right in the center, along Dame Eugenia Charles Blvd (also known as Bayfront).
- Hike to the gurgling Boiling Lake.
- Rappel down rainforest waterfalls in Morne Trois Pitons National Park.
- Swim, snorkel or dive amid crystal bubbles at Champagne Reef.

ST LUCIA

- Cruise ships dock in Castries. Some berths are right in town, others are a fair distance around a point.
- With a few hours, you can hunt for souvenirs in Castries Central Market; hit Reduit Beach or Pigeon Island National Landmark; or experience the thrills of zip-lining in the rainforest.

KINGSTOWN

- Traveling on foot from the cruise-ship dock, you can spend an intriguing day exploring the traditional Caribbean port town of Kingstown.
- Further afield, you can take a day trip by boat to the Falls of Baleine; tour St Vincent's lush interior on a hike or a drive; or jump on a ferry to the stunning island of Bequia.

ST GEORGE'S

- Cruise ships dock right in St George's.
- Popular actvities include exploring St George's, visiting Grand Etang National Park and enjoying Grand Anse Beach.

BRIDGETOWN

- Traveling on foot from the cruise-ship dock you can spend a day exploring Bridgetown.
- Further afield: taste rum at Mount Gay; see sea turtles on a west-coast snorkeling tour; lose yourself in ancient forests and gardens.

the site of political meetings, farmers markets and, more ominously, public executions and a slave market. Nowadays it's got souvenir stalls.

Dominica Museum Museum

(Bayfront near King George V St; admission US$2; ⏲9am-4pm Mon-Fri, to noon Sat) This small but interesting museum gives an overview of the history of Dominica and its people. Informative displays delve into Carib lifestyles, Creole culture and the slave trade.

Public Market Market

(off Hanover St; ⏲6am-5pm Mon-Sat) This bustling riverfront market is a good place to have a bowl of goat water (stew), pick up a bottle of sea moss or put together a picnic. Get lost amid myriad stands; join locals for a beer.

Activities

Many dive shops run whale-watching tours for US$50. Sightings are most common between November and March.

Dive Dominica Diving
(☎448-2188; www.divedominica.com; Castle Comfort Lodge, Coast Rd; 1-/2-tank dive US$55/90) The island's oldest dive shop.

Tours

Ken's Hinterland Adventure Tours Tours
(☎448-4850; www.khattstours.com; Fort Young Hotel, Victoria St; hikes US$35-80) Tours include hikes to Boiling Lake, snorkeling outings, bird-watching in the Syndicate rainforest and waterfalls tours.

Sleeping

Ma Bass Central Guest House Guesthouse $
(☎448-2999; www.mabassdominica.com; 44 Fields Lane; r US$44-70; ❄ 📶) The friendly owner, Theresa Emanuel (better known as Ma Bass), offers true hospitality that's like staying with your auntie. The 10 basic rooms (some fan-only) have vintage home-style decor.

Sutton Place Hotel Hotel $
(☎449-8700; www.suttonplacehoteldominica.com; 25 Old St; s/d from US$75/95; ❄ @ 📶) Many of the rooms at this well-run but

Roseau

Sights
1 Botanic Gardens ... D1
2 Dominica Museum ... B3
3 Old Market ... B3
4 Public Market ... A2

Activities, Courses & Tours
Ken's Hinterland Adventure Tours ... (see 5)

Sleeping
5 Fort Young Hotel ... C3
6 Ma Bass Central Guest House ... C2
7 Sutton Place Hotel ... B2

Eating
8 Calabash ... B2
9 Cocorico Café ... B2
10 Old Stone Grill & Bar ... B2

Drinking & Nightlife
Warner's Bar ... (see 5)

Roseau

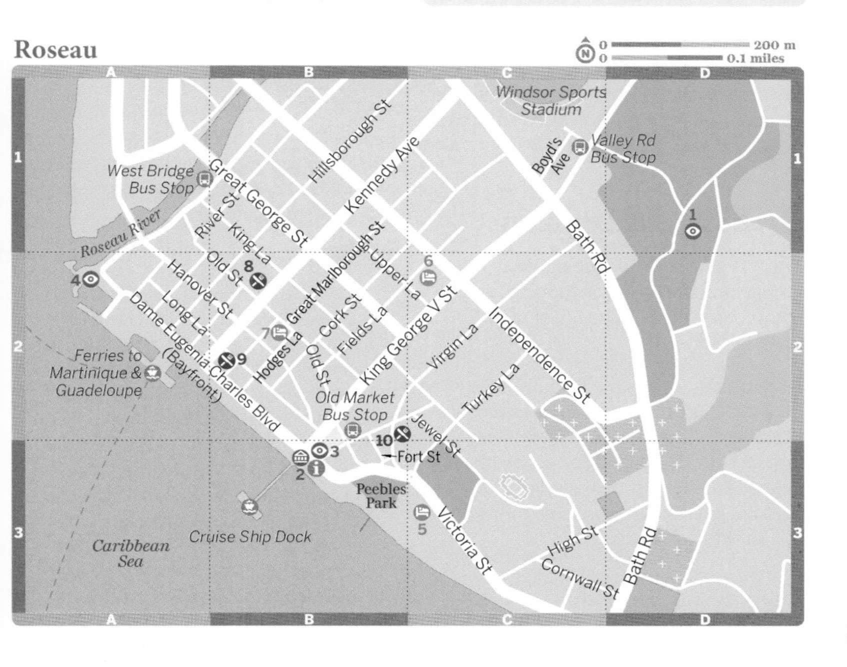

The Best... of Dominica

1 Gliding along the Indian River (p288)

2 Playing in the bubbles of Champagne Reef (p286)

3 Relaxing in the natural hot sulfur springs at (p285)

4 Taking a refreshing dip into crystal-clear Emerald Pool (p288)

5 Soaking up the bustle, beauty and history of Roseau (p280)

basic hotel have four-poster beds; suites have kitchenettes. The bar in the stone cellar recalls the building's 19th-century pedigree and it has a good cafe.

Fort Young Hotel Hotel **$$**
(448-5000; www.fortyounghotel.com; Victoria St; r US$100-250;) The old cannons that decorate this full-service 71-room hotel are a testament to its origin as an 18th-century fort. Now, it's the best option in town; go for an oceanfront room with a balcony.

Eating & Drinking

There are a score of simple places for a drink along the narrow beach heading south of town along the coast road to Castle Point.

Calabash Caribbean **$**
(440-9200; cnr Old St & Kennedy Ave; mains EC$15-40; 7am-8pm Mon-Sat;) Truly gracious service sets this casual upstairs cafe apart. Enjoy simple sandwiches and seafood while gazing over the hubbub in the streets below.

Old Stone Grill & Bar Caribbean **$$**
(440-7549; Castle St; mains US$10-30; 5-10pm) Busy with celebrating locals, gleeful visitors and nervous couples on third dates, this bistro has tables inside and out and makes mean blender drinks. Fare such as fish cakes and jerk pork have a spicy kick.

Cocorico Café French-Creole **$$**
(449-8686; cnr Dame Eugenia Charles Blvd & Kennedy Ave; mains EC$12-40; 8:30am-4:30pm Mon-Fri, to 2pm Sat;) Tousled tourists, gabby girlfriends and bronzed expats enjoy tasty crepes, crisp salads and yummy hot dishes such as the coconut curry chicken. This open-air corner spot always buzzes.

Warner's Bar Bar
(Fort Young Hotel, Victoria St; 11am-11pm) Friday happy hour is the place to ring in the weekend. It has sweeping views over the water, so come for sunset.

Information

Tourist Office (448-2045; www.dominica.dm; Dame Eugenia Charles Blvd; 8am-4pm Mon-Fri) On the ground floor beneath the Dominica Museum.

Roseau Valley

East of Roseau, the Roseau Valley is a ribbon of rural villages giving access to some of Dominica's most dramatic terrain and top wilderness sites.

TRAFALGAR FALLS

Your camera will have a love affair with these misty twin **waterfalls** (admission US$5), whose easy access puts them on the must-see list of just about every visitor to Dominica. If you don't like crowds, come before 10am or after 4pm.

An easy 0.4-mile trail (lots of steps, though) leads to a viewing platform. Water from the upper falls crosses the Titou Gorge before plunging down the sheer 200ft rock face and feeding the hydro-electric plant downhill. The lower falls flow from the Trois Pitons River in the Boiling Lake area.

Following the narrow, rocky trail beyond the platform means negotiating slippery moss-covered boulders, so wear sturdy shoes and watch your step. As a reward, you can cool off in shallow river pools or loll in the warm sulfur springs below the taller fall.

WOTTEN WAVEN

Across the valley from Trafalgar, and linked to it by a road across the River Blanc, Wotten Waven is famous for its natural hot sulfur springs. There are mellow options for dipping in waters and then there's **Screw's Sulfur Spa** (admission EC$25; ⏲10am-10pm), which reflects the lively persona of its Rasta owner.

Sleeping & Eating

As you meander the narrow steep roads in this beautiful valley, you'll pass various simple cafes serving fruit grown out back. Look for tiny guesthouses built from bamboo.

Le Petit Paradis Guesthouse **$**

(☎448-5946; lepetitparadis200@hotmail.com; r US$28-45, meals US$7-20; @ 📶) Choose from 11 simple rooms of varying sizes and comforts at this genial inn in the heart of the valley. The big-hearted owner, Joan, cooks great meals all day, for guests and those passing by. Herbs come from her garden.

Getting There & Away

Buses to the Roseau Valley make the trip from the Valley Rd stop in Roseau to Wotten Waven in about 20 minutes and to Trafalgar in about 30 minutes (check with the driver to make sure you're on the right bus).

MORNE TROIS PITONS NATIONAL PARK

This national park stretches across 17,000 acres of Dominica's mountainous volcanic interior. It's a stunning pastiche of lakes, fumaroles, volcanoes, hot springs and dense tropical forest. Hikes start in the mountain village of Laudat (elevation 1970ft).

Activities

Boiling Lake Hiking

Dominica's pre-eminent trek, and one of the hardest, is the six-hour round-trip to the world's second-largest actively boiling lake (the largest is in New Zealand). Geologists believe the 207ft-wide lake is a flooded fumarole – a crack in the earth that allows hot gases to vent from the molten lava below. The fizzing waters sit inside a deep cauldron and are a spectacular sight.

The hike traverses the aptly named Valley of Desolation, whose sulfur rivers, belching steam vents and geysers evoke post-atomic grace. It then follows narrow ridges, snakes up and down mountains and runs along hot streams. Wear sturdy walking shoes and expect to get wet and muddy.

The strenuous 6-mile hike to the lake begins at Titou Gorge and requires a guide. Ask for a referral at your hotel. The cost should be about US$40 per person.

Titou Gorge Swimming

A swimming hole gives way to this narrow gorge ending at a torrential waterfall. The eerily quiet, short swim through the crystal-clear water is a spooky experience. The gorge is at the Boiling Lake trailhead.

The Waitukubuli National Trail

A new long-distance hiking trail, the **Waitukubuli National Trail** (www.waitukubulitrail.com), links the far south with the far north of the island, hitting all the key beauty spots along the way, from Scotts Head to Boiling Lake and Emerald Pool. Its 115 miles are divided into 14 segments of various lengths and difficulty but each one is designed to be completed in one day. The website has maps and more.

Middleham Falls
Hiking

The trail to Middleham Falls, one of Dominica's highest waterfalls (200ft), takes you on an interesting rainforest walk. The main trailhead is along the Roseau–Laudat road, about 5 miles east of Roseau. The hike starts at 1600ft, climbs to 2200ft and then drops down to the falls. Allow about two to three hours round-trip.

Extreme Dominica
Adventure Tour

(☎295-7272, 295-6828; www.extremedominica.com; canyoning tour US$160) This pro outfit runs exhilarating half-day adventures that have you rappelling down waterfalls and floating in crystal-clear pools at the bottom of deep canyon walls. It also offers scenic hikes and turtle watching.

Getting There & Away

Buses to Laudat (40 minutes) leave from the Valley Rd bus stop in Roseau. A taxi ride from Roseau to Laudat costs EC$80.

South of Roseau

The coastal road south of Roseau takes you down to Mediterranean-flavored Soufriere Bay, dead-ending at Scotts Head in about 30 minutes.

Along the way, **Champagne Reef** is one of Dominica's most unusual underwater playgrounds. Volcanic bubbles emerge from vents beneath the sea floor, making it feel like you're swimming in a giant glass of champagne. Best of all, you can snorkel right off the (rocky) beach.

At the heart of the bay, which is the rim of a sunken volcanic crater, **Soufriere** is a sleepy fishing village whose undisputed 'hot spot' is the **Soufriere Sulfur Springs** (site fee US$5). It's the source of a steaming hot stream in the hills above town whose water is captured in a series of stone pools.

Scotts Head has a gem of a setting along its gently curving shoreline. Activity centers on the waterfront where old men

Left: Trafalgar Falls (p284); Below: Red ginger flower, Roseau
(LEFT) MICHAEL RUNKEL/GETTY IMAGES ©; (BELOW) DANITA DELIMONT/GETTY IMAGES ©

hang out on the porches of pastel-painted houses.

West Coast

The drive along the west coast takes you past Canefield Airport and through several villages and on to Portsmouth.

MERO & SALISBURY

About halfway up the coast, grayish-black **Mero Beach** is the west coast's most popular sandy strand. It's accessed via a narrow one-way road off the main highway. A string of bars serve drinks and meals and rent beach chairs.

There are some beautiful dive sites just a 10-minute boat ride away, including Coral Gardens, Rena's Reef and Whale Shark Reef. **East Carib Dive** (449-6575; www.east-carib-dive.com; Salisbury; 1-/2-tank dives US$50/80) runs trips and snorkeling tours.

Sleeping & Eating

Tamarind Tree Hotel Hotel $$
(449-7395; www.tamarindtreedominica.com; Salisbury; r US$80-165; closed Sep;) This 12-room property run by a Swiss-German couple sits on a seaside cliff amid nicely landscaped grounds. Some rooms have fans, others air-con. There is a shared porch and a rooftop sitting area for stargazing.

Connie's Mero Beach Bar Caribbean $
(Mero Beach; meals EC$12-20; 8am-late, dinner by reservation) A Mero Beach institution, Connie serves snacks, drinks and friendly advice on local attractions. The menu changes daily, but goat curry, steamed fish and fried chicken are typical. The nearby **Romance Cafe** is another excellent spot.

Emerald Pool

Easily accessible **Emerald Pool** (Central Dominica; site fee US$5) takes its name from its lush green setting and clear water. At the base of a 40ft waterfall, the pool is deep enough for a refreshing dip. The 0.3-mile path to get here winds through a rainforest of massive ferns and tall trees. There are two viewpoints – one is a panorama of the Atlantic coast and the other is a great view of Morne Trois Pitons, Dominica's second-highest mountain. The path can get a bit slippery in places. Come before 10am or after 3pm to avoid crowds.

The pool is on the well-maintained road linking Canefield and Castle Bruce. The drive is about 30 minutes from either.

MORNE DIABLOTIN NATIONAL PARK

Established to protect the habitat of the national bird, the Sisserou parrot, and its pretty red-necked cousin, the Jaco parrot, this national park covers some 8242 acres. It's named for Dominica's tallest peak (4747ft).

Activities

Syndicate Parrot Reserve Hiking

(site fee US$5) This easy one-hour loop trail through the Syndicate Rainforest on the western slopes of Morne Diablotin is your best chance to see Dominica's endangered parrots (the best spotting time is in the early morning and late afternoon). Also watch for any of Dominica's four hummingbird species.

To get to the reserve, turn onto the signposted road just north of the village of Dublanc and continue to Syndicate Estate, about 4.5 miles inland.

PORTSMOUTH

POP 3200

Dominica's second-largest town is slightly scruffy but set on attractive Prince Rupert Bay.

Sights & Activities

Indian River River

(site fee US$5) The slow and silent boat trip along this shady mangrove-lined river is a memorable experience as you glide past buttressed bwa mang trees whose trunks rise out of the shallows, their roots stretching out laterally along the riverbanks. Enjoy close-up views of egrets, crabs, iguanas, hummingbirds and other creatures.

Rowers wait at the mouth of the river and charge EC$50 per person for the 1½-hour trip.

Cabrits National Park National Park

(admission US$5; 8am-6pm) Located on a scenic peninsula 1.25 miles north of Portsmouth, this is the site of **Fort Shirley**, an impressive, though ruined, 18th-century British garrison. The park encompasses the surrounding coastal area, as well as the island's largest swamp. It has good views across the bay and serene spots for picnics.

Some of the fort's stone ruins have been cleared and partially reconstructed, while others remain half-hidden in the jungle. The powder magazine has been turned into a small **museum** that has a great model of the island.

Cabrits Dive Center Diving

(445-3010; www.cabritsdive.com; Picard Estate; 1-/2-tank dives US$66/99) Close to some of the island's most spectacular sites, including Toucari Caves and Douglas Bay Point. Most sites are only a short boat ride away. Snorkeling gear rents for US$22 per day, snorkeling trips are US$33.

Sleeping & Eating

Good lodging can be found a short drive north or south of Portsmouth. In town there are simple cafes.

Manicou River Resort Resort **$$**
(☎616-8903; www.manicouriverresort.com; Everton Hall Estate, Tanetane; cottage from US$130;) About 10 minutes north of Portsmouth, this beautiful retreat sits about 400ft above the Caribbean and affords picture-perfect views over the water and the Cabrits. Stay in individual octagonal cottages brimming with unique design details.

Soak up the site's serenity while swinging in a hammock on your balcony or taking a dip in a pool fed by volcanic springwater. Kitchens and beds are both king size.

Getting There & Away

Buses up the west coast leave from the West Bridge bus stop in Roseau. In Portsmouth, buses leave from the town square on Bay Rd.

Northeastern Coast

The narrow road cutting to the east coast from Portsmouth across Dominica's remote and sparsely populated north is a stunning drive past massive ferns, towering palms, wild helliconias and thick banana groves. Budget about two hours for the drive. Numerous scenes from *Pirates of the Caribbean* were filmed in this area.

CALIBISHIE

Calibishie is an attractive fishing village with the best beaches on the island. It makes a good stop for lunch or an overnight stay, particularly if you're catching a morning flight from nearby Melville Hall Airport.

Ask locals for directions to various tiny beaches on coves. A favorite is at **Batibou Bay** (entrance fee US$5) at the end of a 1km bumpy dirt road; after heavy rains it's often only accessible by 4WD. This coconut palm-fringed crescent has good swimming and snorkeling with a coral reef just offshore; there's a cafe.

Sleeping & Eating

Jacoway Inn B&B **$$**
(☎445-8872; www.calibishie.net; r incl breakfast from US$85;) This two-room B&B is run by the irrepressible Carol Ann. Enjoy plenty of elbow room amid artsy decor, quality furnishings, a kitchenette and fresh fruit and flowers. The upstairs unit has a big balcony with views out to sea. The home-cooked breakfasts are memorable. It's high above the village, up a steep road. Look for the sign.

Veranda View B&B **$$**
(☎613-9493; www.lodgingdominica.com; r incl breakfast US$65-105;) This brightly decorated three-room inn is right on the sand and has great beachfront vistas. The owner is a consummate host and excellent cook (delicious dinners are EC$30).

Mero Beach (p287)
WALTER BIBIKOW/GETTY IMAGES ©

Weekly Pass

Numerous natural and historic sites on Dominica charge US$5 for admission. You can instead purchase a weekly pass good for all the sites for $12, a great deal!

Information

Tourist Office (☎445-8344; www.calibishiecoast.com; ⏰9am-5pm Mon-Fri) Internet access (EC$5 per hour) and good info on the many little places to stay in the region.

MARIGOT & PAGUA BAY

Sprawling Marigot encompasses Melville Hall Airport and several neighborhoods strung along the highway. Aside from the gas station (the only one for miles), there's little to make you want to stop. Instead, push on to gorgeous Pagua Bay, which has a rocky beach suitable for bodysurfing.

Sleeping & Eating

Hibiscus Valley Inn Guesthouse $$

(☎445-8195, 225-3965; www.hibiscusvalley.com; r US$42-150, meals US$13-20; 📶) This convivial rainforest lodge 15 minutes from Melville Airport has a range of rooms: a 'simple room' with shared facilities down by the river; a 'nature bungalow' with a veranda for lounging in a hammock; or a hotel standard room with air-con, TV and fridge. Tours include a popular tubing trip down the Pagua River.

Pagua Bay House Inn $$$

(☎445-8888; www.paguabayhouse.com; r from US$200, mains from US$15; ❄📶) These luxe rooms feature industrial-flavored facades and warm wooden interiors. Rates include use of kayaks and boogie boards. The open-air **Bar & Grill** has views across the road to the pounding surf. Ceviche, Caesar salad and fish tacos are the lunch treats, while dinners include steaks and lobster. It's a popular daytime stop.

Champagne Reef (p286)

Carib Territory

The 3700-acre Carib Territory, which begins around the village of Bataka and continues south for 7.5 miles, is home to most of Dominica's 2200 Caribs – properly known as Kalinago. It's a rural area with cultivated bananas, breadfruit trees and wild heliconia growing along the roadside. Many houses are traditional wooden structures on log stilts, but there are also simple cement homes and, in the poorer areas, shanties of corrugated tin and tar paper.

The roadside **Cassava Bakery** in Salybia sells delicious traditional Carib bread hot from the oven (EC$5). It's crunchy, cake-like and made from coconut and cassava.

ST LUCIA

POP 181,000

Noted for its oodles of small and luxurious resorts that drip color and flair, St Lucia is really two islands in one. Rodney Bay in the north offers modern comforts amid a beautiful bay. In the south, Soufrière is at the heart of a gorgeous region of old plantations, hidden beaches and the geologic wonder of the impossibly photogenic Pitons.

Castries

The main city of St Lucia is worth a stop as you transit from one of the islands to the other. Its best feature is the soaring Morne Fortune (2795ft) as its backdrop. Most of the city's historic buildings were destroyed by major fires between 1785 and 1948, but it makes for an interesting stroll.

The markets mostly sell tat to cruise-ship passengers, but you can find interest back in the recesses. If possible, avoid the charmless area of town along Jeremie St and the main port area.

Sights

Cathedral of the Immaculate Conception Cathedral

(Laborie St; 8am-5pm) The city's Catholic cathedral, built in 1897, is a grand stone structure that has a splendidly painted interior of trompe l'oeil columns and colorfully detailed biblical scenes. The island's patron saint, St Lucia, is portrayed directly

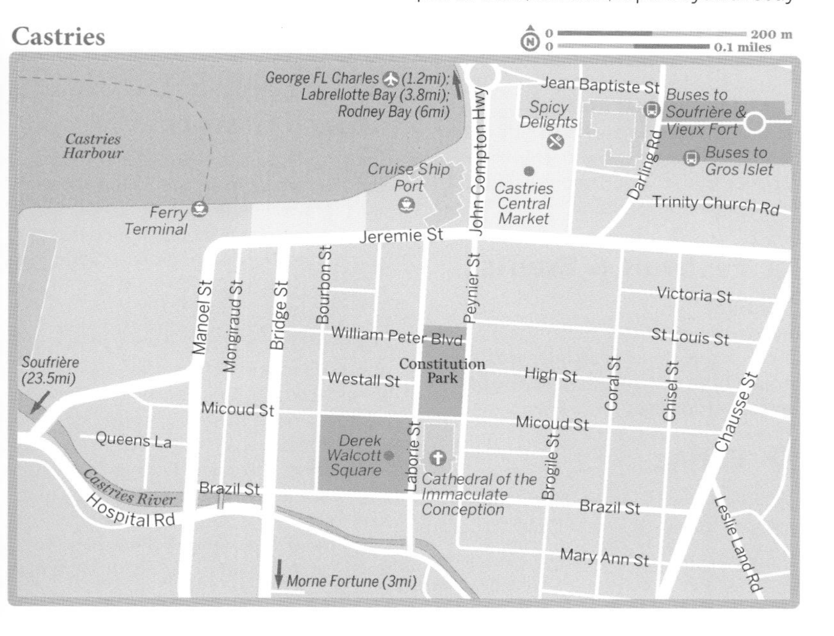

Detour: The East Coast

A 30-minute drive from Castries transports you to yet another world, along the Atlantic-battered east coast, where you can experience a St Lucia that's very Creole, laid-back and little visited.

While this coast lacks the beaches of the west, it makes up for it with lovely bays backed by spectacular cliffs, a rocky shoreline pounded by thundering surf, and a handful of picturesque fishing towns, including **Dennery** and **Micoud**.

above the altar. When children's choirs are practicing, it's magical.

Derek Walcott Square Square
This lovely square is named for local writer Derek Walcott, who won the Nobel Prize for literature in 1992. It's a quiet park surrounded by a handful of attractive 19th-century wooden buildings.

Castries Central Market Market
(Jeremie St) Head to the north side of the central market, where you'll find fresh produce from the rich countryside and other authentic items.

Festivals & Events

Carnival Carnival
(www.luciancarnival.com; Jul) The biggest show on the island's calendar. Castries' streets buzz with music, costume parades and calypso.

Eating

For good rotis and local dishes, try the stalls on the north side of Castries Central Market.

Spicy Delights Caribbean $
(Castries Central Market; mains EC$12-25; 8am-3pm Mon-Sat) One of several simple cafes serving great local food hidden under a portico on the north side of the market. This is the place for 'figs & salt,' a stew of salt cod and boiled green bananas that's much better than it looks.

Pink Plantation House Creole $$
(452-5422; Chef Harry Dr, Morne Fortune; mains EC$40-75; 11:30am-3pm Mon-Fri, 6:30-9pm Fri, 9am-noon Sun) This art gallery housed in a splendid colonial mansion sitting on a lush property doubles as a restaurant. The views from the veranda are to die for. The Sunday brunch, at EC$60, is unmissable. Wonderful cocktails, too.

Shopping

There's little reason to browse the junk-filled tourist stalls lining the port area. Look further afield.

Eudovic's Art Studio Woodcarvings
(452-2747; www.eudovicart.com; Morne Fortune; 8am-4:30pm Mon-Fri, 8am-2pm Sat & Sun) Vincent Joseph Eudovic is a renowned master carver, and his studio at Morne Fortune is a magnificent art gallery, 3 miles south of the center.

Around Castries

Going north past the airport along Gros Islet Rd from Vigie Peninsula the ocean-side highway snakes its way to Rodney Bay. This stretch is far busier and more built-up than any other areas in St Lucia.

Rodney Bay & Gros Islet

About 10km north of Castries, the vast horseshoe of Rodney Bay boasts the island's most diverse tourist facilities. Within the bay is a large, artificial lagoon and marina, flanked by Rodney Bay Village, a somewhat bland assemblage of bars, restaurants, shops and more.

Far more interesting is the fishing village of Gros Islet to the north. Here the historic streets are lined with rum shops and fishing shacks draped with drying nets.

 Beaches

Reduit Beach Beach
This long stretch of white sand is the most popular beach on the island. The sea ranges from turquoise to azure, the waves are benign and there are plenty of beach activities and cafes at hand. The central part of the beach gets mobbed so head to the south end on the far side of the vast Rex Resort. It's less crowded, and has shade and a good beach bar.

 Activities

There are several dive sites and snorkeling spots of note off the northwestern coast. Day sail and sunset cruises are hugely popular, with many operators.

Scuba Steve's Diving Diving
(450-9433; www.scubastevesdiving.com; Gros Islet; discover dive US$80;) Offers dives across the island and snorkel trips (from US$35).

Endless Summer Cruises Cruises
(450-8651; www.stluciaboattours.com; Rodney Bay Marina; sunset cruise from US$60) A popular operator with a range of cruises.

 Sleeping

Bay Guesthouse Guesthouse $
(450-8956; www.bay-guesthouse.com; Bay St, Gros Islet; r US$55-125;) Within easy walking distance of Gros Islet, this waterfront guesthouse is amazing value. It's run by a charming couple who have a great insight into the needs of travelers. Rooms range from compact to spacious, some have stunning views. The grounds have hammocks.

East Winds Inn Resort $$$
(452-8212; www.eastwinds.com; La Brelotte Bay, Gros Islet; all-inclusive per night from US$700;) Understated yet beautiful, relaxed yet luxurious, this all-inclusive resort is one of St Lucia's most appealing beachside resorts. It has a mere 30 rooms spread over a garden- and bird-filled site. Service is superb, as is the food.

Portsmouth from Manicou River Resort (p289)

NICK LEDGER/GETTY IMAGES ©

Forest Thrills

Enjoy the rainforest from a Tarzan perspective? Just 30 minutes east of Rodney Bay, **Rainforest Adventures** (**458-5151; www.rainforestadventure.com; Chassin; admission from US$76; 9am-3pm Tue-Fri & Sun**) has zip-lines through the trees. For the less adventurous, it offers a 1½-hour aerial 'tram' ride over the canopy and bird-watching tours.

Ginger Lily Hotel Hotel $$$
(**458-0300; www.thegingerlilyhotel.com; Reduit Beach Ave; r from US$190;**) An excellent alternative to the bigger resorts nearby, Ginger Lily Hotel is functional, intimate and blissfully quiet. The 11 rooms have balconies and terraces but no sea views. Reduit Beach is just across the road.

Eating & Drinking

RODNEY BAY

Rodney Bay has dozens of midrange restaurants offering all types of food. A strip of bars keeps people hopping from one to the next until the early hours.

Spinnakers Beach Bar & Restaurant Caribbean $
(**452-8491; www.spinnakersbeachbar.com; Reduit Beach; mains EC$25-90; 11am-10pm**) Right on Reduit Beach, this venue is a catch-all for locals, cruise-shippers and seemingly everybody else. The views out to sea from the open-air tables are why people go on holiday.

Delirious Bar
(**Rodney Bay Village; 11am-late Mon-Sat**) Come for rollicking times on the terrace and good cocktails. One of several on the inland nightlife strip.

GROS ISLET

On Friday nights (and to a lesser extent Thursday) the weekly **jump-up** gets going. Stalls sell fresh fish, grilled chicken and other delights. The music plays at full volume and there's dancing in the streets.

Seafood Grills Seafood $
(**Bay St, Gros Islet; meals from EC$15; 5-10pm**) A rotating string of open-air joints across from the water offer excellent seafood grills most nights of the week. They are ultra-casual: wait for a plate of barbecued fresh fish, get a few sides, then find a spot in the dark at a picnic table. Wash it all down with a cold brew.

Flavours of the Grill Caribbean $$
(**450-9722; Mare Therese St, Gros Islet; mains EC$25-45; 11am-10pm Mon-Sat**) This intimate eatery, in a colorful, quirky Creole home in the center of Gros Islet, offers refined versions of Caribbean classics. The seafood is locally caught.

Pigeon Island

This former island was joined to the mainland in the 1970s when a sandy causeway was constructed; it's one of Rodney Bay's best sights.

Pigeon Island National Landmark (**www.slunatrust.org; adult/child EC$16/2.50; ticket booth 9am-5pm**) has a fascinating range of historic sites scattered across the bucolic former 'island.' Its spicy history dates back to the 1550s, when St Lucia's first French settler, Jambe de Bois (Wooden Leg), used the island as a base for raiding passing Spanish ships. Two centuries later, British admiral George Rodney fortified Pigeon Island, using it to monitor the French fleet on Martinique.

Pigeon Island is a fun place to explore, with paths winding around the remains of barracks, batteries and garrisons whose partially intact stone buildings create a ghost-town effect. At the top of Fort Rodney Hill, you'll find a small but well-preserved fortress, a few rusting cannons and cardiac-arresting views.

On the south side, there are two small **beaches** with water sports. A much larger beach outside the grounds is often overrun with tour groups.

Eating

Jambe De Bois Caribbean $

(Pigeon Island National Landmark; mains EC$10-25; 9am-10pm Tue-Sun, to 5pm Mon) Locals, yachties and frequent visitors know they'll get a delicious meal and a wonderful view of the bay. Pick out a table on the breezy veranda; on Saturday and Sunday nights it has live music. You can access the cafe even when the ticket office is closed.

The Northern Tip

Once you've left bustling Rodney Bay, life becomes more sedate as you head toward the island's northernmost reaches. On Cap Estate the hilly terrain is dotted with chichi villas, large estates and the island's only public golf course. From there it's an easy drive downhill to secluded **Cas En Bas Beach**. On the wilder side of the island, the winds and surf here can be lively.

Activities

Cas En Bas Beach and Smugglers Cove both have a small water-sports center that rents out sailboats, kayaks, windsurfers and snorkeling gear (from US$25 per hour).

Cas En Bas always has a stiff breeze, which makes it an excellent (yet largely undiscovered) kitesurfing spot.

Kitesurfing St Lucia Kitesurfing

(714-9589; www.kitesurfingstlucia.com; Cas En Bas Beach; lessons from US$120, rental per half day from US$50; hours vary) Offers lessons (from US$80 for two hours) and rentals (from US$35).

Sleeping & Eating

Cotton Bay Village Resort $$$

(456-5700; www.cottonbayvillage.com; Cas En Bas; r from US$350;) Overlooking Cas En Bas Beach, this resort caters to sophisticated couples and active families while, at the same time, offering cozy privacy to honeymooners. It features 75 spacious units, a vast pool and the beach right out front.

Marjorie's Beach Bar & Restaurant Caribbean $

(520-0001; Cas En Bas Beach; mains from EC$50; 11am-4pm) Feel the sand between your toes at this funky cafe on the sand. Enjoy tasty Creole dishes and wicked rum cocktails.

Western St Lucia

As the road heads south from Castries, it encounters the rising topography of the island – twisting and turning around hairpin corners and steep hills – and uncluttered ocean views. Passing through

Pigeon Island (left)
FLAVIO VALLENARI/GETTY IMAGES ©

the tiny fishing villages of Anse La Raye and Canaries, and the banana plantations that surround them, the real St Lucia comes to the fore.

MARIGOT BAY

Deep, sheltered Marigot Bay is an exquisite example of natural architecture. Sheltered by towering palms and the surrounding hills, the narrow inlet is said to have once hidden the entire British fleet from French pursuers. Yachts play the same trick these days – the bay is a popular place to drop anchor and hide away for a few nights. Enjoy nearby beaches.

 Sleeping & Eating

Inn On The Bay B&B **$$$**
(451-4260; www.saint-lucia.com; Marigot Bay; r from US$245;) Outstandingly positioned atop a secluded hill (views!), this peach of a place, run by a Canadian couple, features five bright and spacious rooms that open onto a pool and a sunset-friendly deck. A free shuttle takes you to the bay.

Julietta's Restaurant & Bar Caribbean **$$**
(458-3224; Marigot Bay Rd; mains EC$25-80; 11am-9pm) Overlooking the bay from the top of the hill, Julietta's offers exceptional views. Enjoy fresh fish and other casual fare.

Rainforest Hideaway Fusion **$$$**
(451-4485; www.rainforesthideawaystlucia.com; Marigot Bay; menus EC$145-180; 5-10pm) This stylish restaurant is perfect for a tête-à-tête. Subdued lighting, elegant furnishings and a breezy deck overlooking the bay will rekindle the faintest romantic flame. The emphasis is on local dishes with a contemporary twist. It's accessible by a small ferry from the docks.

ANSE LA RAYE

Heading south along the coast from Marigot Bay, the winding road snakes its way through this tiny and evocative fishing village. Usually quiet, everything changes for **Seafood Friday**. Street stalls sell fish at unbeatable prices; the party gets a bit wild and goes most of the night.

Soufrière and the Pitons (right)

PAUL BAGGALEY/GETTY IMAGES ©

SOUFRIÈRE & THE PITONS

If one town were to be the heart and soul of St Lucia, it would have to be Soufrière. Its attractions include a slew of colonial-era edifices scattered amid brightly painted wooden storefronts and a bustling seafront.

The surrounding landscape is little short of breathtaking: the sky-scraping towers of rock known as the Pitons stand guard over the town. Jutting from the sea, covered in vegetation and ending in a summit that looks otherworldly, these are St Lucia's iconic landmarks.

The area boasts beauty above and below the water as well as historic and natural sights aplenty.

Climbing Gros Piton

If you have time for only one trek during your stay, choose the Gros Piton (2617ft) climb. Starting from the hamlet of Fond Gens Libres, you walk mostly through a thick jungle. The final section is very steep, but the reward is a tremendous view of southern St Lucia and the densely forested mountains of the interior. Allow roughly four hours there and back. A guide is mandatory; contact **Gros Piton Nature Trail Guides** (286-0382; guide US$30).

Climbing Petit Piton is discouraged by local authorities because some sections involve clambering on near-vertical slabs of rock.

Beaches

Anse Chastanet Beach

Stretched out in front of the resort of the same name, Anse Chastanet is a fine curving beach and it's an easy 1-mile walk from Soufrière. The sheltered bay is protected by high cliffs. The snorkeling just offshore is some of the best on the island; hassle-free access is through the resort.

Anse Mamin Beach

A dreamy, secluded enclave of golden sand edges a gently curved cove that's about a 10-minute walk north of Anse Chastanet, or about 30 minutes from town.

Malgretoute Beach Beach

South of Soufrière along the Vieux Fort Rd, take the small road toward the Viceroy Resort. The reward is this lovely light-sand beach with some good snorkeling just offshore. It's just north of looming Petit Piton.

The nearby much-hyped **Sugar Beach** is made with imported sand and requires a long walk through the unwelcoming walled enclave of the Viceroy Resort.

Sights

Morne Coubaril Estate Adventure Park

(459-7340; www.stluciaziplining.com; off Vieux Fort Rd; adult/child EC$18/9, zip-lining US$69; 8am-4pm) This 18th-century estate, off the Vieux Fort road, about half a mile north of Sulphur Springs, offers a great insight into the plantation world that dominated this country for so long. Zip-lines let you sail through the forest, with Petit Piton forming a perfect backdrop.

Diamond Falls Botanical Gardens & Mineral Baths Gardens

(459-7565; www.diamondstlucia.com; adult/child EC$15/7.50, baths from EC$12.50; 10am-5pm Mon-Sat, 10am-3pm Sun) Wander amid tropical flowers and trees, at this old estate. Mineral baths date from 1784, when they were built atop hot springs so that the troops of France's King Louis XVI could take advantage of their therapeutic effects. It's 1 mile east of Soufrière town center.

Activities

The waters off Soufrière, which have been designated a marine park, are a magnet for divers of all levels. There's a good balance of reef dives, drop-offs and easy dives, as well as a couple of wrecks.

Tet Paul Nature Trail Nature Trail
(www.soufrierefoundation.org; off Vieux Fort Rd; tour adult/child EC$12.50/5; 9am-5pm) Don't miss this community-run nature trail. During the 45-minute tour, a guide will show you an organic farm and take you to a lookout; the view of the Pitons that jab the skyline is stunning but even better are the insights into traditional local life. It's signposted, 3.1 miles south of Soufrière.

Action Adventure Divers Diving
(459-5599; www.aadivers.org; Hummingbird Beach Resort; 2-tank dive US$95) Offers a wide range of trips.

Mystic Man Tours Boat Trips
(459-7783; www.mysticmantours.com; Bridge St, Soufrière; tours from US$30; 8am-4pm Mon-Sat) Boat excursions in the area, from whale-watching and snorkeling trips to sunset cruises and deep-sea fishing outings, are on offer.

Sleeping

Most places to stay are fairly isolated, so a rental car is advised. Some hotels provide shuttle services to nearby beaches.

Fond Doux Resort & Plantation Resort $$
(459-7545; www.fonddouxestate.com; off Vieux Fort Rd; cottages from US$180;) Hidden in the hills to the south of Soufrière, this 250-year-old working cocoa plantation is a great place to unwind. Eleven tastefully refurbished historic cottages are surrounded by tropical gardens. The restaurant, **Jardin Cacao**, grows most of its food on the estate.

Hummingbird Beach Resort Resort $$
(459-7232; www.istlucia.co.uk; Soufrière; r US$90-250;) Friendly, low-key and peaceful, this modest resort is a short walk from both town and Anse Chastanet. The best-value rooms have no view, but for just a bit more you can enjoy ocean vistas and Piton views.

Crystals Boutique Hotel $$$
(285-1984; www.stluciacrystals.com; Soufrière; r from US$190;) Indian and Caribbean touches, woodcarved furnishings, and a treehouse bar are just some of the features at this offbeat retreat. No two cottages are alike; most come with a private plunge pool. The views of the Pitons and the valley of Soufrière are mesmerizing.

Ladera Resort $$$
(459-7323; www.ladera.com; off Vieux Fort Rd; ste incl breakfast from US$500;) The location is one of the best in St Lucia: an 1100ft-high ridge with full-frame views of the Pitons and the ocean. The spacious rooms have a rich, naturalistic design and their own plunge pools; there's also a spa. It's 2.5 miles south of town.

Eating & Drinking

Most hotels and resorts have in-house restaurants and bars that are also open to nonguests. Many have stunning food, views or both.

Martha's Tables Caribbean $$
(459-7270; off Vieux Fort Rd, Malgretoute; meals from US$15; 11:30am-2pm Mon-Fri) Just up the hill from Malgretoute Beach, this homestyle restaurant is in Martha's actual home. Each day she prepares a spread of excellent comfort food using local flavors. Grab a plastic chair and enjoy.

Orlando's Caribbean $$$
(459-5955; www.orlandosrestaurantstl.com; Cemetery Rd; mains from US$25; 7:30-10am & noon-2pm Wed-Mon) Chef Orlando Sachell made a name for himself basically inventing the concept of farm-to-table cuisine at some of St Lucia's best resorts. Now he has his own fine restaurant right in Soufrière. The breakfast and lunch menu changes constantly but the high level of service doesn't. Book in advance.

The South Coast

On the road to Vieux Fort, **Choiseul**, a little village south of Soufrière, has an active handicraft industry, and a roadside arts-and-crafts center.

At the very southern tip of the island, **Vieux Fort**, the island's second-largest town, lies on a vast plain onshore from where the azure waters of the Caribbean blend with those of the rough Atlantic Ocean. Right off the end of the runway at Hewanorra International Airport, **Sandy Beach** is great for kitesurfing and windsurfing. Get gear from **Reef Kite & Surf** (☎454-3418; www.slucia.com/kitesurf; Sandy Beach, Anse des Sables, Vieux Fort; rentals per half-day from US$60).

ST VINCENT & THE GRENADINES

POP 109,500

Just the name St Vincent and the Grenadines (SVG) evokes visions of exotic, idyllic island life. Imagine an island chain in the heart of the Caribbean Sea, uncluttered by tourist exploitation; with white-sand beaches on deserted islands, sky-blue water gently lapping the shore and barely a soul around.

St Vincent

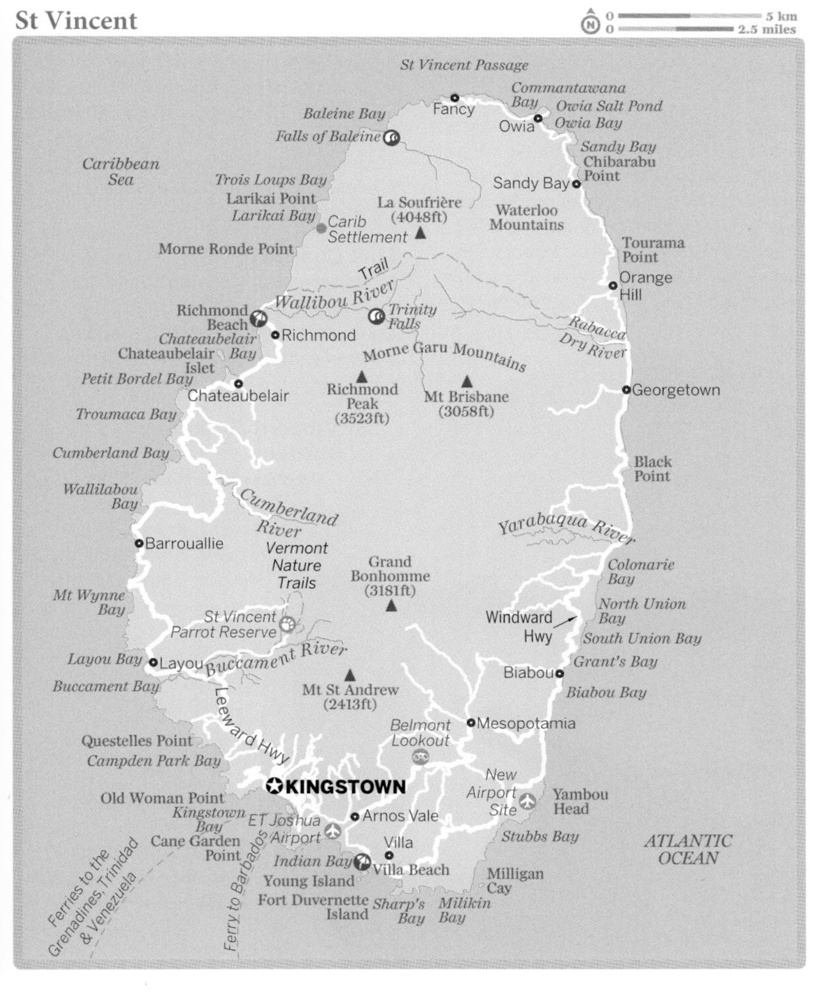

St Vincent

POP 101,000

St Vincent is the largest island and the hub that most travelers will pass through on their visit to SVG. Though not uninspiring, the allure of the Grenadines pulls most visitors away from here quickly.

The beaches are on the average side and the frenetic pace of Kingstown and its unpolished edges inspires many to head out to the calm of the Grenadines. But the island is fascinating for exploring. The verdant rainforested interior has good hiking options, and vast banana plantations provide a timeless spectacle.

KINGSTOWN

POP 32,300

Rough cobblestone streets, arched stone doorways and covered walkways conjure up a Caribbean of banana boats and colonial rule. Kingstown heaves and swells with a pulsing local community that bustles through its narrow streets and alleyways. Steep hills surround the town, amplifying the sounds of car horns, street vendors and the music filtering through the crowd.

The nearby towns of Villa and Indian Bay are where you will find the majority of the resorts on the island.

Sights

The cobblestone streets, shipping agencies and rum shops around Sharpe St feel unchanged in a century.

Save your real beach time for the idyllic white sands of the Grenadines, but for a local dip, look for the narrow strips of sand amid small coves at **Villa Beach**.

Public Market Market

(**6am-3pm**) There are some permanent stalls in the market building but the real action is on the streets outside. Bananas in shapes and sizes that will never get slapped with a multinational brand label are found in profusion. It's liveliest on Saturday mornings.

Fort Charlotte Fort

(**daylight**) Just north of the city and standing proudly atop a 660ft ridge, Fort Charlotte (1806) offers commanding views of both town and the Grenadines to the south.

St Vincent Botanic Gardens Gardens

(**Montrose Rd; admission EC$5; 6am-6pm**) The oldest botanical gardens in the western hemisphere, the St Vincent Botanic Gardens are lovingly tended and provide an oasis of calm that's only half a mile north from the frenzy of Kingstown.

Tours

Baleine Tours Guided Tour

(**457-4089, 315-608-7118; www.sites.google.com/site/whalbich/home; adult/child**

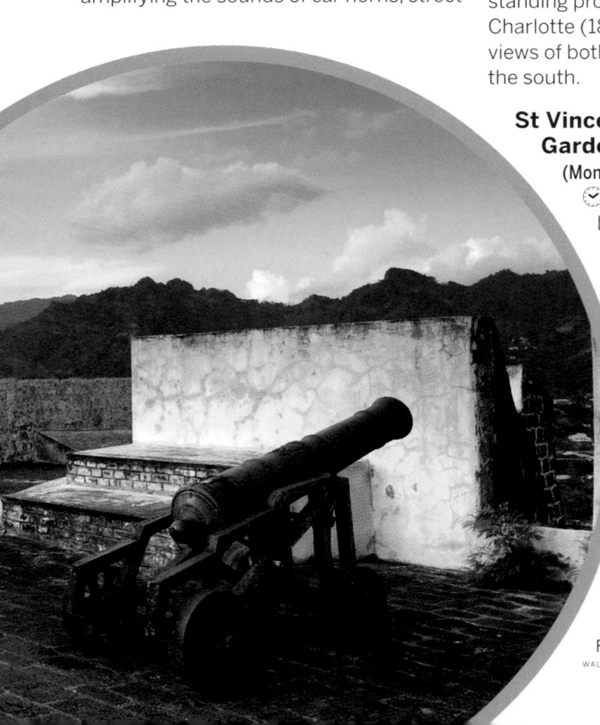

Fort Charlotte

WALTER BIBIKOW/GETTY IMAGES ©

Kingstown

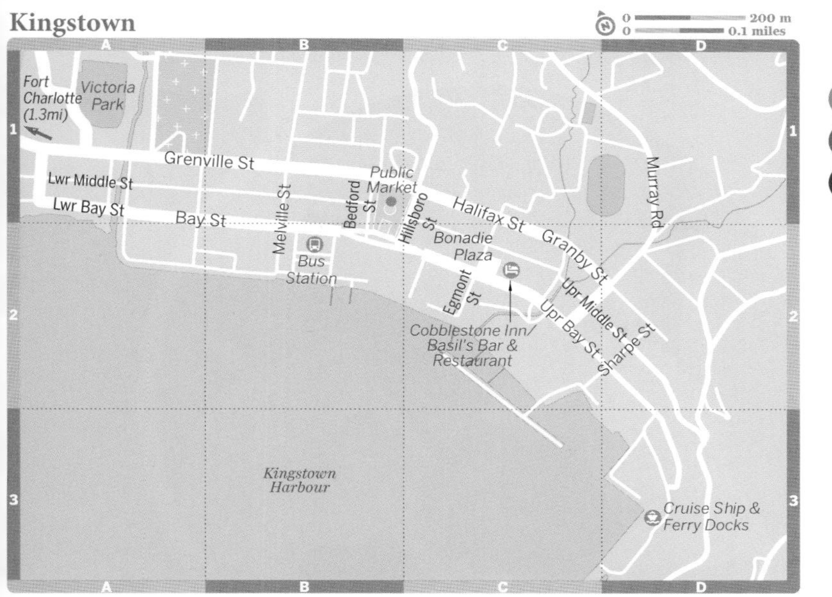

from US$80/40) A much-lauded outfit that takes people on a boat along the west coast for a day that includes swimming at the Baleine Falls, lunch at a *Pirates of the Caribbean* site and other stops on the lush and wild shore.

Festivals & Events

Vincy Mas Carnival
(end of Jun or early Jul) *The* big yearly event in St Vincent. This enormous carnival culminates in a street party in Kingstown with steel bands, dancers and drinks.

Sleeping

The majority of options are in the beachside communities of Indian Bay and Villa.

Beachcombers Hotel Resort **$$**
(458-4283; www.beachcombershotel.com; r US$100-200; @) This is a real find on the west side of Villa. Multicolored buildings dot the landscape in true Caribbean style. The best rooms have large verandas overlooking the harbor and islands.

Cobblestone Inn Hotel **$$**
(456-1937; www.thecobblestoneinn.com; Upper Bay St, Kingstown; r from US$100; @)
The Cobblestone Inn was built from the shell of an 1814 cobblestone warehouse and modernized into a comfy urban hotel. The 26 rooms are nicely fitted out.

Young Island Resort Resort **$$$**
(458-4826; www.youngisland.com; Young Island; r incl meals from US$480; @)
It's only 200yd offshore from Villa, but the vaguely heart-shaped private Young Island is a whole world away. The 29 units here include sexy villas, some with plunge pools, killer views and everything you need to forget about the little hotel ferry back to St Vincent.

Eating & Drinking

There are some good, simple restaurants in Kingstown serving local fare. Impromptu bars rule the streets as the Saturday market wanes in the afternoon.

Most hotels have good restaurants open to nonguests.

Below: Model maker, Mauvin's Model Boat Shop (p305); **Right:** Port Elizabeth (right)
(BELOW) WALTER BIBIKOW/GETTY IMAGES ©; (RIGHT) MICHELE WESTMORLAND/GETTY IMAGES ©

Basil's Bar & Restaurant

International $$

(☎457-2713; Cobblestone Inn, Upper Bay St; mains from EC$30; ⏰8am-late) If the food weren't so good you might think you'd entered a pirate's dungeon, given the moody lighting and stone walls. Food spans American and Caribbean favorites; the lunch buffet is great. It has Kingstown's classiest bar.

French Veranda

French $$$

(☎453-1111; www.marinershotel.com; Mariners Hotel, Villa; mains US$20-40; ⏰noon-10pm) The name says it all: the food is French and it's served on a lovely veranda with sweeping views in a mood of casual elegance.

Getting There & Around

A new airport may open in 2015 on the east side of the island.

The cruise ship and ferry docks are at the south end of Kingstown Harbour.

The bus station is near the fish market on Bay St, although buses can also be hailed along the road.

WINDWARD HIGHWAY

The windward (east) coast of St Vincent is a mix of wave-lashed shoreline, quiet bays and small towns. The black-sand **beaches** meld into the banana plantations and the lush vegetation grows up into the hilly interior.

As you head north, you really start to get off the beaten track. The jungle gets a bit thicker, the road a bit narrower, and towering **La Soufrière** volcano (4048ft) begins to dominate the skyline.

Continuing on you will hit **Sandy Bay**, a sizable village that has the island's largest concentration of Black Caribs. North is Owia Bay and the village of **Owia**, where you'll find the **Salt Pond**, a group of tidal pools protected from the crashing Atlantic by a massive stone shield. This is a popular swimming hole with crystal-clear waters and a view of St Lucia to the north.

LEEWARD HIGHWAY

The Leeward Hwy runs north of Kingstown along St Vincent's west coast for 25 very slow miles, ending at Richmond Beach. Offering some lovely scenery, the road climbs into the mountains as it leaves Kingstown, then winds through the hillside and back down to deeply cut coastal valleys that open to coconut plantations, fishing villages and bays lined with black-sand beaches.

Vermont Nature Trails

About a 3-mile drive north of Kingstown is a sign along the Leeward Hwy, pointing east to the **Vermont Nature Trails**, 3.5 miles inland. Here you'll find the Parrot Lookout Trail, a 1.75-mile loop (two hours) that passes through the southwestern tip of the **St Vincent Parrot Reserve**, which is a thick rainforest.

Wallilabou Bay

Just a few years ago, the small village of Wallilabou was one of the most recognizable places in all of SVG. Various parts of the first *Pirates of the Caribbean* movie were filmed here in 2002. Today the last vestiges of the sets are crumbling away, but you can relax in buccaneer spirit at ramshackle **Tony's Bar** (Wallilabou Bay; 9am-very late) right on the sand.

Bequia

POP 5400

Bequia (pronounced 'beck-way') is the most perfect island in the whole Grenadines. Stunning beaches dotting the shoreline, accommodations to fit most budgets and a slow pace of life all help to create an environment that is unforgettable. There are fine restaurants, shops that retain their local integrity and enough golden sand and blue water to keep everybody blissful.

PORT ELIZABETH

POP 2600

The appealing little town of Port Elizabeth is little more than a line of shops rimming the beach of Admiralty Bay backed by a

Detour: Falls of Baleine

It's the stuff of tropical fantasies: a 60ft waterfall crashes down a fern-dappled rock in a silvery arc into a lovely wide freshwater pool below. The gorgeous Falls of Baleine, at the isolated northwestern tip of the island, are accessible only by boat tour.

natural amphitheater of green hills. The harbor is often packed with yachts from the world over.

Activities

Wandering the island enjoying the beaches is the top way to let the days slip past. Further afield, day trips to nearby islands are popular.

You don't have to go far for great diving on Bequia – there are some top sites just on the edge of Admiralty Bay. Trips to Tobago Cays are a highlight for many.

Friendship Rose Boating
(☎495-0886; www.friendshiprose.com; day trips adult/child from US$150/75) This 80ft vintage schooner is a beautiful example of boat building and once served as a mail boat. Now it runs day trips throughout the Grenadines to various islands including Mustique and the Tobago Cays.

Bequia Dive Adventures Diving
(☎458-3826; www.bequiadiveadventures.com; Belmont; 2-tank dive US$105) Dives throughout the Grenadines.

Ramblers Hiking Tours Hiking
(☎430-0555; www.hiking-bequia.com; hikes per person from US$25) Explore the green hills and flower-scented trails of Bequia.

Festivals

Blessing of the Whaleboats Cultural
Held on the last Sunday in January, on Bequia. Few realize that Bequians still harvest a few whales each year.

Easter Regatta Sailing
Around Easter, this is SVG's main sailing event.

Sleeping & Eating

Bequia has a lot of holiday rentals.

Rambler's Rest Guesthouse $
(☎430-0555; www.accommodation-bequia.com; Port Elizabeth; r US$33-110; wifi) This haven just above the docks is run by the irrepessible Donnaka, a splendid host and gentleman. He has two simple rooms (there's a shared kitchen and terrace with great views) and a larger two-bedroom apartment. He delights in taking guests on walks and runs Ramblers Hiking Tours.

DeckHouse Bequia Inn $$
(☎570-6590; www.thedeckhousebequia.com; Happy Valley; r from US$150; air-con wifi) Right on the water (it has its own dock) at the west end of Admiralty Bay, this four-room inn is a fabulous deal. Rooms (two with amazing views) are large, nicely fitted out and have outdoor sitting areas. Breakfasts are deliciously stylish and homemade. Nonguests can join at lunch and dinner, for superb meals from a short and changing menu.

It's a 20-minute walk from the docks (with one steep hill), an EC$15 taxi or – best – an EC$20 water taxi ride.

Frangipani Hotel Hotel $$
(☎458-3255; www.frangipanibequia.com; Belmont Walkway; r US$75-275; mains from US$20; wifi) This lodge has 15 rooms and a great waterfront location. The 2nd floor of the vintage main building has pleasantly simple rooms, some sharing bathrooms. Out back are the modern garden units, with stone walls and harbor-view sundecks. The **bar** is a favorite meeting spot; the **restaurant** (Belmont Walkway; mains EC$25-70;

7:30am-9pm) has a hugely popular BBQ (EC$40) some nights.

Fig Tree Caribbean **$$**
(457-3008; www.figtreebequia.com; Belmont Walkway; mains from EC$20; 8am-10pm Nov-Mar, 11am-8pm Apr-Oct, closed Tue) A quarter-mile stroll along the waterfront west of the docks, this open-air restaurant has views to match both the great food and the hospitality of the owner, Cheryl Johnson. Creole touches abound; book ahead for the Friday night fish fry.

Shopping

The artistic community in Bequia obviously draws inspiration from the location. You can browse their wares at the many idiosyncratic little shops. Many locals make beautiful model boats.

Mauvin's Model Boat Shop Model Boats
(Front St; 9am-5pm Mon-Sat) Carefully crafted model boats are made here under a breadfruit tree and sold in a little gallery.

Information

Bequia Tourism Association (458-3286; www.bequiatourism.com; 8:30am-6pm Mon-Fri, 9am-1:30pm Sat, 9am-noon Sun) An excellent resource, located in the small building on the ferry dock. It's staffed by helpful locals.

Getting There & Around

James F Mitchell Airport is near Paget Farm, at the southwest end of the island. The frequent ferries from Kingstown dock right in Port Elizabeth.

Many places are accessible on foot from Port Elizabeth. Everything else is a quick trip by minibus (EC$2 to EC$5). 'Taxis' can be SUVs or open-top pick-ups (EC$10 to EC$30).

Bikes are easily rented; cars cost about US$60 per day.

LOWER BAY

The tiny beachside community of Lower Bay has the best beach on the island: stunningly clear waters of Admiralty Bay spread out in front like a turquoise fan from a base of golden sand. It's never crowded; vendors rent out beach chairs and there's a couple of cute beachfront cafes.

Local Knowledge

Names: Stephen & Sally Ellyatt

OCCUPATION: CHARTER YACHT OWNERS, SAILORS

RESIDENCE: ABOARD OUR SAILBOAT, THE *SILENT WINGS*

1 WHAT'S YOUR FAVORITE ISLAND IN THE GRENADINES?

Bequia. It's got an unspoiled colorful town with quirky Caribbean charm, welcoming local people, a wide range of provisioning shops and restaurants. It's also not touristy, but there are still many things to do such as diving, snorkeling, sailing in local traditional whaling boats and walking.

2 HOW ABOUT MYSTERIOUS MUSTIQUE?

It's an exclusive island that you can only reach by smaller seacraft and small planes. The island has been carefully preserved. There are some beautiful beaches and trails to explore, and you never know who you're going to meet at Basil's Bar!

3 WHAT'S THE BEST NATURAL AREA?

We love Tobago Cays! And all our guests love it too – the beautiful turquoise color of the warm sea never ceases to astound. We swim with turtles and see the iguanas. Some challenging navigation around the reefs only makes this more of a special place.

4 HOW DO YOU KNOW YOU'RE IN PARADISE?

When we're anchored in Saltwhistle Bay in Mayreau. It's a lovely sheltered sandy bay surrounded by palm trees. The swimming's good in the blue water and there are friendly beach cafes and bars.

5 WHAT'S A FAVORITE OFFBEAT PLACE?

Chatham Bay on Union Island, where there is a great anchorage, an interesting sandy beach and a small selection of local bars and restaurants in a pristine natural setting.

FRIENDSHIP BAY

Located over the hill on the southeast coast of the island, the gentle curve of Friendship Bay is about 1.5 miles from Port Elizabeth.

A rarely crowded crescent of sand, the beach here is a top reason to make the strenuous yet short walk over the spine of the island (or wimp out on a short taxi or bus ride). A dense thicket of palms provides shade and that nicely clichéd tropical look.

Sleeping & Eating

Bequia Beach Hotel Resort **$$$**
(458-1600; www.bequiabeach.com; Friendship Bay; r from US$350;) This sprawling low-rise beachfront boutique resort is modestly discreet. Units range from basic garden-view rooms to villas with private pools. **Bagatelle** (dinner mains from US$30; 8am-10pm) is popular locally for its changing menu of freshly prepared local produce and seafood.

SPRING BAY

On a quiet island, this is the quiet end. It's a brief hop over the central spine from Port Elizabeth. Sugar plantations still operate here, and there are good views of the often turbulent waters to the east.

Sanctuary operator Orton King's dream of saving the hawksbill sea turtle from extinction is seeing fruition at the **Old Hegg Turtle Sanctuary** (admission EC$15; 9am-5pm), a hatchery right on the beach.

Sleeping & Eating

Firefly Hotel **$$$**
(458-3414; www.fireflybequia.com; r from US$375;) Just 10 minutes from Port Elizabeth, and you're transported to tranquil luxury. The 10 rooms are tastefully decorated with a minimalist flare, accented with views worthy of royalty. It's set in a working tropical fruit plantation that dates from the 1700s; tours (highly recommended, US$10) are available.

Canouan (right) from the air

MANGINI PHOTOGRAPHY/GETTY IMAGES ©

SVG Ferries

Several ferries link the islands. Note that schedules can change by whim so always confirm timings. Service to outer islands is not daily.

Bequia Express (784-457-3539; www.bequiaexpress.net; one way EC$25) Links St Vincent and Bequia (75 minutes) several times daily on large car ferries.

Jaden Sun (784-451-2192; www.jadeninc.com; St Vincent to Bequia/Canouan/Mayreau/Union Island one way EC$40/90/100/100) Fast ferry linking St Vincent to Bequia, Canouan, Mayreau and Union Island (two hours) five days a week.

MV Admiral (784-458-3348; www.admiraltytransport.com; one way St Vincent-Bequia EC$25) A large car ferry that connects St Vincent and Bequia (75 minutes) two to three times daily.

MV Gem Star (784-457-4157; St Vincent-Union Island one way EC$70) Slow cargo boat from St Vincent to Canouan, Mayreau and Union Island (seven hours), two round-trips each week.

Sugar Reef Boutique Hotel **$$$**
(458-3400; www.sugarreefbequia.com; Spring Bay; r from US$200; closed Sep-Oct) Eight beautiful rooms are scattered about 65 acres fronting a palm-shaded beach. The buildings are elegantly restored plantation-era gems. The popular **cafe** (mains from EC$20; noon-9pm, closed Sep-Oct) is reason enough to stop in. It serves artful smoothies, salads, sandwiches, seafood, treats and more.

Mustique

POP 3000

What can you say about Mustique other than 'Wow!'? First, take an island that offers stunning beaches and everything else you expect to find in paradise, then add to the mix accommodations that defy description or affordability. With prices that exclude all but the super-rich, film stars and burnt-out musicians, this island is the exclusive playground of the uber-affluent.

The documentary *The Man Who Bought Mustique* (2000) tells the unlikely story of Lord Glenconner, the man who turned the island into a playground for the rich. Most visitors not staying in a fabulous retreat come on widely marketed day trips from Bequia. They join the local swells for drinks and more at **Basil's** (488-8350; www.basilsbar.com; 9am-late;), one of the Caribbean's great waterfront bars.

Canouan

POP 1200

Canouan (pronounced 'cahn-oo-ahn') is an interesting place, both historically and aesthetically. This beautiful hook-shaped island has some of the most brilliant beaches in the entire Grenadines chain, and some of the most secluded hideaways too (plus one very large resort).

You'll find lovely **beaches** within a short walk of the tiny main town of Charlestown and the ferry dock. For low-key tropical pleasures, try **Tamarind Beach Hotel & Yacht Club** (458-8044; www.tamarindbeachhotel.com; Charlestown; r US$205-300;) right near town.

Mayreau

POP 400

The compact palm-covered island of Mayreau sits just west of the Tobago Cays. With only a handful of roads, no airport and a smattering of residents, Mayreau is almost the fabled desert isle.

Stop in to the east side of the island (a 20-minute walk from the ferry dock) and you find **Saltwhistle Bay**. A double crescent of beautiful beaches split by a narrow palm-tree-fringed isthmus, it seems to come right out of central casting for tropical ideals. The turquoise water laps both sides of the sandy strip, sometimes only a few feet away. Yachts drop anchor in the bay and the odd day-tripper motors ashore for a bit of lunch and a sandy frolic.

Union Island

POP 3000

Union Island feels like an outpost at the bottom of a country – and that's just what it is. The small port town of **Clifton** has a slightly rough-edged charm and you can easily spend a day wandering its short main street and the surrounding hills. It's an important anchorage for yachts and a transport hub: there are boats to Carriacou in Grenada. It also has decent accommodations, services and just enough nightlife.

Excursions to Tobago Cays are popular. **Grenadines Dive** (458-8138; www.grenadinesdive.com; Clifton; 2-tank dive US$90) runs diving and snorkeling trips.

 Sleeping & Eating

Clifton has the best range of sleeping options south of Bequia. Wander the town for good local places to eat.

Anchorage Yacht Club Hotel Hotel $$
(458-8221; www.anchorage-union.com; Clifton; r US$80-160;) Right at the yacht docks. It's popular with visiting sailors and holidaymakers. The best feature of the otherwise standard rooms are the views of the harbor. The vast terrace bar is popular with people transacting business of all kinds and yacht passengers desperate for dry land.

Lambis Caribbean $
(Clifton; mains from EC$15; 7am-late) The end of many an evening – in more ways than one. This large and somewhat shambolic institution sits in the middle of town and is open to the harbor. Food includes tasty budget-priced curries, stews and fried fish. There's a bar, and a band plays most nights.

Information

Union Island Tourist Bureau (458-8350; Clifton; 9am-noon & 1-4pm Mon-Fri) On the main road near the Customs office. Has good info on Tobago Cays.

Getting Around

Union Island is pretty small and you'll have no trouble exploring on foot. The airport is a short walk from town.

Tobago Cays

With five small islands ringed with coral reefs, the fabled Tobago Cays offer some of the Caribbean's best diving and snorkeling.

The islands sit firmly in a national park and are only accessible via boat on a day trip from one of the Grenadines. And what a day trip it can be – the snorkeling is world class and the white-sand beaches look like a strip of blinding snow. Underwater, sea turtles and parrot fish are just the start of myriad species you'll see. The coral is gorgeous.

You can get a day trip to the Cays from any place in the Grenadines. The best operators are found on Bequia and Union Island. Expect to pay from US$90 to US$200 for a full day out.

GRENADA

POP 105,600

It's not called the Spice Island for nothing; you really can smell the nutmeg in the air on Grenada. And it could be called the Fruit Island for the luscious bounty growing profusely in the green hills. Then again it could be called the Beach Island for the plethora of idyllic sandy strands. We could go on...

Grenada Island

The island of Grenada is an almond-shaped, beach-rimmed gem of a place with 75 miles of coastline surrounding a lush interior, which is filled with tropical rainforest.

ST GEORGE'S

POP 4800

St George's is one of the most picturesque towns in the Caribbean. It's a fabulous place to explore on foot, from handsome old buildings to the the Carenage harbor. Interesting shops and cafes dot the narrow and busy streets.

Sights

Fort George Fort

(Church St; admission EC$5; 7am-5pm)
Grenada's oldest fort was established by the French in 1705 and is the centerpiece of the St George's skyline.You can explore the dank tunnels and climb to the top to see the cannons and bird's-eye views.

Grenada Island

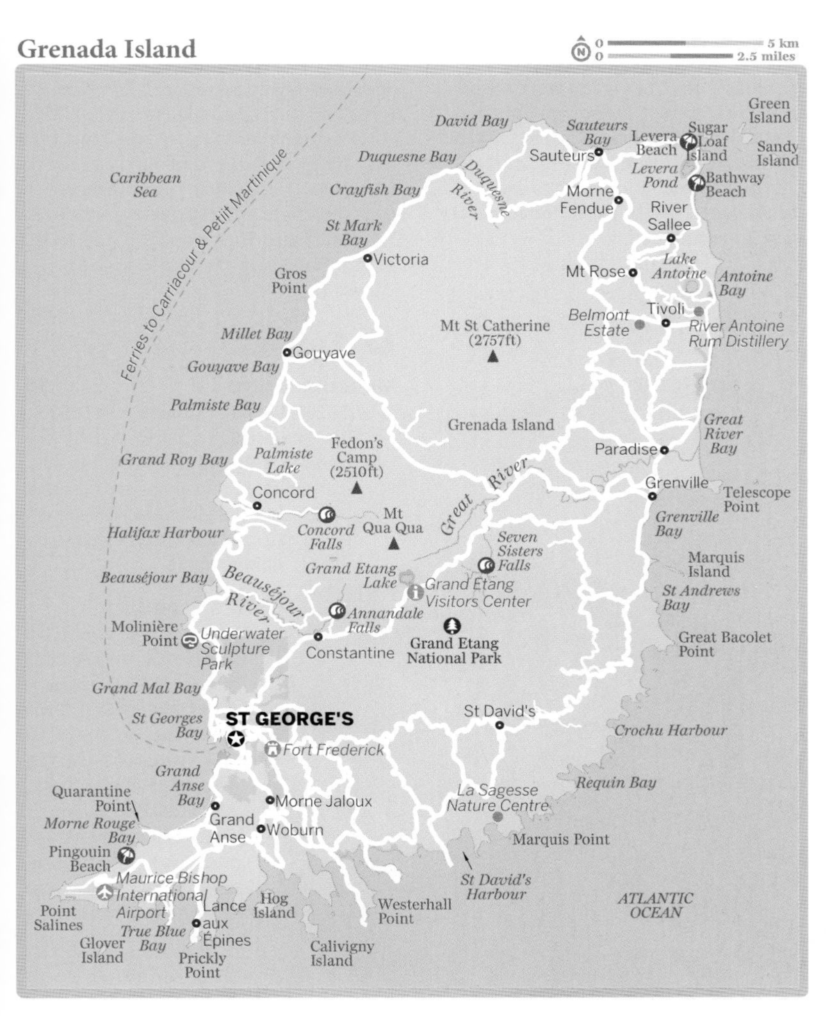

A plaque in the parade ground marks the spot where revolutionary leader Maurice Bishop was executed, which set in motion events that led to the US invasion in 1983.

Cathedral of the Immaculate Conception Cathedral
(**Church St**) Sitting pretty at the top of the capital's hill, St George's Roman Catholic cathedral provides a great vantage point over the town. Though Hurricane Ivan in 2004 all but gutted the structure, it's since been painstakingly restored.

Carenage Harbor
A scenic inlet, the Carenage is a great place for a stroll along the water's edge, taking in the colorful fishing boats and the bustle of supplies being loaded for other islands. At the north end, the sturdy Georgian buildings overlooking the water – including the red-brick **National Library** – have been restored.

Grenada National Museum Museum
(**☎440-3725; cnr Young & Monckton Sts; adult/child EC$5/2.50; ⏰9am-4:30pm Mon-Fri, 10am-1:30pm Sat**) Staffed by enthusiastic members, this museum covers the topsy-turvy history of Grenada. It can easily absorb an hour. On some Friday evenings there are folk performances.

St George's Market Square Market
(**Halifax St**) Busiest on Friday and Saturday mornings, this is the largest market in Grenada, with stalls heaped with produce, spices and the odd bit of local craft.

Fort Frederick Fort
(**Richmond Heights; admission EC$5; ⏰8am-5pm**) Constructed by the French in 1779, Fort Frederick was soon used – paradoxically – by the British to defend against the French. It's the island's best-preserved fort, and offers striking panoramic views. The fort is atop Richmond Hill, 1.25 miles east of St George's on the road to St Paul's.

Eating

Museum Bistro Caribbean **$$**
(**☎416-7266; Monckton St; mains from EC$30; ⏰10am-4pm Mon-Sat**) Upstairs from the Grenada National Museum, this enticing restaurant offers creative and organic lunches. Excellent natural juices, too – try the golden apple.

BB's Crabback Caribbean **$$**
(**☎435-7058; www.bbscrabback.co.uk; The Carenage; mains from US$15; ⏰9am-10pm Mon-Sat**) The namesake waterfront restaurant of celebrity chef and local bon vivant Brian Benjamin, it's on the water with a few other restaurants. Local faves like callaloo soup (a

Fort George (p309), St George's
MICHELE WESTMORLAND/GETTY IMAGES ©

St George's

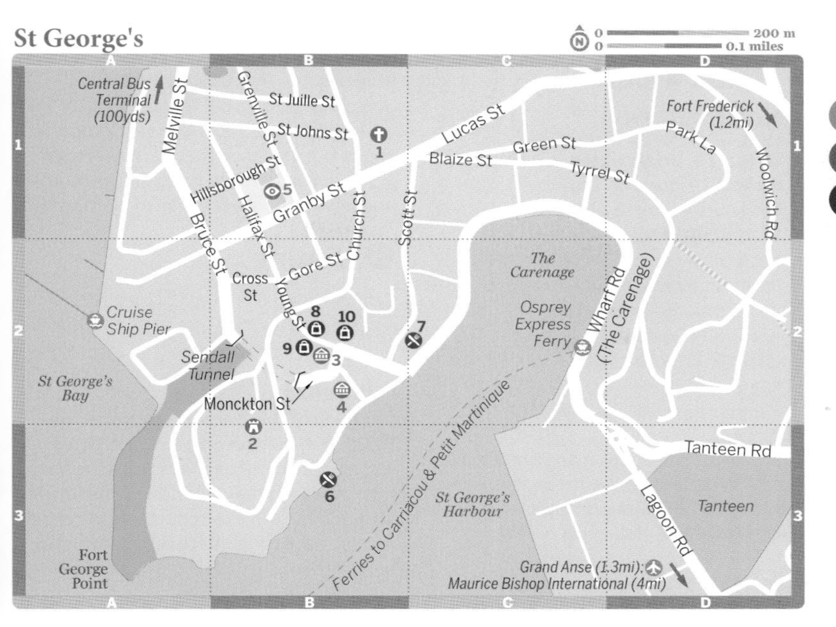

rich stew) and fresh seafood are popular. Fussier appetites can order pancakes and everyone loves the chocolate dessert.

Nutmeg Caribbean $$
(The Carenage; mains EC$12-40; 11am-9pm Mon-Sat) Get above the bustle of the waterfront at this open-air balcony restaurant. Have a roti or traditional meaty main.

Shopping

One of the best reasons to wander the atmospheric streets is to discover little shops selling artful goods unlike those near the cruise-ship docks.

Yellow Poui Art Gallery Art
(440-3001; Young St; 9:30am-3:30pm Tue-Fri, to 1:30pm Sat) This 3rd-floor gallery features work from over 80 local artists.

Tikal Handicrafts
(Young St; 9am-5pm Mon-Fri, to 2pm Sat) Simply put, it's not the usual tourist crap. Tikal has a large and varied selection of crafts, prints, fabrics, books and ceramics.

St George's

Sights
1 Cathedral of the Immaculate Conception ... B1
2 Fort George ... B3
3 Grenada National Museum ... B2
4 National Library ... B2
5 St George's Market Square ... B1

Eating
6 BB's Crabback ... B3
Museum Bistro ... (see 3)
7 Nutmeg ... C2

Shopping
8 Art Fabrik ... B2
9 Tikal ... B2
10 Yellow Poui Art Gallery ... B2

Art Fabrik Textiles
(440-0568; Young St; 9am-5pm Mon-Fri, to 1pm Sat) A small shop filled with beautiful batik creations made right on Grenada. Ask to see the dyeing process.

Getting There & Around

Buses depart from the central terminal in St George's. The longest route goes to Sauteurs (EC$12, 90 minutes).

Underwater Sculptures

Grenada's **Underwater Sculpture Park** is 7ft beneath the surface of the sea, just north of St George's in Molinière Bay. The life-size sculptures include a circle of women clasping hands, a man at a desk and a solitary mountain-biker, all slowly becoming encrusted with coral growth. There are almost 80 works.

St George's is best explored on foot; lose the rental ASAP as the streets in the center are narrow and congested and driving is a huge headache. A taxi to Grande Anse costs about EC$45.

GRAND ANSE

Famous Grand Anse Beach is one of the island's best and is justifiably popular. It's lined with a relaxed assortment of low-rise resorts. Drop by for the day at **Camerhogne Park**, where you can rent a lounger and get a snack.

To escape crowds, look for a little dirt road off Grand Anse Rd, where it turns south right after the Spice Island Beach Resort. It leads to a small parking area and uncrowded sands.

Activities

Aquanauts Grenada Diving
(444-1126; www.aquanautsgrenada.com; 2-tank dives US$110) Runs diving and snorkeling trips around the island.

Sleeping

Coyaba Beach Resort Resort **$$$**
(444-4129; www.coyaba.com; Grand Anse Beach; r from US$300;) Set upon a great stretch of beach, the 80 rooms exude relaxed luxury. The beachfront grounds are beautifully landscaped; there's a spa.

Flamboyant Hotel Resort **$$$**
(444-4247; www.flamboyant.com; Mourne Rouge Bay Rd; r from US$180;) Sprawling down a hill to the southern end of Grand Anse Beach, this vast property spans both sides of the road. There are great sea views from many of the rooms and a fine cafe and bar down by the sand.

Eating

Grand Anse has a range of beachfront restaurants and bars, as well as some interesting indie options.

Umbrellas American **$$**
(439-9149; Grand Anse Beach; mains from EC$20; 11am-10pm;) A stylish two-floor wooden building just back from the sand, with tables on the upper deck and inside. It's good for a frosty cocktail, cold beer or a meal. Salads counterbalance the long burger menu.

Coconut Beach Seafood **$$$**
(444-4644; Grand Anse Beach; mains from US$20; noon-10pm Wed-Mon) French- and Creole-accented seafood is served up inside this old beachfront house or at tables right on the sand. Famous for its lobster, this family-run restaurant puts just the right amount of nutmeg in the rum punch.

MORNE ROUGE BAY

Though just down the way from Grand Anse Beach, this superior stretch of beach is a brilliant example of the snow-white sand and crystal-clear blue water that the Caribbean is known for. Development has so far been modest, so it's uncrowded. It has shade but limited services.

Sleeping

Kalinago Hotel **$$**
(444-5254; www.kalinagobeachresort.com; r from US$150;) This cheerful resort has plain but spacious rooms overlooking the water (and just above the beach), plus a nice oceanside pool.

LaLuna Hotel **$$$**

(433-0001; www.laluna.com; Morne Rouge; cottages from US$550; @) One of the Caribbean's best resorts, there's a simple elegance to these 16 Balinese-inspired cottages with private plunge pools and open-air bathrooms. It's at a secluded end of spectacular Mourne Rouge Bay beach.

POINT SALINES & TRUE BLUE

The filigreed coastline around Point Salines is dominated by Maurice Bishop International Airport. It's notable for the string of lovely beaches to the north of the runway, just off the airport road.

South of the airport, True Blue is a relaxed corner of the island with some nice top-end hotels, good eateries and multiple yacht marinas.

Crowning the peninsula enclosing True Blue Bay, St George's Medical School (SGU) is a sprawling campus inhabited almost exclusively by young Americans seeking offshore medical degrees (notoriously, President Ronald Reagan said he was defending these students when he ordered the American invasion in 1983).

Beaches

Pingouin Beach Beach

(Pink Gin Beach;) Pingouin Beach is a lovely swath of powdery white sand with warm blue waters, good snorkeling and wonderful views over to St George's. It's close to the popular Beach House restaurant, north of the airport.

Sleeping & Eating

True Blue Bay Resort & Marina Hotel **$$$**

(433-8783; www.truebluebay.com; True Blue; r US$20-400; @) Built at the edge of a yacht-filled bay, this family-owned resort is an island favorite, with multi-colored huts that pop off the green grass like a carpet of children's jellybeans lining the hill. Apartments feature full kitchens; the luxurious tower rooms have great views and telescopes to scan the horizon.

Beach House Fusion **$$**

(444-4455; www.beachhousegrenada.com; Portici Bay; mains US$15-40; noon-4pm Mon-Sat Dec-Mar, 6-10pm Mon-Sat year-round) Beautifully set right on the beach, just north of the airport, this casually elegant

Artist Jason de Caires Taylor photographing his statue, *Sienna in Grenada*, at the Underwater Sculpture Park (left)

JASON DE CAIRES/BARCROFT MEDIA/GETTY IMAGES ©

bistro serves a changing menu of salads, sandwiches and complex dinner mains that reflect the island's bounty. Book in advance and ask about the shuttle service.

LANCE AUX ÉPINES

Lance aux Épines (lance-a-peen) is a peninsula that forms the southernmost point of Grenada. It's home to a pretty beach and a marina.

 Sleeping

Lance aux Épines Cottages Hotel $$

(☎444-4565; www.laecottages.com; Lance aux Épines; r from US$160;) Beautiful beach views here are enjoyed by 11 attractive rooms that come complete with kitchens and large living areas. Well set up for families, extras abound including free kayaks.

GRAND ETANG ROAD

Overhung with rainforest and snaking uphill in a series of switchback turns, the Grand Etang Rd shoots right up the island's spine. The mountainous center of the island is often awash with misty clouds, and looks like a lost primordial world, its tangle of rainforest brimming with life – including monkeys that often get a bit too friendly.

Grenada's verdant splendor is on full display here; look for cassava, nutmeg, star fruit, cinnamon, clove, hibiscus, passionfruit, pineapple, avocado, mango, banana, coconut and much more.

Annandale Falls

An idyllic waterfall with a 30ft drop, Annandale Falls is surrounded by a grotto of lush vegetation, and has a large pool where you can take a refreshing swim. It's a two-minute walk from the **visitor center (admission EC$5; 8am-4pm)**. It's a popular day trip for cruise-ship passengers.

Grand Etang National Park

Two and a half miles northeast of Constantine, after the road winds steeply up to an elevation of 1900ft, you enter Grand Etang National Park, a natural wonderland laced with hiking trails. At the **visitor center (☎440-6160; admission EC$5; 8am-4pm)** you can pay your admission, learn a little about the park and get a refreshment.

Annandale Falls

HOLGER LEUE/GETTY IMAGES ©

Hiking trails in the park include the following:

Grand Etang Shoreline This 1½-hour loop walk around Grand Etang Lake is gentle.

Morne La Baye This easy 15-minute walk starts behind the visitor center and takes in native vegetation.

Mt Qua Qua This is a moderately difficult three-hour round-trip hike that leads to the top of a ridge, offering some of the best views of the rainforest.

Seven Sisters Falls This two-hour hike passes seven waterfalls in the rainforest and is considered the best hike in Grenada. It starts 1.25 miles north of the visitor center.

GRENVILLE

Halfway up the east coast, bustling Grenville is the area's agricultural hub, and its busy streets offer a good insight into typical life. Amid a smattering of old stone buildings look for **Melting Pot (mains from EC$12; 10am-8pm Mon-Sat)**, an upstairs cafe on the waterfront with tasty local food.

NORTH OF GRENVILLE

Heading north, the road stays inland from the coast. It's a green and curvaceous drive.

Sights

Belmont Estate Farm

(442-9524; www.belmontestate.net; Belmont; tours EC$10; 8am-4pm, closed Sat) Cocoa is Grenada's main crop and it's celebrated at this 300-year-old working plantation. Among the other crops here: cinnamon, cloves, bay leaf, ginger and nutmeg. Guided tours explain cocoa production, and you can walk the landscaped gardens and have a tasty lunch. The estate is about 2 miles northwest of Tivoli.

River Antoine Rum Distillery Distillery

(442-7109; Tivoli; tours EC$5; 8am-4pm Mon-Fri) River Antoine has produced rum since 1785. Tours here cover all aspects of the smoky, pungent production process, from the crushing of cane to fermentation and distillation. Of course there's tasting.

Detour: Grenville to Gouyave

Head west from Grenville into the deep, green heart of Grenada. A good road wanders sinuously along rushing rivers, over green hills and through thick tropical forests. Along the way you'll see bananas, taro, flowers of all kinds and much more. Fragrant squares of nutmeg dry beside the road, while hummingbirds dart overhead.

The drive will take about 90 minutes; it's easy to literally lose the plot, so use the GPS on your phone or be ready to ask directions of obliging locals.

BATHWAY BEACH & AROUND

From River Sallee, a road leads to Bathway Beach, a lovely stretch of coral sands. At the north end, a rock shelf parallels the shoreline, creating a very long, 30ft-wide sheltered pool that's great for swimming. Stands sell food and drinks.

SAUTEURS

On the northern tip of the island, the town of Sauteurs (whose French name translates as 'Jumpers') is best known for its grim history. In 1651, local Carib families elected to throw themselves off the 130ft-high cliffs that line the coast rather than surrender to the advancing French army.

GOUYAVE

Gouyave, roughly halfway up the west coast from St George's, is a supremely attractive fishing village. It is well worth spending a couple of hours just walking around, having a drink and taking in the ambience.

On Friday evenings from around 7pm, the town comes alive for a rollicking **fish fry**, with vendors selling fresh fish, lobster and all the trimmings from street stalls, and music echoing through the streets.

Sights

Nutmeg Processing Cooperative Factory

(admission US$1; 8am-4pm Mon-Fri) On Gouyave's main road, you can literally smell one of the most important aspects of Grenada's heritage: nutmeg. This large nutmeg processing station is a vast, drafty old facility where workers sort the fragrant and tasty pods. Tours leave constantly and are a bargain.

Row after row of drying racks are covered with the fruit of trees descended from the first nutmeg plants planted here by the British in 1843 to compete with the Dutch half a world away in Indonesia.

Carriacou

POP 9100

The fact that most people don't realize that there are in fact *three* islands in the nation of Grenada is a fitting introduction to Carriacou (carry-a-cou). You won't find cruise ships, big resorts or souvenir shops; this is Caribbean life the way it was 50 years ago: quiet, laid-back and relaxed.

HILLSBOROUGH

POP 5000

Carriacou's gentle pace is reflected in the sedate nature of its largest town, Hillsborough. There's a couple of streets lined with a mixture of modern blocks and classic Caribbean wooden structures. Go for a wander, appreciating glimpses of the turquiose waters at breaks in the buildings.

Sights & Activities

Carriacou Museum Museum

(443-8288; Patterson St; adult/child EC$5/2.50; 9:30am-4pm Mon-Fri) This small, community-run museum has an interesting array of Carib artifacts plus displays on African heritage and the colonial era.

Deefer Diving Diving

(443-7882; www.deeferdiving.com; Hillsborough; 2-tank dives from US$105) The best local dive shop runs trips to SVG's Tobago Cays.

Sleeping & Eating

Wander Hillsborough's main street for good local cafes.

Green Roof Inn Hotel $$

(443-6399; www.greenroofinn.com; r from US$80; **)** Half a mile up the

Nutmeg pods
HOLGER LEUE/GETTY IMAGES ©

Grenada's Chocolate

You can't tour the factory but you can enjoy the very fruit of the local organic cocoa plantations: the **Grenada Chocolate Company** (www.grenadachocolate.com) makes a line of delicious dark chocolate bars that are widely sold. We love the crunchy 'nib-a-licious.'

road from Hillsborough, this is a quiet and beautiful place to stay. The simple rooms have mosquito-netted beds, and some have fab sea views.The **restaurant** (443-6399; mains from EC$60; 5-9pm Tue-Sun;) serves superb meals (the smoked lobaster, OMG!) to match the vista.

Hotel Laurena Hotel $$
(443-8759; www.hotellaurena.com; Main St; r from US$100;) Right in the heart of town, this tidy hotel has rooms in four blocks, some with nice views. The restaurant, **Laurena II** (mains from EC$15; 8am-9pm;), makes for a good, breezy pause and has excellent local fare.

Patty's Deli Market $
(443-6258; Main St; 9am-4:30pm Mon-Fri) Upmarket groceries, from deli meats and cheeses to fresh quiches and cakes, plus wines and excellent sandwiches (EC$15).

Information

Tourist Office (443-7948; Main St; 8am-noon & 1-4pm Mon-Fri) Helpful; located across from the pier.

Getting There & Around

The *Osprey* ferry from St George's docks right in the heart of town, as do boats from Union Island on SVG.

Minivans charge EC$4 to go anywhere on the island from 7am to around sunset. Vehicle rental is about US$60 per day. Taxi drivers charge about EC$200 for a three-hour tour.

NORTH OF HILLSBOROUGH

The northern part of Carriacou is a delightful place to explore, with good scenery and tiny villages.

The first is cute little **Bogles**. Continuing on, the road traverses the crest of **Belvedere Hill**, providing sweeping views of the tiny islands of Petit St Vincent and Petit Martinique.

From here, the route northeast (called the High Rd) leads down to **Windward**, a charming small village where, if you're lucky, locals will be out building a traditional Carriacou sloop.

Sleeping & Eating

Bogles Round House Cafe $$
(443-7841; Bogles; mains from EC$55; restaurant noon-2pm & 6:30-8:30pm Mon, Tue, Thu-Sat, 11-4pm Sun) It is a round house and it's run by award-winning chef Roxanne Russell. The food – European dishes infused with Caribbean flavors – is inventive. Three rustic cottages (from US$100) are scattered around the grounds and there's a small beach.

SOUTH OF HILLSBOROUGH

The biggest reason to venture to this part of the island is the aptly named **Paradise Beach**, a superb stretch of sand bordered by palms and sea-grape trees. Further on, **Tyrrel Bay** is a deep, protected bay. It's a popular anchorage for visiting yachts and there are a couple of cafes.

BARBADOS

POP 285,000

Barbados has it all: beach resorts from humble to grand, smashing nightlife, a Unesco World Heritage capital, Bridgetown, a beautiful interior dotted with gardens, wild surf on the lonely east coast and a proud and welcoming populace.

Bridgetown

POP 108,000

Wandering bustling Bridgetown with its many sights and old colonial buildings can easily occupy a day. There is good

Bridgetown

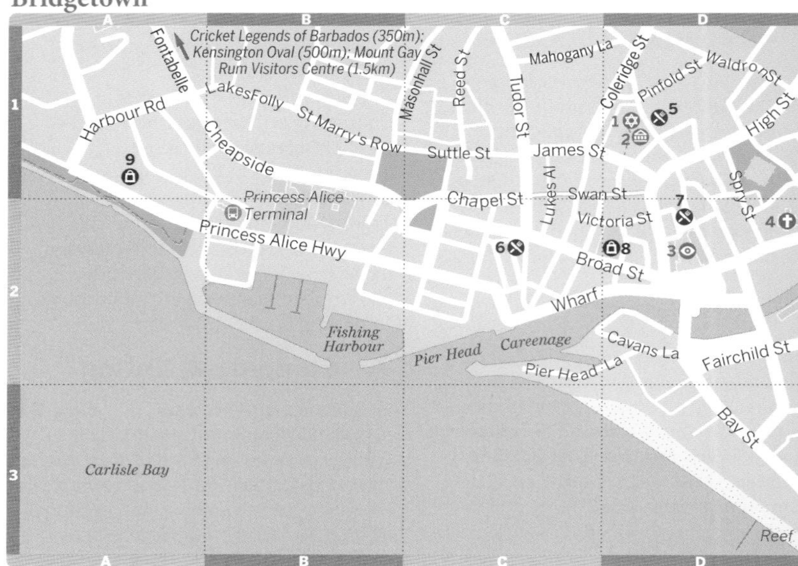

Bridgetown

Sights
1 Barbados Synagogue D1
2 Nidhe Israel Museum D1
3 Parliament Buildings D2
4 St Michael's Cathedral D2

Eating
5 Legendary Fish Cakes D1
6 Mustor's Restaurant C2
7 Parliament Market D2

Shopping
8 Cave Shepherd D2
9 Pelican Craft Village A1

shopping, especially along Broad St and on pedestrian-only Swan St, which buzzes with the rhythms of local culture. The entire downtown area and south to the Garrison was recognized by Unesco in 2012 for its historical significance.

Sights & Activities

Most sights can be reached on foot. Look for the free publication *Bridgetown and Its Garrison,* which is a good guide to the Unesco World Heritage sites.

St Michael's Cathedral — Cathedral

(St Michael's Row; 9am-4pm Sun-Fri, to 1pm Sat) The island's Anglican cathedral was originally completed in 1665 to accommodate 3000 worshippers, but came tumbling down in a hurricane a century later. Today's structure dates from 1789.

Parliament Buildings — Notable Buildings

(museum admission B$10; museum 9am-4pm Mon, Wed-Sat) On the north side of **National Heroes Square** are two stone-block, neo-Gothic-style buildings constructed in 1871. The west-side building with the clock tower contains public offices; the building on the east side houses the Senate and House of Assembly. At the **museum** learn about the island's proud democratic heritage.

Nidhe Israel Museum — Museum

(Synagogue Lane; adult/child B$25/12.50; 9am-4pm Mon-Fri) Housed in a restored 1750 Jewish community center, this museum documents the fascinating story of the Barbados Jewish community. You can also visit the nearby 1833 **Barbados**

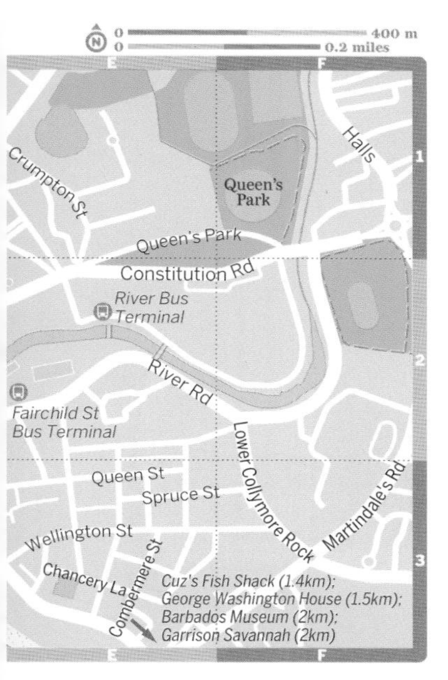

Synagogue (Synagogue Lane; 9am-4pm Mon-Fri).

Eating

Bridgetown is the best place to enjoy genuine local food and genuine local prices.

Mustor's Restaurant Caribbean $
(McGregor St; lunch from B$14; 10am-4pm Mon-Sat) Climb the stairs to a large, plain dining room. Choose from staples such as pork stew and flying fish. Then select the sides – we love the macaroni pie. Finally, hope for an open balcony table.

Legendary Fish Cakes Seafood $
(Magazine Lane; mains from B$4; 10am-4pm Mon-Sat) Salt cod cakes are a local treat and this storefront makes the most beloved version. Light and crispy batter holds the salty goodness inside. Herbs add flavor and depth. Yum.

Parliament Market Caribbean $
(Palmetto St; meals from B$10; 11am-2pm Mon-Sat) A series of small wooden huts behind the Parliament buildings has both produce and lunch items. Some of the region's finest chicken soup comes from a green hut without a sign but with a pile of sugar beets out front.

Shopping

Broad St in the center is the place for shops great and small.

Pelican Craft Village Crafts
(Princess Alice Hwy; 10am-5pm Mon-Sat) This ever-evolving complex of galleries and workshops, between downtown and the cruise-ship terminal, features the works of many local artists.

Cave Shepherd Department Store
(Broad St) The island's grand old department store has well-priced rum and a quality souvenir section. There's a decent book department.

Getting There & Away

Bus stations are scattered through town.

Fairchild Street Bus Terminal (Bridge St) North of Fairchild St; public buses going south and east.

George Washington Slept Here

In 1751, at age 19 – some 38 years before he would become the first US president – George Washington visited Barbados as a companion to his half-brother Lawrence, who suffered from tuberculosis. It was hoped that the tropical climate would prove therapeutic.

The pair rented a house in the Garrison area and stayed on the island for six weeks. The restored **George Washington House** (Bush Hill, Garrison; adult/child B$20/5; 9am-4:30pm Mon-Fri) gives a fascinating glimpse of the trip and the time. As it was, Lawrence never recovered and died the next year.

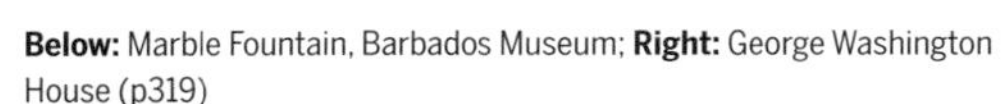
Below: Marble Fountain, Barbados Museum; **Right:** George Washington House (p319)

Princess Alice Terminal (Princess Alice Hwy) At the west end; public buses going north.

River Bus Terminal (Nursery Rd) Minibuses along central and eastern routes.

Around Bridgetown

Most sights are within 5km of Bridgetown's center.

 Sights

Garrison Savannah Area Historic Area

About 2km south of central Bridgetown and inland from Carlisle Bay, the Garrison is part of the World Heritage zone and was the home of the British command in the 1800s. A focal point is the oval-shaped Savannah, which was once parade grounds and is now used for cricket games, jogging and Saturday horse races. Standing along the west side of the Savannah are some of the Garrison's more ornate colonial buildings, where you'll find the world's largest collection of 17th-century cannons.

Barbados Museum Museum

(☎427-0201; www.barbadosmuseum.org; Garrison; adult/child B$15/7.50; ⏰9am-5pm Mon-Sat, 2-6pm Sun) This excellent museum is housed in an early-19th-century military prison. It has engaging displays on all aspects of the island's history, beginning with its early indigenous residents.

 Tours

Mount Gay Rum Visitors Centre Tour

(www.mountgay.com; Spring Garden Hwy; tours US$10; ⏰hourly tours 9:30am-3:30pm Mon-Fri, 10:30am-2:30pm Sat) The aged rums here are some of Barbados' best. The visitor center is about 1km north of Bridgetown Harbour.

Eating

Cuz's Fish Shack Seafood **$**
(Pebbles Beach; mains B$8; 10am-4pm Mon-Sat) The eponymous Cuz doles out stupendously juicy fish cutters (sandwiches) from the beachside food truck.

Entertainment

Cricket matches are played throughout the year at the **Kensington Oval** (274-1200; www.kensingtonoval.org; President Kennedy Dr; 9am-4pm) in Garrison near Bridgetown, which was the site of the final in the 2007 World Cup. Nearby, you can learn about past triumphs at **Cricket Legends of Barbados** (227-2651; Fontabelle; 10am-4pm Mon-Fri).

South Coast

The south coast is the island's midrange tourism epicenter. This virtually uninterrupted stretch of development – and beach – runs from the outskirts of Bridgetown all the way to the airport.

HASTINGS & ROCKLEY

Hastings and Rockley are home to some attractive, popular beaches. Commercialism rules, although there's an attractive new **boardwalk** on the waterfront east of Hastings.

Beaches

Accra Beach Beach
(Hastings Main Rd) The largest beach in the area, it is a picture-perfect crescent of sand. Backed by shade trees, there's moderate surf. The new boardwalk allows you to walk west for more than 3km to Hastings.

Eating & Drinking

Champers Seafood **$$$**
(435-6644; www.champersbarbados.com; Rockley; mains B$50-80; 11:30am-3pm Sun-Fri, 6-9:30pm daily) This longtime favorite

has a dreamy location overlooking Accra Beach. Elegant meals include the usual range of grilled seafood plus fresh pasta. Brits will understand the name means 'Champagne' – drink some in the lower-level lounge.

Mojo Bar

(Hwy 7, Rockley; ⌚11am-late) A big old house by the side of the road, Mojo has a wide open-air veranda plus all sorts of nooks inside for nuzzling your companion or listening to the excellent music. Monday is open-mike night. The burgers are good.

WORTHING

Worthing is a good base if you're on a tight budget but still want to be near the action.

Beaches

Sandy Beach Beach

A nice strip of white powder without a clever name that's well off the main road. The water defines 'turquoise.'

Sleeping

Maraval Guesthouse & Apartments Guesthouse $

(☎435-7437; www.maravalbarbados.com; 3rd Ave; r from US$40, apt US$100-150; wi-fi) On a tiny lane near Sandy Beach, Maraval has six simple rooms with shared bathrooms and in-room sinks in a vintage beach house. There's a kitchen and a pleasant common room. Nearby are several apartments that are right on the beach. All are bargain-priced for Barbados.

Coral Mist Beach Hotel Hotel $$

(☎435-7712; www.coralmistbarbados.com; Hwy 7, Worthing; r US$125-200; air-con, wi-fi, pool) This small and traditional beachfront hotel wins plaudits for its ideal beachfront location. All 32 rooms have kitchen facilities, balconies and views of the blinding-white beach. You can walk to much nearby.

Eating

Worthing has some good inexpensive dining choices; for a special dinner, head down the road to St Lawrence Gap.

Harbor walk, Bridgetown (p317)

Oistins Fish Fry

The fishing village of Oistins is the place to be two nights a week. Featuring soca, reggae, pop and country music, vendors selling barbecued fish and plenty of rum drinking, the legendary **Oistins Fish Fry** (food 6-10:30pm Fri & Sat) draws mobs. It's roughly 60% locals, 40% tourists and there's a joyous electricity in the air on Friday night, which is just a tad more fun than the fish fry's other night, Saturday. It's held in a complex of low-rise modern buildings right on the sand next to the fish market.

Here are some tips to have a great time:

Standard menu Most of the stalls serve the same menu: grilled fish and shellfish, pork chops, ribs and chicken. Sides include macaroni pie, chips, plaintains, grilled breadfruit, garlic bread and more. Unless you specify, you'll get a bit of each side with your main. It costs about B$35 per person.

Standards vary Just because there's more than 30 vendors serving the same menu doesn't mean all are created equal. Go with the crowds, they know.

Party! Buy a cheap and icy bottle of Banks (B$3) and plunge in. Some of the open-air bars like the ever-golden **Lexie's** (Fish Market, Oistins Beach; 24hr) never close. People have been known to lose all inhibitions and even propose!

Carib Beach Bar & Restaurant Cafe $$

(2nd Ave; meals B$20-40; 11am-late) This open-air cafe right on Sandy Beach is the hub of local holiday life. Seafood and burgers are the main items, enjoy 'em at picnic tables on the sand while you watch waves break on the reef offshore or at tables near the bar. There's live music Friday nights.

ST LAWRENCE GAP & DOVER BEACH

The real action here lies along a 1.5km-long road that runs close to the beach and is lined with hotels, bars, restaurants and shops. It's mostly free of traffic, allowing nighttime strolling.

The west end is known as St Lawrence Gap; the east end carries the Dover Beach moniker.

Dover Beach itself has a nice, broad ribbon of white sand that attracts swimmers, bodysurfers and windsurfers.

Sleeping

Accommodations options in the Gap span the gamut from off-beach cheapies to flash resorts.

Southern Palms Beach Club Resort $$$

(428-7171; www.southernpalms.net; St Lawrence Gap; r from US$250;) A traditional beach resort that stays in the pink – literally. Most of the various three-story blocks are decked out in a cheery pink tone. The 92 rooms have large balconies and patios.

Eating & Drinking

One of the pleasures of the Gap is wandering the street at night comparing the many restaurants. Bars range from humble to famously swank.

Sugar Ultra Lounge Club

(420-7662; St Lawrence Gap; 8pm-late) Where Rihanna parties when she's home on holiday. Several other clubs are nearby.

SILVER SANDS

At the southernmost tip of the island, between Oistins and the airport, is the breezy, kitesurfing-mecca of Silver Sands.

Activities

deAction Beach Shop Windsurfing
(☎428-2027; www.briantalma.com; Silver Sands; gear rental per hr from US$60, lessons per day from US$80; ⏰8am-dusk) Run by board-legend Brian Talma, this shop is set on one of the hemisphere's premier spots for windsurfing and kitesurfing. Watch huge kites twirl about the sky while riders hop the waves below with a cold Banks at the cafe.

Zed's Surfing Adventures Surfing
(☎428-7873; www.barbadossurf.com; Surfer's Point; board rental per day US$25, lessons from US$80; ⏰9am-5pm Mon-Sat) Runs tours and classes island-wide.

West Coast

Barbados' west coast has lovely tranquil beaches that are largely hidden by the majority of the island's luxury hotels and walled estates. Known to some as the Platinum Coast, it gets this moniker either from the color of the sand or the color of the credit cards.

In colonial times, the area was a popular holiday retreat for the upper crust of British society. These days, the villas that haven't been converted to resorts are owned by the wealthy and famous. That's on the water side of course. On the *other* side of Hwy 1 are modest huts and simple vacation retreats. Although the beaches are all public, the near constant development means that you only get a few coastal glimpses.

PAYNES BAY

Fringed by a fine stretch of white sand, gently curving Paynes Bay in St James is endlessly popular and is the west coast's most popular spot for swimming and snorkeling (you will almost certainly see sea turtles).

Have your paparazzi moment at the celebrity-studded beach in front of the ultra-exclusive **Sandy Lane** (☎444-2000; www.sandylane.com; Paynes Bay; r from US$1200; ❄📶🏊) hotel – there's public

Andromeda Botanic Gardens (right)

access along the resort's north wall.

HOLETOWN

The first English settlers to Barbados landed at Holetown in 1627. Long a bastion of understated luxury, Holetown has exclusive shops and a charming little nightlife area near the beach.

There's lots of good **snorkeling** in the mellow waters and reefs here.

Sleeping

The Holetown area has some of the island's most vaunted resorts, many in former mansions of the fabulously wealthy.

Coral Reef Club Resort **$$$**
(422-2372; www.coralreefbarbados.com; Holetown; r US$450-900;) This family-owned 88-unit luxury hotel has 5 hectares of gorgeous landscaped grounds surrounding an elegant gingerbread fantasy of a main building.

If You Like... Beautiful Gardens

Goergeous botanical gardens dot the interior of Barbados.

1 **HUNTE'S GARDENS**
(Castle Grant; admission B$30; 9am-5pm) One man's vision of a verdant tropical fantasy.

2 **WELCHMAN HALL GULLY**
(www.welchmanhallgullybarbados.com; Hwy 2, Welchman Hall; adult/child B$24/12; 9am-4pm) A surviving tract of original Barbados tropical rainforest.

3 **FLOWER FOREST**
(433-8152; www.flowerforestbarbados.com; off Hwy 2, Richmond; adult/child B$25/12.50; 8am-4pm) A 20-hectare botanic garden is on the site of a former sugar estate which has many stately mature citrus and breadfruit trees.

4 **ANDROMEDA BOTANIC GARDENS**
(433-9261; http://andromeda.cavehill.uwi.edu; Hwy 3, Bathsheba; adult/child B$25/12.50; 9am-5pm, last admission 4:30pm) A wide collection of tropical plants, including orchids, ferns, water lilies, bougainvillea, cacti and palms.

Eating & Drinking

Holetown's best attribute is its little enclave of bars and restaurants that mix the grand with the pedestrian.

Ragamuffins Caribbean **$$**
(www.ragamuffinsbarbados.com; 1st St; mains from B$50; 6-10pm) Ragamuffins is in a 60-year-old chattel house now filled with personalities. Dishes are all Caribbean with some added attitude. On Sunday there's a drag show.

MT STANDFAST

Popular with hawksbill turtles that feed on sea grasses just off its shore and with the snorkelers that come to watch, Mt Standfast also has a good **beach**.

WESTON

This is the west coast in a nutshell: a fish market and fruit stand on the waterfront with a couple of church steeples as a backdrop. The nearby rum shop, **John Moore Bar**, offers a heady mix of genial local characters and their newfound visitor friends.

MULLINS BEACH

A popular and family-friendly beach along Hwy 1 between Holetown and Speightstown, the waters are usually calm and good for swimming and snorkeling. Drinks from the boisterous cafe are delivered to your beach chair.

Sleeping

Legend Garden Condos Inn $$
(☎422-8369; www.legendcondos.com; Mullins Bay; r US$115-160, 3-night minimum; ❄ 📶 🏊) Fabulous value for the location, across the road and just 200m from the beach. The units here have kitchens and are lovingly decorated by the owners and spread out on spacious grounds.

SPEIGHTSTOWN

Easily the most evocative small town on Barbados, Speightstown combines old colonial charm with a vibe that has more rough edges than the endlessly upscale precincts to the south. Since the main road was moved to the charmless bypass east, traffic is modest, so take time strolling to look up at the battered old wooden facades.

Sights

A radiant vision in white stucco, **Arlington House** (Queen St; adult/child B$25/12.50; ⏲10am-5pm Mon-Fri, 10am-3pm Sat) is an 18th-century colonial house that now houses an engaging museum run by the National Trust.

Eating & Drinking

Fisherman's Pub Caribbean $
(☎422-2703; Queen St; meals from B$15; ⏲11am-late Mon-Sat, noon-4pm Sun) This waterfront cafe is a local institution that serves up fish from the boats floating off the side deck. On Wednesdays there is steel-pan music and a buffet. As the evening wears on, the scene gets more Bajan. Line up for the ever-changing and excellent fare.

Central Barbados

Several roads cross the rolling green hills of the island's interior. There's a wealth of historic and natural sights here and you can spend days winding around small roads far from the crowds.

Surprises abound: you'll round a corner and discover a huge stone 19th-century church or the fascinating plantation-era signal tower at **Gun Hill** (☎429-1358; Fusilier Rd, Salisbury; adult/child B$10/5; ⏲9am-5pm Mon-Sat), which was how the colonials once communicated.

SPEIGHTSTOWN TO BATHSHEBA

The road going into the hills east of Speightstown, Hwy 2, steadily climbs through historic sugarcane fields. The ruins of mills dot the landscape.

At Portland, turn off Hwy 2 and follow a narrow road winding

St Nicholas Abbey (right)
BRENT WINEBRENNER/GETTY IMAGES ©

under a cathedral of huge mahogany trees arching overhead to **St Nicholas Abbey** (www.stnicholasabbey.com; adult/child B$35/20; ⏲10am-3:30pm Sun-Fri), a Jacobean-style mansion that is one of the oldest plantation houses in the Caribbean and a must-see stop on any island itinerary.

About 700m southeast of the abbey, the road passes **Cherry Tree Hill**, which has grand views right across the Atlantic coast.

Rejoin Hwy 2 and head toward the coast, passing through the little town of **Belleplaine**, which has a good cafe. Running along the rugged coast through low sand dunes, the road here is one of the great ocean drives right until you reach Bathsheba.

Eastern Barbados

The wild Atlantic waters of the east coast are far removed from the rest of the island. The population is small, the coast craggy and the waves incessant.

BATHSHEBA

Bathsheba is prime surfing country. It's also good for long beach walks as you contemplate feeling you've reached the end of the world. It's an idyllic image of sand, sea and palm trees.

If you're not an expert swimmer, this is not really the place to go into the water; rather, enjoy the wave-tossed scenery on long beach walks. Note the iconic **Mushroom Rock**, one of several rocks carved into shapes that will cause mycologists to swoon.

Activities

Soup Bowl Surfing

The world-famous reef break known as the Soup Bowl is right off the beach and is one of the best waves in the Caribbean islands. Don't underestimate the break just because the region is not known for powerful surf – Soup Bowl gets big. The best months are August to March.

Sleeping & Eating

Bathsheba's beach has a couple of good cafes.

Sea-U! Guest House Boutique Hotel **$$**

(☎433-9450; www.seaubarbados.com; Tent Bay, Bathsheba; r from US$150; @ wifi) There's an addictive porch here looking out to sea from the hillside location. Cottages and a restaurant pavilion round out the verdant site. Dinner is served daily.

Getting There & Away

A taxi can be negotiated for about B$70 from Bridgetown or the south coast, or catch one of the regular buses from Bridgetown that travel Hwys 2 and 3. The trip takes about 45 minutes.

SURVIVAL GUIDE

Directory A–Z

Accommodations

The following price ranges refer to the cost of a double room during high season (December to April) and, unless otherwise stated, do not include taxes.

$ less than US$75

$$ US$75 to US$200

$$$ more than US$200

Barbados

The south coast generally has smaller and more affordable beach resorts. The west coast is where you'll find the big money. There is every kind of accommodations across the island.

Most hotels add a 7.5% government tax plus a 10% service charge, and many have a minimum stay in high season.

Dominica

Dominica has no big resorts but it does have cottages tucked into the jungle, boutique inns and remote hideaways.

A 10% value-added tax (VAT) and a 10% to 15% service charge are usually added to bills.

Grenada

Grenada has all manner of beach resorts and hotels, large and small.

Practicalities

ELECTRICITY

Barbados 110V, 50Hz; US-style two-pin plugs; also some UK-style sockets.

Dominica 220/240V, 50/60 cycles; North American two-pin sockets.

Grenada 220V, 50 cycles; UK-style three-pin plugs; some US-style two-pin plugs.

St Lucia 220V, 50Hz; three-pronged, UK-style plugs.

SVG 220V to 240V, 50Hz; UK-style three-pin plugs; some resorts have US-style outlets with 110V power.

TIME

Atlantic Standard Time (GMT-4)

TIPPING

A 15% to 20% overall tip is the norm in restaurants; 10% to 15% is often added to the bill. A tip of 15% is usually added to the bill in hotels. A 10% tip is the norm in taxis. Watch for service charges in hotels and resorts.

WEIGHTS & MEASURES

Barbados Metric system.

Dominica, Grenada, St Lucia & SVG Imperial system.

A 10% tax and a 10% service charge are added to most bills.

St Lucia

In addition to boutique hotels and all-inclusive resorts, which form the core of the market, St Lucia offers more offbeat options.

Taxes, which include a 10% service charge and a 10% tax, are added to rates.

SVG

There are a wide range of accommodations options throughout SVG.

A 10% VAT is added to all hotel rooms. A 10% service charge is frequently tacked on to bills – be sure to clarify exactly what price you are being quoted. Prices are in either EC$ or US$, depending on the hotel.

Food

The following price ranges are for the cost of a main course.

Barbados

$ less than B$25

$$ B$25 to B$60

$$$ more than B$60

Dominica, St Lucia & SVG

$ less than EC$30

$$ EC$30 to EC$50

$$$ more than EC$50

Grenada

$ less than US$25

$$ US$25 to US$75

$$$ more than US$75

Health

Barbados There are excellent medical facilities in Barbados. Tap water is safe to drink.

Dominica Roseau, Marigot and Portsmouth have medical facilities. US Centers for Disease Control recommends against drinking tap water on Dominica, although many people do it without any problems. Most, however, prefer the taste of bottled water.

Grenada There is a hospital in St George's. Grenada's tap water is chlorinated and theoretically safe to drink, but many prefer bottled water.

St Lucia You'll find medical facilities in Castries, Vieux Fort and Rodney Bay. Tap water is safe to drink.

SVG There are public and private hospitals throughout the islands. Serious problems will require a trip to St Vincent, if not further. On St Vincent, tap water is generally safe to drink. On the outer islands water comes from rain collection, wells or desalination plants – so the quality can vary and the taste can be unpleasant at times.

Language

English is the main language on all the Windward Islands.

Money

Barbados Barbadian dollars (B$) are used, but larger payments can be made in US dollars. Some tourist places quote rates in US dollars. ATMs are common.

Dominica The Eastern Caribbean dollar (EC$) is used and US dollars are widely accepted. ATMs are few outside of Roseau and Portsmouth.

Grenada The Eastern Caribbean dollar (EC$) is used. Most hotels, shops and restaurants accept US dollars. There are ATMs across Grenada.

St Lucia The Eastern Caribbean dollar (EC$) is the island currency. US dollars are often accepted. ATMs are found in major towns.

SVG The Eastern Caribbean dollar (EC$) is the local currency. All of the major islands, except for Mayreau, have a bank and ATMs. People will always accept US dollars.

Opening Hours

The following are standard business hours across the islands. Exceptions include the smaller islands where hours may be shorter or more erratic.

Banks 9am to 3pm Monday to Friday

Restaurants noon to 9pm

Shops 9am to 5pm Monday to Friday, to 1pm Saturday (in tourist areas to 8pm Monday to Saturday)

Public Holidays

Barbados

In addition to those observed throughout the region, Barbados has the following public holidays:

Errol Barrow Day January 21

Heroes' Day April 28

Labor Day May 1

Emancipation Day August 1

Kadooment Day First Monday in August

UN Day First Monday in October

Independence Day November 30

Dominica

In addition to the holidays observed throughout the region, Dominica has the following public holidays:

Carnival Monday & Tuesday Two days preceding Ash Wednesday (the beginning of Lent, 46 days before Easter)

May Day May 1

Beach, Bathsheba (p327)

August Monday First Monday in August

Independence Day/Creole Day November 3

Community Service Day November 4

Grenada

In addition to those observed throughout the region, Grenada has the following public holidays:

Independence Day February 7

Labor Day May 1

Corpus Christi Ninth Thursday after Easter

Emancipation Days First Monday & Tuesday in August

Thanksgiving Day October 25

St Lucia

In addition to holidays observed throughout the region, St Lucia has the following public holidays:

New Year's Holiday January 2

Independence Day February 22

Labor Day May 1

Corpus Christi Ninth Thursday after Easter

Emancipation Day August 3

Thanksgiving Day October 5

National Day December 13

SVG

In addition to those observed throughout the region, SVG has the following public holidays:

St Vincent & the Grenadines Day January 22

Labor Day First Monday in May

Caricom Day Second Monday in July

Carnival Tuesday Usually second Tuesday in July

Emancipation Day First Monday in August

Independence Day October 27

Telephone

When calling from North America, dial the code plus the local number. From elsewhere dial your country's international access code plus the area code plus the local number. Country codes:

Barbados ☎1-246

Dominica ☎1-767

Grenada ☎1-473

St Lucia ☎1-758

SVG ☎1-784

Visas

Visas to visit the Windward Islands nations are not required for the US, Canada, the EU and most Commonwealth countries.

Waterfront, Bridgetown (p317)

Getting There & Away

Entering the Windward Islands

Visitors to the Windward Islands nations must have a valid passport and – in principle – a round-trip or onward ticket.

Note: if you are planning to transit to your next destination by boat (eg Grenada to St Vincent & the Grenadines) it is a good idea to carry a print-out showing your plans and/or boat reservation. This should mollify any bureaucrats who get curious.

Air

The main airline for regional service within the Windward Islands and to neighboring islands is the oft-maligned Liat (www.liat.com). Flights are often late, and last-minute schedule changes may cause havoc if you have connections with other airlines. Other regional airlines:

Caribbean Airlines **(www.caribbean-airlines.com)** Has regional routes centered on Trinidad.

SVG Air **(www.svgair.com)** Connects St Vincent, Bequia, Canouan, Mustique and Union Island with Barbados and St Lucia.

Barbados

Grantley Adams International Airport **(BGI; www.gaiainc.bb)** is on the island's southeast corner, about 16km from Bridgetown. It is the largest airport in the Eastern Caribbean and the major point of entry for the region.

Barbados is served by major airlines flying from North America and the UK.

Dominica

Most flights arrive at **Melville Hall Airport** (DOM), on the northeast side of the island about a 90-minute drive from Roseau.

There is a cash EC$59 (US$23) departure tax for anyone over age 12 whether by plane or boat. There are no flights to North America or Europe.

The small **Canefield Airport** about 15 minutes north of Roseau handles only regional flights on small aircraft.

Grenada

Maurice Bishop International Airport **(GND; ☎444-4555; www.mbiagrenada.com)** is large and has full services. It has flights from North America and the UK.

Lauriston airport in Carriacou is a very modest affair with limited regional flights.

St Lucia

Confusingly, St Lucia has two airports:

Hewanorra International Airport **(UVF; www.slaspa.com)** In Vieux Fort at the remote southern tip of the island. It handles flights from North America, the UK and Europe plus a few regional flights.

George FL Charles Airport **(SLU; www.slaspa.com)** Conveniently located in Castries but due to the short runway is only served by regional flights on prop planes.

SVG

St Vincent is the main airport for SVG, however tiny **ET Joshua Airport** in Kingstown can only handle small planes, so service is limited to nearby islands such as Barbados and Grenada. The main islands in the Grenadines also have service to Barbados. There is a EC$40 departure tax payable by all departing passengers.

A new airport, Argyle International Airport, is under construction on the east side of St Vincent near Yambou Head but is years behind schedule and may not open until 2015 or later. It will be able to handle jets and flights from North America and beyond.

Sea

The Windward Islands are some of the most popular places to sail in the world. Yacht harbors and charters abound. The one exception is Barbados, where its easterly position and challenging sailing conditions keep it well off the main track for most sailors.

Ferry

L'Express des Îles **(www.express-des-iles.com; adult/child one way from €76/36)** connects Dominica, Guadeloupe, Martinique and St Lucia several times weekly on 300-seater catamarans.

Getting Around

With the exception of L'Express des Îles connecting Dominica and St Lucia and small-boat service between Grenada and SVG, to island-hop within the Windward Islands, you'll have to fly. The main carriers are Liat and SVG Air.

In all the Windward Islands, you drive on the left.

Barbados

Bus It's possible to get to virtually any place on the island by public bus. There are three kinds of bus:

Government-operated public buses Large and blue with a yellow stripe.

Privately operated minibuses Intermediate-sized buses painted yellow with a blue stripe.

Route taxis Individually owned minivans that have 'ZR' on their license plates and are painted white.

All types of bus charge the same fare: B$2 to any place on the island. You should have exact change when you board the government bus, but minibuses and route taxis will make change.

Bus stops are marked with red-and-white signs printed with the direction in which the bus is heading ('To City' or 'Out of City'). Buses usually have their destinations posted on or above the front windshield.

Buses along the main routes, such as Bridgetown to Oistins or Speightstown, are frequent, running from 6am to around midnight. You can get complete schedule information on any route from the Transport Board (☎436-6820; www.transportboard.com).

Car Roads are good on Barbados. Visitors must obtain a temporary driver's license from their car-rental agency (B$10). Most major firms have affiliates at the airport and offices in Holetown.

In addition to a full range of cars, many rent strange, small convertible cars called 'mokes' (they look like the odd car in *Fantasy Island*), which don't have doors. These are an acquired taste. You won't need 4WD.

Taxi Taxis are common at the airport. Some 'official' prices (subject to negotiation) from the airport to the island's main destinations:

Bathsheba B$73

Holetown B$58

Speightstown B$73

Dominica

Bus Travel by bus is the most economical way of getting around. Private minibuses run between major cities from 6am to 7pm Monday to Saturday, stopping as needed along the way. Fares are set by the government and range from EC$1.75 to EC$11.

Car The main island loop road is good. Other roads can be slow going. Drivers need a local license issued by a car-rental agency. It costs US$12 or EC$30 and is valid for one month. Small local rental firms serve the airports. A 4WD is needed for exploring the mountains.

Island Car Rentals (☎255-6844; www.islandcar.dm)

Road Runner Car Rental (☎440-2952; www.roadrunnercarrental.com)

Taxi Fares are regulated by the government, but be sure to confirm the fare with the driver. To order a cab, call the Dominica Taxi Association (☎449-8553). Sample fares from Melville Hall Airport:

Roseau or Portsmouth US$26

Calibishie or Carib Territory US$15

Scotts Head US$34

Castle Comfort US$28

Grenada

Air SVG Air (www.svgair.com) has flights between Grenada and Carriacou.

Boat You can charter a small open boat to take you between Carriacou and Clifton on Union Island in SVG for a negotiable US$100; it's a bumpy (and often wet) 40-minute ride for a maximum of four people.

The *MV Jasper* mail boat runs between Carriacou and Union Island (EC$50, one hour) on a sporadic schedule.

Bus Privately run minivans run a series of set, numbered routes crisscrossing the islands, and are inexpensive and fast. Very fast.

Buses run frequently from around 7am to 7pm, but services start to thin out after 6pm. Buses on all routes run infrequently on Sundays.

Car Main roads on Grenada are good. Purchase a visitor's driving license (EC$30) through rental agencies. Most major firms have agencies on Grenada. You can arrange for pickup at the airport and ferry dock.

Ferry The Osprey (☎440-8126; www.ospreylines.com) is a large, fast boat connecting Grenada, Carriacou and Petit Martinique in less than two hours (per person one way Grenada to Carriacou EC$80, Carriacou to Petit Martinique EC$20). The boats run one to two times daily.

Reservations are rarely required, except on holidays. Tickets from Grenada are purchased on board, and from Carriacou at the office on Main St, Hillsborough. The *Osprey* arrives and departs at the east side of the Carenage in Grenada; and from the Hillsborough pier in Carriacou.

Taxi It's easy to find a cab; rates are negotiable.

St Lucia

Bus Service is via privately owned minivans. They're a cheap way to get around. St Lucia's main road forms a big loop around the island, and buses stop at all towns along the way. They're frequent between main towns and generally run until 10pm (later on Friday). Very few run on Sunday.

If there's no bus stop nearby, you can wave buses down as long as there's space for the bus to pull over. Sample fares from Castries to Gros Islet or Marigot Bay are EC$2.50, and to Soufrière, EC$10.

Route numbers are displayed on the buses, but it's best to check with the driver.

Car The mains roads are good, though explorations will require 4WD. Drivers must have a local driving permit (US$22), which is sold by the car-rental companies. Most major rental firms have franchises here.

Taxi Taxis are available at the airports, the harbor and in front of major hotels. They are not metered but they adhere to standard fares. Sample prices include Castries and Rodney Bay for US$25 and US$90 between Castries and Soufrière. Confirm the fare before getting in.

SVG

Air Flights within SVG are a quick and inexpensive way to shuttle within the Grenadines.

Mustique Airlines (www.mustique.com)

SVG Air (www.svgair.com)

Boat You can charter a small open boat to take you between Clifton on Union Island in SVG and Carriacou, Grenada for a negotiable US$100; it's a bumpy (and often wet) 40-minute ride for a maximum of four people.

The *MV Jasper* mail boat runs between Union Island and Carriacou (EC$50, one hour) on a sporadic schedule. A private boat costs EC$450. Arrange at the Anchorage Yacht Club Hotel (p308) in Clifton.

The main islands of SVG are linked by ferries (p307). You can also get between islands in the Grenadines by chartered small boats and yachts for fees from US$75 to US$400. Get info at docks or with your accommodations.

Bus Crowded minivans provide public transport on St Vincent. When you get to your stop, either tap on the roof or try to get the attention of the conductor. Fares vary by distance, ranging from EC$1 to EC$5.

Car St Vincent is worth exploring by car. Bequia is worth a car for one day. Road conditions are slow, and 30km/h is a good average. A visitor's driver's license costs EC$40.

Avis (☎456-6861; www.avis.com)

Lewis Auto World (☎456-2244; www.lewisautoworld.com)

Taxi Cabs are found on St Vincent and Bequia. Rates are negotiable.

Southern Caribbean

You can feel the heat and the beat of South America in the Southern Caribbean. Venezuela is close to the south and the continent's music and cultures meld with the Caribbean. Yet the vibe of each of these five major islands is different. Trinidad is all business until it comes to its Carnival, an all-consuming debauch that rivals Rio's. Just north, however, Tobago couldn't be more different. It's as mellow and as naturally beautiful as any island further north in the region.

Meanwhile to the west, the ABCs, the distinctly Dutch-flavored troika of islands, are each unique. Aruba is the favorite winter escape for Americans longing for perfect beaches and resorts. Tiny Bonaire simply has some of the world's best diving, with tangible dollops of history and funky vibes adding character. Finally, Curaçao has an intriguing colonial-era main city with natural and beachy escapes.

Wild bromeliads, Tobago (p372)
DEBRA WISEBERG/GETTY IMAGES ©

Southern Caribbean Itineraries

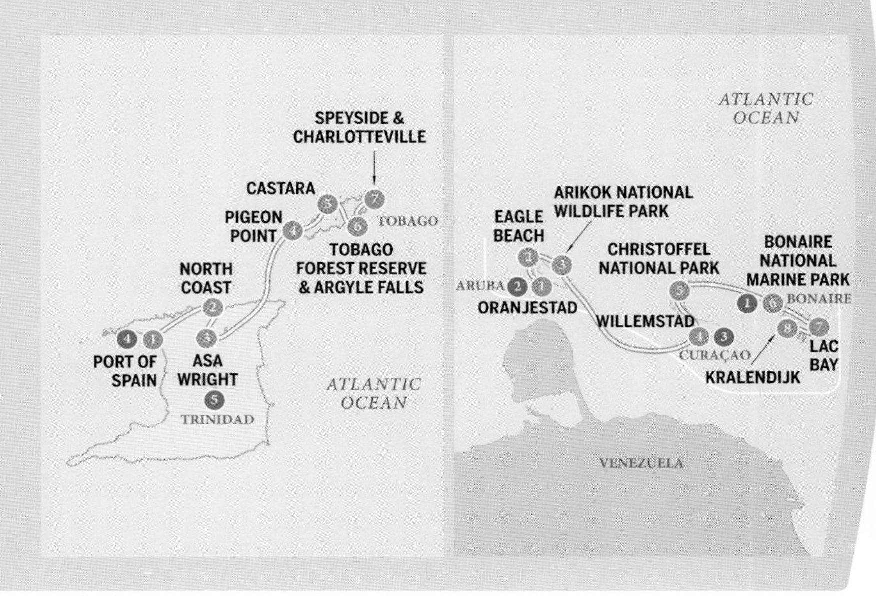

Seven Days

1 Port of Spain (p358) Start in Trinidad. Wander around the green and pleasant Savannah to check out the zoo and botanical gardens, then sample some classic Trini cooking with late lunch at Veni Mange. Once the sun sets, hit the Ariapita Ave bars.

2 North Coast (p369) Head through the hills to Maracas to ride the waves and try a bake and shark lunch, then spend the afternoon checking out the spectacular Las Cuevas and Blanchisseuse beaches.

3 Asa Wright (p368) Take a drive into the cool green jungle of the Northern Range for some truly awesome bird-watching, Creole lunch and a dip in a natural swimming pool.

4 Pigeon Point (p374) Hop over to Tobago to sink your toes into the soft white sand of this picture-perfect beach, or get an adrenaline rush with a kitesurfing session.

5 Castara (p381) Enjoy the laid-back life with a seafood lunch and manta-ray spotting at the main beach, then snorkeling at the neighboring Heavenly Bay.

6 Tobago Forest Reserve & Argyle Falls (p382) Take a walk into the oldest protected forest reserve in the western hemisphere, then defeat the afternoon heat by cooling off in the rushing waters of Argyle Falls.

7 Speyside & Charlotteville (p384) Indulge in a glass-bottom boat ride and some superlative snorkeling at Speyside. After lunch at Jemma's Treehouse, drive over to Charlotteville for swimming and sunset-watching at Pirate's Bay beach.

THIS LEG: 125KM

Ten Days

❶ **Oranjestad** (p338) Aruba's main town is a great place to wander. Spend a day enjoying its cafes and then plunge into local culture at the Aruba Archaeological Museum.

❷ **Eagle Beach** (p341) Loll about on the island's best beach, enjoying the long ribbon of powdery family-friendly sand.

❸ **Arikok National Wildlife Park** (p345) Walk, hike, drive and swim on the wild side, which has a fine new visitors center. You can easily spend a day exploring, from mysterious old gold mines to hidden beaches to picnic spots overlooking the wild surf.

❹ **Willemstad** (p351) On day four make the short hop over to Curaçao, where you can lose a day wandering the fascinating neighborhoods of this Unesco-recognized city. Dutch colonial heritage mixes with the grit of a busy port town. Learn about the legacy of slavery at the excellent Museum Kura Hulanda, then head over to the hot and historic neighborhood of Pietermaai for food and music.

❺ **Christoffel National Park** (p355) Feel the power of the windblown and wave-tossed east coast at this 1800-hectare preserve with a fab museum and some excellent nature walks. Afterwards stop at one of the island's many beaches.

❻ **Bonaire National Marine Park** (p349) On day seven make another short hop to Bonaire, where the entire coast is a Unesco-recognized world treasure of underwater beauty close to shore. Prepare to spend a lot of time diving and snorkeling.

❼ **Lac Bay** (p350) Get above the water at one of the world's premier destinations for windsurfing.

❽ **Kralendijk** (p346) On your last night, step out in Bonaire's main town, which has more than its fair share of great nightspots.

THIS LEG: 284KM

Southern Caribbean Highlights

❶ **Best Diving: Bonaire** (p346) You can wake up in the morning, step out on your hotel room's terrace, don scuba gear and plunge into world-class waters.

❷ **Best Beaches: Aruba** (p338) The pearly sands of Eagle Beach meld right into Palm Beach; just two of the island's great beaches.

❸ **Best History: Curaçao** (p351) Old town Willemstad wears its Unesco recognition with pride. Watch supertankers sail through town then visit old plantation houses.

❹ **Best Nightlife: Port of Spain** (p358) Trinbagonians take their liming seriously, as attested by the capital's bars and clubs.

❺ **Best Festival: Trinidad Carnival** (p359) The biggest, baddest and by far the Caribbean's best, with thousands of revelers partying for two days straight.

Willemstad (p351)

Discover the Southern Caribbean

ARUBA

POP 103,000

Americans from the east coast fleeing winter make Aruba the most touristed island in the southern Caribbean.

And that's not really surprising given that it has miles of the best beaches, plenty of package resorts and a compact and cute main town, Oranjestad, which is ideally suited for the two-hour strolls favored by day-tripping cruise-ship passengers. It's all about sun, fun and spending money.

But venture away from the resorts and you'll find that Aruba offers more. At the island's extreme ends are rugged, windswept vistas and uncrowded beaches.

Fort Zoutman, Oranjestad

WALTER BIBIKOW/GETTY IMAGES ©

Oranjestad

POP 29,000

Aruba's capital is a large island town that combines a mix of local commerce with the breathless pursuit of visitor business. Oranjestad has an appealing mix of old and new structures intermingled with scads of shops, bars and restaurants. At night the town is quiet.

Sights

Oranjestad is good for walking; very little is more than a 10-minute walk from the Yacht Basin.

Aruba Archaeological Museum Museum

(582-8979; www.namaruba.org; Schelpstraat; 10am-5pm Tue-Fri, 10am-2pm Sat & Sun) FREE Grand 1920s colonial buildings house this brilliant new museum. The engaging exhibits range from stone tools found on Aruba dating from 4000 BC to displays detailing Arawak life and the colonial era.

Fort Zoutman Fort

Not much to look at, but what's left dates from the 18th century. Best-preserved is the **Willem III Tower**, built to warn of approaching pirates.

Southern Caribbean

0 100 km
0 50 miles

FORT-DE-FRANCE
MARTINIQUE (FR)
CASTRIES
ST LUCIA
Saltibus
Sandy Bay
St Vincent
KINGSTOWN
ST VINCENT & THE GRENADINES
Grenada Island
Sauteurs
ST GEORGE'S
GRENADA
Caribbean Sea
ARUBA (NETH)
Oranjestad
CURAÇAO (NETH)
BONAIRE (NETH)
St Willibrordus
Kralendijk
Willemstad
Punto Fijo
Coro
La Orchila
Blanquilla
Tobago
Scarborough
TRINIDAD & TOBAGO
Federal Dependencies
Nueva Esparta
La Asuncion
PORT-OF-SPAIN
Carupano
CARACAS
Cumaná
Trinidad
San Fernando
Barquisimeto
Valencia
Barcelona
San Carlos
VENEZUELA
Maturin

Ports of Call

ORANJESTAD

- A long dock can handle several megaships at once, which is good given Aruba's popularity as a cruise-ship destination. Once off the boat, either head off to explore or press into Oranjestad proper (which you can do on free vintage-style trams). Don't be put off by the humdrum collection of shops closest to the pier.
- If you're docked for a few hours, don't miss an excursion to the many sights on the wild Northeast Coast, and time pounding the sand on Eagle Beach, Aruba's best.

KRALENDIJK

- The long dock can handle several megaships at once, which means that Kralendijk's population can triple or more on busy days.
- Options if you're docked for a few hours include enjoying some of the world's best diving and snorkeling; and windsurfing on Lac Bay.

WILLEMSTAD

- Historic, picturesque and compact, Willemstad is a very popular stop for cruise ships.
- With a few hours in port, you can wander Willemstad's Unesco-recognized streets and neighborhoods, and learn of Curaçao's slave heritage at the Museum Kura Hulanda.

PORT OF SPAIN

- The low-key terminal in downtown Port of Spain is a short taxi ride from the zoo, botanical gardens, Queen's Park Savannah and the Ariapita Ave bars and restaurants.
- The pick of the day tours are bird-watching at the Asa Wright Nature Centre and the Caroni Bird Sanctuary, or a north-coast trip that kicks off with wave-jumping and bake-and-shark at Maracas beach.

SCARBOROUGH

- The Scarborough dock is steps away from the market and botanical gardens, though you need a taxi to get to colonial-era Fort King George or to sink your toes in the whiter-than-white sand of Pigeon Point Beach.
- An island tour taking in the Leeward coast beaches and a snorkeling stop at Speyside offers a tantalizing taste of the rest of the island.

Festivals & Events

Carnival Carnival
(**Jan or Feb**) This is a big deal on the islands, where a packed schedule of fun begins right after New Year's Day. Aruba's parades are an explosion of sound and color.

Eating & Drinking

Snack trucks are an island institution. Look for these spotless trucks in the parking lots near the Yacht Basin serving up a range of ultrafresh food from sunset well into the wee hours.

Happy Spot Ice Cream $
(Caya GF Betico Croes; 11am-8pm) More than a dozen blenders are kept busy making milkshakes and fresh juice drinks at the open-air hut on the main shopping drag. Go on, have a triple cone.

Qué Pasa International $$
(583-4888; www.quepasaaruba.com; Wilhelminastraat 18; mains US$12-25; 11am-2pm Mon-Fri, 5-10pm daily;) The accent is Spanish but the language is global at this effusive cafe. A huge upstairs terrace is just the place to settle in for good drinks, conversation and dishes with myriad inspiration. Check out the art gallery and have a glass of chilled white.

Driftwood Seafood $$$
(583-2515; Klipstraat 12; mains US$18-50; 5-10pm Mon-Sat) Toss back too many of the serious cocktails at this 1960s supper club and you'll expect Dean Martin to walk in. It's owned by a local fisherman, and the changing menu reflects what he and his pals have caught. Grilled lobster is simple and simply terrific. The US$26 three-course special is a bargain.

Resort Area

Almost all of Aruba's hotels and resorts are on a long strip along some of the Caribbean's best beaches. Beginning 3km northwest of Oranjestad, the resort area has wide roads, lush landscaping and excellent beaches.

Beaches

Eagle Beach Beach
Fronting a stretch of the Low-Rise Resorts just northwest of Oranjestad, Eagle is a long stretch of white sand that regularly makes lists of the best in the world. Portions have shade trees and you can obtain every service you need here, from a lounger to a cold drink.

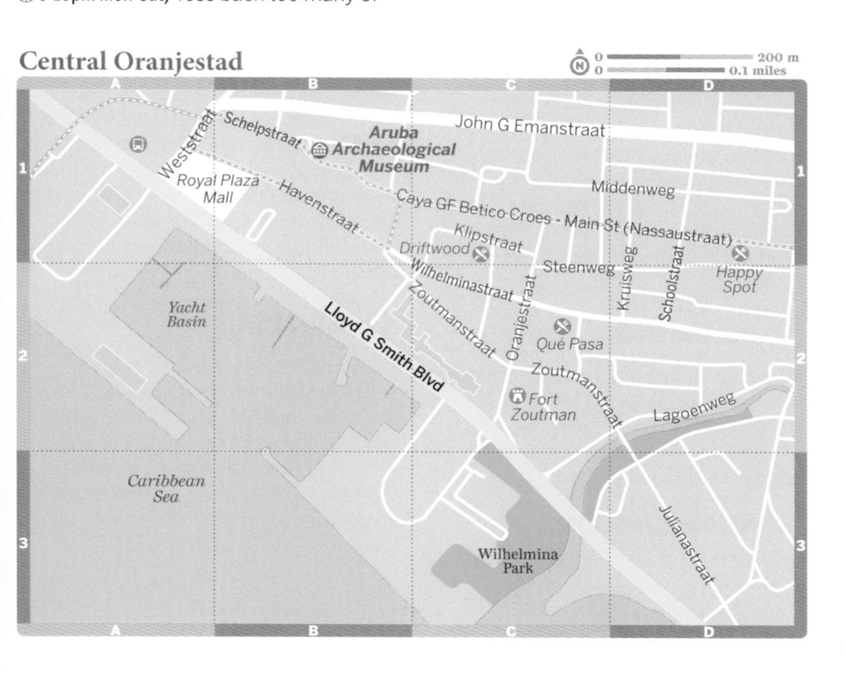

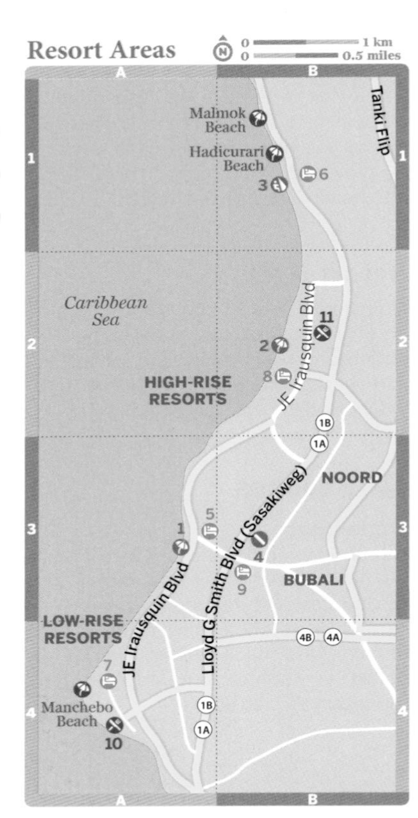

Resort Areas

Sights
- 1 Eagle Beach A3
- 2 Palm Beach B2

Activities, Courses & Tours
- 3 Aruba Active Vacations B1
- 4 Mermaid Sport Divers B3

Sleeping
- 5 Amsterdam Manor Beach Resort A3
- 6 Beach House Aruba B1
- 7 Bucuti Beach Resort A4
- 8 Radisson Aruba Resort B2
- 9 Sasaki Apartments B3

Eating
- 10 Matthew's A4
- 11 Queen's B2

Palm Beach Beach

A classic white-sand beauty, but only for those who enjoy the company of lots of people, as it fronts the High-Rise Resorts. During high season the sands can get jammed, but for some that's part of the scene.

Activities

Aruba has scores of fun activities pegged to its wind and water. All are more energizing than the heavily promoted 4WD tours, ATV tours and numerous other acronym-related tours.

DIVING & SNORKELING

Aruba has some excellent diving around its shores.

Mermaid Sport Divers Diving

(**587-4103; www.scubadivers-aruba.com; Lloyd G Smith Blvd; 2-tank dives from US$75**) Mermaid has a huge range of dive packages plus its own pool for training.

WINDSURFING

Aruba has world-class windsurfing.

Aruba Active Vacations Windsurfing

(**741-2991; www.aruba-active-vacations.com; Hadicurari Beach; rentals per hr from US$25, lessons from US$50**) The island's main windsurfing operator is based on Hadicurari Beach at the Fisherman's Huts, a prime bit of windsurfing water north of the high-rise resorts. A variety of lessons are available. It also does kitesurfing and stand-up paddleboarding for similar rates.

Sleeping

Accommodations on Aruba are ideally suited to the large-resort-seeking tourists the island targets – area names helpfully describe the architecture. The Low-Rise Resorts area mostly fronts Eagle Beach, the island's best. The High-Rise Resorts area has huge hotels affiliated with major chains.

Sasaki Apartments Hotel **$$**
(☎587-7482; www.sasaki-apartments.com; Bubali 143, Noord; r US$100-130; ❄@📶🏊) This simple complex is just a couple of busy roads away (400m) from Eagle Beach. The 24 studio apartments are spare in decor but have fully equipped kitchens. There's a pool and a barbecue grill and you're very close to a huge supermarket and stores.

Bucuti Beach Resort Resort **$$$**
(☎583-1100; www.bucuti.com; Lloyd G Smith Blvd 55B; r US$300-500; ❄📶🏊) One of the classiest choices among the Manchebo Beach low-rises, the 63-room Bucuti has a vaguely Spanish feel. Guest rooms are large, with kitchenettes and deep balconies, many with ocean views. The Tara wing is quite luxurious. There is a cafe in a concrete pirate ship.

Amsterdam Manor Beach Resort Hotel **$$$**
(☎587-1492; www.amsterdammanor.com; JE Irausquin Blvd 252; r US$210-450; ❄@📶🏊) At the north end of Eagle Beach and just across, this 72-unit family-run low-rise resort mimics a Dutch village, without the frosty weather. The recently revamped rooms and buildings come in a variety of shapes and sizes; all have kitchenettes. Some have sizable balconies or terraces with views.

San Nicolas

A small town near the island's ill-placed oil refinery, San Nicolas preserves Aruba's former rough-and-ready character long since banished from Oranjestad.

Baby Beach is a nice curve of sand, with gentle waters.

Charlie's Bar (Zeppenfeldstraat 56; meals US$8-25; ⏰11am-9pm Mon-Sat) is the big draw here. Started in 1941, it is still run by the same family and is a community institution. The walls are lined with a hodgepodge of stuff collected over the decades. The food combines local dishes with plenty of fresh seafood.

Colonial buildings, Oranjestad

DENNIS K. JOHNSON/GETTY IMAGES ©

Radisson Aruba Resort Resort $$$
(586-6555; www.radisson.com/aruba; JE Irausquin Blvd 81; r US$250-600;) The pick of the high-rise resorts. It has extensive, lush grounds. The 359 rooms have a newly freshened relaxed tropical motif and, unlike some other high-rises up here, it has a wide beach.

Eating

Close to the high-rise resorts there is a plethora of development adding upscale malls, chain restaurants and nightlife to the mix. A short walk or drive inland to Noord and you'll find a nice range of locally owned places.

Queen's Caribbean $$
(586-0606; Palm Beach Plaza Mall, JE Irausquin Blvd; mains US$20; 3-11pm) A oasis among the uninspired chains in the high-rise resort area – and one that serves Aruban food. Chef-owner Varella Innocencia is the namesake queen and her specialties include local treats such as *keshi yena* (stuffed Gouda cheese) and her famous chicken stew.

Matthew's Seafood $$
(588-7300; www.matthews-aruba.com; JE Irausquin Blvd 51; mains US$10-40; 7:30am-10pm) Just what you want for a beachy vacation: a beachside restaurant. Enjoy sunsets and more from this large open-air pavilion. Breakfasts have the standards, salads and sandwiches feature at lunch, and dinner has seafood and steaks.

Entertainment

Nightlife in the Low-Rise Resorts area is blissfully sedate. In the High-Rise Resorts area it is focused in and around several high-concept malls with a plethora of mostly chain bars, lounges and cinemas.

Almost every high-rise resort has a **casino**, many of which are surprisingly small. Slot machines are by far the most common game; most are open to 4am.

Left: Beachfront, Aruba; Below: Green iguana on Eagle Beach (p341)
(LEFT) PICARDO/GETTY IMAGES ©; (BELOW) HOLGER LEUE/GETTY IMAGES ©

Northwest Coast

The glitz of the resort area is quickly forgotten in this adjoining region of decent beaches, gracious homes and some significant Aruban landmarks.

Sights & Activities

California Lighthouse Landmark
Near Arashi Beach, this tall sentinel is named for an old shipwreck named *California*, which is *not* the ship of the same name that stood by ineffectually while the *Titanic* sank (despite much local lore to the contrary). The views are great and there's a good daytime cafe.

Sleeping

Almost in the shadow of the generic international resorts just south on Palm Beach, the hotels of the north are a characterful bunch with sunset views and a 30-second walk to the admittedly thin beach.

Beach House Aruba Hotel $$
(586-2384; www.beach-house-aruba.com; Lloyd G Smith Blvd 450; r US$85-350;) Funky doesn't begin to describe this sprawling collection of beach huts set in a dense garden across from Hadicurari Beach. The perfect antidote to the generic resorts.

Arikok National Wildlife Park

Arid and rugged, Arikok National Wildlife Park comprises 20% of Aruba and is the top nonbeach natural attraction.

The park has an impressive **Visitors Center** (585-1234; www.arubanationalpark.org; adult/child US$10/free; ticket sales 8am-3:30pm, park gate to 4pm) at the entrance. Here you'll find displays on the park and its natural features.

The principal road is about 11km long and links the west entrance with the southern one near San Nicolas, allowing a circular tour. Although slow going, it's doable in a budget rental car. Watch out for the many iguanas as you drive and stop once in a while and listen for the bray of **wild donkeys**.

Look for the park's three main types of **trees**: the iconic and bizarrely twisted divi-divi; the *kwihi*, with its tasty sweet-sour long yellow beans; and the *hubada*, which has sharp, tough thorns. Spiky aloe plants abound – see how many of the 70 varieties of cactus you can identify.

At **Boca Prins** on the coast there is a dramatic and dangerous beach in a narrow cove that forms explosive surf.

BONAIRE

POP 16,600

Bonaire's appeal is its amazing reef-lined coast. Entirely designated a national park, the beautiful waters lure divers from across the globe. But while no diving (or snorkeling) initiate will be disappointed, Bonaire also has world-class windsurfing. Although the beaches are mostly slivers of rocky sand, several take on a pink hue from ground coral washed ashore. Away from today's activities are fascinating vestiges of the island's grim legacy of slavery.

Kralendijk

POP 3600

Bonaire's capital and main town has a long seafront that's good for strolling day or night. The smattering of low-rise colonial-era buildings in mustard and pastels add charm.

Sights

Fort Oranje Fort

(museum 8am-noon & 1:30-4:30pm Mon-Fri) FREE Follow the cannons south along the waterfront to a small bastion built in the 1700s by the Dutch and modified often through the years.

Beaches

Bonaire doesn't have many eye-popping beaches but its pint-sized desert-island

Dutch architecture, Bonaire

KIM DAILEY/GETTY IMAGES ©

sibling just offshore, **Kleine Bonaire**, does. Day trips are popular and cost about US$25 for the boat ride.

Sleeping

Unlike other Caribbean islands, Bonaire has few large resorts; instead, hotels are smaller and often excellent value. Online agencies have numerous apartment listings.

Captain Don's Habitat Resort **$$**
(☎717-8290; www.habitatbonaire.com; Kaya Gobernador N Debrot; r & apt US$140-350; ❄@📶🏊) Belying that logo of a pirate flag bearing a skull impaled by a sword, the Captain runs a very comfortable resort. The 85 large units are set on spacious grounds, located 1km north of the town. Air tanks are available 24 hours a day.

Lizard Inn Guesthouse **$$**
(☎717-6877; www.lizardinnbonaire.com; Kaya America 14; r from US$80; ❄📶🏊) Proof that Bonaire offers good-value lodging. Only five minutes' walk from the shore and the center, this tidy compound has 12 basic but comfortable rooms. Some larger units have cooking facilities. The owner is a gem.

Buddy Dive Resort Resort **$$**
(☎717-5080; www.buddydive.com; Kaya Gobernador N Debrot 85; r/apt from US$140/200; ❄@🏊) Divers never had it so good: the reef is right off the deck and there's a drive-through air-tank refill station out front. The more than 70 rooms and apartments are all large.

Carib Inn Guesthouse **$$**
(☎717-8819; www.caribinn.com; Julio A Abraham Blvd; r & apt US$140-180; ❄📶) There are 10 units here in a small compound right on the water; most have kitchens, some are studios and others have one or two bedrooms. You can get your tanks refilled and a dock allows for easy dive-boat pickup. It's a short walk to the center.

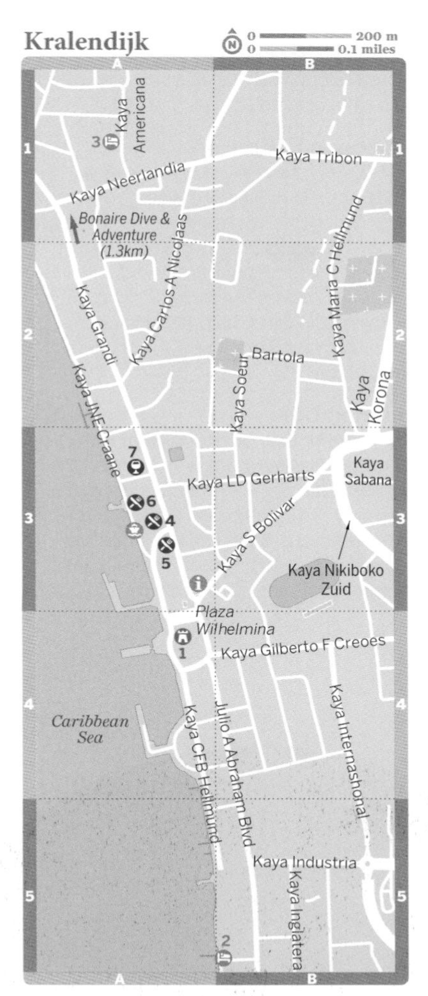

Kralendijk

Sights
1 Fort Oranje A4

Sleeping
2 Carib Inn B5
3 Lizard Inn A1

Eating
4 Donna & Giorgio's A3
5 Mona Lisa A3
6 Rumba Cafe A3

Drinking & Nightlife
7 Little Havana A3

Eating & Drinking

The Kralendijk area has a splendid collection of places to eat.

El Fogon Latino South American $
(717-2677; Kaya Nikiboko Zuid 88; mains US$6-12; 11am-9pm Wed-Mon) Direct from Colombia, this little cafe has tables on a porch or in its breezy dining room. The light and crispy fried dorado fillet is superb, as are the many other meaty plate meals. Skip the potatoes for the succulent fried plantains. It's on the road to Lac Bay.

Rumba Cafe Caribbean $$
(701-0134; Kaya CEB Hellmund 25; mains from US$12; 9am-9pm) Great views from the covered terrace are just the start at this cheery cafe in the heart of town. There are numerous fresh fish dishes as well as some excellent salads. Settle in and watch somnolent life barely pass by.

Donna & Giorgio's Seafood $$
(717-3799; www.donnagiorgio.com; Kaya Grandi 52; mains US$10-30; 9:30am-3pm Mon-Sat, 6:30-10pm Tue & Fri) This open-air restaurant is right in the center. The classic Italian menu has many treats and there are always plenty of specials. Make sure you book.

Mona Lisa Dutch $$$
(717-8718; Kaya Grandi 15; mains US$20-40; 5-10pm Mon-Fri, bar to 2am) This local institution is a tropical version of a traditional Dutch brown cafe. Choose from excellent steaks and seafood displayed on a changing blackboard menu. Book.

Little Havana Bar
(700-5927; www.littlehavanabonaire.com; Kaya Bonaire 4; 5pm-2:30am) A classic atmospheric bar in a historic whitewashed building. Walk through the open doors and you pass back many decades in time. Sit at the rich wooden bar and enjoy a fine Cuban cigar. Enjoy tapas from the adjoining Spanish restaurant at tables out front.

North of Kralendijk

The road north along the coast is like a roller coaster, but in good shape. There are great vistas of the rocky seashore and frequent pullouts for the marked dive sites. About 5km north of Kralendijk the road becomes one way, north, so you are committed at this point. After another 5km you reach a T-junction. To the right is the direct road to Rincon. But turn left (west), following the coast until the road turns sharply inland. Good views of the large inland lake, **Gotomeer**, are off on the left. **Flamingos** stalk about in search of bugs. The road

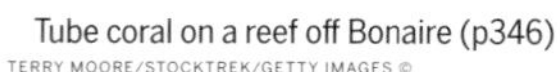

Tube coral on a reef off Bonaire (p346)

Diving & Snorkeling in Bonaire

Bonaire's dive sites are strung along the west side of the island. The closeness of the reefs and the clarity of the waters make for unparalleled access for divers. You can reach more than half of the identified dive sites from shore (or your hotel!).

BONAIRE NATIONAL MARINE PARK

The Unesco World Heritage **Bonaire National Marine Park** (717-8444; www.bmp.org; diving/snorkeling day-pass US$10/2, annual pass US$25/10) covers the entire coast of the island to a depth of 200ft (60m). There are more than 90 named dive sites.

Conservation is taken seriously. Divers new to Bonaire must receive an orientation from a dive operator.

DIVE OPERATORS

Every hotel and resort has a relationship with a dive operator or conversely – like Captain Don's Habitat – is a dive operator with a place to stay. Most offer myriad packages, including many options for snorkelers.

Well-regarded operators include **Bonaire Dive & Adventure** (717-2229; www.bonairediveandadventure.com; Kaya Gobernador N Debrot 77A; 6 days unlimited air or nitrox US$195, boat dive US$33; 8:30am-4:30pm), a free-standing dive operation.

passes through some lush growth and ends in Rincon.

RINCON

Bonaire's second town, Rincon, is rather sleepy and that may simply be because it's old. Over 500 years ago Spaniards established a settlement here because a) it was fertile and b) it was hidden from passing pirates. Most of the residents are descended from slaves, who worked the farms and made the long trek to the salt flats in the south.

Bonaire's harvest festival, **Simadan**, is usually held here in early April, and celebrates traditional dance and food.

Sights

The best sight is the town itself. Homes have a classic Caribbean look and are painted in myriad pastel shades.

Mangazina di Rei Museum
(786-2101; www.mangazinadirei.org; adult/child US$10/5; 9am-5pm Mon-Fri, last tour 4pm) About 1.5km east of Rincon, look for the second-oldest stone building on Bonaire. It has been restored and includes exhibits about its use during the peak of slavery on Bonaire.

Eating

Rose Inn Caribbean $$
(Kaya Guyaba 4; mains from US$10; 11am-3pm Thu-Tue, hours vary) A local institution run by Rose herself. A genial mix of folks enjoy plate lunches of local fare (fish stew, goat, fried chicken etc) at mismatched tables scattered under trees. Service can be erratic, but that's why you're here.

East of Kralendijk

The road from Kralendijk to Lac Bay is a highlight. Off the main road, a branch goes around the north side of the water. Close to the water there are dense mangroves and flocks of flamingos. It's a popular ride for cyclists.

The **Mangrove Info & Kayak Center** (599-790-5353; www.mangrovecenter.com;

Washington-Slagbaai National Park

Covering the northwest portion of the island and comprising almost 20% of the land, Washington-Slagbaai National Park is a great place to explore. Roads are rough and all but impassable after rain, but it's well worth the effort. The terrain is mostly tropical desert, and there is a proliferation of cactuses and birds.

An excellent **information center** (www.stinapa.org; adult/child US$25/free, discount with diving permit; ⌚8am-5pm, last entry at 2:45pm), small **museum** and **cafe** are at the entrance. From here you can take one of two drives: a 2½-hour, 34km route or a 1½-hour, 24km route. There are picnic, dive and swimming stops along the way and a tiny cafe at a remote beach.

Two hikes are best done well before the heat of noon: the 90-minute Lagadishi loop, which takes you past ancient stone walls, a blowhole and the rugged coast; and the two-hour Kasikunda climbing trail, which takes you up a challenging path to the top of a hill for sweeping views.

The park entrance is at the end of a good 4km concrete road from Rincon.

Kaminda Lac 140; boat/kayak tour US$27/46; ⌚Mon-Sat) is right on the mangroves and offers various tours.

LAC BAY

Lac Bay is one of the world's premier **windsurfing** destinations. The windswept shallows are good year-round for beginners; peak conditions are November to July and pros descend in May and June. The powdery beach is good year-round.

At the end of the main road on the south side, **Bonaire Windsurf Place** (☎717-2288; www.bonairewindsurfplace.com; Lac Bay Rd; 2-day rental from US$145, lessons from US$50; ⌚10am-6pm) has all things windsurfing (plus kayaking and paddleboarding). It has a cafe and a good veranda for watching the action on the water.

South of Lac Bay, a paved road follows the flat windward coast, which has pounding surf along a desolate shore littered with flotsam.

South of Kralendijk

The south end of Bonaire is flat and arid, and you can see for many miles in all directions. Multihued salt pans where ocean water evaporates to produce salt dominate the landscape. Metal windmills are used to transfer water out of the ponds. As evaporation progresses, the water takes on a vibrant pink color from tiny sea organisms.

Along the coast you will see the legacy of a vile chapter in Bonaire's past: tiny restored **slave huts**. Living conditions in these minuscule shelters are hard to imagine now, but they were home to hundreds of slaves, who worked in the salt ponds through the 19th century. The four different-colored 10m **pyramids** along the coast are another legacy of the Dutch colonial era. Colored flags matching one of the pyramids were flown to tell ships where they should drop anchor to load salt.

Just north of the slave huts, **Pink Beach** is a long sliver of sand that takes its color from pink coral washed ashore. It's pretty rough and you'll want a thick pad for sunbathing, but the swimming (not to mention the diving and snorkeling) is good. The beach is even better to the south at the **Vista Blue** dive spot.

CURAÇAO

POP 151,900

Go-go Curaçao balances commerce with Unesco-recognized old Willemstad and an accessible beauty, thanks to hidden beaches along a lush coast. It's a wild mix of urban madness, remote vistas and a lust for life.

Willemstad

POP 75,000

Willemstad is both a big city and a small town. Residents live in the hills surrounding Schottegat, and much of the city is sprawling and rather mundane. But this all changes radically in the Unesco-recognized old town.

Sights

The old town of Curaçao is split by Sint Annabaai, which is really a channel to Schottegat. On the west side is Otrobanda, an old workers' neighborhood, which has a mixture of beautifully restored buildings and areas rough around the edges. East of the channel – and linked by the swinging Queen Emma Bridge – is Punda, the old commercial center. North across Queen Wilhelmina Bridge is the old port and warehouse neighborhood of Scharloo.

Diving & Snorkeling in Curaçao

Curaçao's reefs are home to almost 60 species of coral, much of it the hard variety. The main areas for diving are from Westpunt south to St Marie; central Curaçao up and down the coast from St Michiel; and the south, beginning at the Curaçao Sea Aquarium. The latter coast and reefs have been protected as part of the **National Underwater Park**.

PUNDA

Queen Emma Bridge Landmark

One of Punda's sedate pleasures is sitting on the wall along the channel

Salt flats, Bonaire (p346)

Willemstad

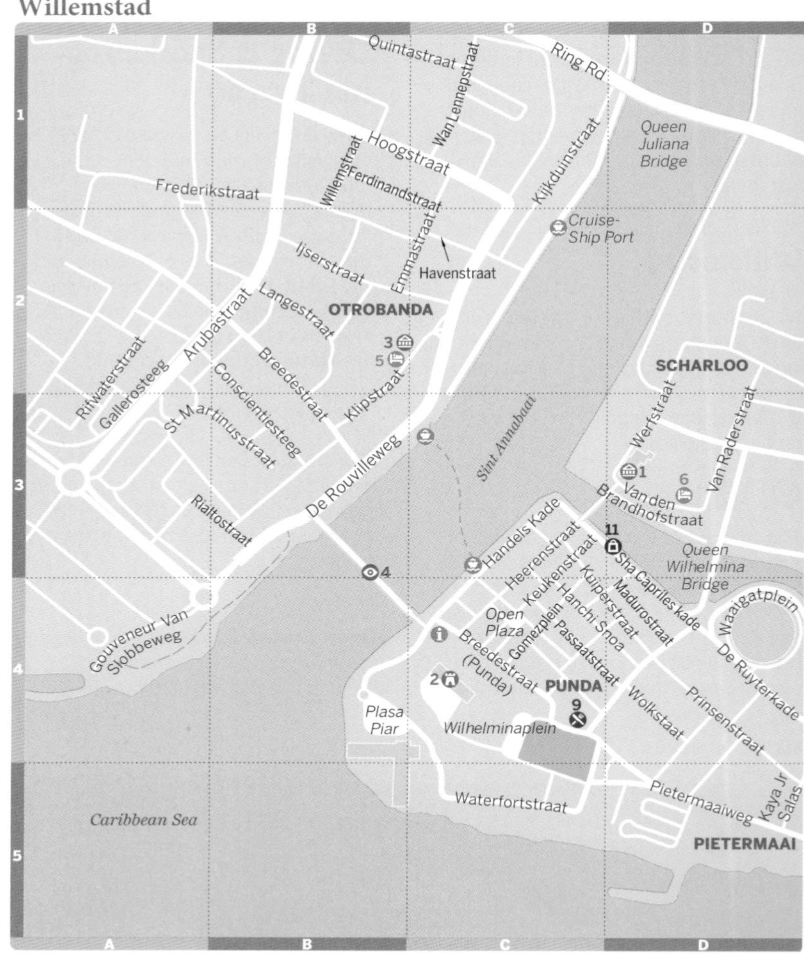

and watching huge ships pass while the Queen Emma Bridge shuttles back and forth to make way. When the bridge is open, two old free **public ferries** nearby cruise into action.

Fort Amsterdam Fort

The much-modified fort is now home to government and official offices. Inside the large courtyard you can soak up the rich colors of the Dutch colonial architecture dating from the 1760s.

Floating Market Market

(Sha Capriles Kade; dawn-dusk) A colorful place to see piles of papayas, melons, tomatoes and much more. The vendors sail their boats the 70km from Venezuela every morning.

OTROBANDA

Follow Wan Lennepstraat uphill into a safe and historic neighborhood for great views of the city and harbor.

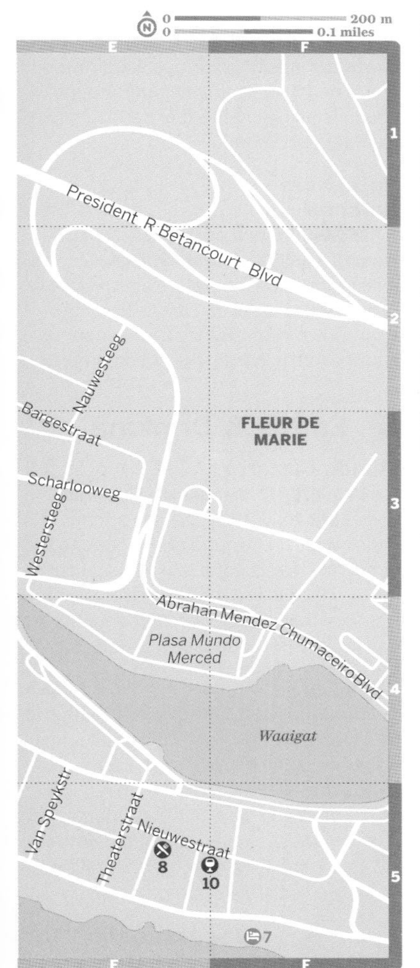

Willemstad

Sights
1 Curaçao Maritime Museum ... D3
2 Fort Amsterdam ... C4
3 Museum Kura Hulanda ... B2
4 Queen Emma Bridge ... B3

Sleeping
5 Hotel Kura Hulanda ... B2
6 Hotel Scharloo ... D3
7 Scuba Lodge ... F5

Eating
8 Mundo Bizzarro ... E5
9 Plein Cafe ... C4

Drinking & Nightlife
10 Miles Jazz Cafe ... E5

Shopping
11 Floating Market ... D3

Museum Kura Hulanda Museum

(☎9-434-7764; www.kurahulanda.com; Klipstraat 9; adult/child NAf18/12.50; ⏲9am-5pm Mon-Sat) One of the best museums in the Caribbean, this is part of the boutique hotel of the same name and is housed in 19th-century slave quarters. The brutal history of slavery in the Caribbean is documented here in superb and extensive exhibits.

SCHARLOO

The docks in the neighborhood are mostly closed, but wander around and you'll see building restorations in progress.

Curaçao Maritime Museum Museum

(☎9-465-2327; www.curacaomaritime.com; Van Den Brandhofstraat 7; adult/child NAf11/5.50, harbor tours adult/child NAf16.50/8.25; ⏲9am-4pm Tue-Sat, harbor tours 2pm Wed & Sat) Engaging displays trace the island's history, detailing how the Dutch West India Company kicked Spain's butt to gain control of the ABCs through to the commercial boom of the 20th century. Well worth the 90-minute time investment are the museum's **harbor tours**. It has a good cafe with views.

PIETERMAAI

Just east of Punda, this equally historic colonial area is becoming the local version of Miami Beach. In the meantime it's a funky mix of decaying mansions, spiffy rehabs, oddball shops and quixotic cafes. The spine, **Nieuwestraat**, is a necessary stroll.

Sleeping

Scuba Lodge
Hotel $$

(☎9-465-2575; www.scubalodge.com; Pietermaaiweg 104; r from US$140, villas from US$575; ❄ 📶) This new hotel exemplifies the exuberant blend of style and funk that is Pietermaai. With its own beach right on the ocean, this small hotel is also close to the center of town. The 32 rooms have luxe touches and mod colors; as the name implies, it offers diving packages.

Hotel Scharloo
Hotel $$

(☎9-465-1012; www.hotelscharloo.com; Van den Brandhofstraat 12; r US$80-150; ❄ 📶) What a find! This historic building has been converted into a 20-room inn. Suites on the top floor of the original building have views of the harbor. More-modest rooms are in a more modern wing in the rear. Some have air-con, others not.

Avila Beach Hotel
Boutique Hotel $$$

(☎9-461-4377; www.avilahotel.com; Penstraat 130; r from US$250; ❄ @ 📶 🏊) The Avila Beach combines rooms in the 18th-century home of a Dutch governor with modern wings of luxurious accommodation. The grounds are elegant and the beach is a fine crescent of sand. It's just east of Pietermaai.

Hotel Kura Hulanda
Boutique Hotel $$$

(☎9-434-7700; www.kurahulanda.com; Langestraat 8; r US$200-400; ❄ @ 📶 🏊) One of Willemstad's best hotels is also a sight in itself. Architect Jacob Gelt Dekker took a run-down neighborhood in Otrobanda and created a village-like hotel complex.

Eating & Drinking

Mundo Bizzarro
Caribbean $$

(☎9-461-6767; 12 Nieuwestraat, Pietermaai; mains US$8-20; ⏰11am-late) The anchor of Pietermaai, the ground floor opens to the street. Inside it's got a faux look of urban decay which is countered by the fine food. Upstairs there's a bar with fab mojitos and live music Wednesday to Saturday.

Plein Cafe
Cafe $$

(Wilhelminaplein 19-23, Punda; meals from NAf10; ⏰7:30am-11pm; 📶) This Dutch cafe and its neighboring twin are so authentic that if it were –1°C (30°F) and raining, you'd think you were in Amsterdam. Waiters scamper among the outdoor tables with trays of drinks and dishes of simple foods.

Miles Jazz Cafe
Bar

(Nieuwestraat 48, Pietermaai; ⏰5pm-2am Mon-Sat) That's Miles as in Davis, one of the inspirations for this stylishly divey nightspot in Pietermaai. Monday is open-mike night.

Punda (p351), Willemstad's old commercial center

Information

On Sundays when cruise ships are in port, many places open that are normally closed for business.

Curaçao's urban mix includes some real poverty. Although street crime is not a huge concern, in some of the recesses of Otrobanda drug-related crime is an everyday problem.

Tourist Information kiosk (Breedestraat; 8am-4pm Mon-Sat, Sun when cruise ship is in port) This kiosk by the Queen Emma Bridge on the Punda side has a wealth of information.

Southeast of Willemstad

Residential neighborhoods make up much of the land immediately south of the center of Willemstad. **Spaanse Water**, a large enclosed bay to rival Schottegat, is an upscale residential area. There's little further south to the tip of Curaçao except arid scrub.

Sights

Curaçao Sea Aquarium Aquarium
(9-461-6666; www.curacao-sea-aquarium.com; Bapor Kibra; adult/child US$21/11; 8am-5pm) On a man-made island, this heavily hyped attraction anchors **BLVD**, a development that includes hotels, bars and artificial beaches. It's home to over 600 marine species including sea lions, stingrays and sharks.

North of Willemstad

Looping around the northern part of Curaçao from Willemstad is central to any visitor's itinerary. Parks, villages and beaches all await discovery. You can do the loop in a day. (Nonstop, the drive takes a little over two hours.)

WEST COAST

There are scores of beautiful **beaches** hidden in coves along the west coast.

To head to the north end of the island via the northwest coast, take the main road, Weg Naar Westpunt (literally, 'road to Westpunt'), 8km from Willemstad to Kunuku Abao, where you turn west onto Weg Naar St Willibrordus. For 18km you drive through some of the most lush countryside in the southern Caribbean.

About 4km past the village, look for signs to the beautiful beach **Kas Abou**.

At Lagún the coast road nears the coast and the first of many fabulous beaches. **Playa Lagún** is a narrow and secluded beach situated on a picture-perfect narrow cove sided with sheer rock faces. There's diving here and a few cafes and apartments.

About 2km on from Lagún is **Landhuis Kenepa**, the main house of another 17th-century plantation. The hilltop site is stunning, but the real importance here is that this was where a slave rebellion started in 1795. A museum here, the **Museo Tula** (9-888-6396; adult/child US$3/1; 9am-4:30pm Tue-Sun), tells this story and explores the African roots of Curaçao.

WESTPUNT

Your journey's goal whether from the west or east; the small village of Westpunt has a beach, **Playa Kalki**, as a worthy reward.

Eating

Jaanchie's Curaçaoan $$
(9-864-0126; Weg Naar Westpunt; mains US$7-20; noon-8pm) Unmissable at the side of the main road. Here you can sample a full menu of island delicacies such as okra soup and goat stew. Some of the meats are rather exotic, but fear not: it all tastes like chicken.

EAST COAST

The windward side of the island is rugged and little developed.

Sights & Activities

Christoffel National Park Park
(9-864-0363; www.christoffelpark.org; Savonet; adult/child US$10/5, tour adult/child US$30/20; 7:30am-4pm Mon-Sat, 6am-3pm Sun, last entrance 90min before closing) This 1800-hectare preserve is formed from three old plantations. The main house for one of the plantations, **Landhuis Savonet**, is at the entrance to the park.

It was built in 1662 by a director of the Dutch West India Company. It's now an excellent **museum** (**www.savonetmuseum.org; Christoffel National Park; adult/child NAf12.50/7.50; ⌚7:30am-4pm**) on the colonial era.

The park has two driving routes over 32km of dirt roads, and sights include cacti, orchids, iguanas, deer, wave-battered limestone cliffs and caves with ancient drawings. Christoffel is about 25km north of Willemstad.

Shete Boka National Park Park

(**Weg Naar Westpunt; admission NAf10; ⌚9am-5pm**) A geologic and oceanic festival. Trails lead from a parking area right off the coast road to natural limestone bridges on the shore, sea-turtle sanctuaries, a big blowhole and isolated little beaches in narrow coves. **Boka Tabla**, a cave in the cliffs facing the water, is the most popular (and closest) walk. It's just northwest of Christoffel National Park.

TRINIDAD & TOBAGO

POP 1.3 MILLION

Trinidad

Put the tourists of Trinidad in a room and you'll have an awkward party: on one side will be wallflower bird-watchers tangled in camera and binocular straps; and on the other – the side with the bar – you'll have the party-hound Carnival fans turning up the music and trying on their spangly costumes.

But here's the secret: there's much more to Trinidad than is seen through binoculars or beer goggles. Of course, the swamps and forests are a bird-watcher's dream, and Port of Spain's Carnival will blow your mind. Yet Trinidad is also replete with verdant hiking and cycling trails, spectacular waterfalls and deserted bays. The rural, untouristed northeast coast harbors rugged beaches of shocking beauty, while the southwest showcases the island's Indian culture, with fragrant curry wafting through the air and flamboyant temples popping up out of nowhere.

With the booming oil and gas industry as its real bread and butter, Trinidad tends to treat tourists in a blasé manner. And to some visitors that's a boon. Genuine adventure awaits you here if you choose to accept.

Shaped like a molar tooth sitting on its side, Trinidad is surrounded by four bodies of water – the Caribbean (north), the Atlantic Ocean (east), the Gulf of Paria (west) and the Columbus Channel (south) – making each coast a little different. The bustling capital of Port of Spain sits along a wide bay on the gulf, and most of the country's better-known attractions are within an

Shete Boka National Park

Trinidad

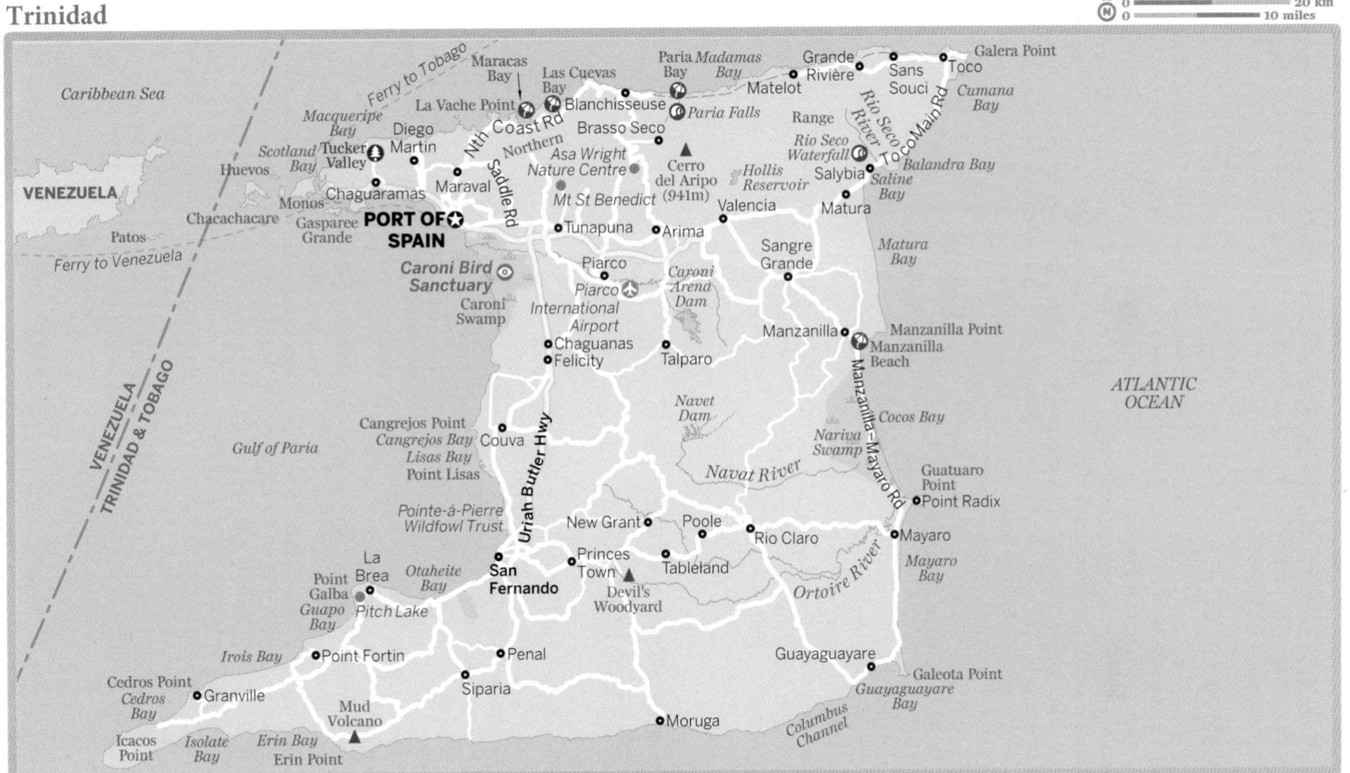
0 20 km
0 10 miles
Caribbean Sea
VENEZUELA
Patos
Ferry to Venezuela
Ferry to Tobago
Huevos
Chacachacare
Monos
Scotland Bay
Macqueripe Bay
Tucker Valley
Chaguaramas
Gasparee Grande
Diego Martin
La Vache Point
Maracas Bay
Las Cuevas Bay
Blanchisseuse
Nth Coast Rd
Northern
Maraval
Saddle Rd
PORT OF SPAIN
Caroni Bird Sanctuary
Caroni Swamp
Asa Wright Nature Centre
Mt St Benedict
Brasso Seco
Tunapuna
Arima
Cerro del Aripo (941m)
Paria Bay
Madamas Bay
Paria Falls
Matelot
Grande Rivière
Sans Souci
Toco
Galera Point
Cumana Bay
Range
Rio Seco River
Rio Seco Waterfall
Toco Main Rd
Balandra Bay
Salybia
Saline Bay
Hollis Reservoir
Valencia
Matura
Matura Bay
Sangre Grande
Piarco
Piarco International Airport
Caroni Arena Dam
Chaguanas
Felicity
Talparo
Manzanilla
Manzanilla Point
Manzanilla Beach
Manzanilla–Mayaro Rd
ATLANTIC OCEAN
Navet Dam
Cocos Bay
Nariva Swamp
Navat River
VENEZUELA
TRINIDAD & TOBAGO
Gulf of Paria
Cangrejos Point
Cangrejos Bay
Lisas Bay
Point Lisas
Couva
Uriah Butler Hwy
Pointe-á-Pierre Wildfowl Trust
New Grant
Poole
Rio Claro
Guatuaro Point
Point Radix
Mayaro
Mayaro Bay
Princes Town
Tableland
Devil's Woodyard
Ortoire River
San Fernando
La Brea
Point Galba
Otaheite Bay
Guapo Bay
Pitch Lake
Irois Bay
Point Fortin
Penal
Siparia
Guayaguayare
Galeota Point
Guayaguayare Bay
Columbus Channel
Moruga
Cedros Point
Cedros Bay
Granville
Mud Volcano
Icacos Point
Isolate Bay
Erin Bay
Erin Point

hour's drive. In fact, you could drive from one side of the country to the other in around three hours, maybe less if you're a pro at bumpy, winding roads.

PORT OF SPAIN

POP 50,500

Spreading back from the Gulf of Paria and cradled by the Northern Range foothills, Port of Spain should be a beautiful city. It does have its aesthetic highlights, including a lovely central green space, the Queen's Park Savannah, and a generous smattering of Hansel-and-Gretel fretworked buildings. But concrete is fast replacing the traditional wood, most of the downtown waterfront is hidden behind grimy warehouses and the relentless traffic is gridlocked. Nonetheless, the explosive development of recent years has done much to make Port of Spain the absorbing place it is today, with an urban insouciance and metropolitan verve that set it apart from the average Caribbean capital. This isn't a city that kowtows to the tourist dollar, and it's all the richer for it. There may not be many designated 'sights' to tick off, but there's plenty of atmosphere in the ruler-straight downtown streets, with their market stalls and shady squares, while the outlying neighborhoods of St James and Woodbrook harbor a host of restaurants and bars. And during Carnival season, huge fetes rock all corners, steel-pan music fills the air around the panyards and the atmosphere is electric. This buzzing city will school you on the most comprehensive partying in the world.

Playing J'ouvert

Trinidad's Carnival opens with Jouvert, a no-holds-barred pre-dawn street party where revelers have permission to indulge in their most hedonistic inclinations, as they welcome in the festivities by playing 'dirty mas.' From 4am, partiers file into the streets, slather themselves and others in mud, paint, oil and even liquid chocolate, and basically go mad while following trucks blasting soca. It's an anarchic scene, so you're best off signing up with an established band like **3Canal** (623-7411; www.3canal.com; 67a Ariapita Ave) or **Chocolate City** (623-4627; chocolatecitycarnival.com; 29 Stone St, Woodbrook), which employ security and lay on drinks and music trucks as well as mud, paint and a basic costume for TT$350 to TT$500.

Sights

Queen's Park Savannah Park

Once part of a sugar plantation, the Savannah is a public park encircled by a 3.7km perimeter road that locals call the world's largest roundabout. In the early evening when the scorching heat subsides, the grassy center is taken up with games of cricket or football, while kids fly kites and joggers crowd the perimeter path and vendors sell cold coconut water.

Magnificent Seven Historic Site

Along the west side of the Queen's Park Savannah are the Magnificent Seven, a line of eccentric and ornate colonial buildings constructed in the early 20th century, and now in various states of repair. From south to north, they are **Queen's Royal College**; **Hayes Court**; **Mille Fleurs**; **Roomor**; the Catholic **Archbishop's Residence**; **White Hall**; and **Stollmeyer's Castle**.

Emperor Valley Zoo Zoo

(www.zstt.org; adult/child TT$20/10; 9:30am-6pm, last entry 5:30pm; P) Just north of Queen's Park Savannah is the 2.5-hectare Emperor Valley Zoo, which opened in 1952. Though small, the zoo has some interesting residents, including indigenous red howler monkeys, ocelots and various snakes including an anaconda found in central Trinidad. A newly landscaped section holds sea otters, flamingos and a butterfly park, while giraffes, warthogs and Bengal tigers are the newest residents.

Trinidad Carnival

With roots in both West Africa and Europe, Carnival is the ultimate indulgence before the sober disciplines of Lent – and everyone's welcome to participate in this big daddy of Caribbean festivals.

Information is available from the **National Carnival Commission of Trinidad & Tobago** (622-1670; www.ncctt.org; 11 St Clair Ave, Port of Spain) and the exhaustive **Trinidad Carnival Diary** (www.trinidadcarnivaldiary.com).

PRE-CARNIVAL HIGHLIGHTS

- Lavish pre-Carnival fetes start on January 1 and continue up till Carnival.
- The Panorama semis and finals see steel-pan bands battle it out on the last two Saturdays before Carnival.
- There are fabulously cute Kiddie Mas parades on the final two Saturdays preceding Carnival.
- Dimanche Gras, on the Sunday before Carnival at Queen's Park Savannah, sees the crowning of Carnival King and Queen and Calypso Monarch finals.

PLAYING MAS

On Carnival Monday and Tuesday, tens of thousands parade and dance in the streets, accompanied by soca trucks with DJs and steel bands. On Monday, players don't wear full costumes, instead hitting the streets in T-shirts or self-made bling. It isn't as glittery and majestic as the Tuesday mas, but it's arguably more of a party. Carnival Tuesday sees revelers decked out in full, glorious costume in a sumptuous and ecstatic display.

To join the parade, you sign up with a 'mas band' such as Tribe, Trini Revellers or Island People. Prices vary (anything from TT$2000 to TT$6000), but cover a costume and two days' parading, often with food and drinks included. You can register directly at mas camps or online; latecomers can usually find costumes via Carnival Junction.

Botanical Gardens Gardens

(6am-6:30pm) FREE Resplendent with exotic trees and plants, and networked by gentle paths, the Botanical Gardens date from 1818. A graceful mansion built in 1875, the adjacent **President's House** (closed to the public), is slated for major repairs, its west wing having collapsed in early 2010.

National Museum & Art Gallery Museum

(www.nmag.gov.tt; cnr Frederick & Keate Sts; 10am-6pm Tue-Sat, 2-6pm Sun) FREE Housed in a classic colonial building, the dusty historical exhibits range from Amerindian settlers to African slaves and indentured Indians. There are also geological displays and explanations of the technology behind oil exploration. The rotating collection of artwork displayed on the top floor gives an excellent introduction to the Trinbago art scene, with pieces from T&T's best-known artists.

Independence Square Neighborhood

The hustle and bustle of downtown culminates along Independence Sq, two parallel streets that flank a central promenade. The commanding 1836 **Roman Catholic Cathedral** caps the promenade's eastern

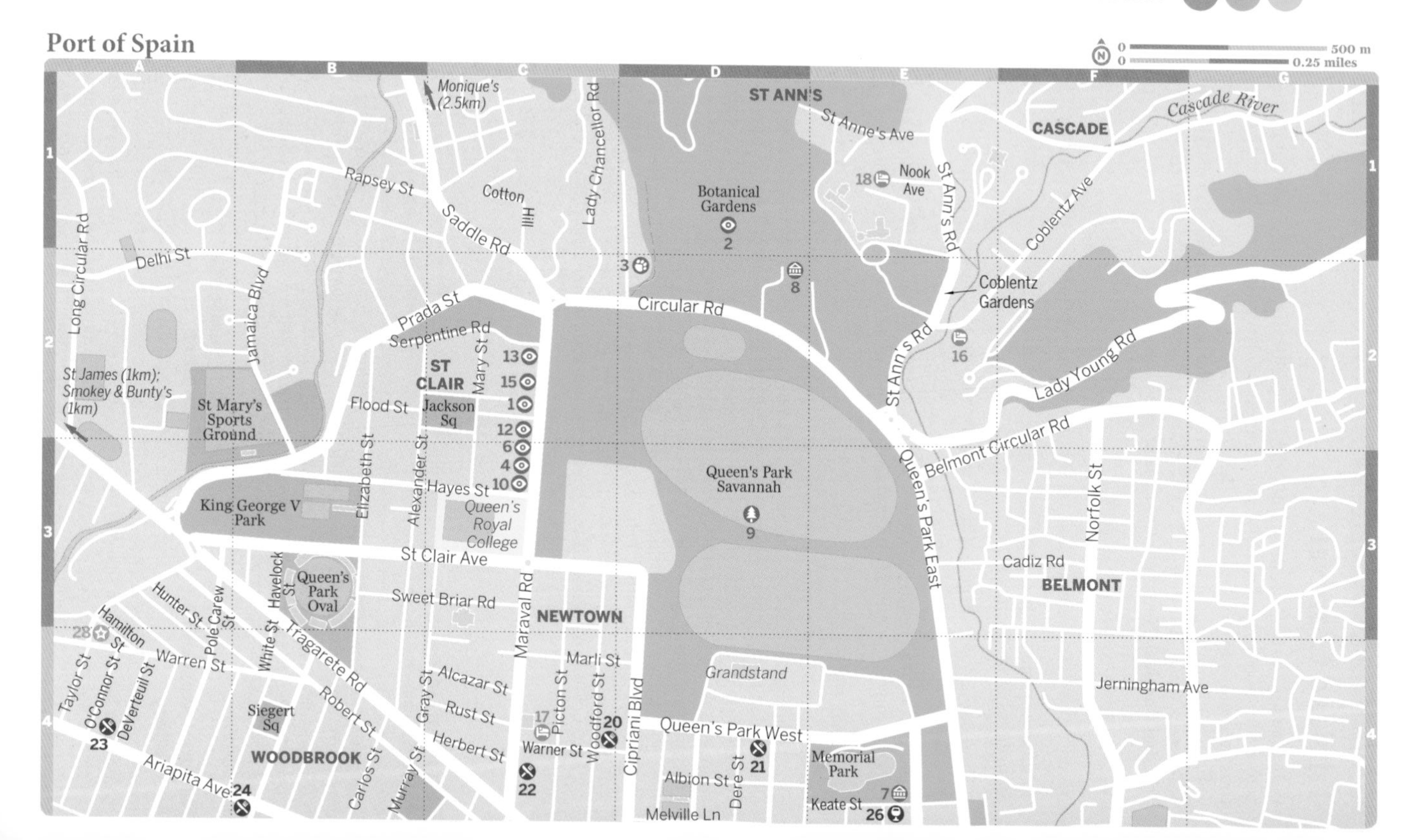
Port of Spain
0 500 m
0 0.25 miles
ST ANN'S
St Anne's Ave
CASCADE
Cascade River
Monique's (2.5km)
Lady Chancellor Rd
Botanical Gardens
2
18
Nook Ave
St Ann's Rd
Coblentz Ave
Rapsey St
Cotton Hill
Saddle Rd
Long Circular Rd
Delhi St
3
8
Coblentz Gardens
Circular Rd
Prada St
Serpentine Rd
Jamaica Blvd
16
St Ann's Rd
Lady Young Rd
ST CLAIR
Mary St
13
15
1
12
6
4
10
St James (1km); Smokey & Bunty's (1km)
St Mary's Sports Ground
Flood St
Jackson Sq
Belmont Circular Rd
Queen's Park Savannah
9
Elizabeth St
Alexander St
Hayes St
King George V Park
Queen's Royal College
Queen's Park East
Norfolk St
St Clair Ave
Cadiz Rd
BELMONT
Hunter St
Pole Carew St
Havelock St
Queen's Park Oval
Sweet Briar Rd
Maraval Rd
NEWTOWN
28
Hamilton St
Warren St
White St
Tragarete Rd
Marli St
Grandstand
Jerningham Ave
Alcazar St
Taylor St
O'Connor St
DeVerteuil St
Siegert Sq
Robert St
Gray St
Rust St
17
Picton St
Woodford St
20
Cipriani Blvd
Queen's Park West
23
WOODBROOK
Carlos St
Murray St
Herbert St
Warner St
21
Memorial Park
Ariapita Ave
24
22
Albion St
Dere St
7
Keate St
Melville Ln
26

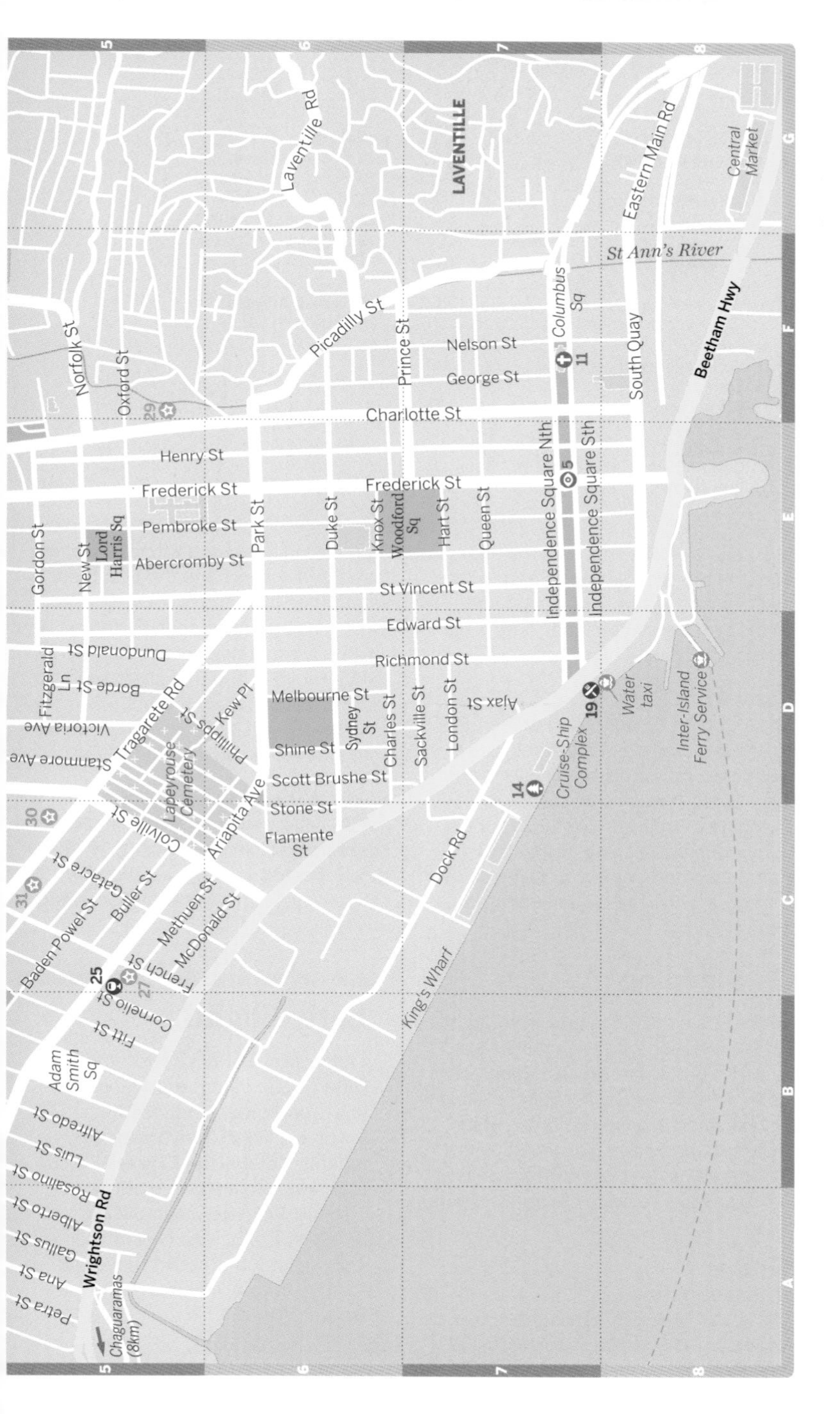
LAVENTILLE
Laventille Rd
Norfolk St
Oxford St
Picadilly St
Prince St
Nelson St
George St
Columbus Sq
St Ann's River
Eastern Main Rd
Central Market
South Quay
Beetham Hwy
Charlotte St
Henry St
Frederick St
Pembroke St
Abercromby St
Lord Harris Sq
Gordon St
New St
Park St
Duke St
Knox St
Woodford Sq
Hart St
Queen St
Independence Square Nth
Independence Square Sth
St Vincent St
Edward St
Richmond St
Dundonald St
Fitzgerald Ln
Borde St
Victoria Ave
Stanmore Ave
Tragarete Rd
Kew Pl
Phillipps St
Lapeyrouse Cemetery
Melbourne St
Sydney St
Charles St
Sackville St
London St
Ajax St
Shine St
Scott Brushe St
Stone St
Flamente St
Ariapita Ave
Colville St
Gatacre St
Buller St
Methuen St
McDonald St
Baden Powel St
French St
Cornelio St
Fitt St
Adam Smith Sq
Alfredo St
Luis St
Rosalino St
Alberto St
Gallus St
Ana St
Petra St
Wrightson Rd
Chaguaramas (8km)
Dock Rd
King's Wharf
Cruise-Ship Complex
Water taxi
Inter-Island Ferry Service

Port of Spain

Sights

1 Archbishop's Residence ... C2
2 Botanical Gardens ... D1
3 Emperor Valley Zoo ... D2
4 Hayes Court ... C3
5 Independence Square ... E7
6 Mille Fleurs ... C3
7 National Museum & Art Gallery ... E4
8 President's House ... D2
9 Queen's Park Savannah ... D3
10 Queen's Royal College ... C3
11 Roman Catholic Cathedral ... F7
12 Roomor ... C2
13 Stollmeyer's Castle ... C2
14 Waterfront Park ... D7
15 White Hall ... C2

Sleeping

16 Carlton Savannah ... E2
17 Forty Winks Inn ... C4
18 Normandie ... E1

Eating

19 Breakfast Shed ... D7
20 Buzo Osteria Italiana ... C4
21 Chaud ... D4
22 Dopson's Roti Shop ... C4
23 More Vino ... A4
24 Veni Mangé ... B4

Drinking & Nightlife

25 Shaker's ... C5
26 Zen ... E4

Entertainment

27 Mas Camp Pub ... C5
28 Phase II Pan Groove ... A4
29 Renegades ... F5
30 Silver Stars ... C5
31 Woodbrook Playboyz ... C5

end; at its western end, past the high-rise blocks of the Nicholas and Central Bank towers, and the statue of cricket hero Brian Lara, the square feeds onto Wrightson Rd, the coastal highway.

Waterfront Park Park

Off Wrightson Rd opposite Independence Sq, the swanky new Waterfront Park is overlooked by high-rise offices and the Hyatt hotel. Though a bit sterile, with its could-be-anywhere waterfalls and manicured landscaping, the waterside promenade does allow you to get close to the gulf, and is a popular liming spot come evening.

Sleeping

Port of Spain holds the bulk of Trinidad's accommodations, and as most of the country's better-known attractions are within an hour's drive, it's quite feasible to stay here and explore the whole island.

During Carnival season, most places offer packages for a set number of days, and raise rates to twice the regular room price.

Culture Crossroads Inn Guesthouse $

(622-3387; www.culturecrossroadstt.com; cnr Bengal & Delhi Sts, St James; s/d US$80/100; P ⊖ ❄ @ ᯤ) Spanking-new place, very professionally run and with easy access to malls, transport and the St James/Woodbrook bars and restaurants. The owner is a legendary soca performer and an effusive source of information on all things Trinidad, and the smart, modern rooms (named after local cultural icons) have plenty of neat little extras to make your stay more comfortable.

Forty Winks Inn Guesthouse $$

(622-0484; www.fortywinkstt.com; 24 Warner St; s/d incl breakfast US$87.50/105; ❄ @ ᯤ) Nicely located in Newtown and very efficiently run, this vibrantly decorated

Early Flight?

The newest of the airport hotels, right on the Piarco roundabout, has experienced some teething problems. Best to stick with the reliable **Holiday Inn Express** (669-6209; www.hiexpress.com/trincitytt; 1 Exposition Dr, Trincity; r from US$133; P ⊖ ❄ ᯤ ≋), with decent rooms, a pool and a free shuttle covering the five-minute drive to and from Piarco Airport.

house has five cheerful rooms and a friendly, intimate atmosphere. There is a patio on top, lush with plants, where you can enjoy the sunset, and breakfast is included.

Normandie Hotel $$

(☎624-1181; www.normandiett.com; 10 Nook Ave; r US$118; P ❄ @ ≈) Tucked into a quiet backstreet, a short walk from the Savannah, this is a lovely retreat, with freshly renovated rooms featuring lots of wood, and good facilities. A popular concert venue at Carnival time, too.

Carlton Savannah Hotel $$$

(☎621-5000; www.thecarltonsavannah.com; Coblentz Ave; r from US$150; P ❄ @ ≈) Super-swanky place just off the Savannah, with classy modern decor and lots of little luxuries in the rooms as well as good in-house dining and drinking; check out the view from the rooftop bar.

Eating

Port of Spain has some truly excellent restaurants, and street food is a big deal here too, with Trini treats available from dusk until late into the night along Western Main Rd in St James, Ariapita Ave in Woodbrook and the southeastern corner of the Savannah.

Breakfast Shed Caribbean $

(Wrightson Rd; mains from TT$40; ⏰breakfast & lunch) Right on the water, Trini women sell homemade food from stalls around the perimeter of an open-air, picnic-benched eating area. The large servings of Trinidadian fare include fish or chicken with macaroni pie, callaloo, plantain and rice. You can grab a fresh cane juice or sea moss shake at Mr Juice's stall.

Dopson's Roti Shop Indian $

(☎628-6141; 25 Maraval Rd, Newtown; roti from TT$20; ⏰6:45am-5:30pm Mon-Fri, 8am-5:30pm Sat) Now in a new and improved location, this renowned little place is a favorite locals' spot – many Trinis claim they make the best roti in Port of Spain here. The fillings are fresh, succulent and generous, and they also cook up a mean traditional breakfast of eggplant and tomato choka, saltfish and smoked herring.

Veni Mangé Caribbean $$

(☎624-4597; www.venimange.com; 67A Ariapita Ave; mains TT$105-145; ⏰11:30am-3pm Mon-Fri, dinner from 7pm Wed & Fri; ✎) West Indian flavor, art, foliage and enthusiasm infuse this vibrant restaurant. Serving Caribbean cuisine with classic French influences, it's one of the best spots for lunch. Try the beef dumplings, the grilled fresh fish with tamarind sauce, or the excellent veggie options.

Trinidad Carnival (p359)

More Vino Japanese, Fusion $$
(622-8466; www.morevino.com; 23 O'Connor St; sushi from TT$68, mains from TT$89; 11am-late Mon-Sat;) This popular wine bar serves up some of the best sushi in town, with all the familiar rolls plus local flavors such as the spicy Maracas, all made right in front of your eyes. Japanese and Thai are also on offer, the wine list is excellent and it's a great spot for a cocktail, too.

Buzo Osteria Italiana Italian $$$
(223-2896; 6 Warner St, Newtown; mains TT$80-275;) Set in a gorgeous old stone building, with a courtyard out back that's ideal for evening cocktails, this is easily one of Trinidad's best restaurants. The Italian chefs cook up authentic meat, seafood and pasta dishes, the pizzas are sublime and the side dishes and desserts inspired. Booking advisable.

Chaud International $$$
(623-0375; www.chaudkm.com; 2 Queen's Park West; mains TT$225-400, tasting menus TT$600-800;) With a ravishing setting in a colonial-era home overlooking the Savannah, this is Trini fine dining at its best. The gourmet creations of local superchef Khalid Mohammed might include lavender-honey glazed duck breast or coriander-crusted yellowfin tuna with a seafood stew. The five- or 10-course tasting menu is unforgettable, but you can also come for the reasonably priced two-course lunch.

Drinking & Nightlife

Port of Spain's drinking scene is concentrated along Ariapita Ave in Woodbrook, with a string of bars pulling in the crowds most nights. Places change quite quickly, so the best plan is to start at Shaker's and work your way west.

Shaker's Bar
(www.shakerstrinidad.com; cnr Ariapita Ave & Cornelio St, Woodbrook; 4pm-midnight Mon, 4pm-2am Tue-Thu, 11am-2am Fri & Sat) This great little bar, with an icy indoor section and a convivial garden, is an excellent liming spot, with good cocktails, and bar snacks too. Look out for the regular live-music performances, usually on Wednesday.

MovieTowne (right), Port of Spain

LATITUDESTOCK · IAN BRIERLEY/GETTY IMAGES ©

Smokey & Bunty Bar

(97 Western Main Rd; ⌚11am-late) St James, just west of central Port of Spain, becomes a hub of activity almost any evening, and this hole-in-the wall watering hole is the center of the action. It's a brilliantly seedy scene: keep your wits about you and enjoy the street theater.

Zen Club

(Keat St; cover from TT$100, often incl drinks; ⌚10pm-late Wed, Fri & Sat) This three-tier club is replete with slick modern decor and features make-out nooks, myriad dance floors, and plenty of pretty young things who shake it all night to soca, hip-hop and other popular beats. A dress code is in effect.

Entertainment

Port of Spain's nightlife is especially happening Thursday through Saturday, but the St James neighborhood is known to always be rocking and the place to find a proper lime when all else fails. Many bars on Ariapita Ave have live music or DJs.

If you'd like someone to accompany you on your first night on the town, contact **Island Experiences (☎625-2410, 756-9677; www.islandexperiencestt.com)** for an evening entertainment tour, which usually includes visits to a couple of panyards, a calypso show and guidance in choosing the best street snacks. About three hours of fun and transportation starts at US$55 per person.

Mas Camp Pub Live Music

(Nu Pub; cnr French St & Ariapita Ave) A taste of old-school Port of Spain, with live calypso several times a week (cover charge varies) often featuring the nation's most celebrated calypsonians. Other nights see anything from karaoke to Latin dance, and there are pool tables out back, too. It has been renamed as the Nu Pub, but it's universally referred to by its original name.

MovieTowne Cinema

(☎627-8277; www.movietowne.com; Audrey Jeffers Hwy, Invaders Bay; tickets adult/child TT$50/40) Besides 10 wide-screen movie

Local Knowledge

Name: Skye Hernandez

OCCUPATION: JOURNALIST AND FORMER EDITOR OF *CARIBBEAN BEAT MAGAZINE*

RESIDENCE: PETIT VALLEY, OUTSIDE PORT OF SPAIN

1 WHERE I GO ON MY DAY OFF

Macqueripe is a small bay in Chaguaramas, within easy reach of where I live in Port of Spain. It's not a stretch-of-white-sand kind of beach, but the water is usually calm and I love the forested area that surrounds it. It's wonderful to be in the ocean and look up to see clear blue skies and huge trees. And sometimes, usually in the afternoons, you can spot dolphins and porpoises far out in the ocean.

2 THE BEST PLACE TO INDULGE IN SOME TRUE TRINBAGO CUISINE

I go to the Breakfast Shed (p362) (it's now named Femmes du Chalet, but nobody ever calls it that) when I'm feeling lazy to cook Sunday lunch: calalloo, baked fish or chicken, stewed pigeon peas, rice and salad. For a great roti I head to Dopson's (p362) on Maraval Rd; goat in a dhalpuri skin is just delicious.

3 THE COOLEST PLACE TO SAMPLE THE LIMING SCENE

For a 'bess' lime, as we say, try Shaker's (p363) on Ariapita Ave. It's relaxed, friendly, has decent bar food and drinks, and it's not hyped up like some of the newer, more clubby-type places.

4 THE MOST MEMORABLE PLACE I'VE COVERED

Lots to choose from but I think with Trinidad, in particular, the most memorable things are festivals rather than places. Steel-band Panorama is certainly one of the most exciting aspects of our Carnival. Following a steel band (or bands) from the early season and hearing the tune evolve to the semi-finals, and then to the finals, is an awesome experience. Being in the Grand Stand of the Queen's Park Savannah for the Panorama finals is something that can bring you to tears.

Panyards

For much of the year, panyards are little more than vacant lots where steel bands store their instruments. Come Carnival season, they become lively rehearsal spaces, pulsating with energy and magnificent sound, with pan-lovers crowding in to buy drinks from the bar and take in the music. It's a window into one of the most important and sacred parts of Trinidad's urban landscape, with aficionados discussing every note and tempo change, and excitement building as the Panorama competition gets closer.

Steel bands start gearing up for Carnival as early as late September, and some rehearse and perform throughout the year. The best way to find out about practice and performance schedules is by asking around. You can also contact **Pan Trinbago** (623-4486; www.pantrinbago.co.tt; Victoria Suites, 14-17 Park St, Port of Spain).

Some popular panyards that welcome visitors:

Phase II Pan Groove (627-0909; Hamilton St)

Renegades (624-3348; 138 Charlotte St)

Silver Stars (633-4733; 56 Tragarete Rd)

Woodbrook Playboyz (628-0320; 27 Tragarete Rd)

theaters, there's also video arcades, a shopping mall, and restaurants and bars arranged around a central courtyard that is a popular liming spot – though it could be in any American suburb. It's west of the center.

Shopping

The central area of Port of Spain, especially around Independence Sq, Charlotte St and Frederick St, is filled with malls and arcades selling everything from spices to fabric by the meter. International shops cluster at the enormous **West Mall** (Western Main Rd), just west of town.

Information

Dangers & Annoyances

Port of Spain has a bad reputation for crime, with robberies and shootings (invariably drug-related) besetting low-income areas such as Laventille, which most travelers never venture into. Nonetheless it's important to use common sense. Busy spots such as Ariapita Ave are safe, but walking solo at night around downtown Port of Spain and across the Savannah is best avoided. It's also a good idea to take a taxi back to your hotel at night rather than walk.

Beware of parking restrictions downtown and in Woodbrook. The street signs can be confusing and police often tow cars, which have to be expensively bailed out at the police station on South Quay. You're better off using a public parking lot (around TT$35 per day).

Medical Services

General Hospital (623-2951; 56-57 Charlotte St) A large full-service public hospital.

St Clair Medical Centre (628-1451; 18 Elizabeth St) A private hospital preferred by expatriates.

Money

The major banks – RBTT, Republic Bank, Royal Bank and First Citizens – all have branches on Park St east of Frederick St, and on Independence Sq. There are also banks in West Mall, Long Circular Mall and on Ariapita Ave. All have 24-hour ATMs.

Tourist Information

Tourism Development Company (TDC; 675-7034; www.gotrinidadandtobago.com) Has a helpful outlet at **Piarco International Airport**

(TDC; ☎669-5196; www.gotrinidadandtobago.com; Piarco International Airport; ⏰8am-4:30pm).

AROUND PORT OF SPAIN

Chaguaramas

The Chaguaramas (sha-gah-*ra*-mus) peninsula was the site of a major US military installation during WWII, and it was fully handed back to Trinidad only in the 1970s. Today the string of marinas along the ocean is a hot spot for yachters, who come here to take advantage of the marina and dry-docking facilities, or wait out the weather – Trinidad lies safely south of the hurricane belt.

The peninsula is a short drive or **water taxi** (☎Port of Spain 624-5137, San Fernando 652-9980; nidco.co.tt; TT$10 Port of Spain-Chaguaramas) ride from the capital; water taxis run regularly Monday to Saturday.

Chaguaramas is also the launching point for tours to a chain of offshore islands, the **Bocas**. Large-group boat tours, as well as hiking, swimming and historical excursions, can be arranged by the **Chaguaramas Development Authority** (☎634-4227; www.chagdev.com). Popular options include the boat trip out to **Gasparee Island** (US$25, three hours), where you can visit caves that drip with stalactites. The most distant, 360-hectare **Chacachacare**, was once a leper colony, and is best visited with **Dolphin Adventures** (☎706-6004; www.dolphinadventures.weebly.com; trips from US$85 per person depending on group size), which offers small-group trips that include a swim in the island's salt pond. It's also a good bet for other Bocas adventures.

Just inland of Chaguaramas town, the 6000-hectare **Tucker Valley** is a popular recreation spot, with picnic grounds, hiking trails and a golf course. The main road through the valley ends at **Macqueripe** (car park TT$20), formerly the swimming spot of American troops and now a pretty place to dive into cool green waters, with views over to the misty Venezuelan coastline; or swing above them by way of the Zip-Itt **zip-line** (☎634-4227; www.chagdev.com; Macqueripe Bay, Tucker Valley; TT$120; ⏰10am-4pm Tue-Fri, 9am-4pm Sat-Sun; 👪) across the bay. Macqueripe has changing rooms (TT$1, open 10am to 6pm), basic refreshments and a children's playground.

Trinidad beachfront

AARON MCCOY/GETTY IMAGES ©

Sleeping

Bight Guesthouse $$
(634-4427; www.peakeyachts.com; Peake's Marina, 5 Western Main Rd; r US$75;) Simple, tidy rooms right on the water make this the nicest midrange option in the area – sit on the porch and enjoy the views of pelicans diving and yachts bobbing. It's good value for the price, too.

CrewsInn Hotel $$$
(634-4384; www.crewsinn.com; Point Gourde; r US$199-224;) As the highest-end option in Chaguaramas, with a pool and resort-like trappings, its bright rooms all have patios and complete amenities, though they are very overpriced.

This hotel-and-marina complex houses the open-air, upscale Lighthouse Restaurant, the main draw of which is the covered deck overlooking the marina.

Eating & Drinking

Sails International $$
(www.sailsrestpub.com; Power Boats Marina; burgers from TT$56, mains TT$195-335; 11am-midnight;) This popular hangout has seating on the water, pool tables inside and a BBQ on Sundays. You can get bar snacks and grilled food here as well as kebabs and local dishes such as callaloo soup and fresh fish or seafood with plentiful sides.

Caffé del Mare Cafe $$
(CrewsInn Marina; quiche from TT$30, salada from TT$79; 8am-8pm Sun-Thu, to 9pm Fri & Sat;) A great stop-off for an ice cream, gooey cake, sweet or savory pastry or slice of quiche. Smoothies, coffee, wine and beer, too, with tables inside or out on the marina front.

Asa Wright Nature Centre

A former cocoa and coffee plantation transformed into an 80-hectare nature reserve, the **Asa Wright Nature Centre** (667-4655; www.asawright.org; adult/child US$10/6; 9am-5pm) blows the minds of bird-watchers, and makes a worthwhile trip even if you can't tell a parrot from a parakeet. Located amid the rainforest of the Northern Range, the center has a lodge catering to birding tour groups, a research station for biologists and a series of hiking trails. Day visitors can only explore on a guided tour (10:30am and 1:30pm); reservations should be made at least 24 hours in advance. Nonguests can also have lunch, with an excellent hot buffet (TT$140, Sunday TT$200) or cheaper snacks like a burger and fries.

Bird species found at the center include blue-crowned motmots, chestnut woodpeckers,

Mockingbird, Tobago
LATITUDESTOCK - IAN BRIERLEY/GETTY IMAGES ©

Bird-Watching

Trinidad and Tobago are excluded from many Caribbean birding books because of the sheer magnitude of additional species here – about 430 in total. Torn from Venezuela, these islands share the diversity of the South American mainland in their swamps, rainforests, ocean islets, lowland forests and savannahs, and the bird-watching is some of the best in the Caribbean.

For references, try *A Guide to the Birds of Trinidad and Tobago* by Richard Ffrench, which has good descriptions but limited plates; or *Field Guide to the Birds of Trinidad and Tobago* by Martyn Kenefyk, Robin Restall and Floyd Hayesm, which has a few more. Detailed plates can also be found in *Birds of Venezuela* by Steven L Hilty.

Best birding spots in Trinidad are Asa Wright Nature Centre, Caroni Bird Sanctuary, Nariva Swamp and Mt St Benedict. In Tobago: Little Tobago and Tobago Forest Reserve.

channel-billed toucans, blue-headed parrots, 14 species of hummingbird and numerous raptors. The sanctuary is also home to a natural swimming pool and to the elusive nocturnal guacharo (oilbird). To protect the oilbirds, tours are limited.

The **lodge (☎667-4655; d per person incl all meals US$340; ❄)** has some rooms in the weathered main house and others in nearby cottages; all are quite simple with private bathrooms. Rates are high but include three ample meals a day, afternoon tea and rum punch each evening.

The center is about a 1½-hour drive from Port of Spain. At Arima, 26km from Port of Spain, head north on Blanchisseuse Rd, turning left into the center after the 7½-mile marker sign. Tour companies such as **Island Experiences (☎621-0407, 756-9677; www.islandexperiencestt.com)** can ferry you here as part of a half- or full-day tour.

NORTH COAST

Winding north from Port of Spain, Saddle Rd becomes the North Coast Rd, climbing over the jungle-slathered mountains of the Northern Range and descending to the Caribbean coastline at Maracas Bay. The road then hugs the seafront for about 15km to the small settlement of Blanchisseuse, after which it passes over a small bridge and narrows into impassability.

Maxi-taxis and route taxis travel to Maracas Bay, but transport to Blanchisseuse is far less frequent; you'll need a car to explore.

Maracas Bay

Just 40 minutes' drive from Port of Spain, Maracas Bay has Trinidad's most popular beach. The wide, white-sand beach, thick with palm trees contrasting against the backdrop of verdant mountains, remains an irresistible lure for both locals and travelers.

Despite the curving headland, the sand is often pounded by waves that serve up good bodysurfing. There are lifeguards, changing rooms (TT$1, open 10am to 6pm), showers, picnic shelters and huts selling cold beers and shark (or the more ecologically sound kingfish) and bake. On weekends the beach gets pretty crowded, but during the week it can feel almost deserted.

Las Cuevas

Just east of Maracas Bay, quieter and less commercial Las Cuevas is another beautiful bay, its wide sweep of sand overhung by cliffs and forest. There's usually good

Caroni Bird Sanctuary

Caroni Bird Sanctuary is the roosting site for thousands of **scarlet ibis**, the national bird of Trinidad and Tobago. In the late afternoon the birds fly in to roost in the swamp's mangroves, giving the trees the appearance of being abloom with brilliant scarlet blossoms. Even if you're not an avid bird-watcher, the sight of the ibis flying over the swamp, glowing almost fluorescent red in the final rays of the evening sun, is not to be missed.

Long, flat-bottomed motorboats, some holding up to 30 passengers, pass slowly through the swamp's channels. The main companies offering tours of the swamp are **Nanan** (☎645-1305; www.nananecotours.com; TT$60) and **Sean Madoo** (☎663-0458; www.madoobirdtours.com; TT$90). Both offer 2½-hour tours, starting at 4pm daily. Reservations are recommended, but if you just show up you should be able to find space on one of the boats.

The sanctuary is off the Uriah Butler Hwy, 14km south of Port of Spain; the turn-off is marked. Many guesthouses and hotels in Port of Spain also arrange trips; a taxi will cost around TT$100.

surfing at its west end, and calmer conditions at its center, where lifeguards patrol. The car park above the sand has changing rooms (TT$1, open 10am to 6pm) and a restaurant serving cold drinks, beers and basic fish or chicken lunches. Take repellant, as the sandflies can be bad here.

Blanchisseuse

POP 800

The road narrows east of Maracas Bay, ending at the tiny village of Blanchisseuse (blan-she-*shuhze*), where the beautiful craggy coastline is dotted with weekend homes. The three beaches aren't the best for swimming, especially in the fall and winter, but the surfing can be pretty good and it's the starting point for some great **hikes**, especially the two-hour walk to spectacular and completely undeveloped **Paria Bay**, which has a waterfall just inland. **Eric Blackman** (☎669-3995) can arrange a guide to Paria or to the luscious **Three Pools**, just 1.5km up the Marianne River from Blanchisseuse.

A professional, well-run hotel, German-operated **Laguna Mar** (☎669-2963; www.lagunamar.com; 65½-mile marker, Paria Main Rd; r TT$440; ❄) comprises three buildings on the hillside at the end of the road, plus a four-bedroom cottage. Just opposite, adjacent to a track down to the beach, the hotel restaurant **Cocos Hut** (mains TT$70-150; ⏰7am-7pm) is a small, cozy spot that's usually the only place in town where you can get a meal, serving up decent fresh fish, lamb or chicken platters.

PITCH LAKE

Some 22km southwest of San Fernando, near the town of La Brea, is **Pitch Lake** (☎651-1232; tours TT$50; ⏰9am-5pm). Once thought of by the Amerindians as a punishment of the gods, this slowly bubbling black 'lake' is perhaps Trinidad's greatest oddity. The 40-hectare expanse of asphalt is around 75m deep at its center, where hot bitumen is continuously replenished from a subterranean fault. One of only three asphalt lakes in the world, it has the single-largest supply of natural bitumen, and as much as 300 tonnes are extracted daily. The lake's surface looks like a clay tennis court covered with wrinkled, elephant-like skin; tour guides sagely take you across via the solid parts. High heels are not recommended. During the rainy season, people sit in its warm sulfurous pools, said to have healing qualities. A visitor center gives some background on the history of the lake.

MANZANILLA & MAYARO

Trinidad's east coast is wild and rural. The mix of lonely beaches with rough Atlantic waters, mangrove swamps and seaside coconut plantations creates dramatic scenery. It's deserted most of the year, except for holidays and weekends, when people flood in to Manzanilla and Mayaro for beachside relaxation, packing coolers with food and splashing about in the gently shelving waters. You get here by way of bustling Sangre Grande (pronounced Sandy Grandy), from where minor roads head down to the Manzanilla–Mayaro Rd.

The Cocal & Nariva Swamp

Running parallel to the beach, the Manzanilla–Mayaro Rd makes for a beautiful drive. It passes through the Cocal, a thick forest of coconut palms whose nuts are shipped all around the island, and which harbor some interesting birds, including red-chested macaws.

Inland of the Cocal, the Ramsar-protected Nariva Swamp covers some 6000 hectares of freshwater wetland. To fully appreciate the area's beauty, book a spot on a kayak tour with **Paria Springs** (☎620-8240; www.pariasprings.com; US$125 incl lunch) or **Caribbean Discovery Tours** (☎624-7281; www.caribbeandiscoverytours.com; US$100-150).

NORTHEAST COAST

'When you out, you out. When you in, you in,' is what they say about the remote northeast. Despite the ruggedly beautiful coastline, waterfalls, hiking trails and swimmable rivers – and the leatherback turtles that lay eggs on the beaches – tourism remains low-key here. Inaccessible from Blanchisseuse, where the north-coast road ends, this quiet region is bounded by Matelot in the north and Matura in the southeast.

It's accessed via the busy little village of Valencia, a short way beyond the end of the Churchill Roosvelt highway, from where the Valencia Main Rd makes a T-junction with the Toco Main Rd, which hugs the northeast coast. Getting here is easiest by far in a taxi or with your own vehicle.

Toco

Sleepy to the point of catatonic, tiny Toco is an attractively battered fishing village of weathered wooden homes. From the main road, Galera Rd heads toward the

Pitch Lake (left), La Brea

beach, a pretty stretch of sand and calm water, with drinks and snacks sold from a couple of stalls. The road ends at the lighthouse that marks **Galera Point**, from which you can see the blue Caribbean sea meeting the green Atlantic.

Grand Riviere

POP 350

The closest the northeast gets to a resort town, Grand Riviere is still a far cry from most Caribbean holiday spots. It's a quiet and peaceful place, rich in natural attractions, from a stunning beach where leatherbacks lay eggs to surrounding rainforest, studded with waterfalls and hiking trails and offering plenty of good bird-watching. A few small-scale resorts have sprung up to cater to lovers of the outdoors, and the village is a fantastic place to get away from it all. The long, wide **beach** shelves steeply down to turbulent waters, but there's calmer swimming to be had at the eastern end, where a clear river flows into the sea.

For other activities, hit up the office of the community-run **Grand Riviere Nature Tour Guide Association** (☎469-1288), in the middle of the village. From March to August, it offers nighttime **turtle-watching** (TT$70, including the required permit) on the beach, as well as year-round **bird-watching** excursions and **hiking** tours (from TT$100) to waterfalls, swimming holes and seldom-visited natural wonders in the area.

The beachside **Mt Plaisir Estate** (☎670-1868; www.mtplaisir.com; r US$145 incl breakfast, restaurant mains US$15-35) was the first hotel in the area. Local art, murals and handcrafted furnishings adorn the quirky but comfortable rooms, and the **restaurant** cooks up divine seafood and local dishes featuring organic fruits and vegetables, plus great homemade bread.

Next door, the compact but decent rooms at **Le Grande Almandier** (☎670-1013; www.legrandealmandier.com; s/d TT$660/864; ❄@) have quaint balconies overlooking the sea, and are a more budget-friendly option. There's also a laid-back cafe and bar.

Tobago

While Trinidad booms with industry and parties all night, tiny Tobago (just 42km across) slouches in a deck chair with a beer in hand watching its crystalline

Beach and pier, Tobago

DEBRA WISEBERG/GETTY IMAGES ©

Tobago

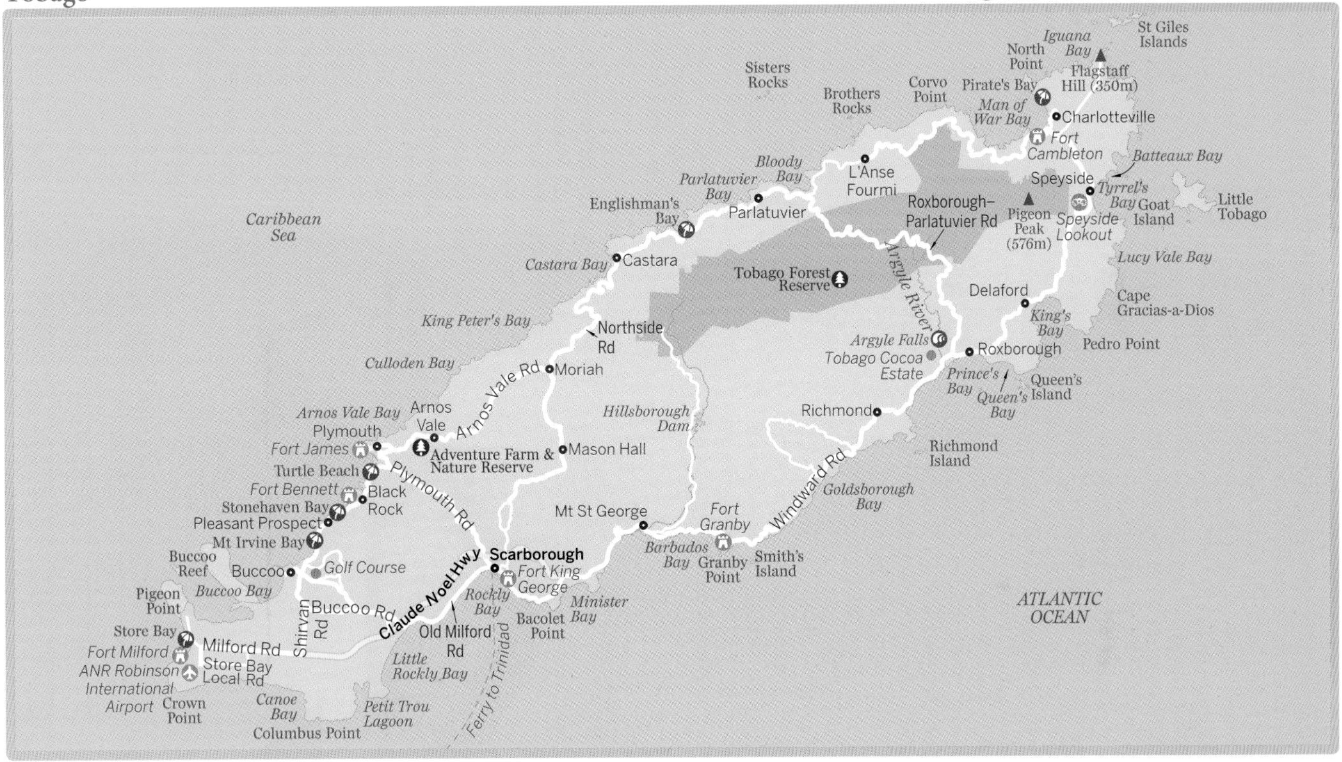
0 10 km
0 5 miles
Caribbean Sea
ATLANTIC OCEAN
St Giles Islands
Iguana Bay
North Point
Flagstaff Hill (350m)
Sisters Rocks
Brothers Rocks
Corvo Point
Pirate's Bay
Man of War Bay
Charlotteville
Fort Cambleton
Batteaux Bay
Bloody Bay
Parlatuvier Bay
L'Anse Fourmi
Speyside
Tyrrel's Bay
Goat Island
Little Tobago
Englishman's Bay
Parlatuvier
Roxborough–Parlatuvier Rd
Pigeon Peak (576m)
Speyside Lookout
Lucy Vale Bay
Castara Bay
Castara
Tobago Forest Reserve
Argyle River
Delaford
Cape Gracias-a-Dios
King's Bay
King Peter's Bay
Northside Rd
Argyle Falls
Tobago Cocoa Estate
Roxborough
Pedro Point
Culloden Bay
Arnos Vale Rd
Moriah
Prince's Bay
Queen's Bay
Queen's Island
Arnos Vale Bay
Arnos Vale
Plymouth
Hillsborough Dam
Richmond
Fort James
Adventure Farm & Nature Reserve
Mason Hall
Richmond Island
Turtle Beach
Plymouth Rd
Fort Bennett
Black Rock
Windward Rd
Goldsborough Bay
Stonehaven Bay
Mt St George
Fort Granby
Pleasant Prospect
Mt Irvine Bay
Barbados Bay
Granby Point
Smith's Island
Buccoo Reef
Buccoo
Golf Course
Claude Noel Hwy
Scarborough
Fort King George
Pigeon Point
Buccoo Bay
Rockly Bay
Minister Bay
Buccoo Rd
Shirvan Rd
Old Milford Rd
Bacolet Point
Store Bay
Milford Rd
Fort Milford
Store Bay Local Rd
ANR Robinson International Airport
Crown Point
Canoe Bay
Little Rockly Bay
Ferry to Trinidad
Petit Trou Lagoon
Columbus Point

waters shimmer in the sun. Though Tobago is proud of its rainforests, fantastic dive sites, stunning aquamarine bays and nature reserves, it's OK with not being mentioned in a Beach Boys song. It accepts its tourists without vigor, but rather with languor, and allows them to choose between plush oceanside hotels or tiny guesthouses in villages where you walk straight to the open-air bar with sandy bare feet, and laugh with the locals drinking rum.

Most of the white-sand beaches and tourist development are centered on the southwestern side of Tobago, starting at Crown Point and running along a string of bays up to Arnos Vale. The lowlands that predominate in the southwest extend to Tobago's only large town, Scarborough. The coast beyond is dotted with small fishing villages and the interior is ruggedly mountainous, with thick rainforest. Divers and snorkelers, and those seeking mellow days, visit the easternmost villages of Speyside and Charlotteville, while birdwatchers head for the Tobago Forest Reserve and the nearby uninhabited islet of Little Tobago.

CROWN POINT

Spread over Tobago's southwest tip, Crown Point is the island's tourist epicenter, offering a relatively wide range of accommodations, restaurants and some nightlife. The attractive beaches and extensive services make many tourists stay put, but anyone wanting a deeper appreciation of Tobago's charms should plan to push eastward to explore other parts of the island.

Beaches

Store Bay Beach

You'll find white sands and good year-round swimming at Store Bay, a five-minute walk from the airport. It's also the main departure point for glass-bottom boat trips to the Buccoo Reef, with hawkers offering these and rides on Jet Skis or banana boats, and renting umbrellas and sun loungers. Facilities include showers/bathrooms (TT$5) and food outlets selling delicious local lunches. Great for families.

Pigeon Point Beach

(admission TT$20; 9am-7pm; P) You have to pay to get access to Pigeon Point, the fine dining of Tobago's beaches, with landscaped grounds, bars, restaurants, toilets and showers spread along plenty of beachfront. The postcard-perfect, palm-fringed beach has powdery white sands and milky aqua water; around the headland, the choppy waters are perfect for windsurfing and kitesurfing with Radical Watersports (p375).

Jetty, Pigeon Point
JOHN HARPER/GETTY IMAGES ©

Activities

DIVING

Stupendous water clarity, giant shoals of tropical fish, stunning corals, a variety of dive sites and excellent operators make diving on Tobago some of the best in the Caribbean. Whether you want to do mellow coral-viewing dives or current-zipping drift dives past huge turtles and sharks, Tobago's got it all. Although serious divers tend to stay at Speyside and Charlotteville, dive operators in Crown Point run trips all over the island. There is a recompression chamber in the east-coast village of Roxborough.

Undersea Tobago Diving
(**631-2626; www.underseatobago.com; dive US$40**) Based at the Coco Reef hotel, this is a reliable dive outfit that places great emphasis on safety and uses top-notch equipment.

R&Sea Divers Diving
(**639-8120; www.rseadivers.com; Toucan Inn, Store Bay Rd; dive US$45**) R&Sea Divers is safe, professional and friendly: this is a Professional Association of Diving Instructors (PADI) facility that's been around for a long time. Staff will pick up divers at any hotel.

OTHER ACTIVITIES

Radical Watersports Water Sports
(**631-5150; www.radicalsportstobago.com; windsurf boards per hr US$45, waterskiing or wake-boarding session US$45, kitesurfing per upwind drop-off US$25, stand-up paddling per hr US$20; 9am-5pm**) Radical Watersports, at the northernmost end of Pigeon Point beach, is the center for wind sports, providing quality rental and lessons. It also rents kayaks and stand-up paddleboards that are perfect for exploring the mangrovey 'No Man's Land' and deserted beaches to the east.

Easy Goers Bikes Cycling
(**681-8025; www.easygoersbikes.com; Milford Rd, Crown Point; mountain bikes per day TT$80**) Right opposite the entrance to Store Bay beach, and offering tours as well as bike rental.

Yoga, Anyone?

Some upscale hotels on Tobago offer yoga classes free to guests, but the best place to take a stretch is the Kariwak Village Holistic Haven, which has a lovely open-air yoga studio, the Ajoupa, where regular Iyengar and Hatha classes are staged, alongside tai chi. Classes cost about TT$100.

Sleeping

Kariwak Village Holistic Haven Hotel **$$**
(**639-8442; www.kariwak.com; Store Bay Local Rd; r from US$150;**) Off Store Bay Local Rd, just a two-minute walk from the airport, Kariwak nestles in lush landscaping. The duplex cabanas line paths that wind through tropical gardens. It's both rustic and refreshing. There's an organic herb garden, two pools (one with waterfall), free yoga and tai chi classes and an excellent restaurant.

Native Abode Guesthouse **$$**
(**631-1285; www.nativeabode.com; 13 Fourth St, Gaskin Bay Rd, Bon Accord; r from US$120;** P) On a tree-filled side street tucked away off Store Bay Local Rd, this is a lovely little place. Rooms are decorated to a very high standard, and are clean, modern and appealing, and have a kitchenette. The owners' garden is a great chill-out spot, filled with fruit trees.

Johnston Apartments Guesthouse **$$**
(**639-8915; www.johnstonapartments.com; Store Bay Rd; r US$105-115;** @) A great location, perched on the cliffs above Store Bay Beach and in walking distance of the Crown Point restaurants and bars. Apartments are neat, clean and modern,

Below: Menu board, Tobago; Right: Vendor, Argyle Falls (p383)
(BELOW) DAN GAIR/GETTY IMAGES ©; (RIGHT) MICHELE WESTMORLAND/GETTY IMAGES ©

with full kitchen. Popular with visiting Trinis.

Conrado Beach Resort Hotel **$$**
(639-0145; www.conradotobago.com; Pigeon Point Rd; r TT$105-130;) On the approach road to Pigeon Point beach, this no-frills resort proves to be excellent oceanside value. Sand and surf are at stumbling distance. The rooms are clean and bright, many with large ocean-view balconies. There is a restaurant and bar onsite.

Coco Reef Resort Resort **$$$**
(639-8572; www.cocoreef.com; d US$326-695; P @) Coco Reef pays elegant homage to luxurious colonial architecture, but a real highlight is the gorgeous Cuban art that lavishes the entire facility. Rooms overlook the white sand of a private beach, and guests enjoy top-tier amenities and excellent service. Rates include breakfast and non-motorized water sports.

Eating

One of the best places to each lunch is at the row of **food huts** opposite the beach at Store Bay, where local women serve delicious dishes like roti, crab and dumplin' and simple plate lunches (TT$30 to TT$60). There's also a cluster of fast-food places at the junction of Milford Rd and Pigeon Point Rd.

Kariwak Village Caribbean **$$**
(639-8442; Kariwak Village Hotel, Store Bay Local Rd; breakfast from TT$70, dinner from TT$170; breakfast, lunch & dinner; P) Beneath the thatched roof and coral-stone walls of this open-air restaurant, the Kariwak chefs create masterpieces of Caribbean and Creole cuisine using fresh ingredients, including organic herbs and vegetables from the garden. Breakfast includes a healthy bowl of fresh fruit, eggs, fish, homemade granola and bread.

The lunch and dinner set menus feature grilled fish and seafood cooked up with plenty of love.

La Cantina Italian $$
(639-8242; http://lacantinapizzeria.com; RBTT Compound, Milford Rd; pizza TT$60-125; noon-2:45pm & 6-9:45pm Mon & Tue, noon-10pm Wed-Sat, 6-9:45pm Sun; P) Tucked into a bank compound off Milford Rd, this buzzing joint cooks up a huge range of authentically Italian pizzas in its wood-fired oven – you can watch the chef spinning dough and adding toppings. Good salads and fast service.

Water Mill International $$
(639-0000; Shirvan Rd; mains TT$145-195; noon-3pm Tue-Sat, 6-10pm Mon-Sat; P) Set in an old sugar mill between Crown Point and Buccoo Bay, with tables under a coral-columned gazebo, this longstanding Tobago restaurant is under new management and offers a wide-ranging and delicious menu, from duck in orange molasses sauce to fish in beurre blanc.

Backyard Cafe Caribbean $$
(639-6274; Milford Rd; mains TT$99-129; noon-8pm Mon-Fri;) It's a treat to visit this colorful roadside cafe that brings a European spin to local ingredients. The dishes are light and flavorful and the juices – like papaya guava – are lovely.

Drinking & Nightlife

Shade Club
(Bon Accord; 6pm-late Wed-Sat) Locals, foreigners and tourists all flock to the open-air Shade for a proper party lime. It's probably the hippest place on the island to wine and grine, though can be a bit of a pick-up joint. Small cover charge Friday and Saturday.

Bago's Bar
(10am-late) Right on the sand where Pigeon Point beach road forks right, this cool little beach bar serves them cold and mixes a mean rum punch. Great for sunset.

Buccoo Reef

Stretching offshore between Pigeon Point and Buccoo Bay, the extensive Buccoo Reef was designated as a marine park in 1973 and a Ramsar site in 2006. The fringing reef boasts five reef flats separated by deep channels. The sheer array of flora and fauna – dazzling sponges, hard corals and tropical fish – makes marine biologists giddy. However, despite the efforts of conservation groups, Buccoo Reef has unfortunately been battered by too much use and not enough protection.

Glass-bottom-boat reef tours are an accessible way to explore Tobago's incredible treasure. Tours leave from Store Bay, Pigeon Point and the village of Buccoo. Most operators charge US$20 per person for a two-hour trip. The boats pass over the reef (much of which is just a meter or two beneath the surface), stop for snorkeling and end with a swim in the **Nylon Pool**, a calm, shallow area with a sandy bottom and clear turquoise waters. All the operators are pretty similar, often playing loud soca and selling drinks on board; you'll be repeatedly approached by touts when on Store Bay beach.

Illusions Bar
(**10am-late**) Pumping soca music into the Crown Point night, this busy bar usually draws a crowd and is a great place to sink a few cold ones.

Information

In Crown Point, there are banks at the airport and along Milford Rd close to Store Bay, all of which have 24-hour ATMs. You'll also find banks and ATMs in Scarborough, and ATMs in Pleasant Prospect, Roxborough, Castara and Charlotteville.

Scarborough General Hospital (**660-4744; Signal Hill; 24hr**) A 15-minute drive from Crown Point.

Tourist Office (**639-0509; ANR Robinson International Airport; 8am-10pm**) The staff provide basic information and can help you book a room or find hiking and bird-watching tour guides.

BUCCOO

Though its narrow strip of white sand is monopolized by fishing boats at the village end, Buccoo's sweeping palm-backed bay is pretty spectacular, though it's more a place to hang out or take a horse ride than throw down your towel. The tiny village itself offers a taste of true local flavor: friendly folks who define laid-back, breathtaking sunsets over the bay, and the infamous Sunday School party every week, staged at the incongruously grand new beach facility.

Activities

Being with Horses (**639-0953; www.being-with-horses.com; 14 Galla Trace, Buccoo; rides from US$85;**) is a small-scale stable offering rides along Buccoo Point and beach. Great for kids, with an intuitive, holistic approach to things equestrian.

Festivals & Events

Easter weekend is a huge deal in Tobago, when everyone flocks to Buccoo for a series of open-air parties and – the highlight of it all – goat races. Taken very seriously, goat racing draws more bets than a Las Vegas casino. The competing goats get pampered like beauty contestants and the eventual champion is forever revered. The partying stretches throughout the weekend and the big races happen on Tuesday.

Sleeping

Miller's Guesthouse Guesthouse $
(☎660-8371; www.millersguesthouse.com; 14 Miller St; s/d US$30/45; ❄ 📶) In a pretty location overlooking Buccoo Bay, the basic singles and doubles are great for budget travelers. A great place for meeting people, and next to a recommended restaurant too.

Eating & Drinking

The main Buccoo Bay Rd has several places selling inexpensive local lunches and dinners, usually based around fish and chicken. There are also a few friendly rum shops dotted around town – just drop in wherever you see a crowd.

El Pescador Seafood $$
(www.leospescador.com; Buccoo Bay Rd; breakfast TT$35-50, lunch & dinner TT$50-320; ⏲breakfast, lunch & dinner) Attached to Miller's Guesthouse, and with tables overlooking Buccoo Bay (offering great sunset views), this friendly place cooks up excellent seafood and meat dishes with a South American twist. Great for a drink, too, with a nice cocktail list.

Entertainment

Sunday School
Music
Lacking any religious affiliation, Sunday School is the sly title for a street party held in Buccoo every Sunday night. Until around 10pm, partygoers are mostly tourists enjoying rum drinks, overpriced barbecue dinners and live steel pan. Later in the night, folks from all over the island come to 'take a wine' or just hang out, with DJs spinning everything from reggae to soca.

LEEWARD ROAD

The stretch of coastline from Mt Irvine Bay to Plymouth has several lovely beaches, a few sizable hotels and a slew of fancy villas hugging the greens of the golf course. Like a sloppy adolescent propping its feet on the table in a fancy living room, Black Rock's tiny Pleasant Prospect is right in the middle. It's a teeny surfer haunt: a cluster of cheap unofficial accommodations, eateries and a few good places to lime.

Beaches

Mt Irvine Beach Beach
This pretty public beach, 200m north of Mt Irvine Bay Hotel, has sheltered picnic tables and changing rooms, plus a good beachside **restaurant**, roti shacks and plenty of shade trees. Surfers migrate here from December to March. You can rent sun loungers, kayaks and surfboards on the beach. Good for families.

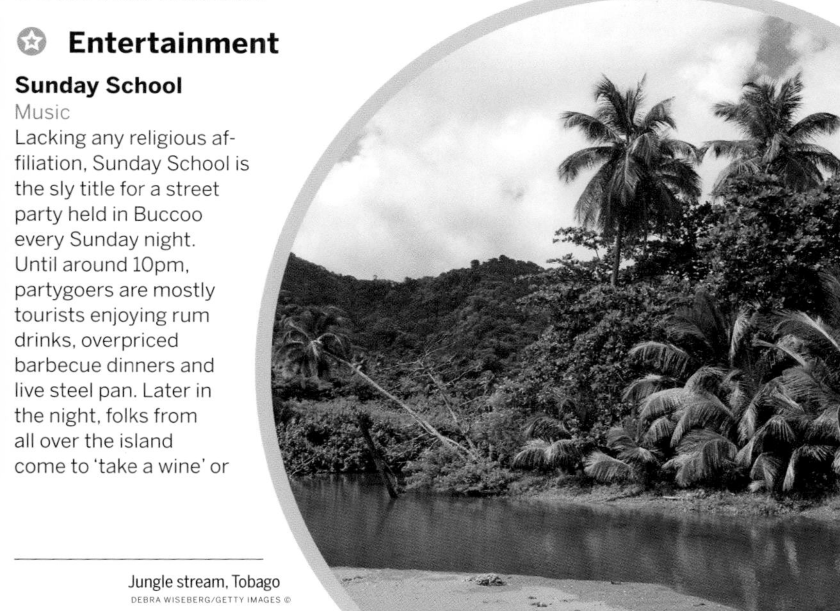

Jungle stream, Tobago
DEBRA WISEBERG/GETTY IMAGES ©

Stonehaven Bay Family Beach

(Grafton Bay; [family icon]) The next beach northeast of Mt Irvine, this fabulous sweep of coarse yellow sand offers some good swimming and bodyboarding. A couple of large-scale hotels overlook the sand, one of which has a beach bar selling lunch and drinks; the eastern end has calmer waters.

Turtle Beach Beach

Another long stretch of yellow-brown sand, with wave-whipped waters shelving sharply off from the beach, this is also one of Tobago's main nesting sites for leatherback turtles. A couple of tour companies offer turtle-watching tours in the March–August season.

Sleeping

Plantation Beach Villas Resort **$$$**

(639-9377; www.plantationbeachvillas.com; villas for 2 people from US$260; P ❄ wifi pool) Right on Stonehaven Beach, this is the nicest of the villa resorts in the area, with tastefully appointed three-bedroom villas, a communal beachside pool and a cute little restaurant and bar. All villas come with a housekeeper who cleans daily and will cook for guests.

Eating & Drinking

Pleasant Prospect has a cluster of local bars, eateries, and even a Rituals coffee shop and Pizza Boys takeaway. **Legger's** (formerly the Ocean Edge Bar) is an unpretentious bar nooked into a cliff overlooking the ocean. It's a great place to snag a beer after a day of sand and surf. It has barbecue Fridays as well. Right across the road, **Moon Over Water** is also a good place to hang with folks.

Fish Pot Seafood **$$**

(635-1728; Pleasant Prospect; mains from TT$70; lunch & dinner Mon-Sat) Very reasonable, this laid-back restaurant specializes in super-fresh, simply prepared seafood (with some chicken and steak dishes), and is equipped with an open-air patio. Excellent homemade bread, too.

Seahorse Inn Restaurant & Bar Caribbean **$$$**

(Seahorse Inn, Stonehaven Bay; mains TT$70-235; lunch & dinner) Sitting alfresco amid a tropical setting overlooking the water,

Englishman's Bay (right), Tobago

with the sound of waves crashing below, this upmarket restaurant specializes in gourmet Creole cuisine.

CASTARA

About a 45-minute drive from Plymouth, Castara is a working fishing village that's popular with tourists not wanting the inundated Crown Point scene. People love the wide, sandy beach, relaxed atmosphere and picturesque setting, but the village is on the cusp of feeling overcrowded itself during high season. Snorkeling is good in the calm Heavenly Bay to the right of the main beach. Ali Baba Tours is based here, providing hiking and boating trips.

Sleeping

Castara Cottage Guesthouse $
(757-1044; www.castaracottage.com; apt US$70-110;) Decked out in rich tropical colors, these three simple apartments are perched on a hillside between Big and Heavenly Bays. Each is equipped with all you need to self-cater, and has pleasant outdoor areas for liming and lounging.

Castara Retreats Resort $$
(766-1010; www.castararetreats.com; r incl breakfast US$125-310;) Beautifully designed wooden villas on a lushly landscaped hillside that offers lovely views of the beach. Each is kitted out in stylish modern decor, and there are even sea views from the beds. Friendly, helpful staff and plenty of privacy.

Naturalist Beach Resort Guesthouse $$
(639-5901; www.naturalist-tobago.com; d apt incl breakfast US$45-125;) This cheerful, family-run place is at beach level on Big Bay, and its cozy apartments include kitchens, fans and air-con, and are all different; some have water views. The newer upstairs units feature lots of local wood and are quite a bit nicer, with shared balconies.

Eating & Drinking

Cascreole Caribbean $
(Big Bay, Castara; mains from TT$50; lunch & dinner) On a wooden deck built over the Big Bay sands, this is all you'd want from a beach bar: ice-cold beers, fresh and delicious fish, plenty of sea breezes and a Thursday night beach bonfire.

Castara Retreats International $$
(766-1010; www.castararetreats.com; Castara; mains TT$110; lunch Wed-Sun, dinner daily) In a beautiful setting on a balcony high over the bay, this is a lovely lunch or dinner choice, with homemade pasta, fresh local juices and excellent seafood. Great for sunset cocktails, too.

Boat House Caribbean $$
(mains TT$60-115; breakfast, lunch & dinner Mon-Fri, lunch & dinner Sun) Between the colorful decor, bamboo detailing and beachside ambience, this restaurant achieves a festive atmosphere. The seafood dishes are accompanied by fresh vegetable side dishes and salad. On Wednesday it has a popular African drumming night with a set menu that includes rum punch.

ENGLISHMAN'S BAY

North of Castara, the road winds past a stretch of coast that's punctuated by pretty beaches and villages, unhurried places with cows grazing at the roadside. The best place to stop is Englishman's Bay, a superb undeveloped beach shaded by stands of bamboo and coconut palms, which draws snorkelers to its gentle waters – a coral reef lies 20m offshore. **Eula's Restaurant** has local fare and rustic toilets.

PARLATUVIER

Just east of Englishman's Bay is Parlatuvier, a tiny fishing village on a striking circular bay. On the hillside just before the village, get postcard-perfect views of the horseshoe bay below from the car park adjacent to Glasgow's Bar.

Tobago Forest Reserve

The paved Roxborough–Parlatuvier Rd crosses the island from Roxborough to Bloody Bay, curving through the Tobago Forest Reserve, established in 1765 and the oldest such reserve in the Caribbean. The 30-minute drive through the reserve passes pretty valleys and mountain views, and is one of the most scenic on the island.

A number of **trailheads** lead off the main road into the rainforest, where there's excellent **bird-watching**. Three-quarters of the way from Roxborough, at **Gilpin Trace**, authorized guides charge TT$160 for a 1½-hour walk, or TT$240 for a two-hour hike to the Main Ridge lookout hut, which affords scenic views of Bloody Bay and the offshore Sisters Rocks. All guides provide interesting commentary on the forest ecosystem and inhabitants, and can lend you rubber boots when it's muddy. For the best birding, aim to arrive at 9am.

Further east, at Bloody Bay, is the Roxborough–Parlatuvier Rd through the Tobago Forest Reserve.

SCARBOROUGH

POP 16,800

Located 15 minutes' drive east of Crown Point, Scarborough is the island's only city, a crowded port with bustling one-way streets and congested traffic. Tobagonians come here to bank, pay bills or go shopping, and though there are some good places to grab a bite and a neat public market, most visitors will want to push onward.

Sights & Activities

Fort King George Fort

FREE Atop a hill at the end of Fort St, this sizable fort was built by the British between 1777 and 1779, and is worth a visit to see its restored colonial-era buildings and magnificent views. Benches under enormous saaman trees allow you to gaze out over Scarborough bay, while cannons line the fort's stone walls, pointing out to sea over palm-covered flatlands below.

The officers' quarters now contain the small but worthy **Tobago Museum** (**639-3970; admission TT$10; 9am-4:30pm Mon-Fri)**, which displays a healthy collection of Amerindian artifacts, maps from the 1600s, military relics, a small geology exhibit and a very interesting collection of watercolor paintings by Sir William Young that depict Tobago from 1807 to 1815.

Eating & Drinking

Ciao Café and Pizzeria Italian $

(Burnett St; mains from TT$60, ice cream from TT$20; 9am-11pm Mon-Sat, 5-11pm Sun;) Both locals and foreigners come to lime at this adorable cafe, which cooks up authentic Italian pizza in a brick oven, plus great panini, coffee and the best homemade gelato in Trinidad and Tobago.

Shore Things Cafe $$

(Old Milford Rd, Lambeau; mains TT$60-120; 11am-6pm Mon-Fri) Even though it's a couple of kilometers west of the city, this is one of the most pleasant oceanside cafes on the island, serving quiche, pizza, salads and fresh juices in a lovely setting overlooking the ocean. Great for teatime cakes, too.

Blue Crab Restaurant Caribbean $$

(639-2737; www.tobagobluecrab.com; cnr Main & Robinson Sts; lunch from TT$55, dinner mains TT$100-165; lunch Mon-Fri, dinner Mon, Wed, Fri by reservation) A family-run restaurant with pleasant alfresco seating (and an air-conditioned dining room) and great West Indian food. You'll have a choice of fresh juice and main dishes such as Creole chicken, fresh fish or garlic shrimp.

Barcode Bar

(www.barcodetobago.com; cover varies; ⏱7pm-late) Overlooking the ocean, with its outdoor deck cooled by sea breezes, this popular bar and nightspot has pool tables and regular special events that draw a big crowd. The karaoke on Thursday is usually pretty popular.

Shopping

For the best selection of local art and crafts in Tobago, head just out of town to Shore Things (p381).

Information

There are branches of Republic Bank and Scotiabank just east of the docks, both equipped with ATMs. There's another ATM right outside the ferry terminal.

Scarborough General Hospital (☎660-4744; Signal Hill; ⏱24hr) Just off the highway on the outskirts of Scarborough, this new facility has an A&E and handles most medical issues on Tobago.

WINDWARD ROAD

East of Scarborough, Tobago's Windward coast is the more rural part of the island, less appealing to tourists thanks to its rough dark-sand beaches. The Windward Rd, which connects Scarborough with Speyside, winds past scattered villages, jungly valleys and white-capped ocean. The further east you go, the more ruggedly beautiful the scenery becomes. Although much of the road is narrow and curvy with a handful of blind corners, it's easliy drivable in a standard vehicle. Journey time from Scarborough to Speyside is 1½ hours.

Just west of Roxborough, the triple-tiered **Argyle Falls (admission TT$40; ⏱7am-5:30pm)** are a far busier affair; go early to skip crowds. On top of admission, you pay one of the resident guides US$10 to lead you on the 20-minute hike up to the falls. Guides swarm the entrance; official guides wear khaki uniforms and carry ID. At 54m, this is Tobago's highest waterfall, cascading down four distinct levels, each with its own pool of spring water.

Speyside (p384), Tobago

SPEYSIDE

The small fishing village of Speyside fronts Tyrrel's Bay, and attracts divers and birders. It's the jumping-off point for excursions to uninhabited Little Tobago island, a bird sanctuary 2km offshore. Protected waters, high visibility, abundant coral and diverse marine life make for choice diving. Nondivers can take glass-bottom boat/snorkel tours. Speyside funnels visitors into high-end, diver-oriented hotels much more than its neighbor Charlotteville, where mixing with the locals is more of a possibility. Above town, the off-road **lookout** has panoramic views out over the islands and reef-studded waters.

Sights & Activities

Little Tobago Nature Reserve

Also known as Bird of Paradise Island (though it isn't home to any of the eponymous birds), Little Tobago was the site of a cotton plantation during the late 1800s, and is now an important seabird sanctuary that offers rich pickings for bird-watchers. Red-billed tropic birds, magnificent frigate birds, brown boobies, Audubon's shearwaters, laughing gulls and sooty terns are some of the species found here. The hilly, arid island, which averages just 1.5km in width, has a couple of short hiking trails with captivating views.

Several operators run glass-bottom-boat trips for US$25. The trip to Little Tobago, a 15-minute crossing, includes bird-watching on the island and snorkeling at Angel Reef. Masks and fins are provided. **Frank's** (660-5438; Batteaux Bay; 10am & 2pm), based at Blue Waters Inn, and **Top Ranking Tours** (660-4904), departing from the beach near Jemma's restaurant, are recommended.

The diving at Little Tobago is some of the region's best. Several dive shops operate in the village; one of the best is **Extra Divers** (660-4852; www.extradiverstobago.eu) at the Speyside Inn hotel.

Sleeping

Speyside Inn Hotel $$

(660-4852; www.speysideinn.com; 189-193 Windward Rd; r incl breakfast US$144;) Quite lovely, this butter-yellow hotel houses bright balcony rooms looking over the ocean, and cottages nestled out back in the jungly landscaping. Extra Divers shop makes its home here, there's a restaurant and bar, and it's often the most animated spot in town (though that's not saying much in quiet Speyside).

Blue Waters Inn Hotel $$$

(660-2583; www.bluewatersinn.com; Batteaux Bay; r incl breakfast from US$245;) The most upscale place to stay

Manta ray, off Speyside
MICHAEL LAWRENCE/GETTY IMAGES ©

and geared to divers, Blue Waters sits on pretty Batteaux Bay, just 1km from the main road. The rooms all have patios and great views. Guests get use of tennis courts, beach chairs and kayaks. There's also a restaurant, bar, spa services and Blue Waters Dive'N, a full-service PADI dive center.

Eating

Jemma's Caribbean **$$**

(mains from TT$70; breakfast & lunch Sun-Fri, dinner Sun-Thu;) Nestled in a tree-house setting and blessed by sea breezes, Jemma's is a standard stop for tour groups and service can be slow. It boasts excellent atmosphere and fresh local food, including fish, chicken and shrimp dishes, and prices are on the higher end. It doesn't serve booze but you are welcome to bring your own.

CHARLOTTEVILLE

There are about four winding kilometers over the mountains from Speyside to Charlotteville, a delightful fishing village nestled in aquamarine Man of War Bay. This secluded town accepts its trickle of off-the-beaten-track tourists with mostly jovial spirits and occasionally apathy. It's more lively than Speyside, and tourist services include a sprinkling of places to stay and eat and an ATM. This may all change, though, with the construction of a new beach facility smack in the middle of the village, which locals are opposing.

Beaches

Man of War Bay Beach

The large, horseshoe-shaped Man of War Bay is fringed by a palm-studded brown-sand beach with good swimming. Roughly in the middle of the beach, you'll find changing facilities (TT$1) and the Suckhole beach bar. The pier towards the eastern end is a nice spot for fishing or sunset-watching.

Pirate's Bay Beach

Walk to the north end of the village, and take the dirt track winding up and around the cliff, and a 10-minute walk brings you to the top of the concrete steps that descend to Pirate's Bay, which offers excellent snorkeling and fantastic beach liming, with locals and visitors making a day of it with coolers and games of beach football. There are no facilities at this secluded beach, so bring your own drinks and food. If you don't fancy walking, ask one of the Man of War Bay fishermen to transport you there and back.

Activities

Shark Shacks Diving

(Charlotteville Adventure Dive Centre; 767-6420; www.shark-shacks.com; dive US$55) Scuba divers should contact Shark Shacks. Right on Man of War Bay, the full-service, PADI-certified dive center rents out full gear and offers a variety of dive trips and certification. Packages include quaint, colorful, clean accommodations.

Sleeping

Man-O-War Bay Cottages Cabin **$**

(660-4327; www.man-o-warbaycottages.com; Charlotteville Main Rd; 1-/3-bedroom cottage US$65/120; @) Plotted in a little botanical garden, with lots of tropical trees, ferns and flowering plants, these 10 simple cottages with kitchens and screened, louvered windows are open to the breeze and sounds of the surf. You'll find them beachside, about five minutes' walk south of the village.

Cholson Chalets Guesthouse **$**

(639-8553; 74 Bay St; apt US$40-88) Cholson Chalets is a clean, well-run place in a well-maintained old building just steps from the ocean. The fresh green-and-white exterior complements the fishing-town vibe. It has nine units of varying size, equipped with kitchens.

Eating & Drinking

G's Caribbean **$**

(Bay St; lunch & dinner) Open when other places in town are closed, this hole-in-the-wall eatery opposite Sharon &

Pheb's has a breezy seaside patio for enjoying the simple meals of fish or chicken and chips, and more elaborate plates with all the local trimmings. Blaring music at weekends from the adjoining bar, too.

Gail's Caribbean **$**
(mains from TT$60; ⏲7pm-late Mon-Sat) Located at the northern end of the waterfront, Gail's serves up freshly caught fish with fantastic local side dishes. Many of the ingredients come straight from Gail's garden.

Sharon & Pheb's Caribbean **$$**
(Bay St; mains from TT$60; ⏲lunch & dinner) Doing great things with fresh fish, shrimp, beef, chicken and vegetables, chef Sharon cooks up delicious local cuisine. There's indoor or outdoor seating.

Practicalities

- **Electricity** All islands: 110V, 60Hz; US-style two- and three-pin plugs are used.
- **Time** Atlantic Standard Time (GMT-4)
- **Tipping** A 15% to 20% overall tip is the norm in restaurants; 10% to 15% is often added to the bill. A tip of 15% is usually added to the bill in hotels. A 10% tip is the norm in taxis. Watch for service charges in hotels and resorts.
- **Weights & Measures** All islands: metric system.

SURVIVAL GUIDE

Directory A–Z

Accommodations

Price ranges for a double room in high season:

$ less than US$75

$$ US$75 to US$200

$$$ more than US$200

ABC

Aruba has all types of accommodations but is especially known for its huge beach resorts. Bonaire has much more intimate hotels and guesthouses, many aimed at divers. Curaçao has a little of everything. Taxes and fees on the islands:

Aruba Hotel taxes and fees are 6% tax plus 10% to 15% service charge.

Bonaire Hotel taxes and fees are US$6.50 per person plus 10% to 15% service charge.

Curaçao Hotel taxes and fees are 7% room tax plus 12% service charge.

Trinidad & Tobago

A 10% service charge and a 15% value-added tax (VAT) can add 35% more to your bill. Most advertised accommodations rates include the tax and service charge, but not always.

Food

ABC

The following price categories are for the cost of a main course:

$ less than US$10

$$ US$10 to US$25

$$$ more than US$25

Trinidad & Tobago

The following price indicators relate to the cost of a main meal:

$ less than TT$30

$$ TT$30 to TT$100

$$$ more than TT$100

Health

There are excellent medical facilities in the ABCs. Tap water is safe to drink.

In Trinidad & Tobago tap water is heavily chlorinated, though it tastes better boiled than fresh from the tap. It can still cause upsets for those unused to it.

Language

Aruba If you only speak English, you won't have a problem on Aruba, although Dutch and Papiamento are the official languages.

Bonaire If you only speak English, you won't have a problem on Bonaire, where most locals are multilingual. Dutch is the official language, but English and Papiamento are spoken widely.

Curaçao If you only speak English, you won't have a problem although Dutch and Papiamento are the official languages.

Trinidad & Tobago English is widely spoken.

Money

Aruba You can pay for just about everything in US dollars on Aruba. Sometimes you will get change back in US currency, other times you will receive it in Aruban florins (Afl).

Bonaire The US dollar (US$) is the official currency.

Curaçao You can pay for just about everything in US dollars in touristed areas. The Netherlands Antillean guilder (NAf) is the official currency.

Trinidad & Tobago The official currency is the Trinidad and Tobago dollar (TT$).

Opening Hours

Outside of tourist areas on Aruba, much is closed on Sunday.

Banks 9am to 4pm Monday to Friday

Restaurants 11am to 10pm

Shops 9am to 6pm Monday to Friday, to 1pm Saturday (in tourist areas to 8pm daily)

Public Holidays

In addition to those observed throughout the region, the islands in this chapter have the following public holidays.

Aruba

GF (Betico) Croes Day January 25

Carnival Monday Monday before Ash Wednesday

National Day March 18

Queen's Birthday April 30

Labor Day May 1

Ascension Day Sixth Thursday after Easter

Bonaire

Ash Wednesday Usually in February, after Carnival

Queen's Birthday April 30

Aruba (p338) from the air

FRANS SELLIES/GETTY IMAGES ©

Labor Day May 1

Ascension Day Sixth Thursday after Easter

Bonaire Flag Day September 6

Curaçao

Carnival Monday Monday before Ash Wednesday

Queen's Birthday April 30

Labor Day May 1

Ascension Day Sixth Thursday after Easter

Flag Day July 2

Trinidad & Tobago

Carnival Monday and Tuesday are unofficial holidays, with banks and most businesses closed.

Spiritual Baptist/Shouter Liberation Day March 30

Indian Arrival Day May 30

Corpus Christi Ninth Thursday after Easter

Labor Day June 19

Emancipation Day August 1

Independence Day August 31

Republic Day September 24

Eid al Fitr (Muslim New Year) Dates vary

Telephone

When calling from North America, dial the country code plus the local number. From elsewhere dial your country's international access code plus the country code plus the local number. Country codes:

Aruba ☎297

Bonaire & Curaçao ☎599

Trinidad & Tobago ☎868

Visas

ABC Visas are not required for citizens of North America, the EU, Australia and many more countries.

Trinidad & Tobago Visas are not necessary for citizens of the US, Canada, the UK or most European countries. Visas are required by citizens of Australia, New Zealand and many other nations.

Getting There & Away

Entering the Southern Caribbean

All visitors need a passport and a return or onward ticket.

Air

Insel Air (www.fly-inselair.com) has a near-monopoly on service linking Aruba, Bonaire and Curaçao. **KLM** (www.klm.com) serves all three from Amsterdam.

Aruba

Reina Beatrix International Airport (AUA; www.airportaruba.com) is a busy, modern airport with plenty of service to North America.

Bonaire

There are a few flights to Bonaire from North America.

Curaçao

Curaçao is well linked to US hubs; KLM flies to Amsterdam. **Liat** (www.liat.

Cruise ship in Willemstad (p351)

com) provides a vital link to Trinidad and the eastern Caribbean.

Hato International Airport (CUR; www.curacao-airport.com) receives international flights. It has a modern terminal with a few cafes and shops after security.

Departure tax (international US$35, Aruba and Bonaire US$9) is included in some tickets but not others.

Trinidad & Tobago

Trinidad is well linked to US hubs. Hometown carrier Caribbean Airlines (625-8246; www.caribbean-airlines.com) has regional flights and serves the US. LIAT (625-9451; www.liatairline.com) serves Barbados, Curaçao and other regional destinations.

ANR Robinson International Airport (TAB; 639-8547; www.crownpointairport.com) Located in Crown Point, 11km southwest of Scarborough, on Tobago. Has regional flights.

Piarco International Airport (www.piarcoairport.com) Located 25km east of Port of Spain, on Trinidad. Has the most international flights.

Sea

Cruise Ship

The ABCs are part of cruise-ship itineraries that cover the southern Caribbean, often on longer 10-day and two-week trips.

Aruba It's not unusual to have more than 10,000 passengers descend on the island in a day. Boats dock at the port in the middle of Oranjestad.

Bonaire Many cruise ships call at Bonaire; on days when more than one arrives, the thousands of visitors almost swamp the island. Boats dock directly at the port in the middle of Kralendijk.

Curaçao Boats dock directly at the cruise-ship port, which is just outside the stunning natural harbor in Willemstad.

Trinidad & Tobago In Trinidad ships dock at the King's Wharf, on ugly Wrightson Rd in Port of Spain, from where you can walk to the downtown area. In Tobago, the cruise ship terminal is adjacent to the ferry terminal in downtown Scarborough.

Departing Aruba

Passengers flying to the US absolutely must check in three hours before flight time. Actually four hours might be better because all US-bound passengers clear customs and immigration *before* they leave Aruba. Most flights back to the US leave during a small time slot in the afternoon and the US-staffed immigration facilities are often mobbed. If possible, try to avoid going home on a weekend, when things are the worst.

Getting Around

All the islands have plenty of international and local car rental firms. Taxis are easily found at airports and cruise ship ports.

Aruba

If you just want to stay at your hotel with only a few forays into Oranjestad and perhaps a hotel-arranged tour, then you won't need a car. Taxis and local buses will get the job done; for freedom to explore Aruba, a car or a bike – at least for a couple of days – is essential.

Bus The main bus depot is right in the center of Oranjestad. Frequent Arubus (787-588-0616; www.arubus.com; fare Afl2.30) serve the hotel areas from Oranjestad.

Car Driving is on the right, you won't need 4WD.

Bonaire

There is no public bus service on Bonaire. However, dive operators will haul you wherever you need to go. You can see all of the island in one or two days of driving, so you might consider renting a car for just that period.

Car Main roads are generally in good condition; however, roads in the national park and other remote spots can be quite rough. Gasoline can be found in Kralendijk. Driving is on the right-hand side.

Curaçao

The best part of a Curaçao visit is exploring the island. You'll want to have your own transport.

Car You won't need 4WD. Driving is on the right-hand side.

Trinidad & Tobago

Air Caribbean Airlines (p388) operates the 20-minute flight between Trinidad and Tobago (one way TT$150).

Boat Inter-Island Ferry Service (☎Tobago 639-2417, Trinidad 625-3055; www.ttitferry.com; adult/child one way TT$50/25; 2½ hours) runs fast catamaran ferries between Queen's Wharf in Port of Spain, Trinidad, and the main ferry dock in Scarborough, Tobago. It's a cheap, comfortable way to travel (unless you're prone to seasickness).

Bus Infrequent, air-conditioned buses travel around Trinidad from Port of Spain. Check online (www.ptsc.co.tt) for schedules. Buses in Tobago cover the whole island but are not very convenient for wider exploration.

Car Driving is on the left side. Port of Spain often has big-city traffic jams.

Maxi-Taxi Maxi-taxis are 12- to 25-passenger minibuses that travel along a fixed route within a specific zone. They're color-coded by route, run 24 hours, are very cheap and are heavily used by the locals. Rides cost TT$2 to TT$12, depending on how far you go.

Best of the Rest

Turks & Caicos (p392)

From posh beachside resorts in Providenciales to the gorgeous remote desert islands of fantasies.

Cayman Islands (p401)

Grand Cayman is one of the Caribbean's top family vacations spots, with one superb beach and oodles of water sports.

Montserrat (p412)

This enchanting and tiny island nation mixes volcanic devastation with pockets of tropical beauty.

Top: Blue iguana (p405), Grand Cayman;
Bottom: Boardwalk, Turks & Caicos (p392)

Turks & Caicos

HIGHLIGHTS

1. **Grace Bay Beach** (p392) Walk the length of the sand to see if it's really twelve miles long like everyone says.
2. **Grand Turk** (p398) Explore a great little colonial town on a great huge beach.
3. **Middle Caicos** (p397) Get lost and debate whether to be found.
4. **Salt Cay** (p396) Watch humpback whales swim past.

Conch shells, Turks & Caicos

The Turks and where? That's the reaction most people have when you mention these tropical isles. Although small in size, they offer a range of experiences. Providenciales gets all the noise and has constant construction along its beautiful main beach. It's an ever-more-popular destination for upscale vacationers looking for low-key fun in the sun.

But everywhere else in the Turks and Caicos (population 32,500) makes Providenciales look like Manhattan. On island after island, you'll find few people, endless white beaches and no end of good diving and snorkeling offshore. Even the nominal capital, cute little colonial Grand Turk, seems like a characterful backwater on any day cruise ships aren't in port.

If you're looking for your desert-island paradise, you might find it here.

CAICOS ISLANDS

The fan of islands that form the main landmass of this nation are the Caicos Islands, which range from the nearly uninhabited East Caicos to the condo-sprouting Providenciales.

Providenciales

POP 23,800

Providenciales, or Provo as it's known locally, is the tourism capital of the Turks and Caicos. It's home to a busy international airport, some fairly rampant development and its crowning glory, miles of beautiful white-sand beaches along its northern coast.

Everything is modern and commercial because it's mostly new. There's no old town – just a few decades ago, this was all salt flats.

Sights

Grace Bay Beach Beach

The biggest attraction on the island is this world-famous stretch of sand, notably long and beautiful even by Caribbean standards. Though it's dotted with hotels and resorts, its sheer size means that finding your own square of paradise is a snap.

Turks & Caicos

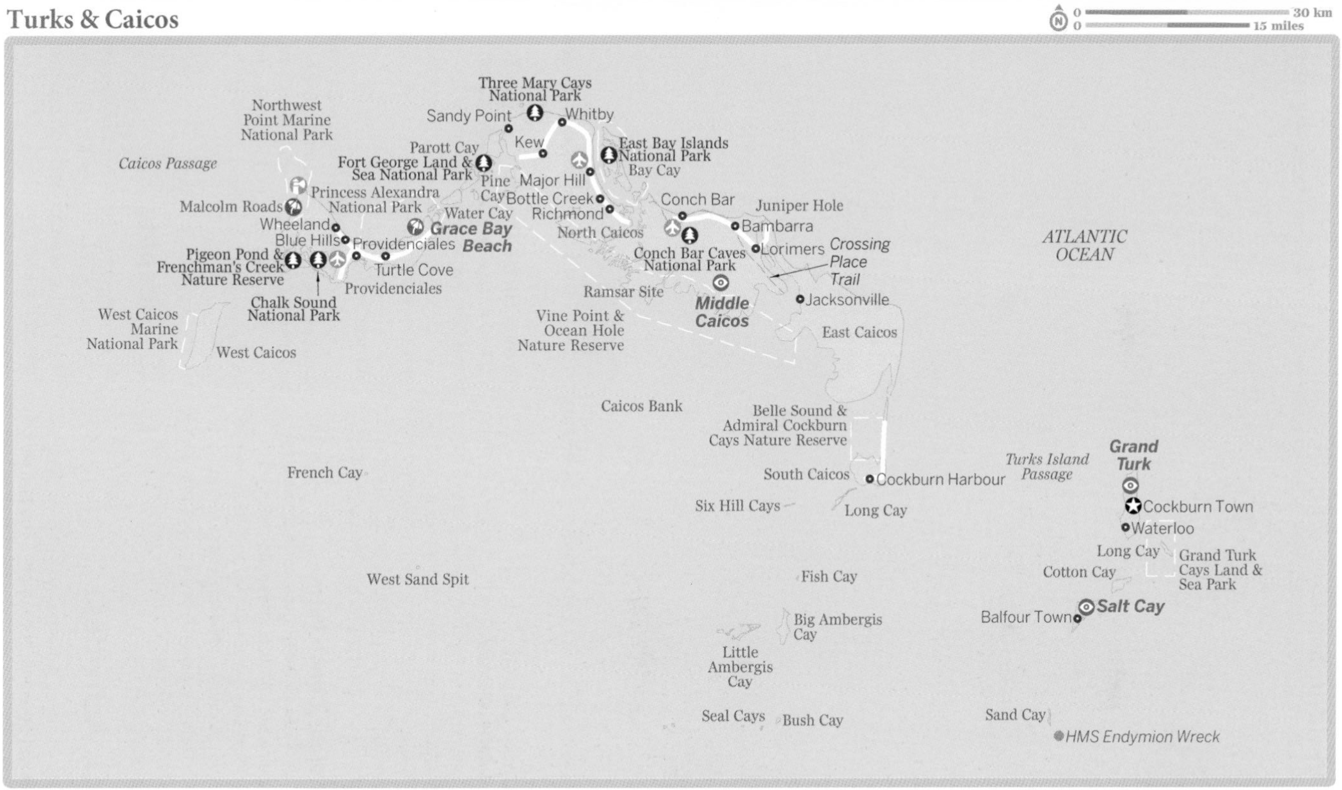

0 — 30 km
0 — 15 miles

ATLANTIC OCEAN
Caicos Passage
Northwest Point Marine National Park
Malcolm Roads
Princess Alexandra National Park
Wheeland
Blue Hills
Providenciales
Grace Bay Beach
Pigeon Pond & Frenchman's Creek Nature Reserve
Chalk Sound National Park
Turtle Cove
Providenciales
West Caicos Marine National Park
West Caicos
Parott Cay
Fort George Land & Sea National Park
Pine Cay
Water Cay
Three Mary Cays National Park
Sandy Point
Whitby
Kew
Major Hill
Bottle Creek
Richmond
North Caicos
East Bay Islands National Park
Bay Cay
Conch Bar
Juniper Hole
Bambarra
Lorimers
Crossing Place Trail
Conch Bar Caves National Park
Ramsar Site
Middle Caicos
Jacksonville
East Caicos
Vine Point & Ocean Hole Nature Reserve
Caicos Bank
Belle Sound & Admiral Cockburn Cays Nature Reserve
South Caicos
Cockburn Harbour
Long Cay
Six Hill Cays
French Cay
West Sand Spit
Fish Cay
Big Ambergis Cay
Little Ambergis Cay
Seal Cays
Bush Cay
Turks Island Passage
Grand Turk
Cockburn Town
Waterloo
Long Cay
Grand Turk Cays Land & Sea Park
Cotton Cay
Salt Cay
Balfour Town
Sand Cay
HMS Endymion Wreck

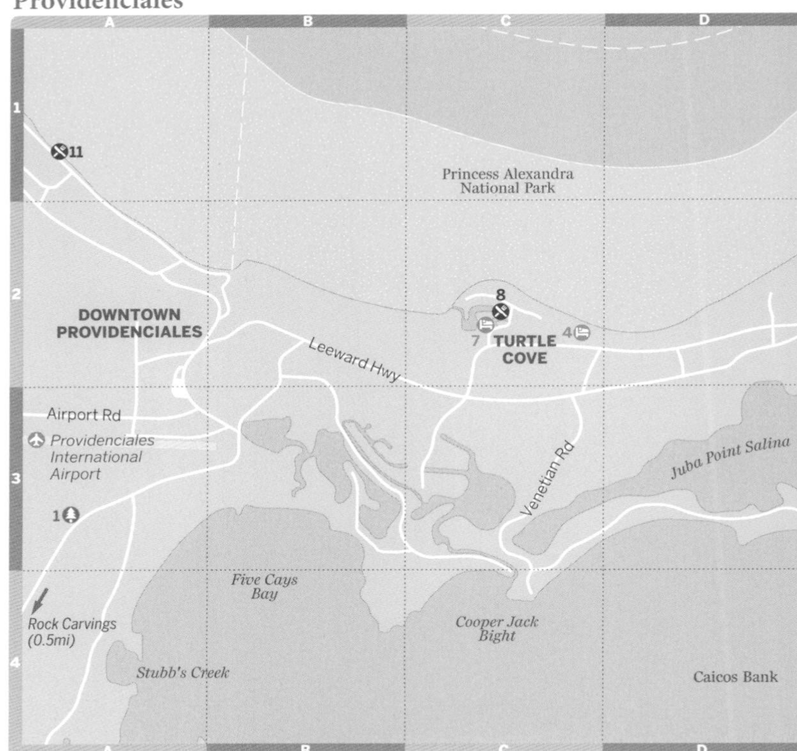

Chalk Sound National Park National Park

The waters of this 3-mile-long bay, 2 miles southwest of downtown, define 'turquoise.' The color is uniform: a vast, unrippled, electric-blue carpet eerily and magnificently studded with countless tiny islets.

Caicos Conch Farm Farm

(946-5643; www.caicosconchfarm.net; tour adult/child US$10/5; 9am-4pm Mon-Fri, to 2:30pm Sat) If you want to see what you've been chowing down on, head to the northeast corner of Provo and have a look at this working conch farm. It's kind of wild, actually.

Activities

There are countless day trips to nearby islands, beaches, snorkeling sites and more.

Provo Turtle Divers Diving

(946-4232; www.provoturtledivers.com; Turtle Cove Marina; 2-tank dive US$130) Offers night dives and more. Also runs seasonal whale-watching tours.

Windsurfing Provo Water Sports

(241-1687; www.windsurfingprovo.tc; Ocean Club East Resort, Grace Bay; windsurfing per hr from US$50; 10am-4pm) A hub of info, gear rental and lessons for windsurfing, kiteboarding, paddleboarding, kayaking and more.

Sleeping

Most of Provo's places to stay are right on Grace Bay Beach. Your main decision is whether you want condo-style, a resort or something else.

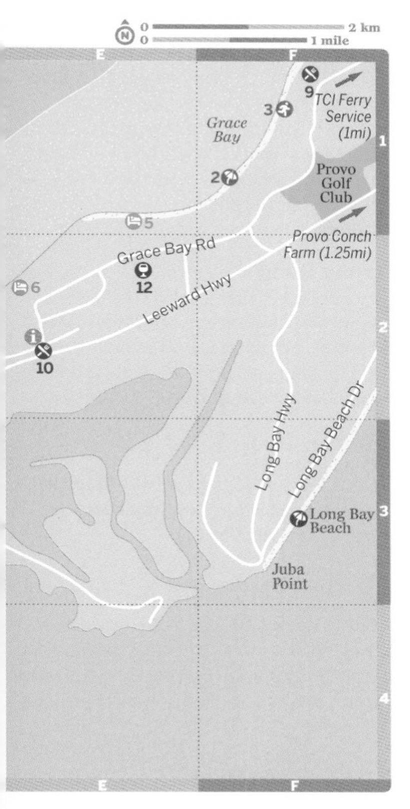

Providenciales

Sibonné Beach Hotel Hotel **$$**
(☎946-5547; www.sibonne.com; Grace Bay; r US$125-250; ❄@📶🏊) Deservedly popular and occupying a divine stretch of sand on Grace Bay, Sibonné is a real anti-resort; the vibe defines mellow. The two cheapest rooms are small but the rest of the choices are roomy and comfy.

Turtle Cove Inn Inn **$$**
(☎946-4203; www.turtlecoveinn.com; Turtle Cove Marina; r from US$140; ❄📶🏊) This older property in the heart of the Turtle Cove Marina is the perfect budget choice on an island where the concept is little known. Rooms are good-sized and some have nice views of the boats. The grounds are a bit ragged.

Point Grace Boutique Hotel **$$$**
(☎946-5096; www.pointgrace.com; off Grace Bay Rd; r from US$500; ❄📶🏊) The 28 rooms and cottages at this modern beachfront resort are sophisticated and luxurious. The vibe here recreates a fantastical colonial-era British estate, although with far better plumbing. Units come in all sizes and amenities include a spa and much more.

Coral Gardens Hotel **$$$**
(☎941-5497; www.coralgardens.com; Turtle Cove; r from US$260; ❄📶🏊) This modern and sleek resort is both relaxed and classy. It's at the quieter western end of Grace Bay. Rooms come in a range of sizes; guests receive free massages. The beachfront cafe Somewhere is very popular.

Eating & Drinking

Provo has a huge range of eating options. Some of the best are run by young chefs and are not on the beach.

Mr Groupers Seafood **$$**
(☎242-6780; 73 Grace Bay Rd; mains from US$15; ⏰11am-10pm) The namesake main dish is succulent and spicy. Other winners among many are the seafood-packed chowder and the various fresh specials. Dining is in an open-air octagonal dining room.

Somewhere Cafe $$

(Coral Gardens, Leeward Hwy, Turtle Cove; mains US$12-25; 8am-10pm) The ideal reward for a walk on the sand is Provo's best beach cafe and bar. Two funky levels are wide open to the water. Choose from tasty breakfasts and casual all-day fare with an accent on Mexican.

Patty's Place Seafood $$

(Blue Hills; mains US$10-20; 10am-9pm) The beach thins out at the west end of the island but it's still worth a trip out to Blue Hills to try one of the simple waterfront cafes along the road. Skip the over-hyped Conch Shack and go another 1.5 miles to this brightly painted house, where fresh seafood is served in simple surrounds.

Coyaba Fusion $$$

(946-5186; www.coyabarestaurant.com; Paradise Inn, off Grace Bay Rd; mains from US$35; 6-10pm Wed-Mon) Coyaba somehow treads the line of fine dining while retaining a relaxed atmosphere. The food is a clever fusion of Caribbean flavors and faithful classics. Chef Paul Newman (no relation) has achieved foodie fame; book in advance.

Baci Ristorante Italian $$$

(941-3044; Harbour Towne Plaza, Turtle Cove; mains US$10-30; noon-2pm Mon-Fri, 6-10pm Mon-Sat) Maritime chic at its best with wrought-iron scrollwork lining the ceilings, all with an authentic Italian-infused flavor overlooking the marina. The casual lunch menu morphs into serious Italian for dinner.

Danny Buoy's Pub

(Grace Bay Rd; 11am-2am) The island's late bar, with a huge terrace, sports on TV and a central spot amid the strip malls that pass for the heart of Provo. A good beer selection and cheap pub grub (until 10pm).

Information

Turks & Caicos Tourism (946-4970; www.turksandcaicostourism.com; Stubbs Diamond Plaza; 9am-5pm Mon-Fri)

Getting There & Around

There is no bus service from Providenciales International Airport. A taxi from the airport to Grace Bay costs US$20 one way for two people. Some resorts arrange transfers.

T&C's Other Islands

Escape from just about everything at these small islands.

East Caicos is the least-inhabited island in the chain. There is a Haitian immigrant community on the island but little else. The beaches are renowned and odds are you will have them all to yourself. However, the only way to get here is by boat charter or your own yacht.

South Caicos is the place to go for unspoilt scuba diving. The waters are pristine and prized for the effort required to get there. The land itself is a windswept wasteland of sand and scrub. South Caicos is connected by air and ferry to Providenciales.

Salt Cay is like the Turks in the 19th century. It's the sort of hideaway that you search your whole life to discover. But while the land is quiet, the sea surrounding the island is awash with life. Turtles, eagle rays and the majestic humpback whale all frequent the waters. **Salt Cay Divers** (241-1009; www.saltcaydivers.tc) is the place to go for info. **Pirate's Hideaway Guesthouse** (244-1407; www.saltcay.tc; Victoria St; r from US$150;) has comfy lodging. You can reach Salt Cay by flight and ferry.

The Cays

The smaller islands around Providenciales are known simply as the Cays, and most of them boast superb beaches and total isolation, being accessible only by a private boat charter.

Fort George Cay is home to the remnants of an 18th-century British-built fort. Divers and snorkelers inspect the gun emplacements slowly becoming one with the sea bottom.

French Cay, south of Providenciales, is an old pirate hideaway now more frequented by migrating birds. Offshore the waters are teeming with stingrays. Nurse sharks gather here in summer.

Parrot Cay is home to one of the Caribbean's most luxurious and exclusive resorts, the eponymous **Parrot Cay** (☎941-7544; www.parrotcay.com; r/ste from US$600/1400; ❄@📶🏊).

North Caicos

POP 1700

While the North Caicos has a distinctive lost-world feel, change is coming – a number of projects are under way to make it the next Providenciales.

Sights & Activities

The Kew area has several historic ruins, including the interesting **Wades Green Plantation**, granted to a British Loyalist by King George III. The owners struggled to grow sisal and Sea Island cotton until drought, hurricanes and bugs drove them out. The plantation lasted a mere 25 years; the owners abandoned their slaves and left. It's a sobering place to visit and worth the effort.

First among many, **Pumpkin Bluff beach** is especially beautiful and the snorkeling is good, with a foundered cargo ship adding to the allure.

Sleeping & Eating

Pelican Beach Hotel Hotel $$
(☎946-7112; www.pelicanbeach.tc; r US$125-200; ⏲Nov-Aug; ❄📶) For those looking for a relaxed, back-to-basics place to stay, this is an excellent option. There is nothing fancy here; plain TV-less rooms sit in a row only a few feet from the beach. Take the half-board option as the food is excellent. Free bicycles for guests.

Whale Spotting

Some 7000 North Atlantic humpback whales use the Turks Island Passage and the Mouchoir Banks, south of Grand Turk, as their winter breeding grounds between February and March. From the beaches of Salt Cay you can watch the whales swim past, or go on a whale-watching trip from Grand Turk.

Silver Palm Restaurant & Bar Caribbean $$
(☎244-4186; Drake Ct, Whitby; mains US$10-25; ⏲8am-9pm Wed-Mon Nov-Jun) Lobster and conch are the specialties here – all of course sourced locally. Informal and friendly, small and intimate, it's located in an old tropical Victorian house.

Getting Around

Al's Rent-a-Car (☎241-1355; www.alsrentacar.com; cars per day from US$75) Essential for exploring.

Middle Caicos

If you're really looking to get away from it all, treat yourself by checking out Middle Caicos. A causeway connects North and Middle, but there are few places to stay on the island and even fewer places to eat, so a day trip is the way to visit.

There are a few tiny settlements dotted along the island; Conch Bar and Bambarra are the largest, but there still isn't much to them. **Bambarra Beach**, however, is possibly the Caribbean beach you've been dreaming about. Impossibly white sand, robin egg–blue water and not a soul around.

TURKS ISLANDS

The Turks group comprises Grand Turk and its smaller southern neighbor, Salt Cay, in addition to several tiny cays. The islands lie east of the Caicos Islands, separated from them by the 22-mile-wide Turks Island Passage.

Grand Turk

Happily lacking the modern development that has enveloped Provo, Grand Turk is a step back in time. At just 6.5 miles long, this dot amid the sea is a sparsely populated, brush-covered paradise. Cockburn Town, the main settlement, has narrow streets frequented by wild donkeys.

Beaches rim the land and calm blue water invites you in for a refreshing swim.

COCKBURN TOWN

POP 3900

You'd be hard pressed to guess that sleepy Cockburn is the capital city of the Turks and Caicos. What it lacks in polish and sophistication it more than makes up for in rustic charm.

The town undergoes a personality transformation when thousands of cruise ship passengers descend.

Beaches

A dirt road leads south to **White Sands Beach**, which is great for snorkelers, and on to lovely pine-shaded **Governor's Beach**, 1.5 miles south of town, a popular place for a picnic and a dip in the sea.

Sights & Activities

Pick up the free *Heritage Walk* pamphlets. **Front St**, which runs along the waterfront, has some magnificent buildings. South of the heart of downtown, **Duke St** narrows off to form a twisting lane of old buildings.

Turks & Caicos National Museum Museum

(946-2160; www.tcmuseum.org; Front St; admission US$7; 9am-1pm Mon-Wed, 1-5pm Thu, also open cruise-ship days) This great little museum has everything from shipwrecks to messages in bottles and crash-landed spacecraft.

Oasis Divers Water Sports

(946-1128; www.oasisdivers.com; Duke St; 2-tank dive from US$95) Runs a huge range of diving and snorkeling tours. Offers humpback-whale spotting in February and March (US$85).

Sleeping & Eating

Bohio Dive Resort & Spa Hotel $$$

(946-2135; www.bohioresort.com; Front St; r from US$210;) Boasts a prime location right on a stunning stretch of sand, excellent-value dive packages and comfortable if unadorned rooms. There are kayaks, sailboats, snorkeling gear and other extras available.

Sand Bar Cafe, Burgers $

(946-1111; Duke St; mains US$8-16; 11am-1am) This small yet lively bar is a popular hot spot with locals, expats and tourists

Port of Call – Grand Turk

Grand Turk is the port of call for most cruises coming to the Turks and Caicos Islands, thanks to a huge facility at the island's south end. On a busy day, two ships will be in port – off-loading nearly 7000 people. To escape the cruise center:

- Book a snorkeling or diving trip in the pristine waters off Grand Turk.
- In February and March join a whale-watching trip to see the magnificent migrating humpbacks.
- Wander the charming old Caribbean streets of Cockburn Town.

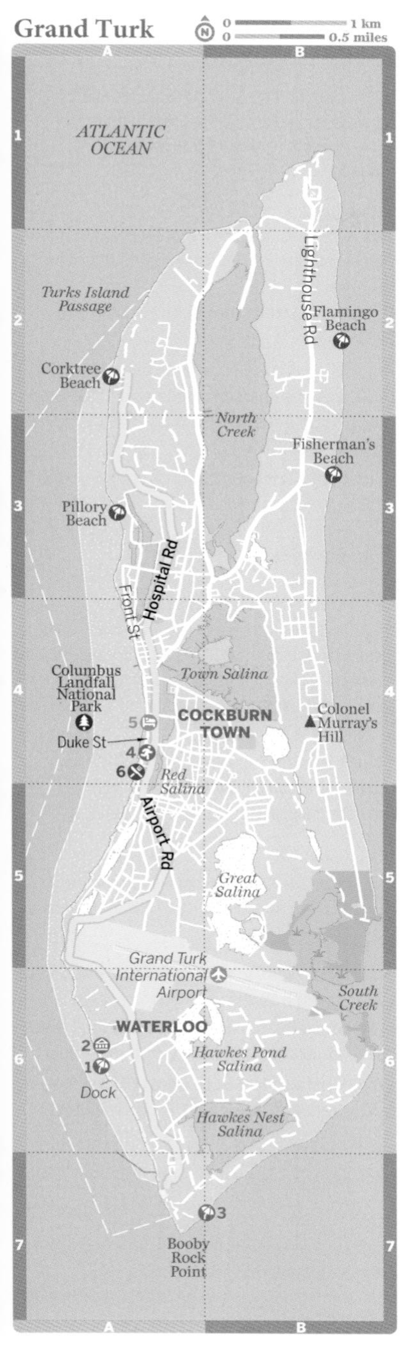

Grand Turk

Sights

1 Governor's Beach ... A6
2 Turks & Caicos National Museum ... A6
3 White Sands Beach ... B7

Activities, Courses & Tours

4 Oasis Divers ... A4

Sleeping

5 Bohio Dive Resort & Spa ... A4

Eating

6 Sand Bar ... A4

alike. The burgers are as good as the beachfront views.

Shopping

The best shopping to be found on the island is in the street stalls that open up on Duke St when the cruise ships are in port. There is a good variety of locally made goods, Haitian artwork and hand-drawn maps.

Getting There & Around

The town center is 1 mile north of the Grand Turk International Airport; a taxi ride from the airport into town costs about US$10.

SURVIVAL GUIDE

Directory A–Z

Accommodations

Accommodations in the Turks and Caicos are mostly in hotels, resorts and apartments/condos. Prices quoted are for high season.

$ US$80 to US$100

$$ US$100 to US$200

$$$ more than US$200

Food

The following price indicators are based on the cost of a main dish.

$ less than US$10

$$ US$10 to US$20

$$$ more than US$20

Practicalities

- **Electricity** 110V, 60Hz. Plug sockets are two- or three-pin US standard.
- **Time** Eastern Standard Time (GMT–5)
- **Tipping** Tip 15% in restaurants and for taxi drivers. However, check your bill, as many restaurants add a service charge automatically.
- **Weights & Measures** Imperial and metric systems are both in use.

Health

There are small hospitals on Provo and on Grand Turk. There are clinics on the smaller islands. The water is safe to drink.

Language

English is universal.

Money

- The US dollar (US$) is the official currency.
- Turks and Caicos crowns and quarters are issued for small change.
- ATMs are found in Providenciales and Grand Turk, but are less common elsewhere.

Public Holidays

In addition to those observed throughout the region, the Turks and Caicos has the following public holidays:

Commonwealth Day March 13
National Heroes' Day May 29
Her Majesty the Queen's Official Birthday June 14 (or nearest weekday)
Emancipation Day August 1
National Youth Day September 26
Columbus Day October 13
International Human Rights Day October 24

Telephone

The country code is ☎1-649.

Visas

No visas are required for citizens of the US, Canada, the UK, Commonwealth countries and most of the EU. Citizens from elsewhere require visas, which can be obtained from British representation abroad.

Getting There & Away

All visitors need a valid passport to enter the country. Proof of onward transportation is required.

Air

There are three airports handling international traffic, but nearly all international flights arrive at Provo.

Grand Turk International Airport (☎946-2233)

Providenciales International Airport (☎941-5670; www.provoairport.com) Has service from major North American hubs and the UK. Being expanded for 2015.

South Caicos International Airport (☎946-4255)

Getting Around

Air

interCaribbean Airways (☎946-4999; www.airturksandcaicos.com) Flies from Providenciales to Grand Turk and South Caicos. Expanding throughout the region, it was formerly called Air Turks & Caicos.

Caicos Express Airways (☎941-5730; www.caicosexpressairways.com) Flights from Providenciales to Grand Turk and Salt Cay.

Bicycle

The islands are flat, making bikes an excellent way to get around. Rentals average US$20 per day.

Boat

TCI Ferry Service (☎946-5406; www.tciferry.com) has two routes:

Providenciales to North Caicos Several times daily (adult/child US$25/15, 30 minutes).

Providenciales to South Caicos Three times weekly (adult/child US$60/45, 30 minutes).

Car

Driving is on the left-hand side.

Taxi

Taxis are available on all the inhabited islands. Cabs are unmetered (though pricing is consistent), so agree on a price before setting out.

Cayman Islands

HIGHLIGHTS

1. **Seven Mile Beach** (p402) The perfect venue for an upscale family vacation.
2. **Stingray City** (p408) Huge, fearless stingrays eat squid out of your hand.
3. **Queen Elizabeth II Botanic Park** (p408) Home to Cayman's huge blue iguanas.
4. **Little Cayman** (p409) A lovely, slow-paced desert isle.

USS Kittiwake (p403), Grand Cayman

What's so surprising about the three Cayman Islands (population 56,800) at first is how un-British they are for a British territory – Grand Cayman seems straight from the US, with ubiquitous SUVs jostling for space at upscale malls and US dollars changing hands as if they were the national currency. Think of it as a much more orderly version of South Florida.

But get away from the crowded commercialism of Grand Cayman's long western coastline and explore the low-key rest of the island. Or visit tiny Cayman Brac and Little Cayman, where crowds are measured in the dozens.

GRAND CAYMAN

POP 52,700

To most of the world, Grand Cayman *is* the Cayman Islands, a glitzy shopping mecca and global financial center where resorts line the fabulous white-sand Seven Mile Beach and the wealthy from around the world spend time sipping cocktails and discreetly playing with their millions. It does have another side – literally – and if you head east, you can escape the mobs.

George Town & Seven Mile Beach

POP 27,000

George Town is the supremely wealthy but surprisingly modest capital of the Cayman Islands. While no doubt cosmopolitan, it's tiny, tidy and easy to walk around.

North of the harbor and town center is Seven Mile Beach, a gorgeous stretch of unbroken white sand where Grand Cayman's tourist industry is concentrated. Most of Grand Cayman's hotels, restaurants and shopping complexes line the island's busiest thoroughfare, West Bay Rd, which travels alongside Seven Mile Beach.

Cayman Islands

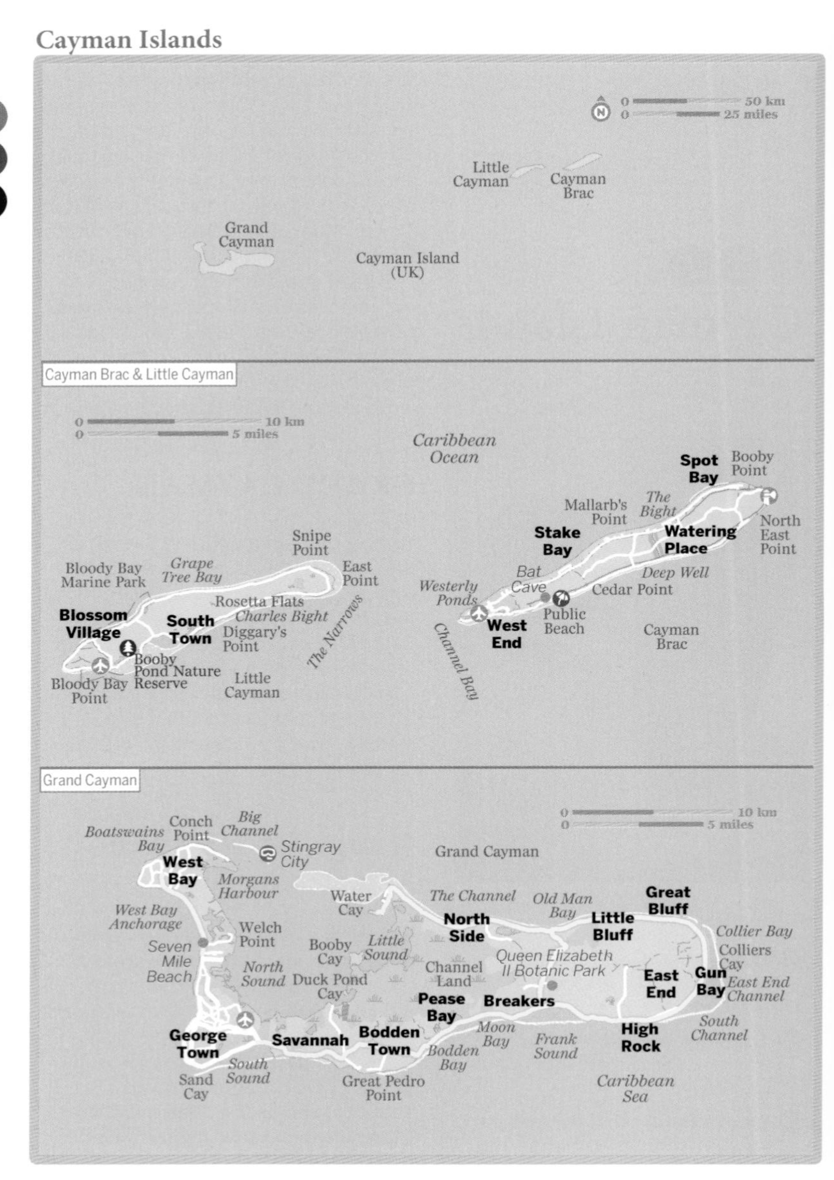

Beaches

Seven Mile Beach Beach

Although it's really only 5.5 miles long, this gorgeous strand of flawless white sand stretches north from George Town and anchors Grand Cayman's tourist industry. It's perfectly maintained, features shady trees in parts and is untrod by vendors.

Port of Call – George Town

Cruise ships anchor off George Town and tenders shuttle passengers by the thousands to and from shore.

With a few hours in port, you can avoid 'Hell' and do the following:

- Frolic on Grand Cayman's superb Seven Mile Beach.
- Pet stingrays while they eat squid directly from your hands at Stingray City.

Sights

There is nothing you can't miss in George Town – it's pleasant enough to stroll around, eat and shop in, but the sights are of minimal interest.

National Gallery of the Cayman Islands Gallery
(945-8111; www.nationalgallery.org.ky; Esterley Tibbetts Hwy; 10am-5pm Mon-Fri, 10am-3pm Sat) FREE Housed in impressive new quarters, the national collection includes contemporary Cayman and Caribbean works.

Activities

DIVING & SNORKELING

Many people coming to Grand Cayman are coming for one thing alone: the great diving. While arguably better, more-pristine sites are available on Cayman Brac and Little Cayman, the diving around Grand Cayman should not be discounted. Popular spots include the **North Wall** and **Stingray City**.

USS Kittiwake Diving
(www.cita.ky) A 76m-long former submarine tender was sunk near West Bay in 2011 and now forms an artificial reef and is a popular dive site.

Eden Rock Diving Center Diving
(949-7243; www.edenrockdive.com; 124 South Church St, George Town; guided 1-/2-tank dives US$70/110) Overlooking the George Town harbor and just three minutes from the cruise-ship tender dock, this outfit is literally above two favorite shore dive spots: Eden Rocks and Devil's Grotto. Both are also good for snorkeling.

WATER SPORTS

Seven Mile Beach has operators with every possible kind of water sports. Windsurfing and kitesurfing are possible at Barkers National Park.

Cayman Kayaks Kayaking Tours
(926-4467; www.caymankayaks.com; tours from adult/child US$30/25) Mangrove tours and nighttime bioluminescent tours, which let you see the eerily glowing water.

Tours

National Trust Culture & Nature Tours
(749-1121; www.nationaltrust.org.ky; 558 South Church St; 9am-5:30pm Mon-Fri, 9am-1pm Sat) Operates some of the most important historical and cultural sites around the island and offers guided tours and hikes.

Sleeping

Much of Seven Mile Beach is covered in condos, hotels and sprawling resorts. Grand Cayman caters to higher-end tourism and places to stay are mostly top end with full services and plenty of family-friendly amenities.

Sunshine Suites Hotel **$$**
(949-3000; www.sunshinesuites.com; 1465 Esterley Tibbetts Hwy, Seven Mile Beach; r from

George Town

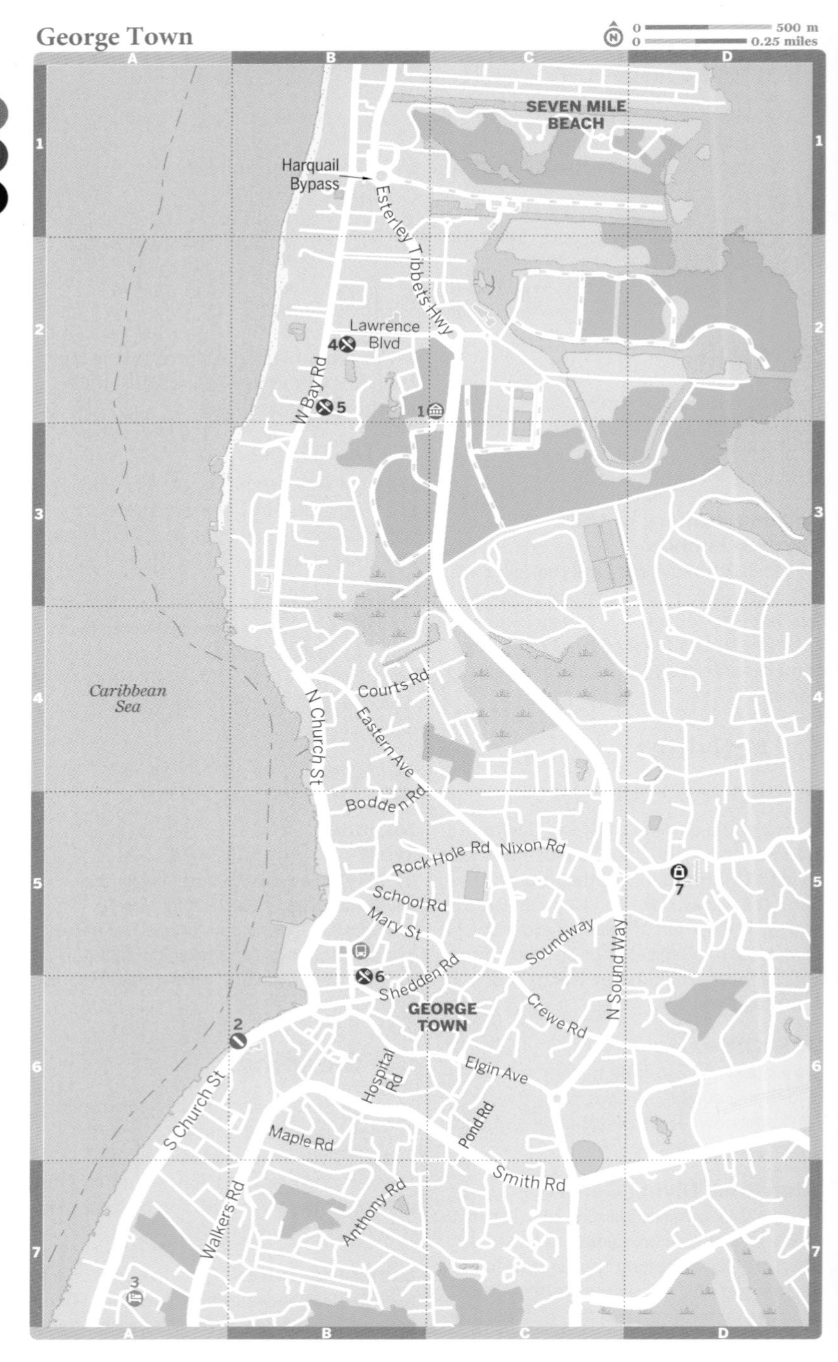
0 500 m
0 0.25 miles
A
B
C
D
1
2
3
4
5
6
7
SEVEN MILE BEACH
Harquail Bypass
Esterley Tibbets Hwy
Lawrence Blvd
W Bay Rd
Caribbean Sea
Courts Rd
N Church St
Eastern Ave
Bodden Rd
Rock Hole Rd
Nixon Rd
School Rd
Mary St
Soundway
N Sound Way
Shedden Rd
GEORGE TOWN
Crewe Rd
Hospital Rd
Elgin Ave
S Church St
Maple Rd
Pond Rd
Smith Rd
Walkers Rd
Anthony Rd
1
2
3
4
5
6
7

CAYMAN ISLANDS

US$170; ❄@📶🏊) This well-run complex of 132 studios and apartments is like a condo with hotel services. Because it's a five-minute walk from the beach, rates are lower. Each unit is equipped with a full kitchen; a small pool lures you in for a dip.

Eldemire's Tropical Island Inn B&B $$
(☎916-8369; www.eldemire.com; Glen Eden Rd, George Town; r from US$140, 1-/2-bedroom ste from US$180/270; ❄@📶🏊) This guesthouse has a large range of accommodations, from very basic rooms for seasonal workers to spacious suites. Suites have kitchens while other guests share a well-equipped common kitchen. There are laundry facilities and bike rentals.

Ritz-Carlton Grand Cayman Resort $$$
(☎943-9000; www.ritzcarlton.com; West Bay Rd, Seven Mile Beach; r from US$350; ❄@📶🏊) The pick of the large resorts is this vast 365-room property located on both sides of West Bay Rd. It's a bit on the gaudy side but despite this, it's undeniably a great place to stay, with two stunning pools, a beautiful stretch of beach, a spa, a private nine-hole golf course and more, including a delicious breakfast buffet.

Discovery Point Club Apartment $$$
(☎945-4724; www.discoverypointclub.com; West Bay Rd, Seven Mile Beach; r from US$260, 1-/2-bedroom ste from US$540/585; ❄@📶🏊) This excellent condo complex is recommended for a comfortable family beach holiday. At the far north end of Seven Mile Beach (in front of a good snorkeling area), all the suites have superb views, balconies or patios and kitchens. The simple rooms are basic.

George Town

Sights
1 National Gallery of the Cayman Islands C2

Activities, Courses & Tours
2 Eden Rock Diving Center B6

Sleeping
3 Eldemire's Tropical Island Inn A7

Eating
4 Cimboco B2
5 Coconut Joe's B2
6 Corita's Copper Kettle B6

Shopping
7 Tortuga Rum Co D5

Blue Iguanas

At up to 1m in length and often with a brilliant azure hide, Grand Cayman's blue iguanas are a moving spectacle that never ceases to amaze. Yet as recently as 2002 there were fewer than a dozen left in the wild. Now their numbers are resurgent thanks to the Blue Iguana Recovery Program, which breeds iguanas and protects habitat. The latest census puts the wild population at 750.

Eating & Drinking

Grand Cayman's dining choices are myriad: from stylish restaurants to simpler cafes producing excellent fresh meals. Don't expect wild nightlife; bars close by 1am, except on Saturday night when they close at midnight!

Corita's Copper Kettle Caribbean $
(☎949-7078; Edward St; meals CI$7-10; ⏰7am-3pm Mon-Sat) This old wooden house right in George Town is home to a fine decades-old Caribbean cafe. The Jamaican-accented fare is hearty, the breakfast sandwich on homemade bread a winner.

Cimboco Bistro $$
(☎947-2782; www.cimboco.com; Marquee Plaza; mains from CI$12; ⏰7:30am-10pm) Always busy, this all-day bistro has a showy open kitchen and a breezy charm. Food emphasizes fresh flavors with an Italian accent (but the breakfast hash has many fans).

Grand Cayman

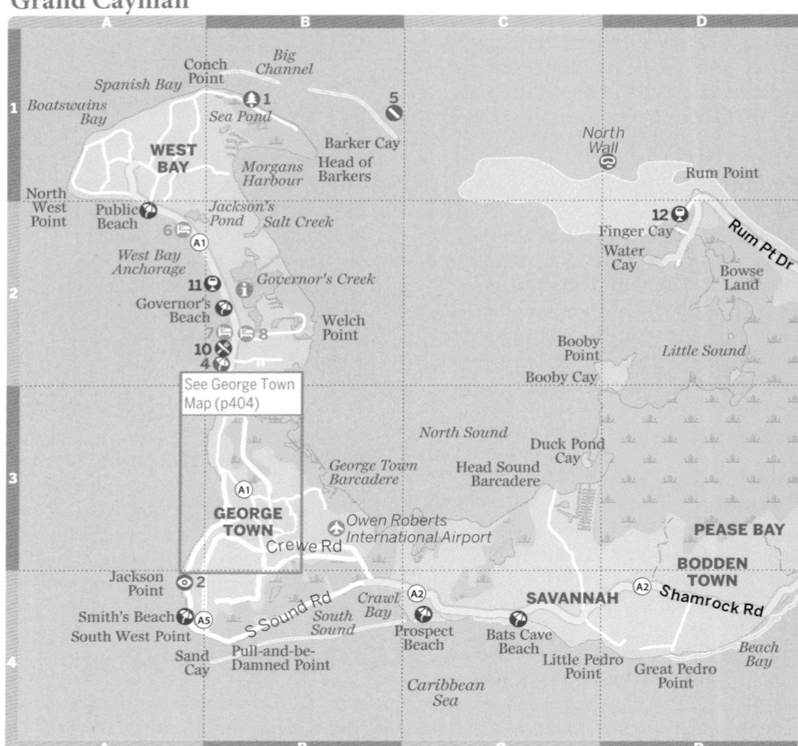

Grand Cayman

Sights

1	Barkers National Park	B1
2	National Trust	A4
3	Queen Elizabeth II Botanic Park	F3
4	Seven Mile Beach	B2

Activities, Courses & Tours

5	Stingray City	B1

Sleeping

6	Discovery Point Club	A2
7	Ritz-Carlton Grand Cayman	B2
8	Sunshine Suites	B2

Eating

9	Chester's Fish Fry	E3
10	Luca	B2

Drinking & Nightlife

11	Tiki Beach	B2
12	Wreck Bar	D2

Coconut Joe's — Cafe $$

(362 West Bay Rd; meals US$8-16; noon-midnight) Dine and drink under a huge poinsettia tree at this casual joint on the east side of the road. Most tables are outside on the terrace and things get lively as the evening progresses. Fish tacos, burgers, salads and more go well with the many beers on tap.

Luca — Italian $$

(623-4550; Caribbean Club, West Bay Rd, Seven Mile Beach; lunch mains from CI$12, dinner mains from CI$25; 10:30am-2:30pm Mon-Fri, 5:30-10pm daily, 11:30am-2pm Sun) Minimalist decor means there's nothing to detract from the sweeping beach views here, except maybe the food. Italian-accented meals include a range of fresh seafood, steaks and pasta.

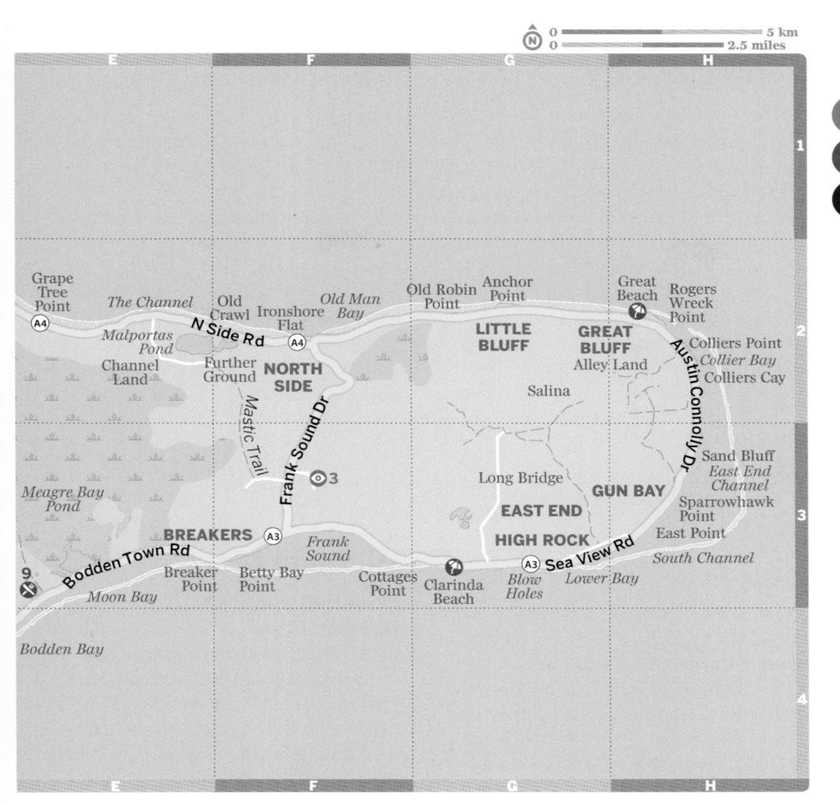

Tiki Beach Cocktail Bar

(☎743-6616; www.tikibeachcayman.net; West Bay Rd; ⏰11am-10pm) Part water-sports center (you can rent snorkel gear), part cafe (it sells sandwiches etc) and full-on bar. The beachside tables have great sunset views and the mixed drink list is long.

Shopping

At the malls clustered around the waterfront, you can buy the usual cruise-ship-port consumer goods such as watches, jewelry and more watches.

Tortuga Rum Co Food

(North Sound Way, George Town; ⏰10am-5pm Mon-Fri) Some 10,000 addictive rum cakes are made here daily. Sure, you can buy them all over the island – and the region – but those at the factory are freshest and the samples the most generous.

Getting There & Around

Bus

The public bus terminal **(Edward St)** serves as the dispatch point for buses to all districts of Grand Cayman.

Taxi

Sample taxi fares from the airport:

- George Town, Southern Seven Mile Beach US$20
- Northern Seven Mile Beach US$40

Stingray City

This stretch of sandy seafloor in Grand Cayman's North Sound is the meeting place for southern stingrays hungry for a meal, and the island's top attraction. As soon as you enter the water, several of the beautiful prehistoric-looking creatures will glide over for some squid.

Studies have shown that the stingrays here have both unusual growth (since they have an unbalanced diet of mostly squid) and have oddball schedules (normally they are nocturnal).

At the simplest, you catch a boat from somewhere along Seven Mile Beach and motor to Stingray City. Tours generally include snorkeling gear and stops, which you don't need for the stingrays but which are useful for exploring deeper areas of North Sound and the North Wall. Three-hour trips start at US$40; operators abound and the offerings are pretty standardized, especially at the 'feed, stroke and go home' level. To avoid the crowds, visit on Sundays (when cruise ships don't dock).

West Bay

North of George Town, West Bay is quietly suburban, and home to the remotely alluring **Barkers National Park** – the first national park in Cayman. Barkers National Park combines low scrub, long sandy beaches and mangroves. Stingray City is 3km east offshore. Heavily promoted trips to **Hell** are really stops in a gift shop parking lot.

Bodden Town

Historic Bodden Town was the capital of the Cayman Islands until George Town scooped that honor in the mid-19th century. It's far removed from the bustle of the west in feel – if not distance – and is a worthy stop for a stroll on any round-island tour. Grab lunch at **Chester's Fish Fry** (563 Bodden Town Rd; mains CI$8-12; 10am-10pm), which has treats grilling all day long.

North Side

The North Side is windswept and uncrowded, providing a direct link to Grand Cayman's past. The drive along the north coast is a highlight.

Sights

Queen Elizabeth II Botanic Park Gardens

(947-9462; www.botanic-park.ky; Frank Sound Dr; adult/child US$10/free; 9am-5:30pm) A veritable treasure trove of the island's native species. The park is home to orchids (in bloom late May through June), parrots and other birds, and nature trails.

The real star here (or should we say stars?) is the **Blue Iguana Recovery Program** (www.blueiguana.ky; tours adult/child incl garden admission US$30/20; tours 11am Mon-Sat), which offers tours of the breeding pens and other areas where the iguanas are encouraged to do what iguanas do.

Rum Point

Swinging in hammocks and snorkeling are the main activities at this quiet **beach**, which draws fans from all over the island. Take some time to explore the trails along the reef-protected shore and mangroves, then enjoy a beachside burger at the fun-filled **Wreck Bar** (Rum Point; meals US$9-20; 10am-5pm Mon-Sat, 10am-6pm Sun).

East End

The East End is the place to head if you want a feel for traditional Caymanian life and don't have the time to visit the sister islands. Here, open space, quiet hamlets and dramatic shoreline are the main features.

LITTLE CAYMAN

POP 170

Tiny Little Cayman (the clue is indeed in the name) is a joy. With more resident iguanas than humans, this delightful island is the place to head for solitude, tranquility and the odd spot of extraordinary diving.

Sights

The sights of Little Cayman are almost entirely natural, whether they be the birds that nest in the wetlands, the iguanas that bask by the road or the marine life on the reef.

Sandy Point Beach

Little Cayman's best beach is a splotch of reef-protected powder that rarely has more than half a dozen people visiting at any one time. There's a tiny pier, limited shade and breaking waves 220yd out.

Activities

Little Cayman has over 60 dive sites marked with moorings. Snorkelers and shore divers find plenty of satisfaction at many well-known sites.

The hotels have diving operations.

Bloody Bay Marine Park Diving

Near the shore and at a depth of only 18ft, **Bloody Bay Wall** plummets vertically into aquamarine infinity as the divers hovering over the abyss wonder whether they are hallucinating.

Jackson's Point Snorkeling

The perfect stop on a round-island bike ride is this series of underwater spots along a mini-wall just 54yd from the narrow strip of rocky sand on the shore.

Sleeping & Eating

For such a small island there's no shortage of low-key resorts here. Most offer favorable diving packages when booked in advance. Most prefer to take week-long bookings.

Paradise Villas Guesthouse **$$**

(948-0001; www.paradisevillas.com; Blossom Village; r from US$185;) You can practically step off the airplane and into your room here (it's a 100yd walk) – but these 12 smart and comfortable cottages are right on the beach and are idyllic with verandas and hammocks coming as standard.

Pirates Point Resort Resort **$$$**

(948-1010; www.piratespointresort.com; Guy Banks Rd; all-inclusive r per person from US$245;) Run by the legendary Gladys Howard, this rustic resort is fantastically located on a pretty beach. There are 11

Cayman Turtle Farm

The heavily marketed **Cayman Turtle Farm** is not the tourist attraction it seems. It's primarily a place where endangered sea turtles are raised to be slaughtered for meat (a practice that has drawn criticism from groups such as the World Society for the Protection of Animals). You'll see them in huge tanks hidden behind fences. In the public area, visitors are encouraged to hold baby turtles, which flap their flippers trying to get back in the water. When we visited it was anything but a Disney-esque experience: there was a dearth of docents with info, signage was skimpy at best and security guards shouted at guests. We can't recommend it.

rooms, all different and strikingly individual, with mosquito nets, large bathrooms and plenty of books to read. The food is excellent; nonguests can book for dinner.

Information

Everything, including an ATM, is clustered in tiny South Town, close to the airport.

Getting There & Around

Tiny **Edward Bodden Airfield** is a short walk from town.

Places to stay can arrange for car rental. Scooten Scooters (**916-4971; www.scootenscooters.com; half-day from US$32; Nov-Jun)** delivers to the airport. Most places loan guests bicycles, the preferred means of local travel. You can circle the island in a few hours.

CAYMAN BRAC

POP 1900

Named after the 'brac' or 'bluff' that makes up much of this cheese wedge of an island, the most easterly of the Cayman Islands is markedly different from both Grand and Little Cayman. The simple reason is that, unlike their cousins, the majority of locals do not work in the tourism industry and life here goes on much as it always has. Come here for a visit for low-key diving, maybe a hike along the Brac and little else.

That's Cayman, Bub

If there's one thing that gets the dander up of locals (in a polite way of course), it's hearing their nation referred to as 'the Caymans.' Don't ask why: they don't know any more than a resident of San Francisco who shudders at hearing 'Frisco' – it's nails on a chalkboard. Preferred terms for the entire country are 'Cayman,' or 'Cayman Islands.' Individual islands are called by their correct names.

Getting There & Around

Flights land at **Gerrard Smith International Airport**. CB Rent-A-Car (**948-2329; www.cbrentacar.com; Gerrard Smith International Airport; 8am-6pm)** has good rates.

SURVIVAL GUIDE

Directory A–Z

Accommodations

Accommodations aren't cheap in Cayman, but are usually of high standard.

Rates quoted are for walk-ins during the high season (mid-December through mid-April) and do not include the 10% government tax and 10% to 15% service tax. Many places will also expect a gratuity for staff.

$ less than US$75

$$ US$75 to US$200

$$$ more than US$200

Food

The following price categories are for the cost of a main course.

$ less than US$10

$$ US$10 to US$25

$$$ more than US$25

Health

There are excellent medical facilities in the Cayman Islands. Tap water is safe to drink.

Language

English is the official language.

Money

- The official currency is the Cayman Islands dollar (CI$), permanently fixed at an exchange rate of CI$0.80 to US$1 (CI$1 equals US$1.25).
- US dollars also accepted.
- Change is given in CI$.

Public Holidays

In addition to those observed throughout the region, Cayman has the following public holidays:

National Heroes' Day Fourth Monday in January

Ash Wednesday Late February

Discovery Day Third Monday in May

Queen's Birthday Second Monday in June

Constitution Day First Monday in July

Remembrance Day Second Monday in November

Telephone

Dial ☎1-345 to reach any number in the Cayman Islands from abroad.

Visas

Not required for citizens of the US, Canada and most European and Commonwealth countries (except Jamaica).

Getting There & Away

Entering the Cayman Islands

All visitors are required to have a valid passport and a return ticket.

Air

Owen Roberts International Airport (**GCM; www.caymanairports.ky**) has flights from North America and the UK.

Getting Around

Air

Each island has an airport.

Cayman Airways Express (**www.caymanairways.com**), a subsidiary of Cayman Airways, provides near-monopoly service between the three islands.

Practicalities

- **Electricity** 110V, 60Hz; US-style two- and three-pin plugs are used.
- **Time** Eastern Standard Time (GMT–5)
- **Tipping** A 10% to 15% tip is the norm in restaurants and taxis. In hotels, 10% is usually added to the bill.
- **Weights & Measures** Imperial system.

Bicycle

Bikes are readily available on all three islands and are often included as part of an accommodations package. Flat terrain, relatively light traffic and near-constant sea access make cycling a pleasure.

Bus

Public minibuses operate across Grand Cayman. Routes radiate out from the bus depot on Edward St in George Town. Service is during daytime. Fares range from CI$2 to CI$3.50.

Car & Motorcycle

- Visitors must obtain a temporary driver's license from their car-rental agency (CI$16).
- Driving is on the left-hand side.

Montserrat

HIGHLIGHTS

1. **Rendezvous Bay** (p412) Montserrat's only white-sand beach
2. **Garibaldi Hill** (p414) Great viewpoint for grasping the extent of volcanic destruction
3. **Oriole Walkway** (p414) An easy walk perfect for birders and nature lovers
4. **National Museum of Montserrat** (p414) An insightful introduction to the island

Soufrière Hills Volcano

Before its lower half became devastated by cataclysmic eruptions of the Soufrière Hills Volcano in 1995, Montserrat was a carefree little island paradise famous as the birthplace of the late Alphonsus Cassell, creator of the soca hit 'Hot, Hot, Hot,' and as the home of Air Montserrat, the famous recording studio founded by Beatles producer Sir George Martin. Sting and Eric Clapton were among the stars who recorded here.

Life changed dramatically on 18 July 1995 when a series of ash falls, pyroclastic flows and mud flows buried the capital, Plymouth, and smaller settlements, farmland and forests. Around 11,000 residents were evacuated and resettled in the north or emigrated to Britain. Today, most tourists come for volcano-related day trips. Driving down the coast, you quickly get a feel for the island's rich tropical life and take in jaw-dropping vistas of the destruction.

The volcano is always a wild card, but by and large, traveling to Montserrat is safe. The island is divided into a Daytime Entry Zone, an Exclusion Zone and a Safe Zone in the north where a new capital is slowly taking shape in Little Bay.

Beaches

Rendezvous Bay Beach

Montserrat's only white sandy beach is a lovely (though facility-free), secluded crescent perfect for swimming, snorkeling and diving. It can only be accessed via a steep 0.7-mile trail from Little Bay or by boat shuttle (one way/round-trip US$15/25) operated by Scuba Montserrat, also based in Little Bay. It also rents kayaks and snorkeling gear.

Sights

Montserrat Volcano Observatory Museum

(MVO; ☎491-5647; www.mvo.ms; adult/child EC$10/free; ⏰10am-3:15pm Mon-Thu)
Scientists at the MVO keep track of the volcano's every belch and hiccup. At the interpretation center, an 18-minute documentary includes riveting live

Montserrat

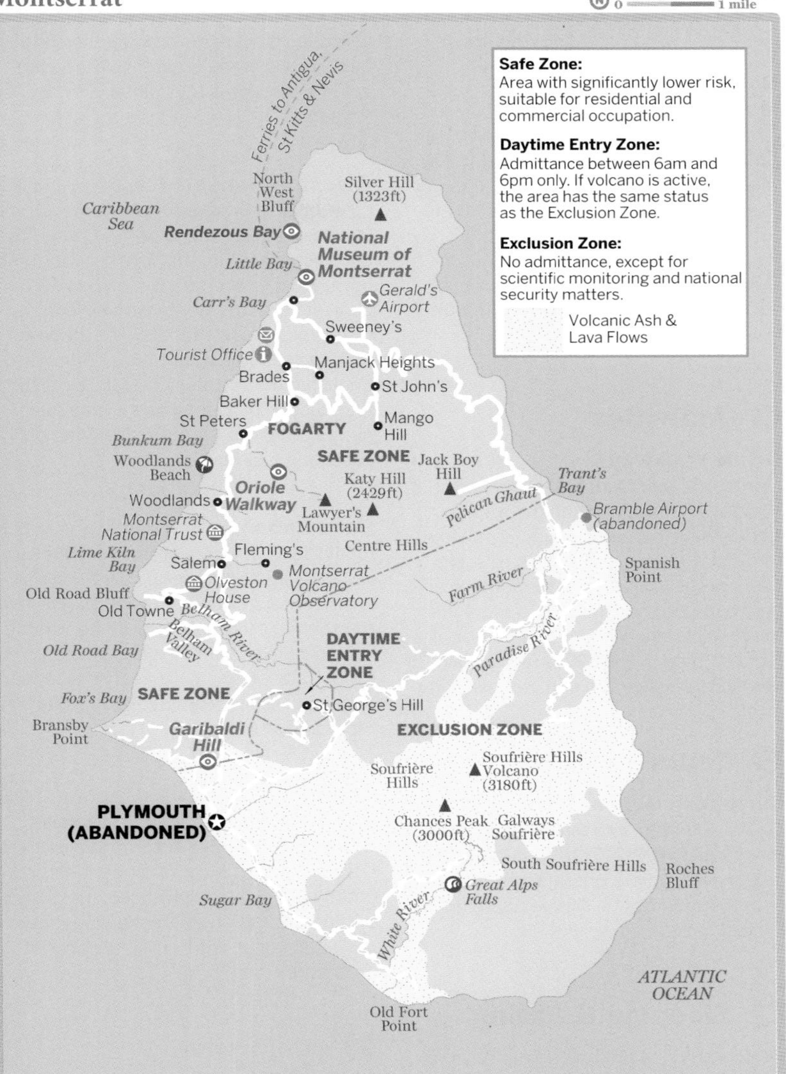

footage of the eruptions and insight into the physical and social upheaval they caused. The terrace offers sweeping views of the volcano, Belham Valley and Plymouth.

Belham Valley Landmark

Now buried under volcanic debris, Belham Valley used to be home to an 18-hole golf course and a three-story building of which only the top floors are still visible. In dry weather it's possible to cross the valley in a 4WD and follow an extremely rough road up **Garibaldi Hill** for sweeping views over what's left of Plymouth.

National Museum of Montserrat Museum
(491-3086; www.montserratnationaltrust.ms; Little Bay; adult/under 12yr EC$5/free; 10am-2pm Mon-Fri) In its new home in Little Bay, the Montserrat National Trust presents exhibits on aspects of island culture and history from Amerindian times to the present. A highlight are the photos and dioramas illustrating pre-eruption Plymouth.

Activities

Oriole Walkway Hiking
Montserrat's most popular hiking trail cuts for 1.3 miles through the tropical Centre Hills to the top of Lawyer's Mountain, from where you'll have bird's-eye views of the island. The tourist office has maps and booklets. For a more in-depth experience, hire local guide James 'Scriber' Daley (492-2943; www.scribersadventures.com) for this and other walking tours.

Tours

Caribbean Helicopters Flights
(268-460-5900; www.caribbeanhelicopters.com; per person US$240) Antigua-based Caribbean Helicopters operates 45-minute flyovers of Soufrière Hills Volcano and the Exclusion Zone.

Sleeping & Eating

Restaurants are few and dinner reservations are recommended.

Gingerbread Hill Guesthouse $$
(491-5812; www.volcano-island.com; St Peters; d US$45-125;) No matter your budget, Clover and David have a bed with your name on it. Choose from the Backpacker Room with outdoor kitchen, the solar-paneled Eco Cottage or the two large and breezy upstairs apartments with stunning ocean views, spacious verandas, full kitchens and ultra-comfy beds. David is the creator of the seven-volume volcano documentary *Pride of Paradise*.

Olveston House Guesthouse $$
(491-5210; www.olvestonhouse.com; Olveston; r US$109-119;) Owned by Sir George Martin, this former wooden home on a former plantation has six charming rooms, some with air-con, others with porch access. The all-day restaurant serves Caribbean-infused English cuisine (mains EC$18 to EC$55). Wednesday barbecue and Friday pub nights are great for eavesdropping on gossiping islanders.

Soca Cabana Caribbean $$
(493-1820; www.socacabana.com; Little Bay; mains EC$30-40; 8am-4pm Sun-Thu, dinner by reservation & 8am-late Fri & Sat) Dance in the sand at this classic beach bar which serves delicious lunches and gets packed for Saturday night karaoke. The wooden bar was rescued from Sir George Martin's recording studio.

Tina's Caribbean $$
(491-3538; Brades Main Rd, Brades; mains lunch EC$25, dinner EC$25-65; 8am-midnight) Locals often pack Tina's air-conditioned cottage, washing down succulent lobster burgers with her homemade ginger beer and finishing up with a slice of coconut cream pie.

Information

The hillside village of Brades has a few small shops, government offices, the post office, a library, a pharmacy and an ATM. Pick up maps and brochures at the **Montserrat Tourist Board** (491-2230; www.visitmontserrat.com; 7 Farara Plaza, Brades; 8am-4pm Mon-Fri) and at the airport.

SURVIVAL GUIDE

Directory A–Z

Accommodations

Rates listed apply to the peak season (December to April) for a double room with private bathroom.

$ less than US$75

$$ US$75 to US$150

$$$ more than US$150

Food

The following price ranges refer to the average cost of one main course. Most places add a 10% service charge.

$ less than EC$30

$$ EC$30 to EC$60

$$$ more than EC$60

Money

Montserrat uses the East Caribbean dollar (EC$) but US dollars are widely accepted.

Public Holidays

In addition to holidays observed throughout the region, Montserrat celebrates the following:

St Patrick's Day March 17

Labor Day May 1

Queen's Birthday First, second or third weekend June

Emancipation Day August 1

Telephone

Montserrat's country code is ☎664.

Getting There & Away

The departure tax for stays over 24 hours is EC$55 or US$21 – cash only.

Air

Tiny Gerald's Airport **(MNI; ☎491-2533)** is served several times daily from Antigua by Fly Montserrat **(☎491-3434; www.flymontserrat.com)** and ABM/SVG Airline **(☎491-4200; www.montserrat-flights.com)**. High winds may delay service for hours or days.

Boat

The on-and-off-again ferry service from Antigua (90 minutes, adult/child round-trip EC$300/150) was on again at the time of writing, as was a weekly ferry from St Kitts & Nevis. Check www.visitmontserrat.com for the latest schedule.

Getting Around

Bus

Minibuses ply the main road in the daytime from Monday to Saturday. There is no schedule and no official stops, so just hail one as it passes.

Car

Unless you're staying for several days, it's easier to hire a car and driver, which should cost no more than US$25 per hour for all passengers. Check www.visitmontserrat.com for a full list of drivers, as well as for car rental agencies should you prefer your own wheels. A compulsory local driver's license (EC$50) can be obtained at the airport, ferry port or the police station in Brades.

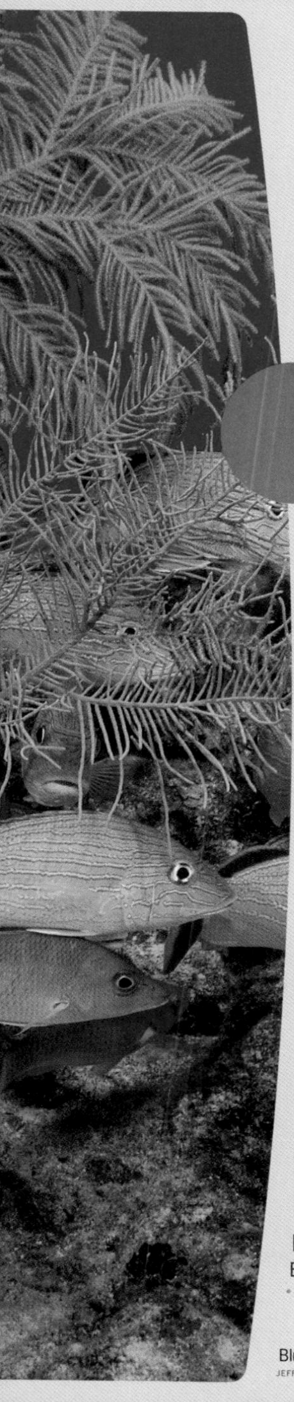

Caribbean Islands In Focus

Blue-striped grunt on a Caribbean reef
JEFF HUNTER/GETTY IMAGES ©

Caribbean Islands Today

“A movement to demand reparations has become official.”

belief systems
(% of population)

if the Caribbean Islands were 100 people

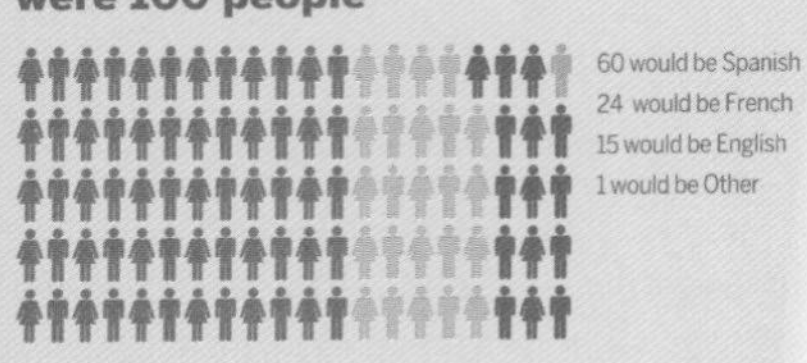

population per sq km

Hawksbill turtle, Turks & Caicos

Reparations

Slavery continues to be an issue in the Caribbean, even though some would think it's a topic that's been relegated to history books. Instead, a movement to demand reparations from countries that got wealthy on the backs of slaves has become official. At a meeting in St Vincent in 2014, leaders from across the region formally agreed to make a legal case to demand compensation.

Although the last slaves were freed in the 19th century, a large portion of the Caribbean's population is descended from slaves. Estimates are fuzzy, but at slavery's peak in the early 1800s, it's thought that the British islands had 2.3 million slaves, the Spanish islands 1.3 million, the French islands 1.1 million and the Dutch islands about 450,000.

Among the arguments for compensation from the current governments of these former colonial outposts is that the ill-effects of slavery (eg bad economic conditions and chronic health conditions) cross generations. Obviously

JEFF HUNTER/GETTY IMAGES ©

the claims – and their size – will be hugely controversial, but with Caribbean leaders agreeing to pursue the money it's bound to stay in the news. And it's noted that Britain set a precedent back when slavery was banned: it paid slave owners for their economic losses.

Economic Woes

Even as other world economies showed signs of recovery after the Global Financial Crisis, the countries of the Caribbean remained in economic doldrums thanks to reduced tourism caused by fiscal problems elsewhere and the countries' own endemic economic weaknesses. In a sign of the problem's depth, once-strong Barbados had to lay off a huge number of government workers. Puerto Rica flirted with bankruptcy as government bondholders scrambled to avoid a debacle like Detroit. Meanwhile, Jamaica barely managed to reach an agreement with the International Monetary Fund for continued economic aid.

The roots of the Caribbean's economic malaise are many, but economists point to the long-term consequences of the independence movement that swept the region over the past few decades. The cost of statehood is hard to spread across an island's small population.

And it's into this sea of red ink that world powers have sailed. All those tiny Caribbean nations add up to a lot of votes in the UN. Taiwan has long sent money to the region, as seen in projects like the new airport on St Vincent. China continues to come on strong, with a huge new stadium for Grenada, factories in Jamaica and much more. Where the US, with its own fiscal austerity issues, fits in to these happenings in its backyard remains to be seen.

Environmental Concerns

The Caribbean's economic problems and desire for foreign investment mean that environmental concerns get short shrift. Besides the long-term uncertainty caused by rising sea levels due to climate change, there are the immediate changes brought on by development. Recent studies have shown that numerous species of sea creatures in the region are in sharp decline, and the stress to coral reefs is immense. The irony is that even as tourists flock to the region for its often jaw-dropping natural beauty, the island governments work against conservation. The hope is that the critical role tourism plays in local economies will help propel efforts to preserve all that is wonderful about the Caribbean. Local initiatives, such as efforts to clean up Puerto Rico's waters, show that progress is possible.

History

The fort of El Morro (p114), Old San Juan

BOB INGELHART/GETTY IMA

Murder, mayhem and bananas. The history of the Caribbean includes every kind of drama – from warring colonial powers to marauding pirates. The stain of slavery is everlasting and almost every aspect of life in the region today is a direct consequence of events through the centuries. Of course where it was once a horrible playground for the ambitious, now it's simply a playground, a definite improvement.

Ahoy Arawaks

The first Caribbeans arrived on the islands closest to South America around 4000 BC. These nomadic hunter-gatherers were followed by waves of Arawaks (a collective term for the Amerindian people believed to be from the Orinoco River Delta around Venezuela and Guyana) who moved north and west, beginning the great tradition of Caribbean island-hopping. Indeed, one of the

1493

Columbus returns on his second voyage, sighting and naming much of the Eastern Caribbean.

Caribbean's recurrent themes, from pre-Columbian times until right now, has been movement of peoples.

Around AD 1200 the peaceable Arawaks were minding their own business when the Caribs from South America started fanning out over the Caribbean. The Caribs killed the Arawak men and enslaved the women, triggering another wave of migration that sent the Arawaks fleeing as far west as Cuba and as far north as the Bahamas. When the Spanish explorers arrived, they dubbed the warfaring people they encountered 'cannibals' (a derivation of the word 'caribal' or Carib), for their reputed penchant for eating their victims. Since the Arawaks had no written language, little of their culture survived, except – thankfully for weary travelers – the hammock.

While many traces of the Caribbean's first people, the Arawaks, were gone at the end of the 15th century, there were still Arawak-speaking people living in regions the Caribs had not yet conquered. These included the Taino, the people whom Columbus first encountered and whose legacy lives on today in Puerto Rico.

And while the Arawak people were mostly gone, their way of life persisted, adopted by new arrivals, whether colonists or slaves. Crops and foods including tobacco, cotton, corn, sweet potatoes, pineapples, cassava (also called manioc or yucca) and tapioca are still island staples today.

Ahoy Columbus

Christopher Columbus led the European exploration of the region, making landfall at San Salvador in the Bahamas on October 12, 1492 – no matter that he thought he was in Asia. He too island-hopped, establishing the first European settlement in the Americas on Hispaniola, today shared by the Dominican Republic and Haiti. Columbus never fully realized that he hadn't discovered islands off the coast of east Asia (a misconception that lives on when an indigenous person is called an 'Indian'). But in his voyages, he did get around. On his first voyage (1492–93) he visited Hispaniola, Cuba and the Bahamas; on his second voyage (1493–94) he made it to much of the Eastern Caribbean starting with Dominica. He took hundreds of slaves, most of whom died before reaching Spain. His third voyage (1498) took him to Trinidad followed by Tobago and Grenada (which he considered part of China), and on his fourth voyage, after revisiting many islands, he ended up stranded in Jamaica for a year.

Discovering new lands gives glory, but what Columbus and subsequent explorers wanted was gold. Legions of Europeans prowled the Caribbean searching for treasure, but it turned out be much further west in Mexico.

That's not to say there weren't riches: the land was fertile, the seas bountiful and the native population, after initial resistance by the toughest of the remaining Caribs, forcibly pliant. The conquistadores set to exploiting it all, violently. Focusing on the

1595
By 1595 the famous English privateers Sir Francis Drake and Jack Hawkins were using the Virgin Islands as a staging ground for attacks on Spanish shipping.

1651
Mass suicide by Caribs in Grenada who preferred to jump off a cliff than be subjugated by the Spanish.

1685
The French Code Noire gives slaves legal protection from murder but also allows for floggings.

Slavery: Life & Legacies

Upon arrival in the Caribbean, slaves were marched to an auction block, exhibited and sold to the highest bidder. On the British and Dutch islands, families were deliberately broken up. Slaves were forced to learn the language of the plantation owners, but they blended their own use of it into a hybrid Creole language that was liberally spiced with African terms. To this day, islanders throughout the Caribbean still slip into Creole. Much West Indian music takes its roots from a spirit of rebellion – most prominent is calypso, a sharp, raplike music that was developed by slaves poking fun at their masters.

biggest islands promising the highest returns, they grabbed land, pillaged and enslaved, settling towns in Cuba, the Dominican Republic, Puerto Rico and Jamaica.

Except for mineral-rich Trinidad, taken early by the Spanish, the Eastern Caribbean was left largely to its own devices until the English washed up on St Kitts in 1623, sparking domino-effect colonization of Barbados, Nevis, Antigua and Montserrat. Not to be outdone, the French followed, settling Martinique and Guadeloupe, while the Dutch laid claim to Saba, Sint Eustatius and St-Martin/Sint Maarten. Over the next 200 years the Europeans fought like children over these islands, and possession changed hands so often that a sort of hybridized culture developed; some islands, like St-Martin/Sint Maarten and St Kitts, were split between two colonial powers.

Origins of Slavery

The Atlantic slave trade had a scale so overwhelming that it depopulated vast tracts of western Africa. From its origins, starting with Portuguese and Spanish colonists in the 1500s, to the final abolition on Cuba in 1886, an estimated 10 million enslaved African people were brought to the Americas.

For the British, who held about 2.3 million slaves, the trade was a lucrative triangular route. Ships sailed from English ports with trinkets and muskets to barter for slaves in Africa. Once the slaves were delivered to the New World, the ships were loaded with sugar, molasses and rum for the journey back to England.

Pirates & War

The Caribbean colonial story is largely one of giant agricultural interests – most notably sugar, but also tobacco, cattle and bananas – fueled by greed and slavery that promoted power struggles between landowners, politicians and the pirates who robbed them. The Bahamas, with hundreds of cays, complex shoals and channels, provided

1776
Sint Eustatius honors an American rebel warship, thus making the Netherlands the first to recognize the US.

1780
A hurricane kills 22,000 from Barbados to St Lucia.

1805
Beaten by the British in Dominica, the French burn Roseau to the ground and flee.

the perfect base for pirates such as Henry Jennings and 'Blackbeard' (Edward Teach), who ambushed treasure-laden boats headed for Europe. On the home front, Britain, Spain and France were embroiled in tiffs, scuffles and all-out war that allowed colonial holdings to change hands frequently. The English took Jamaica in 1655 and held Cuba momentarily in 1762, while the Spanish and French agreed to divide Hispaniola in 1731, creating the Dominican Republic and Haiti of today. The legacies of this period – Santo Domingo's Fortaleza Ozama, the fortresses of Old San Juan and the vibrant mix of cultures – are among the most captivating attractions for travelers.

Loosening Colonial Ties

Except for the Eastern Caribbean, which has historically been more laid-back and easily controlled by its European overseers, colonial infighting had locals plotting rebellion and independence. Haiti was way in front of the curve in declaring independence in 1804, followed by the Dominican Republic in 1844 and Cuba in 1902.

Some islands have opted to maintain strong neo-colonial ties to the parent country, as is the case with the French protectorates of St-Barthélemy, Martinique

Canon protecting the St John's harbour (p186), Antigua

1815
The Treaty of Vienna restores Guadeloupe and Martinique to France.

1834
Britain abolishes slavery throughout its empire; the Dutch follow suit in 1863.

1878
Sweden gives Saint Barthélemy to France, ending its little-remembered colonial ambitions in the Caribbean.

The Best... Forts & Ruins

1 Old San Juan (p114)

2 Brimstone Hill Fortress (p211), St Kitts

3 Fort George (p309), Grenada

4 Pigeon Island (p294), St Lucia

5 Fort Shirley (p288), Dominica

and Guadeloupe, and the commonwealth situation between Puerto Rico and the US. Independence on the one hand and statehood on the other has always had its champions in Puerto Rico, with statehood narrowly losing plebiscites in 1993 and 1998 but on tap for yet another vote again in the near future.

In the post-WWII period, Britain moved to divest itself of its Caribbean colonies by attempting to create a single federated state that would incorporate all of the British-held Caribbean. One advantage of the federation was that it was expected to provide a mechanism for decolonizing smaller islands that the British felt would otherwise be too small to stand as separate entities.

After a decade of negotiation, Britain convinced its Caribbean colonies – Jamaica, Barbados, Trinidad and the British Windward and Leeward Islands – to join together as the West Indies Federation. The new association came into effect in 1958, with the intent that the federation work out the intricacies of self-government during a four-year probationary period before the islands emerged as a single new independent nation in 1962.

Although the West Indies Federation represented dozens of islands scattered across some 2000 miles (3200km) of ocean, the British established Trinidad, at the southernmost end of the chain, to be the governing 'center' of the federation.

For centuries the islanders had related to each other via their British administrators, and the political and economic intercourse between the islands had been quite limited. In the end, the lack of a united identity among the islands, coupled with each island's desire for autonomy, proved much stronger than any perceived advantage in union.

Jamaica was the first to develop a rift with the new association and opted to leave the federation in 1961. Trinidad itself soon followed suit. Both islands were wary of getting stuck having to subsidize the federation's smaller islands, which had a history of being heavily dependent upon British aid. The concept of a smaller federation limped along for a few more years, but after Barbados broke rank and became an independent nation in 1966, the British were forced to go back to the drawing board.

The remaining islands continued to splinter. Dominica and St Lucia gained independence as single-island nations. Antigua, St Vincent, Grenada and St Kitts were each linked with smaller neighboring islands to form new nations.

1916–24
US occupation of the Dominican Republic; also occupies Haiti from 1915–34.

1937
Dominican dictator Rafael Trujillo orders Haitians be killed in retaliation for cattle rustling; 20,000 perish.

1959
Cuban Revolution triumphs, which ripples across the Caribbean. Puerto Rico welcomes many new casino owners.

Anguilla, which was connected with St Kitts and Nevis, rebelled three months after the new state's inauguration in 1967 and negotiated with the British to be reinstated as a Crown Colony. Montserrat also refused to be dispensed with so readily by the British and was allowed to continue as a Crown Colony.

The islands linked to St Vincent and to Grenada also initially grumbled, but they have managed to work out their differences well enough to maintain their unions.

The Dutch, like the British, also hoped to create a single federation of all their Caribbean possessions – Curaçao, Aruba, Bonaire, Sint Maarten, St Eustatius and Saba – collectively known as the Netherlands Antilles. In 1954 a charter was enacted that made these six islands an autonomous part of the Netherlands. Under the charter, island affairs were largely administered by elected officials, although the Dutch continued to hold the purse strings and maintain other controls. The islands were expected to develop the mechanisms for self-rule and move gradually, as a unit, toward full independence from the Netherlands.

But that didn't work out. The islands never considered union as a single nation. Aruba was the first out in 1986 and became a single island state. The remaining five islands each followed over the next 24 years so that today, all six are independent of each other but still linked in some way to the Netherlands.

A Rum-Punch Future

The last 100 years have been a mixed bag for the region. US intervention in countries seen as geostrategically important, particularly Haiti and Cuba, usually does more harm than good. Furthermore, monocrop agriculture – bananas in Jamaica, nutmeg in Grenada – means the islands are at the mercy of heavy weather and market

The Caribbean in Film

The portrayals may not be literal, but you can get a feel for the region's history in movies.

- *1492: Conquest of Paradise* (1992) Somewhat forgotten, this Ridley Scott epic includes a carpet-chewing Gérard Depardieu as the explorer and a haughty Sigourney Weaver as Queen Isabella I.
- *Pirates of the Caribbean* Not exactly documentaries, but the series is great fun and includes scenes shot on St Vincent, Tortuga, Dominica and Puerto Rico.
- *Dr No* (1962) Shows Sean Connery as James Bond in a somnolent post-colonial Jamaica; Ursula Andress provides a good study of vintage regional swimwear.

1967
Anguillans force the Royal St Kitts Police Force off the island for good, declaring independence.

1983
After President Ronald Reagan orders an invasion, 70 Cubans, 42 Americans and 170 Grenadians die.

1986
Aruba leaves the Netherlands Antilles and becomes an autonomous entity.

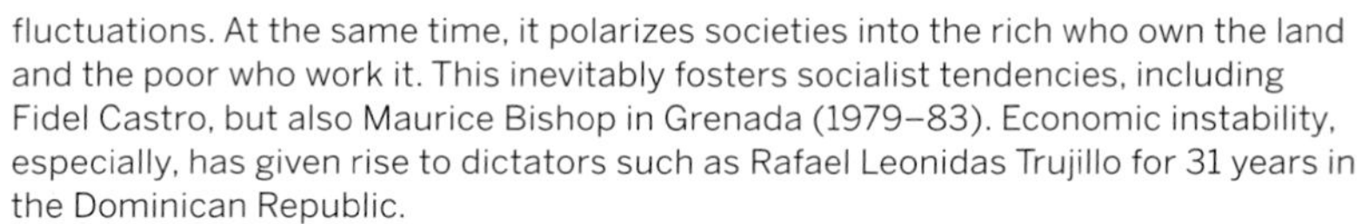

fluctuations. At the same time, it polarizes societies into the rich who own the land and the poor who work it. This inevitably fosters socialist tendencies, including Fidel Castro, but also Maurice Bishop in Grenada (1979–83). Economic instability, especially, has given rise to dictators such as Rafael Leonidas Trujillo for 31 years in the Dominican Republic.

One thing all the islands have in common is tourism, which began taking hold when other sectors of the islands' economies began to crumble, particularly agriculture. Much of tourism's foundation was literally laid in WWII.

St-Martin is a good example. In 1930 the population stood at just 2000. But in 1943 the US Navy built large runways on the island to use as a base in the Caribbean. The French capitalized by using the runways to fly in tourists, by the 1950s bringing the population of St-Martin/Sint Maarten up to about 70,000 and making tourism the number one industry on both sides of the island. The US left similar infrastructure – ports and airfields – across the region which proved useful for the cruise and package-holiday business as it got going in the 1950s.

Crop-leveling hurricanes (eg Gilbert in 1988, Hugo in 1989) spurred some islands to develop tourism industries, while the 1997 World Trade Organization ruling favoring Central American bananas over Caribbean ones forced St Vincent and Martinique to look at diversifying. Far from a panacea, unfettered tourism can wreak havoc on the environment or give rise to societal woes such as prostitution in Cuba. But overall the perception that tourism is a good source of jobs and revenue is widespread. Polls have shown that people in places as diverse as Trinidad and Barbados overwhelmingly say they not only like tourists but that their presence makes everybody's life better. Of course these polls may have been taken when Brobdingnagian cruise ships *weren't* in port.

1994
Lester Bird continues the ruling dynasty started by his father, VC, in 1981.

2004
Hurricane Ivan sweeps through the Caribbean, devastating Grenada.

2008
Presidential candidate Barrack Obama criticizes US companies using the Cayman Islands as a tax dodge.

Family Travel

Beach games, Providenciales (p392), Turks & Caicos

MATT DUTILE/GETTY IMAGES ©

Taking the kids on their first-ever boat ride, building sand castles, wandering rainforest trails or meeting local children – it's simple adventures like these that make the Caribbean such a great region for families. But all islands are not created equal in the fun department. Sure, young adventurers will delight on Dominica, but for good-time sandy fun, there are definitely some other islands to consider first.

Caribbean Islands for Kids

The Caribbean isn't just a huge playground for adults, it's one for kids too. Like any playground some parts are more fun than others. Islands dedicated to adult pursuits, like diving or hiking, might leave little ones out of the action, but plenty more islands have myriad activities for children. Islands with large beach resorts may seem positively designed for kids – at least to the younger mind.

Best Islands for Families

- **Aruba** Large resorts with kids' activities, excellent beaches, mostly calm seas and lots of adventure activities, including water sports.

- **Barbados** Lots of family-friendly beaches in the south and west, and popular kids' surfing lessons.

- **Cayman Islands** Seven Mile Beach is great for families. Large resorts have kids' programs and the water is calm.
- **Puerto Rico** Old San Juan has amazing forts and big resorts cater to families.
- **US Virgin Islands** One of the best destinations for kids. Highlights are abundant and include resort fun and tourist towns with child-friendly allure on all three main islands.

The Best... Family Fun

1 Eagle Beach (p341), Aruba

2 West Coast (p324), Barbados

3 Stingray City (p408), Grand Cayman

4 El Morro (p114), San Juan

5 Maho Bay (p231), US Virgin Islands

Planning

Where to Stay

Resorts offer scores of kid-friendly amenities, but some families prefer staying in simpler places closer to island life. Before booking any lodging, ask for details to assess its appropriateness. For example:

- Does it welcome kids or accept them grudgingly?
- If it's a resort, what sort of kids' activities does it offer?
- Does the room have a DVD player and wi-fi?
- Is there a kitchen or at least a refrigerator, so you can avoid the expense of always eating out?
- Are there safe places where kids can play?
- Even if the beach is nearby, is it across a heavily trafficked street?
- Does it provide cribs, change tables and other baby supplies?
- Does it offer on-site babysitting?

What to Pack

Be prepared for lots of time in the sun and sea. Most lodgings provide beach towels, chairs and umbrellas. You can buy sand pails, snorkel masks and anything else you forget at beach shops in resort areas. Elsewhere you'll need to bring what you want in the diversions department. Bring:

- snorkel gear (especially masks) that you've tested for leaks and proper fit
- water wings and other flotation devices
- pails and shovels
- sturdy reef shoes
- underwater camera
- car seat if driving a lot.

Need to Know

- Changing facilities, cots, high chairs, kids' menus and all the other niceties of family travel are best found at large international resorts. Look for ones with kids' clubs and the like.
- The larger islands will have complete health facilities. They will also have large supermarkets with diapers, familiar treats from home and so on.

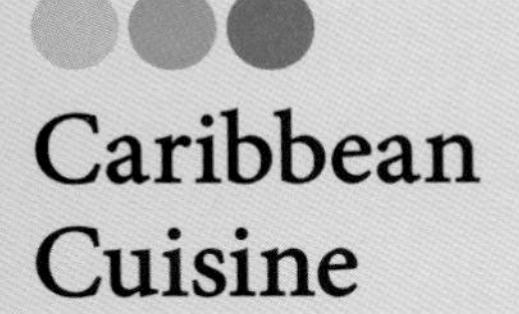

Caribbean Cuisine

Jerk chicken and roasted corn, Jamaica

DEBBI SMIRNOFF/GETTY IMAGES ©

Caribbean cuisine blends fruits and rice, seafood and spice, to create flavors as vibrant as the colors of the islands. Seafood still dripping with saltwater, thrown on the grill and spritzed with lime, has made many a Caribbean travel memory. Meats come in stews or beautifully grilled. Tropical fruits are Caribbean icons. And then there's the rums. Straight or imaginatively mixed to suit your fancy.

Flavors of the Caribbean

Each island has its favorite dishes and you can tell a lot about the island's history by what's favored. Ethnic heritages combine with each island's unique bounty to produce unique tastes.

Antigua

- **Pepperpot** Antigua's national dish is a hearty stew blending meat and vegetables, such as okra, spinach, eggplant, squash and potatoes. It's often served with fungi, which are not mushrooms but cornmeal patties or dumplings.

- **Black pineapple** The local pineapple was first introduced by the Arawaks and is smaller than your garden variety. It's known as 'black' because it's at its sweetest when kind of dark green. It grows primarily on the southwest coast, near Cades Bay.

- **Rock lobster** This hulking crustacean has a succulent tail but no claws and is best served grilled. (And you'll be forgiven if after a few rum punches you're humming a tune by the B-52s while digging in.)

Aruba, Bonaire & Curaçao

- **Cheese** An obvious Dutch legacy, usually eaten straight with a beer. When used in cooking it was traditionally a special treat.
- **Keshi yena** Comes in myriad variations: a cheese casserole with chicken, okra and a few raisins for seasoning. Much better than it sounds.
- **Funchi** Based on cornmeal, it is formed into cakes and fried, mixed with okra and fried, or used as a coating for chicken and fish.
- **Goat (cabrito) stew** A classic dish that most in ABC will say is made best by their own mother. Also appears in curries.
- **Yambo** A Creole gumbo stew with plenty of okra.
- **Frikandel** A classic Dutch deep-fried snack made from ground meat and a lot of pepper.
- **Bitterballen** Another Dutch classic – little deep-fried meaty balls served at roadside stands.
- **Pastechi** Dough pockets filled with meats and/or Dutch cheese, and deep-fried. Popular in curries.
- **Satay** Indonesian skewers of barbecued meat with a savory peanut sauce, via the colonial Dutch.

Barbados

- **Flying fish** Served fried in delicious sandwiches all over the country. It's a mild white fish that is great sautéed or deep-fried.
- **Conkies** A mixture of cornmeal, coconut, pumpkin, sweet potato, raisins and spices, steamed in a plantain leaf.
- **Fish cakes** There are myriad Bajan recipes, made from salt cod and deep-fried. Look for them being sold from food trucks.

Favorites Everywhere

These dishes can be found across the Caribbean.

Callaloo A creamy thick soup or stew blending a variety of vegetables (eg spinach, kale, onions, carrots, eggplant, garlic, okra) with coconut milk and sometimes crab or ham. The base can be spinach-like.

Roti Fiery chutney sets off the curried chicken, beef, conch or vegetable fillings in these burrito-like flat-bread wraps.

Conch Look for farm-raised versions as conch in the wild are endangered. This large pink mollusk is cooked with onion and spices in a stew, fried up as fritters, or sliced raw and served with a lime marinade.

- **Cou-cou** A creamy cornmeal and okra mash.
- **Cutters** Meat or fish sandwiches in a salt-bread roll. Best absolutely fresh and dripping with juice and a dash of hot sauce.
- **Jug-jug** A mixture of cornmeal, green peas and salted meat.
- **Pepper sauce** You'll find variations across the Caribbean but that from Barbados comes in the greatest variety. Done right, it lights your meal's fire without setting your mouth on fire.
- **Bananas** Local varieties are green even when ripe (look for them in markets). Much more complex in flavor than the usual supermarket varieties.

The Best... Places for Good Meals

1 San Juan (p120), Puerto Rico

2 Oistins (p323), Barbados

3 Grand Cayman (p401), Cayman Islands

4 Deshaies (p251), Guadeloupe

5 Bequia (p303), St Vincent & the Grenadines

British Virgin Islands & US Virgin Islands

- **Anegada lobster** Hulking crustaceans plucked from the water in front of your eyes and grilled on the beach in converted oil drums.
- **Fungi** A polenta-like cornmeal cooked with okra, typically topped by fish and gravy.
- **Pate** Flaky fried dough pockets stuffed with spiced chicken, fish or other meat.

Cayman Islands

- **Mannish water** Stewy mixture of yams plus the head and foot of a goat; *may* cure impotency.
- **Tortuga rum cake** A heavy, moist cake available in a number of addictive flavors; makes a great gift to take home.
- **Jelly ice** Chilled coconut water sucked from the shell.

Dominica

- **Fresh fruit** Dominica grows all sorts of fruit, including bananas, coconuts, papayas, guavas and pineapples, and mangoes so plentiful they litter the roadside in places.
- **Sea moss** Nonalcoholic beverage made from seaweed mixed with sugar and spices and sometimes with evaporated milk. It's sold in supermarkets and cafes.

Dominican Republic

- **La Bandera** (the flag) The most typically Dominican meal. Consists of white rice, habichuela (red beans), stewed meat, salad and fried green plantains.
- **Bananas** (guineos) A staple served stewed, candied or boiled and mashed. With plantains, the dish is called *mangú;* with pork rinds mixed in it is called *mofongo* and is nothing like the iconic Puerto Rican version.
- **Fish** Central to the Dominican diet – usually served in one of four ways: *al ajillo* (with garlic), *al coco* (in coconut sauce), *al criolla* (with a mild tomato sauce) or *a la diabla* (with a spicy tomato sauce).

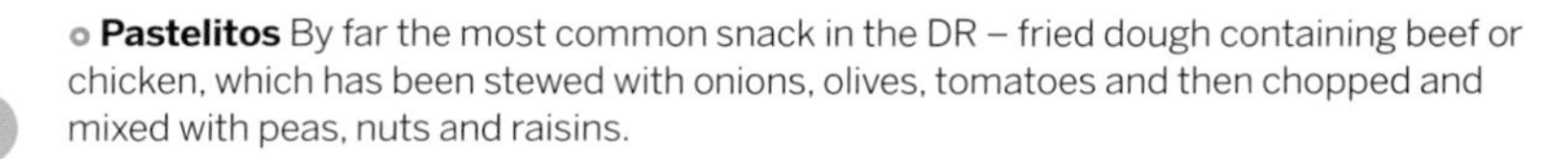

- **Pastelitos** By far the most common snack in the DR – fried dough containing beef or chicken, which has been stewed with onions, olives, tomatoes and then chopped and mixed with peas, nuts and raisins.

Grenada

- **Oil down** Beef and salt pork stewed with coconut milk. Best served with some fresh bread.

- **Saltfish and bake** Seasoned saltfish with onion and veg, and a side of baked or fried bread.

Guadeloupe & Martinique

- **Acras** A universally popular hors d'oeuvre, *acras* are fried fish, seafood or vegetables fritters in tempura. *Acras de morue* (cod) and *crevettes* (shrimp) are the most common and are both delicious.

- **Crabes farcis** Stuffed crabs are a typical local dish. Normally they're stuffed with a spicy mixture of crabmeat, garlic, shallots and parsley that is then cooked in the shell.

- **Blaff** This is the local term for white fish marinated in lime juice, garlic and peppers and then poached. It's a favorite dish in many of Guadeloupe's restaurants.

- **Baguettes** *Oui,* they can thank the French for having the best bread in the region.

- **Creole flavors** The spicy and piquant basis for many a fine dish.

Jamaica

- **Jerk** Jamaica's most well-known dish, jerk is actually a cooking method: smother food in a tongue-searing marinade, then smoke over a wood fire.

- **Seafood** Snapper and parrotfish are popular. A favorite dish is escoveitched fish – pickled in vinegar then fried and simmered with peppers and onions.

- **Breadkinds** A catchall term for starchy sides, from plantains and yam to pancake-shaped cassava bread (bammy) and johnnycakes (fried dumplings).

Top Cocktails

Curaçao Yes, there really is a liquor by the name. It's a startling blue, especially given its orange flavor.

Mudslide A creamy cocktail combining Kahlua, Baileys and vodka – from Grand Cayman.

Painkiller A sweet mix of rum, coconut, pineapple, orange juice and nutmeg.

Rum Punch The ubiquitous drink of the Caribbean. No two versions are alike but the best should combine multiple rums with fresh fruit juice and a dusting of nutmeg.

Ti-punch Short for petit punch, it's the normal *apéro* (aperitif) in Guadeloupe: a mix of rum, lime and cane syrup, but mainly rum.

- **Saltfish & Ackee** Jamaica's national dish, and a delicious breakfast besides. Ackee is a fleshy, somewhat bland fruit; saltfish is, well, salted fish. When mixed together they're delicious, somewhat resembling scrambled eggs.

- **Brown stew** Not a soup, brown stew is another popular method of cooking that involves simmering meat, fish or vegetables in savory-sweet sauce.

- **Patties** Baked shells filled with spicy beef, vegetables and whatever else folks desire. Cheap and filling.

Montserrat

- **Goat water** Montserrat's national dish is far more loved than its dubious-sounding name would suggest. 'Got some?' is a frequent conversation starter and refers to the spicy clove-scented broth accented with floating chunks of goat meat. It's eaten hot with a crusty bread roll.

Puerto Rico

- **Mofongo** A plantain crust encases seafood or steak in this signature dish.

- **Brazo Gitano** The 'Gypsy's Arm' is a huge cake roll, filled with fresh, mashed fruit and sweet cheese.

- **Lechón Asado** Smoky, spit-roasted suckling pig is sold at roadside trucks and is a taste of heaven.

- **Sorullitos de Maíz** Deep-fried corn-meal fritters make an excellent bar snack.

Curaçao liquor, produced in Curaçao

St Kitts & Nevis

- **Stewed saltfish** Official national dish; served with spicy plantains, coconut dumplings and seasoned breadfruit.
- **Pelau** Also known as 'cook-up,' this dish is the Kittitian version of paella: a tasty but messy blend of rice, meat, saltfish, vegetables and pigeon peas.

St Vincent & the Grenadines

- **Fresh produce** St Vincent produces top quality and delicious fruits and vegetables.
- **Savory pumpkin soup** More squash-like than the American Thanksgiving staple; often like a rich stew.
- **Saltfish** Dried fish that has been cured: delicious when made into fishcakes.

Trinidad & Tobago

- **Doubles** Curried *channa* (chickpeas) in a soft fried *bara* (bread).
- **Bake and shark** Seasoned shark steaks, topped with salad and local sauces and served in a floaty fried bake.

Turks & Caicos

Lobster Don't miss tasting the fresh lobster during your stay – traditionally served in a butter sauce with lime, it's the culinary highlight of the country.

Rums of the Caribbean

The Caribbean makes the world's best rum, and while some venture no further than a regular old Cuba libre (rum and cola) or piña colada, a highball of exquisite seven-year-old *añejo* over ice, sipped as the sun sets, is liquid heaven.

- **Antigua** Cavalier and English Harbour are best mixed with fruit juice for a refreshing – if potentially lethal – punch.
- **Barbados** Considered to produce some of the finest in the Caribbean, with Mount Gay being the best-known label.
- **Dominica** Rum connoisseurs crave the local concoction, Macoucherie. Don't be fooled by the plastic bottles or cheap-looking label, it's an undiscovered gem.
- **Dominican Republic** Dozens of local brands are available, but the big three are Brugal, Barceló and Bermudez.
- **Jamaica** Clear and light white rums, flavored rums, brain-bashing overproof rums (rum over 151 proof), deep dark rums, and the rare amber nectar of the finest premium rums.
- **Puerto Rico** The national drink. Though the headquarters of Bacardi are outside San Juan, Puerto Ricans drink locally made Don Q or Castillo.
- **Saba** Known for homemade rums, which are often flavored with locally grown banana, mango, vanilla or 'Saba spice.' Most restaurants and hotels have their own special brew.
- **USVI** Cruzan rum has been St Croix's happy juice since 1760, from light white rum to banana, guava and other tropical flavors.

Cruising the Caribbean

Cruise liner, British Virgin Islands

HOLGER LEUE/GETTY IMAGES ©

More than two million cruise-ship passengers sail the Caribbean annually, making it the world's largest cruise-ship destination. The typical cruise-ship holiday is the ultimate package tour. Other than the effort involved in selecting a cruise, it requires minimal planning – just pay and show up – and for many people this is a large part of the appeal. In just a few days you can get a taste of many islands.

Cruising Today

While the ships get bigger (new ships carry more than 5000 passengers), the amenities also grow, and today ships can have everything from climbing walls and an in-line skating rink to nightclubs and waterfalls.

For the most part, the smaller, 'nontraditional' ships put greater emphasis on the local aspects of their cruises, both in terms of the time spent on land and the degree of interaction with islanders.

Ships sail at night and sit in ports by day, typically 8am to 4pm. Shore excursions span the gamut of activities. You can drop a bundle on an real adventure or just wander the streets of the port town.

Main Routes

While there are variations, cruise itineraries tend to concentrate on three main areas.

Eastern Caribbean

Cruises can last three to seven days, with few days during which you're only at sea due to the profusion of port calls. Some itineraries may venture south to Barbados or even to Aruba, Bonaire and Curaçao; there is much overlap between the eastern and southern itineraries. Islands in the eastern area: Antigua, Bahamas, British Virgin Islands, Dominican Republic, Guadeloupe, Puerto Rico, St Kitts and Nevis, St-Martin/Sint Maarten, Turks and Caicos, US Virgin Islands.

Southern Caribbean

Itineraries are usually at least seven days due to the distance from the main departure ports. There is often some overlap with the eastern Caribbean islands, with stops at the US Virgin Islands common. Islands in the southern area: Aruba, Barbados, Bonaire, Curaçao, Dominica, Grenada, Martinique, St Lucia, St Vincent and the Grenadines, Trinidad and Tobago.

Western Caribbean

Often only five days in length, the western itineraries usually also include Mexican ports, such as Cancun. There are often stops at Puerto Rico and other eastern ports and longer itineraries may include southern stops. Islands in the western area: Cayman Islands and Jamaica.

Ports of Departure

Main departure ports for Caribbean cruises are Fort Lauderdale and Miami, Florida; and San Juan, Puerto Rico. All three cities are well equipped to deal with vast numbers of departing and arriving cruise-ship passengers and are closest to the Caribbean.

Secondary departure ports are typically set up for local markets and won't see the line's biggest or flashiest ships (though some veteran cruisers like that). These include Galveston, Texas; New Orleans, Louisiana; Port Canaveral and Tampa, Florida and even as far north as Baltimore, Maryland and New York City. Cruises from these ports need more time at sea to travel to and from the Caribbean.

What to Pack

Clothes and personal items such as toiletries and medications are the important things to pack. Sundries can be bought at high prices on board or at regular prices in ports of call. Don't forget:

- comfortable, casual cotton wear
- comfortable, cool walking shoes for shore excursions
- waterproof sandals for around the pool and active shore excursions
- khakis, a dress and shirts with collars for evening dining
- outfits for cruises with formal nights (men can often rent tuxes in advance through the cruise line).

Ports of Call

There are many choices of where to visit on a cruise. Note that some cruise lines stop at 'private islands', which are beaches that function as an extension of the shipboard experience. A prime example is 'Labadie', used by ships under the Royal Caribbean umbrella and which is really a walled-off beach on Haiti's north coast.

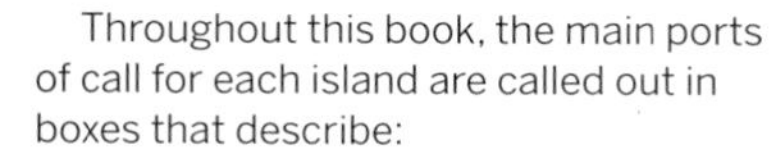

Throughout this book, the main ports of call for each island are called out in boxes that describe:

- whether cruise ships dock on land or if passengers need to ride tenders to port;
- what the harbor area is like;
- where, if anywhere, you can walk to; and
- popular activities during your time ashore.

Tipping

Tipping is usually expected and can add 20% or more to your shipboard account. Many lines have gotten around the discretionary nature of tips (which are the primary wages for the crew) by automatically putting them on your bill in the form of 18% to 20% gratuity fees.

Note, however, that there's often no transparency about how much of these 'gratuities' actually reach the crews, many of whom work 12-hour days, seven days a week.

Costs

The cost of a cruise can vary widely, depending on the season and vacancies. While it will save you money to book early, keep in mind that cruise lines want to sail full, so many will offer excellent last-minute discounts – sometimes up to 50% off the full fare.

You'll pay less for an inside room deep within the ship, but be aware that the really cheap rooms are often claustrophobic and poorly located (be sure to study deck plans). Some packages provide free or discounted airfares to and from the port of embarkation (or will provide a rebate if you make your own transportation arrangements).

Most cruises end up costing US$200 to US$600 per person, per day, including airfare from a major US gateway city. Port charges and government taxes typically add on another US$150 per cruise. Be sure to check the fine print about deposits, cancellation and refund policies, and travel insurance.

Extras on Board

- **Alcoholic drinks** Usually not included in the price of the cruise; a profit center for the lines.
- **Meals** You can still get free and abundant food but ships now have a range of extra-cost restaurants where for, say, US$20 you can get a steak dinner in an exclusive setting. But even fancy coffees now often come with a fee.
- **Activities** Spas, adventure sports, classes; the lines are always looking for new things they can sell to passengers.

Shore Excursions

Numerous guided tours and activities are offered at each port of call, each generally costing US$40 to US$100 or more. These tours are also a major profit earner for the cruise lines so there is great pressure for passengers to join – some reported heavy-handed tactics include cruise lines suggesting that people who booked tours with third parties have been left behind in port. Note the following:

- There is no requirement to book tours via the cruise lines.
- By going outside of the cruise line's shore excursions, travelers can set their own itinerary, avoid less-appealing mandatory stops (for shopping) and save money.

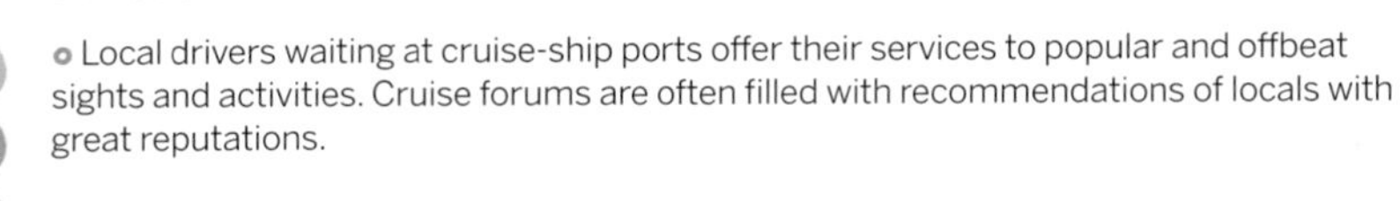

- Find activities and tours in advance and book over the web.
- Local drivers waiting at cruise-ship ports offer their services to popular and offbeat sights and activities. Cruise forums are often filled with recommendations of locals with great reputations.

Booking a Cruise

There are several options for researching and booking a cruise. A cruise line's own website will offer deals or upgrades not found elsewhere and there are big discounts for booking with them up to a year in advance. Large travel-booking sites often have last-minute discounts.

Specialist Cruise Sites

Some specialist websites for cruising have spectacular deals as lines dump trips at the last moment that otherwise would go unsold. Some recommended sites:

Cruise411 (www.cruise411.com)

Cruise.com (www.cruise.com)

Cruise Outlet (www.thecruiseoutlet.com)

Vacations to Go (www.vacationstogo.com) Especially good last-minute deals.

Travel Agencies

Most cities have travel agencies that specialize in cruises; these can be very helpful if you are new to cruising. Try these industry websites for referrals:

American Society of Travel Agents (www.asta.org)

Cruise Lines International Association (CLIA; www.cruising.org)

Useful Resources

Good sources for further cruise information before you book:

Cruise Critic (www.cruisecritic.com) An in-depth site for people who like to cruise. The forums are excellent, with detailed critical opinions and information on ships, islands and more.

Cruise Junkie (www.cruisejunkie.com) A good site providing a well-rounded overview of the industry, including safety and environmental issues.

Cruise Law News (www.cruiselawnews.com) Excellent website that reports on issues facing the cruise-ship industry. Environmental problems, virus outbreaks, industry lobbying and more are covered. A good source for context to all the hype.

Theme Cruises

Old TV shows, science fiction, computers, musicians, (very) minor celebrities, soap operas, sports teams, nudism, politics, LBGT... What these all have in common is that they're all themes for cruises.

Cruise lines sell group space to promoters of theme cruises but typically no theme is enough to fill an entire ship. Rather, a critical mass of people will occupy a block of cabins and have activities day and night just for them, including lectures, autograph sessions, costume balls and performances.

No theme or interest is too obscure or improbable. To find one, simply search your phrase with 'cruise'.

Choosing a Cruise

So many options! So many decisions! Things to consider:

- **Budget** How much can you spend? Can you trade a cabin with a balcony (the most common kind now) for a cheaper, windowless room on a nicer ship for a longer voyage?

- **Style** A mass-market, upscale or specialist cruise? Consider your budget; whether you prefer numerous formal evenings, or to keep things casual; and any special interests you have.

- **Itinerary** Where do you want to go and what ports of call appeal? Do you like the idea of days spent just at sea?

- **Size matters** The megaships are geared for various budgets, so the important decision is how many people you want to sail with. On large ships, you can have 5000 potential new friends and also have the greatest range of shipboard diversions. Small ships, while sometimes exclusive and luxurious, are not always so, and usually lack the flashier amenities (such as climbing walls). Smaller ships will also call at smaller ports on less-visited islands.

- **Season** High season for Caribbean cruising is the same as at resorts in the islands: mid-December to April. The largest number of ships sail at this time and prices are at their highest. At other times there are fewer voyages but prices drop. Storms are more likely to cause itineraries to suddenly change during hurricane season June to November.

- **Demographics** Different cruise lines, and even ships within cruise lines, tend to appeal to different groups. Although cruisers in general tend to be slightly older, some ships have quite a party reputation; others are known for their art auctions and oldies music in the lounges. Also consider if you're looking for a family- or singles-oriented cruise.

Cruise ship at sea, Jamaica

The Best... Ports of Call

1 Bridgetown, Barbados (p317)

2 Roseau, Dominica (p280)

3 St George's, Grenada (p309)

4 Old San Juan, Puerto Rico (p114)

5 Grand Turk, Turks & Caicos (p398)

Sustainable Cruising

Although all travel comes with an environmental cost, by their very size, cruise ships have an outsize effect. Among the main issues:

- **Air pollution** According to UK-based Climate Care, a carbon offsetting company, cruise ships emit more carbon per passenger than airplanes – nearly twice as much – and that's not including the flights that most passengers take to get to their point of departure. Most ships burn low-grade bunker fuel, which contains more sulfur and particulates than higher-quality fuel. The US and Canada are phasing in new regulations to require ships to burn cleaner fuel when they are close to land; however, the industry is fighting this. Small nations in the Caribbean are also being pressured into not adopting these regulations.

- **Water pollution** Cruise ships generate enormous amounts of sewage, solid waste and gray water. While some countries and states have imposed regulations on sewage treatment (with which the cruise lines comply), there's little regulation in the Caribbean. The United Nations instituted a ban on ships dumping solid waste in the water.

- **Cultural impact** Although cruise lines generate money for their ports of call, thousands of people arriving at once can change the character of a town and seem overwhelming to locals and noncruising travelers. In Bonaire, for example, 7000 cruisers can arrive in one day – half the country's population.

What You Can Do

If you're planning a cruise, it's worth doing some research. Email the cruise lines and ask them about their environmental policies – wastewater treatment, recycling initiatives, and whether they use alternative energy sources. Knowing that customers care about these things has an impact. There are also organizations that review lines and ships on their environmental records. These include the following:

Friends of the Earth (www.foe.org/cruisereportcard) Letter grades given to cruise lines and ships for environmental and human health impacts.

US Centers for Disease Control & Prevention (www.cdc.gov) Follow the travel links to the well-regarded sanitation ratings for ships calling in US ports.

Cruise Lines

Cruising is huge business and the major players earn billions of dollars a year. Many lines are actually brands owned by one of the two big players: Carnival and Royal Caribbean control 90% of the market in the Caribbean.

There are also nontraditional cruises, where you can feel the wind at your back on large sailing ships equipped with modern technology.

Popular Cruise Lines

The following cruise lines sail large vessels on numerous itineraries in the Caribbean:

Carnival Cruise Lines (www.carnival.com) The largest cruise line in the world. Its enormous ships offer cruising on myriad Caribbean itineraries.

Celebrity Cruises (www.celebritycruises.com) An important brand of Royal Caribbean, it has huge ships that offer a more upscale experience than Carnival and RCI.

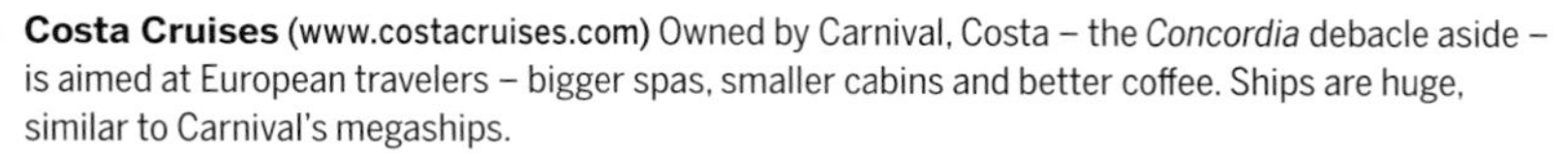

Costa Cruises (www.costacruises.com) Owned by Carnival, Costa – the *Concordia* debacle aside – is aimed at European travelers – bigger spas, smaller cabins and better coffee. Ships are huge, similar to Carnival's megaships.

Crystal Cruises (www.crystalcruises.com) Luxury cruise line with ships carrying about 800 passengers – small by modern standards. Attracts affluent, older clients who enjoy a wide range of cultural activities and formal evenings.

Disney Cruise Line (www.disneycruise.com) Disney's large ships are like floating theme parks, with children's programs and large staterooms that appeal to families.

Holland America (www.hollandamerica.com) Owned by Carnival, Holland America offers a traditional cruising experience, generally to older passengers. It has limited sailings in the Caribbean during the Alaska winter (its summer market).

Norwegian Cruise Line (NCL; www.ncl.com) Offers 'freestyle cruising' on large cruise ships, which means that dress codes are relaxed and dining options more flexible than on other lines. There are lots of extra-fee dining choices.

Princess Cruises (www.princess.com) Owned by Carnival, Princess has large ships that ply the Caribbean and offer a slightly older crowd a range of pampering activities while aboard.

Regent Seven Seas Cruises (www.rssc.com) Smaller ships (maximum 700 passengers) with a focus on luxury cabins and excellent food.

Royal Caribbean International (RCI; www.royalcaribbean.com) The archrival to Carnival has a huge fleet of megaships (some carry more than 5600 people), aimed right at the middle of the market. It has itineraries everywhere in the Caribbean all the time and offers lots of activities for kids.

Nontraditional Cruises

Sea Cloud Cruises (www.seacloud.com) The fleet includes a four-masted, 360ft (110m) ship dating from 1931 and a modern sibling. On both, the sails are set by hand. This German-American company operates luxury cruises in the Eastern Caribbean.

Star Clippers (www.starclippers.com) These modern four-masted clipper ships have tall-ship designs and carry 180 passengers. Itineraries take in smaller islands of the Eastern Caribbean.

Windstar Cruises (www.windstarcruises.com) Windstar's luxury four-masted, 440ft (134m) vessels have high-tech, computer-operated sails and carry less than 400 passengers. Note that the sails aren't the main means of propulsion most of the time.

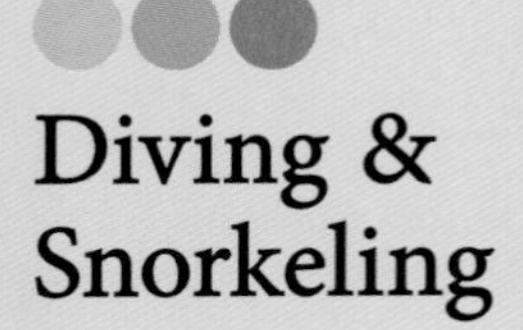

Diving & Snorkeling

Elkhorn coral

STEPHEN FRINK/GETTY IMAGES

Whether you're an experienced diver or slapping on fins for the first time, few places offer such perfect conditions for underwater exploration. The Caribbean Sea is consistently warm – temperatures average 80°F (27°C) – and spectacularly clear waters mean visibility can exceed 100ft (30m). Professional dive operators are as prolific as the postcard-worthy beaches and, whether you skim the surface or plunge far below, the colorful, active marine world delivers an amazing show.

Antigua & Barbuda

Antigua has excellent diving, with coral canyons, wall drops and sea caves hosting a range of marine creatures, including turtles, sharks and barracuda. Popular sites include the 2-mile-long (3km) Cades Reef and Ariadne Shoal. A fun spot for divers and snorkelers is the wreck of the *Jettias,* a 310ft (94m) steamer that sank in 1917 and now provides habitat for fish and coral.

And Barbuda? It's still a secret, word-of-mouth destination, with scores of shipwrecks along its surrounding reef.

Aruba

There is fine diving and snorkeling around the southern shores, with elaborate, shallow reefs and coral gardens ablaze with colorful critters. Wreck fans will love it here too, with a series of plane- and shipwrecks, some of which were sunk intentionally as artificial reefs. Of particular interest is the large German WWII freighter, *Antilla*.

The Best... Diving Areas

1 Réserve Cousteau (p255), Guadeloupe

2 Little Cayman (p409), Cayman Islands

3 Bonaire (p346)

4 Saba Marine Park (p199), Saba

5 St Thomas (p140), US Virgin Islands

Barbados

Barbados cannot compete with its neighboring heavyweights, but it boasts excellent diving nonetheless. The west coast is blessed with lovely reefs, wreathed with soft corals, gorgonians and colorful sponges. There are also a dozen shipwrecks. The largest and most popular, the 111m freighter *Stavronikita,* sits upright off the central west coast in 138ft (42m) of water, with the rigging reaching to within 20ft (6m) of the surface. In Bridgetown's Carlisle Bay, a series of coral-encrusted wrecks lie in only 23ft (7m) of water, making for good snorkeling as well as diving.

Bonaire

Bonaire is one of the most charismatic dive areas in the Caribbean. Since 1979 the crystal-blue canvas that wraps around the island has been a protected haven. Dive boats are required to use permanent moorings and popular dive sites are periodically closed to let the reefs recover. With the exception of Klein Bonaire sites, most dive sites are accessible from shore. Diving is absurdly easy; drive up, wade in, descend, explore. The gently sloping reefs are positively festooned with hard and soft corals, sponges, gorgonians and a dizzying array of tropical fish. A couple of wrecks, including the *Hilma Hooker,* spice up the diving.

British Virgin Islands

The islands huddle to form a sheltered paradise of secluded coves, calm shores and crystal-clear water, which in turn provide outstanding visibility, healthy coral and a wide variety of dive and snorkeling sites. Conservation is taken seriously, and there are lots of permanent mooring buoys.

Salt Island offers one of the Caribbean's best wreck dives: the monster-sized RMS *Rhone* – 310ft (94m) long and 40ft (12m) abeam – sunk in 1867. Amazingly, it's still in good shape and is heavily overgrown with marine life.

Another drawcard is the seascape – expect giant boulders, canyons, tunnels, caverns and grottoes.

Cayman Islands

With more than 250 moored sites, and plenty of shore diving and snorkeling possibilities, diving is the most popular activity in the Cayman Islands. Little Cayman has the finest Caribbean wall diving – along Bloody and Jackson's Bays, sheer cliffs drop so vertically they'll make you gasp in your regulator. The snorkeling here can be fantastic.

The Best... Snorkeling Areas

1 Réserve Cousteau (p255), Guadeloupe

2 Grand Cayman (p401), Cayman Islands

3 Little Tobago (p384), Trinidad & Tobago

4 Tobago Cays (p308), St Vincent & the Grenadines

5 Soufrière (p297), St Lucia

6 Grenada (p308)

Coral and sponges of all types, colors and sizes cascade downward as you slowly descend along the wall.

Grand Cayman has plenty of shallow dives suitable for novices and snorkelers, including the legendary Stingray City, where stingrays can be approached on a sandy seafloor in less than 12ft (4m) of water.

Curaçao

Curaçao ranks among the best diving destinations in the region, with a number of rewarding sites along its southern lee coast. Among the draws are a couple of wrecks in shallow water, including the *Tugboat*, to the southeast – even snorkelers can admire the swirl of life around the boat. One of the coolest dives on Curaçao, Mushroom Forest, is off the west end and peppered with coral mounds on a sandy plateau.

Dominica

The strength of Dominica is its underwater topography. The island's rugged scenery continues below the surface, where it forms sheer drop-offs, volcanic arches, massive pinnacles, chasms, gullies and caves.

Many top dive sites are in the Soufriere Bay marine reserve. Scotts Head Drop-Off, the Pinnacle and the Soufriere Pinnacle are favorites and Champagne Reef, popular with beginners and snorkelers, is a subaquatic hot spring off Pointe Guignard where crystal bubbles rise from underwater vents.

The central west coast is another premier diving area. The topography is not as unique as in the southwest, making the dives less challenging.

Dominican Republic

The Dominican Republic is mostly famous for its kitesurfing and windsurfing, but it shouldn't be sneezed at. There's a wide choice of easy dives lurking off the Península de Samaná on the northeastern coast. Facing the Atlantic, the water there is cooler and visibility is somewhat reduced but the terrain is varied and you'll find a few shipwrecks to keep you happy. All the main dive spots have shallow reefs where nondivers can snorkel.

Grenada

With extensive reefs and a wide variety of marine life, the waters around Grenada offer excellent diving. The southwest coast has the majority of dive sites, with the wreck of the *Bianca C* ocean liner one of the most popular. Other good log entries for wreck buffs include the *King Mitch*, the *Rum Runner* and the *Hema 1*. Molinière Point, north of St George's, has some of Grenada's best snorkeling.

Other top snorkeling spots include Sandy Island off the northeast coast of Grenada, and White Island and (another) Sandy Island off the coast of Carriacou.

Guadeloupe

Guadeloupe's top diving site is the Réserve Cousteau, at Pigeon Island off the west coast of Basse-Terre. This is a protected area, so you can expect myriad tropical fish, turtles and sponges, and a vibrant assemblage of hard- and soft-coral formations. There are also two superb wrecks in the vicinity. The Réserve Cousteau is also a magnet for snorkelers, with scenic spots in shallow, turquoise waters.

For those willing to venture away from the tourist areas, there's Les Saintes. This area is a true gem with numerous untouched sites, striking underwater scenery and a diverse fish population – not to mention the phenomenal Sec Pâté, which consists of two giant pitons in the channel between Basse-Terre and Les Saintes.

Jamaica

So, you want variety? Jamaica's your answer. Sure, nothing is really world-class, but Jamaica offers an assortment of diving experiences. Treasures here include shallow reefs, caverns and trenches, walls, drop-offs and wrecks just a few hundred meters offshore. This is especially true on the north coast from Negril to Ocho Rios, where diving and snorkeling conditions are exceptional. Tip: if you're after less-crowded dive sites, opt for Runaway Bay.

Martinique

Wrecks galore! St-Pierre is a must for wreck enthusiasts. Picture this: more than a dozen ships that were anchored in the harbor when the 1902 volcanic eruption hit now lie on the seabed, at depths ranging from around 30ft to 280ft (10m to 85m).

To the southwest, Grande Anse and Diamant also deserve attention, with a good balance of scenic seascapes, elaborate reef structures and dense marine life.

Puerto Rico

You will find good snorkeling reefs off the coasts of Vieques, Culebra, Fajardo and the small cays east of Fajardo. The cays off the south and east coasts also have good shallow reefs. There's good diving off Rincón and Fajardo, as well as spectacular wall dives out of La Parguera on the south coast.

Saba

This stunning volcanic island might even be more scenic below the ocean's surface. Divers and snorkelers can find a bit of everything (except wrecks): steep wall dives just offshore, submerged pinnacles and prolific marine life, including nurse sharks, stingrays and turtles. The Saba Marine Park has protected the area since 1987 and offers many untouched, buoy-designated diving spots.

St-Barthélemy

St-Barth has healthy, expansive reefs and varied marine line that includes barracuda, gropers, turtles, rays, sea fans, giant barrel sponges and black coral. The best sites lie just off the various islets that are scattered off the island. St-Barth also features a handful of wrecks, adding diving variety.

St Lucia

If you think the above-ground scenery is spectacular in St Lucia, you should see it under the sea. The area near Soufrière boasts spectacular, near-shore reefs, with a wide variety of corals, sponges, fans and reef fish. It's excellent for both diving and snorkeling. Wreck enthusiasts will enjoy *Lesleen,* a 165ft (50m) freighter that was deliberately sunk in 1986.

To the northwest, Rodney Bay is the main jumping-off point to a variety of good dives, although the topography is less impressive than around Soufrière.

St Vincent & the Grenadines

The sparsely inhabited islands and bays shelter thriving offshore reefs. You'll find steep walls decorated with black coral around St Vincent, giant schools of fish around Bequia, and a coral wonderland around Canouan. There's also pure bliss in the Tobago Cays – these five palm-studded, deserted islands surrounded by shallow reefs are part of a protected marine sanctuary and offer some of the most pristine reef diving in the Caribbean. Snorkeling is also superlative.

Arrow crab, Bonaire
JIM WATT/GETTY IMAGES ©

Sint Eustatius

The island's last volcanic eruption was 1600 years ago but you can still see evidence of the lava flow on the seabed, in its deep trenches and fissures. Vestiges of 18th-century colonial Sint Eustatius are also found beneath the surface, such as portions of quay wall that have slipped into the sea. Old ballast stones, anchors, cannons and ship remains have become vibrant coral reefs, protected by the Statia Marine Park.

A collection of ships has also been purposefully sunk over the past 15 years.

Trinidad & Tobago

Tobago is most definitely a diving destination. Situated on the South American Continental Shelf between the Caribbean and Atlantic, the island is massaged by the Guyana and North Equatorial Currents. Also injected with periodic pulses of nutrient-rich water from the Orinoco River, Tobago's waters teem with marine life, including pelagics (read: hammerhead sharks). The variety of corals, sponges and ancient sea fans make this a top destination.

Speyside is the launching pad for Little Tobago island, which is famous for its large brain corals and is also a mecca for snorkelers.

Turks & Caicos

Salt Cay is a diving highlight, where you can dive with humpback whales during their annual migration. Grand Turk has pristine reefs and spectacular wall diving, while the exceptional diving on rarely visited South Caicos is worth the hassle of getting there. There is also diving off Provo, where you can get the chance to see dolphins and numerous reef species.

US Virgin Islands

The sister islands of St Thomas and St John offer top-notch diving and snorkeling conditions, with a combination of fringing reefs and a contoured topography (arches, caves, pinnacles, tunnels and vertical walls). St Croix features a fascinating mix of wreck (Butler Bay shelters no fewer than five wrecks) and wall dives; advanced divers will make a beeline for the aptly named Vertigo dive site.

Weddings & Honeymoons

Wedding setting, Negril (p70), Jamaica

The Caribbean is a world-class destination for love. You can find virtually any kind of experience on one of the islands. If you're getting married, you'll join the numerous couples who've exchanged vows in one of these beautiful places. Because the region is so popular for weddings, most hotels and resorts can offer plenty of planning advice, from arranging the event to getting your license.

Wedding Types

While you can have almost any kind of wedding you want on any island, the island's own personalities definitely make each one better for different kinds of events. A few are especially well-suited to honeymoons that are total escapes.

Grand Affair

Invite everyone you know! Group rates at a large resort mean that you can send out invites far and wide for an event that is not out of reach. Resorts easily organize traditional ceremonies and receptions.

- **Aruba** Plenty of resorts specialize in big weddings . In fact any of the resorts at Palm Beach will easily handle affairs with hundreds of guests. Good airlinks make access easy.

- **Cayman Islands** Plenty of resorts offer good group rates on Seven Mile Beach. Lots of flights make it easy to invite people from all over.

- **Dominican Republic** Big resorts by the dozen mean you have lots of choices for planning a big event. Try Punta Cana; flights can be cheap, easing the fiscal pain on guests.

- **Jamaica** One of the top Caribbean wedding destinations. Some major resorts offer free ceremonies if you book enough rooms, so invite everyone you know. Lots of flights make getting there easy. Consider Treasure Beach and Boston Bay.

- **Puerto Rico** All those huge resorts right on the beach in San Juan are perfect for large ceremonies. Americans will find the marriage legalities are extra simple plus there are lots of good venues for subsidiary events such as rehearsal parties.

- **St-Martin/Sint Maarten** Dutch and French resorts are well versed in hosting fabulous weddings. You can literally choose the kind of accent you want.

The Best... Honeymoons

1 Anguilla (p178)

2 Barbuda (p195)

3 Jamaica (p54)

4 St-Barth (p237)

5 St Lucia (p291)

- **Turks & Caicos** The large resorts on Grace Bay beach will easily absorb scores of friends and family, yet the scale is not so vast that everyone will get lost. The smaller islands offer complete honeymoon escapes.

- **US Virgin Islands** A good place for Americans wary of red tape, or requiring that all their guests have passports. Large resorts have decades of experience with nuptials, yet you can find tiny, intimate places for the honeymoon.

Intimate

Live large in a small, exclusive resort. These can be expensive, so it could limit the number of guests. Luxury boutique resorts will usually handle all details and customize anything.

- **Anguilla** One of the Caribbean's poshest islands is bound to offer everything you'd want for an exclusive and expensive event. Go ahead, rent your own villa with a butler.

- **Antigua & Barbuda** A big range of upscale resorts means this is the place for an exquisite event. It's a popular destination for Brits thanks to good air links and its colonial history. Isolated Barbuda is great for honeymoons.

- **Barbados** A full array of top-end services for any style of wedding; good UK connections make this popular with Brits. The many long-time-open resorts and hotels mean they know just what to do, although the smaller sizes favor more intimate affairs.

- **St-Barthélemy** Excels at small, top-end weddings. Rent a villa with staff for your special day. Also the place to go for a top-end honeymoon.

- **St Kitts & Nevis** Bliss-inducing pampering on Nevis plus the island's own intimate beauty make this a natural for a small and special event.

- **St Lucia** A score of small, luxurious boutique hotels in the gorgeous south are naturals, both for the wedding and the honeymoon.

Big Adventure

Enjoy one of the Caribbean's off-the-beaten-path locations where you can hike, kayak or dive etc. These are good for couples who want a nontraditional ceremony.

- **Bonaire** Perfect for outdoor nuptials with a twist: get married at a small waterfront resort, then go diving with the bridal party. Or, get married underwater.

- **British Virgin Islands** Tortola is the center of Caribbean yachting; great for boat-based weddings or for honeymoons. Get a few of your favorite couples and laze your way through the islands on a chartered yacht.
- **Dominica** With so much outdoors action you might be too pooped to... no, of course not. Hike wild trails in the morning, get hitched in the afternoon. Lots of isolated wilderness retreat getaways.
- **Grenada** Small, secluded lodges with warm hospitality make good choices for smaller events. Some of the tiny beaches such as Anse la Roche are perfect for the sunset love shots.
- **St Vincent & the Grenadines** From chartering a yacht to finding a small, intimate setting on a small intimate island such as Bequia, SVG is good for adding a dash of adventure to your event.

Planning

Size

By their very nature Caribbean weddings tend to limit the number of guests who can attend. Costs and time off for the trip are issues, although some large resorts give very good rates for large wedding parties, so your nuptials could be an excuse for a holiday.

But if you want to gather together just a few friends, then it's easy to find gorgeous locations where you'll enjoy each other's company for days on end.

Style

Large resorts are good places for traditional wedding ceremonies as they can arrange for cakes, flowers, photographers and all the other accoutrements. Trying to organize all the trimmings at a secluded retreat or small lodge, especially while making the arrangements from your home country, may be very difficult. But that may also be the point if you want to shed traditional touches.

Costs

You can quickly go nuts adding treats and options to your sweetest day. Work with hotels and resorts to figure prices and make sure you allow for the licenses, service fees and other extras.

Papers

It is vital that you confirm in advance what you'll need for a marriage license. It varies greatly by country. Get info from the national tourism authority or a resort that specializes in weddings and then double-check it all. Here are just some of the bureaucratic hoops you may need to bound through:

- original birth certificates
- legal proof of divorce or death of previous spouse
- legal proof of the marriage officiant's status
- a local marriage license (up to US$300 or more in some places)
- blood tests.

There can also be delays in processing – some islands need 48 hours or more to process a license request; others require that you be on the island 48 hours or more in advance of the ceremony.

If the red tape proves too much, you can always have the unofficial ceremony of your dreams in the Caribbean while saving the legal ceremony for your home country.

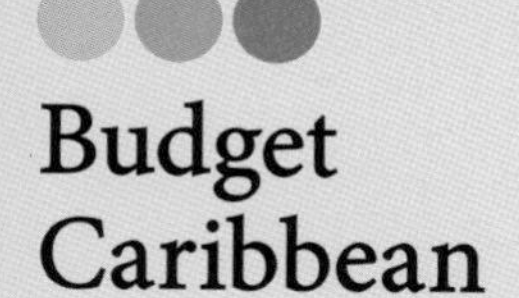

Budget Caribbean

Food market, Oistins (p323), Windward Islands

INGOLF POMPE/GETTY IMAGES ©

The Caribbean is not cheap, but there are ways to get the most bang for your buck with a little forward planning and some savvy choices. In this section, our authors share strategies for saving money, plus we rate the islands for their budget-friendliness. All islands are not created equal in the budget department – some can be much more affordable than others.

Island Budgeting Guide

The following lists have islands categorized by their overall expensiveness. But note that even the most expensive can be more affordable with clever strategies.

Great-Value Islands

These islands are least likely to break the bank.

- **Bonaire** Excellent budget choice. Small resorts on the water cater to divers who are value-conscious.

- **Dominica** One of the Caribbean's best bargains: everything is much cheaper than the region's averages, especially lodging and eating; public transportation is comprehensive.

- **Montserrat** Definitely a budget island: great value and high standards, even at guesthouses.

Local eateries are cheap and excellent. Limited public transportation; taxis are not too expensive.

- **Puerto Rico** In San Juan there's an abundance of hotels: look for internet deals and good rates for apartment rentals. Culebra and Vieques have fine budget options. Good public transportation.
- **Saba** A tiny island with few accommodation choices but some nice ones for around US$100.
- **Sint Eustatius** Although choices are few, limited tourism except for value-conscious divers means accommodation choices are good value, even January to March.
- **Trinidad** Not particularly tourist oriented, so there are many good-value options. Inexpensive in comparison to other islands. Public transportation and street food are cheap and good.
- **Tobago** As in Trinidad, there are many good-value options. Crown Point has the majority of places to stay, and competition keeps prices low.

Islands for All Budgets

You can spend a lot or, well, less on these islands.

- **Antigua** Expensive island: mostly higher-end resorts; few guesthouses and those are not appealing. Rent an apartment and self-cater. Vacation rentals have become more prevalent – try along the southwest coast near Cades Bay. Public transportation is OK in developed areas but rare to the remote east and southeast.
- **Aruba** The beaches are lined with mostly top-end resorts but Eagle Beach – our favorite – does have some good midrange options. Stay 10 minutes' walk from the beach and you can get a good room with a kitchen for about US$100 a night. Public transportation is excellent.
- **Barbados** The west coast with its old-money resorts and mansions can be pricey, although there are good-value apartments 10 minutes from the beaches. The south is filled with budget and midrange choices close to the sand. Good public transportation.
- **British Virgin Islands** Tortola is the secret to budget travel in the BVI. It has a good range of guesthouses and moderate resorts.
- **Curaçao** Budget accommodation in beautiful Willemstad is often not worth the cheap prices, but some better midrange options are opening. Holiday apartments on north-coast beaches are good value. Public transportation is OK.
- **Dominican Republic** The central highlands are better value than elsewhere.

Budget Tips

Here are some of the best ways to save money:

Travel in groups Bring your friends and other couples along with you and rent a villa.

Book far in advance For high season deals.

Book at the last minute For incredible deals as hotels dump empty rooms.

Follow the divers They demand great value near beautiful waters.

Ride buses and ferries You meet folks and may have an adventure.

Live like a local Save money while having a more authentic visit.

Travel sustainably It's the right thing to do and it saves you money.

Travel in low season Prices can drop 40% or more.

Great off-the-beaten-path places to stay: Tubagua Plantation Eco Lodge and Sonido del Yaque; Bahia de Las Águilas. Buses cover the country.

- **Grenada** Generally affordable. There are some modest resorts in and around George Town plus excellent local restaurants. A car will be good for a couple of days' exploration. Carriacou has a few good budget options.
- **The Grenadines** Some islands are quite expensive (eg Mustique) but others such as Bequia have excellent good-value choices. You can walk where you want to go.
- **Guadeloupe** Good budget/midrange options are available throughout the country – think US$70 per night. Good buses; ferries to tiny offshore islands are cheap and fun.
- **Jamaica** Treasure Beach and the south (St Elizabeth parish), plus Port Antonio and the northeast, are fantastic for getting a taste of the 'real' Jamaica outside of the resorts. Public transportation is good albeit adventurous.

The Best... Budget Islands

1 Bonaire (p346)

2 Dominica (p280)

3 Puerto Rico (p109)

4 Trinidad (p356)

5 Tobago (p372)

- **Martinique** Budget/cheap midrange options are available throughout the country – around US$70 per night. Ferries and buses provide good links.
- **St Lucia** Consider staying in midrange places such as inns and guesthouses that are not directly on the beach. Travel in low season.
- **St-Martin/Sint Maarten** Consider staying in the island's towns – such as Philipsburg or Marigot. Shop at local markets (ask the locals where they buy their groceries). Public transportation is just OK.
- **St Vincent** There are some good modest resorts near Kingstown, which also has a good inn in town. Public transportation just OK.
- **Turks & Caicos** Expensive beachfront resorts; the best value is at diving resorts in Providenciales and Grand Turk.
- **US Virgin Islands** Rates are very seasonal, falling 40% or more in slack times. Resorts tend to be pricey; look for holiday apartments online.

Top-End Islands

These are the posh islands of the Caribbean; still, there are ways even these can fit a budget.

- **Anguilla** One of the most exclusive and expensive islands in the Caribbean; not a budget option.
- **Barbuda** At least 50% more expensive than Antigua. The only way to save money is by staying in guesthouses but these are very basic. Getting around is ridiculously expensive.
- **Cayman Islands** Most of the accommodation is on beautiful Seven Mile Beach and is quite expensive. There are more-affordable options off-beach. Public transportation is excellent.
- **Nevis** Stay in Charlestown, which has some reasonably priced eateries. The rest of the island is very expensive but actually good value given the high standards.

- **St-Barthélemy** Prohibitively expensive in high season; other times you might find an affordable villa rental online. Splurge at the luxury restaurants with their €29 'value' meals.
- **St Kitts** Expensive island. Look for online specials at the resorts. Use the decent public transportation and get a room with a kitchen.

Quick Getaways

With competitive airfares from the US and Canada and resorts offering great deals online, several Caribbean islands are well suited to a quick, affordable getaway. Consider the following:

- **Montego Bay, Jamaica** Famous resort town with a huge range of beachside accommodations.
- **Old San Juan, Puerto Rico** Explore forts and beaches by day; wander lively streets by night.
- **St-Martin/Sint Maarten** The choice of a French frolic or Dutch treat.

Live Like a Local

Take time to meet the locals by doing what they do – you'll enjoy a more affordable and authentic experience. Some simple, common-sense tips:

- Eat at lunch wagons or stalls. The local fare is cheap and often incredibly good.
- Drop by a local bar – often the de facto community center. Besides a drink, you'll get all sorts of useful – or wonderfully frivolous – advice.
- Look for community fish fries or barbecues in the Eastern Caribbean.

Survival Guide

Kitesurfing, Anguilla (p178), Leeward Islands
THIERRYDEHOVE.COM/GETTY IMAGES ©

Directory

Book Your Stay Online

For more accommodations reviews by Lonely Planet authors, check out http://hotels.lonelyplanet.com. You'll find independent reviews, as well as recommendations on the best places to stay. Best of all, you can book online.

Accommodations

A wide range of accommodations awaits travelers in the Caribbean, from inexpensive guesthouses and good-value apartments, to elaborate villas and luxury beachside resorts. And there are also plenty of midrange options in between.

Prices

See the individual destination chapter directories for information on the price bands used in reviews.

Seasons

During low season, May to mid-December, rates may be up to 40% less or the property may be closed.

Camping

Camping is limited in the Caribbean and on some islands freelance camping is either illegal or discouraged.

Guesthouses

The closest thing the Caribbean has to hostels, guesthouses are usually great value. Often in the middle of a town or village and rarely alongside a beach, they offer good opportunities for cultural immersion.

Hotels

Across the Caribbean, hotel rooms can range from humdrum to massive 1000-room resorts to glorious villas hovering over the sea.

All-Inclusive Resorts

Born in Jamaica and now prevalent across the Caribbean, all-inclusive resorts allow you to pay a set price and then nothing more once you arrive. You usually get a wristband that allows you free access to the hotel or resort's restaurants, bars and watersports equipment. Many properties have jumped onto the 'all-inclusive' bandwagon, but don't necessarily supply the goods. Be sure to find out exactly what 'all-inclusive' includes. Questions to ask:

- What is the variety and quality of food available?
- How many meals are included?
- Are all drinks included?

Island Sovereignty

The islands by national affiliation (if an island is not mentioned here, it is an independent nation):

- British West Indies – Anguilla, Turks and Caicos, the Cayman Islands, Montserrat (an 'overseas territory') and British Virgin Islands (a crown colony) due to their affiliation with the UK.
- French West Indies – Includes Guadeloupe, St-Martin, St-Barthélemy and Martinique due to their status as départements d'Outre-mer (overseas départements) of France.
- Netherlands Antilles – Historically Aruba, Curaçao, Bonaire, Sint Maarten, Saba and Sint Eustatius. Aruba, Bonaire and Curaçao (often called the ABC Islands) are also known as the Leeward Netherlands Antilles. All the islands maintain affiliation with the Netherlands to a greater and lesser degree.
- USA – Puerto Rico, US Virgin Islands.

- Is 'free alcohol' limited to wine with dinner?
- Are there lots of extra-charge options at mealtimes (steaks etc), meaning that the regular food is uninspiring?
- What activities are included (an extra charge for snorkeling gear is a sign of stinginess)?

Climate

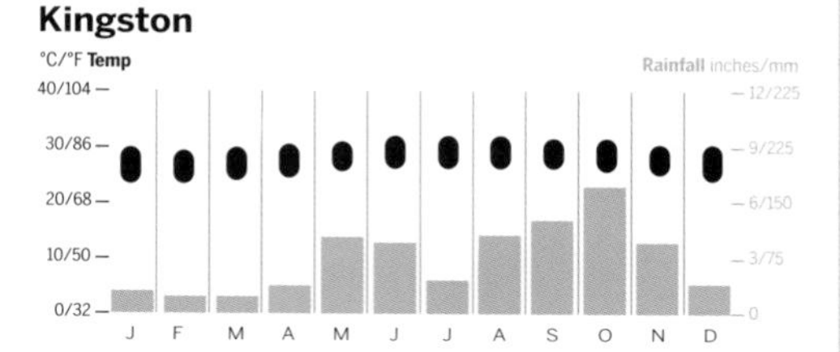

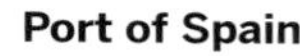

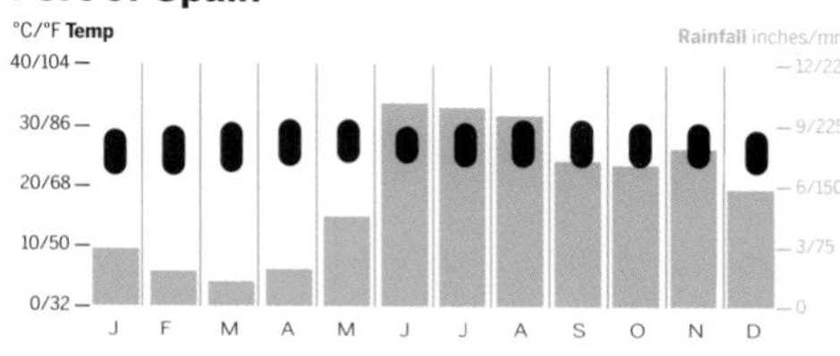

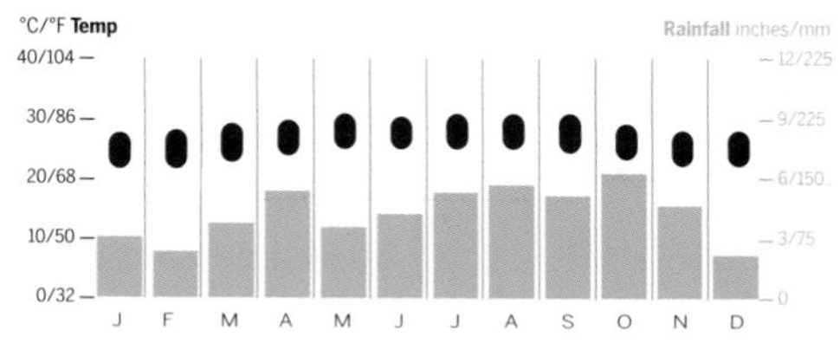

Customs Regulations

All the Caribbean islands allow a reasonable amount of personal items to be brought in duty free, as well as an allowance of liquor and tobacco. Determining what you can take home depends on where you're vacationing and your country of origin. Check with your country's customs agency for clarification.

Electricity

The electric current varies across the islands. See the Practicalities boxes in individual chapter Survival Guides for details.

Gay & Lesbian Travelers

Parts of the Caribbean are not particularly gay-friendly destinations and on many of the islands overt homophobia and machismo is prevalent.

Gay men and lesbians generally keep a low profile, and public hand-holding, kissing and other outward signs of affection are not commonplace. Jamaica is a special case in terms of harassment (and worse) of gay people.

Still, there are several niches for gay travelers. Particularly friendly islands include Aruba, Bonaire, Curaçao, Dominican Republic, Guadeloupe, Martinique, Puerto Rico, Saba, St-Martin/Sint Maarten and the US Virgin Islands.

Health

The availability of medical care and the safety of drinking water varies around the Caribbean. See the 'Survival Guide' sections of individual destination chapters for details.

Insurance

It's foolhardy to travel without insurance to cover theft, loss and medical problems. Start by seeing what your own insurance policy covers; you may find that many aspects of travel in the Caribbean are already covered, but there may be gaping holes.

Worldwide travel insurance is available at www.lonelyplanet.com/travel_services. You can buy, extend and claim online anytime – even if you're already on the road.

Internet Access

Internet access and wi-fi is generally easily found throughout most of the Caribbean.

Legal Matters

Due to the stereotype that pot-smoking is widespread in the Caribbean (it isn't), some visitors take a casual attitude about sampling island drugs.

Be forewarned that drug trafficking is a serious problem throughout the Caribbean and most officials have little to no tolerance of visitors caught using. Penalties vary throughout the islands, but getting caught smoking or possessing marijuana (or any illegal drug for that matter) can result in stiff jail sentences.

Money

US dollars are often accepted in lieu of local currency (and in some cases are the local currency). For details on money and tipping, see the individual destination chapter directories.

Public Holidays

See the individual destination chapter directories for information on holidays on individual islands. Regionwide standard public holidays:

New Year's Day January 1

Good Friday Friday before Easter, late March/early April

Easter Monday Monday after Easter, late March/early April

Whit Monday Eighth Monday after Easter

Christmas Day December 25

Boxing Day December 26

Safe Travel

In terms of individual safety and crime, the situation is quite varied in the Caribbean. It's hard to imagine more tranquil areas than Saba and Sint Eustatius, where most people don't even have locks on their doors.

However, there are places for extra caution, including Pointe-à-Pitre (Guadeloupe), Fort-de-France (Martinique), urban areas of Jamaica, urban areas on St-Martin/Sint Maarten and downtown Port of Spain (Trinidad).

In most areas there is a huge disparity between the income of locals and the (real or perceived) wealth of visitors. If you venture beyond the borders of the tourist areas, you may observe populations devastated by poverty, and a lack of medical supplies and clean water, in places such as Jamaica. Add to this the existence of drug production and trafficking and you can see why crime is a problem in some areas.

Exchange Rates

	US$1	C$1	€1	UK£1
Aruban florin (Afl)	1.80	1.88	2.57	2.94
Barbadian dollar (B$)	2.00	2.10	2.87	3.28
Cayman Islands dollar (CI$)	0.82	0.86	1.18	1.35
Dominican peso (RD$)	37.60	39.48	54.09	61.80
Eastern Caribbean dollar (EC$)	2.70	2.83	3.88	4.44
Euro (€)	0.70	0.73	-	1.14
Jamaican dollar (J$)	85.22	89.21	122.18	139.72
Netherlands Antillean guilder (NAf/ANG)	1.79	1.85	2.53	2.89
Trinidad & Tobago dollar (TT$)	6.35	6.67	9.13	10.44
US dollar (US$)	-	1.05	1.44	1.64

For the latest exchange rates see www.xe.com.

Beware: Manchineel Trees

Manchineel trees grow on beaches throughout the Caribbean. The fruit of the manchineel, which looks like a small green apple, is poisonous. The milky sap given off by the fruit and leaves can cause severe skin blisters, similar to the reaction caused by poison oak. If the sap gets in your eyes, it can result in temporary blindness. Never take shelter under the trees during a rainstorm, as the sap can be washed off the tree and onto anyone sitting below.

Manchineel trees can grow as high as 40ft (12m), with branches that spread widely. The leaves are green, shiny and elliptical in shape. On some of the more visited beaches, trees will be marked with warning signs or bands of red paint. Manchineel is called *mancenillier* on the French islands.

It's advisable to check your own government's travel advisories for the latest information.

Telephone

See the individual destination chapter directories for information on country codes.

Time

Only the Turks and Caicos observe Daylight Savings Time.

- **Eastern Standard Time** (EST; five hours behind GMT) Turks and Caicos, Jamaica, the Cayman Islands, the Dominican Republic.
- **Atlantic Standard Time** (AST; four hours behind GMT) All other islands.

Travelers with Disabilities

Travel in the Caribbean is not particularly easy for those with physical disabilities. Overall there is little or no awareness of the need for easier access onto planes, buses or rental vehicles. One exception is Puerto Rico, where good compliance with the Americans Disabilities Act (ADA) means many sights and hotels have wheelchair accessibility.

Visitors with special needs should inquire directly with prospective hotels for information on their facilities. The larger, more modern resorts are most likely to have the greatest accessibility, with elevators, wider doorways and wheelchair-accessible baths.

While land travel may present some obstacles, cruises are often a good option for travelers with disabilities in the Caribbean. Many cruise lines can coordinate shore-based excursions in tour buses equipped for special needs.

Island Time

In the Caribbean life moves at a slow, loosely regimented pace. You'll often see signs in front of shops, bars and restaurants that say 'open all day, every day' and this can mean several things; the place could truly be open all day every day of the week, but don't count on it. If business is slow, a restaurant, shop or attraction might simply close. If a bar is hopping and the owner's having fun, it could stay open until the wee hours. If the rainy season is lasting too long, a hotel or restaurant might close for a month. In other words, hard and fast rules about opening times are hard to come by.

The only consistent rule is that Sundays are sacred and 'open every day' generally translates to 'open every day except Sunday.'

Visas

Passport and visa requirements vary from island to island. See the individual destination chapter directories for information on visa requirements.

Weights & Measures

Some Caribbean countries use the metric system, others use the imperial system, and a few use a confusing combination of both. See the individual destination chapter directories for information.

Women Travelers

Although the situation varies between islands, machismo is alive and well. Men can get aggressive, especially with women traveling alone. On many islands local men have few qualms about catcalling, hissing, whistling, sucking their teeth or making kissy sounds to get female attention. While much of this is simply annoying, it can make women feel unsafe.

Like it or not, women will generally feel much safer if traveling with a male companion. Women traveling alone need to be sensible and careful – avoid walking alone after dark, heading off into the wilderness on your own, hitchhiking or picking up male hitchhikers. Generally try to avoid any situation where you're isolated and vulnerable. Don't wear skimpy clothing when you're not on the beach – it will just garner you a lot of unwanted attention. Also note that 'harmless flirtation' at home can be misconstrued as a serious come-on in the Caribbean.

Transport

Getting There & Away

This section gives a broad overview about the many options for travel to the Caribbean and ways to get around once you are there. Full details can be found in the destination transport sections.

Flights and tours can be booked online at www.lonelyplanet.com/travel_services.

Entering the Caribbean Islands

Generally your passport is all that's required to enter most Caribbean islands. This holds true for Americans (who will need passports to also return to the US), with the exceptions being Puerto Rico and USVI.

You may be asked to show an onward air ticket (Barbados is known for this) or prove sufficient funds. On islands that ask for your length of stay, always pad the figure so as to avoid having to extend the length of your stay.

Air

Major Caribbean Islands have flights from North America, the only exceptions being ones with airports unable to handle jets. Larger islands also have service from the UK and Europe.

Departure Tax

Some airports charge a departure that is *not* included in the price of the ticket. See the chapter transport sections for details.

Sea

The only way to reach the Caribbean by sea is on a cruise ship (or for a few lucky people on a yacht).

Getting Around

Air

The Caribbean has an extensive network of airlines serving even the smallest islands.

Bicycle

The popularity of cycling in the Caribbean depends on

where you go. Several islands are prohibitively hilly, with narrow roads that make cycling difficult. Others such as Little Cayman are ideal.

 Boat

Getting around the islands by yacht is a fantasy for many. Charters are generally quite easy.

Ferries link some islands within the Caribbean, including the following:

- Anguilla, Saba, St-Martin/Sint Maarten and St-Barthélemy
- British Virgin Islands and US Virgin Islands
- Dominica, Guadeloupe, Martinique and St Lucia
- The Dominican Republic and Puerto Rico

Flying Tips

Our authors learned from experience three things you should remember:

- Try not to arrive on a regional flight in the afternoon when most of the North American and European flights arrive, swamping immigration and customs. We flew from Montserrat to Antigua: the flight was 15 minutes; the wait in immigration lines was 2½ hours.
- Keep anything essential you might need for a few days with you. Luggage often somehow misses your flight – even if you see it waiting next to the plane as you board. It may take days – if ever – to catch up with you.
- Check in early. Bring a book and snack and hang out. We saw people with confirmed seats repeatedly bumped after flights checked in full and their alternative was days later. A two-hour wait is not bad if you're prepared for it. In many airports, you can check in early and then go someplace else like the incredibly fun beach bars near the Sint Maarten airport runway.

Bus

Inexpensive bus service is available on most islands, although the word 'bus' has different meanings in different places. Some islands have full-size buses (Aruba, Barbados et al), while on others a 'bus' is simply a pickup truck with wooden benches in the back.

Whatever the vehicle, buses are a good environmental choice compared to rental cars and they are excellent ways to meet locals. People are generally quite friendly and happy to talk to you about their island. Buses are a good way to hear the most popular local music tracks, often at an amazingly loud volume.

Buses are often the primary means of commuting to work or school and thus are most frequent in the early mornings and from mid- to late afternoon. There's generally a good bus service on Saturday mornings, but Sunday service is often nonexistent.

Car & Motorcycle

Driving in the Caribbean islands can rock your world, rattle your brains and fray your nerves. At first. Soon, you'll get used the often poor road conditions, slow speeds and relaxed adherence to road rules and using your horn to communicate everything from 'Hey, I'm turning right!' to 'Hey, you're cute!' to 'Hey, [expletive] you!'

Driver's License

You'll need your driver's license in order to rent a car. On most of the former British islands, you'll also need to purchase a visitor's driver's license (US$12 to

Island Driving

Offer a lift It's common courtesy on many islands to slow down and offer pedestrians a lift (and is considered obligatory on some).

Beware of goats! Keep an eye out for stray dogs, iguanas, wild horses, chickens and goats, all of which meander aimlessly on the island roads.

Cede the right-of-way Drivers often stop to let others turn or pedestrians to cross even when you don't think it's necessary.

Climate Change & Travel

Every form of transport that relies on carbon-based fuel generates CO_2, the main cause of human-induced climate change. Modern travel is dependent on airplanes, which might use less fuel per mile per person than most cars but travel much greater distances. The altitude at which aircraft emit gases (including CO_2) and particles also contributes to their climate change impact. Many websites offer 'carbon calculators' that allow people to estimate the carbon emissions generated by their journey and, for those who wish to do so, to offset the impact of the greenhouse gases emitted with contributions to portfolios of climate-friendly initiatives throughout the world. Lonely Planet offsets the carbon footprint of all staff and author travel.

US$20) from your car rental agent.

Rental

Car rentals are available on nearly all of the islands, with a few exceptions (usually because they lack roads). On most islands there are affiliates of the international chains, but local rental agencies may have better rates.

Road Rules

Road rules vary by island. In general note that driving conditions may be more relaxed than you are used to.

What side of the road to drive on depends on the island; this can be confusing if you're island-hopping and renting cars on each island. Adding to the confusion, some cars have steering columns on the opposite side of where you'd expect. See destination chapter transport sections for details.

Hitchhiking

Hitchhiking is an essential mode of travel on most islands, though the practice among foreign visitors is uncommon.

If you're driving a rental car, giving locals a lift can be a great form of cultural interaction and much appreciated by those trudging along the side of the road while – comparatively – affluent foreigners whiz past.

Behind the Scenes

Our Readers

Many thanks to the travelers who wrote to us with helpful hints, useful advice and interesting anecdotes:

Ryan Brown, Kevin Charbonneau, Kirsten Grace, Jim Green, Elizabeth Hogan, Bjorn Mellquist, Margaret Niles, Jorrit Noyons, Claudia Ritsert-Clark, Isabella Solca, Eddie Stiel, Abigail Strong-Hammer, Matthew Thompson, Kirsten Vangenechten, Lotte van der Wielen

Author Thanks

Ryan Ver Berkmoes

Huge thanks go to an amazing author team. At LP deep affection for my friends on the old Oakland team, including Kathleen Munnelly and Catherine Craddock. And thanks to Branislava Vladisavljevic and Sarah Reid. And of course I'm grateful to all the people in the Caribbean who helped with my research. And finally, love to Alexis Averbuck, my dream date now and forever at the Oistins fish fry.

Jean-Bernard Carillet

Huge thanks to Jean in Guadeloupe, Régis and Marie, Babeth and Peyo, for all the good time and great rum; and to Chris and Eva for just about everything.

This Book

This 1st edition of Lonely Planet's *Discover Caribbean Islands* guidebook was researched and written by Ryan Ver Berkmoes, Jean-Bernard Carillet, Paul Clammer, Michael Grosberg, Kevin Raub, Brendan Sainsbury, Andrea Schulte-Peevers, Polly Thomas, Luke Waterson and Karla Zimmerman. This guidebook was commissioned in Lonely Planet's Oakland office, and produced by the following:

Destination Editors Sarah Reid, Branislava Vladisavljevic
Commissioning Editor Kathleen Munnelly
Coordinating Editors Andrea Dobbin, Fionnuala Twomey
Product Editor Kate James
Senior Cartographer Mark Griffiths
Book Designer Lauren Egan
Senior Editors Claire Naylor, Karyn Noble
Assisting Editors Katie Connolly, Anne Mulvaney
Assisting Cartographer Corey Hutchison
Cover Researcher Naomi Parker
Thanks to Bruce Evans, Indra Kilfoyle, Martine Power, Dianne Schallmeiner, Angela Tinson, Juan Winata

SEND US YOUR FEEDBACK

We love to hear from travelers – your comments keep us on our toes and help make our books better. Our well-traveled team reads every word on what you loved or loathed about this book. Although we cannot reply individually to your submissions, we always guarantee that your feedback goes straight to the appropriate authors, in time for the next edition. Each person who sends us information is thanked in the next edition, the most useful submissions are rewarded with a selection of digital PDF chapters.

Visit **lonelyplanet.com/contact** to submit your updates and suggestions or to ask for help. Our award-winning website also features inspirational travel stories, news and discussions.

Note: We may edit, reproduce and incorporate your comments in Lonely Planet products such as guidebooks, websites and digital products, so let us know if you don't want your comments reproduced or your name acknowledged. For a copy of our privacy policy visit lonelyplanet.com/privacy.

Behind the Scenes

Paul Clammer

Bless up to those who were great help on the road: David 'Scotty' Scott (Reggae Hostel), Karen Hutchinson (Jamaica Cultural Enterprises), Annie Paul (University of the West Indies), Karin Wilson Edmonds (Yard Edge), Christopher Edmonds (Red Selecter), Josh Chamberlain (Alpha Boys), Nate (driver extraordinaire in Ocho Rios), Carla Gullotta (Drapers San Guest House), Leonard Welsh (Reach Falls) and staff at the Jamaica Conservation & Development Trust. Thanks also to Erin MacLeod for remote input, and Brendan Sainsbury: I owe you both a Red Stripe or three.

Michael Grosberg

Thanks to Carly Neidorf for putting up with my long absences and of course to Kevin Raub. And on the road thanks to the following for their time, guidance, insight and warmth: Patricia Suriel, Omar Rodriguez, Michael Scates, Mark Rodriguez, Tim Hall, Clare and Jeroen Mutsarrs and Lorenzo Sanssani.

Andrea Schulte-Peevers

Fond thanks to all the wonderful friends and strangers who've provided valuable local insights about the Leeward Islands before, during and after my research trip. There's too many of you to mention individually, but you know who you are.

Polly Thomas

Huge thanks to Skye Hernandez for her love, hospitality, laundry services and limitless knowledge of T&T; to Cecily Rugg and Matthew Thomas for unstinting support; and to Dexter, Aaron and Soleil Lewis for just about everything.

Karla Zimmerman

Thanks to the local knowledge interviewees who took the time to talk about their favorite places. Thanks to stalwart LP colleague Ryan Ver Berkmoes, whose good humor didn't fail when I hit him up for info. Thanks most to Eric Markowitz, partner-for-life supremo, who fed me and brought me beer during the write-up phase. You top my Best List.

Acknowledgments

Climate map data adapted from Peel MC, Finlayson BL & McMahon TA (2007) 'Updated World Map of the Köppen-Geiger Climate Classification', *Hydrology and Earth System Sciences*, 11, 1633–44.

Cover photographs
Front: Playa Bonita, Dominican Republic, Tristan Deschamps/Alamy ©
Back: Soufrière & the Pitons, St Lucia, Windward Islands, Robert Harding World Imagery/Alamy ©

Index

A

B

000 Map pages

000 Map pages

D

E

F

000 Map pages

G

H

I

J

K

L

000 Map pages

M

N

O

P

000 Map pages

R

S

T

U

V

000 Map pages

W

Z

NOTES

How to Use This Book

These symbols give you the vital information for each listing:

- Telephone Numbers
- Opening Hours
- Parking
- Nonsmoking
- Air-Conditioning
- Internet Access
- Wi-Fi Access
- Swimming Pool
- Vegetarian Selection
- English-Language Menu
- Family-Friendly
- Pet-Friendly
- Bus
- Ferry
- Metro
- Subway
- London Tube
- Tram

All reviews are ordered in our authors' preference, starting with their most preferred option. Additionally:

Sights are arranged in the geographic order that we suggest you visit them, and within this order, by author preference.

Eating and Sleeping reviews are ordered by price range (budget, mid-range, top end) and within these ranges, by author preference.

Look out for these icons:

No payment required

A green or sustainable option

Our authors have nominated these places as demonstrating a strong commitment to sustainability – for example by supporting local communities and producers, operating in an environmentally friendly way, or supporting conservation projects.

Map Legend

Sights
- Beach
- Buddhist
- Castle
- Christian
- Hindu
- Islamic
- Jewish
- Monument
- Museum/Gallery
- Ruin
- Winery/Vineyard
- Zoo
- Other Sight

Activities, Courses & Tours
- Diving/Snorkelling
- Canoeing/Kayaking
- Skiing
- Surfing
- Swimming/Pool
- Walking
- Windsurfing
- Other Activity/Course/Tour

Sleeping
- Sleeping
- Camping

Eating
- Eating

Drinking
- Drinking
- Cafe

Entertainment
- Entertainment

Shopping
- Shopping

Information
- Post Office
- Tourist Information

Transport
- Airport
- Border Crossing
- Bus
- Cable Car/Funicular
- Cycling
- Ferry
- Monorail
- Parking
- S-Bahn
- Taxi
- Train/Railway
- Tram
- Tube Station
- U-Bahn
- Underground Train Station
- Other Transport

Routes
- Tollway
- Freeway
- Primary
- Secondary
- Tertiary
- Lane
- Unsealed Road
- Plaza/Mall
- Steps
- Tunnel
- Pedestrian Overpass
- Walking Tour
- Walking Tour Detour
- Path

Boundaries
- International
- State/Province
- Disputed
- Regional/Suburb
- Marine Park
- Cliff
- Wall

Population
- Capital (National)
- Capital (State/Province)
- City/Large Town
- Town/Village

Geographic
- Hut/Shelter
- Lighthouse
- Lookout
- Mountain/Volcano
- Oasis
- Park
- Pass
- Picnic Area
- Waterfall

Hydrography
- River/Creek
- Intermittent River
- Swamp/Mangrove
- Reef
- Canal
- Water
- Dry/Salt/Intermittent Lake
- Glacier

Areas
- Beach/Desert
- Cemetery (Christian)
- Cemetery (Other)
- Park/Forest
- Sportsground
- Sight (Building)
- Top Sight (Building)